PURE

JFC Swing

Dr. Satyaraj Pantham

SAMS

201 West 103rd Street, Indianapolis, Indiana 46290

Pure JFC Swing

International Standard Book Number: 0-672-31423-1

Library of Congress Catalog Card Number: 98-87276

Printed in the United States of America

First Printing: February 1999

01   00   99   4   3   2   1

Trademarks

Warning and Disclaimer

EXECUTIVE EDITOR
Tim Ryan

DEVELOPMENT EDITOR
Jon Steever

MANAGING EDITOR
Lisa Wilson

PROJECT EDITOR
George E. Nedeff

COPY EDITOR
Pat Kinyon

INDEXERS
Heather Goens
Christine Nelsen

PROOFREADER
Gene Redding

TECHNICAL EDITOR
Jeff Perkins

SOFTWARE DEVELOPMENT SPECIALIST
Craig Atkins

INTERIOR DESIGN
Karen Ruggles

COVER DESIGN
Anne Jones

LAYOUT TECHNICIANS
Brandon Allen
Timothy Osborn
Staci Somers

Contents at a Glance

Contents

11   TEXT WIDGETS   207

12   SCROLLERS AND SLIDERS   227

PART III SYNTAX REFERENCE

About the Author

Dr. Satyaraj Pantham earned a Ph.D. from the Indian Institute of Science, Bangalore (India), for his research work in Flight Stability and Control. He has worked as a professional programmer for the past nine years, developing software for a variety of systems that range from aircraft to email.

Dr. Pantham has been programming with Java since the beginning of the Java revolution. He currently works as a consultant for Sun Microsystems and IBM. His most recent project at Sun Microsystems involved the development of a Swing-based GUI for MailView/HotJavaViews, a suite of desktop applications meant for the network computer or Java station. His software developmental interests include JFC, design patterns, 2D graphics, solid modeling, and real-time 3D graphics.

Dedication

To Ganesha and Skandha:

The eternal brothers who are Gurus of True Knowledge.

Acknowledgments

Though I would like to take all the credit for writing this book, I must admit that it is the retelling of the work conducted by pioneers. Therefore, first of all, I am very much indebted to the pioneers who created the concepts and the APIs for Swing.

Many thanks go to my associates at Sun Microsystems, especially Kapono Carter for his time to discuss various Swing concepts while I was preparing programs, and Naresh Adoni for reviewing some of the chapters. I would also like to thank my friend Dale Green for his encouragement at critical times.

Special thanks goes to the Sams team for their interest in creating this book. I am extremely thankful to Tim Ryan for his immense interest, suggestions, and tailoring of my ideas to create a book of this type. Thanks to Jon Steever for his development help. I would also like to acknowledge Pat Kinyon for doing excellent editing work. Thanks are also due to Jeff Perkins for reviewing the examples from this book.

Finally, I must thank my family members, Pushpa and Saravan, for the sacrifices that were made while I was working on this book. My wife Pushpa showed a lot of interest and was very involved in editing the enormous number of API methods in the reference portions of this book. It would have been simply impossible for me to create them single-handedly with the time pressure to complete the appendixes.

Tell Us What You Think!

As the reader of this book, *you* are our most important critic and commentator. We value your opinion and want to know what we're doing right, what we could do better, what areas you'd like to see us publish in, and any other words of wisdom you're willing to pass our way.

As the Executive Editor for the Java team at Macmillan Computer Publishing, I welcome your comments. You can fax, email, or write me directly to let me know what you did or didn't like about this book—as well as what we can do to make our books stronger.

When you write, please be sure to include this bookís title and author as well as your name and phone or fax number. I will carefully review your comments and share them with the author and editors who worked on the book.

Fax: 317-817-7070

Email: java@mcp.com

Mail: Tim Ryan
           Executive Editor
           Java
           Macmillan Computer Publishing
           201 West 103rd Street
           Indianapolis, IN 46290 USA

Introduction

This code-intensive reference is written for experienced Java developers who need to quickly learn the concepts and practical uses of JFC Swing in Java 2/JDK 1.2. Because the implementation of Swing components relies on AWT resources such as layout managers and event handling, these topics are also covered here for the sake of completeness. However, you will get the most value from this book if you are already familiar with AWT.

Pure JFC Swing is divided into three parts. Section I, "Conceptual Reference," is an accelerated introduction that explains the features and structure of the Swing Set; how Swing relates to JFC, AWT, and Java 2/JDK 1.2; and some of the fundamental programming techniques you will need to implement Swing components.

Each chapter in Section II, "Technique Reference," contains a concise description of one set of Swing components and well-commented, commercial-quality code that demonstrates how to build sophisticated Swing GUIs. In writing this book, I have placed the emphasis on creating code that you can use directly in your own programs. I have also described the functionality of code modules in each program by using snippet-by-snippet comments and explanations.

Section III, "Syntax Reference," contains four quick reference appendixes. Appendix A, "JFC Swing Quick Reference," is the quick reference for the Swing packages and their classes. Appendix B, "AWT Event Classes Quick Reference," contains material for referencing AWT event classes. These classes are often used in connection with the events fired by Swing components. Appendix C, "Important AWT Classes for Swing," presents the other important AWT classes, such as `Component`, `Container`, and layout managers used in Swing programming. Appendix D, "Accessibility Quick Reference," is the reference material for the Accessibility API.

Programmers who are approaching Swing for the first time and have no prior experience with AWT should pay special attention to the chapters on event handling and layout managers. These two chapters not only cover important Swing topics, but also explain fundamental GUI programming techniques and most of the relevant AWT information needed to use Swing.

Finally, I would like to state that this book presents a careful choice of topics and programs based on what professional developers need, and that each program contains realistic techniques and code that can be used in your daily programming projects. However, because programming is an art and developers can do numerous gymnastics with Swing components, I can't promise that you will find every single use of every Swing component in this book!

Satyaraj Pantham
San Jose, California
January 1999

CHAPTER 1

Swing Overview

The production version of the Java Development Kit 1.2 (also named Java 2) was released in December 1998. JDK 1.2 contains a sophisticated set of graphics and user interface API, called the Java Foundation Classes (JFC), as core packages. An important technology in JFC is Swing, a diverse selection of lightweight components that can be used to build sophisticated user interfaces. Figure 1.1 shows how JFC and Swing relate to JDK 1.2.

Swing components are an enhancement to the existing Abstract Window Toolkit (AWT) components; they are not intended to replace AWT components. Both types of components can be used in the same interface. Swing components range from basic controls such as buttons, check boxes, scrollbars, and sliders to complex widgets like text panes and editor panes.

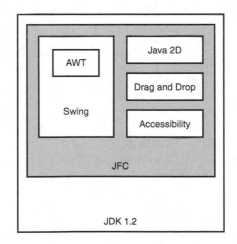

Figure 1.1

JDK 1.2, JFC, and Swing.

> **NOTE**
>
> Swing was first released as an extension API to JDK 1.1 that had to be downloaded separately. With JDK 1.2, JFC and Swing are integrated directly into the JDK. Therefore, you do not need to obtain the Swing set API separately.

JFC Technologies

JFC contains five major technologies, one of which is Swing. JFC also contains the Abstract Window Toolkit (AWT), Accessibility, Drag and Drop, and 2D Graphics. This book focuses on Swing and the Accessibility API. The following is a brief description of the constituents of JFC:

- *Accessibility API*—Assistive technologies (or systems) are useful for disabled people who need additional help to use the user interface. The assistive systems include screen readers, screen magnifiers, and speech recognition systems. The Accessibility API provides an interface that allows assistive technologies to interact and communicate with JFC and AWT components. This chapter will discuss the assistive technologies further and provide a reference in Appendix D, "Accessibility Quick Reference." The related API will also be observed in Swing classes.
- *Abstract Windowing Toolkit*—The Abstract Windowing Toolkit, or AWT, is not new to Java programmers. The AWT is the cornerstone for the JFC itself and is one of the core libraries that was launched with JDK 1.0. In fact, the AWT lays the foundation for the Swing components. While you can create the user interface with Swing components, you still need to use the layout managers and event models supported in AWT. Therefore, this book contains some of the topics such as layout managers and event handling from AWT to help you avoid having to search for information elsewhere. The relevant API quick reference is also provided at the end of the book. If you need more information, please see *JFC Unleashed*, also published by Sams.
- *2D Graphics*—The API in the AWT supports graphics to some extent in Java programming. However, as the Java technology started maturing, the necessity to incorporate a more sophisticated graphics API was recognized. Thus, JDK 1.2 has arrived with 2D graphics that enhance the existing graphics support. The 2D Graphics API can support advanced 2D graphics and imaging.
- *Drag and Drop*—With native platform–capable drag-and-drop, a user with a native application sitting next to a Java application will be able to drag-and-drop between the Java and native applications. The level of precision in the user gesture (drag movement) will be consistent with that of the host native platform.

Swing Features

Swing development has its roots in the Model-View-Controller (MVC) architecture. The MVC-based architecture allows Swing components to be replaced with different data models and views. The pluggable look-and-feel is a result of the MVC architecture. Because Java is a platform-independent language and runs on any client machine, you should be able to harness the look-and-feel of just about any platform. The following is a summary of Swing's key features:

- *Lightweight Components*—Starting with the JDK 1.1, the AWT supports lightweight component development. For a component to qualify as lightweight, it cannot depend on any native system classes, also called "peer" classes. In Swing, most of the components have their own view supported by the Java look-and-feel classes. Thus, the components do not depend on any peer classes for their view.
- *Pluggable Look-and-Feel*—This feature enables the user to switch the look-and-feel of Swing components without restarting the application. The Swing library supports a cross-platform look-and-feel—also called the Java look-and-feel—that remains the same across all platforms wherever the program runs. The native look-and-feel is native to whatever particular system on which the program happens to be running, including Windows and Motif. The Swing library provides an API that gives great flexibility in determining the look-and-feel of applications. It also enables you to create your own look-and-feel.

Swing Packages

The Swing API is organized into a number of packages to support APIs for various categories such as components, pluggable look-and-feel, events, component borders, and so on. The package members (classes and interfaces) and their API methods are given in Appendix A, "JFC Swing Quick Reference." The following is the list of package names in Swing:

```
javax.swing
javax.swing.border
javax.swing.colorchooser
javax.swing.event
javax.swing.filechooser
javax.swing.plaf
javax.swing.plaf.basic
javax.swing.plaf.metal
javax.swing.plaf.multi
javax.swing.table
javax.swing.text
javax.swing.text.html
javax.swing.tree
javax.swing.undo
```

Additionally, there are two more packages to store the look-and-feel classes of the Motif and Windows operating systems. These packages are included with JDK 1.2, but because they deal with operating systems that are outside the domain of Sun Microsystems, the packages are named differently:

```
com.sun.java.swing.plaf.motif.*
com.sun.java.swing.plaf.windows.*
```

The JComponent Class

The class `JComponent` is introduced to serve as the parent of Swing components. This is an abstract class and encapsulates the basic features and operations specific to Swing components. The AWT `Container` class is the parent of `JComponent`, as shown in Figure 1.2. Thus, the AWT lays the foundation for the Swing set of components.

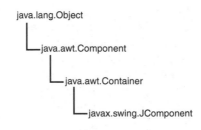

Figure 1.2

The class hierarchy of JComponent.

NOTE

Because Swing components extend from the AWT container, you can expect the components to behave like containers. However, you should make use of this feature judiciously, depending on the component.

The class `JComponent` is the common location for various features of the Swing components. You can refer to the `JComponent` methods that represent these features in Appendix A. The following is a list of these features:

- Accessibility support
- Setting borders around components
- Setting boundaries for components
- Actions for control of multiple components from one point
- Keystroke handling
- Adding change listeners
- Firing property change events
- Aligning components in their display areas
- Autoscrolling
- Setting double buffering

- Assigning dimensions for resizing behavior
- Assigning ToolTips
- Enabling request focus

Swing Components

This section provides an overview of all the Swing components. Swing labels and buttons will be discussed with code details so that they can be used to demonstrate various preliminary concepts such as event handling, containers, layouts, and borders. Table 1.1 lists Swing components and their definitions.

Table 1.1   Swing Components

Component	Definition
JApplet	This class represents Swing applets and hierarchically extends the AWT applet.
JButton	This class represents Swing buttons. These buttons can possess an icon as well as text with suitable (absolute as well as relative) positioning. You can create a button object with any of the constructors supported (see Chapter 8, "Buttons and Check Boxes") as follows: `JButton buttonRef = new JButton(text, icon);` where text and icon are the text label, and the icon is used over the button.
JCheckBox	This class represents check boxes in Swing (see Chapter 8).
JColorChooser	This class represents Swing color choosers. Color choosers are ready-made dialog boxes with a color palette. This topic is covered in Chapter 15, "File Choosers and Color Choosers."
JComboBox	A Swing combo box is an enhancement over the AWT component called Choice. The combo box is a pull-down list with a capability to display the selected item in a display area. You can also enter an item in the display area to edit it into the list (see Chapter 9, "Lists and Combo Boxes").
JDesktopPane	This is a type of container to attach the internal frames in Swing. You can find out more about desktop panes in Chapter 4, "Frames, Panes, and Panels." (Also look for the definition of an internal frame in this table.)
JDialog	This class represents the Swing version of dialog boxes. JDialog extends the AWT dialog box and requires its components to be added to its content pane (see Chapter 14, "Dialog Boxes and Option Panes").
JFileChooser	The class JFileChooser is a dialog box that allows you to open or save information content. Swing file choosers are discussed in Chapter 15.

continues

Table 1.1 continued

Component	Definition
JFrame	This class represents the Swing frame that is more sophisticated than the AWT frame. You can add components in layers, add a menu bar, or paint over the component (through a component called a *glass pane*). Frames are discussed in Chapter 4.
JInternalFrame	Internal frames are attached to a main frame of an application. You can start new sessions by using an internal frame in an application. Internal frames are discussed in Chapter 4.
JLabel	This class represents Swing labels that can display a piece of text as well as icons with suitable positioning. A label object can be created by using the following statement: `JLabel lableRef = new JLabel(text, icon, JLabel.CENTER);` This statement creates a label with the specified `text` and `icon` and their alignment along the horizontal direction (see Chapter 7, "Icons, Labels, and Borders").
JLayeredPane	This class represents the layered panes in Swing. Layered panes create the dimension along the depth of a component. You can position components on each layer of the layered pane. Swing applets and frames contain layered panes by default. Layered panes are discussed in Chapter 4.
JList	The `JList` class represents components that can display a list of items in a user interface. This component uses the M-UI (modified MVC) architecture and lets you deal with list models for sophisticated programming (see Chapter 9).
JMenu	This class represents Swing menus (see Chapter 13, "Menus, Toolbars, and ToolTips").
JMenuBar	This class represents the menu bar over a Swing applet or frame. Chapter 13 covers the details.
JMenuItem	This class represents Swing menu items. Menu items are button-like objects that can trigger specific actions in a program. Swing menu items are also discussed in Chapter 13.
JOptionPane	This class represents the option panes in Swing. Option panes are dialog boxes that display some information to the user or get confirmation from the user so that the program can be executed further based on the choice the user makes. Option panes are discussed in Chapter 14.
JPanel	This class represents Swing panels that have the capability of double buffering along with the ability to group other components. `JPanel` is discussed in Chapter 4.

Component	Definition
JPasswordField	This class represents a text field that does not display the text entered into it, but displays the specified character (such as *) as input is given into the field. Password fields are discussed in Chapter 11, "Text Widgets."
JPopupMenu	This class represents Swing pop-up menus that contain functionality to be accessed with a mouse click (see Chapter 13).
JProgressBar	This class represents progress bars in Swing. You can use a progress bar to indicate the state of some operation. Chapter 17, "Timers and Progress Indicators," discusses progress bars in Swing.
JRadioButton	This class represents Swing radio buttons. By using radio buttons, you can select an option from a given list of mutually exclusive options. Radio buttons are discussed in Chapter 8.
JRadioButtonMenuItem	Radio button menu items are menu items that represent mutually exclusive items. You can select only one item at a time. This topic is presented in Chapter 13.
JScrollBar	Scrollbars are used to scroll a child component horizontally or vertically in a container. Scrollbars are discussed in Chapter 12, "Scrollers and Sliders."
JScrollPane	Swing scroll panes are containers with a ready-made scrolling facility. Scroll panes are discussed in Chapter 12.
JSlider	This class can be used to create slider objects that allow you to select specific values in a specified interval. Swing sliders are discussed in Chapter 12.
JSplitPane	This class represents the split pane in Swing. The split pane provides separation between two components positioned in it. Chapter 4 discusses this topic in detail.
JTabbedPane	This class represents tabbed panes used in Swing. Tabbed panes are space savers used to display child components. The child components can be displayed one tab at a time over multiple tabs. Tabbed panes are discussed in Chapter 4.
JTable	The JTable class represents Swing tables and is discussed in Chapter 10, "Tables."
JTextArea	This class represents text area components in Swing. Text area components allow the editing of multiline plain text. You can find the information in Chapter 11.
JTextPane	This class can be used to create sophisticated editors in Swing applications. A text pane serves as a graphics editor for text as well as pictures. The text pane component is discussed in detail in Chapter 11.

Table 1.1   continued

Component	Definition
JToggleButton	This class represents Swing toggle buttons. Toggle buttons remain depressed when you operate them once. You can make them pop up by operating the button again. Toggle buttons are discussed in Chapter 8.
JToolBar	This class represents Swing toolbar objects. A toolbar is a strip-like area where you can add a set of important buttons or other components so that they are easily accessible. Toolbars can also be made floatable. Chapter 13 discusses the details of Swing toolbars.
JToolTip	This class represents a ToolTip object that can display a small amount of text to indicate the name or purpose of a component. ToolTips are discussed in Chapter 13.
JTree	Trees are used to display hierarchical data in a user interface. This class represents Swing tree objects. Trees are discussed in Chapter 16, "Trees."

Accessibility Support

Assistive, or access, technology is a system that makes a computer program more accessible to users with physical disabilities. Examples of assistive technology are screen magnifiers provided for users with visual impairments, screen readers that synthesize speech and read the content of a screen to the blind, and screen-based keyboards for users who cannot operate the normal keyboards.

Java accessibility support provides an extensible set of APIs that is compact, simple, and easy to use. The accessibility interfaces and classes abridge the user interface components from a Java applet/application to the access or assistive technology (system) that provides access to the applet/application. The quick reference on the accessibility API can be found in Appendix D, "Accessibility Quick Reference." The architecture of an application that implements accessibility support is shown in Figure 1.3.

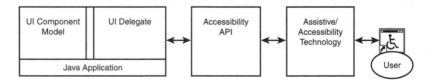

Figure 1.3

The architecture of an application using accessibility support.

In addition to the accessibility API, an assistive technology also requires the necessary accessibility utilities. These utilities locate the objects that implement the accessibility

API, support loading into the Java Virtual Machine, monitor AWT and JFC events, count the top-level Java windows that are open, retrieve the mouse cursor location and the component that has focus, and so on.

NOTE

As an application developer, you don't have to deal with the accessibility utilities; they are used by the developers of assistive technology systems.

CHAPTER 2

Swing Applets

This chapter is a quick introduction to using Swing applets; it discusses the fundamental topics involved in creating Swing applets and how they differ from normal applets. First you will see a "Hello! Swing World" program that implements a Swing applet; then you will study the technical details behind Swing applets.

Hello! Swing World

Listing 2.1 contains a simple Swing program called THello.java. This program simply prints the greeting label "Hello! Swing World" (rather than the same old greeting "Hello! World"). "Hello! Swing World" is coded to function both as an applet and an application, so you will find some extra code statements in the program; otherwise, the program has only one core statement, as follows:

```
getContentPane().add(new JLabel(
        "Hello! Swing World",
        new ImageIcon("AnimSpeaker.gif"),
        JLabel.CENTER));
```

The details of this statement will become clear as you progress through the next few chapters. For now, you can note the animated icon and the greeting label "Hello! Swing World" displayed over the applet or application frame. Also, you may note the class identifiers JApplet and JFrame, which represent Swing applets and Swing frames, respectively. These classes are inherited from the respective AWT classes called Applet and Frame. Figures 2.1 and 2.2 display the output of the program when it is run as an applet and as an application. Note that the output as an applet shows the title bar indicating that the program is being run in an appletviewer. You can also observe the status Applet started in the status bar.

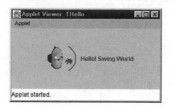

Figure 2.1

The THello applet executed in the appletviewer.

Figure 2.2

The THello program running as an application.

*Listing 2.1   A Simple Swing Applet/Application to Demonstrate JApplet
(THello.java)*

```
// Your first Swing program.

/*
 * <Applet code=THello width=300 height=150>
 * </Applet>
 */

import javax.swing.*; // Import the Swing classes
import java.awt.event.*; // for the WindowAdapter and WindowEvent classes

// This is your Swing applet (by extending JApplet).
public class THello extends JApplet {

    public void init() {
        // Here is the only program statement.
        // Create a string label to display the text as shown here
        // with an icon made from the animated GIF file.
        // The text and icon are centered by using JLabel.CENTER
        // The label is added to the content pane
        // of the applet (see Code Details).
        getContentPane().add(new JLabel(
            "Hello! Swing World",
            new ImageIcon("AnimSpeaker.gif"),
            JLabel.CENTER));
```

```
    }

    // When you run this program as an application.
    // The main method to instantiates the application frame.
    public static void main(String[] args) {
        // Create a Swing frame.
        JFrame f = new JFrame("THello");

        // Create an instance of the THello applet.
        THello helloApplet = new THello();

        // Initialize the applet instance.
        helloApplet.init();

        // Add the applet to the JFrame (to it's content pane).
        f.getContentPane().add(helloApplet);

        // Add the listener to close the frame.
        f.addWindowListener(new WindowEventHandler());

        // Assign the frame size and display it.
        f.setSize(300, 150); // frame: width=300, height = 150
        f.show(); // Display the frame
    }
}

// Class to close the frame and exit the application.
class WindowEventHandler extends WindowAdapter {
    public void windowClosing(WindowEvent e) {
        System.exit(0);
    }
}
```

Code Details

As stated previously, the program can function as both an applet and an application. Thus, you can expect the methods init() as well as main() in the same program. The init() method contains the statement that creates a label with the text "Hello! Swing World" and an animated icon (a speaker sending sound waves). Then the label is added to the applet. The init() method is invoked when you run the program as an applet.

Before you proceed to the code inside the init() method, you should observe two more important features in the program. As you can see, the import statement contains the Swing package as javax.swing.*. This is the key package that contains the Swing classes JApplet and JFrame. Throughout your Swing programming career, you will continually be using this import statement at the top of all your programs.

The other point of interest is that the class THello extends JApplet. This is because the program is a Swing applet and thus extends JApplet, which is the Swing applet class. The applet tag <Applet>...</Applet> at the top of the program allows you to run the file THello.java by using the appletviewer. This avoids the unnecessary creation of another file named THello.html while testing the code. Note that all the applets in this book are tested by using this convention.

Next, coming to the main() method inside the program, you need this to allow the code to function as an application. To create a Swing application, you need to use a JFrame object to contain the label. However, in the case of this program, the applet that contains the "Hello! Swing World" label is added to the frame. This is shown in the following code statement:

```
// Create a Swing frame.
JFrame f = new JFrame("THello");

// Create an instance of THello applet.
THello helloApplet = new THello();

// Initialize the applet instance.
helloApplet.init();

// Add the applet to the JFrame (to its content pane).
f.getContentPane().add(helloApplet);
```

The remaining code statements display the frame with the specified size. The frame also features a window listener to perform a clean exit when closing the frame. One final point is that a component, such as label, is added to something called the "content pane" instead of directly adding it to the applet or frame. A reference to the content pane can be obtained by using the method getContentPane(). You will learn more about the content pane as you progress through the book.

TIP

You can use the wrapper code in this program (allowing the program to function as both an applet and an application) in your other programs that require similar functionality.

Swing Applets

The Swing set introduces its own version of the applet, whose parent is the AWT applet. Swing applets are made more sophisticated so that they can support menu bars and layering of components in the dimension of depth, and allow painting over the components already laid inside the applet.

With support for menu bars, Swing applets can possess a menu bar. The layering of components is essentially placing components in multiple layers overlapping each other. This in turn allows the components to be positioned so that the feeling of depth is created. Swing applets contain a special component called a *layered pane* to achieve this feature.

The other feature that allows painting over components inside the applet can be accomplished by using a component called a *glass pane*. The glass pane is a transparent component that allows the background components to be visible. However, you can paint over the glass pane to make the painting visible in the foreground.

Swing applets are represented by the class JApplet, which is stored in the package javax.swing. You can create a Swing applet by creating a class that extends JApplet. While adding children to it, you need to add them to something called a *content pane*, which receives the applet's children. The Swing library introduces this intermediate container to deal with the complexities involved in mixing up the lightweight and heavyweight components in an applet. The following code statement shows how a component can be added to the content pane inside a Swing applet:

```
// Get a handle on the applet's content pane.
Container contentPane = this.getContentPane();

// You may want to assign a new layout.
contentPane.setLayout(someLayoutObject);

// Add the component to the applet.
contentPane.add(someComponent);
```

You can also obtain references to the applet's layered pane, glass pane, and menu bar by calling the following methods on the applet's instance:

```
public void getLayeredPane()
public void getGlassPane()
public void getJMenuBar()
```

JApplet Example Program

Listing 2.2, TJApplet.java, shows the code to implement a Swing applet that displays a simple label with a border. The resulting applet from this program is shown in Figure 2.3.

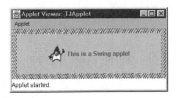

Figure 2.3

A Swing applet displaying a label with a matte border.

Listing 2.2   Swing Applet with a Matte Border (TJApplet.java)

```
// Demonstrates the Swing applets

/*
 * <Applet code=TJApplet width=200 height=100>
 * </Applet>;
 */

import javax.swing.*;
import java.awt.*;

public class TJApplet extends JApplet {

    public void init() {
        // 1. Get a reference to the content pane of the applet.
        Container contentPane = getContentPane();
        // 2. Create a label with an icon and text.
        JLabel label = new JLabel("This is a Swing applet", // text
                            new ImageIcon("Metal.gif"), // icon
                            JLabel.CENTER); // horiz. position

        // 3. Assign a matte border by using an icon and the specified insets.
        label.setBorder(BorderFactory.createMatteBorder(
                        10,  // top inset
                        10,  // left inset
                        10,  // bottom inset
                        10,  // right inset
                        new ImageIcon("border.gif"))); // border icon

        // 4. Add the label to the applet's content pane.
        contentPane.add(label);
    }
}
```

Code Details

TJApplet extends the Swing class JApplet and thus qualifies itself as a Swing applet. Inside the init() method, snippet-1 gets a handle on the applet's content pane. This reference will be used to add any components to the applet.

Snippet-2 creates a Swing label with the specified text label and the icon. Snippet-3 assigns a border to the label. The border is of type matte border and uses an icon for the matte pattern. The border thickness of the four sides of the label is assigned through the respective insets. Snippet-4 is the statement to add the label to the applet. Note that you have to add the label to the applet's content pane rather than the applet itself.

CHAPTER 3

Event Handling

User interface elements fire events in response to user input. These events are propagated down the application to execute the specified functionality. If no functionality has been defined, the events produce no effect.

The AWT in JDK 1.1 introduced the delegation event model to handle user interface events. Because the Swing set is an extension of AWT, Swing components also function based on the delegation event model.

This chapter initially discusses the concepts of the delegation event model and describes the high-level events generated by Swing components. This chapter also explains the corresponding event listeners and the classes needed to create event listeners. Note that most of the Swing components use the classes of AWT events and event listeners. The low-level events generated by the mouse, keyboard, and other devices will be discussed later.

Delegation Model

The delegation event model supports a clean separation between the core program and its user interface. The delegation pattern allows robust event handling that is less error prone due to strong compile-time checking. In addition, the delegation event model improves performance because the toolkit can filter out undesirable events (like high frequency mouse events) that are not targeted to execute any function.

The delegation event model consists of three separate objects to deal with event handling: event sources, events, and listeners. Event sources are any of the user interface components such as buttons, text fields, scrollbars, and sliders. Event sources generate and fire events, and the events propagate until they are finally attended to by their listeners.

Events are objects of specific class types that are extended from the class java.util.EventObject.

Event listeners are objects that implement specific event listener interfaces extended from the root interface java.util.EventListener. The methods implemented inside the listener classes contain the functionality that needs to be executed when the corresponding user interface component is operated.

To attend to the events generated by an event source, the listener object needs to be registered with that source. This is performed by either using the method set*EventType*Listener() or more often add*EventType*Listener() because it supports *multi-casting*. When a source supports multi-casting, multiple listeners can be registered or removed from the source.

Swing Events, Sources, and Listeners

This section explains the Swing sources, the events they generate, and the listener interfaces that are implemented to handle the events.

As discussed in the previous chapter, the Swing library supports a good number of sophisticated user interface components such as buttons, check boxes, radio buttons, text fields, and so on. All these components fire events that are handled by their respective listener classes. Table 3.1 presents the Swing event sources and their corresponding listeners.

NOTE

Swing components also depend on AWT events and listeners in addition to the events and listeners supported in the Swing library.

Table 3.1   Swing Event Sources and Listeners

Swing Sources	Event Listeners
AbstractButton	
JTextField	ActionListener
Timer	
JDirectoryPane	
JScrollBar	AdjustmentListener
JComponent	AncestorListener
DefaultCellEditor	CellEditorListener

Swing Sources	Event Listeners
AbstractButton DefaultCaret JProgressBar JSlider JTabbedPane JViewport	ChangeListener
AbstractDocument	DocumentListener
AbstractButton JComboBox	ItemListener
JList	ListSelectionListener
JMenu	MenuListener
AbstractAction JComponent TableColumn	PropertyChangeListener
JTree	TreeSelectionListener
JPopupMenu	WindowListener

The methods encapsulated by these event classes and listener interfaces are listed in Appendix B, "AWT Event Classes Quick Reference." The specific events fired by the Swing components and the respective listeners will be discussed in detail as you progress through Chapters 8–17 on various source components.

To handle specific events, you need to create a listener class that implements the relevant listener interface. The listener class provides the code for the interface methods as shown in the following:

```
class MyListener implements SomeEventListener {
    public void interfaceMethod1 (SomeEvent se1) {
        // functionality to be executed
    }

    public void intefaceMethod2 (SomeEvent se2) {
        // functionality to be executed
    }

    ...
    ...

}
```

ActionEvent Code Example

Listing 3.1 demonstrates the action events fired by button components. The program creates a Swing applet with a button displayed over it. This button is the source object to generate events of class type `ActionEvent`. There is a listener object of type `ButtonListener` that has been registered with the source object.

Whenever the user clicks the button, the method `actionPerformed()` is executed; this method essentially contains the functionality to be executed when the button is operated. In this example, the enclosed functionality is to ring the bell, as shown in the code. The output from Listing 3.1 is shown Figure 3.1.

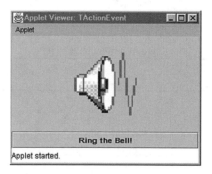

Figure 3.1

An ActionEvent applet demonstrating sources, events, and listeners.

Listing 3.1   ActionEvent Example with One Button That Demonstrates Sources, Events, and Their Listeners (TActionEvent.java)

```
/*
 * <Applet code=TActionEvent width=300 height=200>
 * </Applet>
 */

import javax.swing.*;
import java.awt.*;
import java.awt.event.*;

public class TActionEvent extends JApplet {
    Container container;
    JLabel label;
    Icon speaker;

    public void init() {
        // 1. Get the handle on the applet's content pane.
        container =  this.getContentPane();

        // 2. Create a speaker icon, add it to a Swing
        // label, and add the label to the applet.
```

```
        speaker = new ImageIcon("speaker.gif");
        label = new JLabel(speaker);
        //label.repaint();
        container.add(label);

        // 3. Create a source (button) for the action event.
        JButton source = new JButton("Ring the bell!");
        container.add(source, BorderLayout.SOUTH);

        // 4. Register the action listener with the source.
        source.addActionListener(new ButtonListener());
    }

// 5. Define the listener class.
class ButtonListener implements ActionListener {
    // 6. Interface method that has been implemented.
    public void actionPerformed(ActionEvent ae) {

        // Ring the bell...
        int i=0;
        while (i<10) {
            Toolkit.getDefaultToolkit().beep();

            try {
                Thread.currentThread().sleep(1000);
            } catch(InterruptedException ie) {
                System.out.println("Sleep Interrupted");
            }
            i++;
        }
    }
  }
}
}
```

Code Details

The applet begins by declaring some objects as its data members. In Swing applets the components are not directly added to the applet. Instead, you need to add them to the underlying content pane of the applet. Therefore, snippet-1 obtains a reference to the content pane. Snippet-2 adds a decorative label with a speaker icon.

Snippet-3 creates a Swing button that serves as the source object to originate and fire events of type ActionEvent. Snippet-4, the source object, has been registered by a listener object by invoking the method addActionListener().

Snippet-5 defines the listener class that implements the interface ActionListener. This class provides the code for the method actionPerformed() from the interface. Notice that the method actionPerformed() takes the object of ActionEvent as its argument. Now with this circuit between the source and its listener, the functionality inside the method `actionPerformed()` is executed whenever the source button is pressed.

Low-Level Events

Low-level events are those generated by the mouse and keyboard that represent low-level inputs or window system incidence on a GUI component. Table 3.2 contains a list of low-level events and their corresponding listeners.

Table 3.2 Low-Level Events and Listeners

Event	Listener
java.awt.event.ComponentEvent	java.awt.event.ComponentListener
java.awt.event.ContainerEvent	java.awt.event.ContainerListener
java.awt.event.FocusEvent	java.awt.event.FocusListener
java.awt.event.KeyEvent	java.awt.event.KeyListener
java.awt.event.MouseEvent	java.awt.event.MouseListener
	java.awt.event.MouseMotionListener
java.awt.event.WindowEvent	java.awt.event.WindowListener

The API methods from these classes are given in the quick reference provided in Appendixes A, "JFC Swing Quick Reference," and B.

Low-Level Mouse Events Code Example

Listing 3.2 demonstrates low-level mouse events. The program creates an applet that is registered by a mouse listener. The mouse listener class implements the `MouseListener` interface. The applet displays the mouse status when it enters or exits the applet. Also, if the user clicks, presses, or releases the mouse button, the state of the mouse button and the mouse position will be displayed over the applet. The output of the program is shown in Figure 3.2.

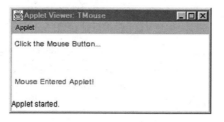

Figure 3.2

A Swing applet demonstrating the low-level mouse events.

Listing 3.2   Low-Level Mouse Events (TMouse.java)
```
// Demonstrates the mouse events (which are low-level events)

/*
 * <Applet code=TMouse width=400 height=200>
 * </Applet>
 */

import javax.swing.*;
import java.awt.*;
import java.awt.event.*;

// 1. Create a Swing applet that implements mouse listener.
public class TMouse extends JApplet
                    implements MouseListener {
    Container container;
    int width, height;
    int x, y;
    int flag;
    String mouseStatus;

    public void init() {
        // 2. Get a reference to the applet's content pane.
        container = this.getContentPane();

        // 3. Initialize the data members.
        x = 0; y = 0;
        width = 2; height = 2; // For a small square to be drawn
        flag = 0;

        // 4. Register the mouse listener with the applet.
        container.addMouseListener(this);
    }

    /*
     * NOTE: The class JApplet contains the update() method
     * to override the same method from the class
     * Component that repairs the container
     * background with its background color and calls
     * the paint() method. The update()in JApplet does not
     * repair the background of the container. It calls the
     * paint() method. You need to use an update() method that repairs
     * the background.
     */
    // 5. The update() method to repair the applet's background.
    public void update(Graphics g) {
```

continues

Listing 3.2   continued

```
      g.setColor(this.getBackground());
      g.fillRect(0, 0, // x and y coordinates
                  getWidth(), // Get the applet's width
                  getHeight()); // Get the applet's height
      paint(g);
   }

   // 6. The paint() method to paint the applet based on the flag.
   public void paint(Graphics g) {
      g.setColor(Color.blue);
      g.drawString("Click the Mouse Button...", 5, 20); // at x=5 & y=20
      g.setColor(Color.red);

      if(flag == 1)
         g.drawString("Mouse Entered Applet!", 5, 80);

      else if(flag == 2)
         g.drawString("Mouse Exited Applet!", 5, 80);

      else if(flag == 3) {
         g.drawString("Mouse Entered Applet!", 5, 80);
         g.fillRect(x, y, width, height);
         g.drawString("Clicked Here!", x, y);
      }

      else if(flag == 4) {
         g.drawString("Mouse Entered Applet!", 5, 80);
         g.fillRect(x, y, width, height);
         g.drawString("Pressed Here!", x, y);
      }

      else if(flag == 5) {
         g.drawString("Mouse Entered Applet!", 5, 80);
         g.fillRect(x, y, width, height);
         g.drawString("Mouse Released!", x, y);
      }
   }

   7. Listener interface method, called when the mouse enters the applet.
   public void mouseEntered(MouseEvent me) {
      flag = 1;
      repaint();
   }

   8. Listener interface method, called when the mouse exits the applet.
   public void mouseExited(MouseEvent me) {
      flag = 2;
```

```
        repaint();
    }

    // 9. Listener interface method, called when the mouse button is clicked.
    public void mouseClicked(MouseEvent me) {
        flag = 3;
        x = me.getX();
        y = me.getY();
        repaint();
    }

    // 10. Listener interface method, called when the mouse button is pressed.
    public void mousePressed(MouseEvent me) {
        flag = 4;
        x = me.getX();
        y = me.getY();
        repaint();
    }

    // 11. Listener interface method, called when the mouse button is released.
    public void mouseReleased(MouseEvent me) {
        flag = 5;
        x = me.getX();
        y = me.getY();
        repaint();
    }
}
```

Code Details

Snippet-1 is the beginning of the applet code. The class TMouse extends JApplet and also functions as a mouse listener by implementing the interface MouseListener. Inside the method init(), snippet-2 obtains a reference to the applet's content pane. Snippet-3 initializes the data members to suitable values. The width and height are the dimensions of a small square that appears when the mouse button is operated over the applet. Snippet-4 shows the statement to register the mouse listener (the applet itself) with the applet.

Snippet-5 shows the code for the update() method where you need to perform the repair work for the applet as the mouse state changes. The applet is basically cleaned up by drawing a rectangle that has been filled with the background color of the applet. This approach has a tendency to slow down the performance that results in flickering of the screen. The practical remedy to control flickering is to use double buffering supported by Swing panels. The Swing panels will be discussed in Chapter 4, "Frames, Panes, and Panels."

Snippet-6 shows the paint() method of the applet. This method is called whenever the mouse status changes. Based on a specific flag that indicates the mouse status, the applet is repainted with the status information.

Snippets 7–11 assign the value of the mouse status flag. These snippets essentially implement the methods from the `MouseListener` interface. The methods `mouseEntered()` and `mouseExited()` simply initialize the flag and call `repaint()`. These methods are invoked when the mouse enters or exits the applet. The other methods (`mouseClicked()`, `mousePressed`, and `mouseReleased()`) are executed when the respective mouse operations are performed. These methods retrieve the mouse coordinates by calling the methods `getX()` and `getY()` on the `MouseEvent` object. This information will be used to display the activation of the mouse button over the applet.

Low-Level Mouse Movement Code Example

Listing 3.3 demonstrates how to handle the low-level mouse movement events—events that are generated when the mouse is moved or dragged. To recognize ordinary mouse movements or mouse movements with a mouse button pressed (dragging the mouse), you need to deal with the interface called `MouseMotionListener`. The listener class implements this interface by defining the interface methods `mouseMoved()` and `mouseDragged()`. This program is an applet that recognizes the state of the mouse motion and displays the status. The output from this program is shown in Figure 3.3.

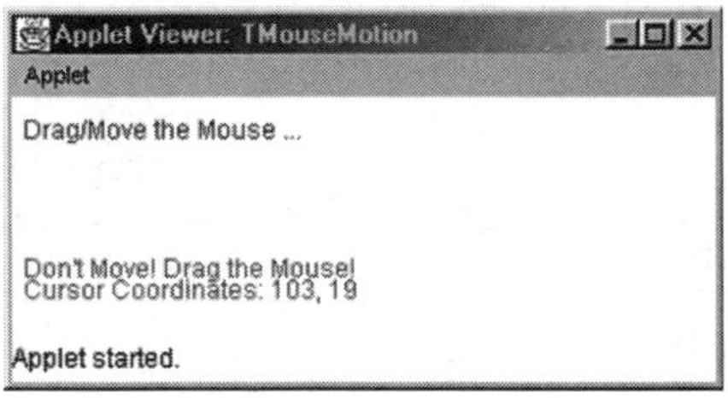

Figure 3.3

An applet demonstrating mouse motion events.

Listing 3.3   Mouse Motion Events (TMouseMotion.java)
```
// Demonstrates mouse motion events.

/*
 * <Applet code=TMouseMotion width=400 height=200>
 * </Applet>
 */

import javax.swing.*;
import java.awt.*;
import java.awt.event.*;

public class TMouseMotion extends JApplet  {
```

```java
int x, y;
int flag;

public void init() {
    // 1. Create an object of the custom listener and register it with
    // the applet.
    CustomListener ct = new CustomListener(this);
    this.addMouseMotionListener(ct);
}


// 2. The update() method to repair the applet's background.
// Warning: This can reduce the performance and lead to flickering.
// The workaround is to use a JPanel attached to the applet.
public void update(Graphics g) {
    g.setColor(this.getBackground());
    g.fillRect(0, 0, getWidth(), getHeight());
    paint(g);
}


// 3. The paint() method to display the mode of mouse motion
// and its location, depending on the flag value.
public void paint(Graphics g) {
    g.setColor(Color.blue);
    g.drawString("Drag/Move the Mouse ...", 5, 20);
    g.setColor(Color.red);

    if(flag == 1) {
        g.drawString("Don't Move! Drag the Mouse!", 5, 85);
        g.drawString("Cursor Coordinates: " + x + ", " + y, 5, 95);
    }
    else if(flag == 2) {
        g.drawString("Don't Drag! Move the Mouse!", 5, 85);
        g.drawString("Cursor Coordinates: " + x + ", " + y, 5, 95);
    }
}
}


// 4. The mouse motion listener.
class CustomListener implements MouseMotionListener {
    TMouseMotion tm;

    public CustomListener(TMouseMotion tm) {
        this.tm = tm;
    }

    // Executed when the mouse is moved.
    public void mouseMoved(MouseEvent me) {
```

continues

Listing 3.3   continued

```
    // Set the flag value
    tm.flag = 1;

    // Get the coordinates of the mouse pointer.
    tm.x = me.getX();
    tm.y = me.getY();

    // Repaint the applet.
    tm.repaint();
}

// Executed when the mouse is dragged.
public void mouseDragged(MouseEvent me) {
    // Set the flag value
    tm.flag = 2;

    // Get the coordinates of the mouse pointer.
    tm.x = me.getX();
    tm.y = me.getY();

    // Repaint the applet.
    tm.repaint();
  }
}
```

Code Details

Inside the `init()` method of the applet, snippet-1 creates a mouse motion listener. This object is registered with the applet so that the applet recognizes the mouse movement. Snippet-2 is the `update()` method that repairs the applet's background and calls the `paint()` method. Snippet-3 defines the `paint()` method that executes the code to draw the motion status of the mouse depending on a flag value.

Snippet-4 defines the mouse motion listener that implements the interface `MouseMotionListener`. You need to implement two methods: `mouseMoved()` and `mouseDragged()`. The implementation code basically sets a value for the status flag and retrieves the coordinates at each position of the mouse as it is moved or dragged. The mouse coordinates are displayed over the applet by calling the `repaint()` method.

Adapters

Most listener interfaces are designed to support multiple event subtypes; thus, they contain multiple abstract methods that need to be implemented by their listener classes. For example, the interface `java.awt.event.MouseListener` contains the methods `mouseClicked()`, `mouseEntered()`, `mouseExited()`, `mousePressed()`, and `mouseReleased()`.

If you do not want to implement functionality for all the methods in an interface, there will be one or more methods left out without any body. To avoid the clutter of empty methods, adapters have been introduced. The adapters are classes that readily implement interfaces with empty methods. In this case, the listener classes simply extend appropriate adapters and only implement the necessary methods to override those in the corresponding adapters. This leads to a cleaner way of handling the necessary events. The following are the adapters used by the Swing listeners:

```
java.awt.event.ComponentAdapter
java.awt.event.ContainerAdapter
java.awt.event.FocusAdapter
java.awt.event.KeyAdapter
java.awt.event.MouseAdapter
java.awt.event.MouseMotionAdapter
java.awt.event.WindowAdapter
```

Adapters Code Example

Listing 3.4 demonstrates the adapters that are used for event handling and the implementation of a key listener. The program is an applet that contains a text field, which is a component where you can enter or display any single line of text. When the applet is displayed, the text field receives the focus, and you can type in some text. The typed text is simply displayed by using a Swing label.

You will notice the `KeyListener` class that extends the class `KeyAdapter` and implements only one method, `KeyTyped()`. This method overrides the one in the adapter class. Note that if the listener class implements the interface `KeyListener`, it needs to implement three methods such as `keyPressed()`, `keyReleased()`, and `keyTyped()`. The program output is shown in Figure 3.4.

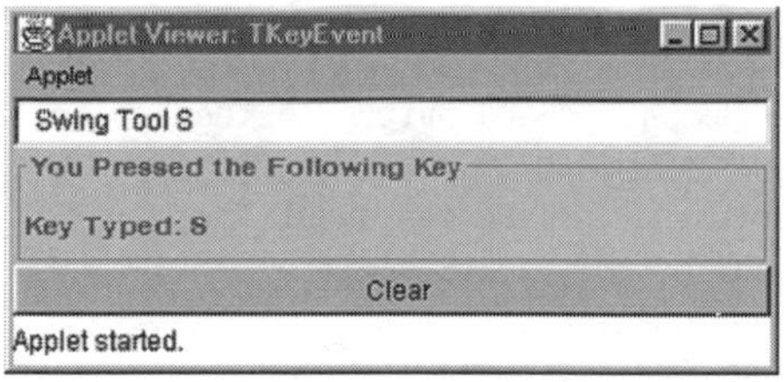

Figure 3.4

A Swing applet demonstrating key adapters.

Listing 3.4   Adapters for Event Handling (TKeyEvent.java)
```
// Demonstrates adapters and key events.

/*
 * <Applet code= TKeyEvent width=350 height=100>
```

continues

Listing 3.4   continued

```
 * </Applet>
 */

import javax.swing.*;
import java.awt.*;
import java.awt.event.*;

public class TKeyEvent extends JApplet {

    Container contentPane;
    JLabel label;
    TextField textField;

    public void init() {
        // 1. Get the handle on the applet's content pane.
        contentPane = this.getContentPane();

        // 2. Create a text field and add a key listener to it.
        textField = new TextField(25); // of 25 char width
        textField.addKeyListener(new MyKeyListener());

        // 3. Create a button object and register an action
        // listener.
        Button button = new Button("Clear");
        button.addActionListener(new ButtonListener());

        // 4. Create a label with the titled border.
        label = new JLabel("Key Typed: Nill");
        label.setBorder(BorderFactory.createTitledBorder(
            "You Pressed the Following Key"));

        // 5. Add the text field and button to the applet's
        // content pane.
        contentPane.setLayout(new BorderLayout());
        contentPane.add("North", textField);
        contentPane.add(label);
        contentPane.add("South", button);

        // 6. Get the focus on to the text field.
        // Note: You can do this only after you add
        // the text field to the container.
        textField.requestFocus();
    }

    // 7. Create the key listener class.
    class MyKeyListener extends KeyAdapter {
        public void keyTyped(KeyEvent e) {
            char c = e.getKeyChar();
```

```
                label.setText ("Key Typed: " + c);
        }
    }

    // 8.   Create the button listener class.
    class ButtonListener implements ActionListener {
        public void actionPerformed(ActionEvent e) {
            //Reset the text components.
            textField.setText("");

            //Return the focus to the text field.
            textField.requestFocus();
        }
    }
}
```

Code Details

Inside the init() method of the applet, snippet-1 gets a reference to the applet's content pane. Snippet-2 creates a text field and adds a key listener to it. Thus, when you type in a character using the keyboard, the key listener responds to it. Snippet-3 creates a button that has been registered by an action listener. Whenever the button is clicked, the text field is cleared so a fresh entry can be made.

Snippet-3 creates a label with a border. Next, all these components are added to the applet's content pane, as shown in snippet-5. Snippet-6 shows the statement that allows the text field to receive focus on starting the applet.

Snippet-7 shows the key listener class that implements the adapter class KeyAdapter. This class implements only one method, keyTyped(), that overrides the same method from the adapter class. You can obtain the character that has been typed by invoking the method getKeyChar() on the object of type KeyEvent. Similarly, other keys such as modifier keys can be retrieved by using the API methods inside the class KeyEvent. Snippet-8 shows the action listener class that supports code for the method actionPerformed(). This method is executed when the button on the applet is operated.

CHAPTER 4

Frames, Panes, and Panels

This chapter discusses how to implement the three categories of Swing containers: frames, panes, and panels. The next chapter will show you how to position various components in a container according to a specified layout.

Frames

A Swing frame is a container that functions as the main window for programs that use Swing components. Swing frames possess a title, a border, and buttons for iconifying, maximizing, and closing the frame.

A Swing frame is represented by the class JFrame, which extends the AWT class Frame (see Figure 4.1). Notice that the Swing frame is a heavyweight container, as is its parent. An instance of JFrame can take advantage of the features of both the JFrame and Frame classes.

WARNING

Although you can invoke the API methods in AWT Frame on a JFrame object, you must watch out for any possible incompatibilities such as improper packing of the frame around its components.

The *content pane* was introduced in Swing to deal with the complexities involved in making lightweight and heavyweight components work together. The content pane basically manages the interior of a Swing frame, which means that you add components to the frame's content pane rather than adding them directly to the frame itself. You will learn more about the content pane as you progress through this chapter.

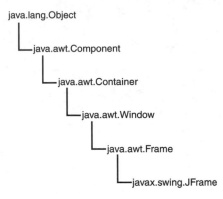

Figure 4.1

The class hierarchy of JFrame.

JFrame Constructors

Following is typical code used to implement a JFrame object and add a component to it:

```
JFrame frame = new JFrame(); // create a frame object
Container contentPane = frame.getContentPane(); // get the content pane
contentPane.setLayout(new SomeLayout()); // if you want to assign
contentPane.add(SomeComponent); // add the component
```

Note that by default the content pane is set to border layout. A layout is the pattern used to display components in a container (see Chapter 5, "Layout Managers," for information about layouts and how they are assigned to a container). Following are the constructors from the class JFrame:

```
public JFrame()
public JFrame(String title)
```

The first constructor creates a new frame that is initially invisible and without a title. The second constructor creates an invisible frame with the specified title. You make the frames appear by invoking the method show(). When closing a frame you can execute either of the following types of closing operations defined in the WindowConstants interface:

```
DO_NOTHING_ON_CLOSE
DISPOSE_ON_CLOSE
```

The first constant does nothing when the windowClosing() method is executed. You must handle the necessary operations, if any, inside the windowClosing() method yourself. The second constant automatically hides and disposes of the frame after invoking any registered listener objects.

These constants are assigned to a frame by invoking the method setDefaultCloseOperation() and using the constants as argument values. The default constant to which the default close operation is set is HIDE_ON_CLOSE, which simply hides the frame.

JFrame Code Example

Listing 4.1 shows an application that displays a Swing frame. The frame contains a label as its only component. The frame is also registered with a window listener to handle the closing of the frame. The output of the frame is shown Figure 4.2.

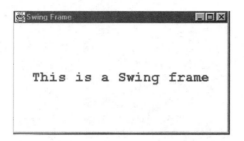

Figure 4.2

A Swing frame (JFrame) with label.

Listing 4.1   JFrame with Label and Window Listener to Handle Closing the Frame (TJFrame.java)

```
// Demonstrates the Swing frames.

import javax.swing.*;
import java.awt.*;
import java.awt.event.*;


class TJFrame extends JFrame {
    Container container = null;

    // 1. Create a Swing frame.
    public TJFrame(String title) {
        super(title);  // set the title for the frame

        // 2. Get the content pane of the frame and
        // configure the frame using its content pane.
        container = this.getContentPane();
        container.setBackground(Color.white);
        container.setForeground(Color.blue);

        // 3. Create a label and add it to the frame.
        JLabel label = new JLabel("This is a Swing frame",
```

continues

Listing 4.1   continued

```
                                    JLabel.CENTER);
        label.setFont(new Font("Sans", Font.PLAIN, 22));
        container.add(label);

        // 4. Add the window listener to close the frame
        // and display it with the specified size.
        addWindowListener(new WindowEventHandler());
        setDefaultCloseOperation(WindowConstants.DISPOSE_ON_CLOSE);
        setSize(350, 200); // width=350, height=200
        show(); // Display the frame
    }

    // 5. The main method.
    public static void main(String[] args) {
        TJFrame frame = new TJFrame("Swing Frame");
    }

    // 6. The listener class to handle closing of the frame.
    class WindowEventHandler extends WindowAdapter {
        public void windowClosing(WindowEvent evt) {
            System.exit(0);
        }
    }
}
```

Code Details

The class TJFrame extends the Swing frame class JFrame. Snippet-1 shows the constructor of the class TJFrame. You can assign a title by calling the constructor of JFrame(title) using super(). Snippet-2 gets a reference to the content pane of the frame. Next it modifies the background and foreground of the frame.

Snippet-3 creates a label object and adds it at the center of the Swing frame by using the content pane. Snippet-4 shows the code to add a window listener to perform the closing of the frame. The snippet also shows the code to resize the frame and display it using the method show(). The other method, setDefaultCloseOperation(), specifies what needs to be done with the frame on closing it. In this case, the frame is disposed of on closing. Snippet-5 shows the main method, and snippet-6 shows the listener class to handle the closing operation of the frame.

Swing Basic Containers

Four new components have been introduced in Swing to deal with the complexities involved in mixing lightweight and heavyweight components in the same container. These new components are the *content pane*, the *layered pane*, the *glass pane*, and an optional *menu bar*. In addition, the *root pane* is a virtual container that contains the content pane, the layered pane, the glass pane, and the menu bar.

Root Pane

Swing containers such as JApplet, JFrame, JWindow, JDialog, and JInternalFrame delegate their duties to the root pane that is represented by the class JRootPane. Note that JInternalFrame is a lightweight container; the others are heavyweight. Because a root pane is made up of a content pane, layered pane, glass pane, and menu bar, contents must be added to one of these root pane members, rather than to the root pane itself. Figure 4.3 depicts how the root pane members are positioned inside the root pane. You can get a reference to the underlying root pane of a container by using the method getRootPane().

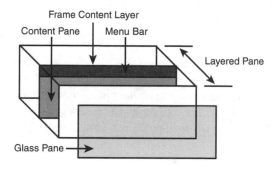

Figure 4.3

The components of the root pane class.

The root pane and its members are all considered to be fundamental in Swing container design. This chapter discusses content panes, glass panes, and layered panes. The implementation of menu bars is discussed in detail in Chapter 13, "Menus, Toolbars, and ToolTips."

NOTE

A root pane cannot have any children. Thus, you should not add any components to a root pane object. Instead, you will add them to the root pane member.

Content Panes

The content pane actually sits on one of the layers of the layered pane. A layered pane contains several layers meant for displaying different Swing components, depending on their overlapping requirements. Figure 4.3 shows the position of the content pane in a layered pane. The content pane is located in a layer specified by the layered pane constant FRAME_CONTENT_LAYER. In fact, the menu bar and the content pane sit on the frame-content layer.

Most Swing components are added to the content pane. You saw how the components were added to a content pane in the previous examples on JFrame and JPanel. The following is typical code used to add a component to a content pane with a specific layout:

```
Container contentPane = swingContainer.getContentPane();
contentPane.setLayout(new SomeLayout());
contentPane.add(new SomeComponent());
```

NOTE

> By default, the content pane is set to the border layout manager.

Glass Panes

The glass pane is a member of the root pane that is used to draw over an area that already contains some components. A glass pane can also be used to catch mouse events because it sits over the top of the content pane and menu bar. Figure 4.3 showed the location of the glass pane in a root pane. Because a glass pane is a member of the root pane, it already exists in a Swing container. However, the glass pane is not visible by default.

NOTE

> You can make a glass pane visible by invoking the method setVisible(true) on a glass pane object. A reference to a glass pane object is obtained by invoking the method getGlassPane() on a container.

Menu Bars

Menu bars are added to the menu bar area, which is a thin rectangular area along the upper edge of the frame content pane layer of the layered pane. The remaining area of this layer is filled with the content pane. Figure 4.3 showed the location of the menu bar in a layered pane. To obtain a reference to the optional menu bar that exists with a Swing frame, you can call the method getJMenuBar() on the container object. For detailed information on creating menu bars, see Chapter 13.

Layered Panes

A layered pane is a container with multiple layers, each of which can be used to add a category of components at different levels of depth (in the third dimension). A component's depth is called its *Z-order positioning*. An object of type Integer specifies the depth at which a component is added. The components at depths specified by higher integers are positioned over the components specified by lower integers. The components positioned in these layers can overlap as required.

A layered pane object is represented by the Swing class JLayeredPane, which extends JComponent, as shown in Figure 4.4. The class is stored in the package javax.swing.

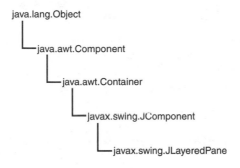

Figure 4.4

The class hierarchy of JLayeredPane.

Layer Details

In addition to using integers to specify the depth of a component, you can use the layer names that are defined by the static constants. There are five convenient layers, defined as follows:

- *Default Layer*—This layer is at the depth specified by the object new Integer(0). The constant DEFAULT_LAYER represents this layer. As the name suggests, this layer is a standard layer to which any component is added by default. The default layer is also the bottommost of the standard layers.
- *Palette Layer*—The palette layer is represented by the constant PALETTE_LAYER and is at the depth specified by the object new Integer(100). This layer is over the top of the default layer. The palette layer is useful to add palettes or floating toolbars. As shown in Chapter 13, the toolbars in Swing can be made floatable.
- *Modal Layer*—The modal layer sits over the top of the palette layer and is represented by the constant MODAL_LAYER. The depth of the modal layer is specified by the depth object new Integer(200). The modal layer is useful to locate dialog boxes that are modal.
- *Pop-up Layer*—The pop-up layer is useful to display pop-ups like menus, ToolTips, and so on that should appear above the component located in the layers discussed previously. The pop-up layer is represented by the constant POPUP_LAYER, which has the depth value new Integer(300).
- *Drag Layer*—The drag layer is represented by the constant DRAG_LAYER, which has the value new Integer(400). When a component is being dragged, reassigning it to the drag layer ensures that it is positioned over every other component. When dragging is finished, the component can be assigned to its original layer.

In addition to these layers, there is a special layer called the frame-content layer to position the content pane and the optional menu bar of the root pane. This layer is specified by the static constant FRAME_CONTENT_LAYER, which has the value new Integer (-30000).

JLayeredPane Code Example

Listing 4.2 shows the program that demonstrates the Swing layered pane. The program is an application with some buttons attached to it. When a button is operated, it adds an internal frame to a specific layer in the layered pane. There is also a Clear button to clear all the internal panes from the main frame. The output of the program is shown in Figure 4.5.

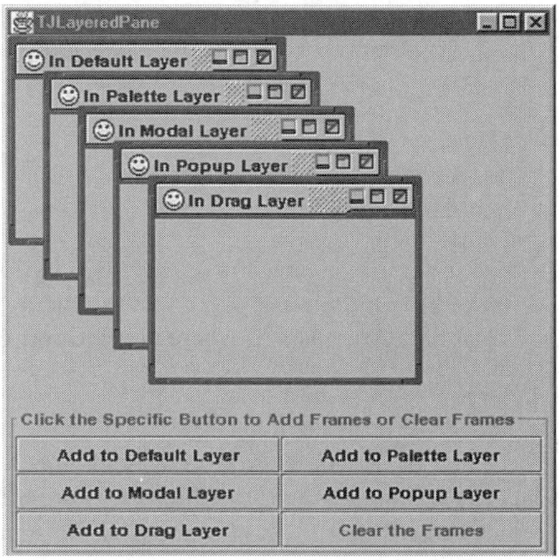

Figure 4.5

Internal frames attached to the Swing layered pane (JLayeredPane).

Listing 4.2   JLayeredPane with Buttons and Internal Frames (TJLayeredPane.java)

```java
// Demonstrates the Swing layered panes.
import javax.swing.*;
import javax.swing.border.*;
import java.awt.*;
import java.awt.event.*;
import java.util.*;

public class TJLayeredPane extends JFrame
                implements ActionListener {
    JButton button;
    JLayeredPane layeredPane;

    static int frameCount = 0;
    static final int xOffSet = 25; // each layer pane x offset
    static final int yOffSet = 25; // each layer pane y offset
```

```java
int numFrames = 1;
// Define arrays for the layered pane constants and their names.
Integer[] layerConstants = { JLayeredPane.DEFAULT_LAYER,
    JLayeredPane.PALETTE_LAYER, JLayeredPane.MODAL_LAYER,
    JLayeredPane.POPUP_LAYER, JLayeredPane.DRAG_LAYER };

String[] layerNames = { "Default Layer", "Palette Layer",
                        "Modal Layer", "Popup Layer",
                        "Drag Layer" };
Vector framesVector = new Vector();


// Constructor.
public TJLayeredPane()    {
    super("TJLayeredPane"); // Assign a title to the frame.
    // 1. Create a panel and assign grid layout with 3 row and 3 columns.
    JPanel panel = new JPanel(new GridLayout(3,3));
    panel.setBorder( // Assign a title border around the panel.
        BorderFactory.createTitledBorder(
            "Click the Specific Button to Add Frames or Clear Frames"));
    // 2. Add the following control buttons to the panel.
    for (int i=0; i<layerNames.length+1; i++) {
        if (i < layerNames.length) {
            button = new JButton("Add to "+layerNames[i] );
            button.setActionCommand(layerNames[i]);
        } else {
            button = new JButton("Clear the Frames");
            button.setActionCommand("Clear");
            button.setForeground(Color.red);
        }
        button.addActionListener(this);
        panel.add(button);
    }
    // 3. Add the panel at the bottom portion of the frame.
    getContentPane().add(panel, BorderLayout.SOUTH);

    // 4. Obtain a handle on the layered pane of the frame.
    layeredPane = getLayeredPane();

    // 5. Code to configure the frame.
    addWindowListener(new WindowEventHandler());
    setDefaultCloseOperation(WindowConstants.DISPOSE_ON_CLOSE);
    setSize(400, 400); // width=400, height=400
    show(); // Display the frame
}


// 6. Whenever a button is clicked.
public void actionPerformed(ActionEvent e) {
    JButton tempButton = (JButton) e.getSource();
```

continues

Listing 4.2   continued

```
        if (tempButton.getActionCommand() == layerNames[0]) { // for default
    ➥layer.
            addInternalFrame(0);
        }
        else if (tempButton.getActionCommand() == layerNames[1]) { // for
    ➥palette layer.
            addInternalFrame(1);
        }
        else if (tempButton.getActionCommand() == layerNames[2]) { // for Modal
    ➥layer.
            addInternalFrame(2);
        }
        else if (tempButton.getActionCommand() == layerNames[3]) { // for pop-
    ➥up layer.
            addInternalFrame(3);
        }
        else if (tempButton.getActionCommand() == layerNames[4]) { // for Drag
    ➥layer.
            addInternalFrame(4);
        }
        else if (tempButton.getActionCommand() == "Clear") {
            //Enumerate the vector elements and dispose all of them.
            for (Enumeration enum = framesVector.elements();
                            enum.hasMoreElements();) {
                ((JInternalFrame) enum.nextElement()).dispose();
            }
            // Set the frame count to zero.
            frameCount = 0;
        }
    }
    // 7. Adds an internal frame to the specified layer.
    public void addInternalFrame(int index) {
        JInternalFrame iFrame = new JInternalFrame(
                    "In " + layerNames[index],
                    true,   // can be resized
                    true,   // can be closed
                    true,   // can be maximized
                    true);  // can be iconified
        // 8. Register the new frame in a vector.
        framesVector.addElement(iFrame);

        // 9. Set the location of the frame.
        iFrame.setLocation(xOffSet*(frameCount),
                        yOffSet*(frameCount++));
        iFrame.setSize(200,150);  // Assign suitable size
        iFrame.setDefaultCloseOperation(iFrame.DO_NOTHING_ON_CLOSE);
        iFrame.setFrameIcon(new ImageIcon("smiley.gif"));
        layeredPane.add(iFrame, layerConstants[index]);
```

```
    }

    // 10. The listener class to handle closing of the frame.
    class WindowEventHandler extends WindowAdapter {
        public void windowClosing(WindowEvent evt) {
            System.exit(0);
        }
    }

    // 11. The main method.
    public static void main(String[] args) {
        TJLayeredPane frame = new TJLayeredPane();
    }
}
```

Code Details

The program TJLayeredPane defines arrays for the layered pane constants and the layer names as data members. Inside the constructor, snippet-1 creates a panel to hold the control buttons to create internal frames and add them to the layered pane layers. Snippet-2 adds the buttons to the panel. The buttons contain the layer names as their labels. When you click a specific button, an internal frame is added to the respective layer. Snippet-3 adds the panel at the bottom portion of the application frame. Snippet-4 obtains a reference to the layered pane associated with the main frame. Snippet-5 shows the code to configure the main frame.

Snippet-6 is the actionPerformed() method, which is invoked whenever a button is clicked. As you can see, when a specific button is clicked, an internal frame is added to the corresponding layer by using the conditional if statement. When you click the Clear button, all the internal frames that have been created are cleared from the main frame.

Snippet-7 shows the actual code to create an internal frame and add it to the specified layer. Snippet-8 registers each new internal frame in a vector. This information is used to clear all internal frames when needed. Snippet-9 defines the location of each frame with the necessary offsets in case an underlying frame exists. Snippet-10 shows the listener class to handle closing the frame. Snippet-11 is the main method that creates the main frame object.

Internal Frames

An internal frame is a container that is similar to the Swing frame, but with one important difference: Internal frames are lightweight. Internal frames support many features like dragging, closing, iconifying, and resizing. They can also possess a title and a menu bar. Internal frames are often used to initiate a new task in a given program. For example, in a word processor, when you begin a new document, it is attached to an internal frame.

An internal frame is represented by the class JInternalFrame, which extends JComponent, as shown in Figure 4.6. The class JInternalFrame is stored in the package javax.swing.

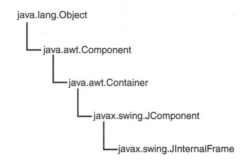

Figure 4.6

The class hierarchy of JInternalFrame.

JInternalFrame Constructors

The following is the list of constructors supported in the class JInternalFrame.

```
public JInternalFrame()
```

creates an object of JInternalFrame without any title. The frame cannot be resized or closed or maximized or iconified.

```
public JInternalFrame(String title)
```

creates an object of JInternalFrame with the specified title. You cannot resize or close, maximize, or iconify the frame.

```
public JInternalFrame(String title,
                      boolean resizable)
```

creates an internal frame with the specified title. You can also specify whether it can be resized or not. However, the frame cannot be closed, maximized, or iconified.

```
public JInternalFrame(String title,
                      boolean resizable,
                      boolean closable)
```

creates an internal frame with the specified title. You can also specify whether it can be resized and closed. However, the frame cannot be maximized or iconified.

```
public JInternalFrame(String title,
                      boolean resizable,
                      boolean closable,
                      boolean maximizable)
```

creates an internal frame with the specified title. You can also control whether it can be resized, closed, or maximized.

```
public JInternalFrame(String title,
                      boolean resizable,
                      boolean closable,
                      boolean maximizable,
                      boolean iconifiable)
```

creates an object of JInternalFrame with the specified title and a control on its resizability, closability, maximizability, and iconifiability.

Desktop Panes

The desktop pane is a special kind of layered pane that is used to create a virtual desktop in Java applications. The main purpose of a desktop pane is to add internal frames. Desktop panes manage the overlapped internal panes to position them in the correct order, depending on the context. Desktop panes also support a desktop manager for the internal frames. You can create a desktop pane object using its only constructor, JDesktopPane().

Desktop Manager

The desktop managers take care of the look-and-feel of the desktop panes and the internal frames. The interface DesktopManager represents the architecture of a desktop manager. The objects of this interface implement code to minimize, maximize, iconify, deiconify, and so on. A desktop pane contains an implementation object of a desktop manager.

Because internal frames are managed by desktop panes, the operations of the desktop manager are exercised on internal frames. The class DefaultDesktopManager is the default implementation of the DesktopManager interface. The default manager object implements the behavior for managing look-and-feel in any of its parents.

Desktop Pane with JInternalFrame Code Example

Listing 4.3 shows an application that creates a Swing frame with a button attached at its lower portion. An internal frame is displayed at the center of the frame. Each time you click the button, the program creates one more internal frame and displays it at the center of the main frame with an offset from the previous frame. The output of the program is shown in Figure 4.7.

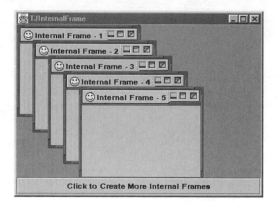

Figure 4.7

A desktop pane displaying internal frames.

*Listing 4.3   JInternalFrame Example—Desktop Pane with Internal Frames
(TJInternalFrame.java)*

```
// Demonstrates the Swing internal frames.

import javax.swing.*;
import java.awt.event.*;
import java.awt.*;

public class TJInternalFrame extends JFrame {
    Container container;
    JButton button;
    JDesktopPane desktop;
    JInternalFrame internalFrame;

    static int frameCount = 1;
    static final int xOffSet = 25;
    static final int yOffSet = 25;

    // 1. Constructor of the frame class.
    public TJInternalFrame() {
        // 2. Give a title to the frame and get its content pane.
        super("TJInternalFrame");
        container = this.getContentPane();

        // 3. Create a button and add it at the lower portion of the
        // frame; also add an action listener.
        button = new JButton("Click to Create More Internal Frames");
        button.addActionListener(new ButtonListener());
        container.add(button, BorderLayout.SOUTH);

        // 4. Create a desktop pane and add an internal frame.
```

```
        desktop = new JDesktopPane(); // holds the internal frame
        container.add(desktop); // add the desktop to the main frame
        createInternalFrame();  // create an internal frame

        // 5. Add the window listener, set the frame size, default close
        // operation and make the frame visible.
        addWindowListener(new WindowEventHandler());
        setDefaultCloseOperation(WindowConstants.DISPOSE_ON_CLOSE);
        setSize(400, 300); // width=400, height=300
        show(); // Display the frame
    }


    // 6. Creates an internal frame and adds it to the desktop pane.
    // Takes care of displaying frames with overlap offsets when called
    // multiple times.
    public void createInternalFrame() {
        // 7. Use a suitable internal frame constructor.
        JInternalFrame iFrame = new JInternalFrame(
                "Internal Frame - " + (frameCount++),
                true,   // can be resized
                true,   // can be closed
                true,   // can be maximized
                true);  // can be iconified

        // 8. Set the location and size, and add it to the desktop pane.
        iFrame.setLocation( xOffSet*(frameCount-2),
                            yOffSet*(frameCount-2));
        iFrame.setSize(200,150);
        desktop.add(iFrame);

        // 9. Let the frame be selected.
        try {
            iFrame.setSelected(true);
        } catch (java.beans.PropertyVetoException ex) {
            System.out.println(
                "Exception while selecting an internal frame");
        }
    }


    // 10. The button (action) listener.
    class ButtonListener implements ActionListener {
        public void actionPerformed(ActionEvent e) {
            createInternalFrame();
        }
    }


    // 11. The listener class to handle closing of the frame.
    class WindowEventHandler extends WindowAdapter {
```

continues

Listing 4.3 continued
```
        public void windowClosing(WindowEvent evt) {
            System.exit(0);
        }
    }

    // 12. The main method.
    public static void main(String[] args) {
        TJInternalFrame frame = new TJInternalFrame();
    }
}
```

Code Details

The program creates a main frame with the title TJInternalFrame. Snippet-1 shows the constructor of the main frame, and snippet-2 sets a title for the frame and gets a handle to its content pane. Snippet-3 creates a button and adds it at the lower portion of the frame. An action listener is also registered with the button.

Snippet-4 creates a desktop pane to add the internal frames. The internal frames are created by the createInternalFrame() method. Snippet-5 adds a window listener to close the frame, configures the main frame by setting its size and default close operation, and makes the frame visible.

Snippets 6–9 show the code to create an internal frame and add it to the desktop pane. The frame is attached at the specified location. Each time the method createInternalFrame() is called, a new frame is created and added to the desktop pane with an offset. The method also selects the new internal frame that has been created. Notice that the method setSelected() throws the exception called PropertyVetoException, so you need to enclose the method in a try...catch statement.

Snippet-10 is the code for the button listener that invokes the method createInternalFrame(). Snippet-11 is the window listener to close the main frame, and snippet-12 shows the main method.

Panels

A panel is a Swing container (a component extension of JComponent) that is often used for grouping components within one area of an applet or a frame. A panel can also be used to group other panels.

Swing panels also support *double buffering*, a technique that helps avoid flickering in animation. If a panel is double buffered before an object is displayed, the object is written to an off-screen memory and then flipped over quickly to the panel. This is a very efficient technique for processing-intensive displays.

Swing panels are represented by the class JPanel, which is stored in the package javax.swing. The class hierarchy of the JPanel class is shown in Figure 4.8. Note that JPanel is a lightweight container.

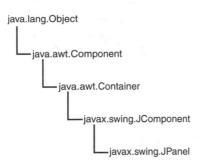

java.lang.Object

java.awt.Component

java.awt.Container

javax.swing.JComponent

javax.swing.JPanel

Figure 4.8

Class hierarchy of the Swing panel class JPanel.

JPanel Constructors

The objects of the Swing panels can be created by using any one of the four constructors given in the class JPanel. The constructors give the provision to control the double-buffering as well as the layout. Following is the list of constructors:

```
public JPanel()
```

creates a double-buffered panel with flow layout.

```
public JPanel(boolean isDoubleBuffered)
```

creates a panel set to flow layout; however, you have an option to control the double buffering by passing the argument value true for having the double buffering or false for not setting the double buffering.

```
public JPanel(LayoutManager layout)
```

creates a double-buffered panel that allows you to assign the layout of interest.

```
public JPanel(LayoutManager layout, boolean isDoubleBuffered)
```

creates a panel with the specified layout. You can also control the double buffering by passing the value true or false.

JPanel Code Example

Listing 4.4 shows an applet that uses four panels to display some labels (see Figure 4.9). Each of the panels is set to the grid layout and is double buffered by default. Note the use of panels to group the components, which is explained in the code comments.

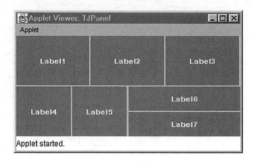

Figure 4.9

An applet displaying the Swing panel.

Listing 4.4   JPanel Used to Create Four Panels with Labels (TJPanel.java)

```
// Demonstrates the Swing panels.

/*
 * <Applet code=TJPanel width=400 height=200>
 *</Applet>
 */

import javax.swing.*;
import java.awt.*;

public class TJPanel extends JApplet {
    Container container = null;

    public void init() {
        // 1. Get a reference to the applet's content pane and
        // assigns a grid layout.
        container = getContentPane();
        container.setLayout(new GridLayout(2,1,2,2));

        // 2. Create four panels with grid layout and specified number
        // of rows and columns. The first two numbers in the
        // GridLayout constructors are the number of rows and columns
        // The next two numbers represent the horizontal and vertical
        // spacing between the components.
        JPanel panel1 = new JPanel(new GridLayout(1,3,2,2));
        JPanel panel2 = new JPanel(new GridLayout(1,2,2,2));
        JPanel panel3 = new JPanel(new GridLayout(2,1,2,2));
        JPanel panel4 = new JPanel(new GridLayout(1,2,2,2));

        // 3. Prepare panel1 with labels 1, 2, and 3.
        setLabel(panel1, "Label1");
        setLabel(panel1, "Label2");
```

```
        setLabel(panel1, "Label3");

        // 4. Prepare panel2 with labels 4 and 5.
        setLabel(panel2, "Label4");
        setLabel(panel2, "Label5");

        // 5. Prepare panel3 with labels 6 and 7.
        setLabel(panel3, "Label6");
        setLabel(panel3, "Label7");

        // 6. Add panel2 and panel3 to panel4.
        panel4.add(panel2);
        panel4.add(panel3);

        // 7. Finally, add panel1 and panel4 to the content pane.
        container.add(panel1);
        container.add(panel4);

    }

    // 8. Supporting method to create and attach a label.
    public void setLabel(Container panel, String text) {
        JLabel label = new JLabel(text, JLabel.CENTER);
        label.setOpaque(true);
        label.setForeground(Color.white);
        label.setBackground(Color.gray);
        panel.add(label);
    }
}
```

Code Details

Snippet-1 gets a reference to the applet's content pane and assigns a grid layout to the applet. Snippet-2 creates four panels; each panel is assigned the grid layout, which has a specified number of rows and columns.

Snippets 3–5 prepare the panels with the prescribed labels. The helping method setLabel() performs this operation as shown in snippet-8. Snippet-6 adds panel2 and panel3 to panel4. Snippet-7 adds panel1 and panel4 to the content pane of the applet.

Split Panes

A split pane is a lightweight Swing container that graphically separates the components that are positioned in it. Split panes can contain *only two* components. Each of the component display areas can be adjusted interactively by the application user. To display the separation of more than two components, you need to nest split panes and components.

Swing split panes are represented by the class `JSplitPane`, which extends `JComponent` as shown in Figure 4.10. The class is stored in the package `javax.swing`.

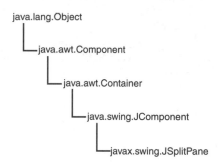

Figure 4.10

The class hierarchy of JSplitPane.

Split panes are of two types: split panes for a horizontal split and those for a vertical split. A horizontal split pane contains a divider that separates two components horizontally. That is, the components are positioned side by side with an adjustable divider between them. The divider can be moved in the horizontal direction. You can specify a split pane object for the horizontal split by using the static integer constant `HORIZONTAL_SPLIT`.

A split pane that supports the vertical split of components contains the components positioned vertically (one over the other). The divider is adjustable in the vertical direction. You can specify a split pane object for the vertical split by using the static integer constant `VERTICAL_SPLIT`.

JSplitPane Constructors

The class `JSplitPane` supports five constructors. Each of the constructors allows the specification of different properties of the split pane object. You can specify the orientation of the split, child components to be added, and whether the resizing of the child component is continuous or not. The following is the list of constructors:

```
public JSplitPane()
```

creates an object that is configured to arrange the child components side by side horizontally with no continuous layout, using two buttons for the components.

```
public JSplitPane(int newOrientation)
```

creates an object that is configured with the specified orientation and no continuous layout. The argument `newOrientation` takes one of the following values:

```
static int HORIZONTAL_SPLIT
static int VERTICAL_SPLIT

public JSplitPane(int newOrientation,
                  boolean newContinuousLayout)
```

creates a new JSplitPane object with the specified orientation and the resizing style of the child components. The first argument is similar to the one in the previous constructor. The second argument specifies whether the child components should be resizable continuously (true) or not (false) while the divider changes position.

```
public JSplitPane(int newOrientation,
                  Component newLeftComponent,
                  Component newRightComponent)
```

creates a new object with the specified orientation and with the specified components. The child components do not perform continuous redrawing.

```
public JSplitPane(int newOrientation,
                  boolean newContinuousLayout,
                  Component newLeftComponent,
                  Component newRightComponent)
```

creates a new object of JSplitPane with the specified orientation and resizing type of child components and with the specified child components.

Continuous Layout Property

As the divider of a horizontal or vertical split pane is adjusted, child components can either be resized continuously for every positional change of the divider before it stops at the final position or be resized on stopping at the final position. This is called continuous layout property.

The continuous layout property can be turned on or off. The child component can be resized by passing the value true for the boolean argument of the method setContinuousLayout(). If the boolean value is set to false, the resizing of the child component takes place only when the divider is left at its final position after adjusting it.

JSplitPane (Horizontal and Vertical) Code Example

Listing 4.5 shows an applet that uses two split panes (one horizontal and the other vertical) nested to display three pictures. Two split panes are needed due to the restriction that a split pane can contain only two components. You can adjust the divider to change the sizes of the pictures. The output of the program is shown in Figure 4.11.

Figure 4.11

A Swing applet displaying pictures in a split pane.

*Listing 4.5   JSplitPane with One Horizontal and One Vertical Split Pane
(TJSplitPane.java)*

```
/*
 * <Applet code=TJSplitPane width=400 height=300>
 * </Applet>
 */

import javax.swing.*;
import java.awt.*;

public class TJSplitPane extends JApplet {
    static int HORIZSPLIT = JSplitPane.HORIZONTAL_SPLIT;
    static int VERTSPLIT = JSplitPane.VERTICAL_SPLIT;
    boolean continuousLayout = true;
    Icon icon1 = new ImageIcon("saravan2.gif");
    Icon icon2 = new ImageIcon("saravan3.gif");
    Icon icon3 = new ImageIcon("ISaravan.gif");

    public void init() {
        // 1. Create a label to display icon1 and add it to a scroll pane.
        JLabel label1 = new JLabel(icon1);
        JScrollPane topLeftComp = new JScrollPane(label1);

        // 2. Create another lable to display icon2 and add it to another
        ➥scroll pane.
        JLabel label2 = new JLabel(icon2);
        JScrollPane bottomLeftComp = new JScrollPane(label2);
```

```
// 3. Create a third label to display icon3 and add it to one more
➥scroll pane.
JLabel label3 = new JLabel(icon3);
JScrollPane rightComp = new JScrollPane(label3);

// 4. Add the scroll panes displaying icon1 and icon2 to a split pane.
JSplitPane splitPane1 = new JSplitPane(VERTSPLIT,
                                       continuousLayout,
                                       topLeftComp,
                                       bottomLeftComp);
splitPane1.setOneTouchExpandable(true); // Provide a collapse/expand
➥widget.
splitPane1.setDividerSize(2); // Divider size.
splitPane1.setDividerLocation(0.5); // Initial location of the divider.

// 5. Add the previous split pane and the scroll pane displaying
// icon3 to an outer split pane.
JSplitPane splitPane2 = new JSplitPane(HORIZSPLIT,
                                       splitPane1, // left comp
                                       rightComp);
splitPane2.setOneTouchExpandable(true); // Provide a collapse/expand
➥widget.
splitPane2.setDividerLocation(0.4); // divider size
splitPane2.setDividerSize(2); // Initial location of the divider.

// 6. Add the outer split pane to the content pane of the applet.
getContentPane().add(splitPane2);
    }
}
```

Code Details

Inside the init() method of the applet, snippet-1 creates a label object to display icon1 and adds it to a scroll pane. Snippets 2 and 3 also create labels to display the respective icons icon2 and icon3 and add them to separate scroll panes.

Snippet-4 adds the scroll panes displaying icon1 and icon2 to a split pane. Snippet-5 adds the split pane and the scroll pane displaying icon3 to another split pane. The latter split pane is added to the content pane of the applet.

Tabbed Panes

A tabbed pane displays a component from a group of components when one of the pane's tabs is selected. The extended portion of the tab, where the selection is made, can have a title, an icon, or both. The tabbed pane helps to save space by displaying each component from a group of multiple components.

The Swing tabbed pane is represented by the class JTabbedPane, which extends JComponent. The class JTabbedPane implements the interfaces Serializable, Accessible and SwingConstants.

JTabbedPane Constructor

The following is the list of constructors supported in the class JTabbedPane:

```
public JTabbedPane()
```

creates an empty tabbed pane. You can add tabs to the tabbed pane by using the method addTab(), which takes one of the tab position constants. See the next constructor for these constants.

```
public JTabbedPane(int tabPlacement)
```

creates an empty TabbedPane with the specified tab placement. The tab placement argument takes one of the values TOP, BOTTOM, LEFT, and RIGHT.

Change Events and Listener

Note that the tabs begin with the index equal to 0 and the *n*-th tab equal to (*n*-1). The tabbed pane object can fire events of type ChangeEvent whenever the selection state has been changed. These events need to be captured by a suitable listener that implements the interface ChangeListener. The code to be executed is enclosed in the method stateChanged().

JTabbedPane Code Example

Listing 4.6 demonstrates how to implement a tabbed pane. The tabbed pane is used to display three aircraft pictures in different maneuvers. You can click the label of a tab to see the corresponding picture. Note how a tabbed pane saves space by displaying the pictures one after the other when the tabs are clicked with the mouse. The output of the program is shown in Figure 4.12.

Figure 4.12

A Swing applet using a tabbed pane (JTabbedPane).

Listing 4.6   JTabbedPane with Three Tabs (TJTabbedPane.java)
```java
// Demonstrates how to implement a tabbed pane.

/*
 * <Applet code=TJTabbedPane width=400 height=300>
 * </Applet>
 */

import javax.swing.*;
import javax.swing.event.*;
import java.awt.*;

public class TJTabbedPane extends JApplet {
    JTabbedPane tabbedPane;
    String[] aircraft = {"Aircraft1.jpg",
                         "Aircraft2.jpg",
                         "Aircraft3.jpg"};
    String[] tips = {"Cruise", "Banking", "Take-off"};

    public void init() {
        // 1. Create a tabbed pane object.
        tabbedPane = new JTabbedPane(JTabbedPane.BOTTOM);
        tabbedPane.addChangeListener(new TabbedPaneListener());

        // 2. Add tabs to the tabbed pane. Each tab displays
        // an aircraft.
        for (int i=0; i<aircraft.length; i++) {
           JLabel label = new JLabel(new ImageIcon(aircraft[i]));
           tabbedPane.addTab("Aircraft-"+(i+1), // Tab text
                             new ImageIcon("smiley.gif"), // Tab icon
                             label,  // component to be displayed
                             tips[i]); // Some tip at the tab
        }

        // 3. Add the tabbed pane to the applet.
        getContentPane().add(tabbedPane);
    }

    // 4. Tabbed Pane listener class.
    class TabbedPaneListener implements ChangeListener {
        int selectedIndex = -1; // -1 = default number less than 0
        JTabbedPane tp;

        public void stateChanged(ChangeEvent ce) {
            tp = (JTabbedPane) ce.getSource();

            // 5. Code to disable a tab that has been selected, and
            // enable the tab that has already been disabled.
```

continues

Listing 4.6   continued

```
            if (selectedIndex == -1 || // if pressed for first time
                selectedIndex != tp.getSelectedIndex()) {
                tp.setEnabledAt(tp.getSelectedIndex(), false);
                if (selectedIndex != -1) // if not the first press
                    tp.setEnabledAt(selectedIndex, true);
            }
            // Store the index of the newly selected tab.
            selectedIndex = tp.getSelectedIndex();
        }
    }
}
```

Code Details

The aircraft pictures and the names of the corresponding maneuvers have been defined
as arrays of strings that are the data members of the applet. Inside the init() method,
snippet-1 creates a tabbed pane. The argument value of the constructor specifies that
the tabs should be at the bottom portion of the tabbed pane. The tabbed pane has also
been registered by a change listener. The change listener contains the code to be
invoked whenever the state of the tab selection is changed.

Snippet-2 creates the labels displaying the aircraft and adds them to different tabs of
the tabbed pane by using the method addTab(). This method takes four arguments: the
text to be shown on the tab, the icon to be displayed on the tab, the component (label)
to be attached at the center of the pane of the tab, and a suitable text tip.

Snippet-3 shows the code to add the tabbed pane to the applet. Snippet-4 is the code
for the change listener. The listener class implements the interface ChangeListener
and encloses the functionality to be executed inside the stateChanged() method.

NOTE

You do not have to handle any events to change over to a new tab by clicking the
tab label.

However, if you wish to execute any functionality when you click a tab, the objects
of ChangeListener can be used. For example, the code implemented inside the
stateChanged() method disables the tab that has been selected and enables the
tab that has been previously disabled. Snippet-5 essentially shows this
functionality.

CHAPTER 5

Layout Managers

A layout is an arrangement of user interface components within a container such as an applet or a frame. To position components according to a specified layout, the Swing tool set primarily depends on the layout classes provided by the earlier Abstract Window Toolkit (AWT). The AWT supports the core technology for layout managers to control the position of each component according to the given layout.

There are five AWT layout managers: flow layout, grid layout, border layout, card layout, and grid bag layout. There are four Swing layout managers. The box layout is the most important and can save you time if you're not familiar with the AWT grid bag layout. The other Swing layout managers are overlay layout, scroll pane layout, and view port layout. These layouts are used by the Swing components; you do not deal with them directly.

This chapter begins with information on how to create a layout manager and assign it to a container such as an applet or a frame, followed by sections on each layout manager. Each of the AWT and Swing layout managers is discussed in detail with suitable demonstration examples. This chapter contains material from the AWT because Swing components are laid out according to the layouts supported in AWT.

Layout Managers

The Abstract Window Toolkit (AWT) supports five classes to deal with different layout scenarios: FlowLayout, GridLayout, BorderLayout, CardLayout, and GridBagLayout. All these classes implement the interface java.awt.LayoutManager and are referred to as layout managers. By using any one of these layout managers, a program can control the arrangement and sizes of components to preserve the appearance of a user interface.

The flow layout and grid layout managers support simple layouts. Use the flow layout to display components in rows at their natural sizes and wrap to the next row at the edge of the container. Alternatively, the grid layout is the suitable manager to display components in rows and/or columns of the same size.

The border layout and card layout managers are meant for more sophisticated programming work. The border layout positions the components based on geographical directions such as north, south, east, west, and center of the container. The card layout positions the components on multiple cards overlapping one another with only one card visible at any point in time.

The grid bag layout is the most sophisticated and versatile of the AWT layout managers. It is somewhat complex to learn, however, and requires some sense of geometry to grasp the underlying idea. You can achieve almost any layout pattern by using the grid bag.

In addition to these layout managers, the Swing tool set provides a box layout, overlay layout, scroll pane layout, and view port layout. The box layout is important because you can use it to create the same layouts generated by the grid bag layout; you can use the box layout in place of the grid bag layout. The other Swing layouts are of less interest here because they are only used by the Swing components themselves; you do not actually need them while building applications.

Assigning a Layout Manager

After a specific layout manager object has been created, you need to assign it to a container so the components can be added to the container according to the layout pattern. The class `Container` (in the package `java.awt`) provides the following two methods to assign a layout manager or to retrieve the layout object that has already been assigned:

```
public void setLayout(LayoutManager layoutObject)
public void LayoutManager getLayout()
```

NOTE

While assigning a layout manager to a Swing applet or frame, you need to assign the layout object to the content pane of the applet or frame rather than directly assigning it to the applet or frame objects.

Laying Out Components

Once a layout manager has been assigned to a container, the components are positioned by using one of the following methods from the class `Container`:

```
public void add(Component comp)
public void add(Component comp,Object constraints)
public void add(Component comp, int index)
public void add(Component comp,Object constraints, int index)
```

In these methods the argument comp is the component to be positioned in the container. The argument constraints is an object that imposes constraints on a component while using specific layout managers such as grid bag layout. The argument index specifies the order in which a component is added to a container. If no index has been specified, the component will be added at the bottom of the stacking list.

You can also remove components from a container by using the following methods that require some of the arguments shown previously.

```
public void remove(int index)
public void remove(Component comp)
public void removeAll()
```

In these methods, removeAll() removes all the components from the container on which it has been invoked.

NOTE

Just as the layout managers are assigned to the content pane of a Swing applet or frame, the components are also added to or removed from the content pane.

Flow Layout Manager

The flow layout manager supports a layout where components are arranged in a row in their natural or preferred sizes. If the arrangement of components won't fit in a single row, the flow layout manager wraps the components to the next row. The procedure continues from top to bottom until all components are placed inside the container. The components can also be specified to be left aligned, right aligned, or centered. By default, components are centered in each row.

FlowLayout Constructors

To create a flow layout manager, any one of the following three constructors can be used:

```
public FlowLayout()
public FlowLayout(int alignment)
public FlowLayout(int alignment,
                  int horizGap,int vertGap)
```

The alignment argument takes one of the three values shown in the following:

```
FlowLayout.LEFT = 0
FlowLayout.CENTER = 1
FlowLayout.RIGHT = 2
```

The horizGap and vertGap arguments are the horizontal and vertical gaps specified in terms of the number of pixels. The horizontal gap is the gap between two adjacent components in a row, and the vertical gap is the gap between components in two adjacent rows. The default value of both arguments is 5 pixels.

Flow Layout Code Example

Listing 5.1 contains a Swing applet that demonstrates how the flow layout manages components. The program creates some buttons and adds them to the applet (see Figure 5.1).

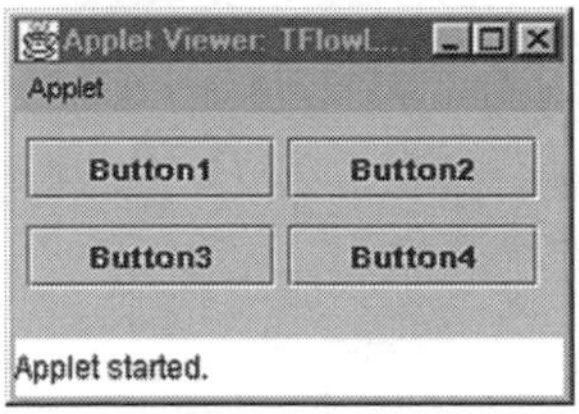

Figure 5.1

A Swing applet demonstrating FlowLayout.

Listing 5.1   FlowLayout (TFlowLayout.java)

```
/*
 * <Applet code=TFlowLayout width=300 height=100>
 * </Applet>
 */

import javax.swing.*;
import java.awt.*;

public class TFlowLayout extends JApplet {
    Container container = null;

    public void init() {
        // 1. Get the handle on applet's content pane.
        container = this.getContentPane();

        // 2. Create the flow layout object and set it for the applet.
        FlowLayout fl = new FlowLayout(FlowLayout.LEFT, 5, 10);
                // horizontal gap = 5 pixels, vertical gap = 10 pixels

        container.setLayout(fl);

        // 3. Create and add some buttons to the applet.
        for (int i=0; i<4; i++) {
            JButton button = new JButton("Button"+(i+1));
            button.setPreferredSize(new Dimension(100,25)); // width=100,
height=25
            container.add(button);
        }
    }
}
```

Code Details

Snippet-1 gets a handle on the applet's content pane. In snippet-2, the applet's content pane is set to the flow layout by using the created flow layout manager object. Snippet-3 is a control loop where the buttons are added to the applet. Notice that the buttons' preferred sizes are changed to accommodate wider labels because the buttons do not fill any extra space.

Notice that the flow layout manager wraps Button3 and Button4 into the next row because it cannot arrange them in the first row with their preferred sizes. However, if you resize the applet as shown in Figure 5.2, you can arrange the buttons in the second row in the first row. The applet also shows the components being left aligned with a 5-pixel horizontal gap and a 10-pixel vertical gap.

NOTE

The flow layout manager tries to place the components in a single row when possible. The appearance of the component layout is subject to change whenever the applet is resized.

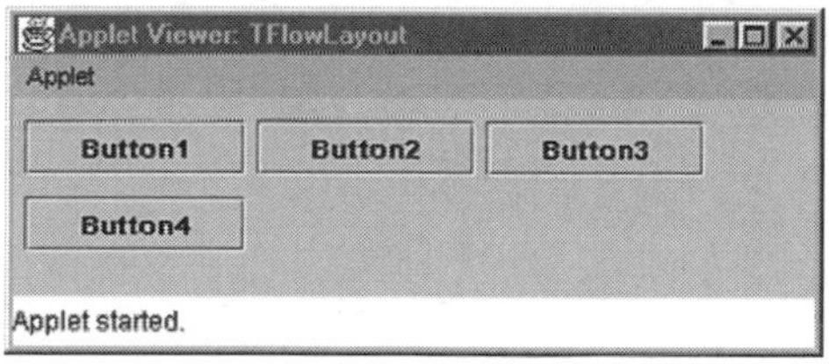

Figure 5.2

The flow layout applet when it has been resized.

Grid Layout Manager

The grid layout manager places the components inside the spaces of a grid pattern attached to the container. All spaces of the grid are of the same size, and the number of grid spaces is decided by specifying the rows and columns of the grid. For example, a grid with two rows and three columns will generate six equal-sized spaces that can take six components. Each user interface component is positioned to fill each of the grid spaces.

The appearance of the layout remains the same even if the container has been resized; the components will also be resized to fill the grid spaces. Any extra gaps between components can be introduced while setting the layout.

GridLayout Constructors

To create an object of type GridLayout, you can use one of the following constructors:

```
public GridLayout(int rows, int columns)
public GridLayout(int rows, int columns,
                  int horizGap, int vertGap)
```

The arguments `rows` and `columns` specify the number of rows and columns to create the grids. At least one of the two arguments must be non-zero. Either a `row` or a column argument specified as zero indicates that any number of components can be arranged in a row or a column. The arguments `horizGap` and `vertGap` specify the respective gaps between grid spaces in number of pixels.

GridLayout Code Example

Listing 5.2 demonstrates the effect of the grid layout manager. The program creates an applet that uses the grid layout manager to form six cells (as three rows and two columns). A Swing button is positioned inside each of the grid cells. Notice that each button fills the entire grid space available (see Figure 5.3).

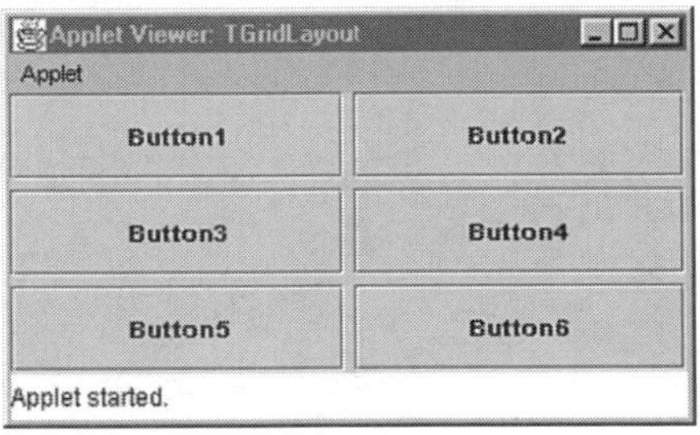

Figure 5.3

The swing applet demonstrating GridLayout.

Listing 5.2   GridLayout (TGridLayout.java)

```
/*
 * <Applet code=TGridLayout width=350 height=150>
 * </Applet>
 */

import javax.swing.*;
import java.awt.*;

public class TGridLayout extends JApplet {
    Container container = null;

    public void init() {
        // 1. Get a handle on the applet's content pane.
        container = this.getContentPane();

        // 2. Assign the grid layout to the content pane.
```

```
GridLayout grid = new GridLayout(3,2, 5,5);
    // rows = 3, cols = 2, horizontal gap =5, vertical gap = 5
container.setLayout(grid);

    // 3. Create and add components to the content pane.
    for (int i=0; i<6; i++)
        container.add(new JButton("Button"+(i+1)));
    }
}
```

Snippet-1 gets a handle on the applet's content pane. Snippet-2 creates an object of type TGridLayout. The constructor takes four argument values: the number of rows and columns and the vertical and horizontal gaps.

Snippet-3 adds the Swing buttons to the resulting six grid spaces. Try resizing the applet and notice that the extra space created is simply filled up by the components.

Border Layout Manager

The border layout manager manages the arrangement of components in a pattern similar to the geographical locations indicated by north, south, east, west, and center. The components fill the respective locations in their natural or preferred sizes with or without gaps. By default, the content pane objects of the Swing applets and frames use the border layout.

The appearance of the layout doesn't change even if the container has been resized. The north and south components can be stretched horizontally, but the preferred height in the vertical direction cannot be altered. Similarly, the east and west components can be stretched vertically, but the preferred width of the components cannot be changed. The component at the center location fills the space available in both horizontal and vertical directions.

BorderLayout Constructors

An instance of the class BorderLayout can be created using any one of the following constructors:

```
public BorderLayout()
public BorderLayout( int horizGap, int vertGap)
```

The horizGap and vertGap arguments specify the horizontal and vertical gaps between components laid out in a container.

Any container that uses the border layout manager requires use of the two-argument method add(Component comp, Object location) from the class java.awt.container to add components.

BorderLayout Code Example

Listing 5.3 demonstrates the border layout by using a Swing applet. By default, the content pane of the Swing applet is already set to the border layout, so you need not explicitly set it to the border layout. The program simply adds some Swing buttons to the applet (see Figure 5.4).

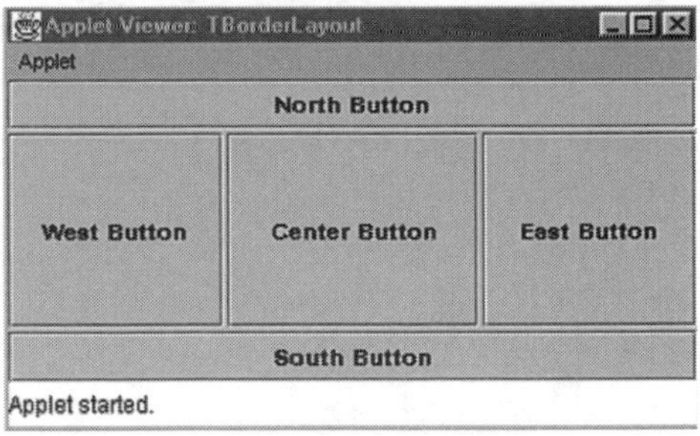

Figure 5.4

The Swing applet using the border layout manager.

Listing 5.3   Border Layout Manager (TBorderLayout.java)

```
/*
<Applet code = TBorderLayout width = 400 height = 250>
</Applet>
*/

import java.awt.*;
import javax.swing.*;

public class TBorderLayout extends JApplet {
    Container container = null;

    public void init() {
        //1. Get a handle on the applet's content pane.
        container = this.getContentPane();
        // container.setLayout(new BorderLayout());
        /* Note: Don't have to explicitly set border layout,
           because the content pane uses border layout
           by default */

        // 2. Give some horizontal and vertical gaps between buttons.
        ((BorderLayout) container.getLayout()).setHgap(2);
        ((BorderLayout) container.getLayout()).setVgap(2);

        // 3. Array that contains border layout constants.
        String[] borderConsts = { BorderLayout.NORTH,
                                  BorderLayout.SOUTH,
                                  BorderLayout.EAST,
                                  BorderLayout.WEST,
                                  BorderLayout.CENTER };
```

```
// 4. Array that contains button names.
String[] buttonNames = { "North Button", "South Button",
                         "East Button", "West Button",
                         "Center Button" };

// 5. Create and add buttons to the container.
for (int i=0; i<borderConsts.length; i++) {
   JButton button = new JButton(buttonNames[i]);

   // You may wish to reset the preferred size of the east
   // and west buttons to display wide labels.
   if (buttonNames[i] == "East Button" ||
       buttonNames[i] == "West Button") {
       button.setPreferredSize(new Dimension(115, 25));
       // width=115, height=25
   }
   container.add(button, borderConsts[i]);
}
}
}
```

Code Details

Snippet-1 gets a handle on the applet's content pane. Because the default layout of the content pane is border layout, you do not have to set it again. Snippet-2 provides some breathing space between components. The method getLayout() returns the layout object that must be cast to the border layout. The other methods, setHgap() and setVgap(), create the horizontal and vertical gaps between the buttons.

Snippets 3 and 4 create two arrays that contain the border layout constants and button names, respectively. Snippet-5 uses this information to create the Swing buttons and adds them to the content pane of the applet. Note that you may have to change the preferred sizes of the east and west buttons to accommodate wide labels.

Card Layout Manager

The CardLayout class supports the layout management of various GUI components on separate cards that are placed one over the other and share the same display area. You can view only one card at a time—the card displayed on the top. Other cards can be brought to display by implementing the methods from the CardLayout class.

CardLayout Constructors

An instance of CardLayout can be created by using one of the following constructors:

```
public CardLayout()
public CardLayout(int horizGap, int vertGap)
```

The second constructor creates a layout with the horizontal and vertical gaps specified by horizGap and vertGap. The horizontal gaps are placed at the left and right edges, and the vertical gaps are placed at the top and bottom edges of the container.

Flipping the Cards

The card layout associates panels, and components are usually grouped inside the panels. The following methods support the flipping of cards to the first and last cards of the container:

```
public void first(Container target)
public void last(Container target)
```

The following are the other methods that allow flipping to the next or previous card from the one that is being displayed:

```
public void next(Container target)
public void previous(Container target)
```

A card can also be displayed by specifying a name tag. If there is no card with such a name tag, no effect is produced. The following is a method from the class CardLayout to display a card by using a name tag:

```
public void show(Container target, String name)
```

In all these methods, the target is the container in which the layout is set.

CardLayout Code Example

Listing 5.4 creates an applet that displays two cards. Each card contains buttons that connect to a Web site. The buttons on the first card connect to JavaSoft, Sun, IBM, and Netscape. The buttons on the second card connect to several aerospace organizations. You can implement these buttons as an exercise. You can also flip between the cards by using the Next and Previous buttons (see Figure 5.5).

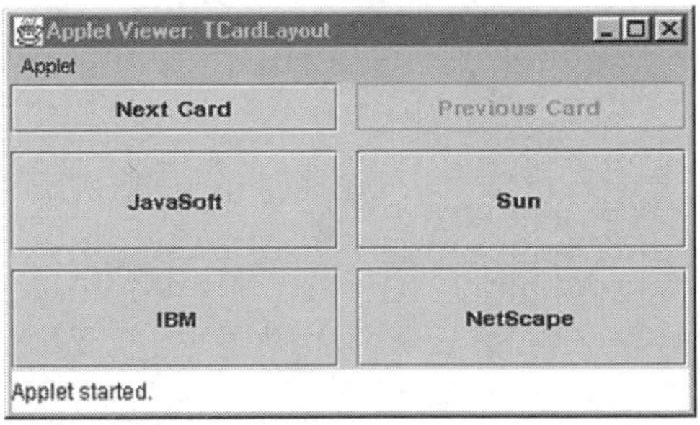

Figure 5.5

An applet that demonstrates the card layout manager.

Listing 5.4   CardLayout (TCardLayout.java)

```
/*
 * <Applet code=TCardLayout width=400 height=200>
 * </Applet>
 */

import javax.swing.*;
import java.awt.*;
import java.awt.event.*;
import java.net.*;

public class TCardLayout extends JApplet {
    // 1. Declare some panel and button references.
    JPanel controlPanel;
    JPanel cardsPanel, swCompPanel, aeroCompPanel;
    JButton nextButton, previousButton;
    JButton javasoftButton, sunButton,
            ibmButton, netscapeButton;
    JButton nasaButton, boeingButton,
            lockheedButton, northropButton;
    URL currentSite = null;

    // 2. Define the string arrays for the sites and site urls.
    String[] swCompSites = {"JavaSoft", "Sun",
                            "IBM", "NetScape"};
    String[] aeroCompSites = {"NASA", "Boeing",
                              "Lockheed", "Northrop"};
    String[] siteURLs = { "http://www.javasoft.com/",
                          "http://www.sun.com/",
                          "http://www.ibm.com/",
                          "http://www.netscape.com/" };

    Container container = null;

    public void init() {
        // 3. Get a handle on the applet's content pane.
        container = this.getContentPane();

        // 4. Create a control panel object.
        controlPanel = new JPanel();
        controlPanel.setLayout(new GridLayout(1,2,10,10));

        // 5. Create and add the next and previous control buttons.
        ButtonListener listener = new ButtonListener();
        nextButton = new JButton("Next Card");
        nextButton.setActionCommand("Next Button");
        nextButton.addActionListener(listener);
        controlPanel.add(nextButton);
```

continues

Listing 5.4   continued

```
    previousButton = new JButton("Previous Card");
    previousButton.setEnabled(false);
    previousButton.setActionCommand("Previous Button");
    previousButton.addActionListener(listener);
    controlPanel.add(previousButton);

    // 6. Create a panel to contain the cards.
    /* Each card will display a set of buttons to
       visit a specific Web site. */
    cardsPanel = new JPanel();
    cardsPanel.setLayout(new CardLayout());
    swCompPanel = new JPanel();
    aeroCompPanel = new JPanel();
    swCompPanel.setLayout(new GridLayout(2,2,10,10));
    aeroCompPanel.setLayout(new GridLayout(2,2,10,10));

    // 7. Add buttons to the these cards.
    for (int i=0; i<swCompSites.length; i++) {
        JButton b = new JButton(swCompSites[i]);
        b.addActionListener(listener);
        b.setActionCommand(swCompSites[i]);
        swCompPanel.add(b);
    }

    for (int i=0; i<aeroCompSites.length; i++) {
        JButton b = new JButton(aeroCompSites[i]);
        b.addActionListener(listener);
        b.setActionCommand(aeroCompSites[i]);
        aeroCompPanel.add(b);
    }

    // 8. Add the company-list panels to cards panel.
    cardsPanel.add("Next Card", swCompPanel);
    cardsPanel.add("Previous Card", aeroCompPanel);

    // 9. Finally, add the control and the cards panels to
    // the applet's content pane.
    ((BorderLayout)container.getLayout()).setVgap(10);
    container.add("North", controlPanel);
    container.add("Center", cardsPanel);
}

// 10. Functionality to be executed when the next-button
// is activated.
public void showNextCard() {
    nextButton.setEnabled(false);
    ((CardLayout) cardsPanel.getLayout()).next(cardsPanel);
    previousButton.setEnabled(true);
}
```

```
// 11. Functionality to be executed when the previous-button
// is activated.
public void showPreviousCard() {
   previousButton.setEnabled(false);
   ((CardLayout) cardsPanel.getLayout()).previous(cardsPanel);
   nextButton.setEnabled(true);
}

// 12. Functionality to display the specific Web page.
public void toDestination(String aSite) {
   System.out.println("Connecting to the web site...");
   try {
       currentSite = new URL(aSite);
   }
   catch (MalformedURLException e) {
      System.out.println("Unknown URL Address: " + aSite);
   }
   getAppletContext().showDocument(currentSite);
}

// 13. The action listener class.
class ButtonListener implements ActionListener {
    public void actionPerformed(ActionEvent ae) {
        JButton tempButton = (JButton) ae.getSource();

        // 14. If the next or previous buttons are pressed...
        if (tempButton.getActionCommand() == "Next Button") {
            showNextCard();
        }
        else if (tempButton.getActionCommand() == "Previous Button") {
            showPreviousCard();
        }

        // 15. If the Web site buttons are pressed...
        for (int i=0; i<swCompSites.length; i++) {
            if (tempButton.getActionCommand() == swCompSites[i])
                toDestination(siteURLs[i]);
        }
    }
}
}
```

Code Details

Snippet-1 shows the declaration of some object references as data members of the applet. The control panel will contain the Next and Previous buttons to flip between the card layout panels. The card's panel will contain the company panels with buttons to take you to those sites. The other reference of type URL temporarily contains the address of the site of your interest.

Snippet-2 creates the arrays that store the names of the computer and aerospace companies. The reference container will provide a handle to the applet's content pane.

Inside the method `init()`, snippet-3 initializes the reference to the content pane. Snippet-4 creates the control panel object and sets it with grid layout. Snippet-5 creates the control buttons to change between the cards. These buttons have been added to the control panel. At this point you don't have to bother with methods that have been operated on the button objects. However, you can note that the method `setEnabled()` can make a button enabled when its argument is `true` or disabled if its argument is `false`. The method `setActionCommand()` allows you to recognize a specific button, by retrieving its string argument, to perform some further operation, as shown in snippet-13.

Snippet-6 creates a cards panel and sets it to the card layout; thus, this panel in turn can contain several panels. The code adds the company panels, containing the buttons to take you to specified sites, to the cards panel. Snippet-7 shows the implementation of buttons for various Web sites. Each `for` loop will initialize the buttons with a specific category of sites such as the computer and aerospace sites.

Snippet-8 adds company panels to the cards panel. Snippet-9 adds the control panel and cards panel to the north and center locations of the applet's content pane.

Snippets 10 and 11 are the implementation of the methods to display the next and previous cards when they are invoked. The methods can also enable or disable the control buttons depending on the context. The method that displays a Web site (when the button on a card has been activated) is shown in snippet-12. The method takes the URL string of the Web site as its argument and creates its `URL` object. This object will be used to display the relevant Web page by invoking the method `showDocument()` on the applet context.

Snippet-13 shows the button listener, where the necessary methods are activated depending on the button that has been clicked. If you click the Next button, the method `showNextCard()` is invoked. To recognize the button that has been clicked, the action command string that has been set by using the `setActionCommand()` will be retrieved by using the method `getActionCommand()`. Then the string will be compared with the reference string. This is in code snippet-14. Snippet-15 loads a specific Web page depending on the button that has been clicked.

Grid Bag Layout Manager

The grid bag layout is one of the most flexible and sophisticated layout managers, and the layout scheme is somewhat involved and complex. The grid bag layout can manage components to span multiple rows and columns, without all the components being the same size. This is done by setting a rectangular grid of cells associated with the container and then placing each component in one or more cells. These cells form the component's display area.

GridBagLayout Constructor

The grid bag layout uses two classes to lay out components: `java.awt.GridBagLayout` and `java.awt.GridBagConstraints`. The constructor

```
public GridBagLayout()
```

creates a new grid bag layout manager that can be set for a container by using the method `setLayout(GridBagLayout gridbag)`.

Grid Bag Constraints

The pattern in which the grid bag layout manager places a component depends on the constraints imposed on the component by using the following method:

```
public void setConstraints(Component comp,
                GridBagConstraints constraint);
```

The constraints are represented by a set of public fields from the class `GridBagConstraints`. These fields can be assigned specific numbers or a set of constants available in the same class. The next sections give descriptions of the fields from the class `GridBagConstraints`.

gridx and gridy

Two coordinates (x, y) are required to position a component, for example a button B1, in a grid of cells. You can then position a corner, preferably the top-left corner, of the button at the specified point (x, y) (see Figure 5.6).

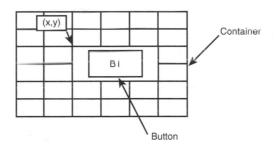

Figure 5.6

Grid of cells with a button positioned in it.

The fields `gridx` and `gridy` represent the x and y coordinates, respectively. `gridx` specifies the number of cells at the left of the component's display area, where the leftmost has `gridx=0`. `gridy` specifies the number of cells at the top of the components display area, where the topmost cell has `gridy=0`. In Figure 5.6, the (x, y) pair is (2, 2).

`gridx` and `gridy` also take the constant `RELATIVE` provided in the `GridBagConstraints` class. The value `RELATIVE` places components next to the previously added component in the specified coordinate direction. By default, both gridx and gridy have the values RELATIVE.

gridwidth and gridheight

After you position the component by using gridx and gridy, the size of the component can be defined. The size of the component is specified in terms of the number of cells it spans in the row and column directions by using the gridwidth and gridheight fields. In Figure 5.6, the values of gridwidth and gridheight for the button are 3 and 2, respectively.

You can also use the value REMAINDER for gridwidth or gridheight to specify that the component be the last one in its row or column, respectively. The other constant, RELATIVE, assigned to gridwidth and gridheight specifies that the component be placed next to the previously added component in the specified row or column. Both gridwidth and gridheight are set to 1 by default.

weightx and weighty

The fields weightx and weighty specify how to distribute the extra horizontal and vertical spaces, respectively, while resizing the container. The weights also play a key role in getting the required appearance for the user interface. The weights can be set to any double type value between 0.0 and 1.0. If a component's specific weight receives a large number, the component occupies extra space in the specified direction. A component that has zero weight receives no extra space. By default, both weightx and weighty are set to 0.

fill

The field fill helps when the component size is smaller than its display area. It specifies how a component is distributed in its display area. You can assign any one of the constants, namely NONE, HORIZONTAL, VERTICAL, or BOTH, to fill. When fill is set to NONE, it indicates that the component should not fill the display area. The constant HORIZONTAL makes the component wide enough to fill the display area in the horizontal direction only. The constant VERTICAL makes the component tall enough to fill the display area in the vertical direction only. Finally, the constant BOTH makes the component fill its display area completely, both horizontally and vertically. By default, the value of fill is set to NONE.

anchor

The field anchor specifies where to anchor a specific component when it is smaller than its display area. Anchoring is specified by using geographical directions. The possible values for this field are NORTH, NORTHEAST, EAST, SOUTHEAST, SOUTH, SOUTHWEST, WEST, NORTHWEST, and CENTER. By default, the component is placed at the center of its display area.

insets

insets is a field of the class type Insets provided in AWT. This field is used to specify the external padding for a component—the space between the component and the boundaries of its display area. The field is set by creating an `Insets` object by using its constructor `Insets(int top, int left, int bottom, int right)`. The argument values `top`, `left`, `bottom`, and `right` are the spaces to be left in the respective directions from the relevant boundaries of the display area. By default, the `insets` field has been set to the object `Insets(0, 0, 0, 0)`; that is, there is no external padding.

ipadx and ipady

`ipadx` and `ipady` specify internal padding—the extra width or height to be added to a component's existing width or height. The resulting extension applies to either side of the component, width or height. Thus the extra width or height of the component will be twice the `ipadx` or `ipady`, respectively. By default, the components do not possess any internal padding.

GridBagLayout Code Example

Listing 5.5 demonstrates how to lay out components in a container by using grid bag layout (see Figure 5.7). The program uses numerical coordinates to position components rather than using the constants `RELATIVE` and `REMAINDER`.

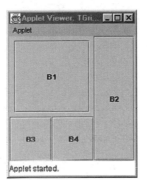

Figure 5.7

A Swing applet with the grid bag layout manager (suitable weights).

Listing 5.5   GridBagLayout (TGridBagLayout.java)

```
/*
 * <Applet code=TGridBagLayout width=200 height=200>
 * </Applet>
 */

import javax.swing.*;
import java.awt.*;

public class TGridBagLayout extends JApplet {
    Container container = null;

    public void init() {
```

continues

Listing 5.5   continued

```java
// 1. Get a handle on the applet's content pane.
container = this.getContentPane();

// 2. Set the container to the grid bag layout and
// define a constraint object.
GridBagLayout gridbag = new GridBagLayout();
container.setLayout(gridbag);
GridBagConstraints c = new GridBagConstraints();

// 3. Common settings for constraint object instant variables.
c.fill = GridBagConstraints.BOTH;

// 4. Settings for button B1.
c.insets = new Insets(5,5,5,5);
c.gridx = 0; c.gridy = 0;
c.gridwidth = 2; c.gridheight = 2;
c.weightx = 1.0; c.weighty = 1.0;
makeButton("B1", gridbag, c);

// 5. Settings for button B2.
c.insets = new Insets(0,0,0,0);
c.gridx = 2; c.gridy = 0;
c.gridwidth = 1; c.gridheight = 3;
makeButton("B2", gridbag, c);

// 6. Settings for button B3.
c.gridx = 0; c.gridy = 2;
c.gridwidth = 1; c.gridheight = 1;
c.weightx = 1.0; c.weighty=0.5;
makeButton("B3", gridbag, c);

// 7. Settings for button B4.
c.gridx = 1; c.gridy = 2;
makeButton("B4", gridbag, c);
}

// 8. Define the function to create and add a button
// according to the constraints.
public void makeButton(String name,
                       GridBagLayout gridbag,
                       GridBagConstraints c) {
    JButton button = new JButton(name);
    gridbag.setConstraints(button, c);
    container.add(button);
}
}
```

Code Details

Listing 5.5 is a Swing applet that places four buttons according to the grid bag layout. In this example, the specific objective is to position the buttons according to the layout configuration shown in Figure 5.7. The button B1 is expected to be a square button, and the button B2 spans from top to bottom at the right edge of the container. The buttons B3 and B4 are also square buttons located one after the other from the lower-left corner of the container.

Snippet-1 inside the method `init()` gets a handle on the applet's content pane. Snippet-2 creates a grid bag layout object and assigns it to the applet. This prepares the applet with a grid pattern attached to it as shown previously in Figure 5.6 (while demonstrating the fields `gridx` and `gridy`).

Next, a grid bag `constraint` object has been defined so that the components can be placed with suitable constraints. Usually it is sufficient to create a single `constraint` object and use it for the components by initializing the constraint fields appropriately. Alternatively, several `constraint` objects can be used for the components or groups of components. The choice depends on the number of components to be placed and the complexity of the layout. The example program uses only one `constraint` object, referred as c, whose fields are manipulated for different buttons.

Snippet-3 initializes the constraint field `fill`, common to all the components. Other constraint fields, such as `gridx`, `gridy`, `gridwidth`, `gridheight`, `weightx`, `weighty`, and so on, will be assigned suitable values for different buttons.

If the required appearance of the layout shown in Figure 5.7 is examined, the coordinates and sizes of display areas of individual buttons can be coded as follows:

```
'B1' button:
    c.gridx = 0; c.gridy = 0;
    c.gridwidth = 2; c.gridheight = 2;

'B2' button:
    c.gridx = 2; c.gridy =0;
    c.gridwidth = 1; c.gridheight = 3;

'B3' button:
    c.gridx = 0; c.gridy = 2;
    c.gridwidth = 1; c.gridheight = 1;

'B4' button:
            c.gridx = 1; c.gridy = 2;
    c.gridwidth = 1; c.gridheight = 1;
```

These constraint settings are shown in the rest of the `init()` method. Finally, the most critical step is to set and tune the fields `weightx` and `weighty` to suitable values. This step creates the required appearance of the layout.

The constraint fields `weightx` and `weighty` are defined by values ranging from 0 to 1.0. If the weights for all components are set to 0, the components pack together at the center of the container as shown in Figure 5.8. The easiest way is to start with all the weights set at 1.0 and then fine-tune them. Figure 5.9 shows the layout when the weights for all the components are set at 1.0.

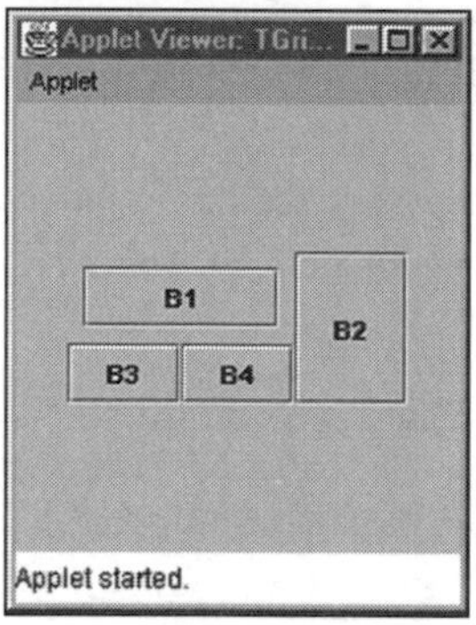

Figure 5.8

A Swing applet with the grid bag layout manager (all weights = 0).

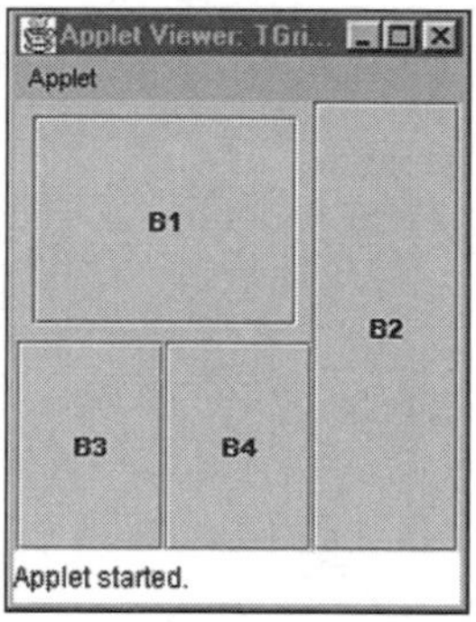

Figure 5.9

A Swing applet with the grid bag layout manager (all weights = 1).

Fine-tuning the weights is a trial and error process with some speculation based on the expected appearance of the user interface. When the applets in Figure 5.7 and Figure 5.9 are compared, the button B1 needs resizing in the y-direction (or height) to make it a square button. Note that the appearance of the button also depends on the dimensions of the container (in this case, the applet width and height equal each other). If the code is observed carefully, the `weighty` of the button B1 has been kept constant; however, the `weighty` of the buttons B3 and B4 is reduced to 0.5. These values can easily be realized if you want to make the height of the button B1 to be just twice the height of the button B3 or B4. The eventual weights will produce the desired effect to create the user interface shown in Figure 5.7.

Snippet-8 deals with the placement of buttons with the imposed constraints. In this connection, the method setConstraints(Component comp, GridBagConstraints (c) is used to impose the prescribed constraints on a component. This statement has been enclosed inside a method makeButton().

The method makeButton() adds each button to the applet by using the add() method.

Figure 5.10 shows the result of the constraints field fill when it has been set to NONE. Because the weights have been fine-tuned, the buttons appear in relevant display areas and remain in their preferred sizes, but they do not fill the entire area. This shows that the assignment of appropriate weights to individual components can control the distribution of extra horizontal and vertical spaces.

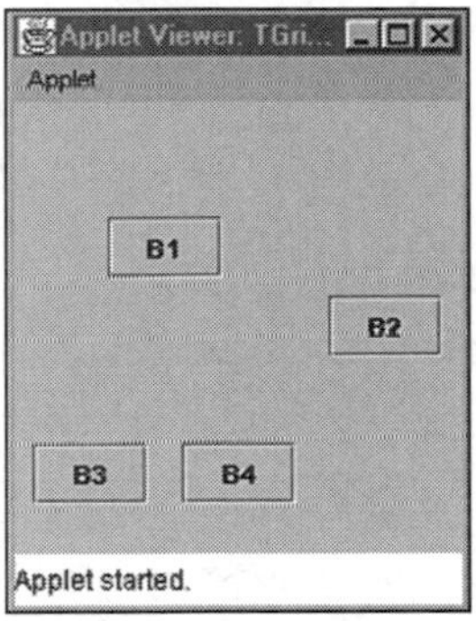

Figure 5.10

A Swing applet with the grid bag layout manager (with suitable weights, but fill = NONE).

Box Layout

By using the grid bag layout discussed earlier, one can achieve almost any kind of sophisticated layout model. In addition to this AWT layout manager, the Swing library introduces another layout called the box layout. The box layout allows creation of sophisticated layouts without the complexities experienced with the grid bag layout. You do not deal with any weights or play around using the trial-and-error approach. Using the box layout is as easy as using the flow layout to lay out components in a container. Containers laid out with box layout can be nested to achieve an effect similar to the grid bag layout.

The box layout patterns are of two types: horizontal and vertical. The horizontal box pattern places the components from left to right in a container. The vertical box pattern places the components from top to bottom. The orientation of the box layout as horizontal or vertical is specified by using the x-axis or y-axis, respectively. Thus, for a given box layout, either the x-axis or the y-axis will be its primary axis.

Whenever a component is added using the box layout, the preferred size of the component is respected. That is, unlike in a grid layout, the box layout allows components to occupy different amounts of space along the primary axis.

In the direction of the non-primary axis, if the components do not have the same dimensions, the box layout attempts to make all the components assume the dimension of the one with the largest value. For example, in a horizontal box layout, if all the components are not of equal heights (dimension along the non-primary axis), the layout manager attempts to make all the components as tall as the tallest component.

If the sizing along the non-primary axis is not possible, the component will be center aligned along that axis; that is, the center of the component will have the same coordinate as the other components in that direction.

The box layout does not wrap any component to the next line if the size of the container is changed. For example, a horizontal box layout with some push buttons in a row will not wrap the buttons to the next line while reducing the size of the container.

The BoxLayout Class

The class `BoxLayout` implements the interface `LayoutManager2` from the Abstract Window Toolkit. This class is a member of the Swing library and has been stored in the package `javax.swing`. The class does not subclass any other significant class except `java.lang.Object`.

You will usually not use the class `BoxLayout` to deal with the box layout; instead, you'll use the class `Box`, explained in the next section. However, the class `BoxLayout` contains some important features to be noted.

To create a box layout manager that lays out components from left to right or top to bottom, use the following constructor:

```
public BoxLayout(Container target, int axis)
```

The `target` is the container for this layout. The `axis` specifies the direction of the box layout, such as horizontal or vertical, and takes any one of the following static constants:

```
static int X_AXIS
static int Y_AXIS
```

The Box Container

The class `Box` represents a lightweight container that can only use the box layout. Trying to assign any other layout manager results in an `AWTError`. The `Box` container allows the components to be laid out either vertically or horizontally by specifying the direction of the layout. A `Box` object is created by using its constructor that takes the axis argument or by using the convenient static methods. The following is the constructor of the `Box` class:

```
public Box(int axis)
```

The argument `axis` takes the value `BoxLayout.X_AXIS` or `BoxLayout.Y_AXIS`. The following are the convenience static methods that do not require any arguments to create a horizontal or vertical box containers respectively:

```
public static Box createHorizontalBox()
public static Box createVerticalBox()
```

The class Box also provides useful methods that add features such as inter-component spacing, component repositioning on resizing of the container, and so on. These features are achieved by using invisible components called glues, fillers, struts, and rigid areas.

A glue component expands as much as necessary to fill the space between its neighboring components in a box layout. This results in the maximum width between components in a horizontal layout and maximum height in the case of a vertical layout. The extra space between components or the components and the container can be evenly distributed by using the glue components. You can create a glue component for the horizontal and vertical layouts by using the following respective static methods:

```
public static Component createHorizontalGlue()
public static Component createVerticalGlue()
```

A strut has a fixed dimension. You use this component to force a certain amount of constant space between two components in a box layout. For example, in a horizontal layout, this component forces a certain amount of gap between two components. A strut can also be used to force the box itself to be of a specified dimension. For example, in a vertical box, a strut can be used to force the width of the box to be of a specified value. Basically a strut has an infinite dimension in the unspecified direction. So for a horizontal strut, the height is not bounded.

A rigid area occupies the specified size. The rigid area components behave similarly to struts. You can specify both the width and the height of the component. The following is the static method that creates a rigid area component:

```
public static Component createRigidArea(Dimension d)
```

A filler allows you to specify the minimum, maximum, and preferred sizes. Fillers are objects of the inner class `Box.Filler`. When a filler is added between two components in a horizontal box, it maintains the specified minimum width and ensures that the container has a minimum height. You can create a filler object as shown in the following:

```
Box.Filler(new Dimension(w1,h1), // minimum size
           new Dimension(w2,h2), // preferred size
           new Dimension(w3, h3)) // maximum size
```

BoxLayout Code Example (Using Invisible Components to Position Other Components)

Listing 5.6 uses the box layout to create an applet that displays the pairs of buttons B1 and B2, B3 and B4, and so on in separate panels to demonstrate the effect of invisible components such as glues, fillers, rigid areas, and struts. Each panel is surrounded by a title bar displaying the corresponding demonstration type (see Figure 5.11). The invisible components have been added either between the buttons, between the buttons and the corresponding panel, or both.

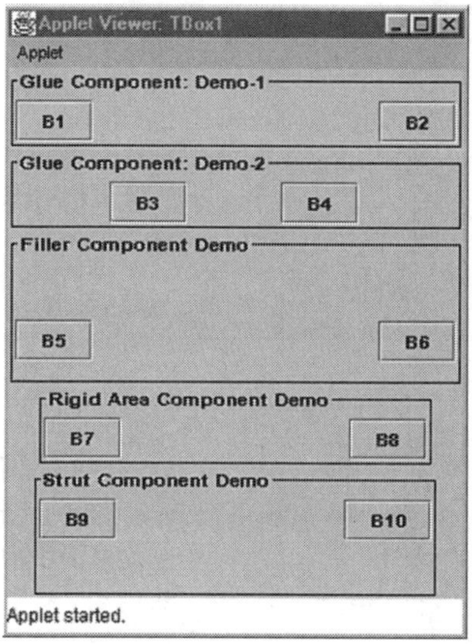

Figure 5.11

Box layout can use invisible components to position other components.

Listing 5.6   BoxLayout Example Using Invisible Components (TBox1.java)

```
// Demonstrates the positioning of components in a box using
// invisible components

/*
 * <Applet code=TBox1 width=300 height=300>
 * </Applet>
 */

import javax.swing.*;
import javax.swing.border.*;
import java.awt.*;

public class TBox1 extends JApplet {
    Container container = null;
```

```
public void init() {
    // 1. Get the handle on the applet's content pane.
    container = getContentPane();

    // 2. Create a vertical box and add it to the applet.
    Box baseBox = Box.createVerticalBox();
    container.add(baseBox);

    // 3. Create the demo panel1 with box layout to display
    // buttons B1 and B2.
    // a) Create the panel and set the box layout.
    JPanel glueDemoPanel1 = new JPanel();
    glueDemoPanel1.setLayout(new BoxLayout(glueDemoPanel1,
                            BoxLayout.X_AXIS));
    // b) Set the title border around the panel.
    TitledBorder border1 = new TitledBorder(
                        new LineBorder(Color.black),
                        "Glue Component: Demo-1");
    border1.setTitleColor(Color.black);
    glueDemoPanel1.setBorder(border1);
    // c) Add the buttons B1 and B2 with a glue component
    // between them.
    glueDemoPanel1.add(new JButton("B1"));
    glueDemoPanel1.add(Box.createHorizontalGlue());
    glueDemoPanel1.add(new JButton("B2"));

    // d) Add the panel to the base box.
    baseBox.add(glueDemoPanel1);

    // 4. Create the demo panel-2, assign box layout and add
    // buttons B3 and B4.
    // a) Create the glue panel 2 and assign the box layout.
    JPanel glueDemoPanel2 = new JPanel();
    glueDemoPanel2.setLayout(new BoxLayout(glueDemoPanel2,
                            BoxLayout.X_AXIS));

    // b) Add a titled border to the panel.
    TitledBorder border2 = new TitledBorder(
                        new LineBorder(Color.black),
                        "Glue Component: Demo-2");
    border2.setTitleColor(Color.black);
    glueDemoPanel2.setBorder(border2);

    // c) Add the buttons B3 and B4 to the panel; also add
    // the glue components between the buttons, and the
    // buttons and panel.
    glueDemoPanel2.add(Box.createHorizontalGlue());
    glueDemoPanel2.add(new JButton("B3"));
```

continues

Listing 5.6   continued

```
glueDemoPanel2.add(Box.createHorizontalGlue());
glueDemoPanel2.add(new JButton("B4"));
glueDemoPanel2.add(Box.createHorizontalGlue());

// d) Add the panel to the base box.
baseBox.add(glueDemoPanel2);

// 5. Create a filler panel and add buttons B5 and B6.
// a) Create the panel object and assign box layout.
JPanel fillerDemoPanel = new JPanel();
fillerDemoPanel.setLayout(new BoxLayout(fillerDemoPanel,
                           BoxLayout.X_AXIS));

// b) Set the titled border to the above panel.
TitledBorder border3 = new TitledBorder(
                          new LineBorder(Color.black),
                          "Filler Component Demo");
border3.setTitleColor(Color.black);
fillerDemoPanel.setBorder(border3);

// c) Add buttons B5 and B6 to the panel; also add the
// filler component between the buttons.
fillerDemoPanel.add(new JButton("B5"));
fillerDemoPanel.add(new Box.Filler(
                   new Dimension(50,75), // Minimum Size
                   new Dimension(50,75), // Preferred Size
                   new Dimension(Short.MAX_VALUE,75)));
                                         // Maximum Value
fillerDemoPanel.add(new JButton("B6"));

// Attach the panel to the base box.
baseBox.add(fillerDemoPanel);

// 6. Create rigid area panel and add buttons B7 and B8.
// a) Create a panel and assign the box layout.
JPanel rigidADemoPanel = new JPanel();
rigidADemoPanel.setLayout(new BoxLayout(rigidADemoPanel,
                           BoxLayout.X_AXIS));

// b) Assign the title border around the panel.
TitledBorder border4 = new TitledBorder(
                          new LineBorder(Color.black),
                          "Rigid Area Component Demo");
border4.setTitleColor(Color.black);
rigidADemoPanel.setBorder(border4);

// c) Add buttons B7 and B8 to the rigid area panel.
// Also add a rigid area in the middle of the buttons.
```

```
        rigidADemoPanel.add(new JButton("B7"));
        rigidADemoPanel.add(Box.createRigidArea(new
Dimension(150,0)));
        rigidADemoPanel.add(new JButton("B8"));

        // d) Add the panel to the base box.
        baseBox.add(rigidADemoPanel);

        // 7. Create the strut panel, assign the box layout, and
        // add the buttons B9 and B10.
        // a) Create the panel and assign the box layout
        JPanel strutDemoPanel = new JPanel();
        strutDemoPanel.setLayout(new BoxLayout(strutDemoPanel,
                                BoxLayout.X_AXIS));

        // b) Set the titled border around the panel.
        TitledBorder border5 = new TitledBorder(
                                new LineBorder(Color.black),
                                "Strut Component Demo");
        border5.setTitleColor(Color.black);

        // c) Add the buttons B9 and B10 to the panel. Also assign
        // the horizontal strut in the middle of the buttons.
        strutDemoPanel.setBorder(border5);
        strutDemoPanel.add(new JButton("B9"));
        strutDemoPanel.add(Box.createHorizontalStrut(150));
        strutDemoPanel.add(new JButton("B10"));

        // d) Add the panel to the base box.
        baseBox.add(strutDemoPanel);
    }
}
```

Code Details

Snippet-1 of the applet TBox1 obtains a reference to its content pane. Snippet-2 creates a vertical box to which the panels created in the next snippets will be added.

Snippet-3 creates the glue demo panel-1 and assigns the horizontal box layout. A title border has been added to the panel with the relevant title showing the demo type. The panel has been attached with the buttons B1 and B2. A glue component has been added between these buttons. You can create a horizontal glue component by calling the static method createHorizontalGlue() in the class Box. Notice that the horizontal glue produces the effect of pushing the buttons B1 and B2 to the edge of the container (see Figure 5.11).

Snippet-4 is similar to snippet-3 except for the additional horizontal glue components that are added between the buttons (B3 and B4) and the panel. The glue components produce the net effect of positioning the buttons with equal spacing as shown in Figure 5.11.

Snippets 5–7 use the invisible components fillers, rigid areas, and struts. Snippet-5 adds the buttons B5 and B6 to a panel with box layout. In addition, a filler component with the specified dimensions for the minimum, maximum, and preferred sizes has been added between the buttons. This component maintains the minimum gap of at least 50 pixels between the buttons. The filler component also ensures that the panel is of a minimum height of 75 pixels (see Figure 5.11).

Snippet-6 adds the buttons B7 and B8 to the relevant panel by using the box layout. A horizontal (0-pixel height) rigid area component with width 200 pixels is added between the buttons. Now the rigid area component always maintains a constant separation of 200 pixels between the buttons (see Figure 5.11).

Snippet-7 uses the horizontal strut in the place of the rigid area component in snippet-6. Notice that the invisible strut also produces the same effect as the rigid area component along the horizontal direction. The only difference is that the horizontal strut has an unlimited height, which makes the panel extend to the remaining portion of the applet (see Figure 5.11).

BoxLayout Code Example (Using Multiple Nesting)

Listing 5.7 demonstrates that the multiple nesting of boxes can produce the effect of a grid bag layout. The layout model is similar to the one shown in the demonstration example in grid bag layout. Thus, the objective of the program is to lay out components to obtain the appearance shown in Figure 5.12.

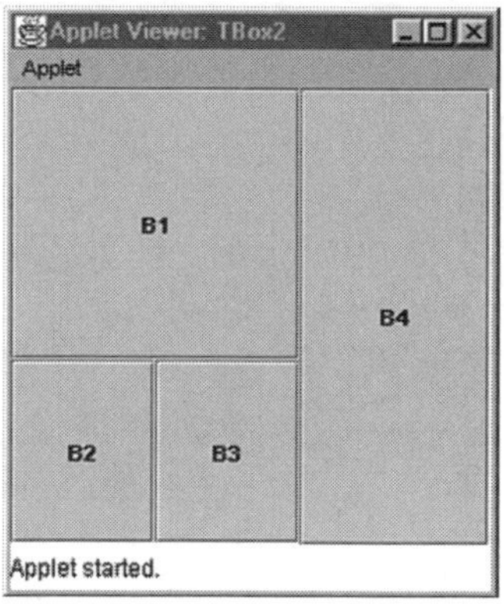

Figure 5.12

The grid bag–like layout achieved with box layout.

Listing 5.7   BoxLayout Example Using Multiple Nesting (TBox2.java)
```
// Multiple-nesting of boxes can produce the effect of
// grid bag layout
```

```
/*
 * <Applet code=TBox2 width=250 height=250>
 * </Applet>
 */

import javax.swing.*;
import java.awt.*;

public class TBox2 extends JApplet {
    Container container = null;

    public void init() {
        // 1. Get the handle on the applets' content pane
        // and set the background color to white.
        container = getContentPane();
        container.setBackground(Color.white);

        // 2. Create a horizontal box and add it to the applet.
        Box baseBox = Box.createHorizontalBox();
        container.add(baseBox);

        // 3. Create a vertical box and add it to the base box.
        Box vBox = Box.createVerticalBox();
        baseBox.add(vBox);

        // 4. Create button B1 and add it to vBox.
        JButton b1 = new JButton("B1");
        b1.setAlignmentX(Component.CENTER_ALIGNMENT);
        b1.setMaximumSize(new Dimension(150,150));
        vBox.add(b1);

        // 5. Create a horizontal box and add it to vBox.
        Box hBox = Box.createHorizontalBox();
        vBox.add(hBox);

        // 6. Create button B2 and add it to hBox.
        JButton b2 = new JButton("B2");
        b2.setAlignmentY(Component.CENTER_ALIGNMENT);
        b2.setMaximumSize(new Dimension(75,100));
        hBox.add(b2);

        // 7. Create another button B3 and add it to hBox.
        JButton b3 = new JButton("B3");
        b3.setAlignmentY(Component.CENTER_ALIGNMENT);
        b3.setMaximumSize(new Dimension(75,100));
        hBox.add(b3);
```

continues

Listing 5.7   continued

```
        // 8. Create the vertical box (vBox1) and
        // add it to the base box.
        Box vBox1 = Box.createVerticalBox();
        baseBox.add(vBox1);

        // 9. Create the button B4 and add it to vBox1.
        JButton b4 = new JButton("B4");
        b4.setAlignmentX(Component.CENTER_ALIGNMENT);
        b4.setMaximumSize(new Dimension(100,250));
        vBox1.add(b4);
    }
}
```

Code Details

Snippet-1 of applet TBox2 gets the handle to its content pane and resets the background color of the container. Snippet-2 creates a horizontal box and adds it to the content pane. This box serves as the base box to which the other components are added.

Snippet-3 creates a vertical box and adds it to the base box. This box will hold the button B1 and a horizontal box. Snippet-4 creates and positions the button B1. Notice that you may have to set the alignment of the button as required. The button is resized to the preferred dimension.

NOTE

If the component does not appear as expected when it has been placed in a box container, you must check the alignment and the resizing of the component.

Snippet-5 creates a horizontal box and adds it to the vertical box. The horizontal box is added with the buttons B2 and B3. Snippets 6 and 7 create and add the buttons B2 and B3 with proper alignment and new size.

Snippet-8 creates a vertical box that is added to the base box. The vertical box is added with the button B4, which spans from the top to the bottom of the applet. Snippet-9 shows the code to create and add the button B4 to the vertical box with a suitable size and alignment.

CHAPTER 6

Swing Design

The Swing component set was created to allow Java developers to rapidly build front-ends for applications by using ready-made and sophisticated widgets. The Swing set has its foundation rooted in the earlier Abstract Window Toolkit (AWT), and it is intended that the new component set must have compatibility with the API in AWT. One of the original goals was to provide an API capable of supporting the look-and-feel of the native system because Java applets or applications, being platform independent, run on a variety of client machines. In addition to this, the language should also have its own special look-and-feel.

To achieve these goals, the Swing team initially adopted the Model-View-Controller (MVC) architecture. This type of approach to building components also allows model-driven programming, so developers can build their own data models to display data through components and hide the complexities involved in fetching the application data. For example, by using model-driven programming to initialize a tree component to display the directory hierarchies from a computer file system, the methods to obtain the file system data can be wrapped in the tree model.

As the work progressed using the MVC architecture, the Swing team realized that a modified design of the MVC was necessary to avoid separating the View and Controller parts that have a close coupling. The first section of this chapter will discuss the modified design.

The next sections of the chapter will present the information on the infrastructure of a component model and the component UI delegate that is basically the remaining portion of a component when its model is removed. Toward the end of the chapter, a demonstration example that emulates the Swing button and its MVC architecture is given.

M-UI: The Simplified MVC

The Model-View-Controller (MVC) architecture has been introduced into the programming world through the language called SmallTalk. Using the MVC approach, a software program with a visual interface can be decomposed into three separate components (see Figure 6.1):

- The Model, which contains the data of the system to be programmed
- The View, which visually displays the data
- The Controller, which transfers the user inputs on the View to the Model by handling the Model data

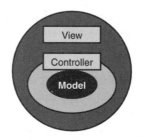

Figure 6.1

The Model-View-Controller separation.

The MVC architecture has a number of advantages:

- The MVC architecture mainly reduces the programming effort required to build systems that present data with multiple views. For example, each Swing component can be supported with different appearances by simply replacing the View portion of the component.
- The MVC architecture also provides a clear separation between the parts that constitute the program. Thus, it allows the problems in each domain to be handled independently.
- The binding between the Model and the View can be performed at runtime rather than at compile time. This allows the user interfaces to change to a new outlook at any time while working with the program.
- Finally, the MVC architecture supports component-based software development in contrast to the monolithic approach.

Due to the merits of MVC architecture, the Swing team initially applied this approach to each of the components they wanted to design. Note that this is in contrast to the MVC architecture traditionally being applied to the entire application. However, very soon the Swing team observed the tight coupling between the Controller and the View. This is due to the fact that writing a flexible controller that handles all types of views is extremely difficult. This led the team to resort to clubbing the View and the Controller. This clubbed portion of each component is called the "UI delegate" of the component. Thus, the MVC architecture has been modified into M-UI architecture.

Component Model

The model of a component represents its data. In Swing, a separate design interface is defined to represent the data model of each component. The interface allows the custom model for a Swing component. Custom models are extremely useful in the case of components that display certain application data. For example, you can define a custom implementation for a Swing tree model to display the file system hierarchy on your computer system. Similarly, information content can be displayed in a text pane according to a suitable format by customizing the model implementation.

Model Types

Component models fall into three categories. There are component models to represent the data of the main application. For example, `TreeModel`, `TableModel`, `ListModel`, `Document`, and `ComboBoxModel` interfaces support the application data models. These model interfaces are useful when building custom models that reduce the programming complexities.

The second type of model stores only GUI-related data such as the button state, selection information, and so on. Examples arc `ButtonModel`, `ListSelectionModel`, and `TableColumnModel`. The third type of model stores data of the application as well as the GUI data. `BoundedRangeModel` is of this type.

Model Changes and Notifications

Through user interaction, the data values from a component model are subjected to change. These changes may have to be reflected in the view of the data. For this purpose, models notify the interested listeners by firing events. Swing models send notifications based on the event model introduced in JavaBeans.

Updating Data View

To generate multiple views for a given data model, the view should not depend on the model. However, if any change takes place in the model data, it should be reflected in the view. To update the view, the listeners must look into the events fired by the model and perform the necessary operations.

NOTE

Normally, it is not necessary to use the model API for every Swing program you write. However, there are occasions where models can help to reduce complexities in programming. This is especially true when you deal with models that represent application data rather than GUI data.

The "UI Delegates"

If the data model is removed from a component, the part that remains is the "UI delegate." The UI delegate is the view and controller clubbed into a single entity. In Swing, UI delegates can be observed as ButtonUI, ComboBoxUI, TreeUI, TableUI, and so on in the package javax.swing.plaf.

The ComponentUI Class

The super class of all the UI delegates is javax.swing.plaf.ComponentUI. The methods in this class perform the installation or uninstallation of the UI. The methods also handle the component geometry and painting. The method installUI() assigns the default attributes of the component (such as its font, color, and border), installs the layout of the component, and adds any event listeners. The method uninstallUI() will undo all the operations performed by the installUI() method.

Pluggable Look-and-Feel

For a language like Java that runs on different platforms, changing the view to that of the current platform makes the user familiar with the Java application. Pluggable look-and-feel gives users an ability to switch the look-and-feel of an application without restarting it. Also, it allows the program to recognize the underlying platform and change the application look-and-feel to be similar to that of the platform.

Developers can create components that can automatically have the appearance and behavior of whatever operating system they happen to be running. Swing components are written in the Java language without using the components from the underlying platform. This facilitates a customizable look-and-feel without relying on the native window system. The pluggable look-and-feel is a natural result of MVC design. Due to the separable nature between the data view and the data model, plugging in another view is easy and straightforward.

The pluggable look-and-feel API in Swing supports the following types of features:

- *Cross-platform or default look-and-feel*—This is also called the Java look-and-feel (previously called the Metal look-and-feel). The cross-platform look-and-feel retains the Java look-and-feel regardless of the platform on which the program is running. When a front end is created by using Swing, the default is set to the Java look-and-feel (unless the default is changed to some other look-and-feel programmatically).

- *System look-and-feel*—This is the look-and-feel of the underlying operating system. The Swing-based front end can be set to any look-and-feel of the underlying platform, such as Motif, Windows, or Macintosh.
- *Dynamically changing look-and-feel*—This feature is a result of the MVC design. You can change the look-and-feel of an application front end at runtime (perhaps by clicking a toolbar button) while the application is running.

Look-and-Feel Packages

Four look-and-feel types can be observed in the Swing library from JDK 1.2. This includes the Java look-and-feel package, which is applied by default. The other look-and-feel packages are Motif type, Windows type, and Macintosh type. The Macintosh type is newly introduced in JDK 1.2, and the supporting library needs to be obtained separately because it is not shipped with the JDK.

The Java look-and-feel package name is `javax.swing.plaf.metal.*`. JDK 1.2 contains the other packages for the Motif look-and-feel and the Windows look-and-feel. The package names for these types are as follows:

```
com.sun.java.swing.plaf.motif.*
com.sun.java.swing.plaf.windows.*
```

This naming convention indicates that the look-and-feel is pertinent to some other operating system outside the domain of Sun Microsystems.

The UIManager Class

The `UIManager` provides the handle to control the look-and-feel of your application. This class contains the static methods to assign a specific look-and-feel to an application or retrieve the current look-and-feel. To assign a particular look-and-feel as the default look-and-feel, you can call the following static methods in the `UIManager` class:

```
public static void setLookAndFeel(String className)
```

This method throws the `ClassNotFoundException` if the assigned look-and-feel could not be found. It can also throw other exceptions such as the `InstantiationException` (if a new instance could not be created), `IllegalAccessException` (if the class is not accessible), and `UnsupportedLookAndFeelException` (if the look-and-feel is not supported).

```
public static void setLookAndFeel (LookAndFeel newLF)
```

This method throws the `UnsupportedLookAndFeelException` if the assigned look-and-feel is not supported.

The other methods of interest retrieve the look-and-feel types and are as follows:

```
public static String getSystemLookAndFeelClassName()
```

This method returns the name of the look-and-feel class that implements the native system look-and-feel. If there is no native look-and-feel, the name of the Java look-and-feel is returned.

```
public static String getCrossPlatformLookAndFeelClassName()
```

This method returns the name of the Java look-and-feel class.

The LookAndFeel Class

LookAndFeel is an abstract class that contains all the basic information for different look-and-feel classes. This class is the root from which the specific look-and-feel classes are extended, as shown in Figure 6.2. The LookAndFeel class has three important duties: identify the current look-and-feel, determine the platform support for a look-and-feel, and build the default look-and-feel table. Programmers who want to build their own look-and-feel must subclass their look-and-feel classes.

```
java.swing.LookAndFeel (abstract)
    └── javax.swing.plaf.basic.BasicLookAndFeel (abstract)
            ├── javax.swing.plaf.metal.MetalLookAndFeel
            ├── com.sun.java.swing.plaf.motif.MotifLookAndFeel
            └── com.sun.java.swing.plaf.windows.WindowsLookAndFeel
```

Figure 6.2

Class hierarchy of specific look-and-feel classes.

In this hierarchy diagram, the concrete classes called `MetalLookAndFeel`, `MotifLookAndFeel`, and `WindowsLookAndFeel` initialize the system color defaults (such as the desktop background, caption colors, text colors, and so on) and specific UI class names for each component, such as `com.sun.java.swing.plaf.motif. MotifButtonUI`.

Dynamic Updating of Look-and-Feel

When an application is running, the look-and-feel can be changed dynamically. However, because a component initializes its UI delegate inside its constructor, the look-and-feel changes that are made at runtime will not automatically propagate to update the UI delegates. Therefore, you need to update the UI delegates programmatically along the containment hierarchy of components.

To handle the dynamic updating of components, Swing provides the static method `updateComponentTreeUI(Component c)` in the class `SwingUtilities`. This method asks each component in the containment hierarchy to call `updateUI()`. Normally, you need to pass the top-level container as the value of the argument for `updateComponentTreeUI(Component c)`. After calling this method, you will also need to validate the container calling the `validate()` method.

Swing Design Emulation Code Example

Listing 6.1 is an example program that emulates the Swing design with a simplified code. This program provides a birds-eye view of the entire design involved with a Swing component. Notice that separate objects represent the component model and its UI delegate. The example component in this program called `MyButton` can be changed between two appearances such as rectangular (the default) and oval shapes by using the pluggable look-and-feel approach. Figure 6.3 shows the default and oval views of `MyButton`.

Figure 6.3

MyButton components in two different look-and-feel presentations (the default and oval shaped).

This program is a combination of three source files, namely `TMyButton.java`, `MyButton.java`, and `MyUIManager.java`. The file `TMyButton.java` contains the application that implements the button `MyButton`. The source file `MyButton` contains the implementation of the `MyButton` component by using Swing design. The file `MyUIManager` contains the code for `MyUIManager` that handles the look-and-feel of the component.

Listing 6.1   Swing Design of a Component Called MyButton (TMyButton.java)
```
// Application program that implements MyButton component.
import javax.swing.*;import java.awt.*;import java.awt.event.*;class TMyButton
extends JFrame {    public TMyButton() {
        // 1. Assign a name to the frame, get the content pane of the
        // frame, and assign white color to the background of the
        // frame.
        super("My Button Frame");
        Container contentPane = this.getContentPane();
        contentPane.setBackground(Color.white);

        // 2. Assign an oval shaped look-and-feel to the buttons.
        // In reality, only the look is altered; the feel is not changed!
```

continues

Listing 6.1   continued

```
        // The default look-and-feel is rectangular and has the
        // program identifier "Default".
        // MyUIManager.setLookAndFeel("Default");
        MyUIManager.setLookAndFeel("Oval");

        // 3. Create a Play button object and set an action command.
        // Also register an action listener.
        MyButton playButton = new MyButton();
        playButton.setText("Play");
        playButton.setActionCommand("playbutton");
        playButton.addActionListener(new ButtonListener());

        // 4. Create a Stop button object and set an action command.
        // Also register an action listener.
        MyButton stopButton = new MyButton("Stop");
        stopButton.setActionCommand("stopbutton");
        stopButton.addActionListener(new ButtonListener());

        // 5. Set the frame to the grid layout and add the Play and
        // Stop buttons.
        contentPane.setLayout(new GridLayout(1,2));
        contentPane.add(playButton);
        contentPane.add(stopButton);

        // 6. Add the window listener to close the frame
        // and display it with the specified size.
        addWindowListener(new WindowEventHandler());
        setDefaultCloseOperation(WindowConstants.DISPOSE_ON_CLOSE);
        setSize(300, 75); // width=300, height=75
        show(); // Display the frame
    }

    // 7. Listener class to close the parent frame.
    class WindowEventHandler extends WindowAdapter {
        public void windowClosing(WindowEvent evt) {
            dispose();
            System.exit(0);
        }
    }

    // 8. Action listener that receives events whenever the Play
    // or Stop button is clicked.
    class ButtonListener implements ActionListener {
        public void actionPerformed(ActionEvent evt) {
            MyButton button = (MyButton) evt.getSource();

            if (button.getActionCommand().equals("playbutton")) {
                System.out.println("You clicked the Play button.");
            }
```

```java
        else if (button.getActionCommand().equals("stopbutton")) {
            System.out.println("You clicked the Stop button.");
        }
    }
}

// 9. The main method.
static public void main(String[] args) {
    new TMyButton();
}
}


// File Name: MyButton.java
// 10.The component called MyButton that is built by using Swing design.
import javax.swing.*;import javax.swing.plaf.*;import java.awt.*;import
java.awt.event.*;
// 11. The component class MyButton is a subclass of JComponent.class MyButton
extends JComponent {    MyButtonModel model = null;
    String text = "";
    Font font = null;
    FontMetrics fontMetrics = null;
    int border = 10;
    boolean buttonPressed = false;

    // 12. MyButton constructor without any arguments.
    public MyButton() {
        this(null);
    }

    // 13. MyButton constructor that takes the text label argument.
    public MyButton(String text) {
        // Assign the data model to the component.
        setModel(new DefaultMyButtonModel());
        // Initialize the text label.
        this.text = text;
        // Obtain the default font.
        font = getFont();
        // If there is no default font, assign a new font.
        if (font == null) {
            font = new Font("SanSerif", Font.BOLD, 14);
        }
        // Retrieve the font metrics of the font.
        fontMetrics = getFontMetrics(font);
        // Register a mouse listener.
        addMouseListener(new ButtonMouseListener());

        // Update the view of the button.
        updateUI();
    }
```

continues

Listing 6.1   continued

```
// 14. Method definition of update.
public void updateUI() {
    // Assign proper look-and-feel for the view depending on the
    // specified look-and-feel.
    if (MyUIManager.getLookAndFeel().equals("Default")) {
        super.setUI(new MyButtonUI());
    }
    else if (MyUIManager.getLookAndFeel().equals("Oval")) {
        super.setUI(new MyButtonOvalUI());
    }
}


// 15. This class is the UI delegate. It has been defined as an
// inner class to simplify the program. This class provides the default
// view of the button.
class MyButtonUI extends ComponentUI {

// 16. Constructor.
public MyButtonUI() {
    repaint(); // Call repaint for further actions.
}

// 17. Retrieve the minimum size of the component.
public Dimension getMinimumSize() {
    int w = fontMetrics.stringWidth(text);
    int h = fontMetrics.getHeight();
    return new Dimension(w+2*border, h+2*border);
}

// 18. Retrieve the preferred size of the component.
public Dimension getPreferredSize() {
    return getMinimumSize();
}

// 19. Retrieve the maximum size of the component.
public Dimension getMaximumSize() {
    return new Dimension(Short.MAX_VALUE, Short.MAX_VALUE);
}

// 20. The update method definition.
public void update(Graphics g, JComponent c) {
    if (c.isOpaque()) {
        g.setColor(c.getBackground());
        g.fillRect(0,0,getWidth(), getHeight());
    }
    paint(g, c);
}
```

```
// 21. The paint method definition.
public void paint(Graphics g, JComponent c) {
    g.setFont(font);

    if (buttonPressed == false) {
        buttonView(g, Color.lightGray, Color.black);
    }
    else {
        buttonView(g, Color.gray, Color.white);
    }
}


// 22. The buttonView method definition.
public void buttonView(Graphics g, Color background, Color foreground) {
    g.setColor(background);
    g.fill3DRect(0,0, getSize().width, getSize().height, true);
    g.setColor(foreground);
    int x = (getSize().width-fontMetrics.stringWidth(text))/2;
    int y = (getSize().height+fontMetrics.getHeight()
                         -fontMetrics.getDescent())/2;
    g.drawString(text, x, y);
}
}


// 23. Implementation of oval shaped look-and-feel for MyButton.
// This view of the button is used as an alternative to its default view.
class MyButtonOvalUI extends ComponentUI {

// 24. Constructor.
public MyButtonOvalUI() {
    repaint();
}

// 25. Retrieve the minimum size of the component.
public Dimension getMinimumSize() {
    int w = fontMetrics.stringWidth(text);
    int h = fontMetrics.getHeight();
    return new Dimension(w+2*border, h+2*border);
}

// 26. Retrieve the preferred size of the component.
public Dimension getPreferredSize() {
    return getMinimumSize();
}

// 27. Retrieve the maximum size of the component.
public Dimension getMaximumSize() {
    return new Dimension(Short.MAX_VALUE, Short.MAX_VALUE);
}
```

continues

Listing 6.1   continued

```java
// 28. The update method definition.
public void update(Graphics g, JComponent c) {
    if (c.isOpaque()) {
        g.setColor(c.getBackground());
        g.fillRect(0,0,getWidth(), getHeight());
    }
    paint(g, c);
}


// 29. The paint method definition.
public void paint(Graphics g, JComponent c) {
    g.setFont(font);

    if (buttonPressed == false) {
        buttonView(g, Color.gray, Color.white);
    }
    else {
        buttonView(g, Color.lightGray, Color.black);
    }
}


// 30. The button view definition.
public void buttonView(Graphics g, Color background, Color foreground) {
    g.setColor(background);
    g.fillOval(0,0, getSize().width, getSize().height);
    g.setColor(foreground);
    int x = (getSize().width-fontMetrics.stringWidth(text))/2;
    int y = (getSize().height+fontMetrics.getHeight()
                            -fontMetrics.getDescent())/2;
    g.drawString(text, x, y);
}
}


// 31. When the user presses or releases the mouse over a button,
// the functionality from the implementation methods from this
// mouse listener class are executed.
class ButtonMouseListener extends MouseAdapter {
    public void mousePressed(MouseEvent evt) {
        requestFocus();
        buttonPressed = true;
        ((MyButton) evt.getSource()).repaint();
    }

    public void mouseReleased(MouseEvent evt) {
        buttonPressed = false;
        ((MyButton) evt.getSource()).repaint();
        ActionEvent actionEvent = new ActionEvent(
                                    MyButton.this,
```

```
                                    ActionEvent.ACTION_PERFORMED,
                                    MyButton.this.getActionCommand());
            processEvent(actionEvent);
        }
    }


    //Supports the action listener.
    ActionListener actionListener;

    // 32. Method to register an action listener with the button.
    public void addActionListener(ActionListener l) {
        actionListener = AWTEventMulticaster.add(actionListener, l);
    }
    // 33. To figure out the action events.
    protected void processEvent(AWTEvent evt) {
        if (evt instanceof ActionEvent) {
            processActionEvent((ActionEvent) evt);
        }
        else {
            super.processEvent(evt);
        }
    }
    // 34. To process the action events.
    protected void processActionEvent(ActionEvent evt) {
        if (actionListener != null) {
            // Execute the action performed from the listener class.
            actionListener.actionPerformed(evt);
        }
    }
    // 35. Method to assign the button model.
    public void setModel(MyButtonModel model) {
        this.model = model;
    }
    // 36. Retrieve the action model.
    public MyButtonModel getModel() {
        return model;
    }
    // 37. Assign the text label to the button.
    public void setText(String text) {
        this.text = text;
        invalidate();
        repaint();
    }
    // 38. Retrieve the text label of the button.
    public String getText() {
        return text;
    }
    // 39. To assign the action command.
    public void setActionCommand(String actionCommand) {
```

continues

Listing 6.1   continued

```
            getModel().setActionCommand(actionCommand);
    }
    // 40. To retrieve the action command.
    public String getActionCommand() {
        String ac = getModel().getActionCommand();
        if (ac == null) {
            ac = getText();
        }
        return ac;
    }
}


// 41. Define a simple button model interface.
interface MyButtonModel {
    public void setActionCommand(String actionCommand);
    public String getActionCommand();
}


// 42. Define the default button model class that implements the
// MyButtonModel interface.
class DefaultMyButtonModel implements MyButtonModel {
    protected String actionCommand = null;
    // 43. Assign an action command.
    public void setActionCommand(String actionCommand) {
        this.actionCommand = actionCommand;
    }
    // 44. Retrieve the action command that has been assigned.
    public String getActionCommand() {
        return actionCommand;
    }
}


// File Name: MyUIManager.java.
// 45. The class MyUIManager. This class figures out the look-and-feel to be
// assigned to a button object. The class contains static method that can
// be invoked from the application class to assign the look-and-feel.
class MyUIManager {
    // Store the look-and-feel string.
    static String lfType = "Default";
    // 46. Assign a new look-and-feel.
    static public void setLookAndFeel(String type) {
        lfType = type;
    }
    // 47. Retrieve the current look-and-feel.
    static public String getLookAndFeel() {
        return lfType;
    }
}
```

Code Details

In program TMyButton.java, snippet-1 assigns a title to the frame, obtains a handle on its content pane, and sets the background of the frame to the color white. Snippet-2 assigns an oval-shaped look-and-feel to the buttons that are attached to the frame. Snippet-3 creates a Play button object and assigns an action command. The snippet also registers an action listener with the button. Snippet-4 performs similar functions for the Stop button.

Snippet-5 prepares the frame with a grid layout of one row and two columns and adds the Play and Stop buttons. Snippet-6 registers a window event handler to close the frame along with other methods to configure the frame. Snippet-7 shows the inner class that represents the window event handler. Snippet-8 is the action listener class that listens to the events fired by the buttons on the frame. Inside the method actionPerformed(), each button is recognized by the action command, and the program prints that the button was clicked on the standard output. Snippet-9 shows the main method that instantiates the class TMyButton.

Snippet-10 (from the source file MyButton.java) shows the code to create the MyButton component by using Swing design. Snippet-11 is the class declaration for MyButton that extends JComponent. Snippets 12 and 13 are the constructors of the class. Notice that while initializing the class, the updateUI() method is called, as shown in snippet-13. Snippet-14 provides the definition of the updateUI() method. Basically, you can find the code to assign a view to the component, depending on the look-and-feel.

Snippet-15 defines the UI-delegate of the component created by using the constructor shown in snippet-16. Snippets 17–19 return the minimum, preferred, and maximum sizes of the component to be laid out. Snippet-20 is the update() method that calls the paint() method to paint the view of the component. Snippet-21 defines the paint() method. The graphics code for the button is operated through a separate method called buttonView(), as shown in snippet-22. Code snippets 23–30 show similar code to define the button view for the oval-shaped look-and-feel.

Snippet-31 shows the listener class to handle the mouse clicks. An object of this class is registered with the button to recognize whenever the button is operated. The class essentially implements the methods mousePressed() and mouseReleased(). Snippet-32 shows the code to register an action listener with the button. The methods under snippets 33 and 34 recognize the action events and process them to activate the actionPerformed() method from the action listener that is registered with the button object.

Snippet 35 and 36 show the methods to assign and retrieve the data model that has already been assigned to the button. Snippets 37 and 38 show the methods to assign and retrieve the text label that is displayed over the button component. Similarly, snippets 39 and 40 are access methods to assign and retrieve the action commands of the button from its button model.

Snippet-41 defines the `MyButtonModel` interface, which contains only two abstract methods. Snippet-42 shows the code for the default buttons model, which implements the interface `MyButtonModel`. Snippets 43 and 44 are the methods that implement the corresponding methods from the interface.

Snippet-45 defines the UI manager of the button. The UI manager is a class called `MyUIManager` and is stored in a separate file called `MyUIManager.java`. The UI manager contains the static methods to assign and retrieve a look-and-feel to the button object.

CHAPTER 7

Icons, Labels, and Borders

Unlike the earlier Abstract Window Toolkit (AWT), the Swing toolkit supports icons that can be used in various components such as labels, buttons, check boxes, and so on.

This chapter examines building your own icons by using the functionality available in graphics context objects (objects of java.awt.Graphics). You will see how to develop icons by using image files that are readily available in Java-supported formats such as GIF and JPEG.

Swing constants are used to position text messages in various components or to set the orientation of the components themselves. This is common to the entire Swing set and applicable to various components presented in this chapter.

In a user interface, short text labels tell the purpose of a specific component. Swing labels are meant for this purpose and support both text strings and icons. This chapter explores Swing labels and how to create them, attach icons, and control the positioning of text and icons. An example shows how to use the supported API in the label class.

The Swing library provides a number of borders that can readily be implemented in an application or an applet to give a decorative appearance to user interfaces. This chapter discusses borders and the implementation of custom borders if none of the Swing borders fulfill your requirements.

Icons

Icons can be displayed on components such as buttons, labels, and menu items to describe the purpose of the component. An icon can be built by using the functionality (such as lines, rectangles, ovals, and so on) provided inside the class java.awt.Graphics or created from a Java-supported image file (such as a .gif or .jpg file).

The Icon Interface

The interface Icon is a design level abstraction that represents an icon to be used in a user interface. The interface has been stored in the package javax.swing. You can create an icon through a custom class that implements the Icon interface. Icons have fixed dimensions of width and height. The following are the three methods from the interface that must be implemented:

```
public abstract void paintIcon(Component c,
                               Graphics g,
                               int x, int y);
public abstract void getIconWidth();
public abstract void getIconHeight();
```

The method paintIcon() paints the picture at the specified coordinates x and y of the icon. The Graphics object is used to invoke the required drawing methods in the implementation code. The Component object restores its properties for painting the background, foreground, and so on.

Creating Icons

Use a class that implements the interface Icon to create an icon. Listing 7.1, a typical implementation class called TestIcon, implements the methods from the interface Icon to create a simple circular icon that is used to indicate the Stop function in a media player (see Figure 7.1).

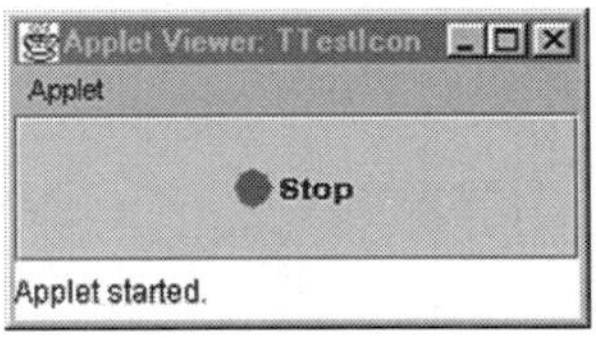

Figure 7.1

A view of the Stop icon of type TestIcon.

Listing 7.1   A Typical Implementation of the Interface Icon (// TestIcon.java)
```
// Shows a class that implements the Icon interface

import javax.swing.Icon;
import java.awt.Graphics;
import java.awt.Color;
import java.awt.Component;

class TestIcon implements Icon {
    int width = 20; // set to some default size
    int height = 20; // set to some default size

    // Constructor without any arguments
```

```
public TestIcon() {
}

// Constructor to specify the icons width and height
public TestIcon(int width, int height) {
    this.width = width;
    this.height = height;
}

// Paint the picture
public void paintIcon(Component c,
                      Graphics g,
                      int x,
                      int y) {
    g.setColor(Color.red);
    g.fillOval(x, y, width, height);
    g.setColor(Color.gray);
    g.drawOval(x, y, width, height);
}

// To retrieve the icon width
public int getIconWidth() {
    return width;
}

// To retrieve the icon height
public int getIconHeight() {
    return height;
}
}
```

The class `TestIcon` implements the complete code for the methods `paintIcon()`, `getIconWidth()`, and `getIconHeight()`. Inside the method `paintIcon()`, two methods from the graphics context are used to draw the circle filled with red color and a gray border. The other two methods return the width and height of the icon. The constructors provide an option to create an icon with the desired size.

Next, you can use the class `TestIcon` to create an icon object as shown in the following:

```
Icon stopIcon = new TestIcon(15, 15);
```

The icon object, `stopIcon`, is of type `Icon`, and is set to the new width and height. Figure 7.1 shows the icon displayed over a Swing button.

Image Icons

You use the class `ImageIcon` from the package `javax.swing` to make an icon from an image file such as *x*.gif or *x*.jpg. The class `ImageIcon` is a ready implementation of the `Icon` interface to produce icons from the specified images. The class provides a list of constructors to create image icons from objects of type `Image` or image files or URLs. The `ImageIcon` class is a direct descendent from the class `java.lang.Object`.

ImageIcon Constructors

The following constructors support different options for creating an icon from a given Java-supported image file:

```
public ImageIcon()
```

This constructor creates a general purpose `ImageIcon` object that can be customized later for a specific image. The customization can be performed by operating the method `setImage(Image image)` on the `ImageIcon` object that has already been created. The method `getImage()` from the same objects returns the relevant image object.

```
public ImageIcon(Image image)
```

This constructor can be used if you have an `Image` object created from a given image source.

```
public ImageIcon(Image image, String description)
```

This constructor is similar to the previous constructor except for the `description` argument. The `description` is any brief text of information that describes the `ImageIcon` object or the image itself. This text is not displayed on the image, but it can be retrieved by using the method `getDescription()` to refer to the icon at any later stage.

```
public ImageIcon(String filename)
```

This constructor creates an icon by using the name of the image file, such as `stop.gif` or `stop.jpg`.

```
public ImageIcon(String filename, String description)
```

This constructor is similar to the previous constructor, with the additional descriptive string.

```
public ImageIcon(URL url)
```

This constructor creates an icon from an image file that resides on a network of computers.

```
public ImageIcon(URL url, String description)
```

This constructor is similar to the previous constructor, with the additional argument for the string `description` about the image.

```
public ImageIcon(byte[] pixelArray)
```

This constructor creates an image icon from an array of pixels in a GIF or JPEG image. The other constructor of this type with a string description is shown in the following:

```
public ImageIcon(byte[] pixelArray, String description)
```

Creating an Image Icon

Creating an icon from a given image file is simpler than using your own implementation of the Icon interface. To create an image icon, you can use one of the ImageIcon constructors such as the following:

```
Icon imageIcon = new ImageIcon("bear.gif");
```

This image icon can be used later in a Swing component to display over it. Figure 7.2 shows the image icon displayed over a Swing label. Swing labels are discussed in the next sections, along with details of how to implement icons with labels.

Figure 7.2

A view of the image icon displayed on a Swing label.

Disabled Image Icons

Whenever a component (such as a button or a check box) is disabled, you can display a grayed-out icon over the component to indicate its disabled state. Disabled icons are grayed out by using a gray filter.

TIP

Normally, Swing component classes take care of setting the disabled icons whenever a component has been disabled. However, there are occasions when you need to do the groundwork to set the disabled icons.

WARNING

In a custom implementation of the interface Icon to create an icon, you need to separately support the code for disabled icons by using the functionality supported in the graphics-context object of type java.awt.Graphics.

The Swing library provides the image filter class GrayFilter to gray out an image. The image filter changes an image into a grayscale image while brightening the image pixels. To create a grayed-out image, you invoke the method createDisabledImage() from GrayFilter by passing the image object as its argument. The following is the typical code:

```
Image image = Toolkit.getDefaultToolkit().getImage("bear.gif");
Image grayImage = GrayFilter.createDisabledImage(image);
Icon grayedIcon = new ImageIcon(grayImage);
```

A grayed-out icon displayed on a Swing label is shown in Figure 7.3. Note that the icon image still reflects its original colors (white and black on the image) shown in Figure 7.2, with the gray shade over the icon.

Figure 7.3

A view of the disabled (grayed-out) image icon.

Swing Constants

The components of the Swing library can require constants to set the position of their text labels or icons. The package javax.swing contains the interface SwingConstants, which provides a list of useful constants. Swing constants also control the orientation of components as horizontal or vertical.

Swing constants are of three groups that represent the box orientation, geographical directions, and horizontal or vertical directions. You use these constants according to the context of their usage. For example, the constants TOP and BOTTOM are used to set the relative location of the text (on a label or button object) with reference to its icon. In the same manner, the constants HORIZONTAL and VERTICAL set the orientation of a scrollbar or slider. The following is the list of Swing constants:

Box-orientation Constants:

```
static int TOP
static int LEFT
static int BOTTOM
static int RIGHT
```

Geographical-direction Constants:

```
static int NORTH
static int NORTH_EAST
static int EAST
static int SOUTH_EAST
static int SOUTH
static int SOUTH_WEST
static int SOUTH
static int NORTH_WEST
static int CENTER
```

The constant CENTER works common to the box-orientation and the geographical-direction constants. The following are the other two constants commonly used to control the orientation of a component:

```
static int HORIZONTAL
static int VERTICAL
```

Swing Labels (JLabel)

A Swing label is a short string of text with or without an associated icon. Swing labels can indicate the purpose of another component such as a text field, slider, and so on. A label cannot be modified directly by the user; it can only be changed inside the program.

A Swing label is a lightweight component that is represented by an object of the class type JLabel. The class JLabel is a direct subclass of JComponent and is stored inside the package javax.swing (see Figure 7.4). The class JLabel also implements the interface SwingConstants.

Swing labels cannot gain the keyboard focus or generate events of any type. They simply display text messages and pictures. The location of the text or picture on a label is controlled by specifying the horizontal and vertical alignments. You can also control the relative position of the text with reference to the icon.

The contents of a label are center aligned in the vertical direction by default. The text message is left aligned in a text-only label, and the image is center aligned horizontally in an image-only label. The default arrangement is that the text is located on the right side of the image, both being aligned in the vertical direction.

JLabel Constructors

To create a label in a program, you use the JLabel constructor that uses suitable arguments for your requirements, such as displaying text only, icon only, an icon in addition to the text, and so on. Swing label objects can be created by using any one of the following constructors:

```
public JLabel();
```

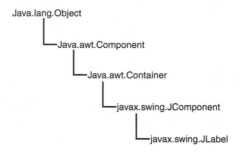

Figure 7.4

The class hierarchy of JLabel.

This constructor creates a JLabel object without any icons or label strings. The label text and the icon can be set by using the public void setIcon(Icon icon) and the public void setText(String text) methods from this class.

```
public JLabel(Icon icon);
```

This constructor creates a JLabel object with the specified icon.

```
public JLabel(Icon icon, int alignment);
```

This constructor is similar to the previous one, except for the additional argument to align the label in the horizontal direction.

```
public JLabel(String text);
```

This constructor creates a JLabel object with the specified text as its label.

```
public JLabel(String text, int alignment);
```

This constructor is similar to the previous one, except for the specified horizontal alignment.

```
public JLabel(String text, Icon icon, int alignment);
```

This constructor creates a JLabel instance with the specified text label, icon, and horizontal alignment.

After a label is created, you can position it in a container according to the layout that is being used. You can control the alignment of a label by invoking the horizontal and vertical alignment functions.

```
public void setHorizontalAlignment(int alignment) and public void
setVerticalAlignment(int alignment)
```

By default, a label is located at the center along the top of the label's display area. Text-only labels are left aligned in the horizontal direction, and icon-only labels are centered horizontally.

You can also specify the position of the text relative to the icon by using the following methods:

```
public void setHorizontalTextPosition(int textPositon)
public void setVerticalTextPosition(int textPositon)
```

By default, both the text and icon are vertically center aligned, but the text is to the right of the icon.

The method `public void setIconTextGap(int iconTextGap)` supports how much space is to be left in terms of pixels between the text and the icon. The default value for this parameter is 4 pixels.

JLabel Code Example

Listing 7.2 creates a simple Swing applet. The applet displays a set of Swing labels with Java icons and a text string (see Figure 7.5). The text string and the icon in each of the labels have been positioned differently by using Swing constants. The program also demonstrates the use of methods from the class `JLabel`.

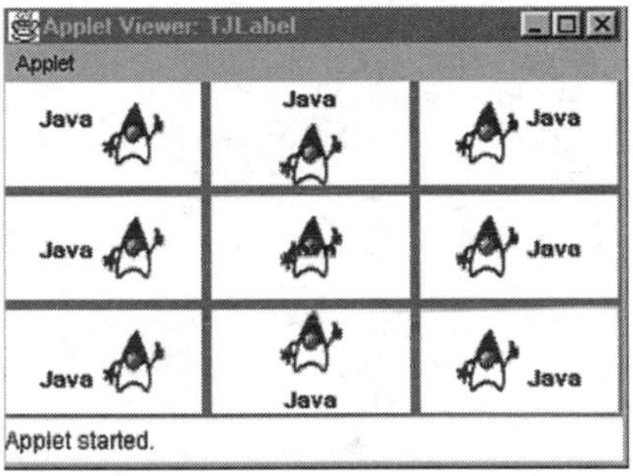

Figure 7.5

An applet displaying Swing labels with icons.

Listing 7.2   JLabel with Labels, Icons, and Constants (TJLabel.java)
```
// Demonstrates the Swing labels, icons, and constants.
/*
 *<Applet code=TJLabel width=400 height=200>
 *</Applet>
 */

import java.awt.*;
import javax.swing.*;
```

continues

Listing 7.2 continued

```java
public class TJLabel extends JApplet {
    Container container = null;
    Icon icon = new ImageIcon("metal.gif");

    public void init() {
        //1. Get a handle on the JApplet's content pane.
        container = getContentPane();

        //2. Create grid layout and set it for the applet and
        //assign a new background color.
        GridLayout grid = new GridLayout(3,3,5,5);
        container.setLayout(grid);
        container.setBackground(Color.gray);

        //3. Invoke the setLabel() method to create and add
        // labels with suitable text and icon positions.
        setLabel(JLabel.LEFT, JLabel.TOP);
        setLabel(JLabel.CENTER, JLabel.TOP);
        setLabel(JLabel.RIGHT, JLabel.TOP);

        setLabel(JLabel.LEFT, JLabel.CENTER);
        setLabel(JLabel.CENTER, JLabel.CENTER);
        setLabel(JLabel.RIGHT, JLabel.CENTER);

        setLabel(JLabel.LEFT, JLabel.BOTTOM);
        setLabel(JLabel.CENTER, JLabel.BOTTOM);
        setLabel(JLabel.RIGHT, JLabel.BOTTOM);
    }

    //4. Create and add labels to the Swing applet.
    public void setLabel(int horizPos, int vertPos) {
        JLabel label = new JLabel("Java",JLabel.CENTER);
        label.setIcon(icon); // Display Java Duke on the label
        label.setHorizontalTextPosition(horizPos);
        label.setVerticalTextPosition(vertPos);
        // Assign new background and foreground colors
        label.setBackground(Color.white);
        label.setForeground(Color.black);
        label.setOpaque(true); // label should not be transparent
        container.add(label);
    }
}
```

Code Details

Listing 7.2 begins with its data fields, such as the declaration of a handle, a named container on the Swing applet's container, and the creation of an icon object. Snippet-1 shows that inside the method `init()` the object reference container is initialized with the applet's content pane object returned by the method `getContentPane()`.

In snippet-2, the applet is set to the grid layout, with nine cells in three rows and three columns, and the applet background is set to the gray color. Snippet-3 of the code invokes the method `setLabel()` nine times to set the labels in the applet.

The method `setLabel()` receives suitable argument values that set the horizontal and vertical positions of the label text with reference to the corresponding icons. For example, the text position in the first label of row one is defined by two arguments: `JLabel.LEFT` positions the text to the left of the icon in the horizontal direction, and `JLabel.TOP` positions the text at the top of the icon in the vertical direction. As a result, the label is positioned at the top-left corner of the icon.

Snippet-4 shows the various steps involved in the method `setLabel()`. The first line of code inside the method creates a `JLabel` object displayed with the text string `Java`. The text string is positioned at the center of the label by using the Swing constant `JLabel.CENTER`. In the next statement, the icon object created as a data field of the applet is attached to the label. The horizontal and vertical positions of the text strings, with reference to the respective icons, are controlled by using the following methods:

```
label.setHorizontalTextPositon(horizPos)
label.setVerticalTextPosition(vertPos)
```

Snippet-4 also shows the statements to set the background and foreground of the labels to the specified colors white and black, respectively. The method `setOpaque()` with its argument value `true` makes each label object opaque. This allows the labels to reflect the colors to which they have been set; otherwise, the labels will simply display the applet's background colors. The output of this program is shown in Figure 7.5.

NOTE

> By default, a Swing label is transparent; therefore, you need to make the label opaque by invoking the method `setOpaque()` and passing the value `true` for its argument.

Borders

A border is basically a margin around the edges of a Swing component. Insets supported in the AWT are meant for a similar purpose. However, Swing borders are more colorful and sophisticated alternatives than the insets in the AWT. The Swing library provides different varieties of borders that provide more impressive appearances to the user interfaces.

The border classes in Swing also use the AWT inset objects in the background. To assign a specific border around a component, you create the border object and assign it to the component by invoking the method

```
public void setBorder(Border border)
```

on the component object. This method overrides any insets that have been directly set to the component.

To create different types of borders, the Swing library supports the design level interface called `Border` and the abstract class named `AbstractBorder`. A number of concrete classes that represent the commonly used borders are also available in the library. The class `BorderFactory` inside the package `javax.swing` contains some convenient methods to create border objects. You can use these methods instead of creating objects from the border classes.

The Border Interface

The interface `Border` is a design level interface that can describe border objects. Thus, classes that represent borders implement this interface. The interface has been stored in the package `javax.swing.border` and contains the following three methods to be implemented:

```
public void paintBorder(Component c, Graphics g,
                        int x, int y,
                        int width, int height)

public Insets getBorderInsets(Component c)

public boolean isBorderOpaque()
```

The method `paintBorder()` is used to paint a border around a specified `Component c` at the location coordinates x and y. The arguments `width` and `height` represent the respective width and height of the painted border. The method `getBorderInsets()` returns the specified insets for the border to be used with `Component c`. The method `isBorderOpaque()` returns `true` or `false` to indicate whether the border should be opaque or transparent. If the return status is `false`, the background color of the container is visible.

The AbstractBorder Class

In addition to the interface `Border`, the package `javax.swing.border` contains a simple abstract class called `AbstractBorder`. This class implements the interface `Border` and represents an empty border with no size. This class is a convenient base class from which other classes are derived. The class `AbstractBorder` contains an overloaded method `getInteriorRectangle()` that is in addition to the methods implemented from the interface `Border`. For further details on this class, you may consult Appendix A, "JFC Swing Quick Reference."

Border Types

The package `javax.swing.border` contains a list of classes for practical borders. You can simply instantiate a specific border class or use the relevant factory method to create a border object. The following sections present the Swing borders that are readily available (see Figure 7.6).

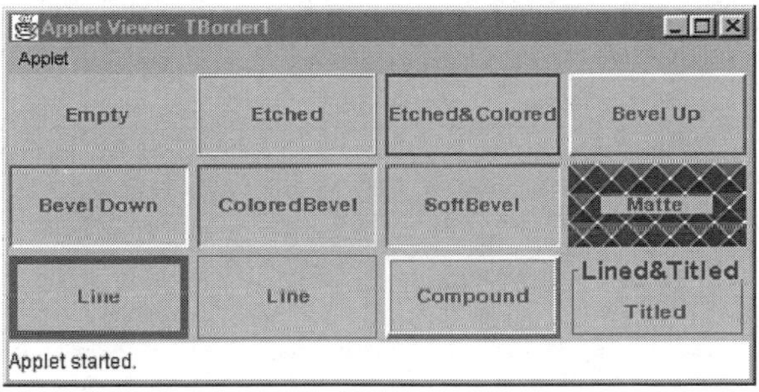

Figure 7.6

An applet displaying labels with Swing borders.

Empty Border

The empty border leaves a transparent margin without any associated drawing (see Figure 7.6). Border objects of this type are represented by the class EmptyBorder and are exact alternatives to using the insets in AWT. The class requires that fields such as top, left, bottom, and right be specified. You can also use an insets object to create an empty border. The following are the constructors for the empty border:

```
public EmptyBorder(int top, int left, int bottom, int right)
public EmptyBorder(Insets insets)
```

Etched Border

An etched border produces either an etched-in or etched-out effect around a component (see Figure 7.6). The etched border is represented by the class EtchedBorder. You can specify the type of etching using the field LOWERED or RAISED. By default, the etched border is of type etched-in.

The etched border can be associated with highlight and shadow colors that can be specified. If no colors are specified for these attributes, the border derives the background colors of the component. To create an etched border, you can use one of the following constructors that require argument values for etched type and highlight and shadow colors:

```
public EtchedBorder()
public EtchedBorder(int etchType)
public EtchedBorder(Color highlight,  Color shadow)
public EtchedBorder(int etchType,
                    Color highlight,  Color shadow)
```

Bevel Border

A bevel border has either a raised or lowered bevel surface as shown in Figure 7.6. The bevel borders are represented by the class BevelBorder, and you use the fields RAISED and LOWERED to make a bevel border raised or lowered. You can use colors for the inner and outer highlights or shadows of a bevel border. The following are the constructors that create bevel borders:

```
public BevelBorder(int bevelType)

public BevelBorder(int bevelType,
                   Color highlight,
                   Color shadow)

public BevelBorder(int bevelType,
                   Color highlightOuter,
                   Color highlightInner,
                   Color shadowOuter,
                   Color shadowInner)
```

Soft Bevel Border

A soft bevel border is a bevel border with softened or rounded corners. The borders of this type are represented by the class SoftBevelBorder. The class SoftBevelBorder extends the class BevelBorder, so you can create soft bevel borders with raised or lowered surfaces. A soft bevel border is created by using any one of the following constructors:

```
public SoftBevelBorder(int bevelType)
public SoftBevelBorder(int bevelType,
                       Color highlight,
                       Color shadow)
public SoftBevelBorder(int bevelType,
                       Color highlightOuter,
                       Color highlightInner,
                       Color shadowOuter,
                       Color shadowInner)
```

Matte Border

A matte border displays a matte pattern. The matte pattern is created by using either a solid color or a tiled icon (see Figure 7.6). The matte borders are of class type MatteBorder, which extends the class EmptyBorder. Solid matte borders are created by using the specified color. Similarly, tiled matte borders are created by using an icon that displays a matte picture. The following constructors create a matte border:

```
public MatteBorder(int top, int left,
                   int bottom, int right,
                   Color color)

public MatteBorder(int top, int left,
                   int bottom, int right,
                   Icon tileIcon)
public MatteBorder(Icon tileIcon)
```

Line Border

A line border is simply a line around a component of a certain thickness and color. A line border object is represented by the class LineBorder, which extends the class AbstractBorder. To create a line border you can use the following static methods:

```
static Border createBlackLineBorder()
static Border createGrayLineBorder()
```

These methods create line border objects with a thickness equal to 1 and with the respective colors. You can also create a line border by using the following constructors:

```
public LineBorder(Color color)
public LineBorder(Color color, int thickness)
```

You need to specify the color of the line. The thickness of the line is optional; if you use the constructor without the thickness argument, the default thickness is of value 1.

Compound Borders

A compound border is composed of two border objects. You can nest an inside border within the insets of an outside border. A compound border is represented by the class CompoundBorder, which extends AbstractBorder. The following constructors create a compound border object:

```
public CompoundBorder()
public CompoundBorder(Border outsideBorder,
                      Border insideBorder)
```

Titled Borders

A titled border is a combination of a title string and any of the borders that have been previously discussed. You control the position of the title with a justification. You can also specify the font and color of the title to be used. All these title attributes are the static fields inside the class TitledBorder, which represents a border with a title. The list of fields is given in the reference provided in Appendix A.

To create a titled border, you need to specify the title and the border. If no border is specified, an etched border is used by default. The following is the list of constructors that create a titled border:

```
public TitledBorder(String title)

public TitledBorder(Border border, String title)

public TitledBorder(Border border, String title,
                    int titleJustification,
                    int titlePosition)
public TitledBorder(Border border, String title,
                    int titleJustification,
                    int titlePosition,Font titleFont)
```

```
public TitledBorder(Border border,String title,
                    int titleJustification,
                    int titlePosition,
                    Font titleFont, Color titleColor)
```

Borders Code Example

The borders discussed so far are demonstrated by the example program shown in Listing 7.3. The program implements an applet that displays a set of labels with borders. Each label will possess a specific type of border.

Listing 7.3   Borders Applet Creates One of Every Type of Border (TBorder1.java)

```
/*
 * <Applet code=TBorder1 width=400 height=200>
 * </Applet>
 */

import javax.swing.border.*;
import javax.swing.*;
import java.awt.*;

public class TBorder1 extends JApplet{
    public void init() {
        // 1. Create an object of panel to contain a label
        // and add it to the applet's content pane.
        LabelPanel panel = new LabelPanel();
        getContentPane().add(panel);
    }
}

// 2. Panel that contains labels with borders.
class LabelPanel extends JPanel {
    Border border;
    JLabel label;

    public LabelPanel() {
        // 3. Assign grid layout (with 3 rows, 4 columns, and
        // 5 pixel horizontal and vertical spacing) to panel.
        setLayout(new GridLayout(3,4,5,5));

        // 4. Create a label with an empty border.
        label = new JLabel("Empty", JLabel.CENTER);
        label.setOpaque(true);
        // Create an empty border object with the specified insets:
        // top = 1; left = 1; bottom = 1; right =1.
        border = new EmptyBorder(1,1,1,1);
        // Assign the border to the label.
```

```
label.setBorder(border);
add(label);

// 5. Create a label with an etched border.
label = new JLabel("Etched", JLabel.CENTER);
label.setOpaque(true);
// Create a raised and etched border.
border = new EtchedBorder(EtchedBorder.RAISED);
label.setBorder(border);
add(label);

// 6. Create a label with an etched border with color.
label = new JLabel("Etched&Colored", JLabel.CENTER);
label.setOpaque(true);
border = new EtchedBorder(EtchedBorder.LOWERED, // Lowered and etched
➥type
                         Color.red, Color.blue); // Hightlight and
➥shadow colors
label.setBorder(border);
add(label);

// 7. Create a label with a bevel border.
label = new JLabel("Bevel Up", JLabel.CENTER);
label.setOpaque(true);
border = new BevelBorder(BevelBorder.RAISED); // Raised bevel type
label.setBorder(border);
add(label);

// 8. Create a label with a lowered bevel border.
label = new JLabel("Bevel Down", JLabel.CENTER);
label.setOpaque(true);
border = new BevelBorder(BevelBorder.LOWERED); // Lowered bevel type
label.setBorder(border);
add(label);

// 9. Create a label with a raised bevel border.
label = new JLabel("ColoredBevel", JLabel.CENTER);
label.setOpaque(true);
border = new BevelBorder(BevelBorder.RAISED, // Raised bevel type
                         Color.gray, Color.yellow); // Hightlight and
➥shadow colors
label.setBorder(border);
add(label);

// 10. Create a label with a soft bevel border.
label = new JLabel("SoftBevel", JLabel.CENTER);
label.setOpaque(true);
```

continues

Listing 7.3   continued

```
        // Create a lowered bevel type border object with softened corners
        // without pointings
        border = new SoftBevelBorder(BevelBorder.LOWERED);
        label.setBorder(border);
        add(label);

        // 11. Create a label with a matte border.
        label = new JLabel("Matte", JLabel.CENTER);
        label.setOpaque(true);
        Icon icon = new ImageIcon("cube.gif");
        // Create a matte border object with the specified insets of
        // top = 20, left = 20, bottom = 20; right = 20 and matte icon
        border = new MatteBorder(20,20,20,20, icon );
        label.setBorder(border);
        add(label);

        // 12. Create a label with a red line border.
        label = new JLabel("Line", JLabel.CENTER);
        label.setOpaque(true);
        border = new LineBorder(Color.red, // Line color = red
                              5); // line thickness = 5.
        label.setBorder(border);
        add(label);

        // 13. Create a label with a gray line border.
        label = new JLabel("Line", JLabel.CENTER);
        label.setOpaque(true);
        // Create a line border with gray color and thickness = 1.
        border = LineBorder.createGrayLineBorder();
        label.setBorder(border);
        add(label);

        // 14. Create a label with a compound border.
        label = new JLabel("Compound", JLabel.CENTER);
        label.setOpaque(true);
        // Create a compound border with a raised bevel border and a raised
        // etched border
        border = new CompoundBorder(
                new BevelBorder(BevelBorder.RAISED),
                new EtchedBorder(EtchedBorder.RAISED));
        label.setBorder(border);
        add(label);

        // 15. Create a label with a titled border with specified
        // border.
        label = new JLabel("Titled", JLabel.CENTER);
        label.setOpaque(true);
        border = new TitledBorder(new LineBorder(Color.red),
```

```
                              "Lined&Titled", // Display title.
                              TitledBorder.DEFAULT_JUSTIFICATION,
// Title justification.

                              TitledBorder.CENTER, // Title location.
                              new Font("Sans", Font.BOLD, 16), // Title
➥font.

                              Color.blue); // Title color.
        label.setBorder(border);
        add(label);


    }
}
```

Code Details

The applet TBorder1 uses a panel that displays a set of Swing labels, each of which is decorated with a border of a specific type. Snippet-1 inside the init() method of the applet creates an instance of the panel and adds it to the applet. Snippet-2 declares a label and a border as data fields of the panel. Snippet-3 assigns the panel to the grid layout.

Snippets 4–15 create labels with their respective borders and add them to the applet. Note that various border objects, such as an empty border, etched border, etched border with color, bevel-up border, bevel-down border, bevel border with color, soft bevel border, matte border, line border, compound border, and titled border are created. The output of this program is shown in Figure 7.6.

Custom Borders

If none of the borders from the Swing library meets your needs, you can create custom borders by using the interface Border or the class AbstractBorder.

To create a custom border, you need to create a custom border class that defines the methods inside the interface Border. The interface Border has already been discussed in an earlier section. Listing 7.4 uses custom borders. The custom border created is made up of a set of four 3D rectangles with a specified color (see Figure 7.7).

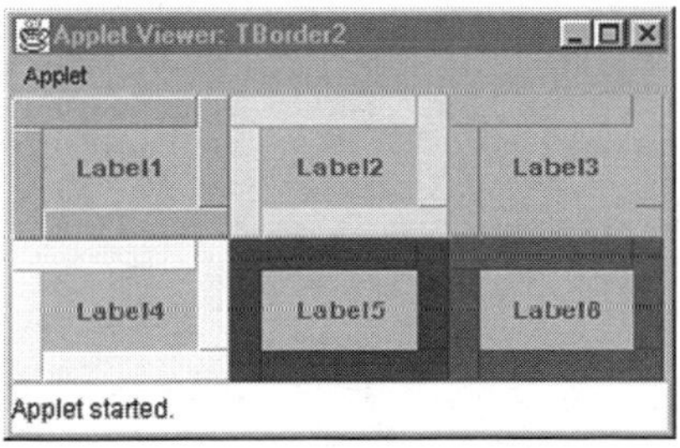

Figure 7.7

An applet displaying labels with custom borders.

Listing 7.4   Custom Borders (TBorder2.java)

```
/*
 * <Applet code=TBorder2 width=300 height=150>
 * </Applet>
 */

import javax.swing.*;
import java.awt.*;
import javax.swing.border.*;

public class TBorder2 extends JApplet {
    public void init() {

        // 1. Get a handle on the applet's content pane.
        // and set the grid layout.
        Container container = this.getContentPane();
        container.setLayout(new GridLayout(2,3)); // 2 rows and 3 columns.

        // 2. Add labels to the applet with decorating
        //     borders created from the class SimpleBorder.

        // 2(a) Create an array of favorite colors.
        Color[] colors = {Color.lightGray, Color.yellow,
                          Color.green, Color.white,
                          Color.blue, Color.red};
        // 2(b) Create labels and add them to the container.
        for (int i=0; i<6; i++) { // Total number of labels = 6.
            JLabel label = new JLabel("Label"+(i+1), JLabel.CENTER);
            label.setOpaque(true);
            container.add(label);
            label.setBorder(new SimpleBorder(15, // Top inset.
                                    15, // Left inset.
                                    15, // Right inset.
                                    15, // Bottom inset.
                             colors[i])); // border color
        }
    }
}

// 3. Define the custom border class called SimpleBorder.
class SimpleBorder implements Border {
    int top;
    int left;
    int bottom;
    int right;
    Color color = null;

    public SimpleBorder(int top, int left, int bottom,
                            int right, Color color) {
```

```
            this.top = top;
            this.left = left;
            this.bottom = bottom;
            this.right = right;
            this.color = color;
    }

    public void paintBorder(Component c, // Component that will contain the
    ➥border.
                            Graphics g,  // Graphics context.
                            int x, int y, // x and y coordinates of the painted
    ➥border.
                            int width, int height) { // Border width and
    ➥height.

        // Create insets around the component to draw the border.
        Insets insets = getBorderInsets(c);

        // Set the border color.
        if (color != null)
            g.setColor(color);

        // Prepare the border by using 3D Rectangles returned by the method.
        // g.fill3Drect(). This method takes the argument values as following:
        g.fill3DRect(0, // x-coordinate
                     0, // y-coordinate
                     width-insets.right, // width
                     insets.top, // height.
                     true); // Rectangle appears to be raised.
        // The following methods also work with the arguments as shown in the
        // previous method call.
        g.fill3DRect(0, insets.top, insets.left,
                        height-insets.top, true);
        g.fill3DRect(insets.left, height-insets.bottom,
                        width-insets.left, insets.bottom, true);
        g.fill3DRect(width-insets.right, 0, insets.right,
                        height-insets.bottom, true);
    }

    public Insets getBorderInsets(Component c) {
        return new Insets(top, left, bottom, right);
    }

    public boolean isBorderOpaque() {
        return true;
    }
}
```

Code Details

The class Tborder2 is a Swing applet displaying six labels with custom borders. Inside the init() method of the applet, snippet-1 gets a handle on the applet's content pane and assigns the layout of type grid layout with two rows and three columns. Snippet-2 defines an array of colors and then adds the labels to the layout. Each of these labels is assigned borders created from the custom class SimpleBorder.

Snippet-3 defines the class SimpleBorder, which implements the interface Border. This class contains the inset arguments top, left, bottom, and right as its fields. The color of the border is declared as a data field. Through the constructor of the class you can initialize these fields.

As you can see inside the class SimpleBorder, the methods from the interface Border are defined. The method paintBorder() creates an insets object by using the method getBorderInsets(). getBorderInsets() returns an insets object with the values top, left, bottom, and right supplied through the constructor.

The graphics context object from the method paintBorder() is then used to set the color of the border to be created. Now you can use the method fill3Drect() to create a 3D rectangle according to the coordinates given in the code. This creates the necessary rectangular border around a label. The other method, isBorderOpaque(), is defined to return true, which makes the border appear with the color that has been assigned. The output from this program is shown in Figure 7.7.

CHAPTER 8

Buttons and Check Boxes

The Swing library provides classes for simple and toggle buttons, and an abstract button that encapsulates certain common functionality of the button classes. The buttons have also been supported for different kinds of pluggable look-and-feel such as Java/Metallic, Motif, and Windows.

Check boxes and radio buttons are components that are functionally parallel to the Swing buttons; however, their graphical view is totally different. Check boxes are often used to turn some attributes on and off in a user interface. Check boxes and radio buttons subclass from the Swing toggle button where their functionality has been encapsulated to a significant extent. This chapter discusses each of these components in detail with examples that demonstrate relevant API methods.

The AbstractButton Class

In general, every GUI component has a certain state and behavior. The behavior common to the regular buttons, check boxes, and radio buttons is enclosed in an abstract class called AbstractButton. Thus, the class AbstractButton encapsulates a rich set of methods. The class AbstractButton is a direct subclass of JComponent and implements the interfaces SwingConstants and ItemSelectable.

TIP

If you have to create any button-like component, you can choose to subclass it from the class AbstractButton (rather than JComponent) to utilize its functionality.

This chapter discusses Swing buttons, represented by the classes JButton and JToggleButton, and check boxes of type JCheckbox and JRadioButton. The class AbstractButton is the parent of all these components with the class-hierarchy relationship shown in Figure 8.1.

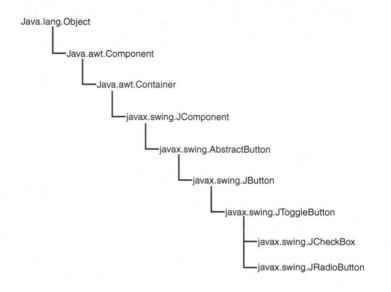

Java.lang.Object

└─Java.awt.Component

  └─Java.awt.Container

    └─javax.swing.JComponent

      └─javax.swing.AbstractButton

        └─javax.swing.JButton

          └─javax.swing.JToggleButton

            ├─javax.swing.JCheckBox

            └─javax.swing.JRadioButton

Figure 8.1

The class AbstractButton and its subclasses.

Anatomy of AbstractButton

The class AbstractButton encapsulates a large number of common methods that are invoked by the objects of its subclasses such as JButton, JToggleButton, JCheckbox, and JRadioButton. Also, because the interface SwingConstants is implemented by the class AbstractButton, the constants can be used inside descendent components. You can find the methods for setting or getting various button attributes and registering listeners with them. The following is a list of the important methods that are often used:

```
public void addActionListener(ActionListener listener)
public void addChangeListener(ChangeListener listener)
public void addItemListener(ItemListener listener)
```

The Swing buttons JButton and JToggleButton fire events that are received by relevant action listeners. The method addActionListener() is a means of registering action listeners with a source component that invokes the method. The method addChangeListener() helps to inform the interested listeners to notify that the state has changed in the event source. The addItemListener() method is commonly used by the objects of `JCheckbox` and `JRadioButton` to register the item listeners whenever an item has been selected or deselected.

In addition to text labels, the Swing buttons also support icons to be displayed over them. Icons for different button contexts, such as when a button has been selected or deselected, disabled or disabled and selected, rolled over or rolled over and selected, can also be changed. The following is a list of methods that provide this support:

```
public void setText(String textLabel)
public void setIcon(Icon icon)
public void setPressedIcon(Icon icon)
public void setRolloverIcon(Icon icon)
public void setSelectedIcon(Icon icon)
public void setDisabledIcon(Icon icon)
public void setRolloverSelectedIcon(Icon icon)
public void setDisabledSelectedIcon(Icon icon)
```

The "set" methods also have their corresponding "get" methods that return the corresponding attributes of the component. For example, the method `setText()` has a corresponding method `getText()` that returns a text of type `String` class.

To align the icon or text horizontally or vertically over its component, you use the following methods that take the Swing constants such as `TOP`, `LEFT`, `BOTTOM`, `RIGHT`, and `CENTER` for the respective positions:

```
setHorizontalAlignment(int swingConstant)
setVerticalAlignment(int swingConstant)
```

The following methods support the positioning of text relative to the icon in the horizontal or vertical direction:

```
public setHorizontalTextPosition(int swingConstant)
public setVerticalTextPosition(int swingConstant)
```

The following are more "set" methods that can be used to set the attributes such as button enabled or disabled, to indicate a shortcut key, to paint the border or focus, and so on:

```
public void setEnabled(boolean value)
public void setKeyAccelerator(int key)
public void setBorderPainted(boolean value)
public void setFocusPainted(boolean value)
public void setMargin(Insets insets)
public void setActionCommand(String command)
```

The following methods return a Boolean value of `true` or `false` depending on the state of the button, such as whether the button has been selected, border painted, focus painted, or rollover enabled:

```
boolean isSelected()
boolean isBorderPainted()
boolean isFocusPainted()
boolean isRolloverEnabled()
```

For a comprehensive list of these methods, refer to Appendix A, "JFC Swing Quick Reference," which covers a large number of classes from different Swing packages. The next sections of this chapter take you to the concrete subclasses of AbstractButton that are displayed in a GUI layout.

Buttons

Swing buttons are represented by the objects of class JButton, and each button is basically an implementation of a push-type button. Unlike AWT buttons, Swing buttons can be displayed with text labels as well as icons. You can also set different icons for different states of the buttons (for example, when the button is pressed or disabled) by using the supporting methods.

The class JButton is a direct subclass of AbstractButton. In fact, a great deal of functionality for JButton has been inherited from AbstractButton. You often invoke most of the methods in the class AbstractButton on a JButton object to, for instance, set a default image or text alignment, register event listeners, and so on.

JButton Constructors

A Swing button is created by using any one of the following constructors:

```
public JButton()
public JButton(String text)
public JButton(Icon icon)
public JButton(String text, Icon icon)
```

The first constructor creates a new button without any text or icon that can be set later to a specific text or icon of interest. The arguments text or icon from the next two constructors specify the text label or the icon to be displayed over the face of the button created by using the specific constructor. The last constructor is useful to specify both the text and icon of the button object while a button is being created.

Action Events and Listeners

The button object fires events that are of the class type ActionEvent. These events can be caught by certain listener objects to perform the processing required.

An action listener class implements the interface ActionListener and provides code for the method actionPerformed(). This is the only method inside the interface ActionListener. To be able to receive the events fired by the button objects, listener objects must be registered with the event sources. You can connect an action listener class with a button source by invoking the method addActionListener() located in the class AbstractButton on a source object. The method addActionListener() takes the button object as its argument value.

Whenever a source button is operated, the action is propagated to invoke the method `actionPerformed()`. Thus the code to be executed whenever a button is operated is enclosed inside this method. The method `actionPerformed()` takes an object of the class `ActionEvent` as its argument value. The class `ActionEvent` contains the methods that retrieve useful information while handling the code inside the method `actionPerformed()`. The methods are as follows:

```
public String getActionCommand()
public int getModifiers()
public String paramString()
```

When an event source creates an action event, it can include a string type action command that gives some details about the event source. The `getActionCommand()` method retrieves the action event's action command. The button example shows how to use `setActionCommand()` and `getActionCommand()`. The method `getModifiers()` retrieves the state of the modifier keys when the action event has been created. The method `paramString()` generates a string that represents the state of the action event.

JButton Code Example

Listing 8.1 demonstrates the use of `JButton`. The program is a Swing applet that shows different "pluggable look-and-feel" views of the `JButton` and utilizes some of the APIs that are operated on the objects of `JButton` (see Figure 8.2). The program also demonstrates the handling of events that are fired by the button objects. When a button is clicked, the appearance of the applet changes to the specific look-and-feel.

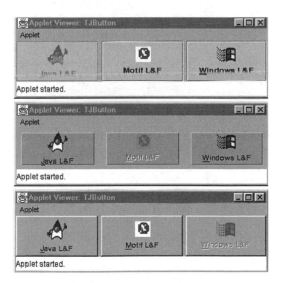

Figure 8.2

The TJButton applet with different pluggable look-and-feels.

Listing 8.1   JButton Used with Different Look-and-Feels (TJButton.java)

```
// Demonstrates the Swing Buttons...
/*
<Applet code=TJButton width=400 height=65>
</Applet>
*/
import java.awt.*;
import javax.swing.*;
import java.awt.event.*;

public class TJButton extends JApplet {
    //1. Declare the Swing buttons.
    JButton button1, button2, button3;
    //2. Icons for the buttons 1, 2, and 3.
    Icon metalIcon = new ImageIcon("metal.gif");
    Icon motifIcon = new ImageIcon("motif.gif");
    Icon windowsIcon = new ImageIcon("windows.gif");
    //3. String forms of different look-and-feel.
    String metallicLF =
        "javax.swing.plaf.metal.MetalLookAndFeel";
    String motifLF =
        "com.sun.java.swing.plaf.motif.MotifLookAndFeel";
    String windowsLF =
        "com.sun.java.swing.plaf.windows.WindowsLookAndFeel";

    public void init() {
        //4. Creating grid layout and setting it for the applet.
        GridLayout grid = new GridLayout(1,3,5,5);
        this.getContentPane().setLayout(grid);
        this.getContentPane().setBackground(Color.lightGray);

        //5. Creating and adding Swing button1.
        button1 = new JButton("Java L&F",metalIcon);
        button1.setVerticalTextPosition(SwingConstants.BOTTOM);
        button1.setHorizontalTextPosition(SwingConstants.CENTER);
        button1.setMnemonic('J');
        button1.setEnabled(false);
        button1.setActionCommand(metallicLF);
        CustomListener cl = new CustomListener(this);
        button1.addActionListener(cl);
        this.getContentPane().add(button1);

        //6. Creating and adding Swing button2.
        button2 = new JButton("Motif L&F",motifIcon);
        button2.setVerticalTextPosition(SwingConstants.BOTTOM);
        button2.setHorizontalTextPosition(SwingConstants.CENTER);
        button2.setMnemonic('M');
        button2.setActionCommand(motifLF);
        button2.addActionListener(cl);
        this.getContentPane().add(button2);
```

```
    //7. Creating and adding Swing button3.
    button3 = new JButton("Windows L&F",windowsIcon);
    button3.setVerticalTextPosition(SwingConstants.BOTTOM);
    button3.setHorizontalTextPosition(SwingConstants.CENTER);
    button3.setMnemonic('W');
    button3.setActionCommand(windowsLF);
    button3.addActionListener(cl);
    this.getContentPane().add(button3);
}

//8. Inner class that supports event handling.
class CustomListener implements ActionListener {
    TJButton testApplet = null;

    public CustomListener(TJButton testApplet) {
        this.testApplet = testApplet;
    }

    public void actionPerformed(ActionEvent evt) {
        //9. For pluggable look-and-feel.
        String LF = evt.getActionCommand();
            try {
                UIManager.setLookAndFeel(LF);
                SwingUtilities.updateComponentTreeUI(testApplet);
                JButton button = (JButton) evt.getSource();
                button.setEnabled(false);
                updateStatus(button);
            } catch (Exception e) {
                System.err.println("Look&Feel not set for "
                                    +LF+" !");
            }
    }
    //10. Updates the status of each button (Enabled/Disabled).
    public void updateStatus(JButton button) {
        if (button == button1) {
            button2.setEnabled(true);
            button3.setEnabled(true);
        }
        else if (button == button2) {
            button1.setEnabled(true);
            button3.setEnabled(true);
        }
        else if (button == button3) {
            button1.setEnabled(true);
            button2.setEnabled(true);
        }
    }
}
}
```

Code Details

Listing 8.1 contains three different objects of type JButton that are shown as its member data in snippet-1. Snippet-2 creates the icon objects that will be set for each of the Swing buttons. Snippet-3 shows a list of string fields, such as metallicLF, motifLF, and windowsLF, which are the string representations of a specific pluggable look-and-feel. This information will be used later to set the required look-and-feel of the applet.

Next, the applet begins with the process of initialization by using the method init(). Snippet-4 creates a layout of type GridLayout and sets it to the Swing applet's content pane. It is important to note that the layout is set to the content pane object and returned by the method getContentPane(), rather than the Swing applet directly.

Snippet-5 creates an object of type JButton with the label "Java L&F" and the icon called metalIcon. The metalIcon has already been created as a data member of the applet. The next couple of lines of code position the text at the specified location on the face of the button with reference to its icon. That is, the text is relatively set at the bottom portion of the button in the vertical direction by using the method setVerticalTextPositon(), and at the center of the button in the horizontal direction by using setHorizontalTextPosition().

The method setMnemonic() supports accelerated keys by underlining the specified letter, "J" in this case. When the applet is displayed, it is shown with the Java/Metallic look-and-feel. Thus, the corresponding button, button1, has been disabled by setting the method setEnabled() to false. In the next line of code, setActionCommand() sets the action command that takes a certain string form of the desired look-and-feel. This method helps to retrieve the look-and-feel at a later stage by using the method getActionCommand(). As will be discussed later, getActionCommand() can be operated on the event object.

The method addActionListener() registers the specified button listener with the button object in snippet-5. The button listener, called CustomListener, receives the events of type ActionEvent that are fired by the source, button1. this. getContentPane().add(button1) adds button1 to the Swing applet's container. Snippets 6 and 7 operate in a similar manner for the other button objects, button2 and button3. These buttons are meant to change the look-and-feel of the Swing applet to the Motif-type and Window-type while the applet is executing.

Snippet-8 shows an inner class that handles the action events fired by the button objects. The listener class implements the interface ActionListener and provides the code for the method actionPerformed(). actionPerformed() is a member of the ActionListener interface and executes its code whenever an ActionEvent object is fired by any one of the source objects of type JButton.

Snippet-9 is the code executed by the method actionPerformed(). getActionCommand() returns the string form of the desired look-and-feel. getActionCommand() is invoked on the ActionEvent object. Note that the string form of look-and-feel has been set previously by using setActionCommand(), which is invoked on a specific button object. The class UIManager controls the look-and-feel of the user interface. The method setLookAndFeel() is the handle to assign a new look-and-feel to the applet TJButton and its components. The value LF is assigned the string form of the requested look-and-feel. You must enclose the setLookAndFeel() method in a try statement to catch a general exception of type Exception or a specific list of exceptions as shown in the following:

```
java.lang.ClassNotFoundException
java.lang.InstantiationException
java.lang.IllegalAccessException
javax.swing.UnsupportedLookandFeelException
```

In these exceptions, the first one is thrown if the look-and-feel class has not been found. The second is thrown if an instance of the class could not be created for some reason because it is an interface or an abstract class. The third exception is thrown if the class is not accessible because it is not public or in a different package. The last is thrown if the look-and-feel is not supported.

The method updateComponentTreeUI() from SwingUtilities is called to update each component in the component-hierarchy to the new look-and-feel. This method takes the object of the applet TJButton as the value of its argument.

When the applet starts, its view appears with the Java/Metallic type look-and-feel. Whenever a button with text "Motif L&F" or "Windows L&F" is clicked, the applet's appearance changes to the respective look-and-feel as shown in the output. The activated buttons are also disabled.

NOTE

When a button is disabled, its icon and label are automatically changed to a gray color by the action of an internal gray filter.

Toggle Buttons

Toggle buttons are similar to the regular buttons discussed previously. There is a minor difference, however. When a toggle button is "pushed-in," its view remains in the pushed-in condition until it is pressed again to "pop-out."

Toggle buttons are represented by the class JToggleButton, which is essentially an encapsulation of a two-state button. JToggleButton is a subclass of AbstractButton. You can invoke any of the methods available in AbstractButton on the objects of JToggleButton. Also note the functionality supported in DefaultButtonModel and the inner class ToggleButtonModel. The class DefaultButtonModel contains the implementation of the model data of a button. Whenever a toggle button is operated, it fires the action events in a way similar to a regular clickable button.

JToggleButton Constructors

A toggle button object can be created by using any one of the eight constructors discussed in this section.

```
public JToggleButton();
public JToggleButton(String textlabel);
public JToggleButton(Icon icon);
public JToggleButton(boolean pressed);
```

The first constructor creates an initially unselected toggle button without setting any text or icon. The second performs the same function as the first with a text label attached to the toggle button. The third constructor creates a toggle button that is in the deselected condition and possesses the specified icon over it. The fourth constructor creates a toggle button that has the specified state as pressed (`true`) or not pressed (`false`).

The following constructors are different combinations of the arguments from these four constructors.

```
public JToggleButton(String textlabel, boolean pressed);
public JToggleButton(Icon icon, boolean pressed);
public JToggleButton(String textlabel, boolean pressed);
```

To create a toggle button with the specified text, image, and pressed state (`true` or `false`), use the following constructor:

```
public JToggleButton(String textlabel, Icon icon,
                     boolean pressed);
```

Toggle Button Code Example

Listing 8.2 shows a simple audio player applet. The applet contains two buttons, Play and Stop, with suitable icons (see Figure 8.3). The icon from the Play button uses an image file, `play.gif`. The Stop button uses the class `TestIcon` from the previous chapter with a slight modification to specify the icon colors. The class `TestIcon` expects you to explicitly pass the colors red and gray for the enabled and disabled icons, respectively. The Play and Stop buttons remain in the pressed-in state whenever they are operated, and pop-out if they are operated again.

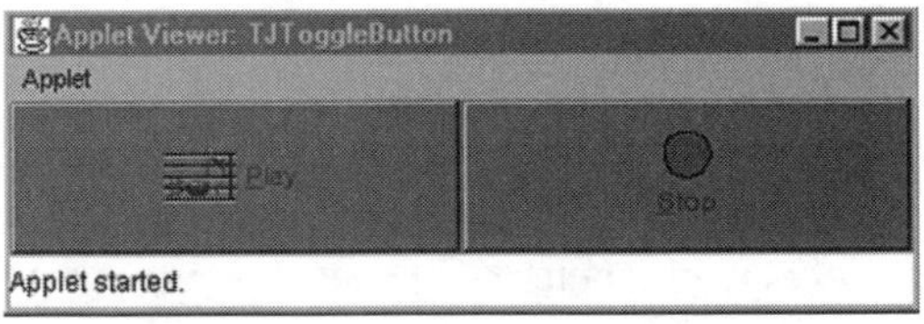

Figure 8.3

The audio player applet created with JToggleButton.

*Listing 8.2   JToggleButton Used to Create a Simple Audio Player
(TJToggleButton.java)*

```java
// Demonstrates the Toggle Buttons...
/*
<Applet code=TJToggleButton width=400 height=75>
</Applet>
*/

import java.awt.*;
import javax.swing.*;
import java.awt.event.*;
import java.applet.*;

public class TJToggleButton extends JApplet {
    // 1. Declare a couple of toggle button references.
    JToggleButton playButton,stopButton;
    // 2. Audio support.
    AudioClip audioClip = null;

    // 3.Icons to be used for the Stop button.
    Icon enabledIcon = new TestIcon(Color.red);
    Icon disabledIcon = new TestIcon(Color.gray);
    String LF = "com.sun.java.swing.plaf.motif.MotifLookAndFeel";

    public void init() {
        // 4. Sets the Motif look-and-feel.
        try {
            UIManager.setLookAndFeel(LF);
        } catch (Exception e) {
            System.err.println("Look and Feel not Initialized!");
        }

        // 5. Create and set the layout.
        GridLayout grid = new GridLayout(1,2);
        this.getContentPane().setLayout(grid);
        this.getContentPane().setBackground(Color.gray);

        // 6. Create and add a Play button.
        ImageIcon playIcon = new ImageIcon("play.gif");
        playButton = new JToggleButton("Play",playIcon);
        playButton.setBackground(Color.lightGray);
        playButton.setForeground(Color.blue);
        playButton.setMnemonic('p');
        CustomListener cl = new CustomListener();
        playButton.addActionListener(cl);
        this.getContentPane().add(playButton);

        // 7. Create and add a Stop button.
        stopButton = new JToggleButton("Stop",enabledIcon);
```

continues

Listing 8.2   continued

```java
        stopButton.setVerticalTextPosition(SwingConstants.BOTTOM);
        stopButton.setHorizontalTextPosition(SwingConstants.CENTER);
        stopButton.setBackground(Color.lightGray);
        stopButton.setForeground(Color.blue);
        stopButton.setMnemonic('s');
        stopButton.addActionListener(cl);
        this.getContentPane().add(stopButton);

        // 8. Initialize the audio clip.
        if (audioClip == null) {
            audioClip = this.getAudioClip(getCodeBase(),
                          "music.au");
        }
    }
    // 9. Listener class for the button objects.
    class CustomListener implements ActionListener {
        public void actionPerformed(ActionEvent e) {
            JToggleButton button = (JToggleButton) e.getSource();
            // 10. If the play button is clicked...
            if (button == playButton) {
                playButton.setEnabled(false);
                if (!stopButton.isEnabled())
                    stopButton.setEnabled(true);
                stopButton.setIcon(enabledIcon);
                audioClip.loop();
            }
            // 11. If the stop button is clicked...
            else if (button == stopButton) {
                stopButton.setEnabled(false);
                stopButton.setIcon(disabledIcon);
                if (!playButton.isEnabled())
                    playButton.setEnabled(true);
                audioClip.stop();
            }
        }
    }
}

/*
 * 12. A class that implements the Icon interface;
 * a slight modification (to display the specified
 * colors) of the TestIcon shown in chapter-7.
 */

class TestIcon implements Icon {
    int width = 20; // default icon-width
    int height = 20;  // default icon-height
    Color fillColor;  // icon color to be specified
```

```
// 13. Constructor that specifies the icon color.
public TestIcon(Color fillColor) {
    this.fillColor = fillColor;
}

// 14. Interface method to paint the icon.
// using the methods in graphics context object
public void paintIcon(Component c,
                      Graphics g,
                      int x,
                      int y) {
    g.setColor(fillColor);
    g.fillOval(x, y, width, height);
    g.setColor(Color.black);
    g.drawOval(x, y, width, height);
}

// 15. Interface method to retrieve the icon width.
public int getIconWidth() {
    return width;
}

// 16. Interface method to retrieve the icon height.
public int getIconHeight() {
    return height;
}
}
```

Code Details

The Swing applet begins by declaring the references for Play and Stop buttons in code snippet-1. These references will be initialized inside the init() method. Snippet-2 declares an object of type AudioClip to support the required audio. Snippet-3 defines a couple of icons called enabledIcon and disabledIcon. These icons will be displayed on the Stop button. Next, the string form of Motif look-and-feel has been defined.

Snippet-4 sets the Motif look-and-feel for the applet by invoking the method setLookAndFeel() from the class UIManager. If the initialization process fails, you need to provide code for catching the exception thrown. Snippet-5 creates GridLayout and assigns it to the applet's content pane.

Snippet-5 initializes an image icon called playIcon and the icon is used to display the playButton object. The Play button is represented by the object of type JToggleButton. You can use the methods setBackground() and setForeground() to initialize the button's background and foreground to the desired colors. The method setMnemonic() provides an accelerated key to start playing the audio player.

The listener object cl of type CustomListener is registered with the playButton object by using addActionListener(). The last line of this snippet adds playButton to the applet's content pane. Snippet-6 creates a Stop button but stopButton does not use an image file as its icon. Instead, it uses the objects of TestIcon class as the required icons for its enabled or disabled states. These icons have already been defined as the member data of this applet. For a view of the class TestIcon, consult Chapter 7, "Icons, Labels, and Borders."

Snippet-7 initializes the audio clip. The reference audioClip is initialized by the return value of the method getAudioClip(). getAudioClip() requires the name of the audio file music.au and its URL as arguments. Note that the class JApplet is a subclass of the AWT class Applet, so you can invoke getAudioClip() from the class Applet.

Snippet-8 creates the listener objects for the Play and Stop buttons by using the class CustomListener. The class implements the interface ActionListener and provides the necessary code to handle the action events inside the method actionPerformed(). Snippet-9 provides the code to perform the music whenever the play button is selected. The statement audioClip.loop() repeatedly runs the music file loaded by the audio clip in a loop. The code also changes the status of the Play and Stop buttons to a new state. Snippet-10 works in a similar manner except that in the last statement of code the statement audioClip.stop() is executed to stop the music whenever the Stop button is selected.

Snippet-12 defines the class TestIcon. The constructor of this class requires the color of the icon, as shown in snippet-13. Snippet-14 creates the icon by using the graphics context object. Snippets 15 and 16 retrieve the width and height of the icon.

Check Boxes

A check box is a small box-like icon that can be checked or unchecked to select or deselect program attributes. A small phrase of text is often used to associate a check box icon to indicate its purpose. Except for their appearance, check boxes function similarly to two-state buttons.

Check boxes are represented by objects of the class JCheckBox, which subclasses from JToggleButton. The class AbstractButton (which is a direct super class for JToggleButton) contains most of the functionality inherited by check boxes.

JCheckBox Constructors

You can create a check box object by using any one of the constructors provided in the class JCheckBox. The constructors allow developers to specify check box icons, associated text, or a combination of both. The initial state of a check box, such as checked or unchecked, can also be specified by using some of the constructors. The following is a list of constructors supported inside the class JCheckBox:

```
public JCheckBox();
public JCheckBox(Icon icon);
public JCheckBox(Icon icon, boolean checked);
```

```
public JCheckBox(String text);
public JCheckBox(String text, boolean checked);
public JCheckBox(String text, Icon icon);
public JCheckBox(String text, Icon icon, boolean checked);
```

The icon argument is the check box icon and is an object of type Icon. The text is any text label of type String. The boolean type argument is true if the check box is to show in the checked condition; for the unchecked condition, the argument value is false.

Item Events and Listeners

Whenever a check box has been selected or deselected, an event of type ItemEvent is fired by the check box object. The item events are commonly fired by component objects that have a number of items to make a selection. The item events contain the affected item and its current state of selection. The following are the methods from the class ItemEvent:

```
public Object getItem()
public ItemSelectable getItemSelectable()
public int getStateChanged()
```

The method getItem() retrieves the item of the item selectable object, such as a check box, when the state of the item selection has changed. The retrieved item can be the item label or an object of type Integer. In the case of check boxes and radio buttons, the retrieved item is the label of the item.

The next method, getItemSelectable(), returns the item selectable object such as a check box or radio button. The purpose of this method is the same as the method getSource() in the class java.util.EventObject. The method getStateChanged() returns either SELECTED or DESELECTED, which are the fields of the selectable object. These fields indicate whether the item has been selected or deselected.

To perform some operation when a check box item is selected, the item events must be captured by a listener class. The method addItemListener() is invoked on the source object by passing the listener object as its argument. The listener class implements the interface java.awt.event.ItemListener and provides the code for the method itemStateChanged() from the interface. The method itemStateChanged() receives the objects of type ItemEvent and contains the code to be executed whenever the item is selected.

Check Box Code Example

A number of methods in a check box object have been inherited from the class AbstractButton. Listing 8.3 demonstrates some of these methods and shows how to handle the item events fired by check boxes.

The applet locates three check boxes along its diagonal and positions the text labels at different locations with reference to the check boxes, as shown in Figure 8.4. The applet shows the degree of correctness of your answer when you select a check box. So click all three boxes to make your answer 100 percent! The answer status is shown at the bottom portion of the applet.

Figure 8.4

Applet demonstrating the Swing check boxes (JCheckBox).

Listing 8.3   JCheckBox (TJCheckBox.java)

```
/*
<Applet code=TJCheckBox width=350 height=150>
</Applet>
*/

import java.awt.*;
import javax.swing.*;
import java.awt.event.*;


public class TJCheckBox extends JApplet {
    JLabel label2 = null;

    public  void init() {
        //1. Obtain a handle on the JApplet container.
        Container container = this.getContentPane();

        //2. Set the layout.
        container.setLayout(new GridLayout(5, 1));

        //3. Create the radio buttons.
        JCheckBox cBox1, cBox2, cBox3;
        cBox1 = new JCheckBox("Light-weight!");
        cBox2 = new JCheckBox("Ready-made!");
        cBox3 = new JCheckBox("Easy-to-use!");

        //4. Add the item listener to the check boxes.
```

```
        CheckBoxListener listener = new CheckBoxListener();
        cBox1.addItemListener(listener);
        cBox2.addItemListener(listener);
        cBox3.addItemListener(listener);

        //5. Set the text position of each button.
        cBox1.setHorizontalTextPosition(SwingConstants.LEFT);
        cBox1.setVerticalTextPosition(SwingConstants.BOTTOM);
        cBox2.setHorizontalTextPosition(SwingConstants.CENTER);
        cBox2.setVerticalTextPosition(SwingConstants.BOTTOM);
        cBox3.setHorizontalTextPosition(SwingConstants.RIGHT);
        cBox3.setVerticalTextPosition(SwingConstants.BOTTOM);

        //6. Set the position of each button in its display area.
        cBox1.setHorizontalAlignment(SwingConstants.LEFT);
        cBox2.setHorizontalAlignment(SwingConstants.CENTER);
        cBox3.setHorizontalAlignment(SwingConstants.RIGHT);

        //7. Create a couple of label to notify what to do and
        // what happened.
        Font font = new Font("Monospaced", Font.ITALIC, 16);
        JLabel label1 = new JLabel("The JFC/Swing Widgets are:");
        label1.setFont(font);
        label2 = new JLabel("Select the Check Boxes...");
        label2.setFont(font);

        //8. Finally, addeach component to the Swing applet.
        container.add(label1);
        container.add(cBox1);
        container.add(cBox2);
        container.add(cBox3);
        container.add(label2);
    }
    //9. Listener class for check boxes.
    class CheckBoxListener implements ItemListener {
        private double n = 0.0;
        public void itemStateChanged(ItemEvent evt) {
            n = n + 100.0/3.0;
            label2.setText("Your Answer is "
                        + new Double(n).toString()
                        + "% Correct!");
            JCheckBox cBox = (JCheckBox) evt.getSource();
            cBox.setEnabled(false);
        }
    }
}
```

Code Details

Snippet-1 creates a reference, `container`, of type `Container` and then initializes it with the content pane object returned by the method `getContentPane()`. The container serves as a handle to add various components to the Swing applet. Snippet-2 sets the grid layout for the applet.

Snippet-3 creates three check box objects with suitable text labels. Snippet-4 creates a common event listener object, `listener`, and registers it with the check box objects, `cBox1`, `cBox2`, and `cBox3`.

In snippet-5, the text labels of the check boxes are positioned by using the methods `setHorizontalTextPosition()` and `setVerticalTextPosition()`. These methods take the Swing constants as their argument values. Snippet-6 provides the code for the horizontal alignment of the check boxes in their display areas. By default, the check boxes align at the center of their display areas in the vertical direction.

Snippet-7 creates a font object that represents a specific text font and then assigns the font to the labels `label1` and `label2`. Snippet-8 adds each of the check box objects to the Swing applet's content pane. By default, the applet appears with the Java/Metallic look-and-feel beause there is no code to provide any specific look-and-feel.

The listener for the check box objects is an inner class shown in snippet-9. The listener class `CheckBoxListener` implements the interface `ItemListener` and, therefore, furnishes the necessary event handling code inside the method `itemStateChanged()`. This method takes the events of type `ItemEvent` as its argument.

Inside the method `itemStateChanged()` is the code segment that computes the percentage value of the correctness of user's input through check boxes. The next statement of code displays a message showing Your Answer is n% correct! where n is the computed percentage value. The remaining portion of the code simply disables a check box. The output of the program when the user checks the check boxes in the first and second rows of the applet is shown in Figure 8.4. When the user checks the third box also, the answer is 100 percent correct!

The check boxes shown in Figure 8.4 can be decorated with different icons rather than the defaults. The icons can be created from image files and then passed into an appropriate check box constructor, as shown in the following:

```
Icon imageIcon = new ImageIcon("iconFile.gif");
JCheckBox checkbox = new JCheckBox("textMessage", imageIcon);
```

Whenever a check box has been selected, the relevant icon will change to its grayed-out form because it has been disabled in the event handler method. Alternatively, if you do not set the check box to the disabled state, you can use another icon to indicate the selected-state. The change over to a selected-state icon can be performed by using the `setIcon()` method inside the event handler method. Figure 8.5 shows the same applet using the check boxes with the specified image icons. Notice that the first check box shows the grayed-out form of the designated icon because the selection has already been made.

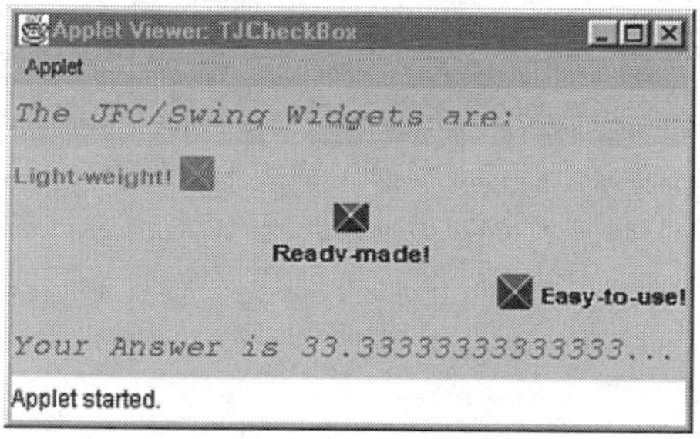

Figure 8.5

The Swing applet showing check boxes with image icons.

Radio Buttons

By default, radio buttons appear with small round-button icons. Radio buttons can possess certain associated text also. Radio buttons are used as a group in which only one button can be selected at a given time. That is, when a button is selected, the remaining buttons in the group are automatically deselected. You can implement these buttons when only one input control should be operated from a set of inputs. For example, in a media player with a set of buttons such a Play, Stop, Fast-Forward, and Rewind, only one button can be selected at a time.

A radio button is an object of the Swing class JRadioButton that subclasses from JToggleButton. Thus, most of the functionality in the class JRadioButton is inherited from the super class of JToggleButton called AbstractButton.

JRadioButton Constructors

You can use any one of the following constructors supported in the class JRadioButton to create a radio button object. The constructors can take a combination of arguments such as the specified icon, an Icon type object, some text as a String type object, and the initial state as true for selected or false for deselected conditions.

```
public JRadioButton();
public JRadioButton(Icon icon);
public JRadioButton(Icon icon, boolean selected);
public JRadioButton(String text);
public JRadioButton(String text, boolean selected);
public JRadioButton(String text, Icon icon);
public JRadioButton(String text, Icon icon,
                    boolean selected);
```

The ButtonGroup Class

JRadioButton objects are grouped together by using an object of another class called ButtonGroup. The class ButtonGroup is located in the package javax.swing. To add a JRadioButton object to a group, you create an object of type ButtonGroup and invoke the method add() on that object. The add() method takes a radio button object as its argument value. The following is a typical code that you use:

```
...
...
// Create radio button objects
JRadioButton radioButton1,radioButton2,radioButton3;
radioButton1 = new JRadioButton();
radioButton2 = new JRadioButton();
radioButton3 = new JRadioButton();

// Create a button group object
ButtonGroup group = new ButtonGroup();

// Add the button objects to the group
group.add(radioButton1);
group.add(radioButton2);
group.add(radioButton3);
...

...
```

NOTE

The class JRadioButton is similar to the class JCheckBox except for their default icons. You can also group objects of type JCheckBox to function similarly to radio buttons. Thus, the radio button component seems to be redundant. At this point, it is important to recollect one of the primary goals of the Swing library—to support users with ready-made widgets for as many GUI components as they can.

Radio Button Code Example

Listing 8.4 demonstrates radio buttons and some of the methods from the class AbstractButton. The applet shows two sets of radio buttons to select a font and a font type (see Figure 8.6). When you select a font or a font type, the selection will be shown on the applet by using a label object. The appearance of the applet has been set to the Motif look-and-feel.

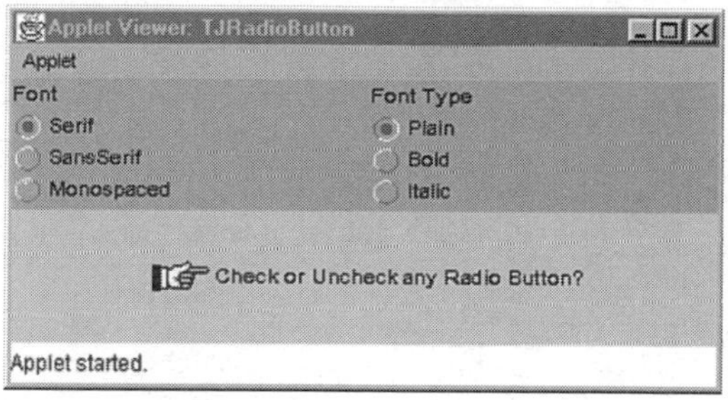

Figure 8.6

An applet demonstrating the Swing radio buttons.

Listing 8.4   JRadioButton Used to Create Two Sets of Radio Buttons (TJRadioButton.java)

```java
/*
 * <Applet code=TJRadioButton width=400 height=150>
 * </Applet>
 */
import java.awt.*;
import javax.swing.*;
import java.awt.event.*;

public class TJRadioButton extends JApplet {
    // 1. Declare the object references.
    JRadioButton rButton1, rButton2, rButton3;
    JRadioButton rButton4, rButton5, rButton6;

    JLabel label = null;
    String message = null;
    Font font = null;
    Container container;
    String LF = "com.sun.java.swing.plaf.motif.MotifLookAndFeel";
    public void init() {
        // 2. Set the look-and-feel of the applet to the Motif type.
        try {
            UIManager.setLookAndFeel(LF);
        } catch (Exception e) {
            System.err.println("Look and Feel not Initialized!");
        }
        // 3. Get a handle on the JApplet container.
        container = this.getContentPane();

        // 4. Initialize the font object.
        font = new Font("Serif", Font.PLAIN, 16);

        // 5. Initialize the message.
        message = "Check or Uncheck any Radio Button?";
```

continues

Listing 8.4   continued

```
// 6. Create grid layout and set it for the JApplet.
container.setLayout(new GridLayout(2, 1));

// 7. Create the JRadioButton objects.
rButton1 = new JRadioButton("Serif", true);
CustomListener cl = new CustomListener();
rButton1.addActionListener(cl);

rButton2 = new JRadioButton("SansSerif");
rButton2.addActionListener(cl);

rButton3 = new JRadioButton("Monospaced");
rButton3.addActionListener(cl);

// 8. Form a group with these radio buttons.
ButtonGroup group1 = new ButtonGroup();
group1.add(rButton1);
group1.add(rButton2);
group1.add(rButton3);

// 9. Create the remaining JRadioButton objects.
rButton4 = new JRadioButton("Plain", true);
rButton4.addActionListener(cl);

rButton5 = new JRadioButton("Bold");
rButton5.addActionListener(cl);

rButton6 = new JRadioButton("Italic");
rButton6.addActionListener(cl);

// 10. Form a group with these radio buttons.
ButtonGroup group2 = new ButtonGroup();
group2.add(rButton4);
group2.add(rButton5);
group2.add(rButton6);

// 11. Create a JPanel and main label objects.
JPanel panel = new JPanel();
panel.setLayout(new GridLayout(4, 2));
Icon picture = new ImageIcon("pointer.gif");
label = new JLabel(message, picture, SwingConstants.CENTER);

// 12. Add the radio buttons to JPanel.
panel.add(new JLabel("Font"));
panel.add(new JLabel("Font Type"));
panel.add(rButton1);        panel.add(rButton4);
panel.add(rButton2);        panel.add(rButton5);
panel.add(rButton3);        panel.add(rButton6);
```

```
        // 13. Add JPanel and canvas to the JApplet.
        container.add(panel);
        container.add(label);
    }


    // 14. The item listener class.
    class CustomListener implements ActionListener {
        public void actionPerformed(ActionEvent evt) {
            JRadioButton rButton = (JRadioButton) evt.getSource();
            if (rButton == rButton1) {
                font  = new Font("Serif", font.getStyle(), 16);
                label.setFont(font);
                label.setText("You selected the SERIF font!");
                container.validate();
            }
            else if (rButton == rButton2) {
                font = new Font("SansSerif", font.getStyle(), 16);
                label.setFont(font);
                label.setText("You selected the SANSSERIF font!");
                container.validate();
            }
            else if (rButton == rButton3) {
                font = new Font("Monospaced", font.getStyle(), 16);
                label.setFont(font);
                label.setText("You selected the MONOSPACED font!");
                container.validate();
            }
            else if (rButton == rButton4) {
                font = new Font(font.getName(), Font.PLAIN, 16);
                label.setFont(font);
                label.setText("You selected the PLAIN style!");
                container.validate();
            }
            else if (rButton == rButton5) {
                font = new Font(font.getName(), Font.BOLD, 16);
                label.setFont(font);
                label.setText("You selected the BOLD style!");
                label.validate();
            }
            else if (rButton == rButton6) {
                font = new Font(font.getName(), Font.ITALIC, 16);
                label.setFont(font);
                label.setText("You selected the ITALIC style!");
                container.validate();
            }
        }
    }
}
```

Code Details

Snippet-1 declares six object references that will be initialized later to the objects of type JRadioButton. Next, the snippet declares a label, string, font, and a container. The reference named container will be assigned the Swing applet's content pane. The last statement of the snippet shows the string representation of the Motif look-and-feel.

Inside the method init(), snippet-2 sets the look-and-feel of the applet to the Motif type by invoking the method setLookAndFeel() from the class UIManager. Whenever you set the look-and-feel to a specific type by using the method setLookAndFeel(), you must catch either the general exception of type Exception or the specific types of exceptions thrown. The list of exceptions is given in the Swing button example.

Snippet-3 initializes the container with the content pane object for this applet. Snippet-4 creates a font object for a specific font that will be set for the labels, and snippet-5 assigns a text message to the data member message. Snippet-6 sets the applet to the grid layout. The radio button references declared as data members of the applet are initialized to the radio button objects in snippet-7. The snippet also shows the code that registers a listener object with the radio button objects.

In snippet-8, the radio buttons rButton1, rButton2, and rButton3 are set to form a group by using the object group1 of type ButtonGroup. In a group of radio buttons, only one button can be selected at a time. Snippets 9 and 10 initialize the remaining radio buttons, rButton4, rButton5, and rButton6, to make a group called group2.

Snippet-11 creates a JPanel object called panel and an image icon called picture. The picture icon is a hand pointing to a message that is displayed when a radio button is selected. The last statement of this snippet creates a label of type JLabel to display the message with the pointer hand icon.

Snippet-12 adds all the radio buttons to the panel object. The panel also contains the label objects to indicate the text labels Font and Font Type in the applet. Snippet-13 adds the panel and the label objects created in snippet-11 to the Swing applet.

Snippet-14 shows the inner class CustomListener that contains the event handling functionality. Note that the radio boxes can also fire events of type ActionEvent because JRadioButton is a subclass of AbstactButton. Thus, the inner class implements ActionListener rather than an ItemListener and furnishes the code for actionPerformed().

The body of actionPerformed() contains the code to be executed whenever a radio button is selected. For example, when the radio button rButton1 is selected, the code under the if statement creates a font of type Serif. A label showing You selected the SERIF font! is displayed in the Serif font. That is done by invoking the methods setFont() and setText() on the label object. The method setFont() sets the font for the label to the font type passed as its argument. The method setText() assigns the specified text to the `label` object. The remaining portion of code in snippet-14 is a repetition of these actions whenever the user selects the other radio buttons. Figure 8.6 shows the output when the user selects the font type Serif. Note the Motif look-and-feel of the radio buttons in the applet.

CHAPTER 9

Lists and Combo Boxes

The Swing library provides two components to display a list of items: the list and the combo box. A Swing list is an archive of items displayed in a box that allows the user to select one or more items. This chapter discusses how to create Swing list components by using different types of data models that include simple to sophisticated formats, rendering the cells of a list with icons, list events, and listeners. The chapter will also show how to handle multiple mouse clicks to select items from a list.

The Swing combo box is a small component with a list of items that drops down when a button on its display area is operated. It allows only one item at a time to be selected. This chapter discusses Swing combo box topics such as constructors, data models, and rendering of item cells with icons. A combo box can also be made editable to add an item in its drop-down list, which is also covered in this chapter.

Lists

The Swing list is a box-like component that displays text items in multiple rows, and is useful when you need to display a large number of items. The rows of text are positioned in different cells of a single column. List items are usually scrollable; however, the Swing list components require the implementation of scrolling separately. You can position the list component in a scroll pane to achieve scrolling.

The Swing list components are represented by objects of the class JList. The class JList is stored in the package javax.swing and is a direct subclass of JComponent (see Figure 9.1). The list component has its support distributed into several interfaces and classes: ListModel, Abstract ListModel, DefaultListModel, ListSelectionModel, DefaultListSelectionModel, ListCellRenderer, and so on.

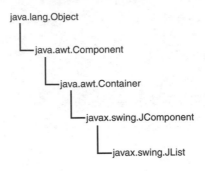

Figure 9.1

The JList class hierarchy.

JList Constructors

You can use any one of the constructors supported in JList to create an object of type JList. The constructors take different types of data models. The following is the list of available constructors:

```
public void JList()
public void JList(Object[] listData )
public void JList(Vector listData)
public void JList(ListModel dataModel)
```

The first constructor uses the default model. However, you can set any data model later by invoking any one of the following methods on the JList object:

```
public void setListData(Object[] listData)
public void setListData(Vector listData)
public void setListData(ListModel dataModel)
```

The second constructor requires data in the form of an array. You can create an array of items and use this constructor to make a list out of them. For example, the following code

```
String[] cities = {"San Jose", "Los Angeles", "San Diego",
                   "San Francisco", "Sacramento"};
JList citiesList = new JList(cities);
```

creates a list object that shows an array of cities.

The constructor with the argument of type Vector is similar to the one with the array-type argument Object. However, by using a vector, you can perform various operations, such as appending more items to the list, by using the functionality provided inside the class java.util.Vector. For example, the following code

```
Vector months = new Vector();
JList list = new JList(months);
```

```
...
months.addElement("January");
...
months.addElement("December");
```

creates a list component with a vector-type data model. You can also add elements to the vector at different levels of code depending on some context or requirement, and the elements that have been added can be displayed in the list component.

The constructor that takes the values of type ListModel is used to show the list data available in complex models. The next section discusses the interface ListModel, shows how to create a data model by using the abstract class named AbstractListModel, and provides an example program that creates a list object by using the data of type ListModel.

Data Models

To display complex models of data in a list component, the Swing library provides the interface ListModel and the classes AbstractListModel and DefaultListModel. The relationships between these representatives of list models are shown in Figure 9.2. The abstract class AbstractListModel readily implements some of the methods from the interface ListModel. The class DefaultListModel is a concrete subclass of AbstractListModel with the readily usable vector-type model.

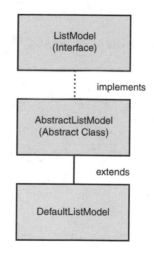

Figure 9.2

The relationships between list model classes.

The ListModel Interface

ListModel provides a design-level interface with a set of methods to be implemented depending on the data model. Because the data items to be shown in the list are indicated by an index, you need to create a class that implements the interface ListModel.

The following are the declarations of methods from the interface ListModel (also see Appendix A, "JFC Swing Quick Reference").

```
public void addListDataListener(ListDataListener l)
public void removeListDataListener(ListDataListener l)
public int getSize()
public Object getElementAt(int index)
```

The method getSize() returns the size of data to be displayed in the list component. The getElementAt() method returns the data value at the specified index of the list. The remaining methods are for registering or removing a data listener from the list model class. The data listener is notified by the data model whenever a change occurs in the data model. The associated event objects are of class type ListDataEvent.

The AbstractListModel Class

To avoid implementing all the methods given in the interface ListModel, the Swing library provides a convenient class called AbstractListModel. This class readily implements the methods addListDataListener() and removeListDataListener() so you only need to implement the methods getElementAt() and getSize().

Typically, you create a class that subclasses from the AbstractListModel and implements the methods getElementAt() and getSize(). Listing 9.1 demonstrates how to use the type ListModel to create a JList object by subclassing the class AbstractListModel. Figure 9.3 shows the output of this code.

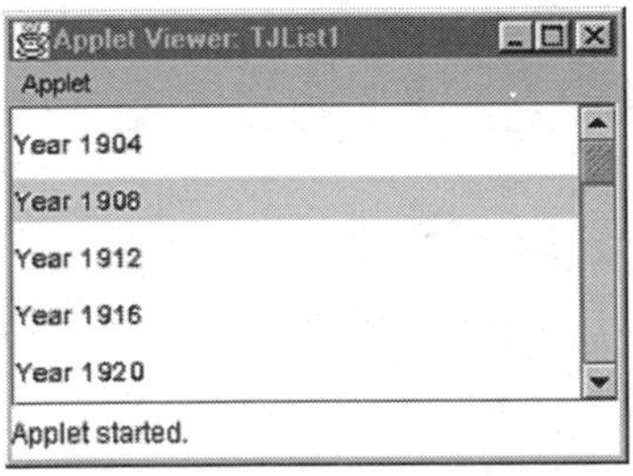

Figure 9.3

JList component that uses the leap year list model.

Listing 9.1   JList Used to Create a Leap Year List (TJList1.java)
```
// Demonstrates how to use the ListModel and JList component

/*
 * <Applet code = TJList1 width = 200 height = 175>
 * </Applet>
 */
```

```
import javax.swing.*;
import java.awt.*;

public class TJList1 extends JApplet {
    // 1. Define the data members.
    JList list = null;
    MyListModel model = null;
    JScrollPane scrollPane = null;
    Container container = null;

    public void init() {
        // 2. Get a handle to the applet's content pane and
        // set the grid layout.
        container = this.getContentPane();
        container.setLayout(new GridLayout(1,1));

        // 3. Create objects of type JList, MyListModel,
        // and JScrollPane and add them hierarchically
        // to the applet as shown.
        model = new MyListModel();
        list = new JList(model);
        scrollPane = new JScrollPane(list);
        container.add(scrollPane);
    }
}

// 4. Custom list data model that generates leap years.
class MyListModel extends AbstractListModel {
    int startYear = 1900;
    int endYear = 2000;
    int leapYear;
    // 5. Returns each list element (leap year).
    public Object getElementAt(int index) {
        index = index + 1; // index starts from 0;
                           // so make it 1.
        if ((startYear+index)%4 == 0)
            return "Year "+(startYear+index);
        else
            return null;
    }

    // 6. Returns the total count of data; that is,
    // total number of years in the present case.
    public int getSize() {
        return (endYear-startYear);
    }
}
```

Code Details

In Listing 9.1, the class `MyListModel` represents a data model that generates the leap years. The class extends `AbstractListModel` and provides the code for the methods `getElementAt()` and `getSize()`. The method `getElementAt()` takes the argument `index`, computes the leap year, and returns it. The method `getSize()` returns the total number of years that provides the number of data points at which the list items have to be computed.

The class `TJList1` declares the references of type `JList`, `MyListModel`, `JScrollPane`, and `Container`. Inside the `init()` method, these references are initialized with their corresponding objects. Note the `JList` constructor using the object of type `MyListModel` as its argument. Next, each of these components are hierarchically added to the other. The list object is added to the scroll pane to support the scrolling facility for the list items, and then the scroll pane is added to the Swing applet's container.

The DefaultListModel Class

The class `DefaultListModel` subclasses from `AbstractListModel` and is currently a list-model implementation of the class `java.util.Vector`. Because there is a `JList` constructor that allows vector-type data models, this class seems to be superfluous. However, this class provides another option for the developers while using the vector-type data models.

Rendering List Cells

A list cell is a narrow horizontal space where a list item is displayed. In addition to the string of text that indicates a list item, you can also render a list cell with a small picture or an image icon. To facilitate the rendering of a cell, the Swing library provides the interface `ListCellRenderer`. The interface contains only one method:

```
public interface ListCellRenderer {
    public Component getListCellRendererComponent (
                            JList list,
                            Object value,
                            int index,
                            boolean isSelected,
                            boolean cellHasFocus);
}
```

The method `getListCellRendererComponent()` returns the component that will be rendered inside the list cell. The argument with the identifier list is the `JList` object for which the cell rendering is being done. The next argument, `value`, is the value returned by the method `getElementAt()` at the specified index in the list model. The `index` is the index to each of the list values. The `boolean` arguments `isSelected` and `cellHasFocus` indicate if the specified cell has been selected or brought to focus respectively.

This interface is implemented by a class that extends a Swing label because a JLabel object can possess text as well as an icon. Shown next is a typical component class for rendering the cells of a list.

```
class MyCellRenderer extends JLabel implements ListCellRenderer {
    Icon [] icons; // array of icons to be used for the list items

    public MyCellRenderer (Icon[] icons) {
        this.icons = icons;
        setOpaque(true);
    }

    // Only method to be implemented from ListCellRenderer.
    public Component getListCellRendererComponent (
                                    JList list,
                                    Object value,
                                    int index,
                                    boolean isSelected,
                                    boolean cellHasFocus) {
        setText(value.toString());
        // Set the icon for each selection using the index.
        if (index < icons.length)
            setIcon(icons[index]);

        // What happens when a selection is made.
        if (isSelected) {
            setBackground(list.getSelectionBackground());
            setForeground(list.getSelectionForeground());
        }
        else {
            setBackground(list.getBackground());
            setForeground(list.getForeground());
        }
        return this;
    }
}
```

In this code, the custom component called MyCellRenderer extends the class JLabel and implements the interface ListCellRenderer. The class data is an array of icons that has been initialized through the constructor. The method getListCellRendererComponent() returns the component of type MyCellRenderer. Inside this method, based on the index, the text labels and icons are set by using the methods setText() and setIcon() from JLabel.

Next you provide the code for what should happen when a certain item has been selected. The methods getSelectionBackground() and getSelectionForeground() return the background and foreground colors that have been set for the JList object. You also need to reset the background and foreground colors of the list cell as given in the previous code.

Rendering List Cells with Icons Code Example

Listing 9.2 uses the class MyCellRenderer to display icons in a Swing list. The program creates an applet that displays a list of computer components by using the Swing list (see Figure 9.4).

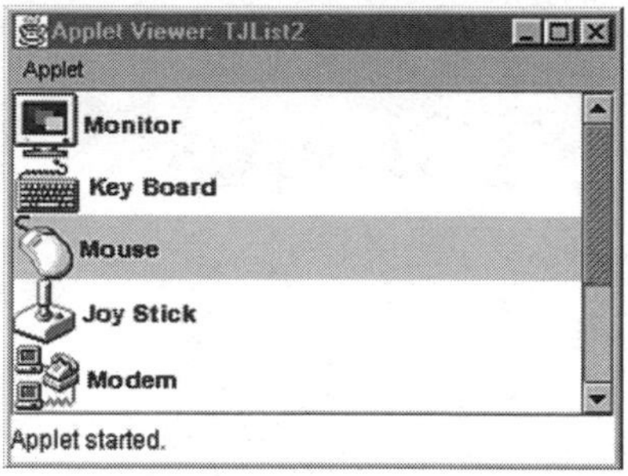

Figure 9.4

The Swing list cells rendered with icons.

Listing 9.2   JList Creates List Cells with Icons (TJList2.java)

```
/*
 * <Applet code=TJList2 width=200 height=150>
 * </Applet>
 */

import javax.swing.*;
import java.awt.*;

public class TJList2 extends JApplet {
    // 1. Labels for the list items.
    String[] ComputerComps = {"Monitor", "Key Board", "Mouse",
                              "Joy Stick", "Modem", "CD ROM",
                              "RAM Chip", "Diskette"};

    // 2. Create icons for selections and make an array.
    Icon icon1 = new ImageIcon("monitor.gif");
    Icon icon2 = new ImageIcon("keyboard.gif");
    Icon icon3 = new ImageIcon("mouse.gif");
    Icon icon4 = new ImageIcon("joystick.gif");
    Icon icon5 = new ImageIcon("modem.gif");
    Icon icon6 = new ImageIcon("cdrom.gif");
    Icon icon7 = new ImageIcon("ramchip.gif");
    Icon icon8 = new ImageIcon("diskett.gif");
    Icon[] icons = {icon1, icon2, icon3, icon4,
                    icon5, icon6, icon7, icon8};

    public void init() {
```

```
        // 3. Create a list object to display the computer
        //     components.
        JList list = new JList(ComputerComps);

        // 4. Render the list cells with icons.
        list.setCellRenderer(new MyCellRenderer(icons));

        // 5. Add the list to the applet's content pane
        //     through a scrollpane.
        getContentPane().add(new JScrollPane(list));
    }
}


// 6. Class that renders the list cells with icons.
class MyCellRenderer extends JLabel implements ListCellRenderer {
    Icon[] icons;

    public MyCellRenderer (Icon[] icons) {
        this.icons - icons;
        setOpaque(true);
    }

    // 7. Method that must be implemented from the interface
    //     ListCellRenderer.
    public Component getListCellRendererComponent (
                        JList list,
                        Object value,
                        int index,
                        boolean isSelected,
                        boolean cellHasFocus) {

        // 8. Set the text for the label.
        if (value != null) {
            String text = value.toString();
            setText(text);
        }

        // 9. Set the icon for each selection cell
        //     indicated by the index.
            setIcon(icons[index]);

        // 10. What happens when a selection is made.
        if (isSelected) {
            setBackground(list.getSelectionBackground());
            setForeground(list.getSelectionForeground());
        }

        // NOTE: This step is very important; otherwise, the
```

continues

Listing 9.2   continued

```
        // selection colors don't render as expected!
        else {
            setBackground(list.getBackground());
            setForeground(list.getForeground());
        }

        // 11. Finally, return this rubber stamp component.
        return this;
    }
}
```

Code Details

Snippets 1 and 2 show the data members of the applet. Snippet-1 defines an array of text strings, each string being the name of a computer component. Snippet-2 creates a bunch of icons of the computer components. These icons are in an array named icons.

Inside the method init(), snippet-3 creates a list object with the array of computer components passed as the argument to its constructor. Snippet-4 uses the method setCellRenderer() to assign the object of type MyCellRenderer to the list object that has been created. Snippet-5 adds the list component to the applet's content pane through a scroll pane object. The scroll pane provides the necessary scrolling facility, in case there are too many items to display through the applet's window.

Snippet-6 shows the rendering class, MyCellRenderer. Note that the rendering component works like a rubber stamp to paint a list cell with an icon and text. The component identifies each cell based on the argument index of the method getListCellRendererComponent(). When you execute this program and bring the mouse focus on to an item, the applet appears as shown in Figure 9.4.

List Selections and Events

In a list component, an item or a set of items is selected to perform some further operations. In connection with selecting list items, the Swing library supports the interface ListSelectionModel and the class DefaultListSelectionModel. There is also a class called ListSelectionEvent to represent the selection events and an interface called the ListSelectionListener to receive the events.

The interface ListSelectionModel represents the current state of selection, and the class DefaultListSelectionModel provides the default data model for the list selections. Although these models exist, you rarely deal with them because the selection methods supported in the class JList are sufficient for most of the common requirements.

Selection Modes

There are three different modes in which item selection can be made. The following is a list of selection modes that are encapsulated as data fields inside the interface ListSelectionModel:

```
static int SINGLE_SELECTION
static int SINGLE_INTERVAL_SELECTION
static int MULTIPLE_INTERVAL_SELECTION
```

By setting the SINGLE_SELECTION mode, you can select only one list item at a time. The mode SINGLE_INTERVAL_SELECTION is used to select a contiguous range of items at once. This selection type is executed by holding the Shift key down and selecting the items. The other mode, called MULTIPLE_INTERVAL_SELECTION, allows for the selection of one or more contiguous ranges of indices at a time. This type of selection is made by holding down the Ctrl key. A selection mode can be assigned to a JList component by invoking the method setSelectionMode().

Selection Methods

The class JList supports a list of set and get methods to deal with various selection attributes of the list component. The following is a brief description of some of the set methods that are commonly used:

```
void setSelectedIndex(int index)
void setSelectedIndices(int[] indices)
void setSelectedValue(Object object, boolean shouldScroll)
```

The methods with the index or indices arguments set the specified list item or items in the selected state. The integer array of indices makes single selections in a contiguous fashion. The method setSelectedValue() requires a value such as an array element, for example cities[i], to make a selection. You can also pass the boolean argument true to allow the list to scroll up or down and display the selected item through the view port.

The interface JList and the class DefaultListSelectionModel support methods to deal with multiple list selections. To make multiple list selections, you can use the anchor and lead indices of the selection items and use the following methods:

```
void setAnchorSelectionIndex(int index)
void setLeadSelectionIndex(int index)
```

To check the selection status (selected or not selected) of all the list items or the item at the specified index, you can use the following respective methods available in the class JList:

```
boolean isSelectionEmpty()
boolean isSelectedIndex(int index)
```

The class JList also provides methods to change the background and foreground colors of item selections. These methods are as follows:

```
void setSelectionBackground(Color c)
void setSelectionForeground(Color c)
```

Selection Events and Listeners Code Example

When a selection has been made or a change to the selection occurs, the selection model of a list component fires events of the class type `ListSelectionEvent`. These events are captured by a listener class that implements the interface `ListSelectionListener`. You can register a selection listener to a list component by using the method

```
void addListSelectionListener(ListSelectionListener listener)
```

which is provided in the interface `ListSelectionModel`, the class `DefaultListSelectionModel`, or by using the convenience method provided in the class `JList`.

The interface `ListSelectionListener` contains only one method, `valueChanged()`, that needs to be defined inside the implementing class. This method takes the events of type `ListSelectionEvent` through its argument. The program given in Listing 9.3 demonstrates these concepts. The output of this program is shown in Figure 9.5.

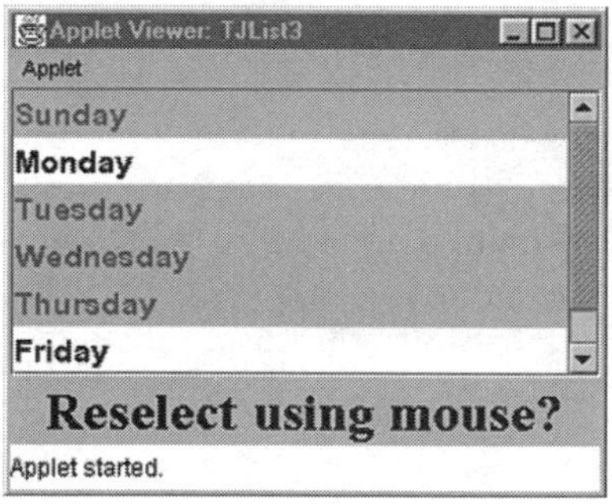

Figure 9.5

An applet demonstrating item selection from a Swing list.

Listing 9.3   List Item Selection (TJList3.java)

```
// Demonstrates the item-selection from a list widget
/*
 * <Applet code=TJList3 width=300 height=200>
 *</Applet>
 */
import javax.swing.*;
import javax.swing.event.*;
import java.awt.*;

public class TJList3 extends JApplet {
    // 1. Declare the required references.
    JList list = null;
```

```
JLabel label = null;
Container c = null;

// 2. Create the arrays for the list selections.
String[] weekdays = {
    "Sunday", "Monday", "Tuesday", "Wednesday",
    "Thursday", "Friday", "Saturday" };
int[] holidays = {0, 6}; //Indices for sunday&saturday

public void init() {
    // 3. Get the handle on the applet's content pane.
    c = this.getContentPane();

    // 4. Create a list object.
    list = new JList(weekdays);
    Font f1 = new Font("SansSerif", Font.BOLD, 16);
    list.setFont(f1);
    list.setSelectionMode(
        ListSelectionModel.MULTIPLE_INTERVAL_SELECTION);
    list.setSelectedIndices(holidays);
    list.addSelectionInterval(2, 4);
    list.setSelectionBackground(Color.blue);
    list.setSelectionForeground(Color.white);

    // 5. Registering a listener class.
    ListSelectionListener l = new MyListener();
    list.addListSelectionListener(l);

    // 6. Add the list to a scroll pane and finally to the applet.
    JScrollPane sp = new JScrollPane(list);
    c.add(sp);

    // 7. Create a label object.
    label = new JLabel("Reselect using mouse?", JLabel.CENTER);
    Font f2 = new Font("Serif", Font.BOLD, 26);
    label.setFont(f2);
    label.setOpaque(true);
    label.setBackground(Color.lightGray);
    label.setForeground(Color.black);
    c.add(label, BorderLayout.SOUTH);
}

// 8. JList selection event listener class.
class MyListener implements ListSelectionListener {
    public void valueChanged(ListSelectionEvent evt) {
        label.setText((String) list.getSelectedValue());
    }
}
}
```

Code Details

Snippet-1 declares references of type JList, JLabel, and Container. Snippet-2 defines a string array of weekdays and an integer array of holidays.

Inside the method init(), snippet-3 gets a handle on the applet's content pane. Snippet-4 creates a JList object with the data model of weekdays. Then you see some of the JList methods in action. The method setSelectionMode() initiates the mode of selection by using the constant MULTIPLE_INTERVAL_SELECTION. setSelectedIndices() takes the array named holidays, Sunday, and Saturday to set them selected when the applet has been displayed. You also find the methods setSelectionBackground() and setSelectionForeground() to control the foreground and background colors of the selected items.

Snippet-5 creates an object of type ListSelectionListener and registers it with the list object by using the method addListSelectionListener(). Because the JList component does not have a ready-made scrolling facility, snippet-6 positions the component in a scroll pane and then in an applet. Snippet-7 shows a label that also has been added to the applet.

Snippet-8 is the list selection listener class that implements the interface ListSelectionListener and provides the code for the method valueChanged(). Whenever a list item is selected, an event of type ListSelectionEvent is fired by the component. This is handled by the method valueChanged() to display the text that represents the selected item. The method getSelectedValue() retrieves the list item that has been selected. The applet displays the multiple selections that have been set in Listing 9.3. However, you can select any day or days of interest by operating the mouse and the keyboard (Ctrl key).

Multiple Mouse Clicks

To select an item from a list component, it is convenient to double-click the mouse on the item. There is no readily available method that can be used from the list classes to handle multiple mouse clicks. However, it is easy to handle mouse clicks by utilizing the method getClickCount() from the event class MouseEvent. The method getClickCount() returns the number of mouse clicks whenever a user clicks the mouse. You can enclose the code to be executed as the body of a control statement that checks the specified number of mouse clicks.

Listing 9.4 demonstrates a typical implementation of handling double-clicks of a mouse. The program uses two list components, one showing the list of Java products and the other to represent a shopping cart. When you double-click the mouse on a Java product to be purchased, the item will be added to the shopping cart as shown in Figure 9.6.

After the list of purchased items is added to the shopping cart, you can place the order by clicking the Order Now button. A Delete Item button has also been provided that removes a specified item from the shopping cart. To execute this, you bring the focus on an item from the shopping cart with a single mouse click and then click the Delete Item button. You can use this applet in a Web page for online shopping.

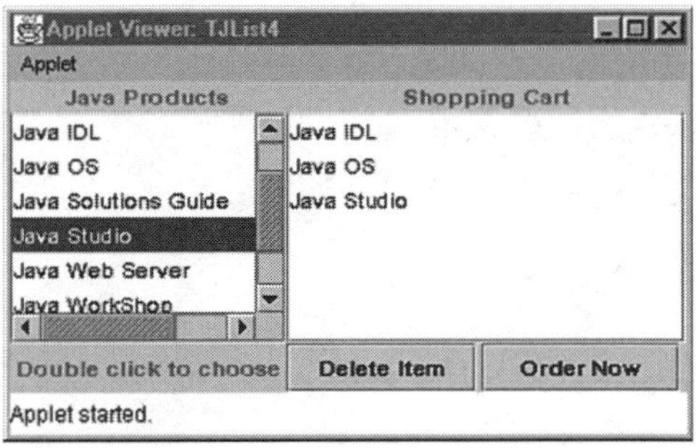

Figure 9.6

Online shopping applet demonstrates the use of double mouse clicks to select a list component.

Listing 9.4   Using Double Mouse Clicks to Select List Components (TJList4.java)

```java
// Demonstrates the List component and double mouse clicks

/*
 * <Applet code = TJList4 width = 400 height = 200>
 * </Applet>
 */
import javax.swing.*;
import java.awt.*;
import java.awt.event.*;
import java.util.Vector;

public class TJList4 extends JApplet {
    // 1. Data members.
    JList prodList = null;
    JList cartList = null;
    String[] products = {
            "Internet Access PlusPack2.0",
            "Java Developer's Companion CD",
            "Java IDL", "Java OS",
            "Java Solutions Guide", "Java Studio",
            "Java Web Server", "Java WorkShop",
            "JavaScope", "JavaSTAR" };
    Container container = null;
    GridBagLayout gridbag = null;
    GridBagConstraints c = null;
    Vector vector = new Vector();
```

continues

Listing 9.4   continued

```
        JScrollPane scrollPane2 = null;
        int index;
        JButton button1, button2;

        public void init() {
            // 2. Prepare the JApplet layout.
            container = this.getContentPane();
            gridbag = new GridBagLayout();
            c = new GridBagConstraints();
            container.setLayout(gridbag);

            // 3. Necessary labels.
            c.fill = GridBagConstraints.BOTH;
            c.gridx = 0; c.gridy = 0;
            c.gridwidth = 2; c.gridheight = 1;
            c.weightx = 0; c.weighty = 0;
            setLabel("Java Products");

            c.gridx = 2;
            setLabel("Shopping Cart");

            // 4. Create a list of Java products.
            c.gridx = 0; c.gridy = 1;
            c.weightx = 1; c.weighty = 1;
            prodList = new JList(products);
            MyMouseListener mListener = new MyMouseListener();
            prodList.addMouseListener(mListener);
            JScrollPane scrollPane1 = new JScrollPane(prodList,
                        JScrollPane.VERTICAL_SCROLLBAR_ALWAYS,
                        JScrollPane.HORIZONTAL_SCROLLBAR_AS_NEEDED);
            gridbag.setConstraints(scrollPane1, c);
            container.add(scrollPane1);

            // 5. Create another list object called cartList.
            c.gridx = 2;
            cartList = new JList();
            scrollPane2 = new JScrollPane(cartList,
                        JScrollPane.VERTICAL_SCROLLBAR_AS_NEEDED,
                        JScrollPane.HORIZONTAL_SCROLLBAR_AS_NEEDED);
            gridbag.setConstraints(scrollPane2, c);
            container.add(scrollPane2);

            // 6. Another label indicating what to do.
            c.gridx = 0; c.gridy = 2;
            c.weightx = 0; c.weighty = 0;
            setLabel("Double click to choose");

            // 7. Add a button to delete items.
            c.gridx = 2; c.gridwidth = 1;
            c.fill = GridBagConstraints.NONE;
```

```
        button1 = new JButton("Delete Item");
        ButtonListener bl = new ButtonListener();
        button1.addActionListener(bl);
        gridbag.setConstraints(button1, c);
        container.add(button1);

        // 8. A Button to order items.
        c.gridx = 3;
        c.ipadx = 10;
        button2 = new JButton("Order Now");
        gridbag.setConstraints(button2, c);
        container.add(button2);

        container.validate();
    }

    // 9. Supporting method for labels.
    public void setLabel(String text) {
        JLabel label = new JLabel(text, SwingConstants.CENTER);
        gridbag.setConstraints(label, c);
        container.add(label);
    }

    // 10. Listener class that recognizes multiple mouse clicks.
    class MyMouseListener extends MouseAdapter {
        public void mouseClicked(MouseEvent me) {
            if (me.getClickCount() == 2) {
                index = prodList.locationToIndex(me.getPoint());
                prodList.setSelectedIndex(index);
                prodList.setSelectionBackground(Color.blue);
                prodList.setSelectionForeground(Color.white);
                vector.addElement(products[index]);
                cartList.setListData(vector);
                cartList.repaint();
                scrollPane2.repaint();
            }
        }
    }

    // 11. Button listener to delete items from the shopping cart.
    class ButtonListener implements ActionListener {
        public void actionPerformed(ActionEvent ae) {
            Object srcButton = (JButton) ae.getSource();
            if (srcButton == button1 && !cartList.isSelectionEmpty()) {
                index = cartList.getSelectedIndex();
                vector.remove(index);
                cartList.repaint();
}
            }
        }
    }
}
```

Code Details

Snippet-1 declares the required data members. `prodList` and `cartList` are the object references to be used for the list of Java products and the list representing the shopping cart. The list of products is an array of strings called `products`. The other data members of the snippet create the layout references, a vector-type reference, a scroll pane, and a couple of buttons. The vector-type reference is the handle for the data model that has been used for the shopping cart.

Inside the `init()` method, the initial layout preparation has been done for the grid bag layout by using the code shown in snippet-2. Snippet-3 attaches the labels to the applet to indicate the Java products and the shopping cart.

Snippet-4 initializes the product list reference by using the constructor that takes the array of strings. The resulting list object is added to a scroll pane before adding the scroll pane to the applet's content pane. Snippet-5 creates a list instance representing the shopping cart. This list is created in the same manner, except for using the constructor without any arguments, and is added to the applet.

Snippet-6 attaches a label to the applet to indicate what to do with the product list. Snippets 7 and 8 create push-type buttons. These buttons are used either to delete an item from the shopping cart or to place an order once the purchase list has been finalized. Snippet-9 makes labels according to the grid bag layout.

In snippet-10, the inner class `MyMouseListener` encloses the code for what happens when the mouse has been clicked on an item in the product list. A mouse listener object is registered with the product list object given in snippet-4. The listener class implements the method `mouseClicked()` to handle the events. Inside this method, multiple clicks of the mouse are obtained by using the method `getClickCount()`.

The `if` statement checks if the mouse has been clicked twice based on the return value of the method `getClickCount()`. If the click count is equal to two, a batch of methods from the class `JList` are executed to perform various operations on the product list and cart list objects.

The method `locationToIndex()` returns the index of an item in the product list by taking the coordinates in the list object. The coordinates are supplied to the method by passing the object of type `Point` returned by the method `getPoint()` in the class `MouseEvent`. Once the index to a list item has been obtained, the item with that index can be selected by using the method `setSelectedIndex()` that takes the index as its argument. The other methods, `setSelectionBackgound()` and `setSelectionForeground()`, set the selected item with the specified colors for the respective features. An item with the same index in the product list is added to the vec-tor object by using the method `addElement()`. The `vector` object is then used to initialize the data for the cart list object.

Snippet-11 implements a button listener to handle what should happen when the button to delete an item is clicked. Inside the code handler `actionPerformed()`, the `if` statement checks whether the button is the one meant to delete an item, and an item is selected. Then, by using the index of the item, the item is removed from the `vector` object or, in turn, from the shopping cart. The method `getSelectedIndex()` in the class `JList` returns the index of the selected item. The last statement of code repaints the cart list object with the modified data. When this program is executed, it displays an applet that can be used in a Web page.

Combo Boxes

A combo box is a narrow strip-like display area with a pull-down list attached to it. The right end of the display area has a small button where the user can open the associated list by using the mouse. An item in the list can be selected so that it will be shown in the display area. Depending on the number of items present in the list and the number of items to be viewed at a time, the pull-down list is supported with scrollbars. Combo boxes are often seen on toolbars.

TIP

Because a combo box is a narrow strip-like component, you can use it as an alternative to the Swing `JList` component if the space available to position the component is limited. However, note that the combo boxes can support the selection of only one item at a time.

A combo box is a lightweight and better alternative to the "choice" component available in the AWT. In addition to supporting the selection of items, a combo box can also be made editable. With an editable combo box, the user can enter an item in its display area that will be stored in the pull-down list.

A Swing combo box is represented by an object of the class `JComboBox`. The class `JComboBox` is a direct subclass of `JComponent` (see Figure 9.7) and is stored in the package `javax.swing`. The features of a combo box have been distributed into different supporting classes such as `ComboBoxModel`, `ComboBoxEditor`, `ListCellRenderer`, and so on, which are discussed with demonstration examples in the next sections.

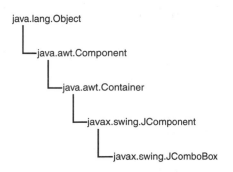

Figure 9.7

The class hierarchy of JComboBox.

JComboBox Constructors

A Swing combo box object is created by using a default data model or by using a specified model through the following constructors:

```
public JComboBox()
public JComboBox(ComboBoxModel dataModel)
```

The constructor without any arguments uses the default data model and can later be set to a specific model by using the method `setModel()` from the class `JComboBox`. The other constructor uses the data model represented by the design interface `ComboBoxModel`. Custom data models are discussed in the next section.

In addition to the previously discussed models of data, you can use the data available in the structure of an array or as a vector of items. The following constructors support these data structures to create combo box objects:

```
public JComboBox(Object[] arrayData)
public JComboBox(Vector vectorItems)
```

The argument `arrayData` represents an array of data members, for example,

```
String[] fonts = {"Times Roman", "Arial",
                 "Courier New", "Book Antiqua"};
```

The argument `vectorItems` from the other constructor is an object of type `java.util.Vector`.

Events and Listeners

Combo box objects can fire two types of events that are of the class types `ItemEvent` and `ActionEvent`. Whenever a selection state has been changed in the pull-down list, it fires an event of type `ItemEvent`. For example, if you select an item or add an item to the list, the state of selection changes and an event is fired. The item events are commonly fired by components that implement the interface `ItemSelectable`.

The item events that are fired are received by an object of type `ItemListener`. The listener class must provide the code for the interface method `itemStateChanged()`. Thus, whenever a combo box selection has been made, the code to be executed must be enclosed in this method.

In addition to firing the item events, combo boxes can also fire `ActionEvents` whenever the state of their item list changes. The action events are received by action listeners that implement the interface `ActionListener` and provide the code for the method `actionPerformed()`. Handling item events and action events is discussed at length in Chapter 8, "Buttons and Check Boxes."

JComboBox Model

As already shown in one of the constructors of `JComboBox()`, the interface `ComboBoxModel` allows you to create combo box objects by using sophisticated data models. The interface `ComboBoxModel` represents a generic data model and extends `ListModel`. Thus, you must implement the methods from both interfaces to create certain data models. The following are the additional methods that require implementation from the interface `ComboBoxModel`:

```
public void setSelectedItem(Object anItem)
public Object getSelectedItem()
```

The `setSelectedItem()` takes the general argument value of type `Object` that can be assigned to a selection variable in an implementation class. The `getSelectedItem()` returns the selection value through its implementation.

To create a custom data model, you have to create a class that implements the interface `ComboBoxModel`; this class represents the data model of interest. An object of the class can be passed as the argument value to the combo box constructor that takes the objects of type `ComboBoxModel`.

While creating a class that implements the interface `ComboBoxModel`, you can avoid implementing all the abstract methods from the interface `ListModel`. To achieve this, create a class, for example `MyComboBoxModel`, that extends the class `AbstractListModel` and implements the methods from the interface `ComboBoxModel` based on the hierarchy of relationships shown in Figure 9.8.

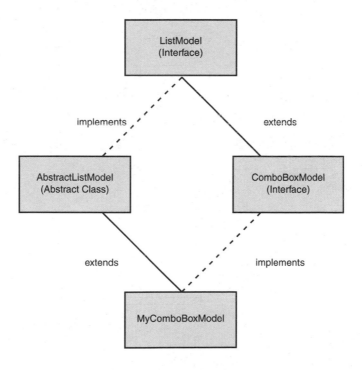

Figure 9.8

The implementation hierarchy for a custom model.

The class `MyComboBoxModel` requires only two extra methods to be implemented from the abstract class `AbstractListModel`. These methods are in addition to the two methods inside the interface `ComboBoxModel`.

JComboBox Code Example

Listing 9.5 demonstrates how to use a custom model to create a combo box object. The output of this program is displayed in Figure 9.9.

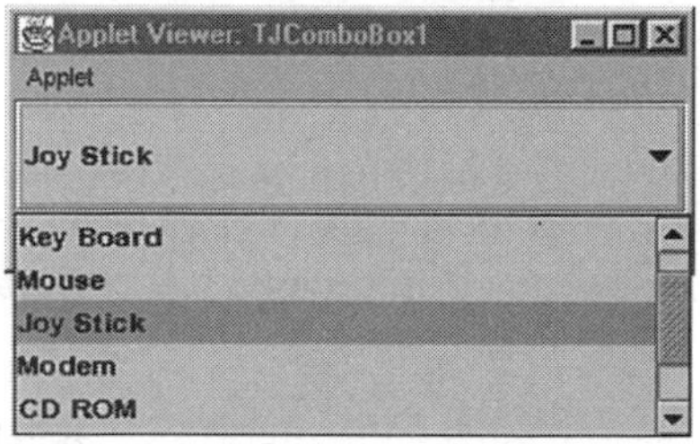

Figure 9.9

JComboBox using the custom model.

Listing 9.5   JComboBox Using the Custom Model (TJComboBox1.java)

```
/*
 * <Applet code=TJComboBox1 width=400 height=50>
 * </Applet>
 */

import javax.swing.*;
import javax.swing.event.*;

public class TJComboBox1 extends JApplet {
    public void init() {
        // 1. Create a combo box with the custom model.
        JComboBox cbox = new JComboBox(new MyComboBoxModel());

        // 2. Set the number of rows to be visible.
        cbox.setMaximumRowCount(5);

        // 3. Add the combo box object to the applet's content pane.
        getContentPane().add(cbox);
    }
}

// 4. Custom data model for the combo box.
class MyComboBoxModel extends AbstractListModel
                      implements ComboBoxModel {
    String[] ComputerComps = {"Monitor", "Key Board", "Mouse",
                              "Joy Stick", "Modem", "CD ROM",
```

```
                    "RAM Chip", "Diskette"};
String selection = null;

// Methods implemented from the class AbstractListModel
public Object getElementAt(int index) {
    return ComputerComps[index];
}

public int getSize() {
    return ComputerComps.length;
}

public void setSelectedItem(Object anItem) {
    selection = (String) anItem; // to select and register an
}                                // item from the pull-down list

// Methods implemented from the interface ComboBoxModel
public Object getSelectedItem() {
    return selection; // to add the selection to the combo box
}
}
```

Code Details

The Swing applet, `TJComboBox1`, simply creates and displays a combo box that uses the custom data model named `MyComboBoxModel`. Snippet-1 creates a combo box object with the custom model. Snippet-2 prescribes the number of items that must be visible from the pull-down list of the combo box. The last statement of code inside the `init()` method adds the combo box object to the applet.

Snippet-4 shows the class `MyComboBoxModel`, which defines the custom data model. You can observe that this class extends the class `AbstractListModel`, to conserve the code, and implements the interface `ComboBoxModel`. The class contains two data members. The data field `ComputerComps` defines an array of string labels to be displayed in the pull-down list of the combo box. The other field selection is an intermediate variable that stores the selected item in the pull-down list.

Next, the methods `getElementAt()` and `getSize()` are implemented from the class `AbstractListModel`, and the methods `getSelectedItem()` and `setSelectedItem()` are implemented from the interface `ComboBoxModel`.

As you have seen with the list components, the method `getElementAt()` is implemented to return the item label at the given index. The method `getSize()` returns the number of items to be placed in the pull-down list. Note that this information is used to prepare the pull-down list of the combo box.

After the pull-down list of components is ready, the model supports user selection of an item in the pull-down list that will be displayed in the text field of the combo box. This functionality is achieved by implementing the other two methods from the interface `ComboBoxModel`. The method `setSelectedItem()` must be implemented to store an item that has already been selected by using the intermediate variable such as `selection`. The other method, `getSelectedItem()`, must be implemented to return the item that has been selected. Then the item will be shown in the combo box display. Try selecting an item in the pull-down list to make it display as expected.

Rendering Item Cells

You have already seen how to render list cells by using icons. List objects have basically used an implementation of the design-level interface called `ListCellRenderer`. The same interface is used to render the item cells of the pull-down list of a combo box.

The interface `ListCellRenderer` expects you to implement the code for its only method `getListCellRendererComponent()`. This method returns a component that serves as a rubber stamp to render cells of the pull-down list. Inside the method `getListCellRendererComponent()`, you need to handle the setting of text labels and icons and the colors for mouse focus on a list cell.

JComboBox with Labels and Icons Code Example

Listing 9.6 demonstrates how to render a combo box with labels as well as icons (see Figure 9.10).

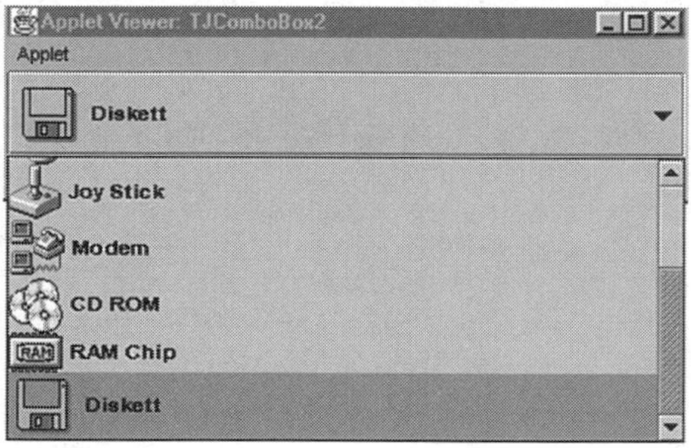

Figure 9.10

JComboBox items rendered with icons and labels.

Listing 9.6   JComboBox Items Rendered with Icons and Labels (TJComboBox2.java)

```
/*
 * <Applet code=TJComboBox2 width=400 height=50>
 * </Applet>
 */

import javax.swing.*;
import javax.swing.event.*;
```

```java
import java.awt.*;

public class TJComboBox2 extends JApplet {
    // 1. Labels for the combo box pull-down list.
    String[] ComputerComps = {"Monitor", "Key Board", "Mouse",
                              "Joy Stick", "Modem", "CD ROM",
                              "RAM Chip", "Diskette"};
    // 2. Create icons for selections and make an array.
    Icon icon1 = new ImageIcon("monitor.gif");
    Icon icon2 = new ImageIcon("keyboard.gif");
    Icon icon3 = new ImageIcon("mouse.gif");
    Icon icon4 = new ImageIcon("joystick.gif");
    Icon icon5 = new ImageIcon("modem.gif");
    Icon icon6 = new ImageIcon("cdrom.gif");
    Icon icon7 = new ImageIcon("ramchip.gif");
    Icon icon8 = new ImageIcon("diskett.gif");
    Icon[] icons = {icon1, icon2, icon3, icon4,
                    icon5, icon6, icon7, icon8};
    public void init() {
        // 3. Create a combo box with the custom model.
        JComboBox cbox = new JComboBox(ComputerComps);
        cbox.setRenderer(new MyCellRenderer(icons));

        // 4. Set the number of rows to be visible.
        cbox.setMaximumRowCount(5);

        // 5. Add the combo box object to the applet's content pane.
        getContentPane().add(cbox);
    }
}


// 6. Class that renders the list cells with icons.
class MyCellRenderer extends JLabel implements ListCellRenderer {
    Icon[] icons;

    public MyCellRenderer (Icon[] icons) {
        this.icons = icons;
        setOpaque(true);
    }

    // 7. Method that must be implemented from the interface.
    public Component getListCellRendererComponent (
                    JList list,
                    Object value,
                    int index,
                    boolean isSelected,
                    boolean cellHasFocus) {
```

continues

Listing 9.6   continued

```
        // 8. Set the text for the label.
        if (value != null) {
            String text = value.toString();
            setText(text);
        }

        // 9. Set the icon for each selection cell indicated
        //    by the index.
        if ((index != -1) && (index < icons.length)) {
            setIcon(icons[index]);
        }

        // 10. What happens when a selection is made.
        if (isSelected) {
            setBackground(list.getSelectionBackground());
            setForeground(list.getSelectionForeground());
        }

        // NOTE: This step is very important; otherwise, the
        // selection colors don't render as expected!
        else {
            setBackground(list.getBackground());
            setForeground(list.getForeground());
        }

        // 11. Finally, return this rubber stamp.
        return this;
    }
}
```

Code Details

Listing 9.6 is a Swing applet that creates a combo box and attaches it to the applet. Snippet-1 shows a data field of the applet that is an array of string labels. These labels will be used to render the list cells of the combo box. Snippet-2 creates a bunch of icon objects and stores them in an array of type `Icon`. These icons will also be used to render the list cells in addition to the labels.

Inside the `init()` method, a combo box object has been created by using the constructor that receives the array of string labels as its argument value. Next, the combo box object is set by using the method `setRenderer()` with a rendering object that is created by using the class `MyCellRenderer`. This class extends the class `JLabel` and implements the interface `ListCellRenderer`. Thus, the class serves as a rubber stamp that contains a label and an icon.

Snippet-4 sets the pull-down list of the combo box to display the specified number of items. This is achieved by using the method `setMaximumRowCount()`. Snippet-5 adds the combo box object to the content pane of the applet.

Snippet-6 shows the class `MyCellRenderer`. Inside this class, you must implement the method `getListCellRendererComponent()`, which contains some important parameters as its arguments. Each of these arguments carry certain important information for the rendering of list cells of the combo box. The argument of `type` list is the pull-down list of the combo box, the `value` is the label to be rendered, and the `integer` type index is the pointer to specify list cells of the combo box. The `boolean` argument `isSelected` provides the information about whether the specified list cell has been selected. Similarly, the `boolean` field `cellHasFocus` specifies if the specified cell has received focus.

Snippet-8 sets the text for the `MyCellRenderer` component by using the method `setText()`. Note that this component is a type of Swing label object because it extends `JLabel`. In a similar manner, snippet-9 sets the icons based on the parameter named index. This snippet uses `setIcon()` from the parent classes.

Snippet-10 sets the background and foreground colors of the specified list cell when a selection has been made. Whenever the selection colors have been rendered, you must explicitly reset the background and foreground of the cells that have not been selected. This functionality is handled in the `else` clause of the control statement.

Finally, as in snippet-11, you need to return the rubber stamp component that is made up of `JLabel` attributes. This component is used by the combo box to render its list cells with the specified labels and icons.

Editable Combo Boxes

One of the important features of combo boxes is that they can be made editable. That is, the user can enter any text in the display area of a combo box, and that text will be added to the pull-down list when the user presses the Enter key.

By default, Swing combo boxes are non-editable; however, you can make them editable by invoking the following method on the combo box object:

```
public void setEditable(boolean trueOrFalse)
```

To find out at any stage of your code whether a specific combo box is editable, you can invoke the following method on that object:

```
public boolean isEditable()
```

The method `isEditable()` returns `true` if the combo box is editable or `false` if it is not.

To paint or edit an item into the editor of a combo box, the component uses a default editor that is of type `ComboBoxEditor`. `ComboBoxEditor` is a design interface that allows the creation of any specific editor of interest. The following is a list of methods to be defined in a class that implements the interface:

```
public Component getEditorComponent()
public void setItem(Object anObject)
```

```
public Object getItem()
public void selectAll()
public void addActionListener(ActionListener l)
public void removeActionListener(ActionListener l)
```

The method getEditorComponent retrieves the component that has been used to edit an item. This component gives the handle on the editor to change its attributes such as background and foreground colors, fonts, and so on. The method setItem() assigns the item to be edited into the combo box list. The complementary method getItem() simply retrieves the edited item. The other method, selectAll(), makes all the items to be selected from the editor.

The method addActionListener() registers an object of type ActionListener to the editor. An action event is generated whenever an edited item changes. The other method, removeActionListener(), removes the listener object that has already been registered. After a custom editor is created, you can set it to a combo box by invoking the following method:

```
public void setEditor(ComboBoxEditor customEditor)
```

The current editor of a combo box can be retrieved by using the following method:

```
public ComboBoxEditor getEditor()
```

The editor that has been set for a combo box can be configured to display a default item by invoking this method

```
public void ConfigureEditor(ComboBoxEditor editor,
                            Object anItem)
```

on the combo box instance.

The default combo box editor uses the Swing JTextField as its component for editing, so you really don't have to deal with an implementation of the interface ComboBoxEditor. However, for any exceptional needs, you may have to use an editor class that implements the ComboBoxEditor interface.

Editable JComboBox Code Example

Listing 9.7 demonstrates how to create an editable combo box. The text that has been edited is added at the top of the pull-down list when you press the return key (see Figure 9.11). The code is also capable of filtering out the duplicate items in the combo box list.

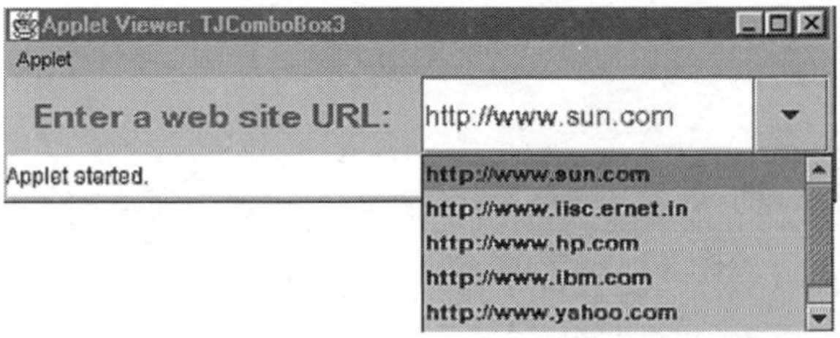

Figure 9.11

Applet displaying an editable combo box.

Listing 9.7   Editable JComboBox (TJComboBox3.java)
```java
// Demonstrates editable combo boxes

/*
 * <Applet code=TJComboBox3 width=450 height=50>
 *</Applet>
 */

import javax.swing.*;
import java.awt.*;
import java.awt.event.*;

public class TJComboBox3 extends JApplet {
    // 1. Declare the references.
    JComboBox cbox = null;
    Container c = null;

    // 2. Define an array of sites to be shown in the
    // combo box pull-down list, by default.
    String[] defaultSites = {
         "http://www.sun.com", "http://www.iisc.ernet.in",
         "http://www.hp.com",  "http://www.ibm.com",
         "http://www.yahoo.com", "http://www.news.com"};
    String defaultEdit = "http://www.javasoft.com";

    public void init() {
        // 3. Get a handle on the applet's content pane.
        // and prepare the container with grid layout
        c = this.getContentPane();
        c.setLayout(new GridLayout(1,2));

        // 4. Create the combo box with the list of default sites.
        cbox = new JComboBox(defaultSites);
        cbox.setOpaque(true);

        // 5. Make the combo box editable.
```

continues

Listing 9.7   continued

```
        cbox.setEditable(true);

        // 6. Configure the combo box editor.
        cbox.configureEditor(cbox.getEditor(), defaultEdit);

        // 7. Rows to be visible without scrollbars.
        cbox.setMaximumRowCount(5);

        // 8. Set the combo box editor colors and font.
        ComboBoxEditor cboxEditor = cbox.getEditor();
        Component editorComp = cboxEditor.getEditorComponent();
        editorComp.setBackground(Color.white);
        editorComp.setForeground(Color.blue);

        Font f1 = new Font("Dialog", Font.PLAIN, 16);
        editorComp.setFont(f1);

        // 9. Font for the combo box popup list.
        cbox.setFont(f1);

        // 10. Register the action listener.
        cbox.addActionListener(new CboxListener());

        // 11. A label to indicate what to do.
        JLabel label = new JLabel("Enter a web site URL:",
                                  JLabel.CENTER);
        label.setFont(new Font("SansSerif", Font.BOLD, 18));

        // 12. Finally...
        c.add(label);
        c.add(cbox);
    }

    class CboxListener implements ActionListener {
        public void actionPerformed(ActionEvent evt) {
            // Helpful flag
            boolean isItemPresent = false;

            // 13. Check if the item already exists in the pop-up list.
            for (int i=0; i<cbox.getItemCount(); i++) {
                if (cbox.getItemAt(i).equals(cbox.getSelectedItem())) {
                    isItemPresent = true;
                    break;
                }
            }

            // 14. If the item is not present in the pop-up list...
            if (!isItemPresent) {
```

```
                    cbox.insertItemAt(cbox.getSelectedItem(), 0);
                    isItemPresent = false;
                }
            }
        }
    }
}
```

Code Details

Listing 9.7 begins by declaring a combo box reference as its data member. The other reference of type `Container` provides the handle to the applet's content pane. Snippet-2 defines a list of default sites; when you start the program, these sites appear in the combo box drop-down list. The other data variable, `defaultEdit`, is to be displayed in the editable area of the combo box.

Inside the `init()` method, snippet-3 gets a handle on the applet's content pane and prepares the applet with a grid layout of one row and two columns. Snippets 4 and 5 create the combo box object and make it editable by using the `JComboBox` method `setEditable()` with its argument as `true`.

Snippet-6 executes another `JComboBox` method called `configureEditor()`. This method is used to set the combo box editor to the default text. Note that you need to supply the argument values of type `ComboBoxEditor` and `Object`.

The method `setMaximumRowCount()` in snippet-7 prepares the drop-down list of the combo box to display the specified number of items. Snippet-8 gets a handle on the default combo box editor by invoking the method `getEditor()` on the combo box object. By using the handle on the combo box editor, you can create an editor component of type `Component` by using the method `getEditorComponent()`. After you obtain this component, you modify the attributes by using the API supported in the class `Component`. Thus, the editor background and foreground colors are prescribed to the white and blue colors, respectively. This snippet also sets the font of the editor to the new font as given.

Snippet-9 assigns the new font to the drop-down list. Note the objects on which you have to invoke the method `setFont()` to assign the font to the combo box editor and the drop-down list. Snippet-10 registers an action listener with the combo box object. Snippet-11 creates a label object with the specified font. Finally, snippet-12 adds these objects to the applet's content pane.

Inside the combo box listener class, snippet-13 checks if an item that has been edited already exists in the drop-down list of the combo box. The method `getItemCount()` returns the number of items present in the drop-down list. The method `getItemAt()` returns the item at the specified index. This item will be compared to the item entered in the combo box. When you press the return key, the method `getSelectedItem()` returns the item entered in the combo box editor. Then, the flag `isItemPresent` is set to `true` if the item is already present in the drop-down list.

Snippet-14 inserts an item at the specified index of the combo box drop-down list. The method `insertItemAt()` takes two arguments, such as the item to be inserted and the location index.

CHAPTER 10

Tables

A table can display data in rows and columns format in a user interface. A table can also optionally allow editing.

Swing table models are powerful, flexible, and easy enough to implement that they are often preferable to the default models. For the details of table classes and methods, see the quick reference in Appendix A, "JFC Swing Quick Reference."

Simple Tables

Swing tables are represented by the class JTable that extends the class JComponent (see Figure 10.1) and is stored in the package javax.swing. This section demonstrates how to create simple tables by using two of the table constructors.

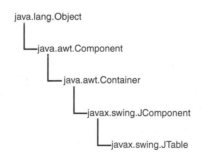

Figure 10.1

The JTable class hierarchy.

JTable Constructors

There are seven constructors supported in the JTable class, with various arguments to generate tables. You can optionally specify the number of rows and columns in a table, table model, table column model, selection model, and so on. The following is the list of constructors and their descriptions:

```
public JTable()
```

creates a JTable object that is initialized with a default data model, a default column model, and a default selection model.

```
public JTable(int numRows, int numColumns)
```

creates a JTable with the specified number of rows and columns with empty cells. The table object uses the default table model.

```
public JTable(Object[][] rowData, Object[] columnNames)
```

creates a JTable to display the values in a two-dimensional array specified by rowData. The column names are specified by the array called columnNames.

```
public JTable(TableModel dm, TableColumnModel cm, ListSelectionModel sm)
```

creates a JTable that is initialized with the specified data model dm, column model cm, and the selection model sm. You can use this constructor to create a sophisticated table.

```
public JTable(TableModel dm, TableColumnModel cm)
```

creates a JTable that is initialized with dm as the data model and cm as the column model. A default model is used as the selection model for this table object.

```
public JTable(TableModel dm)
```

creates a JTable that is initialized with the specified data model dm. The default models are used for the column model and selection model.

```
public JTable(Vector rowData, Vector columnNames)
```

creates a JTable to display the data stored in vectors. The data structure for the rows of the table is the vector of vectors, and the column names is simply a vector. This constructor is useful if you are storing some data (that can be displayed in a table) using vectors in a program.

To quickly implement an elementary table, you can choose the previous constructor that uses only the rows and columns or use the constructor that requires the arrays of data. Note that the tables that are created by using these constructors have certain inherent drawbacks. Basically, these tables only allow data of type String. Also, the tables become editable, which may not be acceptable. To overcome these drawbacks, you need to implement tables by using the custom models as shown in the next section.

Table Header

A table header is the top portion of each column in a table where the column title is displayed. In Swing, the column header is represented by the class JTableHeader. You

can retrieve the header of a table object by calling the method getTableHeader().
There is another method called getDefaultTableHeader() that returns the table header when no other header has been assigned. A different table header can be assigned by using the class setTableHeader().

Resizing Columns

By default, the tables created in Swing allow resizing of columns. You can interactively adjust the width of a column by dragging the mouse on a column line. The behavior of columns during resizing can be controlled by using the following constants:

```
static int AUTO_RESIZE_OFF
```

does not allow any column width to change.

```
static int AUTO_RESIZE_ALL_COLUMNS
```

controls the resizing of all columns in a proportionate manner. Thus the column spacing appears the same even after resizing.

```
static int AUTO_RESIZE_NEXT_COLUMN
```

controls in such a way that when a column is adjusted, the next column gets adjusted in the opposite direction.

```
static int AUTO_RESIZE_SUBSEQUENT_COLUMNS
```

preserves the total width by changing the width of the subsequent columns.

```
static int AUTO_RESIZE_LAST_COLUMN
```

adjusts only the last column during resizing. The remaining columns remain unchanged.

Simple Table Code Example

Listing 10.1 creates a very simple table and adds it to an applet. The program uses the table constructor that requires the number of rows and columns to be specified. Notice that the table is editable by default. The output of this program is shown in Figure 10.2.

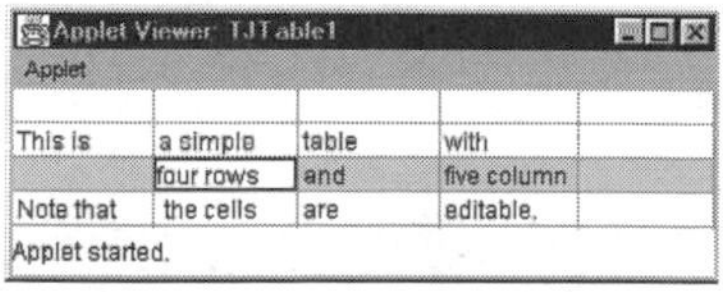

Figure 10.2

A simple table with four rows and five columns.

Listing 10.1   Simple Table (TJTable1.java)
```
// Demonstrates how to create a simple table with the
// specified number of rows and columns.

/*
 * <applet code = TJTable1 width = 350 height = 150>
 * </applet>
 */

import javax.swing.*;

public class TJTable1 extends JApplet {
    public void init() {
        // 1. Create a table using the number of rows and
        // columns and add it to the content pane.
        JTable table = new JTable(4,5); // 4 rows & 5 columns

        getContentPane().add(table);
    }
}
```

Code Details

Listing 10.1 is an applet that shows a simple table of four rows and five columns. There are only two statements inside the `init()` method. In snippet-1, the first statement creates a table using the constructor `JTable(int rows, int columns)`. The second statement adds the table to the content pane of the applet.

Table Built with Arrays Code Example

Listing 10.2 shows one more program that creates a Swing table using data available in arrays. The column array is simply an array of headings to be displayed in each column. The rows are represented by an array of arrays because each row itself is an array of data items to be displayed. The table has been positioned in an applet. The output of this program is shown in Figure 10.3.

NOTE

The table header needs to be explicitly added at the top portion of the container. It does not appear by simply adding the table to its container.

Name	Size (Bytes)	Date	Directory
AUTOEXEC....	149	09-11-98	false
REAL	DIR	12-11-97	true
WINDOWS	DIR	03-24-97	true
COMMAND....	92879	07-11-97	false

Figure 10.3

A table created by using arrays of data.

Listing 10.2   Table Created Using Arrays of Data (TJTable2.java)

```java
// Demonstrates how to create a simple table with the
// specified row data and column data.

/*
 * <applet code = TJTable2 width = 350 height = 100>
 * </applet>
 */

import javax.swing.*;
import java.awt.*;
import java.util.*;

public class TJTable2 extends JApplet {
    // Create an array of names to be displayed in the table
    // header.
    String[] columnNames = {"Name", "Size (Bytes)", "Date", "Directory"};

    // Create an array of row data (each row is an array) to be
    // displayed in the rows of the table.
    Object[][] rowData = {
        {"AUTOEXEC.BAT", "149", "09-11-98", new Boolean(false)},
        {"REAL", "DIR", "12-11-97", new Boolean(true)},
        {"WINDOWS", "DIR", "03-24-97", new Boolean(true)},
        {"COMMAND.COM", "92879", "07-11-97", new Boolean(false)}};

    public void init() {
        // 1. Create a table by using the row and column data.
        JTable table = new JTable(rowData, columnNames);

        // 2. Add the table column header and the
        // table to the content pane of the applet.
        getContentPane().add(table.getTableHeader(), BorderLayout.NORTH);
        getContentPane().add(table);
    }
}
```

Code Details

In Listing 10.2, the data to be displayed in a table has been stored in arrays. The column data is simply an array of strings called columnNames. The row data is an array of arrays, where each array contains the data for a particular row.

Inside the init() method, snippet-1 creates a table object by using the data defined in arrays. In snippet-2, the table is added to the content pane of the applet. The column header that contains the titles is also added to the top portion of the applet to display the table completely.

NOTE

If you do not use a scroll pane to display a table, you need to explicitly add the table header at the top of the content pane.

Table Models

The previous section showed how to create trees by using data that is available in arrays. In practice, however, the data may be available in a more complex form. To create tables using complex data formats, you need to depend on table models. In fact, developers must consider using table models extensively to realize the full potential of Swing tables. Fortunately, creating custom table models in Swing is easier than you might expect.

The package `javax.swing.table` supports the design level interface for a Swing table called `TableModel`. The `TableModel` interface contains the following methods to be implemented:

```
public void addTableModelListener(TableModelListener l)
```

adds a listener to the list that's notified each time a change to the data model occurs.

```
public Class getColumnClass(int columnIndex)
```

returns the lowest common denominator `Class` in the column.

```
public int getColumnCount()
```

returns the number of columns managed by the data source object.

```
public String getColumnName(int columnIndex)
```

returns the name of the column at `columnIndex`.

```
public int getRowCount()
```

returns the number of records managed by the data source object.

```
public Object getValueAt(int rowIndex, int columnIndex)
```

returns an attribute value for the cell at `columnIndex` and `rowIndex`.

```
public boolean isCellEditable(int rowIndex, int columnIndex)
```

returns `true` if the cell at `rowIndex` and `columnIndex` is editable.

```
public void removeTableModelListener(TableModelListener l)
```

removes a listener from the list that's notified each time a change to the data model occurs.

```
public void setValueAt(Object aValue, int rowIndex, int columnIndex)
```

assigns an attribute value for the record in the cell at `columnIndex` and `rowIndex`.

Default Table Model

By default, a table object uses the data model of class type `DefaultTableModel`. This class implements the previous interface `TableModel` and extends the class `AbstractTableModel`. You can retrieve the default table model object by calling the method `getModel()` when no other model has already been assigned.

TIP

> Often you do not have to use the default model because custom table models are easy to create, but flexible and powerful enough to represent complex data.

Abstract Table Model

The Swing library also supports a class called `AbstractTableModel` to allow developers to create custom table models easily. The custom table model class can extend `AbstractTableModel`, and requires you to implement only the following methods:

```
public int getRowCount();
public int getColumnCount();
public Object getValueAt(int row, int column);
```

Table Model Event and Listeners

The events of type `TableModelEvent` are fired whenever a table data model has changed. These events are listened to by the objects that implement the interface `TableModelListener`. The interface contains the method `tableChanged()`, which contains the code to be executed whenever the data model undergoes some change.

You can also know precisely where the data changes have taken place. For this purpose you can invoke the methods supported in the event class `TableModelEvent`. For the list of methods, see Appendix A.

Custom Table Model Code Example

Listing 10.3 shows the program that uses the custom table model to obtain the files and subdirectories from the specified directory. The application displays the contents of the home directory on your computer by using the Swing table. You can also view the contents of another directory by entering the path in the text field shown at the top portion of the frame. The output of the program is shown in Figure 10.4.

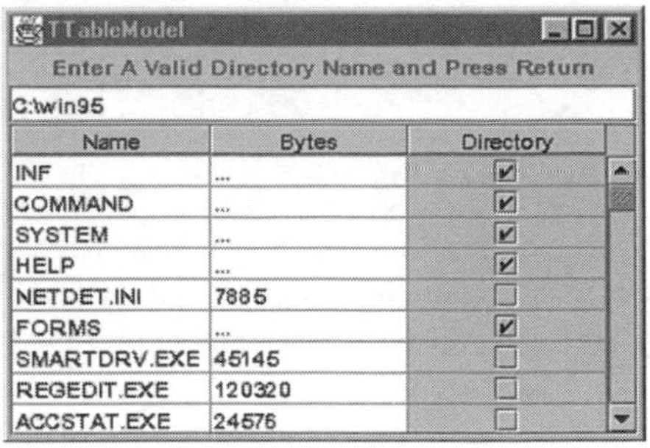

Figure 10.4

A table generated by using a custom model.

Listing 10.3   Custom Table Model (TTableModel.java)
```
// Demonstrates a custom table model.

import javax.swing.*;
import javax.swing.table.*;
import javax.swing.event.*;
import java.awt.*;
import java.awt.event.*;
import java.io.File;

public class TTableModel extends JFrame {
    Container container;
    JTable table;
    JScrollPane scrollPane;
    JLabel label;
    JTextField textField;

    public TTableModel() {
        // 1. Assign a title to the frame and get
        // the handle on the content pane.
        super("TTableModel");
        container = this.getContentPane();

        // 2. Create a label and text field and add
        // them to a panel.
        label = new JLabel(
            "Enter A Valid Directory Name and Press Return",
            JLabel.CENTER);
        textField = new JTextField();
        textField.addActionListener(new TextFieldListener());
        JPanel panel = new JPanel(new GridLayout(2,1));
        panel.add(label);
        panel.add(textField);
```

```
        // 3. Get the root/system home. Use this home directory
        // to create a file object that is used by the directory
        // or file system model construct the table model. Also
        // display the home directory in the text field.
        String home = System.getProperty("user.home");
        table = new JTable(new DirectoryModel(new File(home)));
        table.createDefaultColumnsFromModel();
        textField.setText(home);

        // 4. Add the panel and table to the container.
        container.add(BorderLayout.NORTH, panel);
        container.add(new JScrollPane(table));

        // 5. Frame settings.
        // Add the window closing listener.
        addWindowListener(new WindowEventHandler());
        setDefaultCloseOperation(WindowConstants.DISPOSE_ON_CLOSE);
        setBackground(Color.white);
        setSize(350, 300);   // Frame width=350, height=300
        show(); // Display the frame
    }

    // 6. Window event handler.
    class WindowEventHandler extends WindowAdapter {
        public void windowClosing(WindowEvent evt) {
            System.exit(0);
        }
    }

    // 7. The main method.
    public static void main(String[] args) {
        TTableModel frame = new TTableModel();
    }

    // 8. Text field listener.
    class TextFieldListener implements ActionListener {
        public void actionPerformed(ActionEvent e) {
            // 9. Get the next directory name entered in
            // the text field, prepare the model, and display
            // the table by assigning the new data.
            DirectoryModel model = new DirectoryModel(
                        new File(textField.getText()));
            table.setModel(model);
        }
    }
}
```

continues

Listing 10.3   continued

```
// 10. The "Directory" or "FileSystem" model.
class DirectoryModel extends AbstractTableModel {
    File directory;
    String[] members;
    int rowCount;

    // 11. Model constructor.
    public DirectoryModel(File dir) {
        directory = dir; // Hold the directory
        members = dir.list(); // Get the list of files
                              // and subdirectories
        if (members != null)
            // Table rows = No. of entities inside the directory
            rowCount = members.length;
        else {
            // If the memeber list is null, row count should be zero.
            rowCount = 0;
            // This can happen if an invalid directory is entered
            // in the text field.
            System.out.println("Not a valid directory!");
        }
    }

    // 12. Retrieve the number of rows for the table to be prepared.
    public int getRowCount() {
        return members != null? rowCount:0;
    }

    // 13. Similarly, retrieve the column count.
    public int getColumnCount() {
        return members != null? 3:0;
    }

    // 14. Retrieve each of the table values at the specified
    // row and column.
    public Object getValueAt(int row, int column) {
        if (directory == null || members == null) {
            return null;
        }

        File fileSysEntity = new File(directory, members[row]);

        switch(column) {
        case 0:
            return fileSysEntity.getName();
        case 1:
            if (fileSysEntity.isDirectory()) {
                return "...";
```

```
            }
            else {
                return new Long(fileSysEntity.length());
            }
        case 2:
            return fileSysEntity.isDirectory()? new Boolean(true):
                                                new Boolean(false);
        default:
            return "";
        }
    }


    // 15. Retrieve the column names to be used in the table header.
    public String getColumnName(int column) {
        switch(column) {
            case 0:
                return "Name";
            case 1:
                return "Bytes";
            case 2:
                return "Directory";
            default:
                return "";
        }
    }


    // 16. Retrieve the class types of the entries in
    // each of the table columns.
    public Class getColumnClass(int column) {
        Class returnClass = String.class;
        if (column == 2)
            returnClass = Boolean.class;
        return returnClass;
    }
}
```

Code Details

Inside the constructor of the frame TTableModel, snippet-1 assigns a title to the frame and initializes a reference to its content pane. Snippet-2 creates a label and text field and adds them to a panel. The text field enables the user to input a valid directory name to view its contents.

Snippet-3 retrieves the home directory as a string and assigns it to the custom model called DirectoryModel as a file object (see snippet-10). The custom model is used by the tree object that has been created. The method createDefaultColumnsFromModel() clears any existing columns and creates columns based on the values returned by the methods getColumnCount() and getColumnClass() from the table model.

Snippet-4 shows the code to add the panel (created in snippet-2) and the table to the frame. Notice that the table is added to the frame through a scroll pane. Snippet-5 shows the configuration associated with the frame object. Snippet-6 is the event handling code to close the frame. Snippet-7 is the main method where the frame instance is created, and snippet-8 is the text field listener class. The text field fires "action" events when an entry is validated. Inside the `actionPerformed()` method, the program fetches the directory path as a string and creates the directory model by using the new directory path. Then the table is assigned the refreshed data model to display the contents of the new directory.

Snippet-10 shows the custom model called `DirectoryModel` that extends `AbstractTableModel`. If you extend a class from the `AbstractTableModel`, you need not implement all the methods from the `TableModel` interface. Snippet-11 shows the constructor for the custom model class. By using this constructor, a copy of the directory is stored in the class. The class also stores the contents of the directory by using an array called `members` and the number of entities (`rowCount`) inside the directory. Notice that inside the `else` clause of the snippet, you need to set the row count to zero in case the user enters a directory name that does not exist.

Snippet-12 shows the method that retrieves the number of rows to be used for the table. Similarly, snippet-13 retrieves the count of the columns. If there are some members in a directory, there will be three columns with column headers such as `Name`, `Bytes`, and `Directory`. If there are no members, the column count is zero.

Snippet-14 shows the crucial method `getValueAt()` that returns the data value for each cell of the table at the specified row and column. This method initially checks whether the directory or its members exit. If they do not exist, the method returns `null`. If they exist, the method creates a `File` object using the directory name and its member at the specified row. Then, for the first column, it returns the directory or filename. Similarly, for the renaming columns, the method returns the information such as the file size and the `boolean` objects as to whether it is a directory or a file.

Snippet-15 retrieves the column titles to be displayed in the table header. Snippet-16 retrieves the class types of the data items in each of the table columns. This method controls the way the entry should be displayed. For example, if you specify the data to be of class type `Boolean` as shown in the code, the output appears with a check box with a suitable selection status (see the output figure in Figure 10.4). Compare this output with the output shown in Figure 10.3, where the `boolean` value is displayed as a string when the program uses the default table model.

Table Selections

Swing tables not only display data, but also allow the selection of data by using the mouse or keyboard. The user can essentially select a row, column, or an individual cell to edit. These selection modes can also be controlled by turning them on or off by using a suitable `boolean` flag. The tables also allow the implementation of checking or removing selections.

You can change the background and foreground colors of the selections using the following methods:

```
public void setSelectionBackground(Color selectionBackground)
public void setSelectionForeground(Color selectionForeground)
```

The following methods control the selection of rows or columns or individual cells:

```
public void setRowSelectionAllowed(boolean flag)
public void setColumnSelectionAllowed(boolean flag)
public void setCellSelectionEnabled(boolean flag)
```

Given a closed interval specified by certain indexes (such as index0 and index1), you can use the following methods to make the rows or columns be selected in the interval:

```
public void setRowSelectionInterval(int index0, int index1)
public void setColumnSelectionInterval(int index0, int index1)
```

To remove a selection in the closed interval of the specified indexes (index0 and index1), you can use the following methods:

```
public void removeRowSelectionInterval(int index0, int index1)
public void removeColumnSelectionInterval(int index0, int index1)
```

For other API methods supported to check the selections, obtain indexes for the selections, and so on, see Appendix A.

Table Selection Model

To handle the selection process, tables depend on the model represented by the interface ListSelectionModel. This model has already been discussed in Chapter 9, "Lists and Combo Boxes." To get a reference to the row selection model, you can call the method getSelectionModel() on the table object. To get the reference to the column selection model, you need to call the getSelectionModel() on the column model of the table. The column model can be retrieved by using the method getColumnModel() on the table object.

Because tables depend on ListSelectionModel, you can expect the selection modes such as *single selection*, *single contiguous interval selection*, or *multiple interval selection*, represented by the constants SINGLE_SELECTION, SINGLE_INTERVAL_SELECTION, and MULTIPLE_INTERVAL_SELECTION. To work with the single contiguous interval selection or multiple interval selection, you need to use the Shift or Alt key. One of the selection modes can be assigned to the selection model by invoking the method setSelectionMode(), which takes these constants as argument values.

Table Selection Events and Listeners

Whenever a selection is made, the events of type ListSelectionEvent are fired. These events need to be attended by objects that implement the interface ListSelectionListener. The implementation class provides the code for the method valueChanged(). This method is invoked whenever a new selection has been made.

Table Selection Code Example

Listing 10.4 demonstrates the selection of table cells. The program creates a simple table displaying the indices of table cells. When the user clicks the mouse in a cell, the selection process is indicated by displaying the selected cell index at the bottom portion of the frame. The output of the code is shown in Figure 10.5.

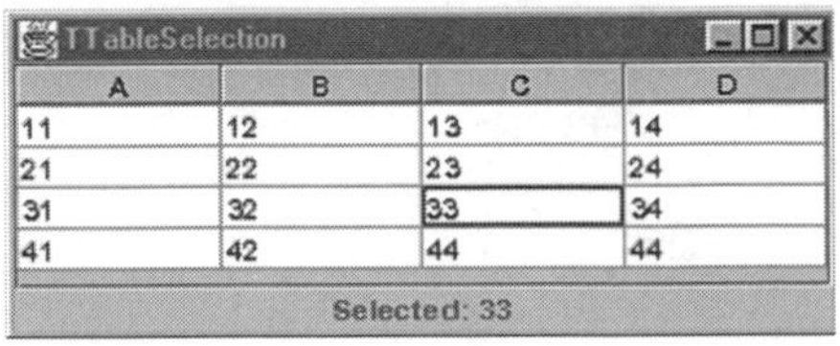

Figure 10.5

Program output to demonstrate table selections.

Listing 10.4   Table Selections (TTableSelection.java)

```java
// Demonstrates the implementation of table selections.
import javax.swing.*;import javax.swing.table.*;import
javax.swing.event.*;import java.awt.*;import java.awt.event.*;public class
TTableSelection extends JFrame
                        implements ListSelectionListener {
    Container container;
    JTable table;
    JScrollPane scrollPane;
    JLabel label;

    String[] columnTitles = {"A", "B", "C", "D"};
    Object[] [] rowData = {
        {"11", "12", "13", "14"},
        {"21", "22", "23", "24"},
        {"31", "32", "33", "34"},
        {"41", "42", "44", "44"}};

    public TTableSelection() {
        // 1. Assign a title to the frame and get
        // the handle on its content pane.
        super("TTableModel");
        container = this.getContentPane();

        // 2. Instantiate the label and table objects.
        label = new JLabel("", JLabel.CENTER);
        table = new JTable(rowData, columnTitles);

        // 3. Registering for cell selection.
        table.setCellSelectionEnabled(true); // selection enabled
        // Obtain a reference to the table selection model
```

```
        ListSelectionModel cellSelectionModel =
            table.getSelectionModel();
        // Assign the selection mode.
        cellSelectionModel.setSelectionMode(
            ListSelectionModel.SINGLE_SELECTION);
        // Add the listener to the table selection model.
        cellSelectionModel.addListSelectionListener(this);

        // 4. Add the panel and table to the container.
        container.add(BorderLayout.SOUTH, label);
        container.add(new JScrollPane(table));

        // 5. Frame settings.
        // Add the window closing listener.
        addWindowListener(new WindowEventHandler());
        setDefaultCloseOperation(WindowConstants.DISPOSE_ON_CLOSE);
        setBackground(Color.white);
        setSize(350, 150);  // Frame width=350, height=150
        show(); // Display the frame
    }

    // 6. Window event handler.
    class WindowEventHandler extends WindowAdapter {
        public void windowClosing(WindowEvent evt) {
            System.exit(0);
        }
    }

    // 7. List selection listenter method to be implemented.
    public void valueChanged(ListSelectionEvent e) {
        int rows, columns;
        String selectedData = null;

        int[] selectedRow = table.getSelectedRows();
        int[] selectedColumns = table.getSelectedColumns();

        for (int i=0; i<selectedRow.length; i++) {
            for (int j=0; j<selectedColumns.length; j++) {
                selectedData = (String) table.getValueAt(
                    selectedRow[i], selectedColumns[j]);
            }
        }
        label.setText("Selected: " + selectedData);
    }

    // 8. The main method.
    public static void main(String[] args) {
        TTableSelection frame = new TTableSelection();
    }
}
```

Code Details

Inside the constructor of the frame, snippet-1 assigns a title and obtains a handle on the frame's content pane. Snippet-2 instantiates the label and table objects. Snippet-3 shows the code to enable the selection process and registers a listener to receive the selection events. To register the selection listener, you need to obtain a reference to the table selection model. Snippet-4 adds the label and table to the frame.

Snippet-5 shows the code to configure the frame. Snippet-6 is the window event handler to close the window. Snippet-7 is the method that has been implemented from the list selection listener. You need to enclose the code to be executed whenever a table selection is made. Snippet-8 is the main method where the main frame is created.

Editing Table Cells

In addition to displaying data, Swing tables can also support editing of data. This feature is extremely useful to store data in a database. Swing tables are sophisticated to the extent that you can attach other data editing components like combo boxes, lists, and so on. You can also use a check box component to edit the `boolean` state (`true` or `false`) of an attribute. By default, Swing tables use a text field as their editor.

To edit a table, you need to deal with the `TableModel` to suitably implement the method `isCellEditable()`. This method must return the value `true` for a given cell that needs to be made editable. You also need to implement the method `setValueAt()`, which is called whenever a cell value has been changed and needs validation. Finally, when a new data item has been edited, the table model notifies its listeners to update the view of the table.

Editable Table Code Example

Listing 10.5 is an application that demonstrates the editable tables. The program basically creates a table that contains column header displaying the name, weight, blood group, and age group of a list of people. By default, the table appears with the data introduced in the program. Figure 10.6 displays the editable table generated by this program.

In the table cells, you can edit the data of people. Notice that the blood group can be selected and edited into a table cell by selecting from the combo box associated with each cell in the Blood Group column. The last column of the table displays the check boxes to edit a proper Boolean value.

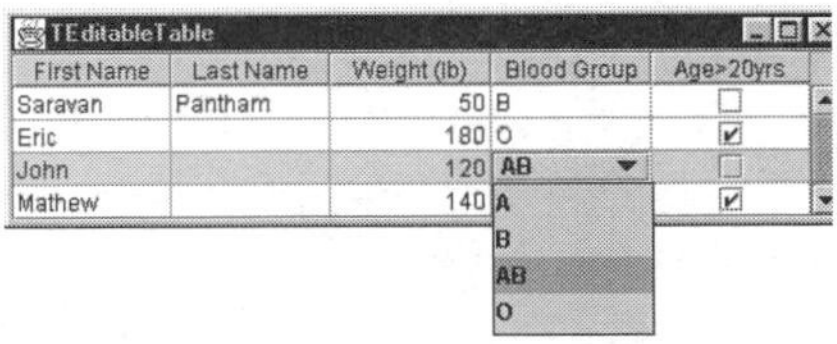

Figure 10.6

Program output to demonstrate table selections.

Listing 10.5   Editable Tables (TEditableTable.java)
```java
// Demonstrates the editable property of Swing tables.

import javax.swing.*;
import javax.swing.table.*;
import javax.swing.event.*;
import java.awt.*;
import java.awt.event.*;

public class TEditableTable extends JFrame {
    Container container;
    JTable table;
    JScrollPane scrollPane;
    JLabel label;
    JTextField textField;

    public TEditableTable() {
        // 1. Assign a title to the frame and get
        // the handle on the content pane.
        super("TEditableTable");
        container = this.getContentPane();

        // 2. Define the data to be displayed in the table.
        String[] columnTitles = {
            "First Name", "Last Name", "Weight (lb)", "Blood Group",
            ➥"Age>20yrs"};
        Object[][] dataEntries = {
            {"Saravan", "Pantham", new Integer(50), "B", new Boolean(false)},
            {"Eric", "", new Integer(180), "O", new Boolean(true)},
            {"John", "", new Integer(120), "AB", new Boolean(false)},
            {"Mathew", "", new Integer(140), "A", new Boolean(true)},
            };

        // 3. Assign the table model object to a table object.
        TableModel model = new EditableTableModel(columnTitles, dataEntries);
        table = new JTable(model);
        table.createDefaultColumnsFromModel();

        // 4. Create a combo box and use it as an editor for the
        // blood group column.
        String[] bloodGroups = {"A", "B", "AB", "O"};
        JComboBox comboBox = new JComboBox(bloodGroups);
        table.getColumnModel().getColumn(3).setCellEditor(
            new DefaultCellEditor(comboBox));

        // 5. Add the above panel and table to the container.
        container.add(new JScrollPane(table));
```

continues

```
        // 6. Frame settings.
        // Add the window closing listener.
        addWindowListener(new WindowEventHandler());
        setDefaultCloseOperation(WindowConstants.DISPOSE_ON_CLOSE);
        setBackground(Color.white);
        setSize(450, 150);  // Frame width=450, height=150
        show(); // Display the frame
    }

    // 7. Window event handler.
    class WindowEventHandler extends WindowAdapter {
        public void windowClosing(WindowEvent evt) {
            System.exit(0);
        }
    }

    // 8. The main method.
    public static void main(String[] args) {
        TEditableTable frame = new TEditableTable();
    }
}

//
class EditableTableModel extends AbstractTableModel {
    String[] columnTitles;
    Object[][] dataEntries;
    int rowCount;

    // 9. Model constructor.
    public EditableTableModel(String[] columnTitles, Object[][] dataEntries) {
        this.columnTitles = columnTitles;
        this.dataEntries = dataEntries;
    }

    // 10. Retrieve the number of rows for the table to be prepared.
    public int getRowCount() {
        return dataEntries.length;
    }

    // 11. Similarly, retrieve the column count.
    public int getColumnCount() {
        return columnTitles.length;
    }

    // 12. Retrieve each of the table values at the specified
    // row and column.
    public Object getValueAt(int row, int column) {
        return dataEntries[row][column];
```

```
    }

    // 13. Retrieve the column names to be used in the table header.
    public String getColumnName(int column) {
        return columnTitles[column];
    }

    // 14. Retrieve the class types of the entries in
    // each of the table columns.
    public Class getColumnClass(int column) {
        return getValueAt(0, column).getClass();
    }

    // 15. Allow all the table cells to be editable.
    public boolean isCellEditable(int row, int column) {
        return true;
    }

    // 16. Assign the data entered to the data model.
    public void setValueAt(Object value, int row, int column) {
        dataEntries[row][column] = value;
    }
}
```

Code Details

The constructor of the frame TEditableTable, snippet-1 assigns a title and obtains a handle to the content pane of the frame. Snippet-2 defines the default data to be displayed in the table cells. Snippet-3 assigns the table model to the table object that is created. The table model implements the methods to make the table editable. Snippet-5 adds the table to the content pane of the main frame. Snippet-6 configures the main frame, and snippet-7 is the event handler to closing the window. Snippet-8 shows the main method.

CHAPTER 11

Text Widgets

With the advent of Swing, text components rise above the simple text field and text area components. The Swing library introduces one more simple component, called the password field, and two advanced components, called editor pane and text pane, that deal with styled text. Although handling styled text is complex, the Swing library uses wrappers over complex features to make the common tasks easily implemented.

The Swing library provides a comprehensive framework to deal with almost all practical text handling through graphical user interfaces. Now you can easily handle single-line plain text, multi-line plain text, and multi-line styled text. Text fields support single-line plain text, and password fields are meant for inputting secret information that should not be directly visible in the text field. The text area component supports multi-line plain text, while the editor pane and text pane are meant for advanced text handling with multi-line styled text. In addition to these components, there are a number of other supporting classes and interfaces to deal with the information model, colors, styles, events, and so on.

The JTextComponent Class

The class JTextComponent is the parent for text components in Swing. Thus, it provides a large number of API methods common to text components, particularly the methods to assign a content or document model to a component and the methods to assign a view and controller. The class also provides API calls to handle undo and redo actions, keymaps and bindings, and caret changes. A comprehensive list of these API calls is given in Appendix A, "JFC Swing Quick Reference."

The Document Interface

The document is the content model for Swing text components. Thus, text components make use of an object of document to store their data. The document is described by the design level interface called `Document`. The interface is stored in the package named `javax.swing.text`.

The information content of a component is stored in a document as elements. These elements implement the interface `Element`, which is stored in the package `javax.swing.text`. Each of these elements possesses attributes such as font, size, color, and so on to describe their style.

Text Fields

The Swing text field can be used to display or edit a single line of plain text. The component appears similar to the AWT text field; however, the Swing text field is a lightweight component. A text-field object is created by using the class `JTextField`, which is a direct subclass of `JTextComponent`. Thus, the functionality of `JTextField` spreads into `JTextComponent` and `JComponent`. `JTextField` objects can fire the action and mouse events that can be captured by a registered listener.

JTextField Constructors

You can create an object of type `JTextField` by using any of the constructors supported in `JTextField` with different arguments. An `int` type argument is meant for specifying the number of columns or field-width of the text field. A String type argument initializes the text field with the specified text and gives a way to display a default text string. A Document type argument specifies the content model for the text storage. The following is a list of constructors that are supported by the class `JTextField`:

```
public JTextField();
public JTextField(String text);
public JTextField(int fieldWidth);
public JTextField(String text, int fieldWidth);
public JTextField(Document docModel, String text,
                  int fieldWidth);
```

JTextField Code Example

Listing 11.1 is a sample program, `TJTextField.java`, which demonstrates the implementation of a Swing text field in a program. You can edit any text in the upper text field and press Enter to get this entry displayed in the lower text field. If you click the Clear button, the text fields are cleared for a fresh entry. The output of this program is shown in Figure 11.1.

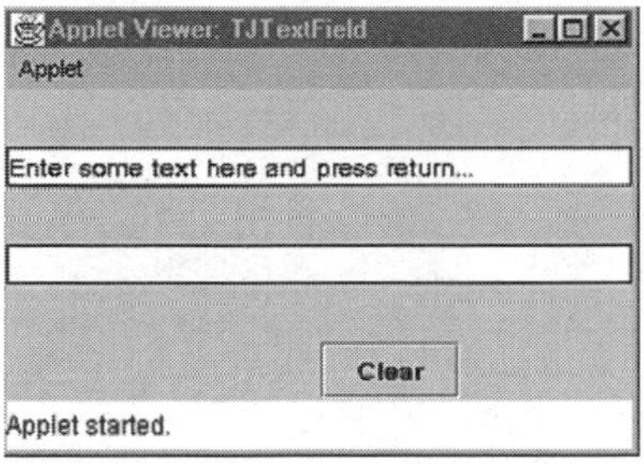

Figure 11.1

An applet displaying Swing text fields.

Listing 11.1   JTextField Components and a Clear Button (TJTextField.java)
```
// Demonstrates Swing text fields.

/*
 * <Applet code = TJTextField width = 300 height = 150>
 * </Applet>
 */

import javax.swing.*;
import java.awt.*;
import java.awt.event.*;

public class TJTextField extends JApplet {
    Container container;
    JTextField textField1, textField2;

    public void init() {
        // 1. Get the handle on the applet's content pane.
        container = this.getContentPane();

        // 2. Prepare the applet with vertical box layout.
        container.setLayout(new BoxLayout(container, BoxLayout.Y_AXIS));

        // 3. Create two text-fields and a button.
        textField1 = new JTextField(
            "Enter some text here and press return", // Initial string
            20); // 20 columns width
        // Add an action listener to this text field.
        textField1.addActionListener(new TextFieldListener());
```

continues

Listing 11.1   continued

```
        // Assign a line border with black color.
        textField1.setBorder(BorderFactory.createLineBorder(Color.black));

        textField2 = new JTextField(20);    // 20 columns width.
        // Assign a line border with blue color.
        textField2.setBorder(BorderFactory.createLineBorder(Color.blue));

        JButton button = new JButton("Clear");
        // Add an action listener to this button.
        button.addActionListener(new ButtonListener());

        // 4. Add text-fields and button to the applet's content pane.
        container.add(Box.createVerticalGlue()); //Add a glue component.
        container.add(textField1); // Add the textfield1.
        container.add(Box.createVerticalGlue()); // Add another glue component.
        container.add(textField2); // add the textfield2
        container.add(Box.createVerticalGlue()); // Add another glue component.
        container.add(button); // Add the button.
    }

    // 5. The text field listener class.
    class TextFieldListener implements ActionListener {
        public void actionPerformed(ActionEvent e) {
            // Retrieve the text entered in textfield1
            // and assign it the other textfield.
            textField2.setText(e.getActionCommand());
        }
    }

    // 6. The button listener class.
    class ButtonListener implements ActionListener {
        public void actionPerformed(ActionEvent e) {
            // Clear both the text fields.
            textField1.setText("");
            textField1.requestFocus(); // Get the focus back
            textField2.setText("");
        }
    }
}
```

Code Details

Inside the init() method, snippet-1 gets a handle to the applet's content pane. Snippet-2 assigns a vertical box layout to the applet. The code to create two text fields and a button is shown in snippet-3. Notice that `textfield1` is registered by an action listener called `TextFieldListener`. The Clear button is also registered by an action listener called `ButtonListener`. Snippet-4 adds these components to the applet's content pane.

Snippet-5 shows the listener class `TextFieldListener`, which implements the interface `ActionListener`. If you press the Enter key when the focus is over a text field, the text field fires an action event. This event can be handled as shown in snippet-5.

Inside the `actionPerformed()` method, the text from `textfield1` is assigned to `textfield2`. The method `getActionCommand()` returns the text field entry because the text field has not been assigned any action command by using the method `setActionCommand()`. The method `setText()` assigns the retrieved text to `textfield2`. Snippet-6 shows the code for the button listener. This listener class shows the code to clear the text fields whenever the Clear button is clicked.

Password Fields

The password field component is similar to the text field in that a single line of text is edited without showing the actual characters; but a default or specified echo character is displayed for each character typed inside the text field. As the name suggests, you can add this component for entering any secret password in a dialog box.

A password field object is created by using `JPasswordField` provided in the `javax.swing` package. `JPasswordField` is a direct subclass of `JTextField`. The constructors inside `JPasswordField` are very much parallel to those of `JTextField`. The following is the list of constructors from the `JPasswordField`:

```
public JPasswordField();
public JPasswordField(String text);
public JPasswordField(int fieldWidth);
public JPasswordField(String text, int fieldWidth);
public JPasswordField(Document docModel, String text,
                      int fieldWidth);
```

As you have seen for the constructors of `JTextField`, the argument `fieldWidth` represents the number of columns assigned for the password field. In practice, the value for this argument is 6. The `String` type argument is the secret text assigned for default usage. The `Document` is the model of the text document used for the password field.

JPasswordField Code Example

Listing 11.2 creates a sample applet that contains a password field for inputting the secret text and a text field for the username. When the user enters a password, the character x is made to echo in the password field. This character is assigned as an alternative to the default character *. The output of this program is shown in Figure 11.2.

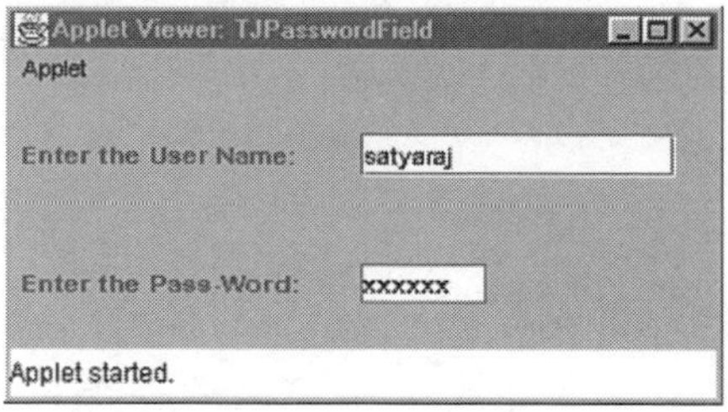

Figure 11.2

A Swing applet displaying the text field and password field.

Listing 11.2   JPasswordField and JTextField components (TJPasswordField.java)

```java
// Demonstrates Swing password fields.

/*
 * <Applet code=TJPasswordField width=350 height=125>
 * </Applet>
 */

import javax.swing.*;
import java.awt.*;

public class TJPasswordField extends JApplet {
    Container container;

    public void init() {
        // 1. Get the handle on the applet's content pane.
        container = this.getContentPane();

        // 2. Set the applet background color and layout.
        container.setBackground(Color.lightGray);
        GridBagLayout gridbag = new GridBagLayout();
        container.setLayout(gridbag);
        GridBagConstraints c = new GridBagConstraints();
        c.insets = new Insets(5,5,5,5); // top, left, bottom, right
        c.weightx = 1; c.weighty = 1;

        // 3. Create the component objects
        // and add them to the applet using grid bag layout.
        c.fill = c.BOTH;
        c.gridx = 0; c.gridy = 0;
        c.gridwidth = 1; c.gridheight = 1;
```

```
JLabel label1 = new JLabel("Enter the Username: ");
gridbag.setConstraints(label1, c);
container.add(label1);

c.gridx = 0; c.gridy = 1;
JLabel label2 = new JLabel("Enter the Pass-Word: ");
gridbag.setConstraints(label2, c);
container.add(label2);

c.fill = c.NONE;
c.anchor = c.WEST;
c.gridx = 1; c.gridy = 0;
JTextField textField = new JTextField("satyaraj", 15);
gridbag.setConstraints(textField, c);
container.add(textField);

c.gridx = 1; c.gridy = 1;
JPasswordField passwordField = new JPasswordField(6);
passwordField.setBorder(BorderFactory.createLineBorder(Color.red));
gridbag.setConstraints(passwordField, c);
container.add(passwordField);

// 4. Set an echo character for the password field.
// Note: The default character is "*".
passwordField.setEchoChar('x');
    }
}
```

Code Details

In Listing 11.2, snippet-1 gets a reference to the content pane of the applet. Snippet-2 assigns the applet to the grid bag layout. A `JTextField` object called `textField` and a password field object called `passwordField` are created. Two `JLabel` objects, called `label1` and `label2`, specify the purpose of the text field and the password field components. The positioning of these components inside the applet is shown in snippet-3.

The text field is displayed with the default text `satyaraj`, which is a username shown by default. The username can be changed if needed. The password field is six characters wide and initially empty. You may notice that when you type each character inside the password field, the character x is echoed in its display area. This is attained by invoking the `setEchoChar(char c)` on the object `passwordField`. Also note that if you do not assign any echo character, the default character * is echoed. Snippet-4 shows the code to change the echo character.

Text Area

The Swing text area is a lightweight alternative for the AWT text area component. Using text area, multiple rows of plain text can be displayed or edited. The text area can also be controlled for the read and write permissions of the users. If a content model (that implements the interface Document) is readily available, you can assign the model to the text area object.

Any Swing text area component is an object of type JTextArea. The class JTextArea is a subclass of JTextComponent and thus inherits a significant functionality from the parent class. While working with text area components, you may often need to use the methods from the classes JTextComponent and JComponent.

JTextArea Constructors

To instantiate an object of JTextArea, you can use any of the following constructors with the arguments of choice:

```
public JTextArea();
public JTextArea(String text);
public JTextArea(int rows, int columns);
public JTextArea(String text, int rows, int columns);
public JTextArea(Document doc);
public JTextArea(Document doc, String text,
                 int rows, int columns);
```

The String type argument text is meant for the initial text message to be displayed inside the text area. The argument rows inside the constructors is the number of rows of text, and the argument columns is the number of columns spanned by the text message.

The argument Document provides a way to assign a specific document model to the text area. The Document is a design-level interface that needs to be implemented in a class depending on the selected document model. If no document model is specified, a default model is automatically considered for the component. At any point later in the program, you can assign the document model by using the method setDocument(Document docModel) from JTextComponent.

JTextArea contains a list of "set" methods such as setColumns(int columns), setFont(Font font), setRow(int rows), setTabSize(int tabSize), and their corresponding "get" methods. The "get" methods return the values of different attributes.

The method append(String text) attaches the argument string text to the end of the current text in the text area, and insert(String text, int position) inserts the text at the specified column. You can also substitute any text in place of existing text inside the text area by using the method replaceRange(String text, int startPosition, int endPosition). In addition to the methods discussed so far, JTextArea makes use of a large number of methods from the class JTextComponent for editing purposes.

Caret Events and Listeners

Whenever a caret changes its position or if text is selected, a caret event is fired by a text component. The class CaretEvent supports the methods getDot() and getMark() to retrieve the current location and the end position of a text selection, respectively.

All listener objects to this event must implement the interface `CaretListener`. This interface requires the method `caretUpdate(CaretEvent e)` to be implemented. The method is invoked whenever the caret position is updated.

JTextArea Code Example

Listing 11.3 is a sample program that demonstrates the API methods from the class `JTextArea`. The contents of the text area may be manipulated by using the text field and the buttons displayed. You can enter any text inside the text field and press the Insert button to insert it at the caret location. You also can select a text segment and press the Delete button to delete it. The other buttons are used for cut, copy, and paste operations. You can select a text segment by sweeping the mouse over the text and then clicking the Cut button to delete the selected text. This text is placed on the system clipboard. The Copy button is also used for a similar purpose, except that the text is not deleted. When the Paste button is operated, the text located on the clipboard is pasted at the caret location. The output of the program is displayed in Figure 11.3.

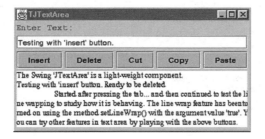

Figure 11.3

The Swing text area.

Listing 11.3   JTextArea and Edit Buttons (TJTextArea.java)
```java
// Demonstrates the Swing text area.

import javax.swing.*;
import java.awt.*;
import java.awt.event.*;

public class TJTextArea extends JFrame {
    // 1. Declare the references for the following objects.
    Container container;
    JLabel label = null;
    JTextField textField = null;
    JTextArea textArea = null;
    JButton insertButton = null;
    JButton deleteButton = null;
```

continues

Listing 11.3   continued

```
    JButton cutButton = null;
    JButton copyButton = null;
    JButton pasteButton = null;

    public TJTextArea() {
        // 2. Assign a name to the frame and obtain a handle
        // on the frame's content pane.
        super("TJTextArea");
        container = this.getContentPane();

        // 3. Create the fonts for label and text area.
        Font labelFont = new Font("SanSerif", Font.BOLD, 14);
        Font textFont = new Font("Dialog", Font.PLAIN, 12);

        // 4. Use the gridbag layout for the applet.
        GridBagLayout gridbag = new GridBagLayout();
        container.setLayout(gridbag);
        GridBagConstraints c = new GridBagConstraints();

        // 5. Add a label.
        c.fill = c.BOTH;
        c.insets = new Insets(2,2,2,2);
        c.gridx = 0; c.gridy = 0;
        c.gridwidth = 5; c.gridheight = 1;
        c.anchor = c.WEST;
        c.weightx = 1.0; c.weighty = 1.0;
        label = new JLabel("Enter Text: ");
        label.setFont(labelFont);
        gridbag.setConstraints(label, c);
        container.add(label);  // add the label

        // 6. Add a text field.
        c.anchor = c.CENTER;
        c.gridx = 0; c.gridy = 1;
        textField = new JTextField();
        gridbag.setConstraints(textField, c);
        container.add(textField);  // add the text-field

        // 7. Add the Insert button.
        c.gridx = 0; c.gridy = 2;
        c.gridwidth = 1; c.gridheight = 1;
        c.fill = c.BOTH;
        insertButton = new JButton("Insert");
        insertButton.setBackground(Color.lightGray);
        gridbag.setConstraints(insertButton, c);
        container.add(insertButton);  // add insert button
```

```
ButtonListener inButtonListener = new ButtonListener();
insertButton.addActionListener(inButtonListener);

// 8. Add the Delete button.
c.gridx = 1; c.gridy = 2;
deleteButton = new JButton("Delete");
deleteButton.setBackground(Color.lightGray);
gridbag.setConstraints(deleteButton, c);
container.add(deleteButton); // add the delete button
ButtonListener dlButtonListener = new ButtonListener();
deleteButton.addActionListener(dlButtonListener);

// 9. Add the Cut button.
c.gridx = 2; c.gridy = 2;
cutButton = new JButton("Cut");
cutButton.setBackground(Color.lightGray);
gridbag.setConstraints(cutButton, c);
container.add(cutButton); // add the cut button
ButtonListener ctButtonListener = new ButtonListener();
cutButton.addActionListener(ctButtonListener);

// 10. Add the Copy button.
c.gridx = 3; c.gridy = 2;
copyButton = new JButton("Copy");
copyButton.setBackground(Color.lightGray);
gridbag.setConstraints(copyButton, c);
container.add(copyButton); // add the copy button
ButtonListener cpButtonListener = new ButtonListener();
copyButton.addActionListener(cpButtonListener);

// 11. Add the Paste button.
c.gridx = 4; c.gridy = 2;
pasteButton = new JButton("Paste");
pasteButton.setBackground(Color.lightGray);
gridbag.setConstraints(pasteButton, c);
container.add(pasteButton); // add the paste button
ButtonListener psButtonListener = new ButtonListener();
pasteButton.addActionListener(psButtonListener);

// 12. Add the text area.
c.gridx = 0; c.gridy = 3;
c.gridwidth = 5; c.gridheight = 1;
c.weightx = 1.0; c.weighty = 1.0;
c.anchor = c.CENTER;
c.fill = c.BOTH;
String someText = "The Swing 'JTextArea' is a " +
```

continues

Listing 11.3   continued

```
                        "light-weight component.";
    textArea = new JTextArea(someText, // To be displayed initially
                             6, // Number of rows.
                             30); // Number of columns.
    textArea.setFont(textFont);
    textArea.setBackground(Color.white);
    textArea.setSelectionColor(Color.yellow);
    textArea.setTabSize(5); // The tab size.
    textArea.setLineWrap(true); // Wrap the line at the container end.
    gridbag.setConstraints(textArea, c);
    container.add(textArea); // Add the text area.

    // 13. Add the window listener to close the frame
    // and display it with the specified size.
    addWindowListener(new WindowEventHandler());
    setDefaultCloseOperation(WindowConstants.DISPOSE_ON_CLOSE);
    setSize(400, 200); // width=400, height=200
    show(); // Display the frame.
}

// 14. Button listener class.
class ButtonListener implements ActionListener {
    public void actionPerformed(ActionEvent e) {
        JButton b = (JButton) e.getSource();
        if (b == insertButton) {
            try {
                // Insert text at the caret position. The text is
                // is retrieved from the text field by using getText().
                textArea.insert(textField.getText(),
                                textArea.getCaretPosition());
            }
            catch (IllegalArgumentException excep) {
            }
        }
        else if (b == deleteButton) {
            textArea.replaceSelection(""); // Selected text is deleted.
        }
        else if (b == cutButton) {
            textArea.cut(); // Cut operation.
        }
        else if (b == copyButton) {
            textArea.copy(); // Copy operation.
        }
        else if (b == pasteButton) {
            textArea.paste(); // Paste operation.
        }
```

```
        }
    }

    // 15. The listener class to handle closing of the frame.
    class WindowEventHandler extends WindowAdapter {
        public void windowClosing(WindowEvent evt) {
            System.exit(0);
        }
    }

    // 16. The main method.
    public static void main(String[] args){
        new TJTextArea();
    }
}
```

Code Details

Snippet-1 shows the declaration of a list of data members to be used in the frame class. Inside the constructor of the frame TJTextArea, snippet-2 assigns a title to the frame and then obtains a reference to its content pane. Snippet-3 defines the fonts to be used for the text over the label and the text inside the text area.

Snippet-4 creates a grid bag layout object and assigns it to the frame through its content pane. Snippet-4 also creates an object of grid bag constraints. Snippet-5 adds the text field at the top portion of the frame. Snippet-6 adds a text field below the label. Snippets 7–11 add the buttons used for the insert, delete, cut, copy and paste operations. Each of these buttons is registered by an action listener.

Snippet-12 shows the code to add the text area at the bottom portion of the frame. The text area object is created by using the constructor that takes the initial text to be displayed, the number of rows, and the number of columns as its argument values. The other methods of interest in the code are setTabSize() and setLineWrap(). These methods control the cursor movement, when the Tab key is pressed, and the line wrapping at the end of the container. Snippet-13 shows the code to configure the frame.

Snippet-14 is the action listener that contains the functionality to be executed when one of the buttons attached to the frame is operated. Snippets 15 and 16 show the event handler to close the frame and the main method to create the frame object.

Editor Kits

A text component uses an editor kit to handle and organize actions such as cut, copy, paste, and so on. Thus, you can depend on editor kits rather than coding all actions from basics. Editor kits are also capable of recognizing document formats such as plain type and HTML type. Swing text support provides the editor kits such as DefaultEditorKit, StyledEditorKit, and HTMLEditorKit. DefaultEditorKit is the parent for StyledEditorKit and manages editing actions for plain text.

StyledEditorKit manages the editing actions for styled text. HTMLEditorKit organizes the actions for HTML language editing. This class descends from StyledEditorKit.

Editor Panes

The Swing editor pane is used to edit or display data content such as HTML, RTF, and so on. The editor pane uses the editor kit of type EditorKit to get the editing resources. Also the editor kit determines the content type to be edited in the editor pane. Thus, a suitable editor kit is required for an editor pane to deal with a specific type of information content.

A Swing editor pane object is represented by the class JEditorPane, which extends JTextComponent. Thus, you can make use of the core functionality supported in JTextComponent. The classes JEditorPane and the JTextComponent are stored in the respective packages javax.swing and javax.swing.text.

JEditorPane Constructors

The JEditorPane class supports three constructors to create its objects. You can specify the information content to be displayed by using the string form (of type String) of its URL or by specifying the URL object itself.

If you use the constructor that does not take any content while creating an editor pane, the information can be assigned at a later stage by using the method setPage(). setPage() exists in two overloaded forms; it can be used with the string form of the URL or the URL object itself.

Following are the constructors from the class JEditorPane:

```
public JEditorPane()
```

creates a JEditorPane object that has the document model set to null.

```
public JEditorPane(URL initialPage)
                throws IOException
```

creates a JEditorPane object based on the specified URL object of the content. The constructor throws an input-output exception if the URL is null or not accessible.

```
public JEditorPane(String url)
                throws IOException
```

creates a JEditorPane object based on a string containing a URL specification for the input. As in the previous constructor, you need to catch the input-output exception.

JEditorPane Code Example

Listing 11.4 is a sample program that implements JEditorPane to display the HTML content specified by the given URL. You can enter the URL string inside the text field. The program fetches the corresponding information content and displays it inside the editor pane. So this is a stripped down version of a browser program. The program output is shown in Figure 11.4.

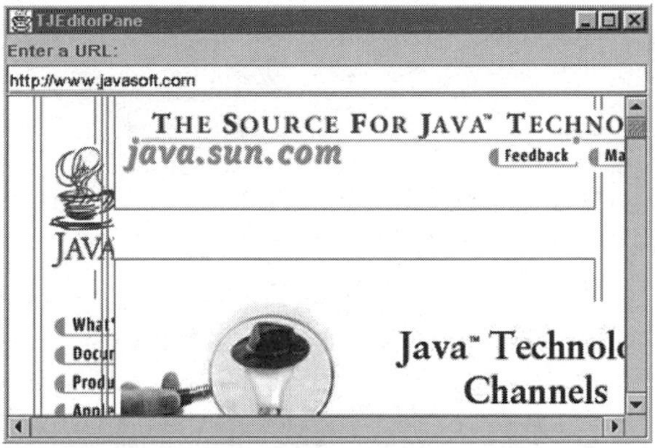

Figure 11.4

Demonstration of a Swing editor pane.

Listing 11.4   JEditorPane Displaying a Web Page (TJEditorPane.java)
```
// Demonstrates the Swing editor pane.

import javax.swing.*;
import javax.swing.event.*;
import java.awt.*;
import java.awt.event.*;
import java.net.*;

public class TJEditorPane extends JFrame {
    JTextField textField;
    JEditorPane editorPane;

    public TJEditorPane () {
        // 1. Assign a title to the frame and obtain
        // a reference to the frame's content pane.
        super("TJEditorPane");
        Container container = this.getContentPane();

        // 2. Create a label and attach it to a panel.
        JLabel label = new JLabel("Enter a URL: ");
        JPanel panel = new JPanel(new GridLayout(2,1));
        panel.add(label);

        // 3. Create a text field and add it to the panel.
        textField = new JTextField();
```

continues

Listing 11.4   continued

```
        textField.addActionListener(new TextFieldListener());
        panel.add(textField);

        // 4. Add the panel to the content pane.
        container.add(panel, BorderLayout.NORTH);

        // 5. Create an editor pane and add it to the content pane
        // through a scroll pane.
        editorPane = new JEditorPane();
        JScrollPane scrollPane = new JScrollPane(editorPane);
        container.add(scrollPane);

        // 6. Add the window listener to close the frame
        // and display it with the specified size.
        addWindowListener(new WindowEventHandler());
        setDefaultCloseOperation(WindowConstants.DISPOSE_ON_CLOSE);
        setSize(350, 200); // width=350, height=200
        setBackground(Color.lightGray);
        setForeground(Color.black);
        show(); // Display the frame

        // 7. Get the focus to textField.
        textField.requestFocus();
    }

    // 8. The text field listener class.
    class TextFieldListener implements ActionListener {
        public void actionPerformed(ActionEvent ae) {
            URL pageURL = null;

            // 9. Create the URL object for the text that has been
            // entered in the text field.
            try {
                pageURL = new URL(textField.getText());
            } catch (MalformedURLException me) {
                System.out.println("MalformedURL");
            }

            // 10. Assign the page to the editor pane so that the
            // page is displayed.
            try {
                editorPane.setPage(pageURL);
            } catch (java.io.IOException ioe) {
                System.out.println("IOException while loading page");
            }
        }
    }
}
    // 11. The main method.
```

```
        public static void main(String[] args) {
            new TJEditorPane();
        }

        // 12. The listener class to handle closing of the frame.
        class WindowEventHandler extends WindowAdapter {
            public void windowClosing(WindowEvent evt) {
                System.exit(0);
            }
        }
}
```

Code Details

Inside the constructor of the frame TJEditorPane, snippet-1 assigns a title to the frame and obtains a reference to the frame's content pane. Snippet-2 creates a label and attaches it to a panel object. Snippet-3 creates a text field object and attaches it to the pane. Snippet-4 attaches the panel to the content pane.

Snippet-5 creates an editor pane object and attaches it to the content pane through a scroll pane. Snippet-6 shows the code to configure the frame and display it. Snippet-7 brings the focus to the text field once it is initialized in the main frame.

Snippet-8 shows the text field listener class. Inside the actionPerformed() method, snippet-9 creates a URL object from the string specification of the resource location. The string specification is retrieved from the text field. Snippet-10 shows the code to assign the URL object to the editor pane to load and display the information content.

Text Panes

The text pane is a lightweight component that supports styled text. You can display multiline text with various character styles and paragraph alignments and display icons and other user interface components. You can embed images into the running text. Thus, the component can be used to build an advanced word processor that contains a number of features for displaying text and graphics.

To display styled text, you need to attach styles (for characters or paragraphs) to the attribute sets and then set the attributes to the text pane. You can assign the character and paragraph attributes to a text pane by using the methods setCharacterAttributes(AttributeSet aset, boolean b) and setParagraphAttributes(AttributeSet aset, boolean b). The boolean value suggests whether the currently existing attributes must be replaced entirely (true) or not (false).

The text pane is represented by the class JTextPane and is a subclass of JEditorPane. The class is stored in the package javax.swing.

JTextPane Constructors

To create an instance of JTextPane, you can use any one of the two provided constructors. There is a constructor without any arguments that assigns a default

StyledEditorKit. No document model is readily available in the instance; you need to assign a document model of type Document in your program. The other constructor allows you to specify the document model. The following are the two constructors that are supported:

```
public JTextPane()
public JTextPane(StyledDocument doc)
```

Undo and Redo Support

To provide the undo and redo features, an object of the Swing class UndoManager needs to be instantiated. This object manages the undoable edits that occur in the document model of a text component. The document fires events of type UndoableEditEvent that needs to be listened to by a registered listener.

The listener class must implement the interface UndoableEditListener and provide code for the method undoableEditHappened(). Inside this method, you can add an edit to the undo-manager object by calling the method addEdit(). You can obtain the undoable edit by calling the method getEdit() on the edit event that has been fired.

JTextPane Code Example

Listing 11.5 is a sample program that implements JTextPane to display styled text. The styled text contains an icon of Java Duke and a banner containing some text. The output of this program is shown in Figure 11.5.

Figure 11.5

Demonstration of a Swing text pane.

Listing 11.5   JTextPane Displaying Styled Text (TJTextPane.java)

```
// TJTextPane.java/* * <Applet code=TJTextPane.class width=400 height=300>
 * </Applet>
 */

import javax.swing.*;
import javax.swing.text.*;
import java.awt.*;
```

```
public class TJTextPane extends JApplet {
    JTextPane textPane = null;
    MutableAttributeSet centerAlign;
    MutableAttributeSet charStyle1, charStyle2, charStyle3;

    public void init() {
        // 1. Create a text pane object.
        textPane = new JTextPane();

        // 2. Prepare the paragraph attribute for center alignment.
        centerAlign = new SimpleAttributeSet();
        StyleConstants.setAlignment(centerAlign,
                                StyleConstants.ALIGN_CENTER);

        // 3. Prepare the character attribute set called style1.
        charStyle1 = new SimpleAttributeSet();
        StyleConstants.setFontFamily(charStyle1, "Serif");
        StyleConstants.setFontSize(charStyle1, 75);

        // 4. Prepare another character attribute set called style2.
        charStyle2 = new SimpleAttributeSet();
        StyleConstants.setFontSize(charStyle2, 35);
        StyleConstants.setUnderline(charStyle2, true);
        StyleConstants.setForeground(charStyle2, Color.red);
        StyleConstants.setBold(charStyle2, true);
        StyleConstants.setItalic(charStyle2, true);

        // 5. Prepare one more character attribute set called style3.
        charStyle3 = new SimpleAttributeSet();
        StyleConstants.setFontSize(charStyle3, 20);

        // 6. Get a reference to the content model of the text pane.
        Document contentModel = textPane.getDocument();

        try {
            // 7. Assign a position to the caret.
            textPane.setCaretPosition(contentModel.getLength());
            // Insert the Java Duke icon.
            textPane.insertIcon(new ImageIcon("javaIcon1.gif"));

            // 8. Assign character attributes to the text pane.
            textPane.setCharacterAttributes(charStyle1, false);
            // Assign paragraph attributes to the text pane
            textPane.setParagraphAttributes(centerAlign, true);

            String javaText = "Java\n";
            // 9. Insert the string in the content of text pane.
```

continues

Listing 11.5   continued

```
            contentModel.insertString(contentModel.getLength(),
                                  javaText, charStyle1);

            // 10. Assign new character attributes to the text pane.
            textPane.setCharacterAttributes(charStyle2, true);

            String coolText = "JFC Swing is Cool!\n";
            // 11. Insert the string in the content of text pane.
            contentModel.insertString(contentModel.getLength(),
                                  coolText, charStyle2);

            // 12. Assign new character attributes to the text pane.
            textPane.setCharacterAttributes(charStyle3, true);

            String doneText = "Done!";
            // 13. Insert the string in the content of text pane.
            contentModel.insertString(contentModel.getLength(),
                                  doneText, charStyle3);
        } catch(BadLocationException blexcep) {
            System.err.println("Exception while inserting the string.");
            blexcep.printStackTrace();
        }

        // 14. Add the text pane to a scroll pane.
        JScrollPane scrollPane = new JScrollPane(textPane);
        // 15. Finally, add the scroll pane to the content pane.
        getContentPane().add(scrollPane);
    }
}
```

Code Details

Inside the constructor of the frame TJTextPane, snippet-1 creates a text pane object. Snippet-2 prepares the paragraph attribute set to align the information at the center of the text pane. Snippet-3 prepares the character attribute set to assign the Serif font of size 75. Similarly, snippets 4 and 5 also prepare different attribute sets to be assigned to the characters in the content.

Snippet-6 obtains a reference to the content model of the text pane. Snippet-7 shows the statement to position the caret and inserts the icon of Java Duke. Snippet-8 assigns the character and paragraph attribute sets to the text pane. Snippet-9 shows the statement to insert the text string into the content model of the text pane. Snippets 10–13 show steps similar to those in snippets 8 and 9. Snippets 14 and 15 show the code to add the text pane to the frame by using a scroll pane.

CHAPTER 12

Scrollers and Sliders

Messages, images, and drawings are often displayed in a GUI container such as an applet or an application frame. If the object, referred to as a subcomponent, to be displayed is larger in size than its container, you need a mechanism that supports part-by-part display of the object. A scrollbar is a display mechanism that allows users to scroll a subcomponent in horizontal and vertical directions.

The scrolling of a subcomponent is the process of repainting the appropriate portion of the subcomponent in the viewable area depending on the direction of the scrollbar motion. This chapter discusses the internals of a scrollbar and gives an example that reveals how the scrollbar parameters change when a scrollbar is being adjusted.

The chapter also discusses another practical mechanism called a scroll pane. Scroll panes are ready-made panels with the required scrollbars already attached to them, and are simpler to implement than scrollbars.

Sliders are close to scrollbars in terms of their view and other internal properties, but they are meant for a different purpose. Sliders are used to set a parameter to a specific value within a continuous range of values of a specified interval. This chapter covers slider objects by using an example that emulates a media player panel.

Scrollbars

A scrollbar contains a scroll knob that slides along a bar attached with small end-buttons. The scroll knob helps to smoothly scroll the subcomponent to be displayed by a desired amount, and the end-buttons support line-by-line scrolling in the indicated directions. A mouse click on the remaining bar-like portion controls block-by-block scrolling inside the view port.

> **TIP**
>
> You may prefer to use a scroll pane rather than a scrollbar to provide scrolling of a given subcomponent. Comparatively, scrollbars require extra coding effort to implement than scroll panes.

The Swing scrollbar is a lightweight object of the class type `JScrollBar`. The class `JScrollbar` is stored in the package `javax.swing` and is a direct subclass of `JComponent`. The scrollbar field orientation specifies whether the scrollbar direction should be horizontal or vertical and takes the constant values `JScrollBar.HORIZONTAL` or `JScrollBar.VERTICAL`. The other fields `unitIncrement` and `bockIncrement` take the values that control the line-by-line or block-by-block adjustment of the subcomponent inside the display area or view port. The adjustment values are limited by the maximum or minimum values of a scrollbar.

> **TIP**
>
> Often the functionality supported inside the class `JScrollBar` is sufficient to implement scrollbars.

The other parameters that specify a scrollbar object are its minimum and maximum values, the instant or current value, and the extent of the viewable area. Note that the extent is the visible amount of the display area in effect. These values are to be assigned by using a `JScrollBar` constructor with an argument or by using the relevant set methods.

JScrollBar Constructors

The class `JScrollBar` contains the following constructors to create a scrollbar object:

```
public JScrollBar();
public JScrollBar(int orientation);
public JScrollBar(int orientation,
                  int value,
                  int extent,
                  int minimum,
                  int maximum);
```

The argument orientation in the constructors specifies whether the scrollbar is horizontal or vertical. The `value` is the initial or current value of the scrollbar. The `extent` is the visible extent or amount of the display area. The `minimum` and `maximum` are the respective minimum and maximum values of the scrollbar.

Adjustment Events and Listeners

When a scrollbar is adjusted, it fires adjustment events that are objects of the event class `AdjustmentEvent`. A class that implements the interface `AdjustmentListener` receives these events. The event listener class is registered with the source scrollbar by invoking the method `addAdjustmentListener()` on the scrollbar object. The method `addAdjustmentListener()` takes the listener object as its argument value.

The listener class must implement the method `adjustmentValueChanged()` from the interface, which takes the `AdjustmentEvent` object as its argument value. The code to be executed when the scrollbar is being adjusted is enclosed in this method.

The class `AdjustmentEvent` contains the following methods that can be used to retrieve some useful parameters:

```
public Adjustable getAdjustable()
public int getAdjustmentType()
public int getValue()
```

The method `getAdjustable()` returns the adjustable object that has fired the event. The next method `getAdjustableType()` retrieves an adjustment type such as the following:

```
UNIT_DECREMENT
UNIT_INCREMENT
BLOCK_DECREMENT
BLOCK_INCREMENT
TRACK
```

The method `getValue()` retrieves the current value in the adjustment event.

JScrollBar Example

Listing 12.1 is a Swing applet that demonstrates the usage of `JScrollBar` constructors and reveals how some of the important properties of a scrollbar change whenever it is being adjusted (see Figure 12.1). The applet also shows the relevant scrollbar APIs in action.

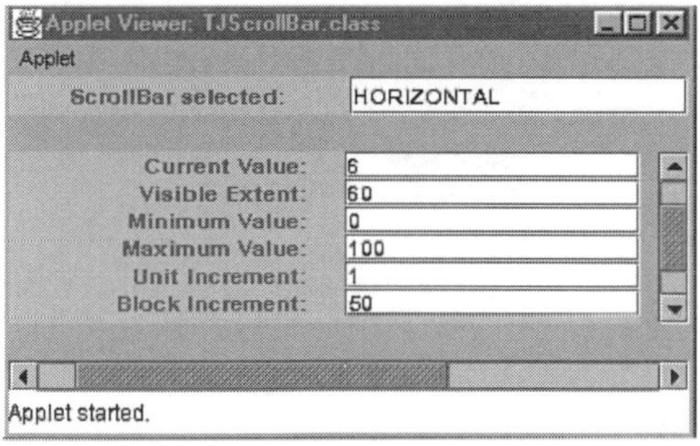

Figure 12.1

Swing applet displaying the JScrollBar attributes.

Listing 12.1   JScrollBar (TJScrollBar.java)

```
/*
 * <Applet code = TJScrollBar.class width = 400 height = 200>
 * </Applet>
 */
import javax.swing.*;
import java.awt.*;
import java.awt.event.*;

public class TJScrollBar extends JApplet {
    // 1. Create references to two scrollbars.
    JScrollBar horizSBar = null;
    JScrollBar vertiSBar = null;
    // 2. Create the other necessary text fields and a panel.
    JPanel panel1 = null; JPanel panel2 = null;
    JTextField tf = null;
    JTextField tf1 = null; JTextField tf2 = null;
    JTextField tf3 = null; JTextField tf4 = null;
    JTextField tf5 = null; JTextField tf6 = null;

    public void init() {
        // 3. Get a handle to the applet's container.
        Container c = this.getContentPane();
        c.setBackground(Color.lightGray);

        // 4. Create horizontal and vertical scrollbar objects.
        horizSBar = new JScrollBar(JScrollBar.HORIZONTAL,
                               20, 60, 0, 100);
        horizSBar.setBlockIncrement(50);
        ScrollBarListener hsbListener = new ScrollBarListener();
        horizSBar.addAdjustmentListener(hsbListener);

        vertiSBar = new JScrollBar();
        vertiSBar.setOrientation(JScrollBar.VERTICAL);
        vertiSBar.setValue(10);
        vertiSBar.setVisibleAmount(30);
        vertiSBar.setMinimum(0);
        vertiSBar.setMaximum(50);
        ScrollBarListener vsbListener = new ScrollBarListener();
        vertiSBar.addAdjustmentListener(vsbListener);


        // 5. Create a panel object panel1.
        JPanel panel1 = new JPanel();
        panel1.setLayout(new GridLayout(1, 2));
        // 6. Create a label and text field objects.
        // and fix them to panel1
        JLabel label = new JLabel("ScrollBar selected:",
                               JLabel.CENTER);
```

```
        tf = new JTextField();
        panel1.add(label); panel1.add(tf);

        // 7. Create a panel object panel2.
        JPanel panel2 = new JPanel();
        GridLayout gridLayout = new GridLayout(6, 2);
        gridLayout.setHgap(20);
        panel2.setLayout(gridLayout);

        // 8. Create the following labels and text fields, and
        // fix them to the panel2.
        JLabel label1 = new JLabel("Current Value:", JLabel.RIGHT);
        JLabel label2 = new JLabel("Visible Extent:", JLabel.RIGHT);
        JLabel label3 = new JLabel("Minimum Value:", JLabel.RIGHT);
        JLabel label4 = new JLabel("Maximum Value:", JLabel.RIGHT);
        JLabel label5 = new JLabel("Unit Increment:", JLabel.RIGHT);
        JLabel label6 = new JLabel("Block Increment:", JLabel.RIGHT);
        tf1 = new JTextField();
        tf2 = new JTextField();
        tf3 = new JTextField();
        tf4 = new JTextField();
        tf5 = new JTextField();
        tf6 = new JTextField();
        panel2.add(label1); panel2.add(tf1);
        panel2.add(label2); panel2.add(tf2);
        panel2.add(label3); panel2.add(tf3);
        panel2.add(label4); panel2.add(tf4);
        panel2.add(label5); panel2.add(tf5);
        panel2.add(label6); panel2.add(tf6);

        // 9. Set the border layout for the applet's content pane
        // and add the panels and scrollbars as give next.
        BorderLayout borderLayout = new BorderLayout();
        borderLayout.setHgap(10);
        borderLayout.setVgap(20);
        c.setLayout(borderLayout);
        c.add("North", panel1);
        c.add("Center", panel2);
        c.add("South", horizSBar);
        c.add("East", vertiSBar);
}

// 10. A listener class that handle the scrollbar adjustment events
class ScrollBarListener implements AdjustmentListener {
        public void adjustmentValueChanged(AdjustmentEvent evt) {
            JScrollBar sBar = (JScrollBar) evt.getSource();

            if (sBar.getOrientation() == 0) {
                tf.setText("HORIZONTAL");
```

continues

Listing 12.1   continued

```
            tf1.setText(Integer.toString(sBar.getValue()));
            tf2.setText(Integer.toString(sBar.getVisibleAmount()));
            tf3.setText(Integer.toString(sBar.getMinimum()));
            tf4.setText(Integer.toString(sBar.getMaximum()));
            tf5.setText(Integer.toString(sBar.getUnitIncrement()));
            tf6.setText(Integer.toString(sBar.getBlockIncrement()));
        }
        else if (sBar.getOrientation() == 1) {
            tf.setText("VERTICAL");
            tf1.setText(Integer.toString(sBar.getValue()));
            tf2.setText(Integer.toString(sBar.getVisibleAmount()));
            tf3.setText(Integer.toString(sBar.getMinimum()));
            tf4.setText(Integer.toString(sBar.getMaximum()));
            tf5.setText(Integer.toString(sBar.getUnitIncrement()));
            tf6.setText(Integer.toString(sBar.getBlockIncrement()));
        }
    }
  }
}
```

Code Details

Snippet-1 decalres two object references, `horizSBar` and `vertiSBar`, of type `JScrollBar`. Snippet-2 creates some necessary references of type `JPanel` and `JTextField`. Snippet-3 gets a handle on the applet's content pane. It also sets a new background color, light gray, for the applet by using the handle to the content pane.

Snippet-4 initializes the horizontal and vertical scrollbar references created earlier. The horizontal scrollbar `horizSBar` is created by using the five arguments constructor from the class `JScrollBar`. The arguments specify the scrollbar orientation, initial value, visible extent, and the minimum and maximum values of the scrollbar. The block increment by which the subcomponent must be scrolled up or down has been set in the next statement by using the method `setBlockIncrement()`. The horizontal scrollbar has been registered by an adjustment listener object `hsbListener` by using the method `addAdjustmentListener()`.

Next, the vertical scrollbar with reference `vertiSBar` is created by using the constructor without any arguments. Then the scrollbar attributes are set to specific values by using the API methods `setOrientation()`, `setValue()`, `setVisibleAmount()`, `setMinimum()`, and `setMaximum()`. The last statements in the code snippet register the scrollbar listener `vsbListener`.

Snippet-5 creates a panel object, `panel1`, with a grid layout. Snippet-6 creates and adds a label and text field to the panel. Snippet-7 creates another panel named `panel2` with a grid layout. Snippet-8 creates a set of labels and text fields and adds them to `panel2`. Snippet-9 sets the Swing applet to the border layout, and the panels are added with one at the center and the other at the north side according to the layout. The horizontal and vertical scrollbars are added at the south and east sides of the applet.

Snippet-10 sets the listener class to handle the adjustment events. The listener class ScrollBarListener implements AdjustmentListener and, thus, provides the code for the interface method adjustmentValueChanged(). This method takes the objects of type AdjustmentEvent as its argument values. The body of the method adjustmentValueChanged() provides the code to display the scrollbar chosen as horizontal or vertical and then reveals the values of the attributes of the selected scrollbar.

The method getOrientation() returns the scrollbar orientation constants 0 or 1 to indicate whether it is horizontal or vertical. The other get methods in the code simply return the current value, visible extent, minimum and maximum values, and unit and block increments of the scrollbars shown in the output of the applet.

Scroll Panes

A scroll pane is used to display a child component with a built-in scrolling facility. The scrolling of a child component, when its size is larger than the available view port, is performed in horizontal or vertical directions by using the scrollbars associated with the scroll pane. Scroll panes are very easy to implement because the adjustment events fired by the scrollbars are already taken care of by the scroll pane object. The scroll panes display as much of the child component as the space permits.

A Swing scroll pane is an object of type JScrollPane that extends from the class JComponent. While implementing a scroll pane in your program, you can use another helping class called JViewport. JViewport is a representation of a rectangular display window or view port that has a certain position and boundaries. The view port can also be added with a suitable border (see the JScrollPane API in Appendix A, "JFC Swing Quick Reference"). JViewport works like a view finder of a camera. When you slide the scrollbars of a scroll pane, the view port is moved so that you can see specific portion of the target object.

Sometimes you may need to apply double buffering to avoid flickering of an image (child component). In this case, use a JPanel that supports double buffering and then add the child component to the JPanel object.

Swing scroll panes also contain corner components and column and row headers. The corner components can be added at each of the available corner spaces of the scroll pane. Each of the row and column headers is a JViewport object that you need to specify. The column header view port scrolls left and right, tracking the left-right scrolling of the main view port, and the row header scrolls in the corresponding direction.

Scroll Pane Constants

A number of scroll pane constants are provided by the public interface ScrollPaneConstants. The class JScrollPane implements this interface for setting the associated horizontal and vertical scrollbars. Given next are some of the scroll pane constants that are be commonly required. These constants are self explanatory to display the scrollbars as the scrollbars should be shown always, on an as-needed basis, or never. On the as-needed basis, a scrollbar is shown whenever a subcomponent is larger than its view port.

```
HORIZONTAL_SCROLLBAR_ALWAYS
HORIZONTAL_SCROLLBAR_AS_NEEDED
HORIZONTAL_SCROLLBAR_NEVER

VERTICAL_SCROLLBAR_ALWAYS
VERTICAL_SCROLLBAR_AS_NEEDED
VERTICAL_SCROLLBAR_NEVER
```

JScrollPane Constructors

You can use any one of the following constructors provided in JScrollPane class to create a scroll pane object:

```
JScrollPane();
JScrollPane(Component childComponent);
JScrollPane(int vertSBarPolicy, int horizSBarPolicy);
JScrollPane(Component childComponent,
            int vertSBarPolicy,
            int horizSBarPolicy);
```

In these constructors, the argument childComponent is the subcomponent object to be displayed. The other arguments horizSBarPolicy and vertSBarPolicy describe the scheme to be used to show the scrollbars in the scroll pane. These arguments take the policy constants provided inside the interface ScrollPaneConstants, listed in the previous subsection.

Scroll Pane Example

Listing 12.2 displays a simple image and a scroll pane (see Figure 12.2). It is important to note the simplicity of the code that has been used to implement a scroll pane. You do not need to separately handle any adjustment events.

Listing 12.2   JScrollPane (TJScrollPane.java)

```
/*
 * <Applet code = TJScrollPane.class width = 300 height = 200>
 * </Applet>
 */
import javax.swing.*;
import java.awt.*;

public class TJScrollPane extends JApplet {
    // 1. Create a scroll pane object and the other
    // necessary objects.
    JScrollPane scrollPane = null;
    JLabel label = null;  // Not a canvas for JScrollPane!
    JPanel panel = null;  // supports double buffering
    Icon icon = null;

    public void init() {
        // 2. Get a handle on the JApplet's container.
```

```
Container container = getContentPane();
container.setLayout(new GridLayout(1,1));

// 3. Create a Swing label and a panel for double buffering.
icon = new ImageIcon("saravan.gif");
label = new JLabel(icon);
panel = new JPanel();
panel.add(label);

// 4. Create a scroll pane and add the panel to it.
scrollPane = new JScrollPane(panel,
            JScrollPane.VERTICAL_SCROLLBAR_ALWAYS,
            JScrollPane.HORIZONTAL_SCROLLBAR_AS_NEEDED);

// 5. Add the scroll pane to the contentpane of JApplet.
container.add(scrollPane);
    }
}
```

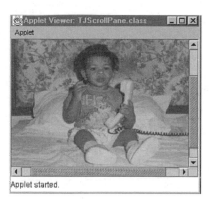

Figure 12.2

JScrollPane showing an image.

Code Details

Snippet-1 declares an object reference of type JScrollPane, and other helpful object references of type JLabel, Icon, and JPanel. Snippet-2 provides the code to create a handle to the content pane of the Swing applet. The applet has also been set to the layout of type GridLayout.

Snippet-3 initially creates an image icon from the given image file and then adds the icon to a label object. After the label object is ready, you can add it to the JScrollPane object snippet-4 creates. In the present program, however, the label object is added to a panel of type JPanel. The object of JPanel supports double buffering that controls flickering of the image. Snippet-4 adds the panel object to the scroll pane object through its constructor.

The constructor also takes the Swing pane constants listed previously to always show the vertical scrollbars. The horizontal scrollbars are displayed only when the width of the image is larger than that of the view port. Finally, snippet-5 adds the scroll pane to the content pane of the Swing applet.

Sliders

A slider is a control mechanism with a pointer knob that can slide on a continuous range of values to select a specific value of the parameter for which the widget has been used. Sliders are often seen in media players to adjust the audio volume, channel frequencies, contrast or brightness of picture, and so on.

The Swing class JSlider is a direct subclass of JComponent and represents the slider widgets. The class JSlider also implements the interface SwingConstants. The slider component can be painted with tick marks by specifying values for its fields majorTickSpacing and minorTickSpacing from the class JSlider. You can also specify the labels for tick marks by using the method setPaintLabels() set to true.

JSlider Constructors

You can create a slider object by using any one of the following constructors:

```
public JSlider();
public JSlider(int orientation,
               int minimum, int maximum,
               int Value);
```

These constructors without any arguments create a horizontal slider with the numerical range from 0 to 100 and an initial value of 50. The argument orientation decides if the slider is horizontal or vertical and takes the value JSlider.HORIZONTAL or JSlider.VERTICAL. The other arguments specify the minimum and maximum values of the slider parameter and the initial value of the slider in the given sequence.

Slider Events and Listeners

Whenever a slider knob is moved, the component fires an event of type ChangeEvent that can be detected by a listener class. The listener class implements the interface

ChangeListener. Any class that implements the interface ChangeListener must provide code for the public method stateChanged(). Thus, the code to be executed whenever a slider knob is moved is enclosed in this method.

The method stateChanged() receives the events of type ChangeEvent. Except for the methods inherited from the java.util.EventObject and java.lang.Object, the ChangeEvent does not contain any methods of its own.

JSlider Code Example

The Swing applet shown in Figure 12.3 demonstrates the APIs from the class JSlider. The applet emulates the control panel of an audio player. The panel contains a set of two vertical sliders that represents the volume controls for left and right channels. The instant value of an individual channel is displayed inside the text field provided above the volume widget.

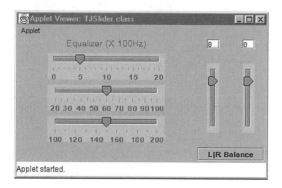

Figure 12.3

Swing applet showing an audio system control panel using JSlider.

The toggle button at the bottom of the volume controls is provided to balance the volume levels of the left and right channels. When the button is pressed, the value of the right channel automatically gets adjusted to that of the left channel. In the pressed-in condition of the balance button, whenever a volume knob is adjusted, the other knob automatically is adjusted such that both the audio levels remain the same. The other set of three horizontal sliders represents a 3-band equalizer showing tick mark labels for the audio frequency spectrum. The code for this applet is given in Listing 12.3.

Listing 12.3   Jslider Audio Control Panel (TJSlider.java)
```
// Demonstrates the Swing slider widget...
/*
 * <Applet code = TJSlider.class width = 400 height = 200>
 * </Applet>
```

continues

Listing 12.3   continued
```
 */
import javax.swing.*;
import javax.swing.event.*;
import java.awt.*;
import java.awt.event.*;

public class TJSlider extends JApplet {
    // 1. Declare the required JSlider references.
    JSlider slider = null;
    JSlider slider1 = null;
    JSlider slider2 = null;
    JSlider slider3 = null;
    JSlider slider4 = null;
    JSlider slider5 = null;

    // 2. Other necessary fields
    JTextField textField = null;
    JTextField textField1 = null;
    JTextField textField2 = null;
    GridBagLayout gridbag = null;
    GridBagConstraints c = null;
    Container container = null;
    boolean buttonPressed = false;

    public void init() {
        // 3. Get a handle on the container of JApplet
        // and assign the color and layout model.
        container = this.getContentPane();
        container.setBackground(Color.lightGray);
        gridbag = new GridBagLayout();
        container.setLayout(gridbag);

        // 4. Constraints for the layout
        c = new GridBagConstraints();
        c.weightx = 1.0; c.weighty = 1.0;
        c.fill = GridBagConstraints.NONE;
        c.insets = new Insets(4, 4, 4, 4);

        // 5. Label showing ëEqualizer (x 100Hz)
        c.gridx = 0; c.gridy = 0;
        c.gridwidth = 1; c.gridheight = 1;
        c.ipadx = 150;
        Font font = new Font("Helvetica", Font.BOLD, 14);
        JLabel label = new JLabel("Equalizer (X 100Hz)",
                                  JLabel.CENTER);
        label.setFont(font);
        gridbag.setConstraints(label, c);
```

```
container.add(label);

// 6. Create horizontal slider1.
c.gridy = 1;
setSlider(JSlider.HORIZONTAL, true,
        0, 20, 5, 5, 1);
slider3 = slider;
slider3.setLabelTable(slider3.createStandardLabels(5));
slider3.setPaintLabels(true);

// 7. Create horizontal slider2.
c.gridy = 2;
setSlider(JSlider.HORIZONTAL, true,
        20, 100, 60, 10, 5);
slider4 = slider;
slider4.setLabelTable(slider4.createStandardLabels(10));
slider4.setPaintLabels(true);

// 8. Create horizontal slider3.
c.gridy = 3;
setSlider(JSlider.HORIZONTAL, true,
        100, 200, 150, 20, 10);
slider5 = slider;
slider5.setLabelTable(slider5.createStandardLabels(20));
slider5.setPaintLabels(true);

// 9. Create the toggle button for the volume balance.
c.ipadx = 0;
c.gridx = 1; c.gridy = 4;
c.gridwidth = 2; c.gridheight = 1;
setButton("L¦R Balance");

// 10. Create volume slider1.
c.ipady = 75;
c.gridy = 1;
c.gridwidth = 1; c.gridheight = 3;
setSlider(JSlider.VERTICAL, false, 0, 10, 8);
slider1 = slider;

// 11. Create volume slider2.
c.gridx = 2; c.gridy = 1;
setSlider(JSlider.VERTICAL, false, 0, 10, 8);
slider2 = slider;

// 12. Create textfield1 for the volume slider1.
c.ipadx = 0; c.ipady = 0;
c.gridx = 1; c.gridy = 0;
c.gridwidth = 1; c.gridheight = 1;
```

continues

Listing 12.3   continued

```
        setTextField(slider1);
        textField1 = textField;

        // 13. Create textfield2 for the volume slider2.
        c.gridx = 2;
        setTextField(slider2);
        textField2 = textField;
}
    // 14. Creates a slider object.
    public void setSlider(int orientation,
                          boolean paintTicks,
                          int minimumValue, int maximumValue,
                          int initValue) {
        setSlider(orientation, paintTicks,
                  minimumValue, maximumValue, initValue, 0, 0);
    }

    // 15. Overload the previous above.
    public void setSlider(int orientation,
                          boolean paintTicks,
                          int minimumValue, int maximumValue,
                          int initValue,
                          int majorTickSpacing,
                          int minorTickSpacing) {
        slider = new JSlider(orientation,
                             minimumValue, maximumValue,
                             initValue);
        slider.addChangeListener(new SliderListener());
        slider.setPaintTicks(paintTicks);
        slider.setMajorTickSpacing(majorTickSpacing);
        slider.setMinorTickSpacing(minorTickSpacing);
        gridbag.setConstraints(slider, c);
        container.add(slider);
    }

    // 16. Create the toggle button for the balance of channels.
    public void setButton(String name) {
        JToggleButton button = new JToggleButton(name);
        button.setBackground(Color.lightGray);
        gridbag.setConstraints(button, c);
        button.addActionListener(new ButtonListener());
        container.add(button);
    }

    // 17. Create text field objects.
    public void setTextField(JSlider slider) {
        textField = new JTextField(2);
        textField.setText(Integer.toString(slider.getValue()));
```

```
        gridbag.setConstraints(textField, c);
        container.add(textField);
    }

    // 18. Button listener for the channel balance
    class ButtonListener implements ActionListener {
        public void actionPerformed(ActionEvent actEvt) {
            JToggleButton buttonTemp = (JToggleButton)
                                    actEvt.getSource();
            buttonPressed = buttonTemp.isSelected();
            slider2.setValue(slider1.getValue());
        }
    }

    // 19. The slider knob position change listener
    class SliderListener implements ChangeListener {
        public void stateChanged(ChangeEvent chngEvt) {
            updateTextField(slider1.getValue(),
                            slider2.getValue());

            JSlider sliderTemp = (JSlider) chngEvt.getSource();
            if(buttonPressed) {
                if(sliderTemp == slider1) {
                    slider2.setValue(slider1.getValue());
                }
                else if(sliderTemp == slider2) {
                    slider1.setValue(slider2.getValue());
                }
            }
        }
    }

    public void updateTextField(int currValue1, int currValue2) {
        textField1.setText(Integer.toString(currValue1));
        textField2.setText(Integer.toString(currValue2));
    }
}
```

Code Details

Snippet-1 of the code declares the references for the slider objects to be used in the applet. Snippet-2 shows the declaration of other necessary objects such as text fields, layout related objects, and so on. Snippet-3 obtains a handle to the content pane by using the method getContentPane(). It also changes the background color of the applet to light gray. Then the applet is configured for laying out components by using the grid bag layout.

Snippet-4 initializes the constraint fields that are common to all the component objects that will be added in the next snippets of code. Snippets 5–13 prescribe the constraints for various components of the applet, and then invokes the respective methods to create the component objects. Snippets 14–17 provide methods that actually create the required component objects and then fix them to the applet according the specified layout constraints.

Snippet-18 provides the listener class for the toggle button. The listener class called `ButtonListener` implements the interface `ActionListener`. The class provides the code for the method `actionPerformed()` that takes the objects of type `ActionEvent` as its argument values. The method body provides the code that gets a temporary reference to the toggle button object and stores the selection state of the toggle button in a `boolean` variable `buttonPressed`. The last statement of the method sets the value of `slider2` (right channel) with the value returned by `slider1` (left channel).

Snippet-19 handles the events fired by the volume slider objects. The inner class `SliderListener` implements `ChangeListener` and provides the code for the method `stateChanged()`. The method `stateChanged()` takes the objects of type `ChangeEvent` as the values for its argument. Essentially the class `SliderListener` supports the functionality on what happens when the knob of `slider1` or `slider2` is adjusted. The method `stateChanged()` calls the method `updateTextField()`, which updates the values of the text fields above the sliders whenever the sliders are adjusted. The remaining portion of the code in the method `stateChanged()` handles what happens when the balance button is pressed and the sliders are adjusted. Inside the `if` and `else...if` clauses, the code shows that the instant value of `slider1` is always adjusted whenever the knob of `slider2` is moved, and vice versa.

CHAPTER 13

Menus, Toolbars, and ToolTips

Menus, toolbars, and ToolTips are standard GUI components. When you click on an item in a menu bar, a drop-down menu with sub-tasks is opened. Pop-up menus enable you to click the right mouse button and have a menu appear. A toolbar gathers components together (usually buttons with icons on them) that all deal with some critical functionality. A ToolTip is a small piece of text that pops up when the user's mouse pointer pauses over an interface component.

Menu Bars and Menus

A menu bar is a narrow rectangular component that is positioned at the top edge of an applet or a frame. The menu bar contains the labels of drop-down menus that will be attached to it. Figure 13.1 displays a Swing menu bar.

Figure 13.1

A Swing menu bar and menu.

Figure 13.1 also shows the separators used to clearly differentiate one set of operations from another. A separator is simply a separating line drawn on a menu as shown in the figure. The separator in the figure separates the set of operations such as creating a new document (New), opening an existing file (Open), and closing a file (Close) from the other set of operations such as saving a file with multiple options (Save or Save As).

The Swing menu bar is a lightweight component that is represented by an object of the Swing class JMenuBar. The class JMenuBar extends from the class JComponent, and is stored in the package javax.swing. Swing menus are represented by the class JMenu that is stored in the same package as JMenuBar. The class JMenu is an extension of the class JMenuItem, which in turn is an extension of the class AbstractButton. Figure 13.2 shows the class hierarchy of JMenuBar and JMenu.

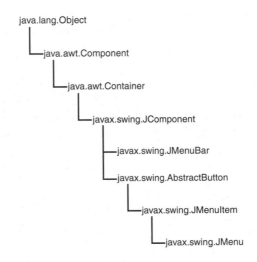

Figure 13.2

The class hierarchy of JMenuBar and JMenu.

JMenuBar Constructors

There is only one constructor available to create a menu bar in your application or applet. Typically, you need to create a menu bar, create a list of menus and add them to the menu bar, and then add the menu bar to the application frame or applet. To add the menu bar to its container, you need to use the add() method. The following is the menu bar constructor:

```
public JMenuBar()
```

JMenu Constructors

Once a menu bar has been created, you can add menus to it by using the following constructors:

```
public JMenu()
public JMenu(String label)
public JMenu(String label, boolean torn_offStatus)
```

The first constructor creates a menu without any label and can be set to any label by using the method setText() from the parent class AbstractButton. The next constructor creates a menu with a text label attached to it. The third constructor performs the same function except for its additional boolean parameter. The boolean parameter is meant to declare whether the menu is torn-off or not—torn-off menus are menus with their own look-and-feel.

JMenuBar and JMenu Code Example

Listing 13.1 demonstrates the Swing menu bar and menu objects. The output of the program is shown in Figure 13.3. The program creates a menu bar and menus and uses some of the API methods in JMenuBar and JMenu to add certain features to these components. The menu bar is added to the applet, while the menus are added to the menu bar.

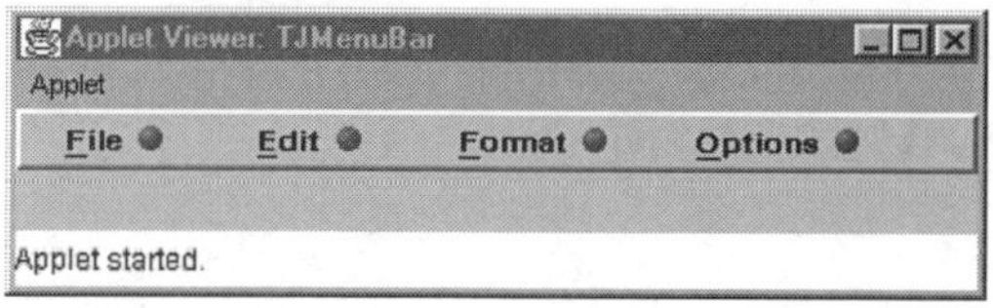

Figure 13.3

A Swing menu bar (JMenuBar) displaying the menu labels (JMenu).

Listing 13.1   JMenuBar with JMenu (TJMenuBar.java)

```
// Demonstrates the Swing menu bar and menus

/*
 * <Applet code=TJMenuBar width=450 height=50>
 * </Applet>
 */

import javax.swing.*;
import javax.swing.border.*;
import java.awt.*;

public class TJMenuBar extends JApplet {
    public void init() {
        // 1. Get the handle on the applet's content pane.
        Container container = this.getContentPane();

        // 2. Create a menu bar with bevel border and
        // add it to the applet.
        JMenuBar menuBar = new JMenuBar();
        menuBar.setBorder(new BevelBorder(BevelBorder.RAISED));
        container.add(menuBar, BorderLayout.NORTH);
```

continues

Listing 13.1   continued

```
        // 3. Create menus for a simple editor.
        JMenu fileMenu = new JMenu("File", true);
        JMenu editMenu = new JMenu("Edit");
        JMenu formatMenu = new JMenu("Format");
        JMenu optionsMenu = new JMenu("Options");

        // 4. Add the menus to the menu bar.
        menuBar.add(fileMenu);
        menuBar.add(editMenu);
        menuBar.add(formatMenu);
        menuBar.add(optionsMenu);

        // 5. Get the handle on each menu to the normal and
        // selected icons and the mnemonic (short-cut) key.
        for (int i=0; i<menuBar.getMenuCount(); i++) {
            JMenu menu = menuBar.getMenu(i);  // returns the menu
            menu.setIcon(new ImageIcon("red.gif"));

            // Set mnemonic key.
            String text = menu.getText(); // gets the menu label
            menu.setMnemonic(text.charAt(0)); // at first char
        }
    }
}
```

Code Details

Snippet-1 obtains the handle on its content pane. Snippet-2 creates the menu bar object and attaches it to the applet. The menu bar is also assigned a raised bevel border. Snippet-3 creates the necessary menus, and snippet-4 adds these menus to the menu bar.

Snippet-5 assigns icons and mnemonic keys to each of the menus by using the count of the menus retrieved by the method `getMenuCount()` from the menu bar object. To obtain each menu from the menu bar, the method `getMenu()` is invoked on the menu bar object. The output from this program is shown in Figure 13.3.

Menu Items

A menu item is essentially a kind of button located in a drop-down menu. When the end user selects a menu item, the action associated with the menu item is performed. A menu item can be used to open another menu where more menu items are located.

The menu items are represented by the class `JMenuItem`. This class is a subclass of `AbstractButton`, and is stored in the package `javax.swing`. Extending the class `JMenuItem` are two more important children named `JCheckBoxMenuItem` and `JRadioButtonMenuItem`. Figure 13.4 shows the class hierarchy of these components.

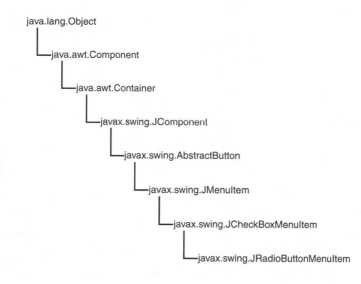

Figure 13.4

Class hierarchy among menu item components.

JMenuItem Constructors

The Swing menu item can be created with simple text, an icon, or both. You can also specify the mnemonic key. Typically, you create a menu item and then add it to a menu. The following is the list of constructors supported to create menu item objects:

```
public JMenuItem()
public JMenuItem(Icon icon)
public JMenuItem(String text)
public JMenuItem(String text, Icon icon)
public JMenuItem(String text, int mnemonic)
```

JMenuItem Code Example

Listing 13.2 creates an applet that contains a menu bar, menus, submenus, and menu items. You can click the Options menu to open the submenus further (see Figure 13.5).

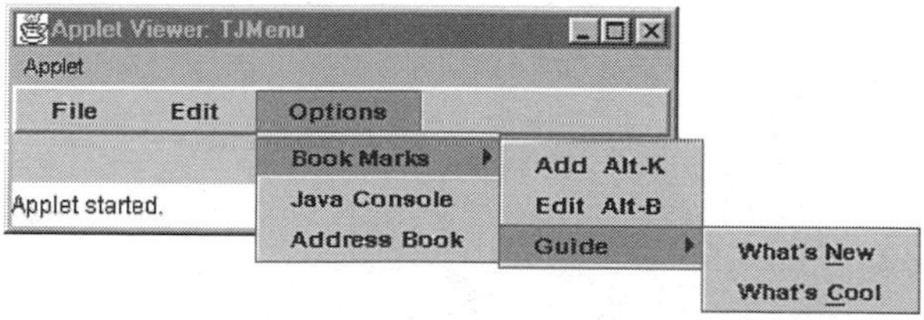

Figure 13.5

The Swing applet displaying menus, submenus, and menu items.

Listing 13.2   JMenu with JMenuItem (TJMenu.java)
```
// Demonstrates the Swing menus, submenus, and menu items

/*
 * <Applet code=TJMenu width=450 height=50>
 * </Applet>
 */

import javax.swing.*;
import javax.swing.border.*;
import java.awt.*;
import java.awt.event.*;

public class TJMenu extends JApplet {

    public void init() {
        // 1. Get the handle on the applet's content pane.
        Container container = this.getContentPane();

        // 2. Add a menu bar to the applet.
        JMenuBar menuBar = new JMenuBar();
        menuBar.setBorder(new BevelBorder(BevelBorder.RAISED));
        menuBar.setBorderPainted(true);
        container.add(menuBar, BorderLayout.NORTH);

        // 3. Add the File menu and its menu items .
        JMenu fileMenu = new JMenu("File", true);
        menuBar.add(fileMenu);

        // 4. Add the submenus to the File menu.
        fileMenu.add(new JMenuItem("New"));
        fileMenu.add(new JMenuItem("Open"));
        fileMenu.addSeparator();
        fileMenu.add(new JMenuItem("Save"));
        fileMenu.add(new JMenuItem("Sava As"));
        fileMenu.addSeparator();
        fileMenu.addSeparator();

        // 5. Add the Edit menu and its menu items.
        JMenu editMenu = new JMenu("Edit");
        menuBar.add(editMenu);

        // 6. Add the submenus to the edit menu.
        editMenu.add(new JMenuItem("Undo"));
        editMenu.addSeparator();
        editMenu.add(new JMenuItem("Cut"));
        editMenu.add(new JMenuItem("Copy"));
        editMenu.add(new JMenuItem("Paste"));
```

```
// 7. Create and add the Options menu and submenus
// and their items.
JMenu optionsMenu = new JMenu("Options");
menuBar.add(optionsMenu);

// 8. Add the submenus to the Options menu.
JMenu bookMarksMenu = new JMenu("Book Marks");
optionsMenu.add(bookMarksMenu);

// 9. Add the submenus to the Book Marks menu.
JMenuItem addMI = new JMenuItem("Add  Alt-K");
bookMarksMenu.add(addMI);
JMenuItem editMI = new JMenuItem("Edit  Alt-B");
bookMarksMenu.add(editMI);
JMenu guideMenu = new JMenu("Guide");
bookMarksMenu.add(guideMenu);

// 10. Add the submenus to the Guide menu.
JMenuItem whatIsNewMI = new JMenuItem("What's New");
whatIsNewMI.setMnemonic('N');
guideMenu.add(whatIsNewMI);
JMenuItem whatIsCoolMI = new JMenuItem("What's Cool");
whatIsCoolMI.setMnemonic('C');
guideMenu.add(whatIsCoolMI);

// 11. Finally, add two more submenus to the Options menu.
JMenuItem javaConsoleMI = new JMenuItem("Java Console");
optionsMenu.add(javaConsoleMI);
JMenuItem addressBookMI = new JMenuItem("Address Book");
optionsMenu.add(addressBookMI);
    }
}
```

Code Details

Inside the init() method of the applet, snippet-1 gets the handle on the applet's content pane. Snippet-2 creates a menu bar and attaches it at the upper portion of the applet. Snippets 3 and 4 create the file menu and its menu items. The file menu is then added to the applet. Similarly, snippets 5 and 6 create the Edit menu and its menu items.

Snippets 7–10 are of considerable interest. Snippet-7 creates the menu title Options and adds it to the menu bar. Snippet-8 creates the Book Marks submenu and adds it to the options menu. Snippet-9 creates the submenus for the Book Marks menu. Snippet-10 creates and adds the menu items to one of the submenus named Guide. Snippet-9 has already created the submenu Guide. Snippet-11 simply adds two more submenus to the Options menu.

Check Box Menu Items

Check box menu items are those that appear similar to check boxes. You can select or deselect a menu item by checking or unchecking the associated icons. Check box menu items are commonly used to select or deselect a set of program attributes.

Check box menu items are represented by the class JCheckBoxMenuItem. These are also created in the same manner as the regular menu items and then added to their menus.

```
public JCheckBoxMenuItem()
public JCheckBoxMenuItem(Icon icon)
public JCheckBoxMenuItem(String text)
public JCheckBoxMenuItem(String text, Icon icon)
public JCheckBoxMenuItem(String text, boolean state)
public JCheckBoxMenuItem(String text, Icon icon,
                         boolean state)
```

In this list of constructors, the first one creates a check box menu item that has not been selected initially and does not possess any text or set icon. The next constructor creates a check box menu item that has not been selected but possesses the set icon. The third constructor creates a deselected check box menu item with the specified text. The fourth constructor is similar to the third one except for the specified icon that will be set. The fifth constructor creates the check box menu item with the specified text and state of selection. The last constructor is the most versatile one; you can specify the text, icon, and the state of selection.

Radio Button Menu Items

Radio button menu items are similar to check box menu items; however, you can select only one item at a time from a group of radio button menu items. Thus if you select one radio button menu item, the other selected item gets deselected. These components are used when the end user needs to select only one item at a time from an available list of items.

To implement a radio button menu item in your program, you typically create a radio button by using one of its constructors and add the component to a group by using the object of type ButtonGroup. The following is a list of constructors to create an object of JRadioButtonMenuItem:

```
public JRadioButtonMenuItem()
public JRadioButtonMenuItem(Icon icon)
public JRadioButtonMenuItem(String label)
public JRadioButtonMenuItem(String label, Icon icon)
```

These constructors create radio button menu items that have not been selected initially. You can use a specific icon for the component by using the argument of type Icon. The argument named label is the menu items' text labels that can be supplied.

JCheckBoxMenuItem and JRadioButtonMenuItem Code Example

Listing 13.3 demonstrates how to implement the check box menu items and radio button menu items. The program is an applet with a menu bar and its menus. The Options menu contains the Fonts and Others submenus. When you click the Fonts menu, three radio button menu items are displayed. The radio button menu items represent the fonts from which only one can be selected at a time. Similarly, when you click the Others options menu, a list of advanced options is displayed. The options are represented by check box menu items from which you can make an arbitrary number of selections. The output of this program is shown in Figure 13.6.

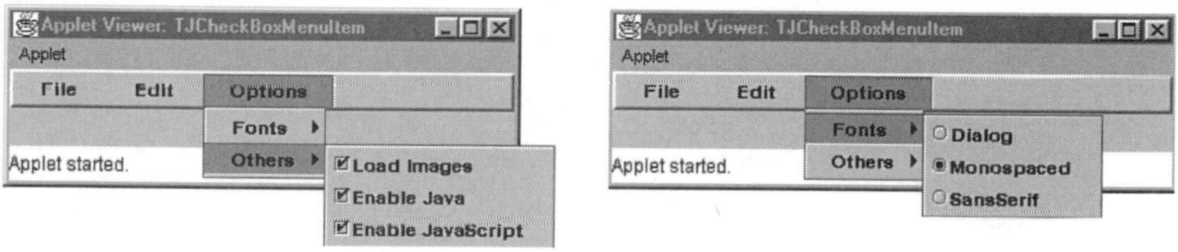

Figure 13.6

The Swing applet showing the check box menu items (left) and radio button menu items (right).

Listing 13.3   JCheckBoxMenuItem and JRadioButtonMenuItem (TJCheckBoxMenuItem.java)

```java
// Demonstrates the check box menu items
// and radio button menu items

/*
 * <Applet code=TJCheckBoxMenuItem width=450 height=50>
 * </Applet>
 */

import javax.swing.*;
import javax.swing.border.*;
import java.awt.*;
import java.awt.event.*;

public class TJCheckBoxMenuItem extends JApplet {

    public void init() {
        // 1. Get the handle on the applet's content pane.
        Container container = this.getContentPane();

        // 2. Create a menu bar and add it to the applet.
        JMenuBar menuBar = new JMenuBar();
```

continues

Listing 13.3   continued

```
menuBar.setBorder(new BevelBorder(BevelBorder.RAISED));
//menuBar.setBorderPainted(true);
container.add(menuBar, BorderLayout.NORTH);

// 3. Create and add the File menu and its menu items.
JMenu fileMenu = new JMenu("File", true);
menuBar.add(fileMenu);

// 4. Create the Edit menu and its menu items
// and add them to the menu bar.
JMenu editMenu = new JMenu("Edit");
menuBar.add(editMenu);

// 5. Create the Options menu, submenus, and their items.
JMenu optionsMenu = new JMenu("Options");
menuBar.add(optionsMenu);

// 6. Create and add the Fonts options menu to the
// Options menu.
JMenu fontsOptionsMenu = new JMenu("Fonts");
optionsMenu.add(fontsOptionsMenu);

// 7. Create radio button menu items and add them
// to the Fonts option menu.
JRadioButtonMenuItem rbItem;
ButtonGroup group = new ButtonGroup();
String[] rbLabels = {"Dialog", "Monospaced", "SansSerif"};
for (int i=0; i<rbLabels.length; i++) {
    rbItem = new JRadioButtonMenuItem(rbLabels[i]);
    fontsOptionsMenu.add(rbItem);
    group.add(rbItem);
}

// 8. Create and add the Others options menu to the
// Options menu.
JMenu advancedOptionsMenu = new JMenu("Others");
optionsMenu.add(advancedOptionsMenu);

// 9. Create and add the check box menu items to the
// Others options menu.
JCheckBoxMenuItem cbItem;
String[] cbLabels =  {"Load Images", "Enable Java",
                      "Enable JavaScript"};
for (int i=0; i<cbLabels.length; i++) {
    cbItem = new JCheckBoxMenuItem(cbLabels[i]);
    advancedOptionsMenu.add(cbItem);
}
    }
}
```

Code Details

Snippet-1 gets the handle on the applet's content pane. Snippet-2 creates a menu bar and adds it to the applet. Snippets 3–5 create different menus and add them to the menu bar. Snippet-6 creates the Fonts submenu and adds it to the Options menu.

The radio button menu objects are created inside the `for` loop in snippet-7. The radio button menu items have been added to the Fonts menu. Notice that you need to group the radio button menu items as shown in the snippet.

Snippet-8 creates the Others menu and adds it to the Options menu. Snippet-9 creates the check box menu items and adds them to the Others menu. When the program is executed, the output is as shown in Figure 13.6.

Pop-up Menus

A pop-up menu is context-sensitive and contains a series of options. The menu shows up when the secondary mouse button (usually the right button) is pressed in an applet or frame window. The user moves the cursor over a hot area defined by the developer to make the menu pop up.

Pop-up menus are often used by expert users as a shortcut for accessing important options. These menus minimize mouse travel by making the options available at the cursor location. Often pop-up menus contain the critical properties of an application.

NOTE

Pop-up menus are not meant for the options that are not available elsewhere in the system.

Swing pop-up menus are represented by the class `JPopupMenu`, which is stored in the package `javax.swing`. The class `JPopupMenu` is a direct descendent from the class `JComponent` as shown in Figure 13.7.

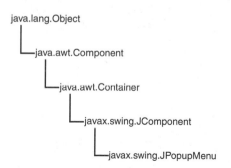

Figure 13.7

The class hierarchy of JPopupMenu.

JPopupMenu Constructors

You need to use one of the following JPopupMenu constructors to create a pop-up menu:

```
public JPopupMenu()
public JPopupMenu(String label)
```

The argument label of type String takes any text string that serves as a title for the pop-up menu.

The created menu object can be added with the menu items of type JMenuItem. Because the pop-up menus appear at the press of a mouse button, a mouse listener is registered with the component with which the pop-up menu will be shown. Then the pop-up menu is displayed by using its show method, which will be invoked when the mouse is pressed and released.

JPopupMenu Code Example

Listing 13.4 creates a pop-up menu and demonstrates how to use it in a text-area component. The example also demonstrates some of the methods from the class JPopupMenu. The output from the code listing is shown in Figure 13.8.

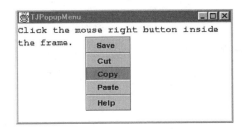

Figure 13.8

A text window displaying a pop-up menu.

Listing 13.4   Text Window That Displays a JPopupMenu (TJPopupMenu.java)
```
// Demonstrates the Swing pop-up menus

import javax.swing.*;
import java.awt.*;
import java.awt.event.*;

public class TJPopupMenu extends JFrame {
    JPopupMenu popupMenu;
    JMenuItem saveItem, cutItem, copyItem, pasteItem,
             helpItem;
    JTextArea textArea;
    Container container;

    public TJPopupMenu() {
```

```
// 1. For frame closing.
this.addWindowListener(new FrameClosing());

// 2. Get a handle on the frame's content pane.
container = this.getContentPane();

// 3. Create and add the text area to the content pane.
textArea = new JTextArea("Click the mouse right button inside "
                        + "\nthe frame.");
textArea.setFont(new Font("Monospaced", Font.PLAIN, 14));
container.add(textArea);

// 4. Create a pop-up menu.
popupMenu = new JPopupMenu("Test Popup Menu");

// 5. Create menu items and add them to the pop-up menu.
// Also add some separators as shown in the code.
saveItem = new JMenuItem("Save");
popupMenu.add(saveItem);

popupMenu.addSeparator();

cutItem = new JMenuItem("Cut");
popupMenu.add(cutItem);

copyItem = new JMenuItem("Copy");
popupMenu.add(copyItem);

pasteItem = new JMenuItem("Paste");
popupMenu.add(pasteItem);

popupMenu.addSeparator();

helpItem = new JMenuItem("Help");
popupMenu.add(helpItem);

// 6. Add the mouse listener to the content pane.
PopupMenuListener pml = new PopupMenuListener();
textArea.addMouseListener(pml);
}

// 7. Mouse listener class.
class PopupMenuListener extends MouseAdapter {
public void mousePressed(MouseEvent me) {
showPopup(me)
}

public void mouseReleased(MouseEvent me) {
    showPopup(me);
```

continues

Listing 13.4   continued

```
        }

        private void showPopup(MouseEvent me) {
            if (me.isPopupTrigger()) {
                popupMenu.show(me.getComponent(),
                                   me.getX(), me.getY());
            }
        }
    }

    // 8. Window listener.
    class FrameClosing extends WindowAdapter {
    public void windowClosing(WindowEvent e) {
                System.exit(0);
        }
    }

    // 9. The main method.
    public static void main(String[] args) {
        TJPopupMenu frame = new TJPopupMenu();
        frame.setTitle("TJPopupMenu");
        frame.setSize(350, 150);
        frame.setVisible(true);
    }
}
```

Code Details

Listing 13.4 creates an application frame, TJPopupMenu, that contains a text area. When you click the right button of the mouse, a pop-up menu is displayed at the point where the mouse has been clicked.

Inside the class TJPopupMenu, some objects are declared as its data members by using three Swing component types: JPopupMenu, JMenuItem, and JTextArea. The other data member, named container, serves as a reference for the frame's content pane.

The constructor TJPopupMenu performs a major activity. Snippet-1 registers a window listener with the frame to contain the code to be executed when the frame has been closed. Snippet-2 gets a handle on the frame's content pane. Next, snippet-3 creates a text area object and adds it to the frame.

Snippet-4 creates a pop-up menu object, and snippet-5 creates some menu items such as Save, Cut, Copy, Paste, and Help. These menu items have been added to the pop-up menu by invoking the add() method on the popupMenu object. The add() method takes a menu item as its argument. The pop-up menu is also added with separators by using the addSeparator() method that has been invoked on the menu object.

Snippet-6 creates a mouse listener object called `PopupMenuListener`. Snippet-7 defines the corresponding class. Then the mouse listener is registered with the text area object. Note that the text area is the component you need to click for the pop-up menu to appear. Inside the class `PopupMenuListener`, the method `showPopup()` contains the code that executes when the mouse has been pressed or released. To display the pop-up menu, the following method is invoked on the menu object:

```
void show(Component component, int x, int y)
```

This method displays the pop-up menu inside the component at the specified coordinate location x and y. The method `getComponent()` in the method `showPopup()` returns the component in which the mouse has been pressed and released. The methods `getX()` and `getY()` return the coordinate locations of the mouse pointer. Snippet-8 shows the listener class to close the window. Snippet-9 is the main method in which you create an instance of the frame.

Toolbars

A toolbar is a component that displays a collection of actions, commands, or function controls. The commonly observed components in a toolbar are pushbuttons. A toolbar is usually positioned near the top edge of an applet or a frame.

Toolbars are useful to display frequently used components. You can display critical functions also, such as Save, in a toolbar to enable the end user to quickly find them. A toolbar can be made movable or floatable. A floatable toolbar is also referred as a palette. To create a toolbar object, you use the class `JToolBar`, which represents the toolbars. The class is stored in the package `javax.swing`. The `JToolBar` class is a lightweight component that extends `JComponent` as shown in Figure 13.9.

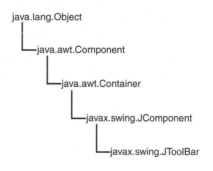

Figure 13.9

The class hierarchy of JToolBar.

JToolBar Constructor

There is only one constructor available for the class `JToolBar`, and the constructor contains no arguments:

```
public JToolBar()
```

To create a toolbar and add a button, typically you do the following:

```
JToolBar toolBar = new JToolBar();
JButton button = new JButton();
toolBar.add(button);
```

You can also add a button that dispatches an action of type Action to a toolbar by using the method add(Action action). This method returns a button object.

Toolbar Separators

A toolbar-specific separator provides disjoining between toolbar components to give better visibility for a specific functionality. A separator can be added to a toolbar by invoking the method addSeparator() on the toolbar object.

NOTE

The toolbar-specific separators are not the regular separators created by using the class JSeparator. The toolbar-specific separators are represented by the class Separator, which is an inner class of JToolBar.

JToolBar Code Example

Listing 13.5 demonstrates some functionality of the class JToolBar. The sample program shows a toolbar embedded with some sample buttons with icons (see Figure 13.10).

The toolbar that has been created is floatable; that is, the toolbar can be dragged to any location on the screen. If you want the toolbar to be non-floatable or fixed to its container at a specific location, execute the following set method with its argument value set to false:

```
JToolBar toolBar = new JToolBar();
toolBar.setFloatable(false);
```

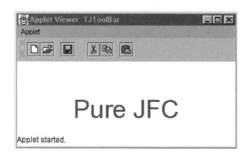

Figure 13.10

Applet showing a horizontal toolbar.

Listing 13.5   JToolBar with Buttons and Icons (TJToolBar.java)

```java
/*
 * <Applet code=TJToolBar width=350 height=150>
 * </Applet>
 */

import javax.swing.*;
import java.awt.*;

public class TJToolBar extends JApplet {
    //1. Create some icons for buttons.
    Icon newIcon = new ImageIcon("new.gif");
    Icon openIcon = new ImageIcon("open.gif");
    Icon saveIcon = new ImageIcon("save.gif");
    Icon cutIcon = new ImageIcon("cut.gif");
    Icon copyIcon = new ImageIcon("copy.gif");
    Icon pasteIcon = new ImageIcon("paste.gif");
    public void init() {

        //2. Get the handle on the applets' content pane.
        Container container = this.getContentPane();

        //3. Create a toolbar object.
        JToolBar toolBar = new JToolBar();

        //4. Set the margin between toolbar border and its comps.
        toolBar.setMargin(new Insets(5,5,5,5));

        //5. Create some toolbar buttons.
        JButton button1 = new JButton(newIcon);
        JButton button2 = new JButton(openIcon);
        JButton button3 = new JButton(saveIcon);
        JButton button4 = new JButton(cutIcon);
        JButton button5 = new JButton(copyIcon);
        JButton button6 = new JButton(pasteIcon);

        //6. Add the buttons to the toolbar with separators.
        toolBar.add(button1);
        toolBar.add(button2);
        toolBar.addSeparator();
        toolBar.add(button3);
        toolBar.addSeparator();
        toolBar.addSeparator();
        toolBar.add(button4);
        toolBar.add(button5);
        toolBar.addSeparator();
        toolBar.add(button6);
```

continues

Listing 13.5   continued

```
        //7. Make a panel with a label.
        JPanel panel = new JPanel();
        JLabel label = new JLabel("Pure JFC", JLabel.CENTER);
        label.setPreferredSize(new Dimension(350,100));
        label.setBackground(Color.white);
        label.setFont(new Font("Dialog", Font.PLAIN, 40));
        label.setOpaque(true);
        panel.add(label);

        //8. Add these components to the applet.
        container.add(toolBar, BorderLayout.NORTH);
        container.add(panel, BorderLayout.CENTER);
    }
}
```

Code Details

The applet TJToolBar defines a set of icons as its data members in code snippet-1. These icons will be used to display them on the buttons that will be created. Inside the init() method, snippet-2 shows the code to get a handle on the applet's content pane.

Snippet-3 creates a toolbar object, and snippet-4 sets some breathing space between the toolbar border and its components. Snippet-5 creates six buttons and adds these buttons to the toolbar. Observe that the sets of buttons have been separated by the toolbar separators.

The panel and its contents created in snippet-7 simply fill the applet. Snippet-8 adds the toolbar and the panel to the applet. The toolbar object has been added to the north side of the border layout.

TIP

For the toolbar to work properly while floatable, use the border layout and add the toolbar to one of its four sides.

Figure 13.10 shows the output of the program; observe that the toolbar has been initially located at the top edge of the applet. The toolbar contains four sets of buttons separated by toolbar separators. The first and third sets contain two buttons each, while the second and the fourth contain only one each. In the first set, the buttons are chosen to create a new document or open an existing file. The second set shows the button to save a file. The third and fourth sets are to execute cut, copy, and paste functions.

Figure 13.11 shows the applet when its toolbar has been relocated to the left side of its display area. The relocation of the toolbar is achieved by pressing the mouse on the rough or dotted portion of the toolbar and dragging it.

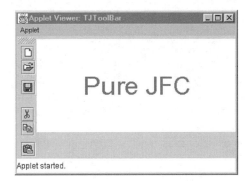

Figure 13.11

The applet showing the toolbar vertically located.

Figure 13.12 shows the applet when the toolbar is totally moved out of the applet. Notice that the toolbar contains a window of its own.

Figure 13.12

The applet showing the toolbar located outside its boundary.

Actions Common to Multiple Controls

Most applications have multiple controls for executing the same functions. For example, in a word processor the cut command is usually executed from different controls such as menu items, toolbar buttons, and sometimes through the menu items in a pop-up menu. In Swing, to execute an action code through two or more controls, you do not have to create multiple listeners and register them with the respective event sources. The Swing library furnishes a simplified system to deal with such common actions.

An `Action` common to two or more components is represented by a listener class that implements the interface `javax.swing.Action`. The `Action` interface extends the interface `java.awt.event.ActionListener`. In addition to the `actionPerformed()`

method, this interface contains several abstract methods to display some text string or icon for a button or menu item, to enable or disable the common functionality, and so on. Now all the component controls that need to perform the common action can simply fire events to activate the `actionPerformed()` method inside the common listener. To register the `Action` object with the corresponding sources, you simply make use of the `add()` method with the listener object of type `Action` as its argument value. For example, the method `add(Action action)` from the class `JToolBar` adds a `JButton` object to the toolbar with the listener object of type `Action` registered with the button. Similar `add()` methods are supported in the other classes such as `JMenu` and `JPopupMenu`.

TAction Code Example

Listing 13.6 executes the cut, copy, and paste operations on a piece of text in a text area. The program is created to be an application (see Figure 13.13) because applets cannot interact with the system clipboard. The component controls for the functions of cut, copy, and paste are available in three different sources: menu items in the Edit menu, menu items in the pop-up menu, and toolbar buttons. When these controls are operated, the information is either moved to or read from the clipboard.

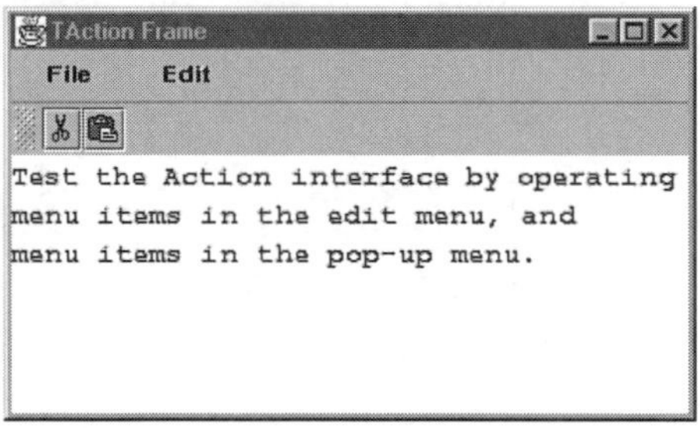

Figure 13.13

Demonstration of handling actions common to multiple controls.

Listing 13.6   Handling Actions Common to Multiple Controls (TAction.java)

```
// Demonstrates how to handle actions common to multiple
// controls such as menu items (in menus and pop-up menus)
// and toolbar buttons.

import javax.swing.*;
import javax.swing.event.*;
import java.awt.*;
import java.awt.event.*;

// The Swing frame class
public class TAction extends JFrame {
    // Declare the data members
    CutAction cutAction = null;
```

```
PasteAction pasteAction = null;
Container container = null;
JPopupMenu popupMenu = null;
JTextArea textArea = null;

// Icons to be used over the toolbar buttons
// and menu items
Icon cutIcon = new ImageIcon("cut.gif");
Icon pasteIcon = new ImageIcon("paste.gif");

public TAction() {
    // 1. Call the super with the prescribed title.
    super("TAction Frame");

    // 2. Get the handle on the frame's content pane.
    container = this.getContentPane();

    // 3. Create a panel and add it at the top of the frame.
    JPanel panel = new JPanel(false);
    container.add(panel, BorderLayout.NORTH);
    panel.setLayout(new GridLayout(2,1));

    // 4. Create a menu bar and attach it to the panel.
    JMenuBar menuBar = new JMenuBar();
    panel.add(menuBar);

    // 5. Create the File and Edit menus.
    JMenu fileMenu = new JMenu("File");
    JMenu editMenu = new JMenu("Edit");

    // 6. Add the menus to the menu bar.
    menuBar.add(fileMenu);
    menuBar.add(editMenu);

    // 7. Create a toolbar and attach it to the panel.
    JToolBar toolBar = new JToolBar();
    panel.add(toolBar);

    // 8. Create the Action objects for the cut and paste.
    // operations
    cutAction = new CutAction("Cut", cutIcon);
    pasteAction = new PasteAction("Paste", pasteIcon);

    // 9. Add the sources of common actions to their parents.
    JMenuItem actionCutItem = editMenu.add(cutAction);
    JMenuItem actionPasteItem = editMenu.add(pasteAction);

    JButton cutButton = toolBar.add(cutAction);
    JButton pasteButton = toolBar.add(pasteAction);
```

continues

Listing 13.6   continued

```
        cutButton.setText("");    // Tool bar buttons need not have
        pasteButton.setText("");  // the labels

        // 10. Create and add the text area to the content pane.
        textArea = new JTextArea("Test the Action interface "
                                +"by operating the tool bar buttons, "
                                +"\nmenu items in the edit menu, and "
                                +"\nmenu items in the pop-up menu.");
        textArea.setFont(new Font("Monospaced", Font.PLAIN, 14));
        container.add(textArea);

        // 11. Create a pop-up menu and add it to the text area.
        popupMenu = new JPopupMenu("Test Popup Menu");
        JMenuItem cutPopupMenuItem   = popupMenu.add(cutAction);
        JMenuItem pastePopupMenuItem = popupMenu.add(pasteAction);

        // 12. Create a pop-up menu listener and register it with
        // text area.
        PopupMenuListener pml = new PopupMenuListener();
        textArea.addMouseListener(pml);

        // 13. To close the frame.
        addWindowListener(new WindowEventHandler());
        setDefaultCloseOperation(WindowConstants.DISPOSE_ON_CLOSE);

        // 14. Set the size of the frame and display it.
        setSize(350, 200);
        show();
    }

    // 15. Cut Action class that extends AbstractAction.
    class CutAction extends AbstractAction {
        public CutAction(String label, Icon icon) {
            super(label, icon);
        }

        public void actionPerformed(ActionEvent ae) {
            textArea.cut();
        }
    }

    // 16.Paste Action class that extends AbstractAction.
    class PasteAction extends AbstractAction {
        public PasteAction(String label, Icon icon) {
            super(label, icon);
        }

        public void actionPerformed(ActionEvent ae) {
            textArea.paste();
```

```
        }
    }

    // 17. The popup menu listener.
    class PopupMenuListener extends MouseAdapter {
        public void mousePressed(MouseEvent me) {
            showPopup(me);
        }

        public void mouseReleased(MouseEvent me) {
            showPopup(me);
        }

        private void showPopup(MouseEvent me) {
            if (me.isPopupTrigger()) {
                popupMenu.show(me.getComponent(),
                                me.getX(), me.getY());
            }
        }
    }

    // 18. Listener class to close the frame.
    class WindowEventHandler extends WindowAdapter {
        public void windowClosing(WindowEvent evt) {
            System.exit(0);
        }
    }

    // 19. The main method.
    public static void main(String[] args) {
        TAction actionFrame = new TAction();
    }
}
```

Code Details

The frame class TAction begins by declaring the action references and other components and icons as data members. Snippet-1, inside the constructor TAction, the parent frame constructor is called with the frame title. Snippet-2 gets the handle to the frame's content pane. Snippet-3 creates a panel with two rows and one column and attaches it to the content pane.

Snippet-4 creates a menu bar and attaches it to the panel. Snippets 5 and 6 create the File and Edit menus and add them to the menu bar, and snippet-7 adds a toolbar to the panel.

Snippets 8 and 9 define the action objects (listeners) that contain the code to execute the cut and paste operations. Passing these action objects into the method add() from JMenu and JToolBar, the corresponding menu items and buttons are created. The menu items appear in the relevant menu (Edit) with the cut and paste action listeners already registered. In the same way, the buttons appear in the toolbar with the cut and paste actions registered with them.

Snippet-10 creates and adds a text area component (with the specified text) to the frame. Snippet-11 creates a pop-up menu, and then creates its menu items by invoking its add() method with the cut and paste action objects (listeners) as argument values.

Snippet-12 shows the listener code to display the pop-up menu. The listener has been registered with the text area. Snippet-13 shows the statement to close the frame, and snippet-14 resizes the frame to the required size and displays it.

Snippets 15 and 16 show the listener class that extend the class AbstractAction. This class implements the interface Action. Note that the method actionPerformed() contains the code to be executed when the corresponding control widgets are operated.

Snippet-17 implements the listener code to display the pop-up menu whenever the right mouse button is pressed and released. Snippet-18 is the listener class to close the frame. Snippet-19 is the main method in which you create the TAction frame.

ToolTips

A ToolTip is text that pops up when the user pauses the mouse pointer over a user interface component. The ToolTip usually contains "what is this" or "how to operate" information of the component. ToolTips are especially useful when a component has no label. For example, buttons on a toolbar contain only icons, in which case ToolTips are needed to indicate their purpose.

TIP

ToolTips should not be longer than a single phrase. Based on human interface experiments, the optimal time for them to appear (when the mouse pointer stops over a component) is about 700 milliseconds.

In Swing, it is very easy to implement standard ToolTips for components. The class JComponent encapsulates the necessary API. Because the Swing components extend JComponent, you can invoke the ToolTip methods on the component objects. The following is the list of the API methods from JComponent:

```
public void setToolTipText(String toolTipText)
```

This method assigns a ToolTip text to the component object on which it has been invoked with the value toolTipText.

```
public String getToolTipText()
```

This method retrieves the ToolTip text of a component that has been assigned by using the previous method.

```
public String getToolTipText(MouseEvent evt)
```

This method returns the ToolTip text of a component (that has already been assigned) based on the location of the mouse operation. This is useful in a component with multiple parts (as in `JTree`, `JTable`, `JTabbedPane`, and so on) that need to be indicated by ToolTips.

```
public Point getToolTipLocation(MouseEvent evt)
```

This method returns the ToolTip location in the receiving component coordinate system. If `null` (the default implementation) is returned, a suitable location is automatically chosen.

Custom ToolTips are rarely required by programmers. To create a ToolTip with a specific outlook, the class `JToolTip` needs to be instantiated. For this purpose, the `JComponent` method

```
public JToolTip createToolTip()
```

is used. The class `JToolTip` is stored in the package `javax.swing`. See Appendix A, "JFC Swing Quick Reference," for a complete list of the methods of `JToolTip`.

JToolTip Code Example

Listing 13.7 shows an applet (see Figure 13.14) with a toolbar containing buttons to perform different operations. The buttons appear only with icons; however, you can add ToolTips to these buttons to indicate their purposes.

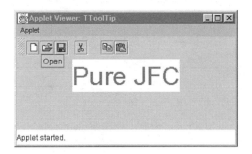

Figure 13.14

Demonstration of ToolTips.

Listing 13.7   TToolTip.java
```
//  Demonstrates the Swing tool tips

/*
 * <Applet code=TToolTip width=350 height=150>
 * </Applet>
 */

import javax.swing.*;
```

continues

Listing 13.7   continued

```
import java.awt.*;

public class TToolTip extends JApplet {
    // Create some icons for buttons.
    Icon newIcon = new ImageIcon("new.gif");
    Icon openIcon = new ImageIcon("open.gif");
    Icon saveIcon = new ImageIcon("save.gif");
    Icon cutIcon = new ImageIcon("cut.gif");
    Icon copyIcon = new ImageIcon("copy.gif");
    Icon pasteIcon = new ImageIcon("paste.gif");

    Icon[] icons = {newIcon, openIcon, saveIcon,
                    cutIcon, copyIcon, pasteIcon};
    String[] toolTips = {"New", "Open", "Save",
                         "Cut", "Copy", "Paste"};

    public void init() {
        // 1. Get the handle on the applet's content pane.
        Container container = this.getContentPane();

        // 2. Create a toolbar object.
        JToolBar toolBar = new JToolBar();

        // 3. Set the margin between the toolbar border and its comps.
        toolBar.setMargin(new Insets(5,5,5,5));

        // 4. Create some buttons and ToolTips
        // and add them to the toolbar. Also add
        // the separators.
        for (int i=0; i<6; i++) {
            JButton button = new JButton(icons[i]);
            button.setToolTipText(toolTips[i]);
            toolBar.add(button);
            if (i == 2 || i == 3 || i == 5)
                toolBar.addSeparator();
            if (i == 3)
                toolBar.addSeparator();
        }

        // 5. Make a panel with a label.
        JPanel panel = new JPanel();
        JLabel label = new JLabel("Pure JFC", JLabel.CENTER);
        //label.setPreferredSize(new Dimension(350,150));
        label.setBackground(Color.white);
        label.setFont(new Font("Dialog", Font.PLAIN, 40));
        label.setOpaque(true);
        panel.add(label);
```

```
    // 6. Add the toolbar and panel to the applet.
    container.add(toolBar, BorderLayout.NORTH);
    container.add(panel, BorderLayout.CENTER);
  }
}
```

Code Details

The applet TToolTip begins by defining a list of icons as data members. These icons are used in the toolbar buttons. In the init() method, snippet-1 gets the handle on the applet's content pane. Snippets 2 and 3 create a toolbar object with the specified margin between the toolbar border and its components.

Next, snippet-4 creates six buttons with the specified icons and attaches them to the toolbar. Notice that the ToolTips have been assigned to the buttons by using the method setToolTipText(). Snippet-5 creates a panel with a label to fill at the center of the applet. Snippet-6 adds the toolbar and the panel to the applet's content pane.

CHAPTER 14

Dialog Boxes and Option Panes

Dialog boxes (also called dialogs) are windows that pop up over a parent window and are used to display feedback messages, confirm actions, receive inputs, display tools, and so on. The Swing library supports a central class called JDialog to create custom dialog boxes.

Additionally, you can use the static methods supported in JOptionPane to create option panes (also called standard dialog boxes) with relatively smaller snippets of code. Option panes can display messages, confirm actions, receive inputs, or contain combinations of these functions.

This chapter first explains the details of implementing custom dialog boxes, and then steps you through creating option panes.

Dialog Boxes (JDialog)

Dialog boxes in the Swing library are represented by the class JDialog, which extends the earlier AWT dialog java.awt.Dialog (see Figure 14.1). JDialog is the main class for creating Swing dialog boxes and is a heavyweight component as is its parent. JDialog is especially useful for creating custom dialog boxes. A content pane serves as the container for all components added to a Swing dialog box; you add components to the content pane as follows:

```
dialogBox.getContentPane().add(someComponent);
```

Because the content pane is in the background of a dialog box, the default layout manager is the border layout.

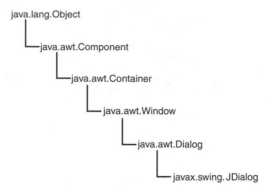

Figure 14.1

The Swing dialog box class hierarchy.

JDialog Constructors

To create a custom dialog box, you can use any of the following constructors supported in the class `JDialog`:

- `public JDialog()`
- `public JDialog(Frame owner)`
- `public JDialog(Frame owner, boolean modal)`
- `public JDialog(Frame owner,String title)`
- `public JDialog(Frame owner, String title,boolean modal)`

`public JDialog()`

creates a non-modal dialog box with no title and parent frame; a default hidden frame is set as the parent of the dialog box. A non-modal dialog box is one that allows input to the parent windows even when the dialog box is active, while a modal dialog prevents input to all other windows in the application until the dialog box is dismissed.

`public JDialog(Frame owner)`

also creates a non-modal dialog box without any title, but with the specified frame as its parent.

`public JDialog(Frame owner, boolean modal)`

creates the specified dialog box type (modal or non-modal), with the specified parent frame, but with no title.

`public JDialog(Frame owner,String title)`

creates a non-modal dialog with the specified title and specified parent frame.

`public JDialog(Frame owner, String title, boolean modal)`

creates a specified dialog box type (modal or non-modal), with the specified title and the specified parent frame.

JDialog Code Example

Listing 14.1 is an applet with a dialog box that displays the current date and time when the user presses a button. This program also demonstrates how to attach Swing dialog boxes to applets rather than frames. The program's output is shown in Figure 14.2.

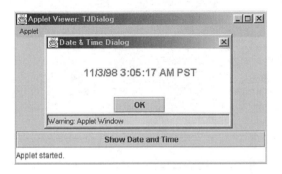

Figure 14.2

Applet displaying a custom Date & Time dialog box using JDialog.

Listing 14.1   Custom Date and Time Dialog Box using JDialog (TJDialog.java)

```
/*
 * <Applet code=TJDialog width=400 height=200>
 * </Applet>
 */

import javax.swing.*;
import java.awt.*;
import java.awt.event.*;
import java.util.*;
import java.text.*;

public class TJDialog extends JApplet implements ActionListener {
    // 1. Declare the underlying frame to which the
    //    dialog is attached.
    Frame frame = null;

    public void init() {
        // 2. Get a handle on the applet's content pane.
        Container container = this.getContentPane();

        // 3. Retrieve the underlying frame of the applet.
        // See snippet-5 for the details of getParentFrame().
```

continues

Listing 14.1   continued

```
        frame = getParentFrame(container);
        // 4. Add a button to bring up the dialog box.
        JButton button = new JButton("Show Date and Time");
        button.addActionListener(this);
        container.add(button, BorderLayout.SOUTH);
    }

    // 5. Retrieve the frame of the applet's container.
    public Frame getParentFrame(Component comp) {
        if (comp instanceof Frame) return (JFrame)comp;

        for (Component c = comp; c != null; c = c.getParent()) {
            // Check only for the Frame, not the JFrame!
            if (c instanceof Frame)
                return (Frame)c;
        }
        return null; // if there are no frames
    }

    // 6. Display the date and time for the current locale.
    public String showDateAndTime() {
        DateFormat dateAndTimeFormat =
                    DateFormat.getDateTimeInstance(
                        DateFormat.SHORT, DateFormat.LONG);
        String dateAndTime = dateAndTimeFormat.format(new Date());
        return dateAndTime;
    }

    // 7. When the button is displayed on the applet is operated…
    public void actionPerformed(ActionEvent ae) {
        String date_time = showDateAndTime();

        // When the applet's button is clicked, create the Swing
        // dialog box and display it.
        DateDialog dialog = new DateDialog(frame, date_time, true);
    }
}

// 8. Create a custom dialog box that extends JDialog
//     with a title and message.
class DateDialog extends JDialog implements ActionListener {
    Icon icon = new ImageIcon("clock.gif");

    public DateDialog(Frame frame, String msg, boolean modal) {
        // 9. Call the JDialog constructor.
        super(frame, "Date & Time Dialog" , modal);

        // 10. Set the background color of DateDialog.
        this.getContentPane().setBackground(Color.white);
```

```
// 11. Create a confirmation button.
JButton button = new JButton("OK");
button.setPreferredSize(new Dimension(80, 25));
button.addActionListener(this);

// 12. Create a label to display the time and date.
JLabel label = new JLabel(msg, icon, JLabel.CENTER);
label.setFont(new Font("Dialog", Font.BOLD, 22));

// 13. Add the message label and OK button to the dialog box.
this.getContentPane().add(label, BorderLayout.CENTER);

Box box = Box.createHorizontalBox();
box.add(box.createHorizontalGlue());
box.add(button);
box.add(box.createHorizontalGlue());
this.getContentPane().add(box, BorderLayout.SOUTH);

// 14. Resize the dialog box and position it at the center of
// the applet.
setSize(300,150);
Dimension dialogDim = getSize();
Dimension frameDim = frame.getSize();
Dimension screenSize = getToolkit().getScreenSize();
Point location = frame.getLocation();
location.translate(
    (frameDim.width-dialogDim.width)/2,
    (frameDim.height-dialogDim.height)/2);
location.x = Math.max( 0, Math.min(location.x,
                    screenSize.width-getSize().width));
location.y = Math.max(0, Math.min(location.y,
                    screenSize.height-getSize().height));

setLocation(location.x, location.y);

this.show();
}

// 15. When the OK button on the dialog box is clicked.
public void actionPerformed(ActionEvent ae) {
    this.dispose();
}
}
}
```

Code Details

Snippet-1 declares the underlying frame of the applet's container. This frame is used as the parent of the dialog box. Inside the init() method, snippet-2 gets a handle on the applet's content pane.

Snippet-3 initializes the applet's data member by retrieving the underlying frame object. Snippet-5 shows the details of the method that is invoked in snippet-3. Basically you need to recursively get the parents of the applet's container and check them to see if any happen to be a frame. If a parent frame is found, this frame is used to attach the dialog box.

Snippet-4 adds a button to the applet and an action listener is registered with the button. Inside the action listener (snippet-7), the current date and time are obtained and displayed by creating the Swing dialog box. The method shown in snippet-6 retrieves the current date and time from the system and formats it according to the current locale.

Snippet-8 creates a Swing dialog box that displays the date and time by using a Swing label. The dialog box will also contain a confirmation button that can be clicked to close the dialog box. The inner class `DateDialog` extends `JDialog` and implements an action listener. In snippet-9, the statement using `super()` creates a modal dialog box of type `JDialog` that is attached to the underlying frame of the applet with the displayed time and date.

Snippets 11–13 create a button and label to be attached to the dialog box. Snippet-14 shows the code to display the dialog box at the center of the applet. For this you need to get the screen size and the dialog box size and use some simple coordinate translation that centers the dialog box. Snippet-15 shows the action listener for the confirmation button displayed on the dialog box. The code to close the dialog box is executed when this button is clicked.

Option Panes (JOptionPane)

The previous section explains that to implement a dialog box using the class `JDialog` you have to explicitly provide code to create a `JLabel`, display any message, hook the dialog to its parent applet or frame, and position the dialog inside the parent frame. Using `JDialog` to implement all your dialog boxes can be cumbersome. Fortunately, the Swing library contains an intermediate class called `JOptionPane`, whose static methods enable you to create option panes (standard dialog boxes) directly with only a few lines of code.

Option panes can be used to display a feedback message or confirmation, or to input information to the application. There is also an option pane called the option dialog box that possesses all the features of the above option panes.

The JOptionPane Class

`JOptionPane` is a convenience class containing the functionality to create option panes that are modal. `JOptionPane` is a direct subclass of `JComponent` and is stored in the package `javax.swing`. The `JOptionPane` static methods are used to create and display option panes of type `JDialog`. The static methods are available in their overloaded forms to create an option pane with the desired list of arguments. The class `JOptionPane` also supports methods to create option panes whose background containers are internal frames.

JOptionPane Constructors

You can create an option pane object with specific arguments to configure the dialog box to be created. By using the created option pane object, you can invoke the method `createDialog()` to create a dialog box. The following is the list of constructors that are available to create the objects of type `JOptionPane`:

```
public JOptionPane()
```

creates an object of `JOptionPane` with the test message `JOptionPane` message.

```
public JOptionPane(Object message)
```

creates an instance of `JOptionPane` to display the specified message by using the plain-message type and the default options delivered by the user interface.

```
public JOptionPane(Object message, int messageType)
```

creates an instance to display the message with the specified `messageType` and the default options. The message type argument takes any one of the values `ERROR_MESSAGE`, `INFORMATION_MESSAGE`, `WARNING_MESSAGE`, `QUESTION_MESSAGE`, or `PLAIN_MESSAGE`, which are fields of the class `JOptionPane`.

```
public JOptionPane(Object message, int messageType,
                   int optionType)
```

creates an instance of `JOptionPane` to display a message with the specified message type (taking any one of the fields given above) and a specified option type such as `DEFAULT_OPTION`, `YES_NO_OPTION`, `YES_NO_CANCEL_OPTION`, `OK_CANCEL_OPTION`. The fifth constructor is similar to the fourth one except for the icon object that is specified.

```
public JOptionPane(Object message, int messageType,
                   int optionType, Icon icon)
```

```
public JOptionPane(Object message, int messageType,
                   int optionType, Icon icon,
                   Object[] options)
```

creates an instance of `JOptionPane` to display a message with the specified message type, option type, icon, and options. None of the options is initially selected.

```
public JOptionPane(Object message, int messageType,
                   int optionType, Icon icon,
                   Object[] options,
                   Object initialValue)
```

creates an instance of `JOptionPane` to display a message with the specified message type, option type, icon, and options, with the initial selection to be specified.

The argument `options` in the preceding constructors is an array of objects of type `Object`. This argument supports a way to use any components other than Swing buttons in a dialog box, or to use Swing buttons with custom labels of interest. Essentially the array is either an array of components or an array of strings. If you pass an array of components as the value of options, the components are displayed over the dialog box instead of regular buttons. In case you pass an array of string labels (of type `String`) as the value of options, the Swing buttons with the prescribed labels are displayed over the dialog box.

NOTE

The `options` objects should contain either some other components or strings. Component objects are added directly to the option pane; string objects are wrapped in a `JButton` and then added. If you provide components, you must ensure that when the component is clicked, the method `setValue()` is invoked to assign the user selection to the option pane.

Creating an Option Pane

After you create an instance of the class `JOptionPane` by using any one of the previously discussed constructors, you can further configure the option pane by using the "set" methods given inside the `JOptionPane` class (see Appendix A, "JFC Swing Quick Reference" for a complete list).

Next, a standard dialog box (also liberally referred as an option pane) of type `JDialog` can be created with the assigned configuration by using the following method from the class `JOptionPane`:

```
public JDialog createDialog(Component parent,
                            String title)
```

This method requires the parent frame to which the dialog box is attached and the title of the dialog box. To create and display a dialog box, you can implement the following code that uses the option pane object:

```
JOptionPane optionPane = new JOptionPane();
JDialog dialog = optionPane.createDialog(parent,
                                         title);
dialog.show();
```

Also, you can directly display the standard dialog boxes (option panes) by using the static "show" methods such as `showMessageDialog()`, `showConfirmDialog()`, `showInputDialog()`, and `showOptionDialog()`. These methods are available in their overloaded forms. Also the "show" methods such as `showInternalMessageDialog()`, `showInternalConfirmDialog()`, `showInternalInputDialog()`, and `showInternal OptionDialog()` are supported to create the standard dialog boxes. These dialog boxes contain the frames of type `JInternalFrame` in their background. The standard dialog boxes will be the topics of interest in the next sections.

Message Dialog Boxes

Message dialog boxes can display any plain-text message in one of five ways: plain message, information, question, error, or warning. The JOptionPane class enables you to create specific message dialogs through the optional use of icons for information, question, error, and warning messages. The exact appearance of each icon conforms to your application's current look-and-feel (Table 14.1).

TABLE 14.1 ICONS FOR MESSAGE TYPES

Message Type	Java LAF	Motif LAF	Windows LAF
ERROR_MESSAGE			
INFORMATION_MESSAGE			
PLAIN_MESSAGE	None	None	None
QUESTION_MESSAGE			
WARNING_MESSAGE			

To display a message dialog box in a program, you can directly use the static method showMessageDialog() with a suitable list of arguments. Alternatively, you can create an object of JOptionPane and invoke createDialog(). The createDialog() method returns a dialog box of type JDialog that is displayed by invoking the method show() on that object. An example will be presented to demonstrate the latter approach shortly.

The following is the list of overloaded methods of showMessageDialog():

```
public static void showMessageDialog(
                Component parent,
                Object message)
```

This method creates and displays a message dialog box with a message confirmation button (OK button) positioned at the bottom of the dialog box. The dialog box has a default title "Confirm," indicating that the user can confirm the message displayed by clicking the OK button. This confirmation title has nothing to do with any critical confirmation (in the form of a question); it exists only to make the user click the button to close the dialog box after reading the message. The argument parent is the frame in which the dialog is displayed. If this is null, or if the parent has no frame, a defaultFrame is used, and the dialog box is displayed at the center of the screen. The next argument message is the message string to be displayed.

```
public static void showMessageDialog(
                    Component parent,
                    Object message,
                    String title,
                    int messageType)
```

This method displays a dialog box with the specified message using a default icon determined by the `messageType` parameter `ERROR_MESSAGE`, `INFORMATION_MESSAGE`, `WARNING_MESSAGE`, `QUESTION_MESSAGE`, or `PLAIN_MESSAGE`. You can also specify the title to be displayed at the top of the dialog box.

```
public static void showMessageDialog(
                    Component parent,
                    Object message,
                    String title,
                    int messageType,
                    Icon icon)
```

This method evokes a dialog box displaying the specified message and title. You can specify the icon to be displayed rather than using the default determined by the argument `messageType`.

NOTE

The parameter `messageType` determines the look-and-feel of the dialog box, depending on its type. For example, the default icons displayed on a dialog box are determined by the parameter `messageType`.

Message Option Pane Code Example

Listing 14.2 creates an option pane to display the date and time on your system as shown in Figure 14.3. The program creates the message dialog box by using the option pane object and displays the dialog box by using the method `show()` invoked on dialog object. Since this program displays the date and time, just as the one given in Listing 14.1, you can compare these programs to observe the reduction in the size of code by using a standard dialog box.

Figure 14.3

An applet displaying the message option pane.

Listing 14.2   Date and Time Message Option Pane (TJOptionPane1.java)

```
/*
 * <Applet code=TJOptionPane1 width=400 height=75>
 * </Applet>
 */

import javax.swing.*;
import java.awt.*;
import java.awt.event.*;
import java.util.*;
import java.text.*;

public class TJOptionPane1 extends JApplet {
    Container container = null;

    public void init() {
        // 1. Get a handle on the applet's content pane.
        container = this.getContentPane();

        // 2. Add a box to the content pane.
        Box box = new Box(BoxLayout.X_AXIS);
        container.add(box);

        // 3. Create a button and add it to the box.
        JButton button = new JButton("Show Date and Time");
        button.setPreferredSize(new Dimension(200,25));
        button.addActionListener(new ButtonListener());
        box.add(Box.createGlue());
        box.add(button);
        box.add(Box.createGlue());
    }

    // 4. Listener class that displays a message dialog box.
    class ButtonListener implements ActionListener {
        String title = "Example Message Dialog";
        int messageType = JOptionPane.INFORMATION_MESSAGE;
        int optionType = JOptionPane.DEFAULT_OPTION;
        Object message = null;
        Object[] options = {ìThanksî};
        String dateAndTime = null;

        public void actionPerformed(ActionEvent e) {
            // 5. Obtain the date and time.
            dateAndTime = showDateAndTime();
            message = "The Time is " + dateAndTime;
```

continues

Listing 14.2   continued

```
        // 6. Create an option pane with specified attributes.
        JOptionPane pane = new JOptionPane(message,
                                           messageType,
                                           optionType,
                                           null,
                                           options);

        // 7. Create and show the dialog box to display the message.
        JDialog dialog = pane.createDialog(container, title);
        dialog.show();

        // 8. Reset the message to null.
        message = null;
    }

    // 9. Obtain the current date and time with the format
    // of the current locale.
    public String showDateAndTime() {
        DateFormat formatter = DateFormat.getDateTimeInstance(
                                    DateFormat.SHORT,
                                    DateFormat.LONG);

        String dateAndTime = formatter.format(new Date());
        return dateAndTime;
    }
  }
}
```

Code Details

TJOptionPane1 is a Swing applet that displays a message option pane created by using
the class TJOptionPane. The applet declares the reference to its content pane as a data
field. Inside the init() method, snippet-1 initializes the reference to the content pane
by obtaining the content pane object. Snippet-2 adds a box to the applet, and snippet-
3 adds a button to the box. A message dialog box with the current date and time appears
when the user operates the button.

Snippet-4 shows the beginning of the listener class. Inside the method
actionPerformed(), snippet-5 retrieves the date and time according to the format of
the current locale. Snippet-9 shows the details on how the date and time are retrieved.

Snippets 6 and 7 are of considerable interest. Snippet-6 creates an object of type
JOptionPane that takes the argument values such as the message to be displayed, message type, option type, icon (as null in this case), and options. The message to be displayed is the current date and time, and the message type is INFORMATION_MESSAGE as
defined in the list of data members of the listener class.

Notice that the options pane uses a button with the custom label Thanks! instead of
making use of the OK button that appears by default. To achieve this, the option pane

object has been created with the constructor that contains the argument options. The parameter `options` takes an array of objects as its value.

Snippet-7 creates and displays the dialog box with the message passed to the `JOptionPane` object. The static method `createDialog()` takes the parent container and the title of the dialog box as its argument value. When you run this program and click the button of the resulting applet, a dialog box is popped up with the current date and time, as shown in Figure 14.3.

Confirmation Dialog Boxes

Dialog boxes are not meant only for displaying feedback messages; they can also be the means of posing questions to the end user. The end user can then answer or confirm by clicking a button such as Yes, No, or Cancel. To display confirm dialog boxes, the Swing library supports a set of overloaded "show" methods as given in the following:

```
public static int showConfirmDialog(
                Component parentComponent,
                Object message)
```

This method creates and displays a modal dialog box with the options Yes, No, and Cancel. The dialog box contains the default title "Select an Option." The argument `parentComponent` determines the frame to which the dialog box is attached. If the value of the parent frame is `null` or if the `parentComponent` has no supporting frame, a default frame will be used and the dialog box will be displayed at the center of the screen. The other argument message is the string to be displayed in the dialog box. This method returns an integer `0`, `1`, or `2` when the user selects the options Yes, No, or Cancel, respectively.

```
public static int showConfirmDialog(
                Component parentComponent,
                Object message,
                String title,
                int optionType)
```

This method brings up a modal dialog box where the number of choices is determined by the `optionType` parameter. The argument `parentComponent` determines the frame in which the dialog box is displayed. The next argument message is the string object to be displayed inside the dialog box. You can also specify the title on the dialog box. The remaining argument specifies the options available on the dialog box such as `YES_NO_OPTION` or `YES_NO_CANCEL_OPTION`. The dialog box returns an integer `0`, `1`, or `2` for the respective option Yes, No, or Cancel that is selected.

```
public static int showConfirmDialog(
                Component parentComponent,
                Object message,
                String title,
                int optionType,
                int messageType)
```

This method allows you to specify the message type in addition to the argument list given in the previous method. The argument `messageType` specifies the type of message indicated by the constants `ERROR_MESSAGE`, `INFORMATION_MESSAGE`, `WARNING_MESSAGE`, `QUESTION_MESSAGE`, or `PLAIN_MESSAGE`. The choice of one of these constants will set an appropriate icon on the dialog box. This method also returns the integer value `0`, `1`, or `2`, depending on the selection made by the user.

```
public static int showConfirmDialog(
                    Component parentComponent,
                    Object message,
                    String title,
                    int optionType,
                    int messageType,
                    Icon icon)
```

This method is similar to the preceding one except for the additional argument `icon`. This parameter allows you to specify the icon of interest on the dialog box. This method also returns `0`, `1`, or `2` for the respective selections Yes, No, or Cancel made by the end user.

Confirmation Option Pane Code Example

Listing 14.3 demonstrates a confirmation option pane. The example is an applet that uses a confirmation dialog box to confirm if the date also needs to be displayed (see Figure 14.4). If the user chooses the Yes button, both the current date and time are displayed (see Figure 14.5). On the other hand, if the user chooses the No button, only the current time is displayed.

Figure 14.4

Applet displaying the confirmation option pane.

Figure 14.5

Pressing Yes invokes a message option pane displaying the time and date.

Listing 14.3   TJOptionPane2.java

```
/*
 * <Applet code=TJOptionPane2 width=400 height=75>
 * </Applet>
 */

import javax.swing.*;
import java.awt.*;
import java.awt.event.*;
import java.util.*;
import java.text.*;

public class TJOptionPane2 extends JApplet {
    Container container = null;

    public void init() {
        // 1. Get a handle on the applet's content pane.
        container = this.getContentPane();

        // 2. Add a box to the content pane.
        Box box = new Box(BoxLayout.X_AXIS);
        container.add(box);

        // 3. Add a button to the box.
        JButton button = new JButton("Show Time");
        button.setPreferredSize(new Dimension(150,25));
        button.addActionListener(new ButtonListener());
        box.add(Box.createGlue());
        box.add(button);
        box.add(Box.createGlue());
    }

    // 4. The listener class.
    class ButtonListener implements ActionListener {
        // 5. Argument values for the confirmation dialog box.
        Object confirmText = "Do You Wish To See Date Also?";
        String confirmTitle = "Date Confirmation Dialog";
        int optionType = JOptionPane.YES_NO_OPTION;
        int messageType1 = JOptionPane.QUESTION_MESSAGE;

        // 6. Argument values for the message dialog box.
        Object information = null;
        String title = "Message Display Dialog";
        int messageType2 = JOptionPane.INFORMATION_MESSAGE;


        // 7. Option selected.
        // If the selection is 'yes', selectedValue = 0;
```

continues

Listing 14.3   continued

```
        // If the selection is 'No', selectedValue = 1;
        int selectedValue;

    public void actionPerformed(ActionEvent e) {
        // 8. Display the confirmation dialog box.
        selectedValue = JOptionPane.showConfirmDialog(container,
                             confirmText, confirmTitle,
                             optionType, messageType1);

        // 9. Fetch the time or date and time.
        information = fetchInformation();

        // 10. Display the message.
        JOptionPane.showMessageDialog(container,
                                  information, title,
                                  messageType2);
    }

    // 11. Returns the time or date and time depending
    // on the Yes or No choice made.
    public String fetchInformation() {
        DateFormat formatter = null;

        if (selectedValue == 0) {  //If it is Yes.
            formatter = DateFormat.getDateTimeInstance(
                              DateFormat.SHORT,
                              DateFormat.LONG);
        }
        else if(selectedValue == 1) {  //If it is No.
            formatter = DateFormat.getTimeInstance(
                                  DateFormat.LONG);
        }

        // Format the time or date and time and return.
        return(formatter.format(new Date()));
    }
  }
}
```

Code Details

TJOptionPane2 is a Swing applet. The method init() simply displays a button that can be operated to see the current time or date and time. Snippet-1 gets a handle on the applet's content pane, and snippet-2 adds a box to the content pane. Snippet-3 shows the code that adds a button to the box with an action listener to display the necessary dialog box.

Snippet-4 initiates the listener class named ButtonListener. Snippets 5 and 6 show the data members of the listener class. The data members are the argument values for the confirmation dialog box and the message dialog box. Snippet-7 declares the variable `selectedValue` that stores the confirmation status such as Yes or No.

Inside the method `actionPerformed()`, snippet-8 creates and displays the confirmation dialog box that has been implemented. The confirmation dialog box displays the value of the argument `confirmText`, with the Yes and No buttons indicated by the argument value `optionType`. When the user chooses one of these buttons, the selection status is stored as 0 or 1 in the parameter `selectedValue`. Snippet-9 fetches the information returned by the method `fetchInformation()` shown in snippet-11. The method `fetchInformation()` returns the information based on the value of `selectedValue`.

In snippet-10, the information that has been retrieved is displayed in a message dialog box. Note that all the dialog boxes created by using the class `JOptionPane` are modal. Thus, the confirmation dialog created in Listing 14.3 waits until the user gives input to it.

Input Dialog Boxes

An input dialog box is one that gathers information in the form of input from the user. This information is used to set the application's attributes. The Swing library supports the input dialog boxes through the class `JOptionPane`; however, these dialog boxes are also objects of type `JDialog`.

The input dialog boxes receive input from the user through an intermediate component such as a text field, combo box, or list. In Swing, an input dialog box appears with a suitable component that is determined by the user interface manager. You can use an input dialog box in a program by directly invoking the static "show" methods that are supported inside the class `JOptionPane`. Following is the list of these methods:

```
public static String showInputDialog(Object message)
```

This method displays a question-message dialog box requesting input from the user. The dialog box makes use of the default frame so it is centered on the screen. The argument message specifies the message to be displayed.

```
public static String showInputDialog(
                Component parentComponent,
                Object message)
```

This method is also similar to the preceding method except for the specified parent frame to which the dialog box will be attached at its center. The argument `parentComponent` specifies the parent component of the dialog, and message is the message to be displayed.

```
public static String showInputDialog(
                Component parentComponent,
                Object message,
                String title,
                int messageType)
```

This method is similar to the previous two methods, but you can additionally specify the title and the message type. The title is a string of text to be displayed in the title bar of the dialog box. The other additional parameter messageType takes the values such as ERROR_MESSAGE, INFORMATION_MESSAGE, WARNING_MESSAGE, QUESTION_MESSAGE, or PLAIN_MESSAGE. These values determine the dialog box icon to bring the required look-and-feel of the dialog box.

```
public static Object showInputDialog(
                    Component parentComponent,
                    Object message,
                    String title,
                    int messageType,
                    Icon icon,
                    Object[] selectionValues,
                    Object initialSelectionValue)
```

This method prompts the user for input through a modal dialog box where the initial selection, possible additional selections, and all other options shown in the preceding method can be specified. The user chooses from the list of selectionValues. If the value of this parameter is null, the user can input any value of interest, usually by means of a JTextField.

The other additional parameter (when compared to the previous methods), initialSelectionValue, is the initial value with which to prompt the user. The UI decides the best possible way to display the selection values, which is usually by means of one of the components such as JComboBox, JList, or JTextField. Whenever the user inputs a value and confirms it, the method returns that value as a string. If the user selects the Cancel button, the method returns the value null.

The icon is the icon to be displayed over the dialog box. The other arguments of the method such as parentComponent, message, title, and messageType are as given and explained in the previous method.

Input Option Pane Code Example

Listing 14.4 demonstrates how to create an input option pane. The program is an applet that prompts the user for input through a dialog box. The input is provided by selecting an option from the display list of a combo box (see Figure 14.6). Once the selection is confirmed, a message dialog box pops up displaying the requested information (see Figure 14.7).

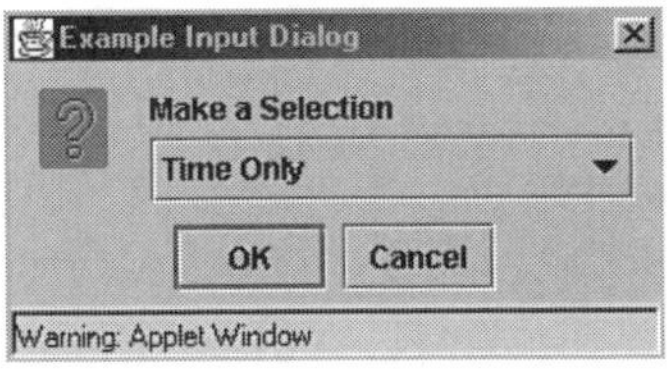

Figure 14.6

Applet displaying the input option pane.

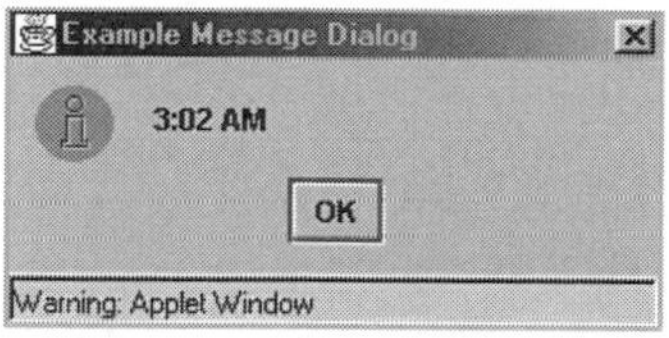

Figure 14.7

A message dialog box.

Listing 14.4   TJOptionPane3.java

```
/*
 * <Applet code=TJOptionPane3 width=400 height=75>
 * </Applet>
 */

import javax.swing.*;
import java.awt.*;
import java.awt.event.*;
import java.util.*;
import java.text.*;

public class TJOptionPane3 extends JApplet {
    Container container = null;

    public void init() {
        // 1. Get a handle on the applet's content pane.
        container = this.getContentPane();

        // 2. Add a box to the content pane.
        Box box = new Box(BoxLayout.X_AXIS);
        container.add(box);

        // 3. Add a button to display the time.
        JButton button = new JButton("Click Me");
        button.setPreferredSize(new Dimension(150,25));
        button.addActionListener(new ButtonListener());
        box.add(Box.createGlue());
        box.add(button);
        box.add(Box.createGlue());
    }

    // 4. The button listener class.
    class ButtonListener implements ActionListener {
        // 5. Argument values for the option pane dialog box.
        String title1 = "Example Input Dialog";
        String message1 = "Make a Selection";
        int messageType1 = JOptionPane.QUESTION_MESSAGE;
```

continues

Listing 14.4   continued

```
    Icon icon = null;
    Object[] options = {"Date Only", "Time Only",
                        "Date and Time"};
    Object optionSelected = options[1];

    // 6. Selection status of check box.
    Object selectedValue;
    // This field stores the selection made in the check box
    // as a string when you press the 'ok' button. If you press
    // the 'cancel' button, the 'null' value is received.

    // 7. Argument values for the message dialog box.
    Object message2 = null;
    String title2 = "Example Message Dialog";
    int messageType2 = JOptionPane.INFORMATION_MESSAGE;

    public void actionPerformed(ActionEvent e) {
        // 8. Display the input dialog box to make a selection.
        selectedValue = JOptionPane.showInputDialog(
                            container, message1, title1,
                            messageType1,
                            null, options, options[1]);

        // 9. Get the date, time, or date and time.
        if (selectedValue != null) {  // i.e., if not 'cancel'
            message2 = getInformation();

            // 10. Finally, display the message dialog box.
            JOptionPane.showMessageDialog(container, message2,
                                          title2, messageType2);
        }
    }

    // 11. Method to retrieve the information.
    public String getInformation() {
        DateFormat formatter = null;

        if (selectedValue == "Time Only") {
            formatter = DateFormat.getTimeInstance(
                            DateFormat.SHORT);
        }
        else if (selectedValue == "Date Only") {
            formatter = DateFormat.getDateInstance(
                            DateFormat.SHORT);
        }

        else if (selectedValue == "Date and Time") {
            formatter = DateFormat.getDateTimeInstance(
```

```
                                    DateFormat.SHORT,
                                    DateFormat.SHORT);
            }

            // Now format the time or date and time and return.
            String information = formatter.format(new Date());
            return information;
        }
    }
}
```

Code Details

The program creates an applet called TJOptionPane3. Inside the method init() of the applet, snippet-1 gets a handle on the applet's content pane. Snippets 2 and 3 add a button to the applet through the box container. When the user clicks the button, an input dialog box with multiple options appears. The relevant code is implemented inside the class that represents a button listener.

Snippet-4 shows the beginning of the listener class. Snippet-5 implements the parameters to be passed as the values of the arguments for the input dialog box. The parameter options defines the options available in the pull-down list of the combo box displayed over the input dialog box. The other parameter, optionSelected, indicates the value to be displayed in the combo box by default.

Snippet-6 shows the parameter that stores the selected value. The selected value from the pull-down list of the combo box is of type String. Snippet-7 shows the parameters for creating the message dialog box; the message dialog box appears when the user makes a selection through the input dialog box.

Inside the method actionPerformed(), snippet-8 shows how to display the input dialog box with a message and a combo box with a list of options to be selected. Snippet-9 retrieves the information returned by the method getInformation().

NOTE

The input dialog returns null if the user presses the Cancel button in the dialog box.

Snippet-10 pops up the message dialog box with the information that has been retrieved. The output from the program is shown in Figure 14.6 when the input dialog box pops up. Once the user provides the input by making a selection, the message dialog box containing the requested information is displayed. Figure 14.7 shows the applet with the message dialog box.

Option Dialog Boxes

An option dialog box is one that possesses the features of all the dialog boxes such as message, confirmation, and input. That is, the layout features of these dialog boxes have been gathered in a single dialog box.

To implement an option dialog box in a program, you can invoke the following static method on the class JOptionPane, which directly creates and displays an option dialog box:

```
public static int showOptionDialog(
                    Component parentComponent,
                    Object message,
                    String title,
                    int optionType,
                    int messageType,
                    Icon icon,
                    Object[] options,
                    Object initialValue)
```

This method brings up a modal dialog box with a specified title, message, and icon. The argument parentComponent is the frame in which the dialog box is displayed. If this parameter is specified as null or if the parentComponent has no frame, a default frame will be used.

The messageType parameter is primarily used to supply a default icon for the look-and-feel. The initial choice is determined by the parameter initialValue, and the set of possible options is determined by the parameter optionType. If optionType is YES_NO_OPTION or YES_NO_CANCEL_OPTION and the options parameter is null, the options are supplied by the look-and-feel. The other parameter options allow the user to use components other than buttons. Also, the parameter is useful to display buttons with any string labels of interest. For more information about these parameters, see the description of "show" methods of the previous dialog boxes.

CHAPTER 15

File Choosers and Color Choosers

In addition to the option panes discussed in Chapter 14, the Swing library readily supports two more standard dialog boxes: a file chooser and a color chooser. The Swing file choosers are alternatives to the AWT file dialog boxes. The file chooser class contains the methods to create the Open and Save dialog boxes, and it supports the Swing dialog boxes for making use of custom file views and file filters. The Swing color choosers display a dialog box with controls that allow the user to choose any sophisticated color. There is no AWT equivalent for this component.

The file and color chooser classes are similar to the option panes discussed in the previous chapter. When you invoke a certain method on a chooser object, an object of a Swing dialog box is created to display the respective chooser pane.

File Choosers

A file chooser is a dialog box used to select a file from the file system. The Swing file choosers are simple to create, but their functionality is fairly sophisticated. File choosers are created in two forms: dialog boxes for opening files and dialog boxes for saving files.

NOTE

The file choosers don't actually open or save files; they return the file object that has been selected for opening or saving. The user needs to implement the file opening or saving by using the file object that has been returned.

The Swing file chooser is represented by the class JFileChooser that extends JComponent. The class hierarchy of JFileChooser is shown in Figure 15.1. The class JFileChooser is stored in the package javax.swing.

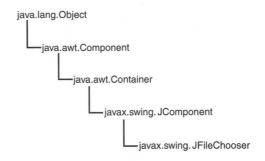

Figure 15.1

Class hierarchy of JFileChooser.

JFileChooser Constructors

To implement a file chooser in an application, create an object of type JFileChooser by using any one of the supported constructors. Note that you can also specify the current directory of type File and the current directory path of type String to file choosers or the custom view of the file system. The custom view specifies the icons to be attached to the file types when they are displayed; these details are discussed in the next section. Following is the list of constructors available inside the class JFileChooser:

```
public JFileChooser()
public JFileChooser(String currentDirectoryPath)
public JFileChooser(File currentDirectory)
public JFileChooser(
    javax.swing.filechooser.FileSystemView
    fileSystemView)
public JFileChooser(File currentDirectory,
    javax.swing.filechooser.FileSystemView
    fileSystemView)
public JFileChooser(String currentDirectoryPath,
    javax.swing.filechooser.FileSystemView
    fileSystemView)
```

```
 public JFileChooser(String currentDirectoryPath)
```

creates a JFileChooser that points to the user's home directory.

```
public JFileChooser(File currentDirectory)
public JFileChooser(
```

and

```
javax.swing.filechooser.FileSystemView
    fileSystemView)
```

use the arguments that specify the path to be displayed by default. You can specify the path as a `File` object as `currentDirectory`, or the `String` object as `currentDirectoryPath`. If a `null` is passed as the value of these arguments, the file chooser will point to the home directory. A file chooser object can also be created by using the information of the custom file view as `fileSystemView`.

The last two constructors

```
public JFileChooser(File currentDirectory,
    javax.swing.filechooser.FileSystemView
    fileSystemView)
```

and

```
public JFileChooser(String currentDirectoryPath,
    javax.swing.filechooser.FileSystemView
    fileSystemView)
```

use the combinations of these arguments to create the file chooser objects.

JFileChooser Code Example

Listing 15.1 demonstrates how to implement the Swing file chooser in a program. The program is an application with a menu bar that allows the user to pull down a file menu. The pull-down menu contains Open and Save As menu items that deploy the corresponding file choosers for file opening or file saving. After selecting a file through the file chooser, one of the confirmation buttons can be selected. The selection status will be displayed in the main frame. Figures 15.2 and 15.3 display the "Open" type and "Save" type file choosers.

Listing 15.1   JFileChooser Application with Open and Save File Choosers (TJFileChooser.java)

```
// Demonstrates the Swing file choosers

import javax.swing.*;
import javax.swing.border.*;
import java.awt.*;
import java.awt.event.*;
import java.io.*;

// 1. The class TJFileChooser frame.
public class TJFileChooser extends JFrame {
    JMenuItem openMI, saveMI, saveAsMI, exitMI;
    JFileChooser fileChooser;
    Container container;
```

continues

Listing 15.1   continued

```
    JLabel label;
    File file, selectedFile;

    public TJFileChooser() {
        // 2. To close the frame.
        this.addWindowListener(new FrameClosing());

        // 3. Get a handle on the frame's content pane.
        container = this.getContentPane();

        // 4. Create a label and add it to the container.
        label = new JLabel();
        container.add(label);

        // 5. Create and add a menu bar.
        JMenuBar menuBar = new JMenuBar();
        menuBar.setBorder(BorderFactory.createEtchedBorder());
        container.add(menuBar, BorderLayout.NORTH);

        // 6. Create and add the file menu and its menu items.
        JMenu fileMenu = new JMenu("File");
        menuBar.add(fileMenu);

        JMenuItem newMI = new JMenuItem("New");
        newMI.setEnabled(false);
        fileMenu.add(newMI);

        openMI = new JMenuItem("Open");
        openMI.addActionListener(new MIActionListener());
        fileMenu.add(openMI);

        fileMenu.addSeparator();

        saveMI = new JMenuItem("Save");
        saveMI.setEnabled(false);
        fileMenu.add(saveMI);

        saveAsMI = new JMenuItem("Save As");
        saveAsMI.addActionListener(new MIActionListener());
        fileMenu.add(saveAsMI);

        fileMenu.addSeparator();
        fileMenu.addSeparator();

        // 7. "Exit" menu item with an action listener.
        exitMI = new JMenuItem("Exit");
        exitMI.addActionListener(new MIActionListener());
        fileMenu.add(exitMI);
```

```
        // 8. Create and add the Edit menu.
        JMenu editMenu = new JMenu("Edit");
        menuBar.add(editMenu);
    }

    // 9. Menu action listener.
    class MIActionListener implements ActionListener {
        public void actionPerformed(ActionEvent ae) {
            JMenuItem menuItem = (JMenuItem) ae.getSource();

            // 10. If the Open menu item is selected.
            if (menuItem == openMI) {
                if (file == null) {
                    // Create a file chooser pointing to the
                    // home directory
                    fileChooser = new JFileChooser();
                }
                else {
                    // Create a file chooser pointing to the
                    // specified file path
                    fileChooser = new JFileChooser(file);
                }

                // Show the dialog box (returns the option selected).
                int selected = fileChooser.showOpenDialog(container);

                // 11. If the Open button over the file chooser is pressed.
                if (selected == JFileChooser.APPROVE_OPTION) {
                    // Get the selected file
                    file = fileChooser.getSelectedFile();

                    // Display the file name in the frame.
                    label.setText("You have selected to open:"+
                    ➥file.getName());
                    label.setHorizontalAlignment(JLabel.CENTER);

                    return;
                }

                // 12. If the Cancel button is pressed.
                else if (selected == fileChooser.CANCEL_OPTION) {
                    label.setText("You have not selected any file to open!");
                    label.setHorizontalAlignment(JLabel.CENTER);
                    return;
                }

            }
```

continues

Listing 15.1   continued

```
              // 13. If the Save menu item is selected.
            else if (menuItem == saveAsMI) {
                  // Here comes your file-saving code...
                  fileChooser = new JFileChooser();
                  int selected = fileChooser.showSaveDialog(container);
                  selectedFile = new File("UNTITLED");
                  fileChooser.setSelectedFile(selectedFile);

                  if (selected == JFileChooser.APPROVE_OPTION) {
                      // Get the selected file
                      selectedFile = fileChooser.getSelectedFile();

                      // Display the selected file name in the frame.
                      label.setText("You have selected to save:"+
                  ➥file.getName());
                      label.setHorizontalAlignment(JLabel.CENTER);

                      return;
                  }
                  else if (selected == fileChooser.CANCEL_OPTION) {
                      label.setText("You have not selected any file to open!");
                      label.setHorizontalAlignment(JLabel.CENTER);

                      return;
                  }
              }

            else if (menuItem == exitMI) {
                  System.exit(0);
              }
          }
      }

    // 14. Listener to close the frame.
    class FrameClosing extends WindowAdapter {
        public void windowClosing(WindowEvent e) {
            System.exit(0);
        }
    }

    // 15. The main method.
    public static void main(String[] args) {
        TJFileChooser frame = new TJFileChooser();
        frame.setTitle("TJFileChooser Example");
        frame.setSize(450, 300);
        frame.setVisible(true);
    }
}
```

Code Details

TJFileChooser.java begins by defining the class TJFileChooser as given in the code snippet-1. Snippet-2 adds a listener that implements the code to close the frame. Snippet-3 gets a handle on the content pane of the application frame.

Snippet-4 creates a label and adds it to the content pane of the frame. Snippet-5 creates a menu bar with the etched border and adds the menu bar at the top of the frame. Snippet-6 provides code to add various menu items to the file menu. Snippet-7 shows the menu item to exit the application. Snippet-8 adds an additional menu called Edit to the menu bar.

Snippet-9 is an action listener that responds when the menu items Open or Save As are activated. If the selected menu item is the Open item, snippet-10 implements what should happen. The code creates a file chooser object and displays the file dialog box to open a file. Notice that the code also preserves the directory path that has been navigated through the file chooser. The next time the file chooser is activated, it appears with the previously selected directory as its current directory level.

Snippet-11 shows the code if the user presses the Open button. The code retrieves the object of the selected file to open by invoking the method getSelectedFile() on the file chooser object. Using this file, an image icon is created and displayed as a label. Snippet-12 is where the actions are implemented when the Cancel button is pressed.

Snippet-13 shows the code when you operate on the Save As menu item. The snippet creates a file dialog box of type "Save" and displays it. When you try to save with a filename, the corresponding file object is returned. You can perform saving the file by using this file object. Snippet-14 is the listener class that implements code to close the frame. Snippet-15 is the main method in which you create the application frame and make it visible.

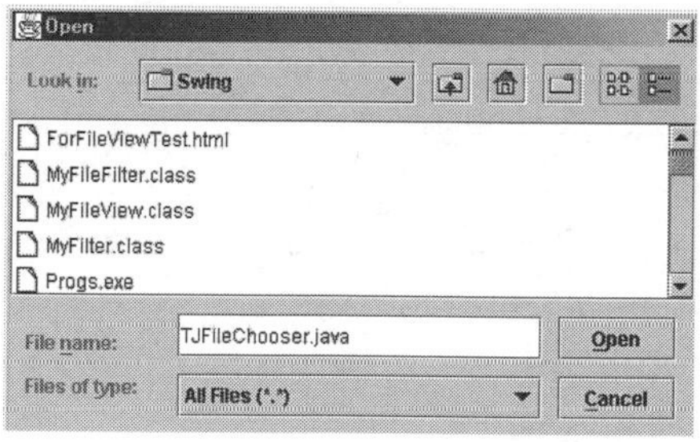

Figure 15.2

The file chooser dialog box that opens a file.

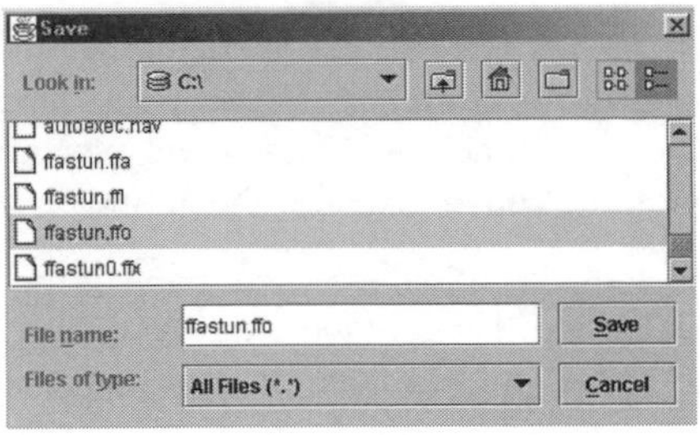

Figure 15.3

The file chooser dialog box that saves a file.

Custom File View

Sometimes in an application the files displayed in a file chooser are associated with icons that are intended to reflect the specific file types. For example, in a program like Paint Shop, the image files are associated with icons specified by the application. The Swing file chooser supports custom views for files by using an abstract class called FileView. This abstract class is stored in the package javax.swing.filechooser.

To apply a specific view to the files in a file chooser, you need to create a class that extends the abstract class FileView. The abstract class contains the following methods:

```
public abstract class FileView {
      public abstract String getName(File f);
      public abstract String getDescription(File f);
      public abstract String getTypeDescription(File f);
      public abstract Icon getIcon(File f);
      public abstract Boolean isTraversable(File f);
}
```

Once the extension class has been created with the methods that override those inside the class FileView, you can apply the custom file view to the file chooser by using the following snippet of code:

```
// Create an object of the custom file view
MyFileView fileView = new MyFileView();
// Assign the file view object to the file chooser object
JfileChooser fileChooser = new JfileChooser();
FileChooser.setFileView(fileView);
```

WARNING

If any of the implemented methods from the custom file view class happen to return null, the file view of the default UI is returned.

An implementation of the `FileView` class to provide a custom file view to a dialog box is demonstrated in Listing 15.2. This listing appears after the following discussion of file filters.

File Filters

A file filter is used to prevent unwanted files from appearing in the list of files displayed by the file chooser. This is very useful when you have many types of files in a single directory but only a specific files are of interest. The Swing file chooser can be associated with a file filter that extends the abstract class `FileFilter`. The abstract class `FileFilter` contains only two methods:

```
public abstract class FileFilter {
    public abstract boolean accept(File f);
    public abstract String getDescription();
}
```

To create a file filter you need to create a class that extends the `FileFilter` class. The extension class implements methods that override the abstract methods by containing the actual code to perform the filtering process. Next you create the filter object and assign it to the file chooser object.

WARNING

Unfortunately, there are two classes in JDK1.2 with the name `FileFilter`. These classes are present in `java.io` and `javax.swing.filechooser` packages. When you access these classes in a program, the compiler gives the necessary warning.

JFileFilter Code Example

Listing 15.2 demonstrates how to implement file filters and provide a custom view for the files. The program basically implements the abstract classes `FileFilter` and `FileView`. The objects of the implementation classes are assigned to the file chooser object. Figure 15.4 shows the output of this program.

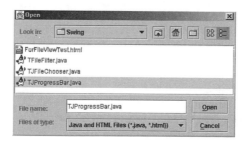

Figure 15.4

The file chooser with a custom view and file filter.

Listing 15.2   JFileFilter with File Filters and Custom File View (TJFileFilter.java)
```
Demonstrates the file filters and custom file view.
import javax.swing.*;
import javax.swing.border.*;
import java.awt.*;
import java.awt.event.*;
import java.io.*;

public class TFileFilter extends JFrame {
    JMenuItem openMI, exitMI;
    JFileChooser fileChooser;
    Container container;
    JLabel label;
    File file, selectedFile;

    public TFileFilter() {
        // 1. To close the frame.
        this.addWindowListener(new FrameClosing());

        // 2. Get a handle on the frame's content pane.
        container = this.getContentPane();

        // 3. create a label and add it to the container.
        label = new JLabel();
        container.add(label);

        // 4. Create and add a menu bar.
        JMenuBar menuBar = new JMenuBar();
        menuBar.setBorder(BorderFactory.createEtchedBorder());
        container.add(menuBar, BorderLayout.NORTH);

        // 5. Create and add the file menu and its menu items.
        JMenu fileMenu = new JMenu("File");
        menuBar.add(fileMenu);

        openMI = new JMenuItem("Open");
        openMI.addActionListener(new MIActionListener());
        fileMenu.add(openMI);

        fileMenu.addSeparator();

        // 6. "Exit" menu item with an action listener.
        exitMI = new JMenuItem("Exit");
        exitMI.addActionListener(new MIActionListener());
        fileMenu.add(exitMI);
    }

    // 7. Menu action listener.
    class MIActionListener implements ActionListener {
```

```java
public void actionPerformed(ActionEvent ae) {
    JMenuItem menuItem = (JMenuItem) ae.getSource();

    // 8. if the "Open"  menu item is selected.
    if (menuItem == openMI) {
        if (file == null) {
            // Create a file chooser pionting to the
            // home directory.
            fileChooser = new JFileChooser();
        }
        else {
            // Create a file chooser pointing to the
            // specified file path.
            fileChooser = new JFileChooser(file);

        }

        // 9. Add a file filter (object of MyFileFilter).
        fileChooser.addChoosableFileFilter(new MyFileFilter());

        // The following statement will assign the new filter
        // discarding the other filters.
        //fileChooser.setFileFilter(new MyFileFilter());

        // 10. Set a custom view for the files (using the object of
        ➥MyFileView).
        fileChooser.setFileView(new MyFileView());

        // 11. Show the dialog box (returns the option selected).
        int selected = fileChooser.showOpenDialog(container);

        // 12. if the Open button over the file chooser is pressed.
        if (selected == JFileChooser.APPROVE_OPTION) {
            // Get the selected file
            file = fileChooser.getSelectedFile();

            // Display the file name in the frame.
            label.setText("You have selected to open:"+
            ➥file.getName());
            label.setHorizontalAlignment(JLabel.CENTER);

            return;
        }

        // 13. if the Cancel button is pressed.
        else if (selected == fileChooser.CANCEL_OPTION) {
            label.setText("You have not selected any file to open!");
            label.setHorizontalAlignment(JLabel.CENTER);
            return;
```

continues

Listing 15.2   continued

```
                    }
              }

              // 14. If the Exit button is pressed.
              else if (menuItem == exitMI) {
                  System.exit(0);
              }
          }
      }

      // 15. Listener to close the frame.
      class FrameClosing extends WindowAdapter {
          public void windowClosing(WindowEvent e) {
              System.exit(0);
          }
      }

      // 16. The main method.
      public static void main(String[] args) {
          TFileFilter frame = new TFileFilter();
          frame.setTitle("TFileFilter Example");
          frame.setSize(450, 300);
          frame.setVisible(true);
      }
}

// 17. Define a file filter class.
class MyFileFilter extends javax.swing.filechooser.FileFilter {

    public boolean accept(File file) {
        if (file.isDirectory()) { // Accept if the file system member is a
        ➥directory
            return true;
        }

        // Retrieve the file name.
        String fileName = file.getName();
        // Note the index of '.' in a file name
        int periodIndex = fileName.lastIndexOf('.');

        // State of acceptence.
        boolean accepted = false;

        if (periodIndex>0 && periodIndex<fileName.length()-1) {
            String extension = fileName.substring(periodIndex+1).toLowerCase();
            if (extension.equals("java"))  // Check if the extension is ".java"
                accepted = true;
```

```
            else if(extension.equals("html")) // Check if the extension is
        ➥.html.
                accepted = true;
        }
        return accepted;
    }

    // Retrieve the description of the filter.
    public String getDescription() {
        return "Java and HTML Files (*.java, *.html))";
    }
}

// 18. Custom file view class.
class MyFileView extends javax.swing.filechooser.FileView {
    // Define the required icon objects.
    ImageIcon javaIcon = new ImageIcon("javaIcon.gif");
    ImageIcon htmlIcon = new ImageIcon("htmlIcon.gif");

    // Retrieve the file name.
    public String getName(File f) {
        return null; // L&F FileView will find this out
                     // of use return f.getName();
    }

    // Retrieve the description of the file.
    public String getDescription(File f) {
        return null; // L&F FileView will find this out
    }

    // Returns the file type as Java.
    public String getTypeDescription(File f) {
        String extension = getExtension(f);
        String type = null;
        if(extension != null) {
            if(extension.equals("java")) {
                type = "Java File";
            }
            if(extension.equals("gif")){
                type = "Html File";
            }
        }
        return type;
    }

    // Retrieve the relevant icon for the file view.
    public Icon getIcon(File f) {
```

continues

Listing 15.2   continued

```
        String extension = getExtension(f);
        Icon icon = null;
        if (extension != null) {
            if(extension.equals("java")) {
                icon = javaIcon;
            }
            if(extension.equals("html")) {
                icon = htmlIcon;
            }
        }
        return icon;
    }
    // Whether a direction is traversable.
    public Boolean isTraversable(File f) {
        return null; //  L&F FileView will find this out
    }

    // Retrieve the extension of a file.
    private String getExtension(File f) {
        String fileName = f.getName();
        int periodIndex = fileName.lastIndexOf('.');
        String extension = null;
        if(periodIndex > 0 &&  periodIndex < fileName.length() - 1) {
            extension = fileName.substring(periodIndex+1).toLowerCase();
        }
        return extension;
    }
}
```

Code Details

In this program, snippets 1–9 and 12–16 create an application similar to the one shown in Listing 15.1. However, snippets 9 and 10 show the code to assign a file filter and file view objects for customization. The method addChoosableFileFilter() assigns the file filter object of type MyFileFilter to the file chooser. This class is capable of displaying only the .java and .html files in the file chooser. The method setFileView() in snippet-10 assigns a custom view for the files displayed in the file chooser.

Snippet-17 defines the class MyFileFilter that extends javax.swing.filechooser. FileFilter. The class FileFilter contains two abstract methods, accept() and getDescription(), to be implemented. The accept() method returns the Boolean state on whether a specific file should be displayed in the file chooser. The getDescription() returns any text that describes the file as "Java and HTML Files."

Snippet-18 defines the custom file view class called MyFileView that extends javax.swing.filechooser.FileView. The custom file view class implements the abstract methods from the FileView class. The methods getName(), getDescription(), and getTypeDescription() return the name of the file, the decription text for the file, and the description of the type of the file, respectively. The method isTraversable() indicates a directory is traversable. The method getIcon() is the vital method that returns the relevant icon to customize the file view.

Color Choosers

The Swing color chooser is a component that displays a control pane to manipulate and select any desired color. The color chooser contains a tabbed pane with the color palette and the RGB sliders used to select a color. You can directly select any desired color from the Swatches pane. If the desired color is not available on the Swatches pane, you can manipulate the sliders over the RGB pane to arrive at the color.

The Swing color chooser pane is represented by the class JColorChooser, which extends JComponent. The class hierarchy of JColorChooser is shown in Figure 15.5. The JColorChooser is located in the package javax.swing.

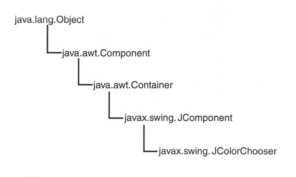

Figure 15.5

Class hierarchy of JColorChooser.

JColorChooser Constructors

To create a color chooser object, you can use any one of the following constructors supported inside JColorChooser:

```
public JColorChooser()
public JColorChooser(Color initialColor)
public ColorChooser(javax.swing.colorchooser.ColorSelectionModel model)
```

In these, the argument initialColor is the initial color with which the color chooser appears when you make it pop up. The first constructor without any arguments creates a color chooser pane with white as the initial color. The next constructor creates the object with the specified initial color. The third constructor creates a color chooser object with the prescribed color selection model. The argument named model is the color selection model of class type ColorSelectionModel. Once you create a color chooser pane, you can display it in a Swing dialog box by using the static methods supported in JColorChooser.

JColorChooser Code Example

Listing 15.3 is a simple drawing applet (see Figure 15.6) that enables you to draw pictures by dragging the mouse over the canvas. When you press the Show Color Chooser button positioned over the applet, a color chooser pane is popped up. You can select any desired color from the color chooser pane. Figure 15.7 shows the Swatches tab of the color chooser pane, and Figure 15.8 shows the RGB tab, which is useful for selecting more sophisticated colors.

Figure 15.6

A simple drawing applet.

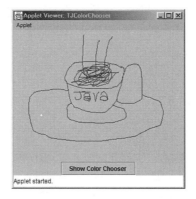

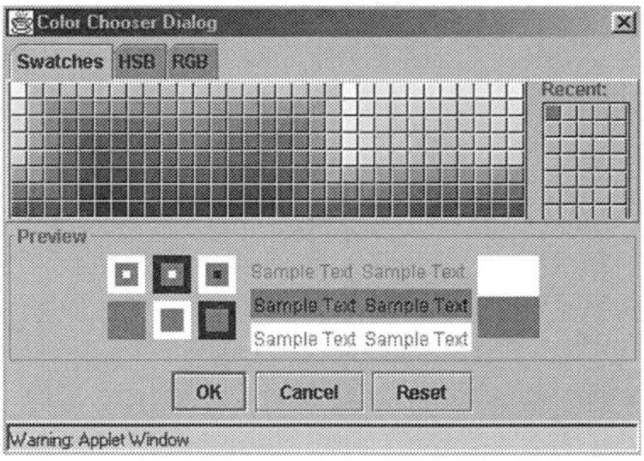

Figure 15.7

The Swatches pane of the color chooser pane displaying the colors palette.

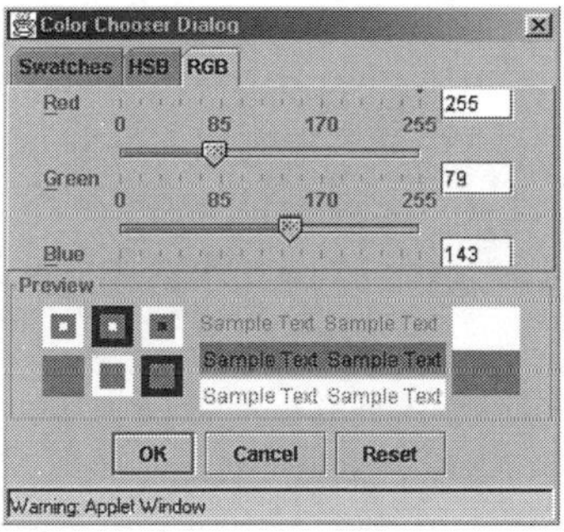

Figure 15.8

The RGB pane to select a fine-tuned color.

Listing 15.3   JColorChooser in a Simple Drawing Applet
(TJColorChooser.java)

```java
/*
 * <Applet code=TJColorChooser width=400 height=400>
 * </Applet>
 */

import javax.swing.*;
import java.awt.*;
import java.awt.event.*;

public class TJColorChooser extends JApplet {
    Container container = null;
    DrawingPanel panel = null;
    JColorChooser colorChooser = null;
    JDialog dialog = null;
    int oldX, oldY, newX, newY;
    Color color = null;

    public void init() {
        // 1. Get a handle on the applet's content pane.
        container = this.getContentPane();

        // 2. Create a drawing panel and add it at the center
        // of the content pane of the applet.

        panel = new DrawingPanel();
        container.add(panel);

        // 3. Add a button at the bottom portion
        // of the applet to display the color chooser pane.
        JButton showButton = new JButton("Show Color Chooser");
        showButton.addActionListener(new ButtonListener());
```

continues

Listing 15.3   continued

```
      Box hBox = Box.createHorizontalBox();
     hBox.add(Box.createHorizontalGlue());
     hBox.add(showButton);
     hBox.add(Box.createHorizontalGlue());
     container.add(hBox, BorderLayout.SOUTH);

     // 4. Create a color chooser object and a dialog box
     //    that displays the color chooser.
     colorChooser = new JColorChooser();
     dialog = JColorChooser.createDialog(
                         container,
                         "Color Chooser",
                         false,
                         colorChooser,
                         new ButtonListener(),
                         new ButtonListener());
}

  // 5. This is where you perform your drawing with
  // the selected color.
  class DrawingPanel extends Panel {
      public DrawingPanel () {
          setBackground(Color.white);
          MyMouseListener mouseListener = new MyMouseListener();
          addMouseListener(mouseListener);
          addMouseMotionListener(mouseListener);
      }

      public void update(Graphics g) {
          g.setColor(color);
          paint(g);
      }

      public void paint(Graphics g) {
         g.drawLine(oldX, oldY, newX, newY);
      }
  }

  // 6. Listener class that responds to all button actions.
  class ButtonListener implements ActionListener {
      public void actionPerformed(ActionEvent e) {
          JButton button = (JButton) e.getSource();

          if (button.getText() equals("Show Color Chooser")) {
              dialog.show();
          }

          if (button.getText().equals("OK")) {
              //dialog.show();
```

```
                    color = colorChooser.getColor();
            }
            else if(button.getText().equals("Cancel")) {
                dialog.dispose();
            }
            // Note: Don't have to handle the actions of the
            // 'Reset' button; this button has been implemented
            // to reset the color to the previously used color.
        }
    }

    // 7. Mouse listener class to draw on the canvas.
    class MyMouseListener extends MouseAdapter
                        implements MouseMotionListener {
        public void mousePressed(MouseEvent e) {
            oldX = e.getX(); oldY = e.getY();
            newX = e.getX(); newY = e.getY();

panel.repaint();
        }

        public void mouseDragged(MouseEvent e) {
            oldX = newX; oldY = newY;
            newX = e.getX(); newY = e.getY();

 panel.repaint();
        }

        public void mouseMoved(MouseEvent e) {}
    }
}
```

Code Details

The applet TJColorChooser begins by declaring the data member as shown in the class. Inside the init() method, snippet-1 gets a handle on the applet's content pane. Snippet-2 creates a drawing panel and adds it at the center of the applet. Snippet-3 creates a button to pop up the Color Chooser dialog box.

Snippet-4 creates an object of JColorChooser. Then a dialog box is created by calling the static method createDialog() from the class JColorChooser. The method createDialog() takes the color chooser object as one of its argument values to display the color chooser inside the dialog box. Snippet-5 defines the class DrawingPanel. DrawingPanel has been registered with the mouse motion listener. The class uses the overridden update() and paint() methods to execute the drawing of lines using the current and previous coordinates of the mouse.

Snippet-6 is the button listener that is common to the Show Color Chooser button and the OK and Cancel buttons over the color chooser panel. When you click the OK button, the selected color is retrieved by invoking the method getColor() on the color chooser object.

NOTE

To achieve a specific color that is not available in the Swatches pane of JColorChooser, select an approximate color in the Swatches pane; then switch to the RGB pane and adjust the sliders to obtain the desired color. You can also use the HSB pane if necessary.

Snippet-7 shows the mouse listener class that contains the functionality to retrieve the mouse coordinates and invoke the paint() method inside the panel. To execute the functionality, you need to either click or drag the mouse.

CHAPTER 16

Trees

A tree is a user interface control used to display a set of hierarchical data. The most common use of a tree is to display the directory structure and associated files of a network drive.

The JTree class is used to create extremely sophisticated, lightweight tree components. The tree design uses a Model-View-Controller (MVC) architecture-based approach. You can execute certain functionality by making selections on the nodes of the tree component; the tree component fires events that need to be received to execute the required functionality.

Swing trees display default look-and-feel–specific icons for each of their nodes. However, you can implement custom rendering for the node cells of the tree widget to customize the look-and-feel. Swing trees also support editable node cells.

Creating Trees

The fundamental object in a tree is called a *node*, which represents a data item in the given hierarchical set. Thus, a tree is composed of one or more nodes. The *root node*, or simply *root*, is the top node of the hierarchical data.

Nodes inside the root node are called *child nodes*, or simply *nodes*. Nodes that contain no child nodes are called *leaf nodes*. Each node that is not a leaf can have an arbitrary number of children, including no (zero) children. In each row of a tree, you will find a node or a leaf node. In each column you will find the nodes whose respective parents reside in the previous column.

For example, in a Windows NT file system, the root node would be c:\. The files in c:\ itself and all the subdirectories represent child nodes. The files in these subdirectories cannot deploy further and thus are the leaves of the files system tree.

Tree and Node Classes

A Swing tree has its functionality distributed into several classes. However, there is only one class, JTree, that is central to all classes. The class JTree represents the tree component and is stored in the package javax.swing. The class hierarchy of JTree is shown in Figure 16.1.

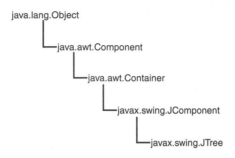

java.lang.Object

└─ java.awt.Component

└─ java.awt.Container

└─ javax.swing.JComponent

└─ javax.swing.JTree

Figure 16.1

The class hierarchy of JTree.

A Swing tree is built from its nodes, which are objects of type TreeNode. The TreeNode is an interface that is stored in the package javax.swing.tree. The interface contains methods that return information about a node such as its parent, if it is a leaf, and its child count. There is another interface called the MutableTreeNode that extends TreeNode. This interface simply adds more abstract methods.

Rather than directly implementing these interfaces, you can use the class DefaultMutableTreeNode, which provides the default implementation of the interface MutableTreeNode. This class extends java.lang.Object. If you want to construct a tree from its nodes, you can create nodes of type DefaultMutableTreeNode and specify the root of the nodes to the JTree object through its constructor. For the list of methods from the node interfaces and the class DefaultMutableTreeNode, consult Appendix A, "JFC Swing Quick Reference."

Following are the constructors of DefaultMutableTreeNode that can be used to create a tree node:

```
public DefaultMutableTreeNode()
```

creates a tree node without a parent and any initial children. However, the node allows children to be added.

```
public DefaultMutableTreeNode(Object userObject, boolean allowsChildren)
```

takes a user object and a Boolean flag. The user object userObject is displayed to describe the node. Usually, this is a string object such as C:\WIN95. The Boolean flag allowsChildren specifies whether the node should allow children (true) or if it should be a leaf (false).

```
public DefaultMutableTreeNode(Object userObject)
```

is similar to the preceding constructor, but without any Boolean flag. A node created by using this constructor always allows children to be added to it.

WARNING

The class `DefaultMutableTreeNode` is not thread safe to use its objects in multiple threads. If you want to use this class or a tree of `TreeNodes` in multiple threads, you need to implement your own synchronization (preferably by using the root node of the tree).

Tree Paths

In the package `javax.swing.tree` there is a class called `TreePath`, which is a representation of the path in the tree that takes you to the specified node. Often the information regarding the intermediate nodes between the root and the specified node can be obtained using this class. See Appendix A for the methods from this class.

JTree Constructors

There are different ways to create a Swing tree component by using the constructors of `JTree`. Following are seven constructors available in the class `JTree`:

```
public JTree()
```

creates a Swing tree with the default model. You can assign a different model to the tree object at a later stage by using the method `setModel()`.

```
public JTree(Hashtable value)
```

creates a tree from a hash table without displaying the root of the tree.

```
public JTree(Object[] value)
```

creates a tree with each element of the specified array as the child of the root node that is not displayed.

```
public JTree(TreeModel newModel)
```

creates an instance of Swing tree by using the specified data model.

```
public JTree(TreeNode root,
boolean asksAllowsChildren)
```

creates a `JTree` object with the specified `TreeNode` as its root. You can also specify whether the tree nodes should allow child nodes.

```
public JTree(TreeNode root)
```

creates a tree object with the specified `TreeNode` as its root. The tree can also display the root node.

```
public JTree(Vector value)
```

creates a `JTree` object with each element of the specified vector as the child node of the root node that is not displayed.

JTree Code Example

Listing 16.1 shows the sample code to create a tree object from its nodes. Initially the · tree nodes are created by using the constructors of the class `DefaultMutableTreeNode`. Then the child nodes are added appropriately to their parent nodes in a hierarchical manner. The root of the node system is attached to a tree object. Figure 16.2 displays the output of the program.

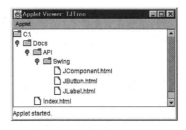

Figure 16.2

An applet displaying the Swing tree.

Listing 16.1   JTree Displaying Its Nodes and Leaves (TJTree.java)

```java
// Demonstrates how to create the Swing tree widget to
// represent hierarchical data.

/*
 * <Applet code = TJTree width = 350 height = 300>
 * </Applet>
 */

import javax.swing.*;
import javax.swing.tree.*;
import java.awt.*;
import java.awt.event.*;

public class TJTree extends JApplet {
    Container container;

    public void init() {
        // 1. Get the handle on applet's content pane.
        container = this.getContentPane();

        // 2. Root node (col0 or root) of the tree.
        DefaultMutableTreeNode root =
            new DefaultMutableTreeNode("C:\\");
```

```java
    // 3. Create the nodes in column 1.
    DefaultMutableTreeNode col11 =
        new DefaultMutableTreeNode("Docs");

    DefaultMutableTreeNode col12 =
        new DefaultMutableTreeNode("README");

    // 4. Add the nodes to the root.
    root.add(col11);
    root.add(col12);

    // 5. Create the nodes in column 2.
    DefaultMutableTreeNode col21 =
        new DefaultMutableTreeNode("API");
    DefaultMutableTreeNode col22 =
        new DefaultMutableTreeNode("index.html");

    // 6. Add the nodes to the node 1 in column 1.
    col11.add(col21);
    col11.add(col22);

    // 7. Create the nodes in column 3.
    DefaultMutableTreeNode col31 =
        new DefaultMutableTreeNode("Swing");

    // 8. Add the node to the node 2 in column 2.
    col21.add(col31);

    // 9. Create the nodes in column 4.
    DefaultMutableTreeNode col41 =
        new DefaultMutableTreeNode("JComponent.html");
    DefaultMutableTreeNode col42 =
        new DefaultMutableTreeNode("JButton.html");
    DefaultMutableTreeNode col43 =
        new DefaultMutableTreeNode("JLabel.html");

    // 10. Add the nodes to the node called Swing.
    col31.add(col41);
    col31.add(col42);
    col31.add(col43);

    // 11. Attach the root (of nodes) to the tree object.
    JTree tree = new JTree(root);

    // 12. Add the tree to a scroll pane and add the scroll pane
    // to the container.
    JScrollPane scrollPane = new JScrollPane(tree);
    container.add(scrollPane);
  }
}
```

Code Details

Listing 16.1 is a Swing applet called TJTree. Inside the method init(), snippet-1 gets the handle on the appletís content pane. Snippet-2 creates the root node of the tree (c:\\ as in a Windows system). The root node can be assumed to exist at column zero of the tree (tree nodes can be viewed as a set of columns). Snippet-3 creates two child nodes (at column level 1) to be added to the root as given in snippet-4.

Snippet-5 creates two more child nodes (at column level 2). These nodes are added to node 1 in column 1, which is the "Docs" node (snippet-6). Snippet-7 creates a node at column level 3 to be added (snippet-8) to node 1 in column 2, which is the API node. Snippet-9 shows the code to create nodes at column level 4 that are added to node 1 of column 3 (snippet-10).

Finally, the roots of the nodes are added to the tree object by using the suitable constructor, as shown in snippet-11. Snippet-12 shows the code to add the tree to a scroll pane that has been added to the applet.

Tree Models

Trees can be used to display much more complex data than that shown in Figure 16.2. The Swing library supports an interface called TreeModel, which is stored in the package javax.swing.tree. The interface models the underlying data of a tree component by implementing the following methods:

```
public Object getRoot()
```

returns the root of the tree.

```
public Object getChild(Object parent,
                       int index)
```

returns the child at the valid argument index in the child array. The argument parent is a node that has been obtained from this data source.

```
public int getChildCount(Object parent)
```

retrieves the count of children of the specified parent. It returns zero if the node is a leaf or there are no children.

```
public boolean isLeaf(Object node)
```

returns true if the specified node is a leaf.

```
public int getIndexOfChild(Object parent,
                           Object child)
```

returns the index of the specified child of the parent.

```
public void valueForPathChanged(TreePath path,
                                Object newValue)
```

notifies the interested parties in the program if the user has changed the data identified by the specified path.

```
public void addTreeModelListener(TreeModelListener l)
```

adds a listener object that will implement certain functionality whenever the tree data has been changed.

```
public void removeTreeModelListener(TreeModelListener l)
```

simply removes the listener object.

By default, a tree component uses the data model represented by the class DefaultTreeModel. An object of DefaultTreeModel contains the model data based on the tree nodes. For the list of methods from this class, see Appendix A.

Model Events and Listeners

Whenever the data of the tree model is subjected to any change, the tree object fires an event of type TreeModelEvent. The model event contains the information regarding the changes to the tree model. These events are received by the listener objects of interface type TreeModelListener.

The listener interface contains the following methods that must be implemented.

```
public void  treeNodesChanged(TreeModelEvent e)
```

is invoked if a node has changed in some way.

```
public void  treeNodesInserted(TreeModelEvent e)
```

is invoked if a node has been inserted into the tree.

```
public void  treeNodesRemoved(TreeModelEvent e)
```

is invoked if a node has been removed from the tree.

```
public void treeStructureChanged(TreeModelEvent e)
```

is invoked if the tree has drastically changed structure from a given node down.

To use the interface TreeModel in a program, you need to implement these methods in a class that represents the data model. An object of the model class can be applied to the tree component through its constructor or by invoking the method setModel() on the tree object.

Custom Tree Model Code Example

In Listing 16.2, the file system on your computer is displayed in a frame by using the Swing tree. The example tree uses an object of the class that implements the interface TreeModel. Note how each of the interface methods are implemented to obtain the directories and files from the file system. The object of the implementation class is assigned to the tree object through its constructor. The output from this program is displayed in Figure 16.3.

Figure 16.3

Displaying the file system by implementing TreeModel.

Listing 16.2   JTree Displaying the File System Hierarchy Using the Custom Tree Model (TTreeModel.java)

```
// Demonstrates how to use custom data models in trees.

import javax.swing.*;
import javax.swing.tree.*;
import javax.swing.event.*;
import java.awt.*;
import java.awt.event.*;
import java.io.File;
import java.util.*;

public class TTreeModel extends JFrame {
    public TTreeModel() {
        super("TTreeModel"); // Give a title to the frame

        // 1. Create an object of FileSystemModel, and create a tree
        // with that model. Add the tree to a scroll pane, and add
        // the scroll pane to the frame.
        FileSystemModel fileSystemDataModel = new FileSystemModel();
        JTree tree = new JTree(fileSystemDataModel);
        JScrollPane scrollPane = new JScrollPane(tree);
        getContentPane().add(scrollPane);

        // 2. Configure the frame and display it.
        addWindowListener(new WindowEventHandler());
        setDefaultCloseOperation(WindowConstants.DISPOSE_ON_CLOSE);
        setSize(300, 250);
        show();
    }

    // 3. The main method.
    public static void main(String [] args) {
        TTreeModel frame = new TTreeModel();
    }
```

```
    // 4. Define a listener class to close the frame.
    class WindowEventHandler extends WindowAdapter {
        public void windowClosing(WindowEvent evt) {
            System.exit(0);
        }
    }
}

// 5. Custom data model that represents the file system data.
class FileSystemModel implements TreeModel {
    private String root;    // The root identifier
    private Vector listeners; // Declare the listeners vector

    public FileSystemModel() {
        // 6. Get the home directory on your system.
        root = System.getProperty("user.home");

        // 7. For Windows 95, root is set to C:\ ("usr.home"
        // retrieves C:\WIN95).
        // You may implement a snippet like this for other OS also
        // like Windows NT, Macintosh, and so on.
        if (System.getProperty("os.name").equals("Windows 95")) {
            File tempFile = new File(root);
            root = tempFile.getParent();
        }

        // 8. Define the listeners vector.
        listeners = new Vector();
    }

    // 9. Retrieves the root of the tree hierarchy.
    public Object getRoot() {
        return (new File(root));
    }

    // 10. Retrieves the members in a directory based on an index.
    public Object getChild(Object parent, int index) {
        File directory = (File) parent;
        String[] directoryMembers = directory.list();
        return (new File(directory, directoryMembers[index]));
    }

    // 11. Retrieves the member count in a directory.
    public int getChildCount(Object parent) {
        File fileSystemMember = (File) parent;
            // fileSystemMember is a directory or file.
```

continues

Listing 16.2   continued

```
        // If a file system member is a directory.
        if (fileSystemMember.isDirectory()) {
            String[] directoryMembers = fileSystemMember.list();

            // Get the count of members in the directory.
            return directoryMembers.length;
        }

        // If the file system member is a file.
        else {
            // Return the member count as zero.
            return 0;
        }
    }

    // 12. Returns the index of a given member in its directory.
    public int getIndexOfChild(Object parent, Object child) {
        File directory = (File) parent;
        File directoryMember = (File) child;
        String[] directoryMemberNames = directory.list();
        int result = -1;

        for (int i = 0; i<directoryMemberNames.length; ++i) {
            if ( directoryMember.getName().equals(
                            directoryMemberNames[i] ) ) {
                result = i;
                break;
            }
        }
        // If no member with such name in the directory.
        return result;
    }

    // 13. Indicates whether a directory member is a tree leaf.
    public boolean isLeaf(Object node) {
        return ((File) node).isFile();
    }

    // 14. Method to add a tree model listener.
    public void addTreeModelListener(TreeModelListener l) {
        if (l != null && !listeners.contains(l)) {
            listeners.addElement(l);
        }
    }

    // 15. Method to remove a tree model listener.
    public void removeTreeModelListener(TreeModelListener l) {
        if (l != null) {
            listeners.removeElement(l);
```

```
        }
    }

    // A dumb method.
    public void valueForPathChanged(TreePath path, Object newValue) {
        // Does Nothing!
    }

    // 16. Additional methods that fire events whenever the model is
    // subjected to change. Possible changes can be nodes
    // inserted, nodes removed, structure changed, and so on.
    public void fireTreeNodesInserted(TreeModelEvent e) {
        Enumeration listenerCount = listeners.elements();
        while (listenerCount.hasMoreElements()) {
            TreeModelListener listener =
                (TreeModelListener) listenerCount.nextElement();
            listener.treeNodesInserted(e);
        }
    }

    public void fireTreeNodesRemoved(TreeModelEvent e) {
        Enumeration listenerCount = listeners.elements();
        while (listenerCount.hasMoreElements()) {
            TreeModelListener listener =
                (TreeModelListener) listenerCount.nextElement();
            listener.treeNodesRemoved(e);
        }

    }

    public void fireTreeNodesChanged(TreeModelEvent e) {
        Enumeration listenerCount = listeners.elements();
        while (listenerCount.hasMoreElements()) {
            TreeModelListener listener =
                (TreeModelListener) listenerCount.nextElement();
            listener.treeNodesChanged(e);
        }

    }

    public void fireTreeStructureChanged(TreeModelEvent e) {
        Enumeration listenerCount = listeners.elements();
        while (listenerCount.hasMoreElements()) {
            TreeModelListener listener =
                (TreeModelListener) listenerCount.nextElement();
            listener.treeStructureChanged(e);
        }

    }
}
```

Code Details

Inside the constructor of the frame TTreeModel, snippet-1 creates an object of the class FileSystemModel. This object is assigned to a tree object through its constructor. Then the tree is displayed in the frame by using a scroll pane. Snippet-2 shows the code to configure and display the application frame.

Snippet-3 shows the main method where the frame object is created. Snippet-4 is the code for the closing operation for the window handler. An object of this class has been registered with the frame as shown in snippet-2.

Snippet-5 shows the tree model class that models the file system data of the computer on which the application runs. Inside the constructor of this class, snippet-6 gets the home directory of the system; the home directory will be the root of the tree component. Snippet-7 shows the code to fetch the root at C:\ rather than C:\WIN95 on a Windows 95 operating system. Similar code may be required to deal with other operating systems. Snippet-8 defines a vector object to contain the model listeners that receive the model events. Model events are generated whenever the data in the tree model is subjected to changes.

Snippets 9–15 show the methods that must be implemented from the interface TreeModel. The method in snippet-9 retrieves information to create the root of the tree. Snippet-10 returns the child node of a specified parent node at the given index. Snippet-11 retrieves the count of nodes (files and directories) in the specified directory. Snippet-12 retrieves the index of a specified node. Snippet-13 confirms whether a given node is a leaf or a non-leaf. Snippets 14 and 15 show the add and remove methods to register listeners with a tree object. Snippet-16 shows the other supporting methods to fire various events.

Interacting with Trees

User interaction with trees is commonly performed in two ways: expanding a tree node to access its inner nodes and leaves, and selecting a leaf node for some further process such as displaying the contents of the file represented by the leaf node.

To deal with the selection of tree nodes, there is a separate interface called the TreeSelectionModel. This interface allows the representation of data of the current tree selection. The class DefaultTreeSelectionModel represents the data model for tree selection. The following are three different modes to select tree nodes:

SINGLE_TREE_SELECTION

In this mode, only one node can be selected at any time.

CONTIGUOUS_TREE_SELECTION

In this mode, you can select multiple nodes, but the paths of these nodes must be adjacent to each other.

`DISCONTIGUOUS_TREE_SELECTION`

This mode also enables you to select multiple nodes without any restrictions. You can assign a new mode to a tree by using the method `setSelectionMode()`.

NOTE

By default, the value of the tree selection mode is `DISCONTIGUOUS_TREE_SELECTION`.

Selection Events and Listeners

To respond to the user interaction of selecting a node, a Swing tree fires an event of type `TreeSelectionEvent`. The class `TreeSelectionEvent` characterizes the change in the selection of the tree. The selection can occur along any tree path.

The selection event needs to be received by a selection listener object that implements the listener interface called `TreeSelectionListener`. The tree selection listeners can figure out the status of the node that has been subjected to selection change. The event and its listener classes have been stored in the package `javax.swing.event`.

Expansion Events and Listeners

When a tree node is expanded, an event of type `TreeExpansionEvent` is fired by the tree object. The class `TreeExpansionEvent` characterizes the expansion or contraction of a node along a tree path. The path of the expanded or contracted node can be received by invoking the path `getPath()` on the event object. This method returns the path object of type `TreePath`. This event is received by an object of the listener class. The listener class implements the interface `TreeExpansionListener`. The event and its listener classes have been stored in the package `javax.swing.event`.

JTree Selection Events Code Example

Listing 16.3 shows an application that demonstrates how to handle tree selection events by using the corresponding listeners. The application frame has been attached with a split pane. The split pane holds two scroll panes: one displaying the tree component and the other containing an editor pane to display the selected HTML file. When you make a selection by clicking the mouse on a tree leaf node, the corresponding file is displayed in the editor pane, as shown in Figure 16.4.

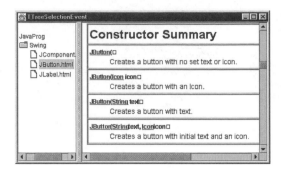

Figure 16.4

JTree node expansions and selections.

Listing 16.3   JTree Node Selections to Display a Document in an Editor Pane (TTreeSelectionEvent.java)

```
// Demonstrates the tree selection events and listeners.
import javax.swing.*;import javax.swing.tree.*;import javax.swing.event.*;
import java.awt.*;
import java.awt.event.*;
import java.net.*;
import java.io.*;

public class TTreeSelectionEvent extends JFrame {
    Container container;
    DefaultMutableTreeNode root;
    JScrollPane treeScrollPane;
    JScrollPane editorScrollPane;
    JEditorPane editorPane;

    public TTreeSelectionEvent() {
        // 1. Get the handle on applet's content pane and
        // create the tree nodes
        super("TTreeSelectionEvent");
        container = this.getContentPane();
        createTreeNodes();

        // 2. Attach the root of the nodes to the tree object
        // and set the tree to the SINGLE SELECTION mode.
        // Also, register a tree selection listener with the
        // tree object to listen to the respective events fired.
        JTree tree = new JTree(root);
        tree.getSelectionModel().setSelectionMode(
            TreeSelectionModel.SINGLE_TREE_SELECTION);
        tree.addTreeSelectionListener(new SelectionListener());

        // 3. Create scroll panes to display the tree, and the
        // editor component. Add the scroll panes to a split pane.
```

```
    // Add the split pane to the applet
    treeScrollPane = new JScrollPane(tree);

    editorPane = new JEditorPane();
    editorScrollPane = new JScrollPane(editorPane);
    JSplitPane splitPane = new JSplitPane(
                            JSplitPane.HORIZONTAL_SPLIT,
                            true,    // Continuous Layout
                            treeScrollPane,
                            editorScrollPane);
    // 4. Add the split pane to the frame.
    container.add(splitPane);

    // 5. Add the window closing listener.
    addWindowListener(new WindowEventHandler());

    // 6. Configure the frame.
    setDefaultCloseOperation(WindowConstants.DISPOSE_ON_CLOSE);
    setSize(350, 250);
    show();
}

// 7. Method that creates the tree nodes.
public void createTreeNodes() {
    // 8. Root node (col0 (col-zero) or root) of the tree.
    root = new DefaultMutableTreeNode("C:\\");

    // 9. Create the nodes in column 1.
    //    and add them to the root
    DefaultMutableTreeNode col11 =
        new DefaultMutableTreeNode("JavaProg");
    root.add(col11);

    // 10. Create the nodes in column 2.
    DefaultMutableTreeNode col21 =
        new DefaultMutableTreeNode("Swing");

    // 11. Add the node to the node 2 in column 2.
    col11.add(col21);

    // 12. Create the nodes in column 3.
    DefaultMutableTreeNode col31 =
        new DefaultMutableTreeNode("JComponent.html");
    DefaultMutableTreeNode col32 =
        new DefaultMutableTreeNode("JButton.html");
    DefaultMutableTreeNode col33 =
        new DefaultMutableTreeNode("JLabel.html");
```

continues

Listing 16.3   continued

```
      // 13. Add the nodes to the node called Swing.
      col21.add(col31);
      col21.add(col32);
      col21.add(col33);
  }

  // 14. Define the tree selection listener.
  class SelectionListener implements TreeSelectionListener {
      URL url;

      // 15. Method that needs to be implemented.
      public void valueChanged(TreeSelectionEvent se) {
          // Obtain the source.
          JTree tree = (JTree) se.getSource();
          // Obtain the selected node.
          DefaultMutableTreeNode selectedNode =
              (DefaultMutableTreeNode)
                  tree.getLastSelectedPathComponent();
          // Obtain the selected node name.
          String selectedNodeName = selectedNode.toString();

          // If the node is a leaf, obtain its URL string.
          if (selectedNode.isLeaf()) {
          String urlString = "file:" +
                             System.getProperty("user.dir") +
                             System.getProperty("file.separator") +
                             selectedNodeName;
          System.out.println(urlString);

          try {
              // Create URL object.
              url = new URL(urlString);
          } catch(MalformedURLException urlex) {
              System.out.println(ìMarlformed URL Exception.î);
          }

          try {
              // Display the resource at the specified URL.
              editorPane.setPage(url);
          } catch(IOException ex) {
              System.out.println("The selected file was not found.");
              System.out.println(ex);
          }
          }
      }
  }
  // 16. Event handler for window closing.
  class WindowEventHandler extends WindowAdapter {
```

```
        public void windowClosing(WindowEvent evt) {
            System.exit(0);
        }
    }
    // 17. The main method.
    public static void main(String[] args) {
        TTreeSelectionEvent frame = new TTreeSelectionEvent();
    }
}
```

Code Details

In Listing 16.3, a Swing frame called TTreeSelectionEvent is defined. Inside the constructor of the frame, snippet-1 gets the handle to the content pane of the frame and
executes the method createTreeNodes(). The code details of this method are given in
the method shown in snippet-7.

Snippet-2 creates the tree object passing the root of the node system. The tree is also
configured to the SINGLE_TREE_SELECTION mode. The method getSelectionModel()
returns the current selection model whose configuration can be changed. The method
setSelectionMode() assigns the new selection mode. Next, a tree node selection listener is registered with the tree object by using the method
addTreeSelectionListener().

Snippet-3 creates a scroll pane and adds the tree object. It also creates an editor pane
to be added to another scroll pane. Next, both the scroll panes are added to a split.
Snippet-4 shows the statement to attach the split pane to the content pane. Snippets 5
and 6 show the code to add a frame-closing listener, and to configure the frame.

Snippets 7–13 define the method createTreeNodes(), which is already invoked in
snippet-1. This method creates a set of node objects and arranges them to form the node
system of the tree.

Snippet-14 defines the node selection listener of the tree that implements the interface
TreeSelectionListener by providing the code for the interface method
valueChanged(). The code inside the method valueChanged() displays the selected
file in the editor pane component that is created in snippet-3. Snippet-16 shows the
class to handle closing of the frame. Snippet-17 is the main method to start the program.

Rendering Tree Node Cells

Each of the tree nodes is associated with a cell to display a text label describing the
node and an image icon. The image icon indicates whether the node is a leaf or a non-
leaf. If it is a non-leaf node, the icon indicates its state, such as whether it is opened or
closed.

By default, Swing trees use an implementation of the interface TreeCellRenderer to
achieve the rendering features of node cells. The default implementation is the class

DefaultTreeCellRenderer. TreeCellRenderer and DefaultTreeCellRenderer are stored in the package javax.swing.tree.

To customize the rendering of node cells of a tree component, the functionality supported in the class DefaultTreeCellRenderer should usually be sufficient. The interface TreeCellRenderer contains the following method:

```
public Component getTreeCellRendererComponent(JTree tree,
                                              Object value,
                                              boolean selected,
                                              boolean expanded,
                                              boolean leaf,
                                              int row,
                                              boolean hasFocus)
```

In addition to implementing this method, the class DefaultTreeCellRenderer supports a number of "set" and "get" methods. Some of the "set" methods will be demonstrated in Listing 16.4.

TIP

The class DefaultTreeCellRenderer supports the "set" methods to customize the icons, text, background, and so on of the tree nodes. You can use these methods at the beginning instead of implementing the TreeCellRenderer interface.

Although the "set" methods are sufficient in many circumstances, there may be times when the methods given in the class DefaultTreeCellRenderer don't meet your requirements. In such situations, you need to create a class that implements the method from the interface TreeCellRenderer. An object of the implementation class can be assigned to the tree object by invoking the method setCellRenderer (TreeCellRenderer renderer) on the tree object.

Node Cell Rendering Code Example

Listing 16.4 demonstrates how to customize the rendering of node cells in a Swing tree. The program is an applet that utilizes the "set" methods supported in the class DefaultTreeCellRenderer. Thus, you initially need to get a reference to the default renderer of the tree component. The program shows how to replace the icons of node cells to those of interest, change the text color of node labels, change the background colors, and so on. The output of the program is shown in Figure 16.5.

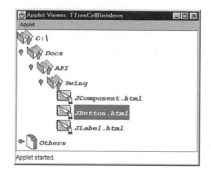

Figure 16.5

Swing applet displaying nodes with custom icons and labels.

Listing 16.4   DefaultTreeCellRenderer Example (TTreeCellRenderer.java)

```
// Demonstrates how to customize the display of
// the tree nodes (or leaves).

/*
 * <Applet code = TTreeCellRenderer width = 350 height = 300>
 * </Applet>
 */

import javax.swing.*;
import javax.swing.tree.*;
import java.awt.*;
import java.awt.event.*;

public class TTreeCellRenderer extends JApplet {
    Container container;

    public void init() {
        // 1. Get the handle on applet's content pane.
        container = this.getContentPane();

        // 2. Root node (col0 or root) of the tree.
        DefaultMutableTreeNode root =
            new DefaultMutableTreeNode("C:\\");

        // 3. Create the nodes in column 1.
        DefaultMutableTreeNode col11 =
            new DefaultMutableTreeNode("Docs");

        DefaultMutableTreeNode col12 =
            new DefaultMutableTreeNode("Others");
```

continues

Listing 16.4   continued

```
// 4. Add the nodes to the root.
root.add(col11);
root.add(col12);

// 5. Create the nodes in column 2.
DefaultMutableTreeNode col21 =
    new DefaultMutableTreeNode("API");

DefaultMutableTreeNode col22 =
    new DefaultMutableTreeNode("Bla...");

// 6. Add these nodes to node 1 in column 1.
col11.add(col21);
col12.add(col22);

// 7. Create the nodes in column 3.
DefaultMutableTreeNode col31 =
    new DefaultMutableTreeNode("Swing");

// 8. Add the node to node 2 in column 2.
col21.add(col31);

// 9. Create the nodes in column 4.
DefaultMutableTreeNode col41 =
    new DefaultMutableTreeNode("JComponent.html");
DefaultMutableTreeNode col42 =
    new DefaultMutableTreeNode("JButton.html");
DefaultMutableTreeNode col43 =
    new DefaultMutableTreeNode("JLabel.html");

// 10. Add the nodes to the node called Swing.
col31.add(col41);
col31.add(col42);
col31.add(col43);

// 11. Attach the root (of nodes) to the tree object.
JTree tree = new JTree(root);

// 12. Get the reference to the existing (default) renderer.
DefaultTreeCellRenderer renderer =
    (DefaultTreeCellRenderer) tree.getCellRenderer();

// 13. Prepare the cell height for the new icons.
tree.setRowHeight(30); // 30 pixels

// 14. Attach the new icons for the leaves nodes when opened,
// and nodes when closed.
```

```
        renderer.setLeafIcon(new ImageIcon("leafIcon.gif"));
        renderer.setOpenIcon(new ImageIcon("fileOpen.gif"));
        renderer.setClosedIcon(new ImageIcon("fileClosed.gif"));

        // 15. Customize the text colors.
        renderer.setFont(new Font("Monospaced", // font name
                                   Font.BOLD|Font.ITALIC, // font type
                                   15)); // Font size.
        renderer.setTextNonSelectionColor(Color.blue);
        renderer.setTextSelectionColor(Color.white);

        // 16. Customize the background of the tree node-cells.
        renderer.setBackgroundNonSelectionColor(Color.white);
        renderer.setBackgroundSelectionColor(Color.gray);
        renderer.setBorderSelectionColor(Color.lightGray);

        // 17. Finally, add the tree to a scroll pane and the scroll pane
        // to the container.
        JScrollPane scrollPane = new JScrollPane(tree);
        container.add(scrollPane);
    }
}
```

Code Details

Inside the init() method of the applet, snippet-1 initializes a reference to the applet's content pane. Snippets 2–11 show the code to create a tree from its nodes (also see Listing 16.1). Snippet-12 is the code statement to obtain a reference to the default tree cell renderer. The method getCellRenderer() returns the renderer of interface type TreeCellRenderer that must be cast into the class type DefaultTreeCellRenderer. This will enable you to use the "set" methods from this class. Snippet-13 prepares the height of the node cell to accommodate the new icons that are slightly larger in size than the default ones.

Snippet-14 shows the code to customize the icons used for the leaves and the nodes that are not leaves. The method setLeafIcon() assigns the specified icon to the cell renderer. The other methods, setOpenIcon() and setClosedIcon(), prescribe the icons for the open and closed states of the non-leaf nodes.

Snippet-15 customizes the font and colors of the text labels in the node cells. The method setFont() assigns the prescribed font to the text label. The next two methods prescribe the color of text when the node is in deselected and selected states.

Snippet-16 customizes the background of the tree node cells for different states of the node, such as selected or deselected. The method setBorderSelectionColor() assigns a new color to the border of the node cells. Notice that in snippets 14–16, you are basically customizing the rendering of node cells by using the reference to the default cell renderer. So the default cell renderer no longer contains the default settings; that is, it has been customized. Finally, snippet-17 adds the tree to a scroll pane that is added to the content pane of the applet.

Editable Tree Nodes

Swing trees support the modification of data items (views) by allowing the user to edit an item name. To deal with editing a tree cell, the Swing library introduces a design level interface called `TreeCellEditor`. This interface represents the abstract model of the cell editor of a tree node. The class `DefaultTreeCellEditor` implements this interface to provide the default model for the cell editor. There is only one method in the interface `TreeCellEditor`:

```
public Component getTreeCellEditorComponent(JTree tree,
                                            Object value,
                                            boolean isSelected,
                                            boolean expanded,
                                            boolean leaf,
                                            int row)
```

To make a tree node editable, you need to invoke the method `setEditable()` on the tree object with its argument value `true`. To activate the text field to perform editing, you have to triple-click the mouse, or double-click it with a pause in between, on a node cell. After the editing is completed, you can press Enter to confirm editing. Note that the tree model fires the event `TreeModelEvent` when the data item has been modified.

In Listing 16.1, the tree component can be made editable simply by adding the following statement in snippet-11:

```
JTree tree = new JTree(root);
tree.setEditable(true);
```

Figure 16.6 shows the output of the program in Listing 16.1 with a node cell activated.

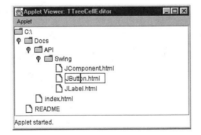

Figure 16.6

Applet displaying a node in the editable state.

The default editor of the tree cell called `DefaultTreeCellEditor` contains sufficient methods to configure the editor as required. For most practical purposes this much functionality should be enough. You can get a reference to the default tree cell editor by invoking the method `getCellEditor()` on the tree object. This method retrieves the cell editor of interface type `TreeCellEditor` that needs to be cast to make the editor class type `DefaultTreeCellEditor`. In case the customization using the default tree cell editor is not enough, you have to implement the interface `TreeCellEditor` on your own to meet the requirements.

CHAPTER 17

Timers and Progress Indicators

Programs often need to perform tasks that involve the periodic execution of certain operations. These tasks are handled in separate threads to allow other processes to be executed simultaneously. For example, to perform an animation, you need to periodically display images at a certain rate and perhaps in a separate thread. The Swing timer encapsulates these functions; it is basically a software device that triggers an action at the specified rate. Timers also use separate threads in the background to execute the task.

This chapter also covers progress bars, progress monitors, and progress monitor input streams. Progress bars are used to indicate the progress of an operation, particularly when the operation is time consuming or the user might think the system has stalled while the operation is still in progress. Progress monitors in Swing pop up a progress dialog box to display the progress of the given operation through a progress bar. The progress monitor input streams are meant for monitoring the progress of reading from the input stream. If the given task takes a certain time before completion, a progress dialog box will pop up to inform the user. In the sections to come, all these topics are discussed and demonstrated using suitable example programs.

Timers

The Swing timer is a software object that is capable of triggering an action to occur at a prescribed rate. The control rate at which the action is performed is specified by the "delay" of the timer. The delay represents the time period, in milliseconds, between two successive actions.

Swing timers are represented by the class Timer, which is a subclass of java.lang.Object. Timers periodically trigger events of type ActionEvent that are listened to by its target listener. The listener class must implement the interface ActionListener and enclose the execution code inside the method actionPerformed(). The target listener is registered with the timer through its constructor.

To use a timer in a program, create a timer object and execute its start() method. The start() method makes the timer fire events in a separate thread and at the specified delay. You can also make the timer fire the event only once by setting the method setRepeats() to false. At any instant, you can stop or restart the timer by invoking the respective methods stop() and restart(). Figure 17.1 depicts the functioning of a timer that periodically executes an action with an initial delay and event delay.

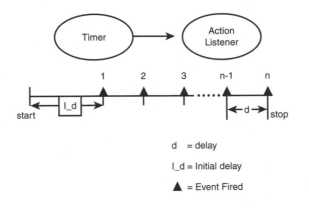

Figure 17.1

The functioning of the Swing timer.

It is possible that the system may become too busy executing the action code inside the method actionPerformed(). If the timer delay is not set sufficiently high, the events will be queued up. When this happens, once the execution of the current action code is complete, the queued up events are executed without the prescribed delay, meaning they are all fired one right after the other. To avoid this situation, Swing timer objects are set by default to coalesce the action code. Coalescing preserves the specified delay between the firing of events. To disable coalescing, call the method setCoalesce() with the Boolean value false.

Timer Constructor

The Swing timer comes with only one constructor, which requires you to specify the delay and the action listener. The action listener implements the interface ActionListener. The following is the constructor from the Timer class:

```
public Timer (int delay, ActionListener listener)
```

Timer Code Example

Listing 17.1 is an applet that displays the label "Swing can flash!" You will find some control buttons that will start, restart, or stop the flashing in different colors of the text label. There is also a toggle button that can be operated to turn off or turn on coalescing. Note that the coalescing is in effect by default. You will also find sliders to change the initial delay and the timer delay to fire events. The output from this program is shown in Figure 17.2.

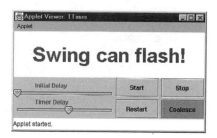

Figure 17.2

An applet demonstrating the Swing timer.

Listing 17.1   Timer (TTimer.java)

```
/*
 * <Applet code=TTimer width=400 height=200>
 * </Applet>
 */

import java.awt.*;
import java.awt.event.*;
import javax.swing.event.*;
import javax.swing.border.*;
import javax.swing.*;

public class TTimer extends JApplet {
    Container container = null;
    Timer timer = null;
    JLabel label = null;
```

continues

Listing 17.1 continued

```
JSlider slider1 = null;
JSlider slider2 = null;
Color[] color = {Color.blue, Color.green, Color.red,
                 Color.yellow, Color.lightGray};

public void init() {
    // 1. Get the handle on the applet's content pane.
    container = this.getContentPane();

    // 2. Create a label and attach it to the applet.
    label = new JLabel("Swing can flash!", JLabel.CENTER);
    label.setBackground(Color.white);
    label.setFont(new Font("Dialog", Font.BOLD, 40));
    label.setOpaque(true);
    container.add(label);

    // 3. Create a horizontal box and attach it at the
    // bottom portion of the content pane.
    Box box = Box.createHorizontalBox();
    container.add(box, BorderLayout.SOUTH);

    // 4. Create a vertical box and add it to the horizontal box.
    Box vbox1 = Box.createVerticalBox();
    box.add(vbox1);

    // 5. Create labels and sliders and attach them to
    // a vertical box.
    JLabel initDelay = new JLabel("Initial Delay", JLabel.CENTER);
    initDelay.setPreferredSize(new Dimension(200, 25));
    vbox1.add(initDelay);
    slider1 = new JSlider(JSlider.HORIZONTAL, 0, 60000, 0);
    slider1.addChangeListener(new SliderListener());
    vbox1.add(slider1);
    JLabel delay = new JLabel("Timer Delay", JLabel.CENTER);
    delay.setPreferredSize(new Dimension(200, 25));
    vbox1.add(delay);
    slider2 = new JSlider(JSlider.HORIZONTAL, 0, 2000, 1000);
    slider2.addChangeListener(new SliderListener());
    vbox1.add(slider2);

    // 6. Create another vertical box and add it to the
    // horizontal box.
    Box vbox2 = Box.createVerticalBox();
    box.add(vbox2);

    // 7. Create a Swing panel with grid layout and add it to
    // the vertical box created in Snippet 6.
```

```
    JPanel panel = new JPanel();
    panel.setLayout(new GridLayout(2,2,5,5));
    vbox2.add(panel);

    // 8. Create Start, Stop, and Restart buttons, and add them
    // to the panel.
    String[] buttonLabels = {"Start", "Stop", "Restart"};
    for (int i=0; i<buttonLabels.length; i++) {
        JButton button = new JButton(buttonLabels[i]);
        button.addActionListener(new ButtonListener());
        panel.add(button);
    }

    // 9. Add a toggle button to the panel.
    JToggleButton toggleButton = new JToggleButton("Coalesce");
    toggleButton.setSelected(true); // since coalesced by default
    toggleButton.addActionListener(new ToggleButtonListener());
    panel.add(toggleButton);

    // 10. Create a timer object with prescribed delay and
    // initial delay retrieved from the corresponding
    // slider objects.
    timer = new Timer(slider2.getValue(), new TimerListener());
    timer.setInitialDelay(slider1.getValue()); //initial delay
}

// 11. Listener class that implements the "action code."
class TimerListener implements ActionListener {
    int i;

    public void actionPerformed(ActionEvent e) {
        if (i == color.length) {
            i = 0;
            label.setForeground(color[i]);
        }
        else {
            label.setForeground(color[i]);
        }
        label.repaint();
        i++;
    }
}

// 12. Button listener that is used to start, stop, or
// restart the timer.
class ButtonListener implements ActionListener {
```

continues

Listing 17.1 continued

```
    public void actionPerformed(ActionEvent e) {
        JButton button = (JButton) e.getSource();

        if (button.getText() == "Start") {
            timer.start();
        }
        else if (button.getText() == "Stop") {
            timer.stop();
        }
        else if (button.getText() == "Restart") {
            timer.restart();
        }
    }
}


// 13. Toggle button listener to change coalescing status.
class ToggleButtonListener implements ActionListener {
    public void actionPerformed(ActionEvent e) {
        if (timer.isCoalesce() == false)
            timer.setCoalesce(true);
        else if (timer.isCoalesce() == true)
            timer.setCoalesce(false);
    }
}


// 14. Slider listener to alter the initial delay or
// timer delay.
class SliderListener implements ChangeListener {
    public void stateChanged(ChangeEvent e) {
        JSlider slider = (JSlider) e.getSource();

        if (slider == slider1) {
            timer.setInitialDelay(slider1.getValue());
        }
        else if (slider == slider2) {
            timer.setDelay(slider2.getValue());
        }
    }
}
}
```

Code Details

The applet TTimer declares various components as its data members. The field color is
an array of display colors that are used to produce the flashing effect. Snippet-1 gets
the handle on the applet's content pane. Snippet-2 creates a Swing label and attaches it
to the content pane. This label will be manipulated later by using a timer to display different colors.

Snippets 3–5 use box containers to position the sliders and the respective indicator labels. Similarly, snippets 6–9 use boxes to add Start, Stop, Restart buttons, and the toggle button for coalescing. Snippet-10 creates a timer object that is assigned with the delay value specified to the respective slider. The timer constructor also takes the target listener that implements the code to be executed. Next, the timer has been assigned the initial delay at which the timer starts if the Start button is operated.

Snippets 11–14 are the listener classes for the timer, push buttons, toggle button, and sliders, respectively. Inside the timer listener, the foreground of the label "Swing can flash!" is assigned different colors to produce the flashing effect. This code is enclosed inside the method `actionPerformed()`. Note that you do not need to create any threads to process the flashing effect of the label; the timer object handles this process in a separate thread.

When you press the Start button, the method `start()` from the timer object is invoked. This functionality has been implemented inside the class `ButtonListener`. The `start()` method causes the code inside `actionPerformed()` to be executed. Similarly, the code for the other methods `stop()` and `restart()` has been enclosed inside the button listener. The toggle button listener assigns the coalescing property according to its status. The class `SliderListener` contains the code to adjust the timer delay and the initial delay of the timer.

Progress Bars

Research on man-machine interaction indicates that users are normally dissatisfied with software response times of more than two seconds. If the delay time is significant, users are likely to conclude that the system has stalled. It is a good idea to use progress bars to make users more comfortable while they wait for software to complete time-consuming tasks.

Progress bars in Swing display the progress in processing through an integer value that is bounded within an interval. Progress bars inform the user of progress by displaying the percentage of completion through a color bar rendering and optionally with the display of its numerical value.

NOTE

Progress bars are good for indicating delays of more than five seconds. If the delay is from one to five seconds, you can use a "system busy" pointer.

Swing progress bars are represented by the class `JProgressBar`, which extends the class `JComponent` as shown in Figure 17.3. The class also implements the interface `SwingConstants`. There is no equivalent to this component in AWT. As with Swing sliders, progress bars are defined by the minimum and maximum values and a current value. That is, the data model can be represented by the interface `BoundedRangeModel`. This data model interface is available inside the package `javax.swing`.

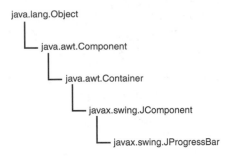

java.lang.Object
    java.awt.Component
        java.awt.Container
            javax.swing.JComponent
                javax.swing.JProgressBar

Figure 17.3

The class hierarchy of JProgressBar.

JProgessBar Constructors

To implement a Swing progress bar in an application, create an object of `JProgressBar` by using any one of its constructors. The constructors may require parameters such as the bounded range data model, orientation, and maximum and minimum values. The following is the list of constructors from the class `JProgressBar`.

```
public JProgressBar()
```

creates a horizontal progress bar with the default values of `0` and `100` for the minimum and maximum values, respectively. These values can be changed by calling the methods `setMinimum()` and `setMaximum()`.

```
public JProgressBar(int orient)
```

creates a progress bar with the specified orientation of `HORIZONTAL` or `VERTICAL`. These attributes are represented by the respective constants from the interface `SwingConstants`. The default values are used for the minimum and maximum values.

```
public JProgressBar(int min, int max)
```

creates a progress bar with the specified minimum and maximum values. By default, the orientation is horizontal.

```
public JProgressBar(int orient, int min, int max)
```

creates a progress bar with the specified orientation and the minimum and maximum values.

```
public JProgressBar(BoundedRangeModel newModel)
```

requires a data model object of type `BoundedRangeModel` that contains the values to specify the range of the progress bar. To view the members of this interface see Appendix A, "JFC Swing Quick Reference." You may want to use the class `DefaultBoundedRangeModel`, which readily implements `BoundedRangeModel` with default settings.

Progress Bar Code Example

Listing 17.2 uses the Swing progress bar to indicate the progress of computation of the specified natural numbers. You can specify the highest number by entering it in a text field displayed over the applet. When you click the Start button, the computation starts and the progress bar instantaneously displays the completion percentage of the computation. The text field in the top-right corner of the applet displays the sum of the natural numbers (see Figure 17.4).

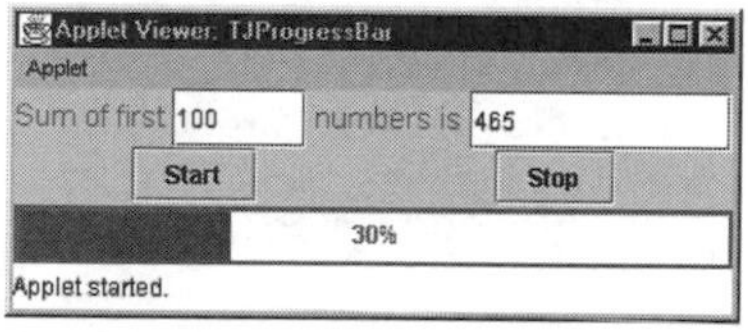

Figure 17.4

An applet displaying a Swing progress bar.

Listing 17.2   A Progress Bar (TJProgressBar.java)

```
/*
 * <Applet code=TJProgressBar width=400 height=100>
 * </Applet>
 */

import javax.swing.*;
import javax.swing.border.*;
import java.awt.*;
import java.awt.event.*;

public class TJProgressBar extends JApplet {
    Container container = null;
    JButton startButton, stopButton;
    JTextField inputTextField, outputTextField;
    JProgressBar pBar = null;
    Timer timer = null;

    static int sum = 0;
    static int counter = 0;

    public void init() {
        // 1. Get the handle on the content pane and
        //      assign the grid layout.
```

continues

Listing 17.2   continued

```
        container = this.getContentPane();
        container.setLayout(new GridLayout(3,1));

        // 2. Add a horizontal box to the container.
        Box hbox1 = Box.createHorizontalBox();
        container.add(hbox1);

        // 3. Add labels and input and output text fields
        //    to the horizontal box.
        hbox1.add(Box.createHorizontalGlue());
        JLabel label1 = new JLabel("Sum of first ", JLabel.LEFT);
        label1.setFont(new Font("Dialog", Font.PLAIN, 15));
        hbox1.add(label1);

        inputTextField = new JTextField("100", 4);
        hbox1.add(inputTextField);

        JLabel label2 = new JLabel(" numbers is ", JLabel.LEFT);
        label2.setFont(new Font("Dialog", Font.PLAIN, 15));
        hbox1.add(label2);

        outputTextField = new JTextField(10);
        hbox1.add(outputTextField);
        hbox1.add(Box.createHorizontalGlue());

        // 4. Add another horizontal box to the container.
        Box hbox2 = Box.createHorizontalBox();
        container.add(hbox2);

        // 5. Add Start and Stop buttons to the container.
        startButton = new JButton("Start");
        startButton.addActionListener(new ButtonListener());
        hbox2.add(Box.createHorizontalGlue());
        hbox2.add(startButton);
        hbox2.add(Box.createHorizontalGlue());
        stopButton = new JButton("Stop");
        stopButton.addActionListener(new ButtonListener());
        hbox2.add(Box.createHorizontalGlue());
        hbox2.add(stopButton);
        hbox2.add(Box.createHorizontalGlue());

        // 6. Create and add a progress bar to the remaining
        //    display area.
        pBar = new JProgressBar();
        pBar.setStringPainted(true);
        Border border = BorderFactory.createLineBorder(Color.red, 2);
        pBar.setBorder(border);
        pBar.setBackground(Color.white);
```

```
        pBar.setForeground(Color.blue);
        pBar.setMinimum(0);

        pBar.setMaximum(Integer.parseInt(inputTextField.getText()));
        container.add(pBar);

        // 7. Create a timer object.
        timer = new Timer(0, new TimerListener());
    }


    // 8. Timer listener that computes the sum of natural numbers,
    //    indicates the computation progress, and displays the result.
    class TimerListener implements ActionListener {
        public void actionPerformed(ActionEvent e) {
            if (Integer.parseInt(inputTextField.getText())> 0){
            counter++;
            sum = sum+counter;
            pBar.setValue(counter);
            outputTextField.setText(Integer.toString(sum));
            }
            else {
                outputTextField.setText("0");
            }

            if (counter >= Integer.parseInt(inputTextField.getText()))
                timer.stop();
        }
    }


    // 9. Button listener that actually starts or stops the
    //    process.
    class ButtonListener implements ActionListener {
        public void actionPerformed(ActionEvent e) {
            JButton button = (JButton) e.getSource();

            if (button.getText() == "Start") {
                outputTextField.setText("");
                if (inputTextField.getText() != " ") {
                    pBar.setMaximum(Integer.parseInt(
                             inputTextField.getText()));
                 sum = 0;
                 counter = 0;
                 timer.start();
                }
            }
            else if (button.getText() == "Stop") {
                timer.stop();
                outputTextField.setText("");
```

continues

Listing 17.2   continued

```
                sum = 0;
                counter = 0;
                pBar.setValue(0);
            }
        }
    }
}
```

Code Details

The applet begins by declaring its content pane, Start and Stop buttons, input and output text fields, a progress bar, and timer as its data members. Inside the init() method, snippet-1 gets a handle on the appletís content pane and assigns the grid layout to the applet. Snippet-2 attaches a horizontal box to the container, to which two labels and input and output text fields are attached in snippet-3.

Snippet-4 adds another horizontal box to the content pane, and snippet-5 attaches the Start and Stop buttons. Snippet-6 creates a progress bar and attaches it at the bottom portion of the applet.

Snippet-8 implements the timer listener. Inside the method actionPerformed(), the sum of the specified natural numbers is computed. The current value of the progress bar is updated and the sum is displayed in the output text field. Snippet-9 shows the button listener that implements the code to start or stop the computation. The snippet also resets the counter and the output text field.

Progress Monitors

To monitor the progress of time-consuming tasks, the Swing library supports a progress monitor. A progress monitor is an object that monitors the progress of the specified task and indicates the state of progress by popping up a dialog box. The dialog box displays a progress bar, which has minimum and maximum values and the current value.

You can use the method setMillisToDecideToPopup() to determine how long the program will take to decide whether or not a progress dialog box should be popped up. The default setting is 500 milliseconds. Once the dialog has popped up, use the method setMillisToPopup() to determine how long the program will wait to begin displaying a status. The longer you have the program wait, the more accurate the status will be once it is displayed. The default setting is 2000 milliseconds.

The Swing progress monitor is represented by the class ProgressMonitor, which extends the class java.lang.Object. The class ProgressMonitor has been stored inside the package javax.swing.

ProgressMonitor Constructor

To create a progress monitor, you can use the ProgressMonitor constructor, which requires information such as the parentComponent to be attached to the progress dialog box, a message to indicate the operation, a note to indicate the state of the operation, and the minimum and maximum bounds of the progress range. Note that the descriptive message indicated by `message` does not change during the progress. The note describing the state of operation can be changed by using the method `setNote()`. The following is the constructor of the class `ProgressMonitor`:

```
public ProgressMonitor(Component parentComponent,
                       Object message,
                       String note,
                       int min,
                       int max)
```

ProgressMonitor Code Example

Listing 17.3 is an applet that computes the sum of natural numbers ending with the specified number. When the Start button is operated, the sum is recursively displayed in the right side text field until it reaches the final sum. A progress bar pops up after the specified time to display the progress in computation (see Figure 17.5). The program essentially uses a progress monitor object to indicate the progress.

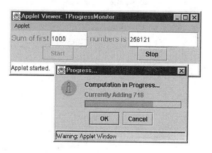

Figure 17.5

An applet displaying the progress monitor.

Listing 17.3   ProgressMonitor (TProgressMonitor.java)

```
/*
 * <Applet code=TProgressMonitor width=400 height=100>
 * </Applet>
 */

import javax.swing.*;
import javax.swing.border.*;
import java.awt.*;
import java.awt.event.*;

public class TProgressMonitor extends JApplet {
    Container container = null;
    JButton startButton, stopButton;
```

continues

Listing 17.3   continued

```
JTextField inputTextField, outputTextField;
ProgressMonitor pMonitor = null;
Timer timer = null;

static int sum = 0;
static int counter = 0;

public void init() {
    // 1. Get the handle on the content pane and
    //      assign the grid layout.
    container = this.getContentPane();
    container.setLayout(new GridLayout(2,1));

    // 2. Add a horizontal box to the container.
    Box hbox1 = Box.createHorizontalBox();
    container.add(hbox1);

    // 3. Add labels and input and output text fields
    //      to the horizontal box.
    hbox1.add(Box.createHorizontalGlue());
    JLabel label1 = new JLabel("Sum of first ", JLabel.LEFT);
    label1.setFont(new Font("Dialog", Font.PLAIN, 15));
    hbox1.add(label1);

    inputTextField = new JTextField("100", 4);
    hbox1.add(inputTextField);

    JLabel label2 = new JLabel(" numbers is ", JLabel.LEFT);
    label2.setFont(new Font("Dialog", Font.PLAIN, 15));
    hbox1.add(label2);

    outputTextField = new JTextField(10);
    hbox1.add(outputTextField);
    hbox1.add(Box.createHorizontalGlue());

    // 4. Add another horizontal box to the container.
    Box hbox2 = Box.createHorizontalBox();
    container.add(hbox2);

    // 5. Add Start and Stop buttons to the container.
    startButton = new JButton("Start");
    startButton.addActionListener(new ButtonListener());
    hbox2.add(Box.createHorizontalGlue());
    hbox2.add(startButton);
    hbox2.add(Box.createHorizontalGlue());
    stopButton = new JButton("Stop");
```

```
        stopButton.addActionListener(new ButtonListener());
        hbox2.add(Box.createHorizontalGlue());
        hbox2.add(stopButton);
        hbox2.add(Box.createHorizontalGlue());

        // 6. Create a timer object.
        timer = new Timer(0, new TimerListener());
    }

    // 7. Timer listener that computes the sum of natural numbers,
    //     indicates the computation progress, and displays the result.
    class TimerListener implements ActionListener {
        public void actionPerformed(ActionEvent e) {
            if (Integer.parseInt(inputTextField.getText())> 0){
            counter++;
            sum = sum+counter;
            pMonitor.setProgress(counter);
            pMonitor.setNote("Currently Adding " + counter);
            outputTextField.setText(Integer.toString(sum));
            }
            else {
                outputTextField.setText("0");
            }

            if (counter >= Integer.parseInt(inputTextField.getText())){
                timer.stop();
                startButton.setEnabled(true);
            }
        }
    }
}

    // 8. Button listener that actually starts or stops the process.
    class ButtonListener implements ActionListener {
        public void actionPerformed(ActionEvent e) {
            JButton button = (JButton) e.getSource();

            if (button.getText() == "Start") {
                startButton.setEnabled(false);
                //9. Create a progress monitor.
                pMonitor = new ProgressMonitor(container,
                                  "Computation in Progress...",
                                  "Note", 0, 100);
                pMonitor.setMillisToPopup(5000);
                outputTextField.setText("");
                if (inputTextField.getText() != " ") {
                    pMonitor.setMaximum(Integer.parseInt(
                                  inputTextField.getText()));
                    sum = 0;
```

continues

Listing 17.3   continued

```
                counter = 0;
                timer.start();
            }
        }
        else if (button.getText() == "Stop") {
            startButton.setEnabled(true);
            timer.stop();
            pMonitor.close();
            outputTextField.setText("");
            sum = 0;
            counter = 0;
        }
    }
  }
}
```

Code Details

Inside the method `init()`, snippet-1 gets a handle on the content pane and prepares for the grid layout with two rows and one column.

Snippet-2 creates a horizontal box and adds it to the container. Snippet-3 creates a couple of labels and input and output text fields and adds them to the horizontal box created in the previous snippet. Snippet-4 creates another horizontal box attached to the container, and snippet-5 adds Start and Stop buttons to the box.

Snippet-6 creates a timer object with no delay. Snippet-7 shows the timer listener to update the sum of natural numbers on each call by the timer object. The method `setProgress()` inside the method `actionPerformed()` updates the current value of the progress bar. The other method, `setNote()`, recursively updates the counter value displayed in the progress dialog box.

Snippet-8 codes what should happen when the Start or Stop button has been chosen. Inside the body of the `if` clause, the progress monitor object is created with the minimum and maximum values of its progress bar. In the next statement, the method `setMillisToPopup()` assigns the time period for the progress monitor to show up after the computation has started. When you click the Stop button, the progress monitor is closed and the computation values are reset.

Progress Monitors for Input Streams

In the Swing library, a separate class called `ProgressMonitorInputStream` has been supported to monitor the progress of reading from an input stream. This class is a kind of monitoring filter and extends from the class `FilterInputStream`, as shown in Figure 17.6. The class is usually applied while an application is reading a file.

The class `ProgressMonitorInputStream` essentially creates a progress monitor dialog box. You can specify when the progress monitor dialog box pops up. The dialog box displays the progress bar indicating the progress of reading the input stream. You do not have to specify the maximum or minimum value of the progress bar, because this information can be figured out by the API from the size of the input resource, such as a file.

Figure 17.6

Class hierarchy of the class ProgressMonitorInputStream.

The progress dialog box contains the buttons displaying the labels OK and Cancel. If you click the OK button, the progress dialog box is closed, but the reading from the input stream continues until completion. If you click the Cancel button, the reading from the input stream is interrupted and an `InterruptedIOException` will be thrown.

NOTE

Like the other input streams, a stream of type `ProgressMonitorInputStream` must also be closed on completion of reading from the specified input stream.

ProgressMonitorInputStream Constructor

To implement a progress monitor input stream filter in your applications, you need to create an object of the class `ProgressMonitorInputStream` by using the following constructor:

```
public ProgressMonitorInputStream(Component parentComponent,
                                  Object message,
                                  InputStream input)
```

This constructor requires arguments such as the descriptive message `parentComponent` to attach the dialog box to be displayed and the input stream object.

ProgressMonitorInputStream Code Example

Listing 17.4 is an application that simply reads a file and writes it on the computer screen. You need to specify the filename, for example `file.txt`, at the command line as in the following:

```
java TProgressMonitorIS <file.txt>
```

The program starts reading the file and, if the reading process takes significant time, a progress monitor dialog box pops up with a progress bar. The time period to pop up can be declared; otherwise, the default time is used. The program uses a frame to serve as the parent for the progress monitor dialog box. When you run this program at the command prompt, the program starts reading the file and displays a progress monitor attached to a frame, as shown in Figure 17.7.

Figure 17.7

An applet displaying the file input progress monitor.

Listing 17.4   ProgressMonitorInputStream (TProgressMonitorIS.java)

```
import javax.swing.*;
import java.awt.*;
import java.awt.event.*;
import java.io.*;

class TProgressMonitorIS {
    static ProgressMonitorInputStream progressInput = null;
    static JFrame frame = null;
    static WindowEventHandler handler = null;

    public static void main(String[] args) {
        // 1. Create a frame and get its content pane.
        frame = new JFrame ("Parent Frame");
        Container container = frame.getContentPane();
        frame.setVisible(true);
        frame.setDefaultCloseOperation(
                    WindowConstants.DISPOSE_ON_CLOSE);
        frame.setSize(350, 200);
        frame.show();

        // 2. Event handler for closing the window.
        handler = new WindowEventHandler();
        frame.addWindowListener(handler);

        // 3. Give the correct usage at the command line.
        //    in case it is needed
```

```
if (args.length != 1) {
    System.out.println("Legal Usage: " +
                "java TProgressMonitorIS <file>");
    System.exit(-1);
}

try {
    // 4. Create a file and file input stream objects.
    File file = new File(args[0]);
    FileInputStream inputStream =  new FileInputStream(file);

    // 5. Create the progress monitor for the input stream.
    progressInput = new ProgressMonitorInputStream(
                        container,
                        "Reading File: " + args[0],
                        inputStream);

    // 6. Get a handle on the progress monitor of the
    // progressInput object, and assign the time periods
    // to decide to pop up and to pop up the dialog box.
    ProgressMonitor monitor =
                progressInput.getProgressMonitor();
    monitor.setMillisToDecideToPopup(0);
    monitor.setMillisToPopup(0);

    // 7. Read the bytes and write on the screen.
    int curByte;
    while((curByte = progressInput.read()) != -1) {
        System.out.print((char) curByte);

        try {
            // 8. Make this thread sleep, if the process
            // is too quick to notice the progress dialog box.
            Thread.sleep(0); // Set this to some value,
                             // say 100, on faster machines
        } catch (InterruptedException ie) {
            System.out.println(
                "Thread Interruption Occurred!");
        }

        // 9. Close the progress input stream filter.
        if(monitor.isCanceled()) {
            progressInput.close();
        }
    }
    10. //Close the progressInputstream.
    progressInput.close();
```

continues

Listing 17.4   continued
```
        } catch (Exception e) {
            System.out.println("....File Reading Interrupted....");
        }
    }
}

// 11. Create the listener class for window closing.
class WindowEventHandler extends WindowAdapter {
    public void windowClosing(WindowEvent evt) {
        System.exit(-1);
    }
}
```

Code Details

Inside the main() method of the application, snippet-1 creates a frame and obtains a handle to its content pane. Snippet-2 registers a listener object (see snippet-11) to close the frame. Snippet-3 gets feedback if the command line syntax is not correct. The code also displays the right syntax to be used.

In snippet-4, a file object and a file input stream object are created. Snippet-5 creates an object of the progress monitor input stream. Note that the constructor requires the object to pop up the parent frame for the progress monitor dialog box. This constructor takes the file input stream as an argument value. In snippet-6, the handle to the progress monitor dialog box is obtained. With this reference, the time periods useful to decide to pop up and to pop up the progress dialog box are assigned. Snippet-7 shows the code to read the bytes from the input stream via the progress monitor. The progress monitor serves as a filter to track the progress of reading the input stream. The code also sends the characters to the computer screen. Snippet-8 shows the code that can be used to control the speed of the current thread to observe the progress dialog box.

Snippet-9 closes the progress monitor input stream if the Cancel button over the progress dialog box is operated. Finally, you need to close the progress monitor input stream, as shown in snippet-10.

APPENDIX A

JFC Swing Quick Reference

This quick reference section has four parts: Appendix A, "JFC Swing Quick Reference," Appendix B, "AWT Event Classes Quick Reference," Appendix C, "Important AWT Classes for Swing," and Appendix D, "Accessibility Quick Reference." Appendix A presents the class hierarchy diagrams and reference material for the classes and interfaces from the Swing packages. However, the details of look-and-feel–specific packages such as javax.swing.plaf.metal, com.sun.java.swing.plaf.motif, and so on have been omitted. For better usability, a short description of each of the interfaces, classes and inner classes has been provided.

How to Use the Quick Reference

Under "Swing Package Details," you will initially find the name of a package followed by its interfaces and classes. Details of packages in the Swing library are presented first, followed by their interface and class details. The classes and interfaces can be accessed by searching alphabetically within a given package.

Quick references covering AWT event classes and important AWT classes are presented in Appendixes B and C. Remember that you need AWT event and layout classes while implementing Swing components. Appendix D presents the quick reference for the Accessibility API included in JFC. To access the classes and interfaces in Appendixes B, C, and D, you can use the same approach detailed in the previous paragraph.

> (**NOTE**
>
> In the class and interface details, if no scope modifier (such as public, protected, or package) is present before a field, constructor or method, you can assume that it is public.

Swing Package Details

The following provides a quick view of the interfaces and classes in the Swing packages.

Package Name: javax.swing

This package contains a set of lightweight Swing components that are platform independent and can be configured to the look-and-feel expected by the user.

Interfaces

Action	MenuElement
BoundedRangeModel	MutableComboBoxModel
ButtonModel	Renderer
CellEditor	RootPaneContainer
ComboBoxEditor	Scrollable
ComboBoxModel	ScrollPaneConstants
DesktopManager	SingleSelectionModel
Icon	SwingConstants
JComboBox.KeySelectionManager	UIDefaults.ActiveValue
ListCellRenderer	UIDefaults.LazyValue
ListModel	WindowConstants
ListSelectionModel	

Classes

AbstractAction	JPanel
AbstractButton	JPasswordField
AbstractListModel	JPopupMenu
BorderFactory	JPopupMenu.Separator
Box	JProgressBar
Box.Filler	JRadioButton
BoxLayout	JRadioButtonMenuItem
ButtonGroup	JRootPane
CellRendererPane	JScrollBar
DebugGraphics	JScrollPane
DefaultBoundedRangeModel	JSeparator
DefaultButtonModel	JSlider

DefaultCellEditor
DefaultComboBoxModel
DefaultDesktopManager
DefaultFocusManager
DefaultListCellRenderer
DefaultListCellRenderer.UIResource
DefaultListModel
DefaultListSelectionModel
DefaultSingleSelectionModel
FocusManager
GrayFilter
ImageIcon
JApplet
JButton
JCheckBox
JCheckBoxMenuItem
JColorChooser
JComboBox
JComponent
JDesktopPane
JDialog
JEditorPane
JFileChooser
JFrame
JInternalFrame
JInternalFrame.JDesktopIcon
JLabel
JLayeredPane
JList
JMenu
JMenuBar
JMenuItem
JOptionPane

JSplitPane
JTabbedPane
JTable
JTextArea
JTextField
JTextPane
JToggleButton
JToggleButton.ToggleButtonModel
JToolBar
JToolBar.Separator
JToolTip
JTree
JTree.DynamicUtilTreeNode
JTree.EmptySelectionModel
JViewport
JWindow
KeyStroke
LookAndFeel
MenuSelectionManager
OverlayLayout
ProgressMonitor
ProgressMonitorInputStream
RepaintManager
ScrollPaneLayout
ScrollPaneLayout.UIResource
SizeRequirements
SwingUtilities
Timer
ToolTipManager
UIDefaults
UIManager
UIManager.LookAndFeelInfo
ViewportLayout

Exception

UnsupportedLookAndFeelException

Package Name: javax.swing.border

This package contains interfaces and classes for drawing sophisticated and impressive borders around Swing components.

Interface

Border

Classes

AbstractBorder	LineBorder
BevelBorder	MatteBorder
CompoundBorder	SoftBevelBorder
EmptyBorder	TitledBorder
EtchedBorder	

Package Name: javax.swing.colorchooser

This package contains interfaces and classes that are used by the JColorChooser component in the javax.swing package.

Interface

ColorSelectionModel

Classes

AbstractColorChooserPanel
ColorChooserComponentFactory
DefaultColorSelectionModel

Package Name: javax.swing.event

This package contains the event interfaces and listener classes for Swing components.

Interfaces

AncestorListener	MenuKeyListener
CaretListener	MenuListener
CellEditorListener	MouseInputListener
ChangeListener	PopupMenuListener
DocumentEvent	TableColumnModelListener
DocumentEvent.ElementChange	TableModelListener
DocumentListener	TreeExpansionListener
HyperlinkListener	TreeModelListener
InternalFrameListener	TreeSelectionListener
ListDataListener	TreeWillExpandListener
ListSelectionListener	UndoableEditListener
MenuDragMouseListener	

Classes

AncestorEvent	MenuEvent
CaretEvent	MenuKeyEvent
ChangeEvent	MouseInputAdapter
DocumentEvent.EventType	PopupMenuEvent
EventListenerList	SwingPropertyChangeSupport
HyperlinkEvent	TableColumnModelEvent
HyperlinkEvent.EventType	TableModelEvent
InternalFrameAdapter	TreeExpansionEvent

```
InternalFrameEvent              TreeModelEvent
ListDataEvent                   TreeSelectionEvent
ListSelectionEvent              UndoableEditEvent
MenuDragMouseEvent
```

Package Name: javax.swing.filechooser

This package contains interfaces and classes used by the JFileChooser component in the javax.swing package.

Classes

```
FileFilter
FileSystemView
FileView
```

Package Name: javax.swing.plaf

This package provides the interfaces and abstract classes that are useful to support pluggable look-and-feel capabilities.

Interface

```
UIResource
```

Classes

```
BorderUIResource
BorderUIResource.BevelBorderUIResource
BorderUIResource.CompoundBorderUIResource
BorderUIResource.EmptyBorderUIResource
BorderUIResource.EtchedBorderUIResource
BorderUIResource.LineBorderUIResource
BorderUIResource.MatteBorderUIResource
BorderUIResource.TitledBorderUIResource
ButtonUI
ColorChooserUI
ColorUIResource
ComboBoxUI
ComponentUI
DesktopIconUI
DesktopPaneU
```

Package Name: javax.swing.plaf.basic

This package provides user interface objects built according to the basic look-and-feel.

Interface

```
ComboPopup
```

Classes

BasicArrowButton
BasicBorders
BasicBorders.ButtonBorder
BasicBorders.FieldBorder
BasicBorders.MarginBorder
BasicBorders.MenuBarBorder
BasicBorders.RadioButtonBorder
BasicBorders.SplitPaneBorder
BasicBorders.ToggleButtonBorder
BasicButtonListener
BasicButtonUI
BasicCheckBoxMenuItemUI
BasicCheckBoxUI
BasicColorChooserUI
BasicComboBoxEditor
BasicComboBoxEditor.UIResource
BasicComboBoxRenderer
BasicComboBoxRenderer.UIResource
BasicComboBoxUI
BasicComboPopup
BasicDesktopIconUI
BasicDesktopPaneUI
BasicDirectoryModel
BasicEditorPaneUI
BasicFileChooserUI
BasicGraphicsUtils
BasicIconFactory
asicInternalFrameTitlePane
BasicInternalFrameUI
BasicLabelUI
BasicListUI
BasicLookAndFeel
BasicMenuBarUI

BasicMenuItemUI
BasicMenuUI
BasicOptionPaneUI
BasicOptionPaneUI.ButtonAreaLayout
BasicPanelUI
BasicPasswordFieldUI
BasicPopupMenuSeparatorUI
BasicPopupMenuUI
BasicProgressBarUI
BasicRadioButtonMenuItemUI
BasicRadioButtonUI
BasicScrollBarUI
BasicScrollPaneUI
BasicSeparatorUI
BasicSliderUI
BasicSplitPaneDivider
BasicSplitPaneUI
BasicTabbedPaneUI
BasicTableHeaderUI
BasicTableUI
BasicTextAreaUI
BasicTextFieldUI
BasicTextPaneUI
BasicTextUI
BasicTextUI.BasicCaret
BasicTextUI.BasicHighlighter
BasicToggleButtonUI
BasicToolBarSeparatorUI
BasicToolBarUI
BasicToolTipUI
BasicTreeUI
BasicViewportUI
DefaultMenuLayoutI

Package Name: javax.swing.plaf.metal

This package contains user interface objects that are built according to the Metal or Java look-and-feel.

Classes

DefaultMetalTheme
MetalBorders
MetalBorders.ButtonBorder
MetalBorders.Flush3DBorder

MetalIconFactory.FolderIcon16
MetalIconFactory.TreeControlIcon
MetalIconFactory.TreeFolderIcon
MetalIconFactory.TreeLeafIcon

```
MetalBorders.InternalFrameBorder        MetalInternalFrameUI
MetalBorders.MenuBarBorder              MetalLabelUI
MetalBorders.MenuItemBorder             MetalLookAndFeel
MetalBorders.PopupMenuBorder            MetalPopupMenuSeparatorUI
MetalBorders.RolloverButtonBorder       MetalProgressBarUI
MetalBorders.ScrollPaneBorder           MetalRadioButtonUI
MetalBorders.TextFieldBorder            MetalScrollBarUI
MetalBorders.ToolBarBorder              MetalScrollButton
MetalButtonUI                           MetalScrollPaneUI
MetalCheckBoxIcon                       MetalSeparatorUI
MetalCheckBoxUI                         MetalSliderUI
MetalComboBoxButton                     MetalSplitPaneUI
MetalComboBoxEditor                     MetalTabbedPaneUI
MetalComboBoxEditor.UIResource          MetalTextFieldUI
MetalComboBoxIcon                       MetalTheme
MetalComboBoxUI                         MetalToggleButtonUI
MetalDesktopIconUI                      MetalToolBarUI
MetalFileChooserUI                      MetalToolTipUI
MetalIconFactory                        MetalTreeUI
MetalIconFactory.FileIcon16
```

Package Name: javax.swing.plaf.multi

This package contains component objects useful for multiplexing look-and-feels by enabling users to combine auxiliary look-and-feels with the default look-and-feel.

Classes

```
MultiButtonUI                           MultiProgressBarUI
MultiColorChooserUI                     MultiScrollBarUI
MultiComboBoxUI                         MultiScrollPaneUI
MultiDesktopIconUI                      MultiSeparatorUI
MultiDesktopPaneUI                      MultiSliderUI
MultiFileChooserUI                      MultiSplitPaneUI
MultiInternalFrameUI                    MultiTabbedPaneUI
MultiLabelUI                            MultiTableHeaderUI
MultiListUI                             MultiTableUI
MultiLookAndFeel                        MultiTextUI
MultiMenuBarUI                          MultiToolBarUI
MultiMenuItemUI                         MultiToolTipUI
MultiOptionPaneUI                       MultiTreeUI
MultiPanelUI                            MultiViewportUI
MultiPopupMenuUI
```

Package Name: javax.swing.table

This package contains interfaces and classes to deal with JTable supported in javax.swing.

Interfaces

TableCellEditor   TableColumnModel
TableCellRenderer   TableModel

Classes

AbstractTableModel   DefaultTableModel
DefaultTableCellRenderer   JTableHeader
DefaultTableCellRenderer.UIResource TableColumn
DefaultTableColumnModel

Package Name: javax.swing.text

This package contains the interfaces and classes that deal with Swing text components.

Interfaces

AbstractDocument.AttributeContext   Highlighter.Highlight
AbstractDocument.Content   Highlighter.HighlightPainter
AttributeSet   Keymap
AttributeSet.CharacterAttribute   MutableAttributeSet
AttributeSet.ColorAttribute   Position
AttributeSet.FontAttribute   Style
AttributeSet.ParagraphAttribute   StyledDocument
Caret   TabableView
Document   TabExpander
Element   ViewFactory
Highlighter

Classes

AbstractDocument
AbstractDocument.ElementEdit
AbstractWriter
BoxView
ComponentView
CompositeView
DefaultCaret
DefaultEditorKit
DefaultEditorKit.BeepAction
DefaultEditorKit.CopyAction
DefaultEditorKit.CutAction
DefaultEditorKit.DefaultKeyTypedAction
DefaultEditorKit.InsertBreakAction
DefaultEditorKit.InsertContentAction

```
DefaultEditorKit.InsertTabAction
DefaultEditorKit.PasteAction
DefaultHighlighter
DefaultHighlighter.DefaultHighlightPainter
DefaultStyledDocument
DefaultStyledDocument.AttributeUndoableEdit
DefaultStyledDocument.ElementSpec
DefaultTextUI
EditorKit
ElementIterator
FieldView
GapContent
IconView
JTextComponent
JTextComponent.KeyBinding
LabelView
LabelView2D
LayeredHighlighter
LayeredHighlighter.LayerPainter
ParagraphView
PasswordView
PlainDocument
PlainView
Position.Bias
Segment
SimpleAttributeSet
StringContent
StyleConstants
StyleConstants.CharacterConstants
StyleConstants.ColorConstants
StyleConstants.FontConstants
StyleConstants.ParagraphConstants
StyleContext
StyledEditorKit
StyledEditorKit.AlignmentAction
StyledEditorKit.BoldAction
StyledEditorKit.FontFamilyAction
StyledEditorKit.FontSizeAction
StyledEditorKit.ForegroundAction
StyledEditorKit.ItalicAction
StyledEditorKit.StyledTextAction
StyledEditorKit.UnderlineAction
TableView
TabSet
TabStop
```

```
TextAction
Utilities
View
WrappedPlainView
```

Exceptions

```
BadLocationException
ChangedCharSetException
```

Package Name: javax.swing.text.html

This package contains the classes to create HTML text editors.

Classes

BlockView	HTMLEditorKit.LinkController
CSS	HTMLEditorKit.Parser
CSS.Attribute	HTMLEditorKit.ParserCallback
FormView	HTMLFrameHyperlinkEvent
HTML	HTMLWriter
HTML.Attribute	InlineView
HTML.Tag	ListView
HTML.UnknownTag	MinimalHTMLWriter
HTMLDocument	ObjectView
HTMLDocument.Iterator	Option
HTMLEditorKit	ParagraphView
HTMLEditorKit.HTMLFactory	StyleSheet
HTMLEditorKit.HTMLTextAction	StyleSheet.BoxPainter
HTMLEditorKit.InsertHTMLTextAction	StyleSheet.ListPainter

Package Name: javax.swing.tree

This package provides interfaces and classes to deal with JTree from the javax.swing package.

Interfaces

MutableTreeNode	TreeModel
RowMapper	TreeNode
TreeCellEditor	TreeSelectionModel
TreeCellRenderer	

Classes

AbstractLayoutCache	DefaultTreeModel
AbstractLayoutCache.NodeDimensions	DefaultTreeSelectionModel
DefaultMutableTreeNode	FixedHeightLayoutCache
DefaultTreeCellEditor	TreePath
DefaultTreeCellRenderer	VariableHeightLayoutCache

Exception

```
ExpandVetoException
```

Package Name: javax.swing.undo

This package supports undo/redo capabilities in an application such as a text editor.

Interfaces

```
StateEditable
UndoableEdit
```

Classes

```
AbstractUndoableEdit          UndoableEditSupport
CompoundEdit                  UndoManager
StateEdit
```

Exceptions

```
CannotRedoException
CannotUndoException
```

Class and Interface Details

This section gives the details of the following packages:

```
javax.swing
javax.swing.border
javax.swing.colorchooser
javax.swing.event
javax.swing.filechooser
javax.swing.plaf
javax.swing.table
javax.swing.text
javax.swing.text.html
javax.swing.tree
javax.swing.undo
```

javax.swing

Interface Action

```
public abstract interface Action
                  extends ActionListener
```

This interface allows simplified implementation of the common functionality executed by multiple GUI controls such as buttons on a toolbar, menu items from regular and pop-up menus, and so on.

Fields

static String	**DEFAULT**
static String	**LONG_DESCRIPTION**
static String	**NAME**
static String	**SHORT_DESCRIPTION**
static String	**SMALL_ICON**

Methods

void	**addPropertyChangeListener** (PropertyChangeListener listener)
Object	**getValue**(String key)
boolean	**isEnabled**()
void	**putValue**(String key, Object value)
void	**removePropertyChangeListener** (PropertyChangeListener listener)
void	**setEnabled**(boolean b)

Interface BoundedRangeModel

public abstract interface **BoundedRangeModel**

This interface defines the data model for components such as sliders, scrollbars, progress bars, and so on whose minimum and maximum (range) values are bounded.

Methods

void	**addChangeListener**(ChangeListener x)
int	**getExtent**()
int	**getMaximum**()
int	**getMinimum**()
int	**getValue**()
boolean	**getValueIsAdjusting**()
void	**removeChangeListener**(ChangeListener x)
void	**setExtent**(int newExtent)
void	**setMaximum**(int newMaximum)
void	**setMinimum**(int newMinimum)
void	**setRangeProperties**(int value, int extent, int min, int max, boolean adjusting)
void	**setValue**(int newValue)
void	**setValueIsAdjusting**(boolean b)

Interface ButtonModel

public abstract interface **ButtonModel**
                          extends ItemSelectable

This interface defines the design-level model to manipulate various states of Swing buttons.

Methods

```
void     addActionListener(ActionListener l)
void     addChangeListener(ChangeListener l)
void     addItemListener(ItemListener l)
String   getActionCommand()
int      getMnemonic()
boolean  isArmed()
boolean  isEnabled()
boolean  isPressed()
boolean  isRollover()
boolean  isSelected()
void     removeActionListener(ActionListener l)
void     removeChangeListener(ChangeListener l)
void     removeItemListener(ItemListener l)
void     setActionCommand(String s)
void     setArmed(boolean b)
void     setEnabled(boolean b)
void     setGroup(ButtonGroup group)
void     setMnemonic(int akey)
void     setPressed(boolean b)
void     setRollover(boolean b)
void     setSelected(boolean b)
```

Interface CellEditor

```
public abstract interface CellEditor
```

This is a design-level interface that defines the functionality of a cell editor. The cell editors are used by cells of components such as lists, tables, and so on to allow editing.

Methods

```
void     addCellEditorListener(CellEditorListener l)
void     cancelCellEditing()
Object   getCellEditorValue()
boolean  isCellEditable(EventObject anEvent)
void     removeCellEditorListener(CellEditorListener l)
boolean  shouldSelectCell(EventObject anEvent)
boolean  stopCellEditing()
```

Interface ComboBoxEditor

```
public abstract interface ComboBoxEditor
```

This interface defines the methods for the editor that is specifically used by Swing combo boxes.

Methods

```
void        addActionListener(ActionListener l)
Component   getEditorComponent()
```

```
Object      getItem()
void        removeActionListener(ActionListener l)
void        selectAll()
void        setItem(Object anObject)
```

Interface ComboBoxModel

```
public abstract interface ComboBoxModel
                        extends ListModel
```

This interface declares the abstract methods to assign and retrieve the selected data item in a combo box. This functionality is required for combo boxes in addition to that of the list model they use.

Methods

```
Object      getSelectedItem()
void        setSelectedItem(Object anItem)
```

Interface DesktopManager

```
public abstract interface DesktopManager
```

This interface defines the design-level functions of a desktop manager. A desktop manager handles look-and-feel attributes, including closing, resizing, and so on, for desktop panes and internal frames.

Methods

```
void        activateFrame(JInternalFrame f)
void        beginDraggingFrame(JComponent f)
void        beginResizingFrame(JComponent f, int direction)
void        closeFrame(JInternalFrame f)
void        deactivateFrame(JInternalFrame f)
void        deiconifyFrame(JInternalFrame f)
void        dragFrame(JComponent f, int newX, int newY)
void        endDraggingFrame(JComponent f)
void        endResizingFrame(JComponent f)
void        iconifyFrame(JInternalFrame f)
void        maximizeFrame(JInternalFrame f)
void        minimizeFrame(JInternalFrame f)
void        openFrame(JInternalFrame f)
void        resizeFrame(JComponent f, int newX, int newY, int
            newWidth, int newHeight)
void        setBoundsForFrame(JComponent f, int newX, int newY, int
            newWidth, int newHeight)
```

Interface Icon

```
public abstract interface Icon
```

This interface defines the methods for an icon that is commonly used to decorate a Swing component.

Methods

```
int      getIconHeight()
int      getIconWidth()
void     paintIcon(Component c, Graphics g, int x, int y)
```

Interface JComboBox.KeySelectionManager

```
public abstract static interface JComboBox.KeySelectionManager
```

This interface defines a key selection manager to be used by a combo box. The interface contains a method that retrieves the index of the row from the combo box items, if a key and the combo box model are supplied.

Method

```
int      selectionForKey(char aKey, ComboBoxModel aModel)
```

Interface ListCellRenderer

```
public abstract interface ListCellRenderer
```

This interface defines a method to obtain the component that renders the cells of a Swing list with the specified icons and labels. The component functions similarly to a rubber stamp.

Method

```
Component   getListCellRendererComponent(JList list, Object value,
            int index, boolean isSelected, boolean cellHasFocus)
```

Interface ListModel

```
public abstract interface ListModel
```

This interface defines the model for the data that is displayed in a Swing list.

Methods

```
void     addListDataListener(ListDataListener l)
Object   getElementAt(int index)
int      getSize()
void     removeListDataListener(ListDataListener l)
```

Interface ListSelectionModel

```
public abstract interface ListSelectionModel
```

This interface defines the model that stores the selection data for a list component, such as the type of selection, the related indices of selection, and so on.

Fields

```
static int      MULTIPLE_INTERVAL_SELECTION
static int      SINGLE_INTERVAL_SELECTION
static int      SINGLE_SELECTION
```

Methods

```
void        addListSelectionListener(ListSelectionListener x)
void        addSelectionInterval(int index0, int index1)
void        clearSelection()
int         getAnchorSelectionIndex()
int         getLeadSelectionIndex()
int         getMaxSelectionIndex()
int         getMinSelectionIndex()
int         getSelectionMode()
boolean     getValueIsAdjusting()
void        insertIndexInterval(int index, int length, boolean
            before)
boolean     isSelectedIndex(int index)
boolean     isSelectionEmpty()
void        removeIndexInterval(int index0, int index1)
void        removeListSelectionListener(ListSelectionListener x)
void        removeSelectionInterval(int index0, int index1)
void        setAnchorSelectionIndex(int index)
void        setLeadSelectionIndex(int index)
void        setSelectionInterval(int index0, int index1)
void        setSelectionMode(int selectionMode)
void        setValueIsAdjusting(boolean valueIsAdjusting)
```

Interface MenuElement

```
public abstract interface MenuElement
```

This interface is used to move through menus in menu hierarchies and select the items. Components or menu items that are added to a menu must implement this interface.

Methods

```
Component       getComponent()
MenuElement[]   getSubElements()
void            menuSelectionChanged(boolean isIncluded)
void            processKeyEvent(KeyEvent event, MenuElement[]
                path, MenuSelectionManager manager)
void            processMouseEvent(MouseEvent event,
                MenuElement[] path, MenuSelectionManager
                manager)
```

Interface MutableComboBoxModel

```
public abstract interface MutableComboBoxModel
                    extends ComboBoxModel
```

This interface defines a combo box model that can be subject to changes. The interface is simply an extension of the regular combo box model.

Methods

```
void      addElement(Object obj)
void      insertElementAt(Object obj, int index)
void      removeElement(Object obj)
void      removeElementAt(int index)
```

Interface Renderer

```
public abstract interface Renderer
```

This interface defines a renderer that is used to paint the values or labels over a Swing component.

Methods

```
Component    getComponent()
void         setValue(Object aValue, boolean isSelected)
```

Interface RootPaneContainer

```
public abstract interface RootPaneContainer
```

This interface is implemented by components that need to provide access methods for a content pane, glass pane, layered pane, and root pane. You will observe containers such as JApplet, JFrame, JInternalFrame, JDialog, and JWindow implementing this interface.

Methods

```
Container      getContentPane()
Component      getGlassPane()
JLayeredPane   getLayeredPane()
JRootPane      getRootPane()
void           setContentPane(Container contentPane)
void           setGlassPane(Component glassPane)
void           setLayeredPane(JLayeredPane layeredPane)
```

Interface Scrollable

```
public abstract interface Scrollable
```

This interface defines the methods to retrieve the data of various scrollable attributes such as viewport dimensions and increment values of scrolling for a container or component that supports scrolling.

Methods

```
Dimension    getPreferredScrollableViewportSize()
int          getScrollableBlockIncrement(Rectangle visibleRect,
             int orientation, int direction)
```

```
boolean     getScrollableTracksViewportHeight()
boolean     getScrollableTracksViewportWidth()
int         getScrollableUnitIncrement(Rectangle visibleRect,
            int orientation, int direction)
```

Interface ScrollPaneConstants

```
public abstract interface ScrollPaneConstants
```

This interface defines the constants that are commonly used by components that support scrolling.

Fields

```
static String     COLUMN_HEADER
static String     HORIZONTAL_SCROLLBAR
static int        HORIZONTAL_SCROLLBAR_ALWAYS
static int        HORIZONTAL_SCROLLBAR_AS_NEEDED
static int        HORIZONTAL_SCROLLBAR_NEVER
static String     HORIZONTAL_SCROLLBAR_POLICY
static String     LOWER_LEFT_CORNER
static String     LOWER_RIGHT_CORNER
static String     ROW_HEADER
static String     UPPER_LEFT_CORNER
static String     UPPER_RIGHT_CORNER
static String     VERTICAL_SCROLLBAR
static int        VERTICAL_SCROLLBAR_ALWAYS
static int        VERTICAL_SCROLLBAR_AS_NEEDED
static int        VERTICAL_SCROLLBAR_NEVER
static String     VERTICAL_SCROLLBAR_POLICY
static String     VIEWPORT
```

Interface SingleSelectionModel

```
public abstract interface SingleSelectionModel
```

This interface defines the selection model for selecting a single item from a Swing component.

Methods

```
void        addChangeListener(ChangeListener listener)
void        clearSelection()
int         getSelectedIndex()
boolean     isSelected()
void        removeChangeListener(ChangeListener listener)
void        setSelectedIndex(int index)
```

Interface SwingConstants

```
public abstract interface SwingConstants
```

This interface defines a list of constants that are commonly required to position and align a Swing component in its display area.

Fields

static int	**BOTTOM**
static int	**CENTER**
static int	**EAST**
static int	**HORIZONTAL**
static int	**LEADING**
static int	**LEFT**
static int	**NORTH**
static int	**NORTH_EAST**
static int	**NORTH_WEST**
static int	**RIGHT**
static int	**SOUTH**
static int	**SOUTH_EAST**
static int	**SOUTH_WEST**
static int	**TOP**
static int	**TRAILING**
static int	**VERTICAL**
static int	**WEST**

Interface UIDefaults.ActiveValue

public abstract static interface **UIDefaults.ActiveValue**

This class represents an active value that allows storage of an entry in the defaults table. The defaults table is constructed with a suitable "get" method whenever it is accessed.

Method

Object	**createValue**(UIDefaults table)

Interface UIDefaults.LazyValue

public abstract static interface **UIDefaults.LazyValue**

This class represents a lazy value that allows storage of an entry in the defaults table. The table is not constructed until it is accessed for the first time. Lazy values are useful for default values that are expensive to construct and seldom retrieved.

Method

Object	**createValue**(UIDefaults table)

Interface WindowConstants

public abstract interface **WindowConstants**

This interface defines the constants that are used to specify what needs to be done when closing a window. Typically, you need to use these constants when closing a Swing frame or dialog box.

Fields

```
static int      DISPOSE_ON_CLOSE
static int      DO_NOTHING_ON_CLOSE
static int      HIDE_ON_CLOSE
```

Class AbstractAction

```
java.lang.Object
  |
  |
  +--javax.swing.AbstractAction
```

public abstract class **AbstractAction**
                        extends Object
                        implements Action, Cloneable, Serializable

This class is a partial implementation of the interface Action. The access methods are defined with default code. You need only provide the code for the method actionPerformed() in a class that subclasses this abstract class.

Fields

```
protected SwingPropertyChangeSupport    changeSupport
protected boolean                       enabled
```

Constructors

AbstractAction()
AbstractAction(String name)
AbstractAction(String name, Icon icon)

Methods

void	**addPropertyChangeListener** (PropertyChangeListener listener)
protected Object	**clone**() //To clone an abstract action
protected void	**firePropertyChange**(String propertyName, Object oldValue, Object newValue)
Object	**getValue**(String key)
boolean	**isEnabled**()
void	**putValue**(String key, Object newValue)
void	**removePropertyChangeListener** (PropertyChangeListener listener)
void	**setEnabled**(boolean newValue)

Class AbstractButton

```
java.lang.Object
  |
  |
  +--java.awt.Component
      |
      |
```

```
+--java.awt.Container
        |
        +--javax.swing.JComponent
                |
                +--javax.swing.AbstractButton
public abstract class AbstractButton
                extends JComponent
                implements ItemSelectable, SwingConstants
```

This class provides a common place for storing a great deal of functionality of buttons, menu items, and menus. You will note that the Swing JButton, JToggleButton, JCheckbox, JRadioButton, JMenuItem, JMenu, JCheckBoxMenuItem, and JRadioButtonMenuItem extend from this class.

Inner Classes

protected class	AbstractButton.AccessibleAbstractButton
protected class	AbstractButton.ButtonChangeListener

Fields

protected ActionListener	actionListener
static String	BORDER_PAINTED_CHANGED_PROPERTY
protected ChangeEvent	changeEvent
protected ChangeListener	changeListener
static String	CONTENT_AREA_FILLED_CHANGED_PROPERTY
static String	DISABLED_ICON_CHANGED_PROPERTY
static String	DISABLED_SELECTED_ICON_CHANGED_PROPERTY
static String	FOCUS_PAINTED_CHANGED_PROPERTY
static String	HORIZONTAL_ALIGNMENT_CHANGED_PROPERTY
static String	HORIZONTAL_TEXT_POSITION_CHANGED_PROPERTY
static String	ICON_CHANGED_PROPERTY
protected ItemListener	itemListener
static String	MARGIN_CHANGED_PROPERTY
static String	MNEMONIC_CHANGED_PROPERTY
protected ButtonModel	model
static String	MODEL_CHANGED_PROPERTY
static String	PRESSED_ICON_CHANGED_PROPERTY
static String	ROLLOVER_ENABLED_CHANGED_PROPERTY
static String	ROLLOVER_ICON_CHANGED_PROPERTY
static String	ROLLOVER_SELECTED_ICON_CHANGED_PROPERTY
static String	SELECTED_ICON_CHANGED_PROPERTY
static String	TEXT_CHANGED_PROPERTY
static String	VERTICAL_ALIGNMENT_CHANGED_PROPERTY
static String	VERTICAL_TEXT_POSITION_CHANGED_PROPERTY

Constructor

`AbstractButton()`

Methods

void	**addActionListener**(ActionListener l)
void	**addChangeListener**(ChangeListener l)
void	**addItemListener**(ItemListener l)
protected int	**checkHorizontalKey**(int key, String exception)
protected int	**checkVerticalKey**(int key, String exception)
protected ActionListener	**createActionListener**()
protected ChangeListener	**createChangeListener**()
protected ItemListener	**createItemListener**()
void	**doClick**()
void	**doClick**(int pressTime)
protected void	**fireActionPerformed**(ActionEvent event)
protected void	**fireItemStateChanged**(ItemEvent event)
protected void	**fireStateChanged**()
String	**getActionCommand**()
Icon	**getDisabledIcon**()
Icon	**getDisabledSelectedIcon**()
int	**getHorizontalAlignment**()
int	**getHorizontalTextPosition**()
Icon	**getIcon**()
String	**getLabel**() // Deprecated. - Use the method getText()
Insets	**getMargin**()
int	**getMnemonic**()
ButtonModel	**getModel**()
Icon	**getPressedIcon**()
Icon	**getRolloverIcon**()
Icon	**getRolloverSelectedIcon**()
Icon	**getSelectedIcon**()
Object[]	**getSelectedObjects**()
String	**getText**()
ButtonUI	**getUI**()
int	**getVerticalAlignment**()
int	**getVerticalTextPosition**()
protected void	**init**(String text, Icon icon)
boolean	**isBorderPainted**()
boolean	**isContentAreaFilled**()
boolean	**isFocusPainted**()
boolean	**isRolloverEnabled**()
boolean	**isSelected**()

protected void	**paintBorder**(Graphics g)
protected String	**paramString**()
	// This method obtains a string that represents the abstract button.
void	**removeActionListener**(ActionListener l)
void	**removeChangeListener**(ChangeListener l)
void	**removeItemListener**(ItemListener l)
void	**setActionCommand**(String actionCommand)
void	**setBorderPainted**(boolean b)
void	**setContentAreaFilled**(boolean b)
void	**setDisabledIcon**(Icon disabledIcon)
void	**setDisabledSelectedIcon**(Icon disabledSelectedIcon)
void	**setEnabled**(boolean b)
void	**setFocusPainted**(boolean b)
void	**setHorizontalAlignment**(int alignment)
void	**setHorizontalTextPosition**(int textPosition)
void	**setIcon**(Icon defaultIcon)
void	**setLabel**(String label)
	//Deprecated. - Use the method setText(text)
void	**setMargin**(Insets m)
void	**setMnemonic**(char mnemonic)
void	**setMnemonic**(int mnemonic)
void	**setModel**(ButtonModel newModel)
void	**setPressedIcon**(Icon pressedIcon)
void	**setRolloverEnabled**(boolean b)
void	**setRolloverIcon**(Icon rolloverIcon)
void	**setRolloverSelectedIcon**(Icon rolloverSelectedIcon)
void	**setSelected**(boolean b)
void	**setSelectedIcon**(Icon selectedIcon)
void	**setText**(String text)
void	**setUI**(ButtonUI ui)
void	**setVerticalAlignment**(int alignment)
void	**setVerticalTextPosition**(int textPosition)
void	**updateUI**()

Class AbstractListModel

```
java.lang.Object
   |
   |
   +--javax.swing.AbstractListModel
```

public abstract class **AbstractListModel**
                    extends Object
                    implements ListModel, Serializable

This class provides an abstract implementation of the interface ListModel. The classes representing custom data models can extend this class and override its methods.

Field

protected EventListenerList   **listenerList**

Constructor

AbstractListModel()

Methods

void	**addListDataListener**(ListDataListener l)
protected void	**fireContentsChanged**(Object source, int index0, int index1)
protected void	**fireIntervalAdded**(Object source, int index0, int index1)
protected void	**fireIntervalRemoved**(Object source, int index0, int index1)
void	**removeListDataListener**(ListDataListener l)

Class BorderFactory

```
java.lang.Object
   ¦
   +--javax.swing.BorderFactory
```

public class **BorderFactory**
          extends Object

This class represents a factory for a number of standard borders introduced in Swing. You can call a specific static method from this class to get a border object of interest, rather than instantiating the border classes.

Methods

static Border	**createBevelBorder**(int type)
static Border	**createBevelBorder**(int type, Color highlight, Color shadow)
static Border	**createBevelBorder**(int type, Color highlightOuter, Color highlightInner, Color shadowOuter, Color shadowInner)
static CompoundBorder	**createCompoundBorder**()
static CompoundBorder	**createCompoundBorder**(Border outsideBorder, Border insideBorder)
static Border	**createEmptyBorder**()
static Border	**createEmptyBorder**(int top, int left, int bottom, int right)
static Border	**createEtchedBorder**()
static Border	**createEtchedBorder**(Color highlight, Color shadow)
static Border	**createLineBorder**(Color color)
static Border	**createLineBorder**(Color color, int thickness)
static Border	**createLoweredBevelBorder**()
static MatteBorder	**createMatteBorder**(int top, int left, int bottom, int right, Color color)

```
static MatteBorder        createMatteBorder(int top, int left, int bottom,
                            int right, Icon tileIcon)
static Border             createRaisedBevelBorder()
static TitledBorder       createTitledBorder(Border border)
static TitledBorder       createTitledBorder(Border border, String title)
static TitledBorder       createTitledBorder(Border border, String title,
                            int titleJustification, int titlePosition)
static TitledBorder       createTitledBorder(Border border, String title,
                            int titleJustification, int titlePosition,
                            Font titleFont)
static TitledBorder       createTitledBorder(Border border, String title,
                            int titleJustification, int titlePosition,
                            Font titleFont, Color titleColor)
static TitledBorder       createTitledBorder(String title)
```

Class Box

```
java.lang.Object
  |
  +--java.awt.Component
        |
        +--java.awt.Container
              |
              +--javax.swing.Box
```

```
public class Box
          extends Container
          implements Accessible
```

This class represents a lightweight container that has been preassigned with box layout. You can create an object of this class directly and add components using the rules of box layout.

Inner Classes

```
protected class    Box.AccessibleBox
static class        Box.Filler    // An invisible and light-weight
                    component that helps to fill in spacing between
                    components, or container and components.
```

Field

```
protected AccessibleContext   accessibleContext
```

Constructor

```
Box(int axis)
```

Methods

```
static Component      createGlue()
static Box            createHorizontalBox()
```

```
static Component      createHorizontalGlue()
static Component      createHorizontalStrut(int width)
static Component      createRigidArea(Dimension d)
static Box            createVerticalBox()
static Component      createVerticalGlue()
static Component      createVerticalStrut(int height)
AccessibleContext     getAccessibleContext()
void                  setLayout(LayoutManager l)
```

Class Box.Filler

```
java.lang.Object
   |
   +--java.awt.Component
          |
          +--javax.swing.Box.Filler
```

```
public static class Box.Filler
                    extends Component
                    implements Accessible
```

An invisible and lightweight component that helps to fill spacing between components that are laid according to the box layout.

Inner Class

```
protected class Box.Filler.AccessibleBoxFiller
```

Field

```
protected AccessibleContext accessibleContext
```

Constructor

```
Box.Filler(Dimension min, Dimension pref, Dimension max)
```

Methods

```
void                  changeShape(Dimension min, Dimension pref,
                      Dimension max)
AccessibleContext     getAccessibleContext()
Dimension             getMaximumSize()
Dimension             getMinimumSize()
Dimension             getPreferredSize()
```

Class BoxLayout

```
java.lang.Object
   |
   +--javax.swing.BoxLayout
```

```
public class BoxLayout
             extends Object
             implements LayoutManager2, Serializable
```

This class represents a layout manager. You can use this layout as an alternative to the grid bag layout introduced in AWT. Components can be laid out vertically or horizontally, depending on the axis specified for the layout.

Fields

static int	**X_AXIS**	// Specifies that the components be placed from left to right
static int	**Y_AXIS**	// Specifies that the components be placed from top to bottom

Constructor

BoxLayout(Container target, int axis)

Methods

void	**addLayoutComponent**(Component comp, Object constraints)
void	**addLayoutComponent**(String name, Component comp)
float	**getLayoutAlignmentX**(Container target)
float	**getLayoutAlignmentY**(Container target)
void	**invalidateLayout**(Container target)
void	**layoutContainer**(Container target)
Dimension	**maximumLayoutSize**(Container target)
Dimension	**minimumLayoutSize**(Container target)
Dimension	**preferredLayoutSize**(Container target)
void	**removeLayoutComponent**(Component comp)

Class ButtonGroup

```
java.lang.Object
    |
    +--javax.swing.ButtonGroup
```

public class **ButtonGroup**
        extends Object
        implements Serializable

This class represents a mechanism to create a group of buttons from which only one can be selected at a time (mutually exclusive). You need this class to form a group of Swing radio buttons from which selection is mutually exclusive.

Field

protected Vector   **buttons**

Constructor

ButtonGroup()

Methods

void	**add**(AbstractButton b)
Enumeration	**getElements**()

```
ButtonModel    getSelection()
boolean        isSelected(ButtonModel m)
void           remove(AbstractButton b)
void           setSelected(ButtonModel m, boolean b)
```

Class CellRendererPane

```
java.lang.Object
   |
   |
   +--java.awt.Component
             |
             |
             +--java.awt.Container
                      |
                      |
                      +--javax.swing.CellRendererPane
```

```
public class CellRendererPane
            extends Container
            implements Accessible
```

This is a helping class between a cell renderer and the component that uses the renderer. An object of this class is useful to prevent the unwanted invocation of repaint() and invalidate() methods. The class is used by Swing tables, trees, and lists.

Inner Class

```
protected class  CellRendererPane.AccessibleCellRendererPane
```

Field

```
protected AccessibleContext   accessibleContext
```

Constructor

```
CellRendererPane()
```

Methods

```
protected void      addImpl(Component x, Object constraints, int index)
AccessibleContext   getAccessibleContext()
void                invalidate()
void                paint(Graphics g)
void                paintComponent(Graphics g, Component c,
                    Container p, int x, int y, int w, int h)
void                paintComponent(Graphics g, Component c,
                    Container p, int x, int y, int w, int h,
                    boolean shouldValidate)
void                paintComponent(Graphics g, Component c,
                    Container p,  Rectangle r)
void                update(Graphics g)
```

Class DebugGraphics

```
java.lang.Object
   |
   +--java.awt.Graphics
          |
          +--javax.swing.DebugGraphics
```

public class **DebugGraphics**
          extends Graphics

This class supports debugging of graphics. Instances of the class are automatically generated whenever the debug options of a component are changed. You can assign a new option to a component by using the method setDebugGraphicsOptions() in JComponent.

Fields

static int	**BUFFERED_OPTION**
static int	**FLASH_OPTION**
static int	**LOG_OPTION**
static int	**NONE_OPTION**

Constructors

DebugGraphics()
DebugGraphics(Graphics graphics)
DebugGraphics(Graphics graphics, JComponent component)

Methods

void	**clearRect**(int x, int y, int width, int height)
void	**clipRect**(int x, int y, int width, int height)
void	**copyArea**(int x, int y, int width, int height, int destX, int destY)
Graphics	**create**()
Graphics	**create**(int x, int y, int width, int height)
void	**dispose**()
void	**draw3DRect**(int x, int y, int width, int height, boolean raised)
void	**drawArc**(int x, int y, int width, int height, int startAngle, int arcAngle)
void	**drawBytes**(byte[] data, int offset, int length, int x, int y)
void	**drawChars**(char[] data, int offset, int length, int x, int y)
boolean	**drawImage**(Image img, int x, int y, Color bgcolor, ImageObserver observer)
boolean	**drawImage**(Image img, int x, int y, ImageObserver observer)

boolean	**drawImage**(Image img, int x, int y, int width, int height, Color bgcolor, ImageObserver observer)
boolean	**drawImage**(Image img, int x, int y, int width, int height, ImageObserver observer)
boolean	**drawImage**(Image img, int dx1, int dy1, int dx2, int dy2, int sx1, int sy1, int sx2, int sy2, Color bgcolor, ImageObserver observer)
boolean	**drawImage**(Image img, int dx1, int dy1, int dx2, int dy2, int sx1, int sy1, int sx2, int sy2, ImageObserver observer)
void	**drawLine**(int x1, int y1, int x2, int y2)
void	**drawOval**(int x, int y, int width, int height)
void	**drawPolygon**(int[] xPoints, int[] yPoints, int nPoints)
void	**drawPolyline**(int[] xPoints, int[] yPoints, int nPoints)
void	**drawRect**(int x, int y, int width, int height)
void	**drawRoundRect**(int x, int y, int width, int height, int arcWidth, int arcHeight)
void	**drawString**(String aString, int x, int y)
void	**fill3DRect**(int x, int y, int width, int height, boolean raised)
void	**fillArc**(int x, int y, int width, int height, int startAngle, int arcAngle)
void	**fillOval**(int x, int y, int width, int height)
void	**fillPolygon**(int[] xPoints, int[] yPoints, int nPoints)
void	**fillRect**(int x, int y, int width, int height)
void	**fillRoundRect**(int x, int y, int width, int height, int arcWidth, int arcHeight)
static Color	**flashColor**()
static int	**flashCount**()
static int	**flashTime**()
Shape	**getClip**()
Rectangle	**getClipBounds**()
Color	**getColor**()
int	**getDebugOptions**()
Font	**getFont**()
FontMetrics	**getFontMetrics**()
FontMetrics	**getFontMetrics**(Font f)
boolean	**isDrawingBuffer**()
static PrintStream	**logStream**()
void	**setClip**(int x, int y, int width, int height)
void	**setClip**(Shape clip)
void	**setColor**(Color aColor)
void	**setDebugOptions**(int options)
static void	**setFlashColor**(Color flashColor)
static void	**setFlashCount**(int flashCount)
static void	**setFlashTime**(int flashTime)
void	**setFont**(Font aFont)
static void	**setLogStream**(PrintStream stream)

void	**setPaintMode**()
void	**setXORMode**(Color aColor)
void	**translate**(int x, int y)

Class DefaultBoundedRangeModel

```
java.lang.Object
  |
  +--javax.swing.DefaultBoundedRangeModel
```

public class **DefaultBoundedRangeModel**
        extends Object
        implements BoundedRangeModel, Serializable

This class represents a bounded range model that is commonly used by components to display a range of bounded values such as minimum and maximum. The class is a default implementation of the interface BoundedRangeModel.

Fields

protected ChangeEvent	**changeEvent**
protected EventListenerList	**listenerList**

Constructors

DefaultBoundedRangeModel()
DefaultBoundedRangeModel(int value, int extent, int min, int max)

Methods

void	**addChangeListener**(ChangeListener l)
protected void	**fireStateChanged**()
int	**getExtent**()
int	**getMaximum**()
int	**getMinimum**()
int	**getValue**()
boolean	**getValueIsAdjusting**()
void	**removeChangeListener**(ChangeListener l)
void	**setExtent**(int n)
void	**setMaximum**(int n)
void	**setMinimum**(int n)
void	**setRangeProperties**(int newValue, int newExtent, int newMin, int newMax, boolean adjusting)
void	**setValue**(int n)
void	**setValueIsAdjusting**(boolean b)
String	**toString**()

Class DefaultButtonModel

```
java.lang.Object
  |
  +--javax.swing.DefaultButtonModel
```

```
public class DefaultButtonModel
            extends Object
            implements ButtonModel, Serializable
```

This class represents a default data model for the states of Swing buttons. To programmatically manipulate a given state of a button, you need to call the methods from this class.

Fields

protected String	**actionCommand**
static int	**ARMED**
protected ChangeEvent	**changeEvent**
static int	**ENABLED**
protected ButtonGroup	**group**
protected EventListenerList	**listenerList**
protected int	**mnemonic**
static int	**PRESSED**
static int	**ROLLOVER**
static int	**SELECTED**
protected int	**stateMask**

Constructor

DefaultButtonModel()

Methods

void	**addActionListener**(ActionListener l)
void	**addChangeListener**(ChangeListener l)
void	**addItemListener**(ItemListener l)
protected void	**fireActionPerformed**(ActionEvent e)
protected void	**fireItemStateChanged**(ItemEvent e)
protected void	**fireStateChanged**()
String	**getActionCommand**()
int	**getMnemonic**()
Object[]	**getSelectedObjects**()
boolean	**isArmed**()
boolean	**isEnabled**()
boolean	**isPressed**()
boolean	**isRollover**()
boolean	**isSelected**()
void	**removeActionListener**(ActionListener l)
void	**removeChangeListener**(ChangeListener l)
void	**removeItemListener**(ItemListener l)
void	**setActionCommand**(String actionCommand)
void	**setArmed**(boolean b)
void	**setEnabled**(boolean b)
void	**setGroup**(ButtonGroup group)
void	**setMnemonic**(int key)
void	**setPressed**(boolean b)

```
void                setRollover(boolean b)
void                setSelected(boolean b)
```

Class DefaultCellEditor

```
java.lang.Object
    |
    +--javax.swing.DefaultCellEditor
```

public class **DefaultCellEditor**
        extends Object
        implements TableCellEditor, TreeCellEditor, Serializable

This class represents a default cell editor for Swing tables and trees.

Inner Class

protected class   **DefaultCellEditor.EditorDelegate**

Fields

protected ChangeEvent	**changeEvent**
protected int	**clickCountToStart**
protected DefaultCellEditor.EditorDelegate	**delegate**
protected JComponent	**editorComponent**
protected EventListenerList	**listenerList**

Constructors

DefaultCellEditor(JCheckBox x)
DefaultCellEditor(JComboBox x)
DefaultCellEditor(JTextField x)

Methods

void	**addCellEditorListener**(CellEditorListener l)
void	**cancelCellEditing**()
protected void	**fireEditingCanceled**()
protected void	**fireEditingStopped**()
Object	**getCellEditorValue**()
int	**getClickCountToStart**()
Component	**getComponent**()
Component	**getTableCellEditorComponent**(JTable table, Object value, boolean isSelected, int row, int column)
Component	**getTreeCellEditorComponent**(JTree tree, Object value, boolean isSelected, boolean expanded, boolean leaf, int row)
boolean	**isCellEditable**(EventObject anEvent)
void	**removeCellEditorListener**(CellEditorListener l)
void	**setClickCountToStart**(int count)
boolean	**shouldSelectCell**(EventObject anEvent)
boolean	**stopCellEditing**()

Class DefaultComboBoxModel

```
java.lang.Object
    |
    +--javax.swing.AbstractListModel
           |
           +--javax.swing.DefaultComboBoxModel
```

public class **DefaultComboBoxModel**
        extends AbstractListModel
        implements MutableComboBoxModel, Serializable

This class represents the default data model for Swing combo boxes. The class is basically the standard implementation of the interface MutableComboBoxModel.

Constructors

DefaultComboBoxModel()
DefaultComboBoxModel(Object[] items)
DefaultComboBoxModel(Vector v)

Methods

void	**addElement**(Object anObject)
Object	**getElementAt**(int index)
int	**getIndexOf**(Object anObject)
Object	**getSelectedItem**()
int	**getSize**()
void	**insertElementAt**(Object anObject, int index)
void	**removeAllElements**()
void	**removeElement**(Object anObject)
void	**removeElementAt**(int index)
void	**setSelectedItem**(Object anObject)

Class DefaultDesktopManager

```
java.lang.Object
    |
    +--javax.swing.DefaultDesktopManager
```

public class **DefaultDesktopManager**
        extends Object
        implements DesktopManager, Serializable

This class represents the default implementation of the interface DesktopManager. The default implementation supports the basic functions (see the methods) to manage Swing internal frames in a parent container.

Constructor

DefaultDesktopManager()

Methods

```
void                    activateFrame(JInternalFrame f)
void                    beginDraggingFrame(JComponent f)
void                    beginResizingFrame(JComponent f, int direction)
void                    closeFrame(JInternalFrame f)
void                    deactivateFrame(JInternalFrame f)
void                    deiconifyFrame(JInternalFrame f)
void                    dragFrame(JComponent f, int newX, int newY)
                        //Calls setBoundsForFrame() with the new values.
void                    endDraggingFrame(JComponent f)
void                    endResizingFrame(JComponent f)
protected Rectangle     getBoundsForIconOf(JInternalFrame f)
protected Rectangle     getPreviousBounds(JInternalFrame f)
void                    iconifyFrame(JInternalFrame f)
void                    maximizeFrame(JInternalFrame f)
void                    minimizeFrame(JInternalFrame f)
void                    openFrame(JInternalFrame f)
protected void          removeIconFor(JInternalFrame f)
void                    resizeFrame(JComponent f, int newX, int
                        newY, int newWidth, int newHeight)
void                    setBoundsForFrame(JComponent f, int newX,
                        int newY, int newWidth, int newHeight)
protected void          setPreviousBounds(JInternalFrame f, Rectangle r)
protected void          setWasIcon(JInternalFrame f, Boolean value)
protected boolean       wasIcon(JInternalFrame f)
```

Class DefaultFocusManager

```
java.lang.Object
   |
   +--javax.swing.FocusManager
         |
         +--javax.swing.DefaultFocusManager
```

public class **DefaultFocusManager**
        extends FocusManager

This class represents the focus manager that is used by default in Swing.

Constructor

DefaultFocusManager()

Methods

```
boolean     compareTabOrder(Component a, Component b)
void        focusNextComponent(Component aComponent)
void        focusPreviousComponent(Component aComponent)
Component   getComponentAfter(Container aContainer, Component aComponent)
Component   getComponentBefore(Container aContainer, Component aComponent)
```

```
Component    getFirstComponent(Container aContainer)
Component    getLastComponent(Container aContainer)
void         processKeyEvent(Component focusedComponent, KeyEvent anEvent)
```

Class DefaultListCellRenderer

```
java.lang.Object
  |
  +--java.awt.Component
        |
        +--java.awt.Container
              |
              +--javax.swing.JComponent
                    |
                    +--javax.swing.JLabel
                          |
                          +--          javax.swing.DefaultListCellRenderer
```

```
public class DefaultListCellRenderer
           extends JLabel
           implements ListCellRenderer, Serializable
```

This class represents the default cell renderer of the Swing list. The cell renderer component is a Swing label that can display an icon and a text string.

Inner Class

```
static class    DefaultListCellRenderer.UIResource
```

Field

```
protected static Border    noFocusBorder
```

Constructor

```
DefaultListCellRenderer()
```

Methods

```
Component    getListCellRendererComponent(JList list, Object
             value, int index, boolean isSelected, boolean
             cellHasFocus)
```

Class DefaultListCellRenderer.UIResource

```
java.lang.Object
  |
  +--java.awt.Component
        |
        +--java.awt.Container
              |
              +--javax.swing.JComponent
```

```
    |
  +--javax.swing.JLabel
        |
        +--javax.swing.DefaultListCellRenderer
              |
              +--javax.swing.DefaultListCellRenderer.UIResource
```

public static class **DefaultListCellRenderer.UIResource**
               extends DefaultListCellRenderer
               implements UIResource

This class represents a UI subclass of DefaultListCellRenderer that implements UIResource. DefaultListCellRenderer doesn't implement UIResource directly so that applications can safely override the cellRenderer property with DefaultListCellRenderer subclasses.

Constructor
DefaultListCellRenderer.UIResource()

Class DefaultListModel

```
java.lang.Object
  |
  +--javax.swing.AbstractListModel
        |
        +--javax.swing.DefaultListModel
```

public class **DefaultListModel**
        extends AbstractListModel

This class represents the default list model. The class is basically an implementation of the utility java.util.Vector. The class is useful if the list data to be displayed is in the form of a vector.

Constructor
DefaultListModel()

Methods

void	**add**(int index, Object element)
void	**addElement**(Object obj)
int	**capacity**()
void	**clear**()
boolean	**contains**(Object elem)
void	**copyInto**(Object[] anArray)
Object	**elementAt**(int index)
Enumeration	**elements**()
void	**ensureCapacity**(int minCapacity)
Object	**firstElement**()
Object	**get**(int index)

Object	**getElementAt**(int index)
int	**getSize**()
int	**indexOf**(Object elem)
int	**indexOf**(Object elem, int index)
void	**insertElementAt**(Object obj, int index)
boolean	**isEmpty**()
Object	**lastElement**()
int	**lastIndexOf**(Object elem)
int	**lastIndexOf**(Object elem, int index)
Object	**remove**(int index)
void	**removeAllElements**()
boolean	**removeElement**(Object obj)
void	**removeElementAt**(int index)
void	**removeRange**(int fromIndex, int toIndex)
Object	**set**(int index, Object element)
void	**setElementAt**(Object obj, int index)
void	**setSize**(int newSize)
int	**size**()
Object[]	**toArray**()
String	**toString**()
void	**trimToSize**()

Class DefaultListSelectionModel

```
java.lang.Object
   ¦
   ¦
   +--javax.swing.DefaultListSelectionModel
```

public class **DefaultListSelectionModel**
            extends Object
            implements ListSelectionModel, Cloneable, Serializable

This class represents the selection model that is used by list components by default. All the selection-related functionality is stored in this class. If you have to modify the selection process, this is the class you need to subclass with modified methods and assign the subclass object to the list component by using setSelectionModel().

Fields

protected boolean	**leadAnchorNotificationEnabled**
protected EventListenerList	**listenerList**

Constructor

DefaultListSelectionModel()

Methods

void	**addListSelectionListener**(ListSelectionListener l)
void	**addSelectionInterval**(int index0, int index1)
void	**clearSelection**()
Object	**clone**()

protected void	**fireValueChanged**(boolean isAdjusting)
protected void	**fireValueChanged**(int firstIndex, int lastIndex)
protected void	**fireValueChanged**(int firstIndex, int lastIndex, boolean isAdjusting)
int	**getAnchorSelectionIndex**()
int	**getLeadSelectionIndex**()
int	**getMaxSelectionIndex**()
int	**getMinSelectionIndex**()
int	**getSelectionMode**()
boolean	**getValueIsAdjusting**()
void	**insertIndexInterval**(int index, int length, boolean before)
boolean	**isLeadAnchorNotificationEnabled**()
boolean	**isSelectedIndex**(int index)
boolean	**isSelectionEmpty**()
void	**removeIndexInterval**(int index0, int index1)
void	**removeListSelectionListener** (ListSelectionListener l)
void	**removeSelectionInterval**(int index0, int index1)
void	**setAnchorSelectionIndex**(int anchorIndex)
void	**setLeadAnchorNotificationEnabled**(boolean flag)
void	**setLeadSelectionIndex**(int leadIndex)
void	**setSelectionInterval**(int index0, int index1)
void	**setSelectionMode**(int selectionMode)
void	**setValueIsAdjusting**(boolean isAdjusting)
String	**toString**()

Class DefaultSingleSelectionModel

```
java.lang.Object
   |
   +--javax.swing.DefaultSingleSelectionModel
```

public class **DefaultSingleSelectionModel**
        extends Object
        implements SingleSelectionModel, Serializable

This class represents a selection model that functions by default for selecting only one item at a time, for example, in a list component.

Fields

protected ChangeEvent	**changeEvent**
protected EventListenerList	**listenerList**

Constructor

DefaultSingleSelectionModel()

Methods

void	**addChangeListener**(ChangeListener l)
void	**clearSelection**()

```
protected void    fireStateChanged()
int               getSelectedIndex()
boolean           isSelected()
void              removeChangeListener(ChangeListener l)
void              setSelectedIndex(int index)
```

Class FocusManager

```
java.lang.Object
    |
    +--javax.swing.FocusManager
public abstract class FocusManager
                extends Object
```

This class represents the Swing focus manager, which is an abstract class. The default focus manager used in Swing extends this class.

Field

```
static String   FOCUS_MANAGER_CLASS_PROPERTY
```

Constructor

```
FocusManager()
```

Methods

```
static void           disableSwingFocusManager()
abstract void         focusNextComponent(Component aComponent)
abstract void         focusPreviousComponent(Component aComponent)
static FocusManager   getCurrentManager()
static boolean        isFocusManagerEnabled()
abstract void         processKeyEvent(Component focusedComponent,
                      KeyEvent anEvent)
static void           setCurrentManager(FocusManager aFocusManager)
```

Class GrayFilter

```
java.lang.Object
    |
    +--java.awt.image.ImageFilter
            |
            +--java.awt.image.RGBImageFilter
                    |
                    +--javax.swing.GrayFilter
public class GrayFilter
            extends RGBImageFilter
```

This class represents an image-processing filter that simply grays out the subjected image. Grayed-out images are commonly displayed over components that have been disabled.

Constructor

`GrayFilter`(boolean b, int p)

Methods

```
static Image    createDisabledImage(Image i)
int             filterRGB(int x, int y, int rgb)
```

Class ImageIcon

```
java.lang.Object
   |
   +--javax.swing.ImageIcon
```

public class **ImageIcon**
        extends Object
        implements Icon, Serializable

This class represents a specific implementation of the interface Icon. The icons are painted by using GIF or JPEG source files. A media tracker can also monitor the loading status of the image.

Fields

```
protected  static Component    component
protected  static MediaTracker tracker
```

Constructors

```
ImageIcon()
ImageIcon(byte[] imageData)
ImageIcon(byte[] imageData, String description)
ImageIcon(Image image)
ImageIcon(Image image, String description)
ImageIcon(String filename)
ImageIcon(String filename, String description)
ImageIcon(URL location)
ImageIcon(URL location, String description)
```

Methods

```
String          getDescription()
int             getIconHeight()
int             getIconWidth()
Image           getImage()
int             getImageLoadStatus()
ImageObserver   getImageObserver()
protected void  loadImage(Image image)
void            paintIcon(Component c, Graphics g, int x, int y)
void            setDescription(String description)
void            setImage(Image image)
void            setImageObserver(ImageObserver observer)
```

Class JApplet

```
java.lang.Object
   |
   +--java.awt.Component
         |
         +--java.awt.Container
               |
               +--java.awt.Panel
                     |
                     +--java.applet.Applet
                           |
                           +--javax.swing.JApplet
```

```
public class JApplet
            extends Applet
            implements Accessible, RootPaneContainer
```

This class represents the Swing applet that has extended fuctionality over the AWT applet. The Swing applet can support a menu bar, layering of frames to produce the feeling of depth (Z-order), a glass pane over the existing components to allow painting over components, and so on.

Inner Class

```
protected class       JApplet.AccessibleJApplet
```

Fields

```
protected AccessibleContext      accessibleContext
protected JRootPane              rootPane
protected boolean               rootPaneCheckingEnabled
```

Constructor

```
JApplet()
```

Methods

```
protected void        addImpl(Component comp, Object constraints, int index)
protected JRootPane   createRootPane()
AccessibleContext     getAccessibleContext()
Container             getContentPane()
Component             getGlassPane()
JMenuBar              getJMenuBar()
JLayeredPane          getLayeredPane()
JRootPane             getRootPane()
protected  boolean    isRootPaneCheckingEnabled()
protected  String     paramString()
protected  void       processKeyEvent(KeyEvent e)
void                  setContentPane(Container contentPane)
void                  setGlassPane(Component glassPane)
```

void	**setJMenuBar**(JMenuBar menuBar)
void	**setLayeredPane**(JLayeredPane layeredPane)
void	**setLayout**(LayoutManager manager)
protected void	**setRootPane**(JRootPane root)
protected void	**setRootPaneCheckingEnabled**(boolean enabled)
void	**update**(Graphics g)

Class JButton

```
java.lang.Object
   |
   +--java.awt.Component
           |
           +--java.awt.Container
                   |
                   +--javax.swing.JComponent
                           |
                           +--javax.swing.AbstractButton
                                   |
                                   +--javax.swing.JButton
```

public class **JButton**
       extends AbstractButton
       implements Accessible

This class represents the regular push-type Swing button. The button is lightweight and can possess an icon and text with specified positioning and orientation.

Inner Class

protected class   **JButton.AccessibleJButton**

Constructors

JButton()
JButton(Icon icon)
JButton(String text)
JButton(String text, Icon icon)

Methods

AccessibleContext	**getAccessibleContext**()
String	**getUIClassID**()
boolean	**isDefaultButton**()
boolean	**isDefaultCapable**()
protected String	**paramString**()
void	**setDefaultCapable**(boolean defaultCapable)
void	**updateUI**()

Class JCheckBox

```
java.lang.Object
   |
```

```
     +--java.awt.Component
        |
        +--java.awt.Container
           |
           +--javax.swing.JComponent
              |
              +--javax.swing.AbstractButton
                 |
                 +--javax.swing.JToggleButton
                    |
                    +--javax.swing.JCheckBox
```

```
public class JCheckBox
          extends JToggleButton
          implements Accessible
```

This class represents a lightweight check box in Swing.

Inner Class

protected class   **JCheckBox.AccessibleJCheckBox**

Constructors

JCheckBox()
JCheckBox(Icon icon)
JCheckBox(Icon icon, boolean selected)
JCheckBox(String text)
JCheckBox(String text, boolean selected)
JCheckBox(String text, Icon icon)
JCheckBox(String text, Icon icon, boolean selected)

Methods

AccessibleContext	**getAccessibleContext**()
String	**getUIClassID**()
protected String	**paramString**()
void	**updateUI**()

Class JCheckBoxMenuItem

```
java.lang.Object
   |
   +--java.awt.Component
      |
      +--java.awt.Container
         |
         +--javax.swing.JComponent
            |
            +--javax.swing.AbstractButton
               |
               +--javax.swing.JMenuItem
```

```
         |
         |
         +--javax.swing.JCheckBoxMenuItem
public class JCheckBoxMenuItem
            extends JMenuItem
            implements SwingConstants, Accessible
```

This class represents a check box menu item. Check box menu items are used in menus and appear similarly to check boxes. Check box menu items are suitable when multiple options need to be selected.

Inner Class

```
protected class    JCheckBoxMenuItem.AccessibleJCheckBoxMenuItem
```

Constructors

```
JCheckBoxMenuItem()
JCheckBoxMenuItem(Icon icon)
JCheckBoxMenuItem(String text)
JCheckBoxMenuItem(String text, boolean b)
JCheckBoxMenuItem(String text, Icon icon)
JCheckBoxMenuItem(String text, Icon icon, boolean b)
```

Methods

```
AccessibleContext    getAccessibleContext()
Object[]             getSelectedObjects()
boolean              getState()
String               getUIClassID()
protected void       init(String text, Icon icon)
protected String     paramString()
void                 requestFocus()
void                 setState(boolean b)
void                 updateUI()
```

Class JColorChooser

```
java.lang.Object
    |
    |
    +--java.awt.Component
            |
            |
            +--java.awt.Container
                    |
                    |
                    +--javax.swing.JComponent
                            |
                            |
                            +--javax.swing.JColorChooser
public class JColorChooser
            extends JComponent
            implements Accessible
```

This class represents a color chooser pane. You can click a tab to move over to the Swatch, RGB, or HSB pane to select any color.

Inner Class

protected class   **JColorChooser.AccessibleJColorChooser**

Fields

protected AccessibleContext	**accessibleContext**
static String	**CHOOSER_PANELS_PROPERTY**
static String	**PREVIEW_PANEL_PROPERTY**
static String	**SELECTION_MODEL_PROPERTY**

Constructors

JColorChooser()
JColorChooser(Color initialColor)
JColorChooser(ColorSelectionModel model)

Methods

void	**addChooserPanel** (AbstractColorChooserPanel panel)
static JDialog	**createDialog**(Component c, String title, boolean modal, JColorChooser chooserPane, ActionListener okListener, ActionListener cancelListener)
AccessibleContext	**getAccessibleContext**()
AbstractColorChooserPanel[]	**getChooserPanels**()
Color	**getColor**()
JComponent	**getPreviewPanel**()
ColorSelectionModel	**getSelectionModel**()
ColorChooserUI	**getUI**()
String	**getUIClassID**()
protected String	**paramString**()
AbstractColorChooserPanel	**removeChooserPanel** (AbstractColorChooserPanel panel)
void	**setChooserPanels** (AbstractColorChooserPanel[] panels)
void	**setColor**(Color color)
void	**setColor**(int c)
void	**setColor**(int r, int g, int b)
void	**setPreviewPanel**(JComponent preview)
void	**setSelectionModel** (ColorSelectionModel newModel)
void	**setUI**(ColorChooserUI ui)
static Color	**showDialog**(Component component, String title, Color initialColor)
void	**updateUI**()

Class JComboBox

```
java.lang.Object
   |
   +--java.awt.Component
         |
         +--java.awt.Container
               |
               +--javax.swing.JComponent
                     |
                     +--javax.swing.JComboBox
```

public class **JComboBox**
        extends JComponent
        implements ItemSelectable, ListDataListener, ActionListener,
        Accessible

This class represents the Swing combo box. The combo box is a combination of a text field and a pull-down list from which an item can be selected. The selected item is displayed in the text field.

Inner Classes

protected class	**JComboBox.AccessibleJComboBox**
static interface	JComboBox.KeySelectionManager

Fields

protected String	**actionCommand**
protected ComboBoxModel	**dataModel**
protected ComboBoxEditor	**editor**
protected boolean	**isEditable**
protected JComboBox.KeySelectionManager	**keySelectionManager**
protected boolean	**lightWeightPopupEnabled**
protected int	**maximumRowCount**
protected ListCellRenderer	**renderer**
protected Object	**selectedItemReminder**

Constructors

JComboBox()
JComboBox(ComboBoxModel aModel)
JComboBox(Object[] items)
JComboBox(Vector items)

Methods

void	**actionPerformed** (ActionEvent e)
void	**addActionListener** (ActionListener l)
void	**addItem**(Object anObject)

void	**addItemListener** (ItemListener aListener)
void	**configureEditor** (ComboBoxEditor anEditor, Object anItem)
void	**contentsChanged** (ListDataEvent e)
protected JComboBox.KeySelectionManager	**createDefaultKey SelectionManager**()
protected void	**fireActionEvent**()
protected void	**fireItemStateChanged** (ItemEvent e)
AccessibleContext	**getAccessibleContext**()
String	**getActionCommand**()
Object	**getItemAt**(int index)
int	**getItemCount**()
JComboBox.KeySelectionManager	**getKeySelection Manager**()
int	**getMaximumRowCount**()
ComboBoxModel	**getModel**()
ListCellRenderer	**getRenderer**()
int	**getSelectedIndex**()
Object	**getSelectedItem**()
Object[]	**getSelectedObjects**()
ComboBoxUI	**getUI**()
String	**getUIClassID**()
void	**hidePopup**()
void	**insertItemAt**(Object anObject,int index)
protected void	**installAncestor Listener**()
void	**intervalAdded** (ListDataEvent e)
void	**intervalRemoved** (ListDataEvent e)
boolean	**isEditable**()
boolean	**isFocusTraversable**()
boolean	**isLightWeightPopup Enabled**()
boolean	**isPopupVisible**()
protected String	**paramString**()
void	**processKeyEvent** (KeyEvent e)
void	**removeActionListener** (ActionListener l)
void	**removeAllItems**()
void	**removeItem**(Object anObject)

void	**removeItemAt**(int anIndex)
void	**removeItemListener** (ItemListener aListener)
protected void	**selectedItemChanged**()
boolean	**selectWithKeyChar**(char keyChar)
void	**setActionCommand**(String aCommand)
void	**setEditable**(boolean aFlag)
void	**setEditor** (ComboBoxEditor anEditor)
void	**setEnabled**(boolean b)
void	**setKeySelectionManager** (JComboBox. KeySelectionManager aManager)
void	**setLightWeight PopupEnabled**(boolean aFlag)
void	**setMaximumRowCount**(int count)
void	**setModel**(ComboBoxModel aModel)
void	**setPopupVisible**(boolean v)
void	**setRenderer** (ListCellRenderer aRenderer)
void	**setSelectedIndex**(int anIndex)
void	**setSelectedItem**(Object anObject)
void	**setUI**(ComboBoxUI ui)
void	**showPopup**()
void	**updateUI**()

Class JComponent

```
java.lang.Object
    |
    +--java.awt.Component
            |
            +--java.awt.Container
                    |
                    +--javax.swing.JComponent
```

public abstract class **JComponent**
                    extends Container
                    implements Serializable

This class represents the parent (base) class for Swing components where a great deal of functionality common to all the components is present.

Inner Class

class   **JComponent.AccessibleJComponent**

Fields

protected AccessibleContext	**accessibleContext**
protected EventListenerList	**listenerList**
static String	**TOOL_TIP_TEXT_KEY**
protected ComponentUI	**ui**
static int	**UNDEFINED_CONDITION**
static int	**WHEN_ANCESTOR_OF_FOCUSED_COMPONENT**
static int	**WHEN_FOCUSED**
static int	**WHEN_IN_FOCUSED_WINDOW**

Constructor

JComponent()

Methods

void	**addAncestorListener**(AncestorListener listener)
void	**addNotify**()
void	**addPropertyChangeListener**(PropertyChangeListener listener)
void	**addVetoableChangeListener**(VetoableChangeListener listener)
void	**computeVisibleRect**(Rectangle visibleRect)
boolean	**contains**(int x, int y)
JToolTip	**createToolTip**()
void	**firePropertyChange**(String propertyName, boolean oldValue, boolean newValue)
void	**firePropertyChange**(String propertyName, byte oldValue, byte newValue)
void	**firePropertyChange**(String propertyName, char oldValue, char newValue)
void	**firePropertyChange**(String propertyName, double oldValue, double newValue)
void	**firePropertyChange**(String propertyName, float oldValue, float newValue)
void	**firePropertyChange**(String propertyName, int oldValue, int newValue)
void	**firePropertyChange**(String propertyName, long oldValue, long newValue)
protected void	**firePropertyChange**(String propertyName, Object oldValue, Object newValue)
void	**firePropertyChange**(String propertyName, short oldValue, short newValue)

protected void	**fireVetoableChange**(String propertyName, Object oldValue, Object newValue)
AccessibleContext	**getAccessibleContext**()
ActionListener	**getActionForKeyStroke**(KeyStroke aKeyStroke)
float	**getAlignmentX**()
float	**getAlignmentY**()
boolean	**getAutoscrolls**()
Border	**getBorder**()
Rectangle	**getBounds**(Rectangle rv)
Object	**getClientProperty**(Object key)
protected Graphics	**getComponentGraphics**(Graphics g)
int	**getConditionForKeyStroke**(KeyStroke aKeyStroke)
int	**getDebugGraphicsOptions**()
Graphics	**getGraphics**()
int	**getHeight**()
Insets	**getInsets**()
Insets	**getInsets**(Insets insets)
Point	**getLocation**(Point rv)
Dimension	**getMaximumSize**()
Dimension	**getMinimumSize**()
Component	**getNextFocusableComponent**()
Dimension	**getPreferredSize**()
KeyStroke[]	**getRegisteredKeyStrokes**()
JRootPane	**getRootPane**()
Dimension	**getSize**(Dimension rv)
Point	**getToolTipLocation**(MouseEvent event)
String	**getToolTipText**()
String	**getToolTipText**(MouseEvent event)
Container	**getTopLevelAncestor**()
String	**getUIClassID**()
Rectangle	**getVisibleRect**()
int	**getWidth**()
int	**getX**()
int	**getY**()
void	**grabFocus**()
boolean	**hasFocus**()
boolean	**isDoubleBuffered**()
boolean	**isFocusCycleRoot**()
boolean	**isFocusTraversable**()
static boolean	**isLightweightComponent**(Component c)
boolean	**isManagingFocus**()
boolean	**isOpaque**()
boolean	**isOptimizedDrawingEnabled**()
boolean	**isPaintingTile**()
boolean	**isRequestFocusEnabled**()
boolean	**isValidateRoot**()
void	**paint**(Graphics g)
protected void	**paintBorder**(Graphics g)
protected void	**paintChildren**(Graphics g)

```
protected void        paintComponent(Graphics g)
void                  paintImmediately(int x, int y, int w, int h)
void                  paintImmediately(Rectangle r)
protected String      paramString()
protected void        processComponentKeyEvent(KeyEvent e)
protected void        processFocusEvent(FocusEvent e)
protected void        processKeyEvent(KeyEvent e)
protected void        processMouseMotionEvent(MouseEvent e)
void                  putClientProperty(Object key, Object value)
void                  registerKeyboardAction(ActionListener
                      anAction, KeyStroke aKeyStroke, int
                      aCondition)
void                  registerKeyboardAction(ActionListener
                      anAction, String aCommand, KeyStroke
                      aKeyStroke, int aCondition)
void                  removeAncestorListener(AncestorListener listener)
void                  removeNotify()
void                  removePropertyChangeListener
                      (PropertyChangeListener listener)
void                  removeVetoableChangeListener
                      (VetoableChangeListener listener)
void                  repaint(long tm, int x, int y, int width, int height)
void                  repaint(Rectangle r)
boolean               requestDefaultFocus()
void                  requestFocus()
void                  resetKeyboardActions()
void                  reshape(int x, int y, int w, int h)
void                  revalidate()
void                  scrollRectToVisible(Rectangle aRect)
void                  setAlignmentX(float alignmentX)
void                  setAlignmentY(float alignmentY)
void                  setAutoscrolls(boolean autoscrolls)
void                  setBackground(Color bg)
void                  setBorder(Border border)
void                  setDebugGraphicsOptions(int debugOptions)
void                  setDoubleBuffered(boolean aFlag)
void                  setEnabled(boolean enabled)
void                  setFont(Font font)
void                  setForeground(Color fg)
void                  setMaximumSize(Dimension maximumSize)
void                  setMinimumSize(Dimension minimumSize)
void                  setNextFocusableComponent(Component aComponent)
void                  setOpaque(boolean isOpaque)
void                  setPreferredSize(Dimension preferredSize)
void                  setRequestFocusEnabled(boolean aFlag)
void                  setToolTipText(String text)
protected void        setUI(ComponentUI newUI)
void                  setVisible(boolean aFlag)
void                  unregisterKeyboardAction(KeyStroke aKeyStroke)
```

```
void                update(Graphics g)
void                updateUI()
```

Class JDesktopPane

```
java.lang.Object
   |
   +--java.awt.Component
        |
        +--java.awt.Container
             |
             +--javax.swing.JComponent
                  |
                  +--javax.swing.JLayeredPane
                       |
                       +--javax.swing.JDesktopPane
```

```
public class JDesktopPane
             extends JLayeredPane
             implements Accessible
```

This class represents a desktop pane whose parent is a layered pane. The desktop pane provides a virtual desktop. Internal frames are added to layers in the desktop pane. A desktop pane also provides a reference to a desktop manager for the current look-and-feel.

Inner Class

```
protected class    JDesktopPane.AccessibleJDesktopPane
```

Constructor

```
JDesktopPane()
```

Methods

```
AccessibleContext   getAccessibleContext()
JInternalFrame[]    getAllFrames()
JInternalFrame[]    getAllFramesInLayer(int layer)
DesktopManager      getDesktopManager()
DesktopPaneUI       getUI()
String              getUIClassID()
boolean             isOpaque()
protected String    paramString()
void                setDesktopManager(DesktopManager d)
void                setUI(DesktopPaneUI ui)
void                updateUI()
```

Class JDialog

```
java.lang.Object
   |
   +--java.awt.Component
```

```
            |
            +--java.awt.Container
                    |
                    +--java.awt.Window
                            |
                            +--java.awt.Dialog
                                    |
                                    +--javax.swing.JDialog
```

public class **JDialog**
        extends Dialog
        implements WindowConstants, Accessible, RootPaneContainer

This class represents heavyweight Swing dialog boxes. You can use this class to create custom dialog boxes. For standard dialog boxes, use the supported option panes. The objects of JDialog support features such as layering of panes, glass panes, menu bars, and so on. You need to add components to the content pane of the dialog box.

Inner Class

protected class   **JDialog.AccessibleJDialog**

Fields

protected AccessibleContext   **accessibleContext**
protected JRootPane   **rootPane**
protected boolean   **rootPaneCheckingEnabled**

Constructors

JDialog()
JDialog(Frame owner)
JDialog(Frame owner, boolean modal)
JDialog(Frame owner, String title)
JDialog(Frame owner, String title, boolean modal)

Methods

protected void	**addImpl**(Component comp, Object constraints, int index)
protected JRootPane	**createRootPane**()
protected void	**dialogInit**()
AccessibleContext	**getAccessibleContext**()
Container	**getContentPane**()
int	**getDefaultCloseOperation**()
Component	**getGlassPane**()
JMenuBar	**getJMenuBar**()
JLayeredPane	**getLayeredPane**()
JRootPane	**getRootPane**()
protected boolean	**isRootPaneCheckingEnabled**()
protected String	**paramString**()
protected void	**processWindowEvent**(WindowEvent e)
void	**setContentPane**(Container contentPane)

void	**setDefaultCloseOperation**(int operation)
void	**setGlassPane**(Component glassPane)
void	**setJMenuBar**(JMenuBar menu)
void	**setLayeredPane**(JLayeredPane layeredPane)
void	**setLayout**(LayoutManager manager)
void	**setLocationRelativeTo**(Component c)
protected void	**setRootPane**(JRootPane root)
protected void	**setRootPaneCheckingEnabled**(boolean enabled)
void	**update**(Graphics g)

Class JEditorPane

```
java.lang.Object
  |
  +--java.awt.Component
          |
          +--java.awt.Container
                  |
                  +--javax.swing.JComponent
                          |
                          +--javax.swing.text.JTextComponent
                                  |
                                  +--javax.swing.JEditorPane
```

```
public class JEditorPane
          extends JTextComponent
```

This class represents the Swing editor panes. An editor kit associates this component based on the content type specified by a URL. The editor pane is capable of configuring itself (automatically) to display the content.

Inner Classes

protected class	**JEditorPane.AccessibleJEditorPane**
protected class	**JEditorPane.AccessibleJEditorPaneHTML**
protected class	**JEditorPane.JEditorPaneAccessibleHypertextSupport**

Constructors

JEditorPane()
JEditorPane(String url)
JEditorPane(String type, String text)
JEditorPane(URL initialPage)

Methods

void	**addHyperlinkListener**(HyperlinkListener listener)
protected EditorKit	**createDefaultEditorKit**()
static EditorKit	**createEditorKitForContentType**(String type)
void	**fireHyperlinkUpdate**(HyperlinkEvent e)
AccessibleContext	**getAccessibleContext**()
String	**getContentType**()

EditorKit	**getEditorKit**()
EditorKit	**getEditorKitForContentType**(String type)
URL	**getPage**()
Dimension	**getPreferredSize**()
boolean	**getScrollableTracksViewportHeight**()
boolean	**getScrollableTracksViewportWidth**()
protected InputStream	**getStream**(URL page)
String	**getText**()
String	**getUIClassID**()
boolean	**isManagingFocus**()
protected String	**paramString**()
protected void	**processComponentKeyEvent**(KeyEvent e)
void	**read**(InputStream in, Object desc)
static void	**registerEditorKitForContentType**(String type, String classname)
static void	**registerEditorKitForContentType**(String type, String classname, ClassLoader loader)
void	**removeHyperlinkListener**(HyperlinkListener listener)
void	**replaceSelection**(String content)
protected void	**scrollToReference**(String reference)
void	**setContentType**(String type)
void	**setEditorKit**(EditorKit kit)
void	**setEditorKitForContentType**(String type, EditorKit k)
void	**setPage**(String url)
void	**setPage**(URL page)
void	**setText**(String t)

Class JFileChooser

```
java.lang.Object
   |
   +--java.awt.Component
         |
         +--java.awt.Container
               |
               +--javax.swing.JComponent
                     |
                     +--javax.swing.JFileChooser
```

```
public class JFileChooser
          extends JComponent
          implements Accessible
```

This class represents the file choosers in Swing. The objects of this class are dialog boxes that allow the user to open or save a file.

Inner Class

```
protected class    JFileChooser.AccessibleJFileChooser
```

Fields

protected AccessibleContext	**accessibleContext**
static String	**ACCESSORY_CHANGED_PROPERTY**
static String	**APPROVE_BUTTON_MNEMONIC _CHANGED_PROPERTY**
static String	**APPROVE_BUTTON_TEXT _CHANGED_PROPERTY**
static String	**APPROVE_BUTTON_TOOL_TIP_TEXT _CHANGED_PROPERTY**
static int	**APPROVE_OPTION**
static String	**APPROVE_SELECTION**
static int	**CANCEL_OPTION**
static String	**CANCEL_SELECTION**
static String	**CHOOSABLE_FILE_FILTER _CHANGED_PROPERTY**
static int	**CUSTOM_DIALOG**
static String	**DIALOG_TITLE_CHANGED_PROPERTY**
static String	**DIALOG_TYPE_CHANGED_PROPERTY**
static int	**DIRECTORIES_ONLY**
static String	**DIRECTORY_CHANGED_PROPERTY**
static int	**ERROR_OPTION**
static String	**FILE_FILTER_CHANGED_PROPERTY**
static String	**FILE_HIDING_CHANGED_PROPERTY**
static String	**FILE_SELECTION_MODE _CHANGED_PROPERTY**
static String	**FILE_SYSTEM_VIEW_CHANGED_PROPERTY**
static String	**FILE_VIEW_CHANGED_PROPERTY**
static int	**FILES_AND_DIRECTORIES**
static int	**FILES_ONLY**
static String	**MULTI_SELECTION_ENABLED _CHANGED_PROPERTY**
static int	**OPEN_DIALOG**
static int	**SAVE_DIALOG**
static String	**SELECTED_FILE_CHANGED_PROPERTY**
static String	**SELECTED_FILES_CHANGED_PROPERTY**

Constructors

JFileChooser()
JFileChooser(File currentDirectory)
JFileChooser(File currentDirectory, FileSystemView fsv)
JFileChooser(FileSystemView fsv)
JFileChooser(String currentDirectoryPath)
JFileChooser(String currentDirectoryPath, FileSystemView fsv)

Class JFrame

```
java.lang.Object
   |
```

```
+--java.awt.Component
        |
        +--java.awt.Container
                |
                +--java.awt.Window
                        |
                        +--java.awt.Frame
                                |
                                +--javax.swing.JFrame
public class JFrame
          extends Frame
          implements WindowConstants, Accessible, RootPaneContainer
```

This class represents Swing frames that possess extended functionality of the AWT frame. Additional support for layering of components (Z-order), glass panes, menu bars, and content panes can be observed. You need to add the child components to the content pane of the frame object.

Inner Class

protected class   **JFrame.AccessibleJFrame**

Fields

protected AccessibleContext   **accessibleContext**
protected JRootPane   **rootPane**
protected boolean   **rootPaneCheckingEnabled**

Constructors

JFrame()
JFrame(String title)

Methods

protected void	**addImpl**(Component comp, Object constraints, int index)
protected JRootPane	**createRootPane**()
protected void	**frameInit**()
AccessibleContext	**getAccessibleContext**()
Container	**getContentPane**()
int	**getDefaultCloseOperation**()
Component	**getGlassPane**()
JMenuBar	**getJMenuBar**()
JLayeredPane	**getLayeredPane**()
JRootPane	**getRootPane**()
protected boolean	**isRootPaneCheckingEnabled**()
protected String	**paramString**()
protected void	**processKeyEvent**(KeyEvent e)
protected void	**processWindowEvent**(WindowEvent e)
void	**setContentPane**(Container contentPane)
void	**setDefaultCloseOperation**(int operation)

void	**setGlassPane**(Component glassPane)
void	**setJMenuBar**(JMenuBar menubar)
void	**setLayeredPane**(JLayeredPane layeredPane)
void	**setLayout**(LayoutManager manager)
protected void	**setRootPane**(JRootPane root)
protected void	**setRootPaneCheckingEnabled**(boolean enabled)
void	**update**(Graphics g)

Class JInternalFrame

```
java.lang.Object
   |
   +--java.awt.Component
         |
         +--java.awt.Container
               |
               +--javax.swing.JComponent
                     |
                     +--javax.swing.JInternalFrame
```

public class **JInternalFrame**
        extends JComponent
        implements Accessible, WindowConstants, RootPaneContainer

This class represents lightweight Swing internal frames. You create an instance of this class and add it to a desktop pane.

Inner Classes

protected class	**JInternalFrame.AccessibleJInternalFrame**
static class	**JInternalFrame.JDesktopIcon**

Fields

protected boolean	**closable**
static String	**CONTENT_PANE_PROPERTY**
protected JInternalFrame.JDesktopIcon	**desktopIcon**
static String	**FRAME_ICON_PROPERTY**
protected Icon	**frameIcon**
static String	**GLASS_PANE_PROPERTY**
protected boolean	**iconable**
static String	**IS_CLOSED_PROPERTY**
static String	**IS_ICON_PROPERTY**
static String	**IS_MAXIMUM_PROPERTY**
static String	**IS_SELECTED_PROPERTY**
protected boolean	**isClosed**
protected boolean	**isIcon**
protected boolean	**isMaximum**
protected boolean	**isSelected**
static String	**LAYERED_PANE_PROPERTY**
protected boolean	**maximizable**
static String	**MENU_BAR_PROPERTY**

protected boolean	**resizable**
static String	**ROOT_PANE_PROPERTY**
protected JRootPane	**rootPane**
protected boolean	**rootPaneCheckingEnabled**
protected String	**title**
static String	**TITLE_PROPERTY**

Constructors

JInternalFrame()
JInternalFrame(String title)
JInternalFrame(String title, boolean resizable)
JInternalFrame(String title, boolean resizable, boolean closable)
JInternalFrame(String title, boolean resizable, boolean closable,
boolean maximizable)
JInternalFrame(String title, boolean resizable, boolean closable,
boolean maximizable, boolean iconifiable)

Methods

protected void	**addImpl**(Component comp, Object constraints, int index)
void	**addInternalFrameListener** (InternalFrameListener l)
protected JRootPane	**createRootPane**()
void	**dispose**()
protected void	**fireInternalFrameEvent**(int id)
AccessibleContext	**getAccessibleContext**()
Color	**getBackground**()
Container	**getContentPane**()
int	**getDefaultCloseOperation**()
JInternalFrame.JDesktopIcon	**getDesktopIcon**()
JDesktopPane	**getDesktopPane**()
Color	**getForeground**()
Icon	**getFrameIcon**()
Component	**getGlassPane**()
JMenuBar	**getJMenuBar**()
int	**getLayer**()
JLayeredPane	**getLayeredPane**()
JMenuBar	**getMenuBar**() // Deprecated. Use the method getJMenuBar().
JRootPane	**getRootPane**()
String	**getTitle**()
InternalFrameUI	**getUI**()
String	**getUIClassID**()
String	**getWarningString**()
boolean	**isClosable**()
boolean	**isClosed**()
boolean	**isIcon**()

boolean	**isIconifiable**()
boolean	**isMaximizable**()
boolean	**isMaximum**()
boolean	**isResizable**()
protected boolean	**isRootPaneCheckingEnabled**()
boolean	**isSelected**()
void	**moveToBack**()
void	**moveToFront**()
void	**pack**()
protected String	**paramString**()
void	**removeInternalFrameListener** (InternalFrameListener l)
void	**reshape**(int x, int y, int width, int height)
void	**setBackground**(Color c)
void	**setClosable**(boolean b)
void	**setClosed**(boolean b)
void	**setContentPane**(Container c)
void	**setDefaultCloseOperation**(int operation)
void	**setDesktopIcon** (JInternalFrame.JDesktopIcon d)
void	**setForeground**(Color c)
void	**setFrameIcon**(Icon icon)
void	**setGlassPane**(Component glass)
void	**setIcon**(boolean b)
void	**setIconifiable**(boolean b)
void	**setJMenuBar**(JMenuBar m)
void	**setLayer**(Integer layer)
void	**setLayeredPane**(JLayeredPane layered)
void	**setLayout**(LayoutManager manager)
void	**setMaximizable**(boolean b)
void	**setMaximum**(boolean b)
void	**setMenuBar**(JMenuBar m) // Deprecated. Use the method setJMenuBar (JMenuBar m).
void	**setResizable**(boolean b)
protected void	**setRootPane**(JRootPane root)
protected void	**setRootPaneCheckingEnabled**(boolean enabled)
void	**setSelected**(boolean selected)
void	**setTitle**(String title)
void	**setUI**(InternalFrameUI ui)
void	**setVisible**(boolean b)
void	**show**()
void	**toBack**()
void	**toFront**()
void	**updateUI**()

Class JInternalFrame.JDesktopIcon

```
java.lang.Object
  |
  |
```

```
        +— java.awt.Component
             |
        +--java.awt.Container
                 |
                +--javax.swing.JComponent
                         |
                        +--javax.swing.JInternalFrame.JDesktopIcon
public static class JInternalFrame.JDesktopIcon
                extends JComponent
                implements Accessible
```

This class represents the desktop icons of internal frames.

Inner Class

```
protected class    JInternalFrame.JDesktopIcon.AccessibleJDesktopIcon
```

Constructor

JInternalFrame.JDesktopIcon(JInternalFrame f)

Methods

AccessibleContext	**getAccessibleContext**()
JDesktopPane	**getDesktopPane**()
JInternalFrame	**getInternalFrame**()
DesktopIconUI	**getUI**()
String	**getUIClassID**()
void	**setInternalFrame**(JInternalFrame f)
void	**setUI**(DesktopIconUI ui)
void	**updateUI**()

Class JLabel

```
        java.lang.Object
             |
        +--java.awt.Component
                 |
                +--java.awt.Container
                         |
                        +--javax.swing.JComponent
                                 |
                                +--javax.swing.JLabel
public class JLabel
            extends JComponent
            implements SwingConstants, Accessible
```

This class represents lightweight Swing labels that optionally display a text string or an image.

Inner Class

protected class   **JLabel.AccessibleJLabel**

Field

protected Component   **labelFor**

Constructors

JLabel()
JLabel(Icon image)
JLabel(Icon image, int horizontalAlignment)
JLabel(String text)
JLabel(String text, Icon icon, int horizontalAlignment)
JLabel(String text, int horizontalAlignment)

Methods

protected int	**checkHorizontalKey**(int key, String message)
protected int	**checkVerticalKey**(int key, String message)
AccessibleContext	**getAccessibleContext**()
Icon	**getDisabledIcon**()
int	**getDisplayedMnemonic**()
int	**getHorizontalAlignment**()
int	**getHorizontalTextPosition**()
Icon	**getIcon**()
int	**getIconTextGap**()
Component	**getLabelFor**()
String	**getText**()
LabelUI	**getUI**()
String	**getUIClassID**()
int	**getVerticalAlignment**()
int	**getVerticalTextPosition**()
protected String	**paramString**()
void	**setDisabledIcon**(Icon disabledIcon)
void	**setDisplayedMnemonic**(char aChar)
void	**setDisplayedMnemonic**(int key)
void	**setHorizontalAlignment**(int alignment)
void	**setHorizontalTextPosition**(int textPosition)
void	**setIcon**(Icon icon)
void	**setIconTextGap**(int iconTextGap)
void	**setLabelFor**(Component c)
void	**setText**(String text)
void	**setUI**(LabelUI ui)
void	**setVerticalAlignment**(int alignment)
void	**setVerticalTextPosition**(int textPosition)
void	**updateUI**()

Class JLayeredPane

```
java.lang.Object
   |
   +--java.awt.Component
         |
         +--java.awt.Container
               |
               +--javax.swing.JComponent
                     |
                     +--javax.swing.JLayeredPane
```

public class **JLayeredPane**
        extends JComponent
        implements Accessible

This class represents the Swing layered panes. A layered pane creates the feeling of depth. You can call the method getLayeredPane() from Swing applets, frames, dialog boxes, windows, and so on to get a reference to the underlying layered pane objects of the respective containers.

Inner Class

protected class   **JLayeredPane.AccessibleJLayeredPane**

Fields

static Integer	**DEFAULT_LAYER**
static Integer	**DRAG_LAYER**
static Integer	**FRAME_CONTENT_LAYER**
static String	**LAYER_PROPERTY**
static Integer	**MODAL_LAYER**
static Integer	**PALETTE_LAYER**
static Integer	**POPUP_LAYER**

Constructor

JLayeredPane()

Methods

protected void	**addImpl**(Component comp, Object constraints, int index)
AccessibleContext	**getAccessibleContext**()
int	**getComponentCountInLayer**(int layer)
Component[]	**getComponentsInLayer**(int layer)
protected Hashtable	**getComponentToLayer**()
int	**getIndexOf**(Component c)
int	**getLayer**(Component c)
static int	**getLayer**(JComponent c)
static JLayeredPane	**getLayeredPaneAbove**(Component c)
protected Integer	**getObjectForLayer**(int layer)
int	**getPosition**(Component c)

```
int                         highestLayer()
protected int               insertIndexForLayer(int layer, int position)
boolean                     isOptimizedDrawingEnabled()
int                         lowestLayer()
void                        moveToBack(Component c)
void                        moveToFront(Component c)
void                        paint(Graphics g)
protected  String           paramString()
static void                 putLayer(JComponent c, int layer)
void                        remove(int index)
void                        setLayer(Component c, int layer)
void                        setLayer(Component c, int layer, int position)
void                        setPosition(Component c, int position)
```

Class JList

```
java.lang.Object
   |
   +--java.awt.Component
          |
          +--java.awt.Container
                  |
                  +--javax.swing.JComponent
                          |
                          +--javax.swing.JList
```

```
public class JList
            extends JComponent
            implements Scrollable, Accessible
```

This class represents the lightweight Swing lists. A list is a single column of selectable items.

Inner Class

```
protected class     JList.AccessibleJList
```

Constructors

```
JList()
JList(ListModel dataModel)
JList(Object[] listData)
JList(Vector listData)
```

Methods

```
void                        addListSelectionListener
                            (ListSelectionListener listener)
void                        addSelectionInterval(int anchor, int lead)
void                        clearSelection()
protected ListSelectionModel    createSelectionModel()
```

void	**ensureIndexIsVisible**(int index)
protected void	**fireSelectionValueChanged**(int firstIndex, int lastIndex, boolean isAdjusting)
AccessibleContext	**getAccessibleContext**()
int	**getAnchorSelectionIndex**()
Rectangle	**getCellBounds**(int index1, int index2)
ListCellRenderer	**getCellRenderer**()
int	**getFirstVisibleIndex**()
int	**getFixedCellHeight**()
int	**getFixedCellWidth**()
int	**getLastVisibleIndex**()
int	**getLeadSelectionIndex**()
int	**getMaxSelectionIndex**()
int	**getMinSelectionIndex**()
ListModel	**getModel**()
Dimension	**getPreferredScrollable ViewportSize**()
Object	**getPrototypeCellValue**()
int	**getScrollableBlockIncrement** (Rectangle visibleRect, orientation, int direction)
boolean	**getScrollableTracksViewport Height**()
boolean	**getScrollableTracksViewport Width**()
int	**getScrollableUnitIncrement** (Rectangle visibleRect, orientation, int direction)
int	**getSelectedIndex**()
int[]	**getSelectedIndices**()
Object	**getSelectedValue**()
Object[]	**getSelectedValues**()
Color	**getSelectionBackground**()
Color	**getSelectionForeground**()
int	**getSelectionMode**()
ListSelectionModel	**getSelectionModel**()
ListUI	**getUI**()
String	**getUIClassID**()
boolean	**getValueIsAdjusting**()
int	**getVisibleRowCount**()
Point	**indexToLocation**(int index)
boolean	**isSelectedIndex**(int index)
boolean	**isSelectionEmpty**()
int	**locationToIndex**(Point location)
protected String	**paramString**()
void	**removeListSelectionListener** (ListSelectionListener listener)

void	**removeSelectionInterval**(int index0, int index1)
void	**setCellRenderer**(ListCellRenderer cellRenderer)
void	**setFixedCellHeight**(int height)
void	**setFixedCellWidth**(int width)
void	**setListData**(Object[] listData)
void	**setListData**(Vector listData)
void	**setModel**(ListModel model)
void	**setPrototypeCellValue**(Object prototypeCellValue)
void	**setSelectedIndex**(int index)
void	**setSelectedIndices**(int[] indices)
void	**setSelectedValue**(Object anObject, boolean shouldScroll)
void	**sbetSelectionBackground**(Color selectionBackground)
void	**setSelectionForeground**(Color selectionForeground)
void	**setSelectionInterval**(int anchor, int lead)
void	**setSelectionMode**(int selectionMode)
void	**setSelectionModel** (ListSelectionModel selectionModel)
void	**setUI**(ListUI ui)
void	**setValueIsAdjusting**(boolean b)
void	**setVisibleRowCount**(int visibleRowCount)
void	**updateUI**()

Class JMenu

```
java.lang.Object
   |
   +--java.awt.Component
        |
        +--java.awt.Container
             |
             +--javax.swing.JComponent
                  |
                  +--javax.swing.AbstractButton
                       |
                       +--javax.swing.JMenuItem
                            |
                            +--javax.swing.JMenu
```

public class **JMenu**
        extends JMenuItem
        implements Accessible, MenuElement

This class represents the normal Swing menus. Menus contain selectable menu items and menu item separators.

Inner Classes

protected class   **JMenu.AccessibleJMenu**
protected class   **JMenu.WinListener**

Field

protected JMenu.WinListener   **popupListener**

Constructors

JMenu()
JMenu(String s)
JMenu(String s, boolean b)

Methods

JMenuItem	**add**(Action a)
Component	**add**(Component c)
JMenuItem	**add**(JMenuItem menuItem)
JMenuItem	**add**(String s)
void	**addMenuListener**(MenuListener l)
void	**addSeparator**()
protected PropertyChangeListener	**createActionChangeListener** (JMenuItem b)
protected JMenu.WinListener	**createWinListener**(JPopupMenu p)
void	**doClick**(int pressTime)
protected void	**fireMenuCanceled**()
protected void	**fireMenuDeselected**()
protected void	**fireMenuSelected**()
AccessibleContext	**getAccessibleContext**()
Component	**getComponent**()
int	**getDelay**()
JMenuItem	**getItem**(int pos)
int	**getItemCount**()
Component	**getMenuComponent**(int n)
int	**getMenuComponentCount**()
Component[]	**getMenuComponents**()
JPopupMenu	**getPopupMenu**()
MenuElement[]	**getSubElements**()
String	**getUIClassID**()
JMenuItem	**insert**(Action a, int pos)
JMenuItem	**insert**(JMenuItem mi, int pos)
void	**insert**(String s, int pos)
void	**insertSeparator**(int index)
boolean	**isMenuComponent**(Component c)
boolean	**isPopupMenuVisible**()
boolean	**isSelected**()
boolean	**isTearOff**()
boolean	**isTopLevelMenu**()
void	**menuSelectionChanged**(boolean isIncluded)

protected String	**paramString**()
protected void	**processKeyEvent**(KeyEvent e)
void	**remove**(Component c)
void	**remove**(int pos)
void	**remove**(JMenuItem item)
void	**removeAll**()
void	**removeMenuListener** (MenuListener l)
void	**setAccelerator**(KeyStroke keyStroke)
void	**setDelay**(int d)
void	**setMenuLocation**(int x, int y)
void	**setModel**(ButtonModel newModel)
void	**setPopupMenuVisible**(boolean b)
void	**setSelected**(boolean b)
void	**updateUI**()

Class JMenuBar

```
java.lang.Object
   |
   +--java.awt.Component
          |
          +--java.awt.Container
                 |
                 +--javax.swing.JComponent
                        |
                        +--javax.swing.JMenuBar
```

public class **JMenuBar**
        extends JComponent
        implements Accessible, MenuElement

This class represents the Swing menu bar. A menu bar is added with menus. For Swing applets, frames, dialog boxes, and windows, you can call the method getJMenuBar() to obtain a handle to the underlying menu bar.

Inner Classes

protected class   **JMenuBar.AccessibleJMenuBar**

Constructors

JMenuBar()

Methods

JMenu	**add**(JMenu c)
void	**addNotify**()
AccessibleContext	**getAccessibleContext**()
Component	**getComponent**()
Component	**getComponentAtIndex**(int i)
int	**getComponentIndex**(Component c)

JMenu	**getHelpMenu**()
Insets	**getMargin**()
JMenu	**getMenu**(int index)
int	**getMenuCount**()
SingleSelectionModel	**getSelectionModel**()
MenuElement[]	**getSubElements**()
MenuBarUI	**getUI**()
String	**getUIClassID**()
boolean	**isBorderPainted**()
boolean	**isManagingFocus**()
boolean	**isSelected**()
void	**menuSelectionChanged**(boolean isIncluded)
protected void	**paintBorder**(Graphics g)
protected String	**paramString**()
void	**processKeyEvent**(KeyEvent e, MenuElement[] path, MenuSelectionManager manager)
void	**processMouseEvent**(MouseEvent event, MenuElement[] path, MenuSelectionManager manager)
void	**removeNotify**()
void	**setBorderPainted**(boolean s)
void	**setHelpMenu**(JMenu menu)
void	**setMargin**(Insets margin)
void	**setSelected**(Component sel)
void	**setSelectionModel**(SingleSelectionModel model)
void	**setUI**(MenuBarUI ui)
void	**updateUI**()

Class JMenuItem

```
java.lang.Object
   |
   +--java.awt.Component
          |
          +--java.awt.Container
                 |
                 +--javax.swing.JComponent
                        |
                        +--javax.swing.AbstractButton
                               |
                               +--javax.swing.JMenuItem
```

public class **JMenuItem**
        extends AbstractButton
        implements Accessible, MenuElement

This class represents Swing menu items. Menu items function similarly to buttons and fire action events.

Inner Class

protected class   JMenuItem.AccessibleJMenuItem

Constructors

JMenuItem()
JMenuItem(Icon icon)
JMenuItem(String text)
JMenuItem(String text, Icon icon)
JMenuItem(String text, int mnemonic)

Methods

void	**addMenuDragMouseListener** (MenuDragMouseListener l)
void	**addMenuKeyListener**(MenuKeyListener l)
protected void	**fireMenuDragMouseDragged**(MenuDragMouseEvent event)
protected void	**fireMenuDragMouseEntered**(MenuDragMouseEvent event)
protected void	**fireMenuDragMouseExited**(MenuDragMouseEvent event)
protected void	**fireMenuDragMouseReleased**(MenuDragMouseEvent event)
protected void	**fireMenuKeyPressed**(MenuKeyEvent event)
protected void	**fireMenuKeyReleased**(MenuKeyEvent event)
protected void	**fireMenuKeyTyped**(MenuKeyEvent event)
KeyStroke	**getAccelerator**()
AccessibleContext	**getAccessibleContext**()
Component	**getComponent**()
MenuElement[]	**getSubElements**()
String	**getUIClassID**()
protected void	**init**(String text, Icon icon)
boolean	**isArmed**()
void	**menuSelectionChanged**(boolean isIncluded)
protected String	**paramString**()
void	**processKeyEvent**(KeyEvent e, MenuElement[] path, MenuSelectionManager manager)
void	**processMenuDragMouseEvent**(MenuDragMouseEvent e)
void	**processMenuKeyEvent**(MenuKeyEvent e)
void	**processMouseEvent**(MouseEvent e, MenuElement[] path, MenuSelectionManager manager)
void	**removeMenuDragMouseListener** (MenuDragMouseListener l)
void	**removeMenuKeyListener**(MenuKeyListener l)
void	**setAccelerator**(KeyStroke keyStroke)
void	**setArmed**(boolean b)
void	**setEnabled**(boolean b)
void	**setUI**(MenuItemUI ui)
void	**updateUI**()

Class JOptionPane

```
java.lang.Object
     |
     +--java.awt.Component
              |
              +--java.awt.Container
                       |
                       +--javax.swing.JComponent
                                |
                                +--javax.swing.JOptionPane
```

public class **JOptionPane**
        extends JComponent
        implements Accessible

This class represents the Swing option panes. An option pane is an intermediate class that simplifies the use of standard dialog boxes by calling relevant static methods.

Inner Class

protected class   JOptionPane.AccessibleJOptionPane

Fields

static int	**CANCEL_OPTION**
static int	**CLOSED_OPTION**
static int	**DEFAULT_OPTION**
static int	**ERROR_MESSAGE**
protected Icon	**icon**
static String	**ICON_PROPERTY**
static int	**INFORMATION_MESSAGE**
static String	**INITIAL_SELECTION_VALUE_PROPERTY**
static String	**INITIAL_VALUE_PROPERTY**
protected Object	**initialSelectionValue**
protected Object	**initialValue**
static String	**INPUT_VALUE_PROPERTY**
protected Object	**inputValue**
protected Object	**message**
static String	**MESSAGE_PROPERTY**
static String	**MESSAGE_TYPE_PROPERTY**
protected int	**messageType**
static int	**NO_OPTION**
static int	**OK_CANCEL_OPTION**
static int	**OK_OPTION**
static String	**OPTION_TYPE_PROPERTY**
protected Object[]	**options**
static String	**OPTIONS_PROPERTY**
protected int	**optionType**
static int	**PLAIN_MESSAGE**
static int	**QUESTION_MESSAGE**

static String	**SELECTION_VALUES_PROPERTY**
protected Object[]	**selectionValues**
static Object	**UNINITIALIZED_VALUE**
protected Object	**value**
static String	**VALUE_PROPERTY**
static String	**WANTS_INPUT_PROPERTY**
protected boolean	**wantsInput**
static int	**WARNING_MESSAGE**
static int	**YES_NO_CANCEL_OPTION**
static int	**YES_NO_OPTION**
static int	**YES_OPTION**

Constructors

JOptionPane()
JOptionPane(Object message)
JOptionPane(Object message, int messageType)
JOptionPane(Object message, int messageType, int optionType)
JOptionPane(Object message, int messageType, int optionType, Icon icon)
JOptionPane(Object message, int messageType, int optionType, Icon icon,
Object[] options)
JOptionPane(Object message, int messageType, int optionType, Icon icon,
Object[] options, Object initialValue)

Methods

JDialog	**createDialog**(Component parentComponent, String title)
JInternalFrame	**createInternalFrame**(Component parentComponent, String title)
AccessibleContext	**getAccessibleContext**()
static JDesktopPane	**getDesktopPaneForComponent**(Component parentComponent)
static Frame	**getFrameForComponent**(Component parentComponent)
Icon	**getIcon**()
Object	**getInitialSelectionValue**()
Object	**getInitialValue**()
Object	**getInputValue**()
int	**getMaxCharactersPerLineCount**()
Object	**getMessage**()
int	**getMessageType**()
Object[]	**getOptions**()
int	**getOptionType**()
static Frame	**getRootFrame**()
Object[]	**getSelectionValues**()
OptionPaneUI	**getUI**()
String	**getUIClassID**()
Object	**getValue**()
boolean	**getWantsInput**()
protected String	**paramString**()
void	**selectInitialValue**()
void	**setIcon**(Icon newIcon)

void	**setInitialSelectionValue**(Object newValue)
void	**setInitialValue**(Object newInitialValue)
void	**setInputValue**(Object newValue)
void	**setMessage**(Object newMessage)
void	**setMessageType**(int newType)
void	**setOptions**(Object[] newOptions)
void	**setOptionType**(int newType)
static void	**setRootFrame**(Frame newRootFrame)
void	**setSelectionValues**(Object[] newValues)
void	**setUI**(OptionPaneUI ui)
void	**setValue**(Object newValue)
void	**setWantsInput**(boolean newValue)
static int	**showConfirmDialog**(Component parentComponent, Object message)
static int	**showConfirmDialog**(Component parentComponent, Object message, String title, int optionType)
static int	**showConfirmDialog**(Component parentComponent, Object message, String title, int optionType, int messageType)
static int	**showConfirmDialog**(Component parentComponent, Object message, String title, int optionType, int messageType, Icon icon)
static String	**showInputDialog**(Component parentComponent, Object message)
static String	**showInputDialog**(Component parentComponent, Object message, String title, int messageType)
static Object	**showInputDialog**(Component parentComponent, Object message, String title, int messageType, Icon icon, Object[] selectionValues, Object initialSelectionValue)
static String	**showInputDialog**(Object message)
static int	**showInternalConfirmDialog**(Component parentComponent, Object message)
static int	**showInternalConfirmDialog**(Component parentComponent, Object message, String title, int optionType)
static int	**showInternalConfirmDialog**(Component parentComponent, Object message, String title, int optionType, int messageType)
static int	**showInternalConfirmDialog**(Component parentComponent, Object message, String title, int optionType, int messageType, Icon icon)
static String	**showInternalInputDialog**(Component parentComponent, Object message)

static String	**showInternalInputDialog**(Component parentComponent, Object message, String title, int messageType)
static Object	**showInternalInputDialog**(Component parentComponent, Object message, String title, int messageType, Icon icon, Object[] selectionValues, Object initialSelectionValue)
static void	**showInternalMessageDialog**(Component parentComponent, Object message)
static void	**showInternalMessageDialog**(Component parentComponent, Object message, String title, int messageType)
static void	**showInternalMessageDialog**(Component parentComponent, Object message, String title, int messageType, Icon icon)
static int	**showInternalOptionDialog**(Component parentComponent, Object message, String title, int optionType, int messageType, Icon icon, Object[] options, Object initialValue)
static void	**showMessageDialog**(Component parentComponent, Object message)
static void	**showMessageDialog**(Component parentComponent, Object message, String title, int messageType)
static void	**showMessageDialog**(Component parentComponent, Object message, String title, int messageType, Icon icon)
static int	**showOptionDialog**(Component parentComponent, Object message, String title, int optionType, int messageType, Icon icon, Object[] options, Object initialValue)
void	**updateUI**()

Class JPanel

```
java.lang.Object
   |
   +--java.awt.Component
         |
         +--java.awt.Container
               |
               +--javax.swing.JComponent
                     |
                     +--javax.swing.JPanel
```

public class **JPanel**
            extends JComponent
            implements Accessible

This class represents the lightweight Swing panels. Panels are useful for grouping child components. Swing panels can optionally support double buffering.

Inner Class

protected class   **JPanel.AccessibleJPanel**

Constructors

JPanel()
JPanel(boolean isDoubleBuffered)
JPanel(LayoutManager layout)
JPanel(LayoutManager layout, boolean isDoubleBuffered)

Methods

AccessibleContext   **getAccessibleContext**()
String   **getUIClassID**()
protected String   **paramString**()
void   **updateUI**()

Class JPasswordField

```
java.lang.Object
   |
   +--java.awt.Component
          |
          +--java.awt.Container
                 |
                 +--javax.swing.JComponent
                        |
                        +--javax.swing.text.JTextComponent
                               |
                               +--javax.swing.JTextField
                                      |
                                      +--javax.swing.JPasswordField
```

public class **JPasswordField**
         extends JTextField

This class represents the password fields supported in Swing. The component is similar to a text field, except that it does not reveal the characters that are typed. Instead, it displays the character * by default (which can be changed) for each typed character.

Inner Class

protected class   **JPasswordField.AccessibleJPasswordField**

Constructors

JPasswordField()
JPasswordField(Document doc, String txt, int columns)
JPasswordField(int columns)
JPasswordField(String text)
JPasswordField(String text, int columns)

Methods

void	**copy**()
void	**cut**()
boolean	**echoCharIsSet**()
AccessibleContext	**getAccessibleContext**()
char	**getEchoChar**()
char[]	**getPassword**()
String	**getText**()
String	**getText**(int offs, int len)
String	**getUIClassID**()
protected String	**paramString**()
void	**setEchoChar**(char c)

Class JPopupMenu

```
java.lang.Object
   |
   +--java.awt.Component
         |
         +--java.awt.Container
               |
               +--javax.swing.JComponent
                     |
                     +--javax.swing.JPopupMenu
```

public class **JPopupMenu**
        extends JComponent
        implements Accessible, MenuElement

This class represents the Swing pop-up menus. Menu items can be added to this component.

Inner Classes

protected class	**JPopupMenu.AccessibleJPopupMenu**
static class	**JPopupMenu.Separator**

Constructors

JPopupMenu()
JPopupMenu(String label)

Methods

JMenuItem	**add**(Action a)
JMenuItem	**add**(JMenuItem menuItem)
JMenuItem	**add**(String s)
void	**addPopupMenuListener** (PopupMenuListener l)
void	**addSeparator**()
protected PropertyChangeListener	**createActionChangeListener** (JMenuItem b)

protected void	**firePopupMenuCanceled**()
protected void	**firePopupMenuWillBecome Invisible**()
protected void	**firePopupMenuWillBecome Visible**()
AccessibleContext	**getAccessibleContext**()
Component	**getComponent**()
Component	**getComponentAtIndex**(int i)
int	**getComponentIndex**(Component c)
static boolean	**getDefaultLightWeightPopup Enabled**()
Component	**getInvoker**()
String	**getLabel**()
Insets	**getMargin**()
SingleSelectionModel	**getSelectionModel**()
MenuElement[]	**getSubElements**()
PopupMenuUI	**getUI**()
String	**getUIClassID**()
void	**insert**(Action a, int index)
void	**insert**(Component component, int index)
boolean	**isBorderPainted**()
boolean	**isLightWeightPopupEnabled**()
boolean	**isVisible**()
void	**menuSelectionChanged**(boolean isIncluded)
void	**pack**()
protected void	**paintBorder**(Graphics g)
protected String	**paramString**()
void	**processKeyEvent**(KeyEvent e, MenuElement[] path, MenuSelectionManager manager)
void	**processMouseEvent**(MouseEvent event, MenuElement[] path, MenuSelectionManager manager)
void	**remove**(Component comp)
void	**removePopupMenuListener** (PopupMenuListener l)
void	**setBorderPainted**(boolean b)
static void	**setDefaultLightWeightPopup Enabled**(boolean aFlag)
void	**setInvoker**(Component invoker)
void	**setLabel**(String label)
void	**setLightWeightPopupEnabled** (boolean aFlag)
void	**setLocation**(int x, int y)
void	**setPopupSize**(Dimension d)
void	**setPopupSize**(int width, int height)
void	**setSelected**(Component sel)
void	**setSelectionModel** (SingleSelectionModel model)

```
void                        setUI(PopupMenuUI ui)
void                        setVisible(boolean b)
void                        show(Component invoker, int x, int y)
void                        updateUI()
```

Class JPopupMenu.Separator

```
java.lang.Object
   |
   +--java.awt.Component
         |
         +--java.awt.Container
               |
               +--javax.swing.JComponent
                     |
                     +--javax.swing.JSeparator
                           |
                           +--javax.swing.JPopupMenu.Separator
```

public static class **JPopupMenu.Separator**
                extends JSeparator

This class represents a separator that is used to logically group menu items in a pop-up menu.

Constructors

JPopupMenu.Separator()

Methods

```
String     getUIClassID()
```

Class JProgressBar

```
java.lang.Object
   |
   +--java.awt.Component
         |
         +--java.awt.Container
               |
               +--javax.swing.JComponent
                     |
                     +--javax.swing.JProgressBar
```

public class **JProgressBar**
                extends JComponent
                implements SwingConstants, Accessible

This class represents progress bars. A progress bar indicates the progress of execution by displaying a percentage of completion.

Inner Class

protected class   **JProgressBar.AccessibleJProgressBar**

Fields

protected	ChangeEvent	**changeEvent**
protected	ChangeListener	**changeListener**
protected	BoundedRangeModel	**model**
protected	int	**orientation**
protected	boolean	**paintBorder**
protected	boolean	**paintString**
protected	String	**progressString**

Constructors

JProgressBar()
JProgressBar(BoundedRangeModel newModel)
JProgressBar(int orient)
JProgressBar(int min, int max)
JProgressBar(int orient, int min, int max)

Methods

void	**addChangeListener**(ChangeListener l)
protected ChangeListener	**createChangeListener**()
protected void	**fireStateChanged**()
AccessibleContext	**getAccessibleContext**()
int	**getMaximum**()
int	**getMinimum**()
BoundedRangeModel	**getModel**()
int	**getOrientation**()
double	**getPercentComplete**()
String	**getString**()
ProgressBarUI	**getUI**()
String	**getUIClassID**()
int	**getValue**()
boolean	**isBorderPainted**()
boolean	**isStringPainted**()
protected void	**paintBorder**(Graphics g)
protected String	**paramString**()
void	**removeChangeListener**(ChangeListener l)
void	**setBorderPainted**(boolean b)
void	**setMaximum**(int n)
void	**setMinimum**(int n)
void	**setModel**(BoundedRangeModel newModel)
void	**setOrientation**(int newOrientation)
void	**setString**(String s)
void	**setStringPainted**(boolean b)
void	**setUI**(ProgressBarUI ui)
void	**setValue**(int n)
void	**updateUI**()

Class JRadioButton

```
java.lang.Object
   |
   +--java.awt.Component
          |
          +--java.awt.Container
                 |
                 +--javax.swing.JComponent
                        |
                        +--javax.swing.AbstractButton
                               |
                               +--javax.swing.JToggleButton
                                      |
                                      +--javax.swing.JRadioButton
```

```
public class JRadioButton
           extends JToggleButton
           implements Accessible
```

This class represents Swing radio buttons. To group radio buttons, you need to create an object of type ButtonGroup and add each of the radio buttons. Only one button from the button group can be selected at a time.

Inner Class

```
protected class    JRadioButton.AccessibleJRadioButton
```

Constructors

```
JRadioButton()
JRadioButton(Icon icon)
JRadioButton(Icon icon, boolean selected)
JRadioButton(String text)
JRadioButton(String text, boolean selected)
JRadioButton(String text, Icon icon)
JRadioButton(String text, Icon icon, boolean selected)
```

Methods

```
AccessibleContext     getAccessibleContext()
String                getUIClassID()
protected String      paramString()
void                  updateUI()
```

Class JRadioButtonMenuItem

```
java.lang.Object
   |
   +--java.awt.Component
          |
          +--java.awt.Container
                 |
                 +--javax.swing.JComponent
```

```
                          |
                          |
                      +--javax.swing.AbstractButton
                          |
                          |
                      +--javax.swing.JMenuItem
                              |
                              |
                          +--javax.swing.JRadioButtonMenuItem
```

public class **JRadioButtonMenuItem**
        extends JMenuItem
        implements Accessible

This class represents the radio button menu items that are added to Swing menus. Radio button menu items appear similarly to radio buttons, and must be grouped by using a ButtonGroup object. Only one menu item can be selected at a time.

Inner Class

protected class   **JRadioButtonMenuItem.AccessibleJRadioButtonMenuItem**

Constructors

JRadioButtonMenuItem()
JRadioButtonMenuItem(Icon icon)
JRadioButtonMenuItem(Icon icon, boolean selected)
JRadioButtonMenuItem(String text)
JRadioButtonMenuItem(String text, boolean b)
JRadioButtonMenuItem(String text, Icon icon)
JRadioButtonMenuItem(String text, Icon icon, boolean selected)

Methods

AccessibleContext	**getAccessibleContext**()
String	**getUIClassID**()
protected void	**init**(String text, Icon icon)
protected String	**paramString**()
void	**requestFocus**()
void	**updateUI**()

Class JRootPane

```
      java.lang.Object
         |
      +--java.awt.Component
            |
            |
         +--java.awt.Container
               |
               |
            +--javax.swing.JComponent
                  |
                  |
               +--javax.swing.JRootPane
```

public class **JRootPane**
        extends JComponent
        implements Accessible

This class represents the Swing root pane. A root pane is basically a wrapper class around a content pane, glass pane, layered pane, or menu bar. Any responsibility given to a root pane is delegated to one of the underlying classes. Root panes exist in Swing applets, frames, dialog boxes, and windows.

Inner Classes

protected class	**JRootPane**.AccessibleJRootPane
protected class	**JRootPane**.RootLayout

Fields

protected Container	**contentPane**
protected JButton	**defaultButton**
protected javax.swing.JRootPane.DefaultAction	**defaultPressAction**
protected javax.swing.JRootPane.DefaultAction	**defaultReleaseAction**
protected Component	**glassPane**
protected JLayeredPane	**layeredPane**
protected JMenuBar	**menuBar**

Constructor

JRootPane()

Methods

protected void	**addImpl**(Component comp, Object constraints, int index)
void	**addNotify**()
protected Container	**createContentPane**()
protected Component	**createGlassPane**()
protected JLayeredPane	**createLayeredPane**()
protected LayoutManager	**createRootLayout**()
AccessibleContext	**getAccessibleContext**()
Container	**getContentPane**()
JButton	**getDefaultButton**()
Component	**getGlassPane**()
JMenuBar	**getJMenuBar**()
JLayeredPane	**getLayeredPane**()
JMenuBar	**getMenuBar**()
boolean	**isFocusCycleRoot**()
boolean	**isValidateRoot**()
protected String	**paramString**()
void	**removeNotify**()
void	**setContentPane**(Container content)
void	**setDefaultButton**(JButton defaultButton)
void	**setGlassPane**(Component glass)
void	**setJMenuBar**(JMenuBar menu)
void	**setLayeredPane**(JLayeredPane layered)
void	**setMenuBar**(JMenuBar menu)
	// Deprecated. Use the method
	setJMenuBar(JMenuBar menu).

Class JScrollBar

```
java.lang.Object
   |
   +--java.awt.Component
          |
          +--java.awt.Container
                 |
                 +--javax.swing.JComponent
                        |
                        +--javax.swing.JScrollBar
```

public class **JScrollBar**
        extends JComponent
        implements Adjustable, Accessible

This class represents Swing scrollbars. Often Swing scroll panes are used rather than using the scrollbars.

Inner Class

protected class   **JScrollBar.AccessibleJScrollBar**

Fields

protected int	**blockIncrement**
protected BoundedRangeModel	**model**
protected int	**orientation**
protected int	**unitIncrement**

Constructors

JScrollBar()
JScrollBar(int orientation)
JScrollBar(int orientation, int value, int extent, int min, int max)

Methods

void	**addAdjustmentListener**(AdjustmentListener l)
protected void	**fireAdjustmentValueChanged**(int id, int type, int value)
AccessibleContext	**getAccessibleContext**()
int	**getBlockIncrement**()
int	**getBlockIncrement**(int direction)
int	**getMaximum**()
Dimension	**getMaximumSize**()
int	**getMinimum**()
Dimension	**getMinimumSize**()
BoundedRangeModel	**getModel**()
int	**getOrientation**()
ScrollBarUI	**getUI**()
String	**getUIClassID**()
int	**getUnitIncrement**()
int	**getUnitIncrement**(int direction)

int	**getValue**()
boolean	**getValueIsAdjusting**()
int	**getVisibleAmount**()
protected String	**paramString**()
void	**removeAdjustmentListener**(AdjustmentListener l)
void	**setBlockIncrement**(int blockIncrement)
void	**setEnabled**(boolean x)
void	**setMaximum**(int maximum)
void	**setMinimum**(int minimum)
void	**setModel**(BoundedRangeModel newModel)
void	**setOrientation**(int orientation)
void	**setUnitIncrement**(int unitIncrement)
void	**setValue**(int value)
void	**setValueIsAdjusting**(boolean b)
void	**setValues**(int newValue, int newExtent, int newMin, int newMax)
void	**setVisibleAmount**(int extent)
void	**updateUI**()

Class JScrollPane

```
java.lang.Object
   |
   +--java.awt.Component
         |
         +--java.awt.Container
               |
               +--javax.swing.JComponent
                     |
                     +--javax.swing.JScrollPane
```

public class **JScrollPane**
        extends JComponent
        implements ScrollPaneConstants, Accessible

This class represents Swing scroll panes. A scroll pane is a ready-made container that supports optional scrollbars in horizontal and vertical directions, viewports, column and row headers, and other corner components.

Inner Classes

protected class	**JScrollPane.AccessibleJScrollPane**
protected class	**JScrollPane.ScrollBar**

Fields

protected JViewport	**columnHeader**
protected JScrollBar	**horizontalScrollBar**
protected int	**horizontalScrollBarPolicy**
protected Component	**lowerLeft**
protected Component	**lowerRight**

```
protected JViewport        rowHeader
protected Component        upperLeft
protected Component        upperRight
protected JScrollBar       verticalScrollBar
protected int              verticalScrollBarPolicy
protected JViewport        viewport
```

Constructors

JScrollPane()
JScrollPane(Component view)
JScrollPane(Component view, int vsbPolicy, int hsbPolicy)
JScrollPane(int vsbPolicy, int hsbPolicy)

Methods

```
JScrollBar                 createHorizontalScrollBar()
JScrollBar                 createVerticalScrollBar()
protected JViewport        createViewport()
AccessibleContext          getAccessibleContext()
JViewport                  getColumnHeader()
Component                  getCorner(String key)
JScrollBar                 getHorizontalScrollBar()
int                        getHorizontalScrollBarPolicy()
JViewport                  getRowHeader()
ScrollPaneUI               getUI()
String                     getUIClassID()
JScrollBar                 getVerticalScrollBar()
int                        getVerticalScrollBarPolicy()
JViewport                  getViewport()
Border                     getViewportBorder()
Rectangle                  getViewportBorderBounds()
boolean                    isOpaque()
boolean                    isValidateRoot()
protected String           paramString()
void                       setColumnHeader(JViewport columnHeader)
void                       setColumnHeaderView(Component view)
void                       setCorner(String key, Component corner)
void                       setHorizontalScrollBar(JScrollBar horizontalScrollBar)
void                       setHorizontalScrollBarPolicy(int policy)
void                       setLayout(LayoutManager layout)
void                       setRowHeader(JViewport rowHeader)
void                       setRowHeaderView(Component view)
void                       setUI(ScrollPaneUI ui)
void                       setVerticalScrollBar(JScrollBar verticalScrollBar)
void                       setVerticalScrollBarPolicy(int policy)
void                       setViewport(JViewport viewport)
void                       setViewportBorder(Border viewportBorder)
void                       setViewportView(Component view)
void                       updateUI()
```

Class JSeparator

```
java.lang.Object
   |
   +--java.awt.Component
          |
          +--java.awt.Container
                 |
                 +--javax.swing.JComponent
                        |
                        +--javax.swing.JSeparator
```

public class **JSeparator**
           extends JComponent
           implements SwingConstants, Accessible

This class represents the separators used in Swing menus. Separators are used to logically group menu items in a menu.

Inner Class

protected class   **JSeparator.AccessibleJSeparator**

Constructors

JSeparator()
JSeparator(int orientation)

Methods

AccessibleContext	**getAccessibleContext**()
int	**getOrientation**()
SeparatorUI	**getUI**()
String	**getUIClassID**()
boolean	**isFocusTraversable**()
protected String	**paramString**()
void	**setOrientation**(int orientation)
void	**setUI**(SeparatorUI ui)
void	**updateUI**()

Class JSlider

```
java.lang.Object
   |
   +--java.awt.Component
          |
          +--java.awt.Container
                 |
                 +--javax.swing.JComponent
                        |
                        +--javax.swing.JSlider
```

public class **JSlider**

```
extends JComponent
implements SwingConstants, Accessible
```

This class represents Swing sliders. Sliders allow the user to select a specific value from a range between minimum and maximum values.

Inner Classes

```
protected class    JSlider.AccessibleJSlider
```

Fields

```
protected ChangeEvent           changeEvent
protected ChangeListener        changeListener
protected int                   majorTickSpacing
protected int                   minorTickSpacing
protected int                   orientation
protected BoundedRangeModel     sliderModel
protected boolean               snapToTicks
```

Constructors

```
JSlider()
JSlider(BoundedRangeModel brm)
JSlider(int orientation)
JSlider(int min, int max)
JSlider(int min, int max, int value)
JSlider(int orientation, int min, int max, int value)
```

Methods

```
void                        addChangeListener(ChangeListener l)
protected ChangeListener    createChangeListener()
Hashtable                   createStandardLabels(int increment)
Hashtable                   createStandardLabels(int increment, int start)
protected void              fireStateChanged()
AccessibleContext           getAccessibleContext()
int                         getExtent()
boolean                     getInverted()
Dictionary                  getLabelTable()
int                         getMajorTickSpacing()
int                         getMaximum()
int                         getMinimum()
int                         getMinorTickSpacing()
BoundedRangeModel           getModel()
int                         getOrientation()
boolean                     getPaintLabels()
boolean                     getPaintTicks()
boolean                     getPaintTrack()
boolean                     getSnapToTicks()
SliderUI                    getUI()
String                      getUIClassID()
```

int	**getValue**()
boolean	**getValueIsAdjusting**()
protected String	**paramString**()
void	**removeChangeListener**(ChangeListener l)
void	**setExtent**(int extent)
void	**setInverted**(boolean b)
void	**setLabelTable**(Dictionary labels)
void	**setMajorTickSpacing**(int n)
void	**setMaximum**(int maximum)
void	**setMinimum**(int minimum)
void	**setMinorTickSpacing**(int n)
void	**setModel**(BoundedRangeModel newModel)
void	**setOrientation**(int orientation)
void	**setPaintLabels**(boolean b)
void	**setPaintTicks**(boolean b)
void	**setPaintTrack**(boolean b)
void	**setSnapToTicks**(boolean b)
void	**setUI**(SliderUI ui)
void	**setValue**(int n)
void	**setValueIsAdjusting**(boolean b)
protected void	**updateLabelUIs**()
void	**updateUI**()

Class JSplitPane

```
java.lang.Object
   |
   +--java.awt.Component
         |
         +--java.awt.Container
               |
               +--javax.swing.JComponent
                     |
                     +--javax.swing.JSplitPane
```

```
public class JSplitPane
          extends JComponent
          implements Accessible
```

This class represents Swing split panes. Split panes are used to graphically separate two child components in a container.

Inner Class

protected class	**JSplitPane.AccessibleJSplitPane**

Fields

static String	**BOTTOM**
static String	**CONTINUOUS_LAYOUT_PROPERTY**
protected boolean	**continuousLayout**
static String	**DIVIDER**

static String	**DIVIDER_SIZE_PROPERTY**
protected int	**dividerSize**
static int	**HORIZONTAL_SPLIT**
static String	**LAST_DIVIDER_LOCATION_PROPERTY**
protected int	**lastDividerLocation**
static String	**LEFT**
protected Component	**leftComponent**
static String	**ONE_TOUCH_EXPANDABLE_PROPERTY**
protected boolean	**oneTouchExpandable**
protected int	**orientation**
static String	**ORIENTATION_PROPERTY**
static String	**RIGHT**
protected Component	**rightComponent**
static String	**TOP**
static int	**VERTICAL_SPLIT**

Constructors

JSplitPane()
JSplitPane(int newOrientation)
JSplitPane(int newOrientation, boolean newContinuousLayout)
JSplitPane(int newOrientation, boolean newContinuousLayout,
Component newLeftComponent, Component newRightComponent)
JSplitPane(int newOrientation, Component newLeftComponent,
Component newRightComponent)

Methods

protected void	**addImpl**(Component comp, Object constraints, int index)
AccessibleContext	**getAccessibleContext**()
Component	**getBottomComponent**()
int	**getDividerLocation**()
int	**getDividerSize**()
int	**getLastDividerLocation**()
Component	**getLeftComponent**()
int	**getMaximumDividerLocation**()
int	**getMinimumDividerLocation**()
int	**getOrientation**()
Component	**getRightComponent**()
Component	**getTopComponent**()
SplitPaneUI	**getUI**()
String	**getUIClassID**()
boolean	**isContinuousLayout**()
boolean	**isOneTouchExpandable**()
protected void	**paintChildren**(Graphics g)
protected String	**paramString**()
void	**remove**(Component component)
void	**remove**(int index)
void	**removeAll**()

void	resetToPreferredSizes()
void	setBottomComponent(Component comp)
void	setContinuousLayout(boolean newContinuousLayout)
void	setDividerLocation(double proportionalLocation)
void	setDividerLocation(int location)
void	setDividerSize(int newSize)
void	setLastDividerLocation(int newLastLocation)
void	setLeftComponent(Component comp)
void	setOneTouchExpandable(boolean newValue)
void	setOrientation(int orientation)
void	setRightComponent(Component comp)
void	setTopComponent(Component comp)
void	setUI(SplitPaneUI ui)
void	updateUI()

Class JTabbedPane

```
java.lang.Object
    |
    +--java.awt.Component
            |
            +--java.awt.Container
                    |
                    +--javax.swing.JComponent
                            |
                            +--javax.swing.JTabbedPane
```

public class **JTabbedPane**
        extends JComponent
        implements Serializable, Accessible, SwingConstants

This class represents Swing tabbed panes. You can click a tab to change over to a new pane that appears in the same display area. Each pane can contain its own set of child components.

Inner Classes

protected class	**JTabbedPane.AccessibleJTabbedPane**
protected class	**JTabbedPane.ModelListener**

Fields

protected ChangeEvent	**changeEvent**
protected ChangeListener	**changeListener**
protected SingleSelectionModel	**model**
protected int	**tabPlacement**

Constructors

JTabbedPane()
JTabbedPane(int tabPlacement)

Methods

Component	**add**(Component component)
Component	**add**(Component component, int index)
void	**add**(Component component, Object constraints)
void	**add**(Component component, Object constraints, int index)
Component	**add**(String title, Component component)
void	**addChangeListener**(ChangeListener l)
void	**addTab**(String title, Component component)
void	**addTab**(String title, Icon icon, Component component)
void	**addTab**(String title, Icon icon, Component component, String tip)
protected ChangeListener	**createChangeListener**()
protected void	**fireStateChanged**()
AccessibleContext	**getAccessibleContext**()
Color	**getBackgroundAt**(int index)
Rectangle	**getBoundsAt**(int index)
Component	**getComponentAt**(int index)
Icon	**getDisabledIconAt**(int index)
Color	**getForegroundAt**(int index)
Icon	**getIconAt**(int index)
SingleSelectionModel	**getModel**()
Component	**getSelectedComponent**()
int	**getSelectedIndex**()
int	**getTabCount**()
int	**getTabPlacement**()
int	**getTabRunCount**()
String	**getTitleAt**(int index)
String	**getToolTipText**(MouseEvent event)
TabbedPaneUI	**getUI**()
String	**getUIClassID**()
int	**indexOfComponent**(Component component)
int	**indexOfTab**(Icon icon)
int	**indexOfTab**(String title)
void	**insertTab**(String title, Icon icon, Component component, String tip, int index)
boolean	**isEnabledAt**(int index)
protected String	**paramString**()
void	**remove**(Component component)
void	**removeAll**()
void	**removeChangeListener**(ChangeListener l)
void	**removeTabAt**(int index)
void	**setBackgroundAt**(int index, Color background)
void	**setComponentAt**(int index, Component component)
void	**setDisabledIconAt**(int index, Icon disabledIcon)
void	**setEnabledAt**(int index, boolean enabled)

void	**setForegroundAt**(int index, Color foreground)
void	**setIconAt**(int index, Icon icon)
void	**setModel**(SingleSelectionModel model)
void	**setSelectedComponent**(Component c)
void	**setSelectedIndex**(int index)
void	**setTabPlacement**(int tabPlacement)
void	**setTitleAt**(int index, String title)
void	**setUI**(TabbedPaneUI ui)
void	**updateUI**()

Class JTable

```
java.lang.Object
    |
    |
    +--java.awt.Component
            |
            |
            +--java.awt.Container
                    |
                    |
                    +--javax.swing.JComponent
                            |
                            |
                            +--javax.swing.JTable
```

public class **JTable**
        extends JComponent
        implements TableModelListener, Scrollable,
        TableColumnModelListener, ListSelectionListener,
        CellEditorListener, Accessible

This class represents Swing tables. Tables can be considered two-dimensional lists.

Inner Class

protected class	**JTable.AccessibleJTable**

Fields

static int	**AUTO_RESIZE_ALL_COLUMNS**
static int	**AUTO_RESIZE_LAST_COLUMN**
static int	**AUTO_RESIZE_NEXT_COLUMN**
static int	**AUTO_RESIZE_OFF**
static int	**AUTO_RESIZE_SUBSEQUENT_COLUMNS**
protected boolean	**autoCreateColumnsFromModel**
protected int	**autoResizeMode**
protected TableCellEditor	**cellEditor**
protected boolean	**cellSelectionEnabled**
protected TableColumnModel	**columnModel**
protected TableModel	**dataModel**
protected Hashtable	**defaultEditorsByColumnClass**
protected Hashtable	**defaultRenderersByColumnClass**
protected int	**editingColumn**
protected int	**editingRow**
protected Component	**editorComp**

```
protected Color                    gridColor
protected Dimension                preferredViewportSize
protected int                      rowHeight
protected int                      rowMargin
protected boolean                  rowSelectionAllowed
protected Color                    selectionBackground
protected Color                    selectionForeground
protected ListSelectionModel       selectionModel
protected boolean                  showHorizontalLines
protected boolean                  showVerticalLines
protected JTableHeader             tableHeader
```

Constructors

JTable()
JTable(int numRows, int numColumns)
JTable(Object[][] rowData, Object[] columnNames)
JTable(TableModel dm)
JTable(TableModel dm, TableColumnModel cm)
JTable(TableModel dm, TableColumnModel cm, ListSelectionModel sm)
JTable(Vector rowData, Vector columnNames)

Methods

```
void                      addColumn(TableColumn aColumn)
void                      addColumnSelectionInterval(int
                          index0, int index1)
void                      addNotify()
void                      addRowSelectionInterval(int index0, int index1)
void                      clearSelection()
void                      columnAdded(TableColumnModelEvent e)
int                       columnAtPoint(Point point)
void                      columnMarginChanged(ChangeEvent e)
void                      columnMoved(TableColumnModelEvent e)
void                      columnRemoved
                          (TableColumnModelEvent e)
void                      columnSelectionChanged
                          (ListSelectionEvent e)
protected void            configureEnclosingScrollPane()
int                       convertColumnIndexToModel(int viewColumnIndex)
int                       convertColumnIndexToView(int modelColumnIndex)
protected TableColumnModel createDefaultColumnModel()
void                      createDefaultColumnsFromModel()
protected TableModel      createDefaultDataModel()
protected void            createDefaultEditors()
protected void            createDefaultRenderers()
protected ListSelectionModel createDefaultSelectionModel()
protected JTableHeader    createDefaultTableHeader()
static JScrollPane        createScrollPaneForTable(JTable aTable)
                          //  Deprecated. Use the method
```

JScrollPane(aTable).

boolean	**editCellAt**(int row, int column)
boolean	**editCellAt**(int row, int column, EventObject e)
void	**editingCanceled**(ChangeEvent e)
void	**editingStopped**(ChangeEvent e)
AccessibleContext	**getAccessibleContext**()
boolean	**getAutoCreateColumnsFromModel**()
int	**getAutoResizeMode**()
TableCellEditor	**getCellEditor**()
TableCellEditor	**getCellEditor**(int row, int column)
Rectangle	**getCellRect**(int row, int column, boolean includeSpacing)
TableCellRenderer	**getCellRenderer**(int row, int column)
boolean	**getCellSelectionEnabled**()
TableColumn	**getColumn**(Object identifier)
Class	**getColumnClass**(int column)
int	**getColumnCount**()
TableColumnModel	**getColumnModel**()
String	**getColumnName**(int column)
boolean	**getColumnSelectionAllowed**()
TableCellEditor	**getDefaultEditor**(Class columnClass)
TableCellRenderer	**getDefaultRenderer**(Class columnClass)
int	**getEditingColumn**()
int	**getEditingRow**()
Component	**getEditorComponent**()
Color	**getGridColor**()
Dimension	**getIntercellSpacing**()
TableModel	**getModel**()
Dimension	**getPreferredScrollableViewportSize**()
int	**getRowCount**()
int	**getRowHeight**()
int	**getRowMargin**()
boolean	**getRowSelectionAllowed**()
int	**getScrollableBlockIncrement** (Rectangle visibleRect, int orientation, int direction)
boolean	**getScrollableTracksViewportHeight**()
boolean	**getScrollableTracksViewportWidth**()
int	**getScrollableUnitIncrement** (Rectangle visibleRect, int orientation, int direction)
int	**getSelectedColumn**()
int	**getSelectedColumnCount**()
int[]	**getSelectedColumns**()
int	**getSelectedRow**()
int	**getSelectedRowCount**()

int[]	**getSelectedRows**()
Color	**getSelectionBackground**()
Color	**getSelectionForeground**()
ListSelectionModel	**getSelectionModel**()
boolean	**getShowHorizontalLines**()
boolean	**getShowVerticalLines**()
JTableHeader	**getTableHeader**()
String	**getToolTipText**(MouseEvent event)
TableUI	**getUI**()
String	**getUIClassID**()
Object	**getValueAt**(int row, int column)
protected void	**initializeLocalVars**()
boolean	**isCellEditable**(int row, int column)
boolean	**isCellSelected**(int row, int column)
boolean	**isColumnSelected**(int column)
boolean	**isEditing**()
boolean	**isManagingFocus**()
boolean	**isRowSelected**(int row)
void	**moveColumn**(int column, int targetColumn)
protected String	**paramString**()
Component	**prepareEditor**(TableCellEditor editor, int row, int column)
Component	**prepareRenderer**(TableCellRenderer renderer, int row, int column)
void	**removeColumn**(TableColumn aColumn)
void	**removeColumnSelectionInterval**(int index0, int index1)
void	**removeEditor**()
void	**removeRowSelectionInterval**(int index0, int index1)
void	**reshape**(int x, int y, int width, int height)
protected void	**resizeAndRepaint**()
int	**rowAtPoint**(Point point)
void	**selectAll**()
void	**setAutoCreateColumnsFromModel** (boolean createColumns)
void	**setAutoResizeMode**(int mode)
void	**setCellEditor**(TableCellEditor anEditor)
void	**setCellSelectionEnabled**(boolean flag)
void	**setColumnModel**(TableColumnModel newModel)
void	**setColumnSelectionAllowed**(boolean flag)
void	**setColumnSelectionInterval**(int index0, int index1)
void	**setDefaultEditor**(Class columnClass, TableCellEditor editor)
void	**setDefaultRenderer**(Class columnClass, TableCellRenderer renderer)

void	**setEditingColumn**(int aColumn)
void	**setEditingRow**(int aRow)
void	**setGridColor**(Color newColor)
void	**setIntercellSpacing**(Dimension newSpacing)
void	**setModel**(TableModel newModel)
void	**setPreferredScrollableViewportSize** (Dimension size)
void	**setRowHeight**(int newHeight)
void	**setRowMargin**(int rowMargin)
void	**setRowSelectionAllowed**(boolean flag)
void	**setRowSelectionInterval**(int index0, int index1)
void	**setSelectionBackground** (Color selectionBackground)
void	**setSelectionForeground** (Color selectionForeground)
void	**setSelectionMode**(int selectionMode)
void	**setSelectionModel** (ListSelectionModel newModel)
void	**setShowGrid**(boolean b)
void	**setShowHorizontalLines**(boolean b)
void	**setShowVerticalLines**(boolean b)
void	**setTableHeader**(JTableHeader newHeader)
void	**setUI**(TableUI ui)
void	**setValueAt**(Object aValue, int row, int column)
void	**sizeColumnsToFit**(boolean lastColumnOnly) // Deprecated. Use the method sizeColumnsToFit(int).
void	**sizeColumnsToFit**(int resizingColumn)
void	**tableChanged**(TableModelEvent e)
void	**updateUI**()
void	**valueChanged**(ListSelectionEvent e)

Class JTextArea

```
java.lang.Object
   |
   +--java.awt.Component
           |
           +--java.awt.Container
                   |
                   +--javax.swing.JComponent
                           |
                           +--javax.swing.text.JTextComponent
                                   |
                                   +--javax.swing.JTextArea
```

public class **JTextArea**
          extends JTextComponent

This class represents the Swing text area. The text area supports the display and editing of multiline plain text.

Inner Class

protected class   **JTextArea.AccessibleJTextArea**

Constructors

JTextArea()
JTextArea(Document doc)
JTextArea(Document doc, String text, int rows, int columns)
JTextArea(int rows, int columns)
JTextArea(String text)
JTextArea(String text, int rows, int columns)

Methods

void	**append**(String str)
protected Document	**createDefaultModel**()
AccessibleContext	**getAccessibleContext**()
int	**getColumns**()
protected int	**getColumnWidth**()
int	**getLineCount**()
int	**getLineEndOffset**(int line)
int	**getLineOfOffset**(int offset)
int	**getLineStartOffset**(int line)
boolean	**getLineWrap**()
Dimension	**getPreferredScrollableViewportSize**()
Dimension	**getPreferredSize**()
protected int	**getRowHeight**()
int	**getRows**()
boolean	**getScrollableTracksViewportWidth**()
int	**getScrollableUnitIncrement**(Rectangle visibleRect, int orientation, int direction)
int	**getTabSize**()
String	**getUIClassID**()
boolean	**getWrapStyleWord**()
void	**insert**(String str, int pos)
boolean	**isManagingFocus**()
protected String	**paramString**()
protected void	**processComponentKeyEvent**(KeyEvent e)
void	**replaceRange**(String str, int start, int end)
void	**setColumns**(int columns)
void	**setFont**(Font f)
void	**setLineWrap**(boolean wrap)
void	**setRows**(int rows)
void	**setTabSize**(int size)
void	**setWrapStyleWord**(boolean word)

Class JTextField

```
java.lang.Object
   |
   +--java.awt.Component
         |
         +--java.awt.Container
               |
               +--javax.swing.JComponent
                     |
                     +--javax.swing.text.JTextComponent
                           |
                           +--javax.swing.JTextField
```

public class **JTextField**
        extends JTextComponent
        implements SwingConstants

This class represents the lightweight text fields supported in Swing. This component supports the display and editing of single-line plain text.

Inner Class

protected class   **JTextField.AccessibleJTextField**

Field

static String   **notifyAction**

Constructors

JTextField()
JTextField(Document doc, String text, int columns)
JTextField(int columns)
JTextField(String text)
JTextField(String text, int columns)

Methods

void	**addActionListener**(ActionListener l)
protected Document	**createDefaultModel**()
protected void	**fireActionPerformed**()
AccessibleContext	**getAccessibleContext**()
Action[]	**getActions**()
int	**getColumns**()
protected int	**getColumnWidth**()
int	**getHorizontalAlignment**()
BoundedRangeModel	**getHorizontalVisibility**()
Dimension	**getPreferredSize**()
int	**getScrollOffset**()
String	**getUIClassID**()
boolean	**isValidateRoot**()
protected String	**paramString**()

```
void                    postActionEvent()
void                    removeActionListener(ActionListener l)
void                    scrollRectToVisible(Rectangle r)
void                    setActionCommand(String command)
void                    setColumns(int columns)
void                    setFont(Font f)
void                    setHorizontalAlignment(int alignment)
void                    setScrollOffset(int scrollOffset)
```

Class JTextPane

```
java.lang.Object
   |
   +--java.awt.Component
          |
          +--java.awt.Container
                 |
                 +--javax.swing.JComponent
                        |
                        +--javax.swing.text.JTextComponent
                               |
                               +--javax.swing.JEditorPane
                                      |
                                      +--javax.swing.JTextPane
```

public class **JTextPane**
          extends JEditorPane

This class represents the text panes supported in Swing. Text panes support the display and editing of multiline styled text.

Constructors

JTextPane()
JTextPane(StyledDocument doc)

Methods

```
Style                      addStyle(String nm, Style parent)
protected EditorKit        createDefaultEditorKit()
AttributeSet               getCharacterAttributes()
MutableAttributeSet        getInputAttributes()
Style                      getLogicalStyle()
AttributeSet               getParagraphAttributes()
boolean                    getScrollableTracksViewportWidth()
Style                      getStyle(String nm)
StyledDocument             getStyledDocument()
protected StyledEditorKit  getStyledEditorKit()
String                     getUIClassID()
void                       insertComponent(Component c)
void                       insertIcon(Icon g)
protected String           paramString()
```

void	**removeStyle**(String nm)
void	**replaceSelection**(String content)
void	**setCharacterAttributes**(AttributeSet attr, boolean replace)
void	**setDocument**(Document doc)
void	**setEditorKit**(EditorKit kit)
void	**setLogicalStyle**(Style s)
void	**setParagraphAttributes**(AttributeSet attr, boolean replace)
void	**setStyledDocument**(StyledDocument doc)

Class JToggleButton

```
java.lang.Object
   |
   +--java.awt.Component
          |
          +--java.awt.Container
                 |
                 +--javax.swing.JComponent
                        |
                        +--javax.swing.AbstractButton
                               |
                               +--javax.swing.JToggleButton
```

public class **JToggleButton**
        extends AbstractButton
        implements Accessible

This class represents the toggle buttons supported in Swing. A toggle button remains depressed when clicked and pops up to its original position when clicked again.

Inner Classes

protected class	**JToggleButton.AccessibleJToggleButton**
static class	**JToggleButton.ToggleButtonModel**

Constructors

JToggleButton()
JToggleButton(Icon icon)
JToggleButton(Icon icon, boolean selected)
JToggleButton(String text)
JToggleButton(String text, boolean selected)
JToggleButton(String text, Icon icon)
JToggleButton(String text, Icon icon, boolean selected)

Methods

AccessibleContext	**getAccessibleContext**()
String	**getUIClassID**()
protected String	**paramString**()
void	**updateUI**()

Class JToggleButton.ToggleButtonModel

```
java.lang.Object
   |
   +--javax.swing.DefaultButtonModel
           |
           +--javax.swing.JToggleButton.ToggleButtonModel
```

public static class **JToggleButton.ToggleButtonModel**
                    extends DefaultButtonModel

This class represents the button model used by the Swing toggle buttons. The button model contains the button's states.

Constructor

JToggleButton.ToggleButtonModel()

Methods

```
boolean     isSelected()
void        setPressed(boolean b)
void        setSelected(boolean b)
```

Class JToolBar

```
java.lang.Object
   |
   +--java.awt.Component
           |
           +--java.awt.Container
                   |
                   +--javax.swing.JComponent
                           |
                           +--javax.swing.JToolBar
```

public class **JToolBar**
            extends JComponent
            implements SwingConstants, Accessible

This class represents toolbars used in Swing. A toolbar contains components such as buttons, combo boxes, and so on to allow easy access for frequently used controls.

Inner Classes

```
protected class     JToolBar.AccessibleJToolBar
static class        JToolBar.Separator
```

Constructors

JToolBar()
JToolBar(int orientation)

Methods

JButton	**add**(Action a)
protected void	**addImpl**(Component comp, Object constraints, int index)
void	**addSeparator**()
void	**addSeparator**(Dimension size)
protected PropertyChangeListener	**createActionChange Listener**(JButton b)
AccessibleContext	**getAccessibleContext**()
Component	**getComponentAtIndex**(int i)
int	**getComponentIndex**(Component c)
Insets	**getMargin**()
int	**getOrientation**()
ToolBarUI	**getUI**()
String	**getUIClassID**()
boolean	**isBorderPainted**()
boolean	**isFloatable**()
protected void	**paintBorder**(Graphics g)
protected String	**paramString**()
void	**remove**(Component comp)
void	**setBorderPainted**(boolean b)
void	**setFloatable**(boolean b)
void	**setMargin**(Insets m)
void	**setOrientation**(int o)
void	**setUI**(ToolBarUI ui)
void	**updateUI**()

Class JToolBar.Separator

```
java.lang.Object
   |
   +--java.awt.Component
         |
         +--java.awt.Container
               |
               +--javax.swing.JComponent
                     |
                     +--javax.swing.JSeparator
                           |
                           +--javax.swing.JToolBar.Separator
```

public static class **JToolBar.Separator**
                extends JSeparator

This class represents a toolbar-specific separator. The toolbar components can be separated to display them as logical groups.

Constructors

`JToolBar.Separator()`
`JToolBar.Separator(Dimension size)`

Methods

Dimension	`getMaximumSize()`
Dimension	`getMinimumSize()`
Dimension	`getPreferredSize()`
Dimension	`getSeparatorSize()`
String	`getUIClassID()`
void	`setSeparatorSize(Dimension size)`

Class JToolTip

```
java.lang.Object
   |
   +--java.awt.Component
         |
         +--java.awt.Container
               |
               +--javax.swing.JComponent
                     |
                     +--javax.swing.JToolTip
```

public class **JToolTip**
        extends JComponent
        implements Accessible

This class represents ToolTips in Swing. Often you can use the method
`setToolTipText()` from the class JComponent. However, this class is useful to create
a custom ToolTip.

Inner Class

protected class	`JToolTip.AccessibleJToolTip`

Constructor

`JToolTip()`

Methods

AccessibleContext	`getAccessibleContext()`
JComponent	`getComponent()`
String	`getTipText()`
ToolTipUI	`getUI()`
String	`getUIClassID()`
protected String	`paramString()`
void	`setComponent(JComponent c)`
void	`setTipText(String tipText)`
void	`updateUI()`

Class JTree

```
java.lang.Object
   |
   +--java.awt.Component
         |
         +--java.awt.Container
               |
               +--javax.swing.JComponent
                     |
                     +--javax.swing.JTree
```

```
public class JTree
extends JComponent
implements Scrollable, Accessible
```

This class represents Swing trees. A tree object is useful to display hierarchical data such as directories on your computer system.

Inner Classes

protected class	**JTree.AccessibleJTree**
static class	**JTree.DynamicUtilTreeNode**
protected static class	**JTree.EmptySelectionModel**
protected class	**JTree.TreeModelHandler**
protected class	**JTree.TreeSelectionRedirector**

Fields

static String	**CELL_EDITOR_PROPERTY**
static String	**CELL_RENDERER_PROPERTY**
protected TreeCellEditor	**cellEditor**
protected TreeCellRenderer	**cellRenderer**
protected boolean	**editable**
static String	**EDITABLE_PROPERTY**
static String	**INVOKES_STOP_CELL** **_EDITING_PROPERTY**
protected boolean	**invokesStopCellEditing**
static String	**LARGE_MODEL_PROPERTY**
protected boolean	**largeModel**
static String	**ROOT_VISIBLE_PROPERTY**
protected boolean	**rootVisible**
static String	**ROW_HEIGHT_PROPERTY**
protected int	**rowHeight**
static String	**SCROLLS_ON_EXPAND** **_PROPERTY**
protected boolean	**scrollsOnExpand**
static String	**SELECTION_MODEL** **_PROPERTY**
protected TreeSelectionModel	**selectionModel**
protected JTree.TreeSelectionRedirector	**selectionRedirector**

static String	**SHOWS_ROOT_HANDLES _PROPERTY**
protected boolean	**showsRootHandles**
protected int	**toggleClickCount**
static String	**TREE_MODEL_PROPERTY**
protected TreeModel	**treeModel**
protected TreeModelListener	**treeModelListener**
static String	**VISIBLE_ROW_COUNT _PROPERTY**
protected int	**visibleRowCount**

Constructors

JTree()
JTree(Hashtable value)
JTree(Object[] value)
JTree(TreeModel newModel)
JTree(TreeNode root)
JTree(TreeNode root, boolean asksAllowsChildren)
JTree(Vector value)

Methods

void	**addSelectionInterval**(int index0, int index1)
void	**addSelectionPath**(TreePath path)
void	**addSelectionPaths**(TreePath[] paths)
void	**addSelectionRow**(int row)
void	**addSelectionRows**(int[] rows)
void	**addTreeExpansionListener** (TreeExpansionListener tel)
void	**addTreeSelectionListener** (TreeSelectionListener tsl)
void	**addTreeWillExpandListener** (TreeWillExpandListener tel)
void	**cancelEditing**()
void	**clearSelection**()
protected void	**clearToggledPaths**()
void	**collapsePath**(TreePath path)
void	**collapseRow**(int row)
String	**convertValueToText**(Object value, boolean selected, boolean expanded, boolean leaf, int row, boolean hasFocus)
protected static TreeModel	**createTreeModel**(Object value)
protected TreeModelListener	**createTreeModelListener**()
void	**expandPath**(TreePath path)
void	**expandRow**(int row)
void	**fireTreeCollapsed**(TreePath path)
void	**fireTreeExpanded**(TreePath path)
void	**fireTreeWillCollapse**(TreePath path)

void	**fireTreeWillExpand**(TreePath path)
protected void	**fireValueChanged** (TreeSelectionEvent e)
AccessibleContext	**getAccessibleContext**()
TreeCellEditor	**getCellEditor**()
TreeCellRenderer	**getCellRenderer**()
TreePath	**getClosestPathForLocation**(int x, int y)
int	**getClosestRowForLocation**(int x, int y)
protected static TreeModel	**getDefaultTreeModel**()
protected Enumeration	**getDescendantToggledPaths**(TreePath parent)
TreePath	**getEditingPath**()
Enumeration	**getExpandedDescendants**(TreePath parent)
boolean	**getInvokesStopCellEditing**()
Object	**getLastSelectedPathComponent**()
TreePath	**getLeadSelectionPath**()
int	**getLeadSelectionRow**()
int	**getMaxSelectionRow**()
int	**getMinSelectionRow**()
TreeModel	**getModel**()
protected TreePath[]	**getPathBetweenRows**(int index0, int index1)
Rectangle	**getPathBounds**(TreePath path)
TreePath	**getPathForLocation**(int x, int y)
TreePath	**getPathForRow**(int row)
Dimension	**getPreferredScrollableViewport Size**()
Rectangle	**getRowBounds**(int row)
int	**getRowCount**()
int	**getRowForLocation**(int x, int y)
int	**getRowForPath**(TreePath path)
int	**getRowHeight**()
int	**getScrollableBlockIncrement** (Rectangle visibleRect, int orientation, int direction)
boolean	**getScrollableTracksViewport Height**()
boolean	**getScrollableTracksViewportWidth**()
int	**getScrollableUnitIncrement** (Rectangle visibleRect, orientation, int direction)
boolean	**getScrollsOnExpand**()
int	**getSelectionCount**()
TreeSelectionModel	**getSelectionModel**()
TreePath	**getSelectionPath**()
TreePath[]	**getSelectionPaths**()
int[]	**getSelectionRows**()
boolean	**getShowsRootHandles**()
String	**getToolTipText**(MouseEvent event)
TreeUI	**getUI**()
String	**getUIClassID**()

int	**getVisibleRowCount**()
boolean	**hasBeenExpanded**(TreePath path)
boolean	**isCollapsed**(int row)
boolean	**isCollapsed**(TreePath path)
boolean	**isEditable**()
boolean	**isEditing**()
boolean	**isExpanded**(int row)
boolean	**isExpanded**(TreePath path)
boolean	**isFixedRowHeight**()
boolean	**isLargeModel**()
boolean	**isPathEditable**(TreePath path)
boolean	**isPathSelected**(TreePath path)
boolean	**isRootVisible**()
boolean	**isRowSelected**(int row)
boolean	**isSelectionEmpty**()
boolean	**isVisible**(TreePath path)
void	**makeVisible**(TreePath path)
protected String	**paramString**()
protected void	**removeDescendantToggledPaths** (Enumeration toRemove)
void	**removeSelectionInterval**(int index0, int index1)
void	**removeSelectionPath**(TreePath path)
void	**removeSelectionPaths**(TreePath[] paths)
void	**removeSelectionRow**(int row)
void	**removeSelectionRows**(int[] rows)
void	**removeTreeExpansionListener** (TreeExpansionListener tel)
void	**removeTreeSelectionListener** (TreeSelectionListener tsl)
void	**removeTreeWillExpandListener** (TreeWillExpandListener tel)
void	**scrollPathToVisible**(TreePath path)
void	**scrollRowToVisible**(int row)
void	**setCellEditor**(TreeCellEditor cellEditor)
void	**setCellRenderer**(TreeCellRenderer x)
void	**setEditable**(boolean flag)
protected void	**setExpandedState**(TreePath path, boolean state)
void	**setInvokesStopCellEditing**(boolean newValue)
void	**setLargeModel**(boolean newValue)
void	**setModel**(TreeModel newModel)
void	**setRootVisible**(boolean rootVisible)
void	**setRowHeight**(int rowHeight)
void	**setScrollsOnExpand**(boolean newValue)
void	**setSelectionInterval**(int index0, int index1)
void	**setSelectionModel** (TreeSelectionModel selectionModel)
void	**setSelectionPath**(TreePath path)

void	**setSelectionPaths**(TreePath[] paths)
void	**setSelectionRow**(int row)
void	**setSelectionRows**(int[] rows)
void	**setShowsRootHandles**(boolean newValue)
void	**setUI**(TreeUI ui)
void	**setVisibleRowCount**(int newCount)
void	**startEditingAtPath**(TreePath path)
boolean	**stopEditing**()
void	**treeDidChange**()
void	**updateUI**()

Class JTree.DynamicUtilTreeNode

```
java.lang.Object
   |
   +--javax.swing.tree.DefaultMutableTreeNode
          |
          +--javax.swing.JTree.DynamicUtilTreeNode
```

public static class **JTree.DynamicUtilTreeNode**
                extends DefaultMutableTreeNode

This class represents a utility to dynamically create tree nodes specified through data structures such as vectors, arrays, strings, or hashtables.

Fields

protected Object	**childValue**
protected boolean	**hasChildren**
protected boolean	**loadedChildren**

Constructor

JTree.DynamicUtilTreeNode(Object value, Object children)

Methods

Enumeration	**children**()
static void	**createChildren**(DefaultMutableTreeNode parent, Object children)
TreeNode	**getChildAt**(int index)
int	**getChildCount**()
boolean	**isLeaf**()
protected void	**loadChildren**()

Class JTree.EmptySelectionModel

```
java.lang.Object
   |
   +--javax.swing.tree.DefaultTreeSelectionModel
          |
          +--javax.swing.JTree.EmptySelectionModel
```

protected static class **JTree.EmptySelectionModel**
                    extends DefaultTreeSelectionModel

This class represents a kind of `TreeSelectionModel` that does not permit the selection of nodes.

Field

```
protected static JTree.EmptySelectionModel    sharedInstance
```

Constructor

```
protected    JTree.EmptySelectionModel()
```

Methods

```
void                              addSelectionPaths(TreePath[] paths)
void                              removeSelectionPaths
                                  (TreePath[] paths)
void                              setSelectionPaths(TreePath[] pPaths)
static JTree.EmptySelectionModel  sharedInstance()
```

Class JViewport

```
java.lang.Object
    |
    +--java.awt.Component
           |
           +--java.awt.Container
                  |
                  +--javax.swing.JComponent
                         |
                         +--javax.swing.JViewport
```

```
public class JViewport
          extends JComponent
          implements Accessible
```

This class represents the viewport that is, for example, used in a scroll pane. The viewport is the display window to see underlying content. The viewport is scrolled up and down by using scrollbars to view the content that is otherwise not visible.

Inner Classes

```
protected class    JViewport.AccessibleJViewport
protected class    JViewport.ViewListener
```

Fields

```
protected boolean    backingStore
protected Image      backingStoreImage
protected boolean    isViewSizeSet
protected Point      lastPaintPosition
protected boolean    scrollUnderway
```

Constructor

`JViewport()`

Methods

void	**addChangeListener** (ChangeListener l)
protected void	**addImpl**(Component child, Object constraints, int index)
protected boolean	**computeBlit**(int dx, int dy, Point blitFrom, Point blitTo, Dimension blitSize, Rectangle blitPaint)
protected LayoutManager	**createLayoutManager**()
protected JViewport.ViewListener	**createViewListener**()
protected void	**fireStateChanged**()
AccessibleContext	**getAccessibleContext**()
Dimension	**getExtentSize**()
Insets	**getInsets**()
Insets	**getInsets**(Insets insets)
Component	**getView**()
Point	**getViewPosition**()
Rectangle	**getViewRect**()
Dimension	**getViewSize**()
boolean	**isBackingStoreEnabled**()
boolean	**isOptimizedDrawingEnabled**()
void	**paint**(Graphics g)
protected String	**paramString**()
void	**remove**(Component child)
void	**removeChangeListener** (ChangeListener l)
void	**repaint**(long tm, int x, int y, int w, int h)
void	**reshape**(int x, int y, int w, int h)
void	**scrollRectToVisible**(Rectangle contentRect)
void	**setBackingStoreEnabled** (boolean x)
void	**setBorder**(Border border)
void	**setExtentSize**(Dimension newExtent)
void	**setView**(Component view)
void	**setViewPosition**(Point p)
void	**setViewSize**(Dimension newSize)
Dimension	**toViewCoordinates**(Dimension size)
Point	**toViewCoordinates**(Point p)

Class JWindow

```
java.lang.Object
   |
   +--java.awt.Component
          |
          +--java.awt.Container
                 |
                 +--java.awt.Window
                        |
                        +--javax.swing.JWindow
```

```
public class JWindow
            extends Window
            implements Accessible, RootPaneContainer
```

This class represents a Swing window. A Swing window is similar to an AWT window and appears without a title bar, border, or closing and resizing buttons. Underlying the window, a content pane, glass pane, layered pane, and menu bar are supported. You need to add the child components to the underlying content pane, rather than adding them directly.

Inner Class

```
protected class      JWindow.AccessibleJWindow
```

Fields

```
protected AccessibleContext    accessibleContext
protected JRootPane            rootPane
protected boolean              rootPaneCheckingEnabled
```

Constructors

```
JWindow()
JWindow(Frame owner)
```

Methods

```
protected void        addImpl(Component comp, Object constraints, int index)
JRootPane             createRootPane()
AccessibleContext     getAccessibleContext()
Container             getContentPane()
Component             getGlassPane()
JLayeredPane          getLayeredPane()
JRootPane             getRootPane()
protected boolean     isRootPaneCheckingEnabled()
protected String      paramString()
void                  setContentPane(Container contentPane)
void                  setGlassPane(Component glassPane)
void                  setLayeredPane(JLayeredPane layeredPane)
void                  setLayout(LayoutManager manager)
protected void        setRootPane(JRootPane root)
protected void        setRootPaneCheckingEnabled(boolean enabled)
protected void        windowInit()
```

Class KeyStroke

```
java.lang.Object
    |
    +--javax.swing.KeyStroke
```
public class **KeyStroke**
            extends Object
            implements Serializable

This class represents a key stroke that occurs on the keyboard. A keystroke object contains the necessary information, such as the key character, key code, and modifier key.

Methods

boolean	**equals**(Object anObject)
char	**getKeyChar**()
int	**getKeyCode**()
static KeyStroke	**getKeyStroke**(char keyChar)
static KeyStroke	**getKeyStroke**(char keyChar, boolean onKeyRelease)
	//Deprecated. Use the method getKeyStroke(char)
static KeyStroke	**getKeyStroke**(int keyCode, int modifiers)
static KeyStroke	**getKeyStroke**(int keyCode, int modifiers,
	boolean onKeyRelease)
static KeyStroke	**getKeyStroke**(String representation)
static KeyStroke	**getKeyStrokeForEvent**(KeyEvent anEvent)
int	**getModifiers**()
int	**hashCode**()
boolean	**isOnKeyRelease**()
String	**toString**()

Class LookAndFeel

```
java.lang.Object
    |
    +--javax.swing.LookAndFeel
```
public abstract class **LookAndFeel**
                    extends Object

This is an abstract class and represents the look-and feel-of components. This class contains functionality to install or uninstall look-and-feel attributes such as borders, colors, fonts, and so on.

Constructor

LookAndFeel()

Methods

UIDefaults	**getDefaults**()
abstract String	**getDescription**()

abstract String	**getID**()
abstract String	**getName**()
void	**initialize**()
static void	**installBorder**(JComponent c, String defaultBorderName)
static void	**installColors**(JComponent c, String defaultBgName, String defaultFgName)
static void	**installColorsAndFont** (JComponent c, String defaultBgName, String defaultFgName, String defaultFontName)
abstract boolean	**isNativeLookAndFeel**()
abstract boolean	**isSupportedLookAndFeel**()
static Object	**makeIcon**(Class baseClass, String gifFile)
static JTextComponent.KeyBinding[]	**makeKeyBindings**(Object[] keyBindingList)
String	**toString**()
void	**uninitialize**()
static void	**uninstallBorder**(JComponent c)

Class MenuSelectionManager

```
java.lang.Object
   |
   +--javax.swing.MenuSelectionManager
```

public class **MenuSelectionManager**
        extends Object

This class represents a menu selection manager that manages selections in a hierarchy of menus.

Fields

protected ChangeEvent	**changeEvent**
protected EventListenerList	**listenerList**

Constructor

MenuSelectionManager()

Methods

void	**addChangeListener**(ChangeListener l)
void	**clearSelectedPath**()
Component	**componentForPoint**(Component source, Point sourcePoint)
static MenuSelectionManager	**defaultManager**()
protected void	**fireStateChanged**()
MenuElement[]	**getSelectedPath**()

boolean	**isComponentPartOfCurrentMenu**(Component c)
void	**processKeyEvent**(KeyEvent e)
void	**processMouseEvent**(MouseEvent event)
void	**removeChangeListener**(ChangeListener l)
void	**setSelectedPath**(MenuElement[] path)

Class OverlayLayout

```
java.lang.Object
    |
    +--javax.swing.OverlayLayout
```

public class **OverlayLayout**
        extends Object
        implements LayoutManager2, Serializable

This class represents a layout manager that enables the user to layer the components. This layout is automatically used by Swing components. Normally you do not need to deal with this layout manager.

Constructor

OverlayLayout(Container target)

Methods

void	**addLayoutComponent**(Component comp, Object constraints)
void	**addLayoutComponent**(String name, Component comp)
float	**getLayoutAlignmentX**(Container target)
float	**getLayoutAlignmentY**(Container target)
void	**invalidateLayout**(Container target)
void	**layoutContainer**(Container target)
Dimension	**maximumLayoutSize**(Container target)
Dimension	**minimumLayoutSize**(Container target)
Dimension	**preferredLayoutSize**(Container target)
void	**removeLayoutComponent**(Component comp)

Class ProgressMonitor

```
java.lang.Object
    |
    +--javax.swing.ProgressMonitor
```

public class **ProgressMonitor**
        extends Object

This class represents a progress monitor. A progress monitor is used to observe the progress of the execution of a process.

Constructors

ProgressMonitor(Component parentComponent, Object message, String note, int min, int max)

Methods

void	**close**()
int	**getMaximum**()
int	**getMillisToDecideToPopup**()
int	**getMillisToPopup**()
int	**getMinimum**()
String	**getNote**()
boolean	**isCanceled**()
void	**setMaximum**(int m)
void	**setMillisToDecideToPopup**(int millisToDecideToPopup)
void	**setMillisToPopup**(int millisToPopup)
void	**setMinimum**(int m)
void	**setNote**(String note)
void	**setProgress**(int nv)

Class ProgressMonitorInputStream

```
java.lang.Object
   |
   +--java.io.InputStream
          |
          +--java.io.FilterInputStream
                 |
                 +--javax.swing.ProgressMonitorInputStream
```

public class **ProgressMonitorInputStream**
        extends FilterInputStream

This class represents a monitor that specifically observes the reading of data from an input stream.

Constructor

ProgressMonitorInputStream(Component parentComponent, Object message, InputStream in)

Methods

void	**close**()
ProgressMonitor	**getProgressMonitor**()
int	**read**()
int	**read**(byte[] b)
int	**read**(byte[] b, int off, int len)
void	**reset**()
long	**skip**(long n)

Class RepaintManager

```
java.lang.Object
   |
   +--javax.swing.RepaintManager
```

public class **RepaintManager**
        extends Object

This class optimizes the number of repaint calls by collapsing multiple requests into a single repaint operation, as in the case of repainting tree nodes.

Constructor

`RepaintManager()`

Methods

void	`addDirtyRegion`(JComponent c, int x, int y, int w, int h)
void	`addInvalidComponent`(JComponent invalidComponent)
static RepaintManager	`currentManager`(Component c)
static RepaintManager	`currentManager`(JComponent c)
Rectangle	`getDirtyRegion`(JComponent aComponent)
Dimension	`getDoubleBufferMaximumSize`()
Image	`getOffscreenBuffer`(Component c, int proposedWidth, int proposedHeight)
boolean	`isCompletelyDirty`(JComponent aComponent)
boolean	`isDoubleBufferingEnabled`()
void	`markCompletelyClean`(JComponent aComponent)
void	`markCompletelyDirty`(JComponent aComponent)
void	`paintDirtyRegions`()
void	`removeInvalidComponent`(JComponent component)
static void	`setCurrentManager`(RepaintManager aRepaintManager)
void	`setDoubleBufferingEnabled`(boolean aFlag)
void	`setDoubleBufferMaximumSize`(Dimension d)
String	`toString`()
void	`validateInvalidComponents`()

Class ScrollPaneLayout

```
java.lang.Object
  |
  +--javax.swing.ScrollPaneLayout
```

```
public class ScrollPaneLayout
         extends Object
         implements LayoutManager, ScrollPaneConstants, Serializable
```

This class represents a layout manager that is automatically used by JScrollPane. Normally you need not have to deal with this layout directly.

Inner Class

static class	`ScrollPaneLayout.UIResource`

Fields

protected JViewport	`colHead`
protected JscrollBar	`hsb`
protected int	`hsbPolicy`
protected Component	`lowerLeft`

```
protected Component        lowerRight
protected JViewport        rowHead
protected Component        upperLeft
protected Component        upperRight
protected JViewport        viewport
protected JScrollBar       vsb
protected int              vsbPolicy
```

Constructor
```
ScrollPaneLayout()
```

Methods
```
void                   addLayoutComponent(String s, Component c)
protected Component    addSingletonComponent(Component oldC, Component newC)
JViewport              getColumnHeader()
Component              getCorner(String key)
JScrollBar             getHorizontalScrollBar()
int                    getHorizontalScrollBarPolicy()
JViewport              getRowHeader()
JScrollBar             getVerticalScrollBar()
int                    getVerticalScrollBarPolicy()
JViewport              getViewport()
Rectangle              getViewportBorderBounds(JScrollPane scrollpane)
                       // Deprecated. Use the method
                       JScrollPane.getViewportBorderBounds().
void                   layoutContainer(Container parent)
Dimension              minimumLayoutSize(Container parent)
Dimension              preferredLayoutSize(Container parent)
void                   removeLayoutComponent(Component c)
void                   setHorizontalScrollBarPolicy(int x)
void                   setVerticalScrollBarPolicy(int x)
void                   syncWithScrollPane(JScrollPane sp)
```

Class ScrollPaneLayout.UIResource
```
java.lang.Object
   |
   +--javax.swing.ScrollPaneLayout
          |
          +--javax.swing.ScrollPaneLayout.UIResource
```
```
public static class ScrollPaneLayout.UIResource
                    extends ScrollPaneLayout
                    implements UIResource
```

This class represents the UI resource of ScrollPaneLayout.

Constructor
```
ScrollPaneLayout.UIResource()
```

Class SizeRequirements

```
java.lang.Object
   |
   |
   +--javax.swing.SizeRequirements
```

public class **SizeRequirements**
            extends Object
            implements Serializable

This class contains functionality to compute the size and position of components.

Fields

float	**alignment**
int	**maximum**
int	**minimum**
int	**preferred**

Constructors

SizeRequirements()
SizeRequirements(int min, int pref, int max, float a)

Methods

static int[]	**adjustSizes**(int delta, SizeRequirements[] children)
static void	**calculateAlignedPositions**(int allocated, SizeRequirements total, SizeRequirements[] children, int[] offsets, int[] spans)
static void	**calculateTiledPositions**(int allocated, SizeRequirements total, SizeRequirements[] children, int[] offsets, int[] spans)
static SizeRequirements	**getAlignedSizeRequirements** (SizeRequirements[] children)
static SizeRequirements	**getTiledSizeRequirements** (SizeRequirements[] children)
String	**toString**()

Class SwingUtilities

```
java.lang.Object
   |
   |
   +--javax.swing.SwingUtilities
```

public class **SwingUtilities**
            extends Object
            implements SwingConstants

This class contains a number of utility methods that are useful in applications that make use of Swing components.

Methods

`static Rectangle[]`	**computeDifference**(Rectangle rectA, Rectangle rectB)
`static Rectangle`	**computeIntersection**(int x, int y int width, int height, Rectangle dest)
`static int`	**computeStringWidth**(FontMetrics fm, String str)
`static Rectangle`	**computeUnion**(int x, int y, int width, int height, Rectangle dest)
`static MouseEvent`	**convertMouseEvent**(Component source, MouseEvent sourceEvent, destination)
`static Point`	**convertPoint**(Component source, int x, int y, Component destination)
`static Point`	**convertPoint**(Component source, Point aPoint, Component destination)
`static void`	**convertPointFromScreen**(Point p, Component c)
`static void`	**convertPointToScreen**(Point p, Component c)
`static Rectangle`	**convertRectangle**(Component source, Rectangle aRectangle, Component destination)
`static Component`	**findFocusOwner**(Component c)
`static Accessible`	**getAccessibleAt**(Component c, Point p)
`static Accessible`	**getAccessibleChild**(Component c, int i)
`static int`	**getAccessibleChildrenCount**(Component c)
`static int`	**getAccessibleIndexInParent**(Component c)
`static AccessibleStateSet`	**getAccessibleStateSet**(Component c)
`static Container`	**getAncestorNamed**(String name, Component comp)
`static Container`	**getAncestorOfClass**(Class c, Component comp)
`static Component`	**getDeepestComponentAt**(Component parent, int x, int y)
`static Rectangle`	**getLocalBounds**(Component aComponent)
`static Component`	**getRoot**(Component c)
`static JRootPane`	**getRootPane**(Component c)
`static void`	**invokeAndWait**(Runnable doRun)
`static void`	**invokeLater**(Runnable doRun)
`static boolean`	**isDescendingFrom**(Component a, Component b)
`static boolean`	**isEventDispatchThread**()
`static boolean`	**isLeftMouseButton**(MouseEvent anEvent)
`static boolean`	**isMiddleMouseButton**(MouseEvent anEvent)
`static boolean`	**isRectangleContainingRectangle** (Rectangle a, Rectangle b)
`static boolean`	**isRightMouseButton**(MouseEvent anEvent)
`static String`	**layoutCompoundLabel**(FontMetrics fm, String text, Icon icon, int verticalAlignment, int horizontalAlignment, int verticalTextPosition, int horizontalTextPosition, Rectangle viewR, Rectangle iconR, Rectangle textR, int textIconGap)

```
static String              layoutCompoundLabel(JComponent c,
                           FontMetrics fm, String text, Icon
                           icon, int verticalAlignment,
                           int horizontalAlignment, int
                           verticalTextPosition,
                           int horizontalTextPosition,
                           Rectangle viewR, Rectangle iconR,
                           Rectangle textR, int textIconGap)
static void                paintComponent(Graphics g, Component
                           c, Container p, int x, int y, int w,
                           int h)
static void                paintComponent(Graphics g, Component
                           c, Container p, Rectangle r)
static void                updateComponentTreeUI(Component c)
static Window              windowForComponent(Component aComponent)
```

Class Timer

```
java.lang.Object
  |
  +--javax.swing.Timer
```

```
public class Timer
            extends Object
            implements Serializable
```

This class represents a timer that controls the repetition of an action at the specified rate.

Field

```
protected EventListenerList    listenerList
```

Constructor

```
Timer(int delay, ActionListener listener)
```

Methods

```
void               addActionListener(ActionListener listener)
protected void     fireActionPerformed(ActionEvent e)
int                getDelay()
int                getInitialDelay()
static boolean     getLogTimers()
boolean            isCoalesce()
boolean            isRepeats()
boolean            isRunning()
void               removeActionListener(ActionListener listener)
void               restart()
void               setCoalesce(boolean flag)
```

```
void               setDelay(int delay)
void               setInitialDelay(int initialDelay)
static void        setLogTimers(boolean flag)
void               setRepeats(boolean flag)
void               start()
void               stop()
```

Class ToolTipManager

```
        java.lang.Object
           |
           +--java.awt.event.MouseAdapter
                  |
                  +--javax.swing.ToolTipManager

public class ToolTipManager
              extends MouseAdapter
              implements MouseMotionListener
```

This is a helping class to manage ToolTips of various UI components in an application.

Inner Classes

```
protected class    ToolTipManager.insideTimerAction
protected class    ToolTipManager.outsideTimerAction
protected class    ToolTipManager.stillInsideTimerAction
```

Fields

```
protected boolean   heavyWeightPopupEnabled
protected boolean   lightWeightPopupEnabled
```

Methods

```
int                 getDismissDelay()
int                 getInitialDelay()
int                 getReshowDelay()
boolean             isEnabled()
boolean             isLightWeightPopupEnabled()
void                mouseDragged(MouseEvent event)
void                mouseEntered(MouseEvent event)
void                mouseExited(MouseEvent event)
void                mouseMoved(MouseEvent event)
void                mousePressed(MouseEvent event)
void                registerComponent(JComponent component)
void                setDismissDelay(int microSeconds)
void                setEnabled(boolean flag)
void                setInitialDelay(int microSeconds)
void                setLightWeightPopupEnabled(boolean aFlag)
                    // Deprecated. Use the method
                    setToolTipWindowUsePolicy(int).
void                setReshowDelay(int microSeconds)
static ToolTipManager  sharedInstance()
void                unregisterComponent(JComponent component)
```

Class UIDefaults

```
java.lang.Object
   |
   +--java.util.Dictionary
          |
          +--java.util.Hashtable
                 |
                 +--javax.swing.UIDefaults
```

public class **UIDefaults**
        extends Hashtable

This class represents a table of default values for the look-and-feel of Swing components. The values are accessed by applications through the UI manager.

Inner Classes

static interface   **UIDefaults.ActiveValue**
static interface   **UIDefaults.LazyValue**

Constructors

UIDefaults()
UIDefaults(Object[] keyValueList)

Methods

void	**addPropertyChangeListener** (PropertyChangeListener listener)
protected void	**firePropertyChange**(String propertyName, Object oldValue, Object newValue)
Object	**get**(Object key)
Border	**getBorder**(Object key)
Color	**getColor**(Object key)
Dimension	**getDimension**(Object key)
Font	**getFont**(Object key)
Icon	**getIcon**(Object key)
Insets	**getInsets**(Object key)
int	**getInt**(Object key)
String	**getString**(Object key)
ComponentUI	**getUI**(JComponent target)
Class	**getUIClass**(String uiClassID)
Class	**getUIClass**(String uiClassID, ClassLoader uiClassLoader)
protected void	**getUIError**(String msg)
Object	**put**(Object key, Object value)
void	**putDefaults**(Object[] keyValueList)
void	removePropertyChangeListener (PropertyChangeListener listener)

Class UIManager

```
java.lang.Object
   |
   +--javax.swing.UIManager
```

```
public class UIManager
           extends Object
           implements Serializable
```

This class represents a UI manager whose responsibility is to monitor the current look-and-feel and its defaults. This is the class you need to use to assign a new look-and-feel.

Inner Classes

static class   **UIManager.LookAndFeelInfo**

Constructor

UIManager()

Methods

static void	**addAuxiliaryLookAndFeel** (LookAndFeel laf)
static void	**addPropertyChangeListener** (PropertyChangeListener listener)
static Object	**get**(Object key)
static LookAndFeel[]	**getAuxiliaryLookAndFeels**()
static Border	**getBorder**(Object key)
static Color	**getColor**(Object key)
static String	**getCrossPlatformLookAnd FeelClassName**()
static UIDefaults	**getDefaults**()
static Dimension	**getDimension**(Object key)
static Font	**getFont**(Object key)
static Icon	**getIcon**(Object key)
static Insets	**getInsets**(Object key)
static UIManager.LookAndFeelInfo[]	**getInstalledLookAndFeels**()
static int	**getInt**(Object key)
static LookAndFeel	**getLookAndFeel**()
static UIDefaults	**getLookAndFeelDefaults**()
static String	**getString**(Object key)
static String	**getSystemLookAndFeel ClassName**()
static ComponentUI	**getUI**(JComponent target)
static void	**installLookAndFeel**(String name, String className)
static void	**installLookAndFeel** (UIManager.LookAndFeelInfo info)
static Object	**put**(Object key, Object value)
static boolean	**removeAuxiliaryLookAndFeel** (LookAndFeel laf)

static void	**removePropertyChangeListener** (PropertyChangeListener listener)
static void	**setInstalledLookAndFeels** (UIManager.LookAndFeelInfo[] infos)
static void	**setLookAndFeel**(LookAndFeel newLookAndFeel)
static void	**setLookAndFeel**(String className)

Class UIManager.LookAndFeelInfo

```
java.lang.Object
   |
   |
   +--javax.swing.UIManager.LookAndFeelInfo
```

public static class **UIManager.LookAndFeelInfo**
                    extends Object

This is a helping class to provide information of the look-and-feel to configure menus for application start up and so on.

Constructor

UIManager.LookAndFeelInfo(String name, String className)

Methods

String	**getClassName**()
String	**getName**()
String	**toString**()

Class ViewportLayout

```
java.lang.Object
   |
   |
   +--javax.swing.ViewportLayout
```

public class **ViewportLayout**
            extends Object
            implements LayoutManager, Serializable

This class represents a layout manager that is automatically used by viewport objects. Normally you do not have to use this class directly.

Constructor

ViewportLayout()

Methods

void	**addLayoutComponent**(String name, Component c)
void	**layoutContainer**(Container parent)

```
Dimension    minimumLayoutSize(Container parent)
Dimension    preferredLayoutSize(Container parent)
void         removeLayoutComponent(Component c)
```

Class UnsupportedLookAndFeelException

```
java.lang.Object
   |
   +--java.lang.Throwable
        |
        +--java.lang.Exception
             |
             +--javax.swing.UnsupportedLookAndFeelException

public class UnsupportedLookAndFeelException
          extends Exception
```

This class represents an exception that is thrown if the specified look-and-feel classes are not found in the user's computer system.

Constructor

```
UnsupportedLookAndFeelException(String s)
```

javax.swing.border

Interface Border

```
public abstract interface Border
```

This is a design-level interface to represent a border around the edges of a component.

Methods

```
Insets     getBorderInsets(Component c)
boolean    isBorderOpaque()
void       paintBorder(Component c, Graphics g, int x, int y, int width,
           int height)
```

Class AbstractBorder

```
java.lang.Object
   |
   +--javax.swing.border.AbstractBorder

public abstract class AbstractBorder
                 extends Object
                 implements Border, Serializable
```

This class represents an abstract border that serves as a base class for various border classes.

Constructor

`AbstractBorder()`

Methods

Insets	**getBorderInsets**(Component c)
Insets	**getBorderInsets**(Component c, Insets insets)
static Rectangle	**getInteriorRectangle**(Component c, Border b, int x, int y, int width, int height)
Rectangle	**getInteriorRectangle**(Component c, int x, int y, int width, int height)
boolean	**isBorderOpaque**()
void	**paintBorder**(Component c, Graphics g, int x, int y, int width, int height)

Class BevelBorder

```
java.lang.Object
    |
    +--javax.swing.border.AbstractBorder
            |
            +--javax.swing.border.BevelBorder
```

public class **BevelBorder**
          extends AbstractBorder

This class represents a bevel border that is either raised or lowered.

Fields

protected int	**bevelType**
protected Color	**highlightInner**
protected Color	**highlightOuter**
static int	**LOWERED**
static int	**RAISED**
protected Color	**shadowInner**
protected Color	**shadowOuter**

Constructors

BevelBorder(int bevelType)
BevelBorder(int bevelType, Color highlight, Color shadow)
BevelBorder(int bevelType, Color highlightOuter, Color highlightInner, Color shadowOuter, Color shadowInner)

Methods

int	**getBevelType**()
Insets	**getBorderInsets**(Component c)
Insets	**getBorderInsets**(Component c, Insets insets)
Color	**getHighlightInnerColor**(Component c)

Color	**getHighlightOuterColor**(Component c)
Color	**getShadowInnerColor**(Component c)
Color	**getShadowOuterColor**(Component c)
boolean	**isBorderOpaque**()
void	**paintBorder**(Component c, Graphics g, int x, int y, int width, int height)
protected void	**paintLoweredBevel**(Component c, Graphics g, int x, int y, int width, int height)
protected void	**paintRaisedBevel**(Component c, Graphics g, int x, int y, int width, int height)

Class CompoundBorder

```
java.lang.Object
  |
  +--javax.swing.border.AbstractBorder
        |
        +--javax.swing.border.CompoundBorder
```

public class **CompoundBorder**
            extends AbstractBorder

This class represents a compound border. For a compound border, two border objects are combined into a single border by nesting an inner border within the insets of an outer border.

Fields

protected Border	**insideBorder**
protected Border	**outsideBorder**

Constructors

CompoundBorder()
CompoundBorder(Border outsideBorder, Border insideBorder)

Methods

Insets	**getBorderInsets**(Component c)
Insets	**getBorderInsets**(Component c, Insets insets)
Border	**getInsideBorder**()
Border	**getOutsideBorder**()
boolean	**isBorderOpaque**()
void	**paintBorder**(Component c, Graphics g, int x, int y, int width, int height)

Class EmptyBorder

```
java.lang.Object
  |
  +--javax.swing.border.AbstractBorder
        |
        +--javax.swing.border.EmptyBorder
```

```
public class EmptyBorder
              extends AbstractBorder
              implements Serializable
```

This class represents an empty border with the specified insets.

Fields

```
protected int    bottom
protected int    left
protected int    right
protected int    top
```

Constructors

```
EmptyBorder(Insets insets)
EmptyBorder(int top, int left, int bottom, int right)
```

Methods

```
Insets     getBorderInsets(Component c)
Insets     getBorderInsets(Component c, Insets insets)
boolean    isBorderOpaque()
void       paintBorder(Component c, Graphics g, int x, int y, int width,
           int height)
```

Class EtchedBorder

```
java.lang.Object
   |
   +--javax.swing.border.AbstractBorder
          |
          +--javax.swing.border.EtchedBorder
public class EtchedBorder
              extends AbstractBorder
```

This class represents an etched border that can be etched in or etched out.

Fields

```
protected int      etchType
protected Color    highlight
static int         LOWERED
static int         RAISED
protected Color    shadow
```

Constructors

```
EtchedBorder()
EtchedBorder(Color highlight, Color shadow)
EtchedBorder(int etchType)
EtchedBorder(int etchType, Color highlight, Color shadow)
```

Methods

Insets	**getBorderInsets**(Component c)
Insets	**getBorderInsets**(Component c, Insets insets)
int	**getEtchType**()
Color	**getHighlightColor**(Component c)
Color	**getShadowColor**(Component c)
boolean	**isBorderOpaque**()
void	**paintBorder**(Component c, Graphics g, int x, int y, int width, int height)

Class MatteBorder

```
java.lang.Object
   |
   +--javax.swing.border.AbstractBorder
        |
        +--javax.swing.border.EmptyBorder
             |
             +--javax.swing.border.MatteBorder
```

public class **MatteBorder**
        extends EmptyBorder

This class represents a matte-like border that is painted by using either a solid color or an icon.

Fields

protected Color	**color**
protected Icon	**tileIcon**

Constructors

MatteBorder(Icon tileIcon)
MatteBorder(int top, int left, int bottom, int right, Color color)
MatteBorder(int top, int left, int bottom, int right, Icon tileIcon)

Methods

Insets	**getBorderInsets**(Component c)
boolean	**isBorderOpaque**()
void	**paintBorder**(Component c, Graphics g, int x, int y, int width, int height)

Class SoftBevelBorder

```
java.lang.Object
   |
   +--javax.swing.border.AbstractBorder
        |
        +--javax.swing.border.BevelBorder
             |
             +--javax.swing.border.SoftBevelBorder
```

```
public class SoftBevelBorder
            extends BevelBorder
```

This class represents a bevel with softened corners. This is a subclass of `BevelBorder`.

Constructors

SoftBevelBorder(int bevelType)
SoftBevelBorder(int bevelType, Color highlight, Color shadow)
SoftBevelBorder(int bevelType, Color highlightOuter, Color highlightInner,
Color shadowOuter, Color shadowInner)

Methods

Insets	**getBorderInsets**(Component c)
boolean	**isBorderOpaque**()
void	**paintBorder**(Component c, Graphics g, int x, int y, int width, int height)

Class TitledBorder

```
java.lang.Object
    |
    +--javax.swing.border.AbstractBorder
        |
        +--javax.swing.border.TitledBorder
```

```
public class TitledBorder
            extends AbstractBorder
```

This class represents a titled border. The title position can be controlled using the supported fields.

Fields

static int	**ABOVE_BOTTOM**
static int	**ABOVE_TOP**
static int	**BELOW_BOTTOM**
static int	**BELOW_TOP**
protected Border	**border**
static int	**BOTTOM**
static int	**CENTER**
static int	**DEFAULT_JUSTIFICATION**
static int	**DEFAULT_POSITION**
protected static int	**EDGE_SPACING**
static int	**LEFT**
static int	**RIGHT**
protected static int	**TEXT_INSET_H**
protected static int	**TEXT_SPACING**
protected String	**title**
protected Color	**titleColor**

```
protected Font          titleFont
protected int           titleJustification
protected int           titlePosition
static int              TOP
```

Constructors

TitledBorder(Border border)
TitledBorder(Border border, String title)
TitledBorder(Border border, String title, int titleJustification,
int titlePosition)
TitledBorder(Border border, String title, int titleJustification,
int titlePosition, Font titleFont)
TitledBorder(Border border, String title, int titleJustification,
int titlePosition, Font titleFont, Color titleColor)
TitledBorder(String title)

Methods

```
Border          getBorder()
Insets          getBorderInsets(Component c)
Insets          getBorderInsets(Component c, Insets insets)
protected Font  getFont(Component c)
Dimension       getMinimumSize(Component c)
String          getTitle()
Color           getTitleColor()
Font            getTitleFont()
int             getTitleJustification()
int             getTitlePosition()
boolean         isBorderOpaque()
void            paintBorder(Component c, Graphics g, int x, int y,
                int width, int height)
void            setBorder(Border border)
void            setTitle(String title)
void            setTitleColor(Color titleColor)
void            setTitleFont(Font titleFont)
void            setTitleJustification(int titleJustification)
void            setTitlePosition(int titlePosition)
```

javax.swing.colorchooser

Interface ColorSelectionModel

public abstract interface **ColorSelectionModel**

This interface represents the selection model for the color choosers in Swing.

Methods

```
void    addChangeListener(ChangeListener listener)
        //Adds listener as a listener to changes in the model.
```

```
Color     getSelectedColor()
void      removeChangeListener(ChangeListener listener)
          //Removes listener as a listener to changes in the model.
void      setSelectedColor(Color color)
          //Sets the model's selected Color to color.
```

Class AbstractColorChooserPanel

```
java.lang.Object
  |
  +--java.awt.Component
        |
        +--java.awt.Container
              |
              +--javax.swing.JComponent
                    |
                    +--javax.swing.JPanel
                          |
                          +--javax.swing.colorchooser.AbstractColorChooserPanel
public abstract class AbstractColorChooserPanel
                    extends JPanel
```

This is an abstract class to represent the superclass for the Swing color choosers. To add an additional color chooser panel to the Swing color chooser, you need to extend your class from this class.

Constructor

```
AbstractColorChooserPanel()
```

Methods

```
protected abstract void    buildChooser()
protected Color            getColorFromModel()
ColorSelectionModel        getColorSelectionModel()
abstract String            getDisplayName()
abstract Icon              getLargeDisplayIcon()
abstract Icon              getSmallDisplayIcon()
void                       installChooserPanel(JColorChooser enclosingChooser)
                           //This get called when the panel is added
                           to the chooser.
void                       paint(Graphics g)
void                       uninstallChooserPanel(JColorChooser
                           enclosingChooser)
                           //This get called when the panel is removed
                           from the chooser.
abstract void              updateChooser()
                           //Override this method to update your ChooserPanel.
                           This method will be automatically called when the
                           model's state changes.
```

Class ColorChooserComponentFactory

```
java.lang.Object
   |
   +--javax.swing.colorchooser.ColorChooserComponentFactory
public class ColorChooserComponentFactory
          extends Object
```

This class represents a factory to produce accessory objects for insertion into Swing color choosers.

Methods

```
static AbstractColorChooserPanel[]    getDefaultChooserPanels()
static Jcomponent                     getPreviewPanel()
```

Class DefaultColorSelectionModel

```
java.lang.Object
   |
   +--javax.swing.colorchooser.DefaultColorSelectionModel
public class DefaultColorSelectionModel
          extends Object
          implements ColorSelectionModel, Serializable
```

This class represents the default implementation of the interface ColorSelectionModel.

Fields

```
protected ChangeEvent       changeEvent
                            //Only one ChangeEvent is needed per model
                            instance since the event's only (read-only)
                            state is the source property.
protected EventListenerList listenerList
```

Constructors

```
DefaultColorSelectionModel()
//Default constructor.
DefaultColorSelectionModel(Color color)
//Initializes selected Color to color
```

Methods

```
void              addChangeListener(ChangeListener l)
                  //Adds a ChangeListener to the model.
protected void    fireStateChanged()
                  //Run each ChangeListener's stateChanged() method.
Color             getSelectedColor()
void              removeChangeListener(ChangeListener l)
                  //Removes a ChangeListener from the model.
void              setSelectedColor(Color color)
```

javax.swing.event

Interface AncestorListener

```
public abstract interface AncestorListener
                    extends EventListener
```

This interface represents the ancestor listener. The implementation class is notified whenever there is a change in a component or its ancestors. The change can be component movement, component visibility, and so on.

Methods

```
void    ancestorAdded(AncestorEvent event)
void    ancestorMoved(AncestorEvent event)
void    ancestorRemoved(AncestorEvent event)
```

Interface CaretListener

```
public abstract interface CaretListener
                    extends EventListener
```

This interface represents a caret listener. The implementation class is notified whenever the caret position in a text component is changed.

Method

```
void    caretUpdate(CaretEvent e)
```

Interface CellEditorListener

```
public abstract interface CellEditorListener
                    extends EventListener
```

This interface represents the cell editor listener. The implementation class is notified whenever there is a confirmed new edit in the cell.

Methods

```
void editingCanceled(ChangeEvent e)
void editingStopped(ChangeEvent e)
```

Interface ChangeListener

```
public abstract interface ChangeListener
                    extends EventListener
```

This interface represents change listeners. The implementation class is notified through an object of ChangeEvent whenever there is a change in the component selection.

Method

```
void stateChanged(ChangeEvent e)
```

Interface DocumentEvent

```
public abstract interface DocumentEvent
```

This interface represents a document event. Implementations of this interface store the document changes whenever the document is being modified.

Inner Classes

static interface	DocumentEvent.ElementChange
static class	DocumentEvent.EventType

Methods

DocumentEvent.ElementChange	getChange(Element elem)
Document	getDocument()
int	getLength()
int	getOffset()
DocumentEvent.EventType	getType()

Interface DocumentEvent.ElementChange

public abstract static interface DocumentEvent.ElementChange

This is an accessory interface that represents the changes made to an element of a document.

Methods

Element[]	getChildrenAdded()
Element[]	getChildrenRemoved()
Element	getElement()
int	getIndex()

Interface DocumentListener

public abstract interface DocumentListener
                        extends EventListener

This interface represents a document listener. The implementation class is notified whenever changes take place in the content of the document.

Methods

void	changedUpdate(DocumentEvent e)
void	insertUpdate(DocumentEvent e)
void	removeUpdate(DocumentEvent e)

Interface HyperlinkListener

public abstract interface HyperlinkListener
                        extends EventListener

This interface represents a hyperlink listener. The implementation class is used to notify events of type HyperlinkEvent whenever the hypertext receives an action such as a mouse click.

Method

void	hyperlinkUpdate(HyperlinkEvent e)

Interface InternalFrameListener

```
public abstract interface InternalFrameListener
                    extends EventListener
```

This interface represents an internal frame listener. The implementation class is notified whenever an event of type InternalFrameEvent is fired by an internal frame. This interface functions analogously to the WindowListener used in AWT.

Methods

```
void    internalFrameActivated(InternalFrameEvent e)
void    internalFrameClosed(InternalFrameEvent e)
void    internalFrameClosing(InternalFrameEvent e)
void    internalFrameDeactivated(InternalFrameEvent e)
void    internalFrameDeiconified(InternalFrameEvent e)
void    internalFrameIconified(InternalFrameEvent e)
void    internalFrameOpened(InternalFrameEvent e)
```

Interface ListDataListener

```
public abstract interface ListDataListener
                    extends EventListener
```

This interface represents a list data listener. The implementation class is notified whenever a change occurs to the data in a list component.

Methods

```
void    contentsChanged(ListDataEvent e)
void    intervalAdded(ListDataEvent e)
void    intervalRemoved(ListDataEvent e)
```

Interface ListSelectionListener

```
public abstract interface ListSelectionListener
                    extends EventListener
```

This interface represents the list selection listener. The implementation class is notified whenever a change occurs in the selection value of a list component.

Method

```
void valueChanged(ListSelectionEvent e)
```

Interface MenuDragMouseListener

```
public abstract interface MenuDragMouseListener
                    extends EventListener
```

This interface represents a menu mouse-drag listener. The implementation class is notified whenever a dragged mouse enters, exits, or is released in the display area of a menu.

Methods

```
void    menuDragMouseDragged(MenuDragMouseEvent e)
void    menuDragMouseEntered(MenuDragMouseEvent e)
```

```
void     menuDragMouseExited(MenuDragMouseEvent e)
void     menuDragMouseReleased(MenuDragMouseEvent e)
```

Interface MenuKeyListener

```
public abstract interface MenuKeyListener
                    extends EventListener
```

This interface represents a menu key listener. The implementation class is notified whenever a key is pressed, released, or typed with the menu focus.

Methods

```
void     menuKeyPressed(MenuKeyEvent e)
void     menuKeyReleased(MenuKeyEvent e)
void     menuKeyTyped(MenuKeyEvent e)
```

Interface MenuListener

```
public abstract interface MenuListener
                    extends EventListener
```

This interface represents a listener for menu events. The implementation class is notified whenever a menu is selected, deselected, or cancelled.

Methods

```
void     menuCanceled(MenuEvent e)
void     menuDeselected(MenuEvent e)
void     menuSelected(MenuEvent e)
```

Interface MouseInputListener

```
public abstract interface MouseInputListener
                    extends MouseListener, MouseMotionListener
```

This interface represents a mouse input listener. The implementation class is notified whenever the mouse enters or exits a component; when the mouse is pressed, released, or clicked on a component; or when the mouse is moved or dragged on a component.

Interface PopupMenuListener

```
public abstract interface PopupMenuListener
extends EventListener
```

This interface represents a pop-up menu listener. The implementation class is notified whenever a pop-up menu becomes visible or invisible or is cancelled.

Methods

```
void     popupMenuCanceled(PopupMenuEvent e)
void     popupMenuWillBecomeInvisible(PopupMenuEvent e)
void     popupMenuWillBecomeVisible(PopupMenuEvent e)
```

Interface TableColumnModelListener

```
public abstract interface TableColumnModelListener
extends EventListener
```

This interface represents a table column model listener. The implementation class is notified whenever a change occurs in the data of the table column model.

Methods
```
void    columnAdded(TableColumnModelEvent e)
void    columnMarginChanged(ChangeEvent e)
void    columnMoved(TableColumnModelEvent e)
void    columnRemoved(TableColumnModelEvent e)
void    columnSelectionChanged(ListSelectionEvent e)
```

Interface TableModelListener
```
public abstract interface TableModelListener
extends EventListener
```

This interface represents a table model listener. The implementation class is notified whenever a change occurs in the data of the table model.

Method
```
void    tableChanged(TableModelEvent e)
```

Interface TreeExpansionListener
```
public abstract interface TreeExpansionListener
                    extends EventListener
```

This interface represents a tree expansion listener. The implementation class is notified whenever a tree expands or collapses a node along a path.

Methods
```
void    treeCollapsed(TreeExpansionEvent event)
void    treeExpanded(TreeExpansionEvent event)
```

Interface TreeModelListener
```
public abstract interface TreeModelListener
extends EventListener
```

This interface represents a tree change listener. The implementation class is notified whenever a change occurs in the nodal data of a tree.

Methods
```
void    treeNodesChanged(TreeModelEvent e)
void    treeNodesInserted(TreeModelEvent e)
void    treeNodesRemoved(TreeModelEvent e)
void    treeStructureChanged(TreeModelEvent e)
```

Interface TreeSelectionListener
```
public abstract interface TreeSelectionListener
                    extends EventListener
```

This interface represents a tree selection listener. The implementation class is notified whenever the selection value changes in a tree.

Method
```
void      valueChanged(TreeSelectionEvent e)
```

Interface TreeWillExpandListener
```
public abstract interface TreeWillExpandListener
                        extends EventListener
```

This interface represents a tree expansion listener. The implementation class is notified whenever a tree expands or collapses a node.

Methods
```
void      treeWillCollapse(TreeExpansionEvent event)
void      treeWillExpand(TreeExpansionEvent event)
```

Interface UndoableEditListener
```
public abstract interface UndoableEditListener
                        extends EventListener
```

This interface represents an undoable edit listener. The implementation class is notified whenever some undoable edits are performed in a text component.

Method
```
void      undoableEditHappened(UndoableEditEvent e)
```

Class AncestorEvent
```
      java.lang.Object
        ¦
        +--java.util.EventObject
              ¦
              +--java.awt.AWTEvent
                    ¦
                    +--javax.swing.event.AncestorEvent

public class AncestorEvent
          extends AWTEvent
```

This class represents an ancestor event that is fired whenever there is a change in the component or its ancestor.

Fields
```
static int      ANCESTOR_ADDED
static int      ANCESTOR_MOVED
static int      ANCESTOR_REMOVED
```

Constructor
```
AncestorEvent(JComponent source, int id, Container ancestor,
Container ancestorParent)
```

Methods
```
Container      getAncestor()
Container      getAncestorParent()
Jcomponent     getComponent()
```

Class CaretEvent

```
java.lang.Object
   |
   +--java.util.EventObject
          |
          +--javax.swing.event.CaretEvent
public abstract class CaretEvent
                   extends EventObject
```

This class represents a caret event that is used to notify that the caret has changed its location in a text component.

Constructor

CaretEvent(Object source) Creates a new CaretEvent object.

Methods

abstract int   **getDot**()
abstract int   **getMark**()

Class ChangeEvent

```
java.lang.Object
  |
  +--java.util.EventObject
        |
        +--javax.swing.event.ChangeEvent
public class ChangeEvent
          extends EventObject
```

This class represents a change event. The change events are fired to notify that the selection state has changed in the event source.

Constructor

ChangeEvent(Object source)

Class DocumentEvent.EventType

```
java.lang.Object
   |
   +--javax.swing.event.DocumentEvent.EventType
public static final class DocumentEvent.EventType
                             extends Object
```

This class is a supporting class for the typesafe enumeration of document event types.

Fields

static DocumentEvent.EventType   **CHANGE**
static DocumentEvent.EventType   **INSERT**
static DocumentEvent.EventType   **REMOVE**

Method

String   **toString**()

Class EventListenerList

```
java.lang.Object
   |
   +--javax.swing.event.EventListenerList
```

public class **EventListenerList**
        extends Object
        implements Serializable

This class represents an event listener list by using an array.

Field
protected Object[]   **listenerList**

Constructor
EventListenerList()

Methods
void	**add**(Class t, EventListener l)
int	**getListenerCount**()
int	**getListenerCount**(Class t)
Object[]	**getListenerList**()
void	**remove**(Class t, EventListener l)
String	**toString**()

Class HyperlinkEvent

```
java.lang.Object
   |
   +--java.util.EventObject
          |
          +--javax.swing.event.HyperlinkEvent
```

public class **HyperlinkEvent**
        extends EventObject

This class represents a hyperlink event. Hyperlink events are fired whenever some action occurs over a hyperlink in an HTML document.

Inner Class
static class **HyperlinkEvent.EventType**

Constructors
HyperlinkEvent(Object source, HyperlinkEvent.EventType type, URL u)
HyperlinkEvent(Object source, HyperlinkEvent.EventType type, URL u, String desc)

Methods
String	**getDescription**()
HyperlinkEvent.EventType	**getEventType**()
URL	**getURL**()

Class HyperlinkEvent.EventType

```
java.lang.Object
  |
  +--javax.swing.event.HyperlinkEvent.EventType
public static final class HyperlinkEvent.EventType
                    extends Object
```

This is an accessory inner class that defines the static event types as ENTERED, EXITED, and ACTIVATED to specify the hyperlink events.

Fields

```
static HyperlinkEvent.EventType    ACTIVATED
static HyperlinkEvent.EventType    ENTERED
static HyperlinkEvent.EventType    EXITED
```

Method

```
String    toString()
```

Class InternalFrameAdapter

```
java.lang.Object
  |
  +--javax.swing.event.InternalFrameAdapter
public abstract class InternalFrameAdapter
                    extends Object
                    implements InternalFrameListener
```

This class represents an abstract adapter that can be extended to create a listener class to receive the internal frame events.

Constructor

```
InternalFrameAdapter()
```

Methods

```
void    internalFrameActivated(InternalFrameEvent e)
void    internalFrameClosed(InternalFrameEvent e)
void    internalFrameClosing(InternalFrameEvent e)
void    internalFrameDeactivated(InternalFrameEvent e)
void    internalFrameDeiconified(InternalFrameEvent e)
void    internalFrameIconified(InternalFrameEvent e)
void    internalFrameOpened(InternalFrameEvent e)
```

Class InternalFrameEvent

```
java.lang.Object
  |
  +--java.util.EventObject
        |
        +--java.awt.AWTEvent
              |
              +--javax.swing.event.InternalFrameEvent
```

```
public class InternalFrameEvent
            extends AWTEvent
```

This class represents an internal frame event that is fired when an internal frame is subjected to operations such as opening or closing, activating or deactivating, iconifying or deiconifying, and so on.

Fields

```
static int      INTERNAL_FRAME_ACTIVATED
static int      INTERNAL_FRAME_CLOSED
static int      INTERNAL_FRAME_CLOSING
static int      INTERNAL_FRAME_DEACTIVATED
static int      INTERNAL_FRAME_DEICONIFIED
static int      INTERNAL_FRAME_FIRST
static int      INTERNAL_FRAME_ICONIFIED
static int      INTERNAL_FRAME_LAST
static int      INTERNAL_FRAME_OPENED
```

Constructor
InternalFrameEvent(JInternalFrame source, int id)

Method
```
String      paramString()
```

Class ListDataEvent

```
java.lang.Object
   |
   +--java.util.EventObject
          |
          +--javax.swing.event.ListDataEvent
```

```
public class ListDataEvent
            extends EventObject
```

This class represents a list data event that is fired whenever the data from the model of a list component changes.

Fields

```
static int      CONTENTS_CHANGED
static int      INTERVAL_ADDED
static int      INTERVAL_REMOVED
```

Constructor
ListDataEvent(Object source, int type, int index0, int index1)

Methods
```
int      getIndex0()
int      getIndex1()
int      getType()
```

Class ListSelectionEvent

```
java.lang.Object
  |
  +--java.util.EventObject
        |
        +--javax.swing.event.ListSelectionEvent
```

public class **ListSelectionEvent**
            extends EventObject

This class represents the list selection event that is fired whenever there is a change in the selection of the list item.

Constructor

ListSelectionEvent(Object source, int firstIndex, int lastIndex, boolean isAdjusting)

Methods

int	**getFirstIndex**()
int	**getLastIndex**()
boolean	**getValueIsAdjusting**()
String	**toString**()

Class MenuDragMouseEvent

```
java.lang.Object
  |
  +--java.util.EventObject
        |
        +--java.awt.AWTEvent
              |
              +--java.awt.event.ComponentEvent
                    |
                    +--java.awt.event.InputEvent
                          |
                          +--java.awt.event.MouseEvent
                                |
                                +--javax.swing.event.MenuDragMouseEvent
```

public class **MenuDragMouseEvent**
            extends MouseEvent

This class represents a menu mouse-drag event that is fired whenever a mouse is dragged over a menu.

Constructor

MenuDragMouseEvent(Component source, int id, long when, int modifiers, int x, int y, int clickCount, boolean popupTrigger, MenuElement[] p, MenuSelectionManager m)

Methods

```
MenuSelectionManager      getMenuSelectionManager()
MenuElement[]             getPath()
```

Class MenuEvent

```
java.lang.Object
  |
  +--java.util.EventObject
        |
        +--javax.swing.event.MenuEvent
```

```
public class MenuEvent
extends EventObject
```

This class represents the menu event that is fired whenever a menu component is opened, selected or canceled.

Constructor

MenuEvent(Object source)

Class MenuKeyEvent

```
java.lang.Object
  |
  +--java.util.EventObject
          |
          +--java.awt.AWTEvent
                |
                +--java.awt.event.ComponentEvent
                      |
                      +--java.awt.event.InputEvent
                            |
                            +--java.awt.event.KeyEvent
                                  |
                                  +--javax.swing.event.MenuKeyEvent
```

```
public class MenuKeyEvent
          extends KeyEvent
```

This class represents a key event that is used to notify the registered listeners whenever a menu has received a key event.

Constructor

MenuKeyEvent(Component source, int id, long when, int modifiers,
int keyCode, char keyChar, MenuElement[] p, MenuSelectionManager m)

Methods

```
MenuSelectionManager      getMenuSelectionManager()
MenuElement[]             getPath()
```

Class MouseInputAdapter

```
java.lang.Object
   |
   +--javax.swing.event.MouseInputAdapter
```

```
public abstract class MouseInputAdapter
                     extends Object
                     implements MouseInputListener
```

This is an adapter class that is used to create a mouse input listener that extends this class. The extended class contains only the necessary methods that override the methods in the adapter.

Constructor
```
MouseInputAdapter()
```

Methods
```
void    mouseClicked(MouseEvent e)
void    mouseDragged(MouseEvent e)
void    mouseEntered(MouseEvent e)
void    mouseExited(MouseEvent e)
void    mouseMoved(MouseEvent e)
void    mousePressed(MouseEvent e)
void    mouseReleased(MouseEvent e)
```

Class PopupMenuEvent

```
java.lang.Object
   |
   +--java.util.EventObject
         |
         +--javax.swing.event.PopupMenuEvent
```

```
public class PopupMenuEvent
          extends EventObject
```

This class represents a pop-up menu event that is fired whenever a pop-up menu is made visible or invisible or cancelled.

Constructor
```
PopupMenuEvent(Object source)
```

Class SwingPropertyChangeSupport

```
java.lang.Object
   |
   +--java.beans.PropertyChangeSupport
         |
         +--javax.swing.event.SwingPropertyChangeSupport
```

```
public final class SwingPropertyChangeSupport
                extends PropertyChangeSupport
```

This is a utility class for the property change support in Swing. This class extends the JavaBean class PropertyChangeSupport, which supports bounded properties.

Constructor
`SwingPropertyChangeSupport`(Object sourceBean)

Methods
void	**addPropertyChangeListener**(PropertyChangeListener listener)
void	**addPropertyChangeListener**(String propertyName, PropertyChangeListener listener)
void	**firePropertyChange**(PropertyChangeEvent evt)
void	**firePropertyChange**(String propertyName, Object oldValue, Object newValue)
boolean	**hasListeners**(String propertyName)
void	**removePropertyChangeListener**(PropertyChangeListener listener)
void	**removePropertyChangeListener**(String propertyName, PropertyChangeListener listener)

Class TableColumnModelEvent

```
java.lang.Object
   |
   +--java.util.EventObject
          |
          +--javax.swing.event.TableColumnModelEvent
```

public class **TableColumnModelEvent**
extends EventObject

This class represents the table column model event that is fired to notify the registered listeners that the data model of a table column has changed by adding, removing, or moving a column.

Fields
protected int	**fromIndex**
protected int	**toIndex**

Constructor
`TableColumnModelEvent`(TableColumnModel source, int from, int to)

Methods
int	**getFromIndex**()
int	**getToIndex**()

Class TableModelEvent

```
java.lang.Object
   |
   +--java.util.EventObject
          |
          +--javax.swing.event.TableModelEvent
```

public class **TableModelEvent**
            extends EventObject

This class represents the table model event that is fired to notify the registered listeners that the data model of the table has changed.

Fields

static int	**ALL_COLUMNS**
protected int	**column**
static int	**DELETE**
protected int	**firstRow**
static int	**HEADER_ROW**
static int	**INSERT**
protected int	**lastRow**
protected int	**type**
static int	**UPDATE**

Constructors

TableModelEvent(TableModel source)
TableModelEvent(TableModel source, int row)
TableModelEvent(TableModel source, int firstRow, int lastRow)
TableModelEvent(TableModel source, int firstRow, int lastRow, int column)
TableModelEvent(TableModel source, int firstRow, int lastRow, int column, int type)

Methods

int	**getColumn**()
int	**getFirstRow**()
int	**getLastRow**()
int	**getType**()

Class TreeExpansionEvent

```
java.lang.Object
   |
   +--java.util.EventObject
          |
          +--javax.swing.event.TreeExpansionEvent
```

public class **TreeExpansionEvent**
            extends EventObject

This class represents the tree expansion event that is fired to identify an expansion path in a tree.

Field

protected TreePath **path**

Constructor

TreeExpansionEvent(Object source, TreePath path)

Method

TreePath **getPath**()

Class TreeModelEvent

```
java.lang.Object
   |
   +--java.util.EventObject
          |
          +--javax.swing.event.TreeModelEvent
```
```
public class TreeModelEvent
          extends EventObject
```

This class represents a tree model event that is fired whenever the data model of the tree changes.

Fields
```
protected int[]        childIndices
protected Object[]     children
protected TreePath     path
```

Constructors
```
TreeModelEvent(Object source, Object[] path)
TreeModelEvent(Object source, Object[] path, int[] childIndices,
Object[] children)
TreeModelEvent(Object source, TreePath path)
TreeModelEvent(Object source, TreePath path, int[] childIndices,
Object[] children)
```

Methods
```
int[]        getChildIndices()
Object[]     getChildren()
Object[]     getPath()
TreePath     getTreePath()
String       toString()
```

Class TreeSelectionEvent

```
java.lang.Object
   |
   +--java.util.EventObject
          |
          +--javax.swing.event.TreeSelectionEvent
```
```
public class TreeSelectionEvent
          extends EventObject
```

This class represents the tree selection event that is fired whenever a change takes place in the tree selection.

Fields
```
protected boolean[]    areNew
protected TreePath     newLeadSelectionPath
```

```
protected TreePath      oldLeadSelectionPath
protected TreePath[]    paths
```

Constructor

TreeSelectionEvent(Object source, TreePath[] paths, boolean[] areNew,
TreePath oldLeadSelectionPath, TreePath newLeadSelectionPath)

TreeSelectionEvent(Object source, TreePath path, boolean isNew,
TreePath oldLeadSelectionPath, TreePath newLeadSelectionPath)

Methods

```
Object        cloneWithSource(Object newSource)
TreePath      getNewLeadSelectionPath()
TreePath      getOldLeadSelectionPath()
TreePath      getPath()
TreePath[]    getPaths()
boolean       isAddedPath()
boolean       isAddedPath(TreePath path)
```

Class UndoableEditEvent

```
java.lang.Object
   |
   +--java.util.EventObject
          |
          +--javax.swing.event.UndoableEditEvent
```

public class **UndoableEditEvent**
            extends EventObject

This class represents an undoable edit event that is fired whenever an undoable edit occurs in a text component.

Constructor

UndoableEditEvent(Object source, UndoableEdit edit)

Method

```
UndoableEdit    getEdit()
```

javax.swing.filechooser

Class FileFilter

```
java.lang.Object
   |
   +--javax.swing.filechooser.FileFilter
```

public abstract class **FileFilter**
                    extends Object

This class represents an abstract filter to display only the specified files in a file chooser. To create a file filter, you need to override the methods from this class by using an implementation subclass.

Constructor
```
FileFilter()
```

Methods
```
abstract boolean     accept(File f)
abstract String      getDescription()
```

Class FileSystemView

```
java.lang.Object
    |
    |
    +--javax.swing.filechooser.FileSystemView
```

```
public abstract class FileSystemView
                      extends Object
```

This class represents the view of the file system on your computer.

Constructor
```
FileSystemView()
```

Methods
```
File                    createFileObject(File dir, String filename)
File                    createFileObject(String path)
abstract File           createNewFolder(File containingDir)
File[]                  getFiles(File dir, boolean useFileHiding)
static FileSystemView   getFileSystemView()
File                    getHomeDirectory()
File                    getParentDirectory(File dir)
abstract File[]         getRoots()
abstract boolean        isHiddenFile(File f)
abstract boolean        isRoot(File f)
```

Class FileView

```
java.lang.Object
    |
    |
    +--javax.swing.filechooser.FileView
```

```
public abstract class FileView
                      extends Object
```

This class represents the view of the files that are displayed in the file chooser. Subclass this class to assign different icons for different categories of files.

Constructor
```
FileView()
```

Methods
```
abstract String      getDescription(File f)
abstract Icon        getIcon(File f)
abstract String      getName(File f)
abstract String      getTypeDescription(File f)
abstract Boolean     isTraversable(File f)
```

javax.swing.plaf

The classes in this package simply serve as the pluggable look-and-feel interfaces for the respective components. For example, the class ButtonUI represents the pluggable look-and-feel interface for the component JButton.

Interface UIResource

public abstract interface **UIResource**

This is a design-level interface that is used to represent objects created by ComponentUI delegates. You will find the class BorderUIResource and its inner classes implementing this interface.

Class BorderUIResource

```
java.lang.Object
    |
    +--javax.swing.plaf.BorderUIResource
```

public class **BorderUIResource**
           extends Object
           implements Border, UIResource, Serializable

This class represents a UIResource border object, which provides a wrapper around a border instance.

Inner Classes

static class	**BorderUIResource.BevelBorderUIResource**
static class	**BorderUIResource.CompoundBorderUIResource**
static class	**BorderUIResource.EmptyBorderUIResource**
static class	**BorderUIResource.EtchedBorderUIResource**
static class	**BorderUIResource.LineBorderUIResource**
static class	**BorderUIResource.MatteBorderUIResource**
static class	**BorderUIResource.TitledBorderUIResource**

Constructor

BorderUIResource(Border delegate)

Methods

static Border	**getBlackLineBorderUIResource**()
Insets	**getBorderInsets**(Component c)
static Border	**getEtchedBorderUIResource**()
static Border	**getLoweredBevelBorderUIResource**()
static Border	**getRaisedBevelBorderUIResource**()
boolean	**isBorderOpaque**()
void	**paintBorder**(Component c, Graphics g, int x, int y, int width, int height)

Class BorderUIResource.BevelBorderUIResource

```
java.lang.Object
   |
   +--javax.swing.border.AbstractBorder
        |
        +--javax.swing.border.BevelBorder
             |
             +--javax.swing.plaf.BorderUIResource.BevelBorderUIResource
```

public static class **BorderUIResource.BevelBorderUIResource**
                        extends BevelBorder
                        implements UIResource

Constructors

BorderUIResource.BevelBorderUIResource(int bevelType)
BorderUIResource.BevelBorderUIResource(int bevelType, Color highlight,
Color shadow)
BorderUIResource.BevelBorderUIResource(int bevelType, Color highlightOuter,
Color highlightInner, Color shadowOuter, Color shadowInner)

Class BorderUIResource.CompoundBorderUIResource

```
java.lang.Object
   |
   +--javax.swing.border.AbstractBorder
        |
        +--javax.swing.border.CompoundBorder
             |
             +--
```
javax.swing.plaf.BorderUIResource.CompoundBorderUIResource

public static class **BorderUIResource.CompoundBorderUIResource**
                        extends CompoundBorder
                        implements UIResource

Constructor

BorderUIResource.CompoundBorderUIResource(Border outsideBorder,
 Border insideBorder)

Class BorderUIResource.EmptyBorderUIResource

```
java.lang.Object
   |
   +--javax.swing.border.AbstractBorder
        |
        +--javax.swing.border.EmptyBorder
             |
             +--javax.swing.plaf.BorderUIResource.EmptyBorderUIResource
```

public static class **BorderUIResource.EmptyBorderUIResource**
                        extends EmptyBorder
                        implements UIResource

Constructors

`BorderUIResource.EmptyBorderUIResource`(Insets insets)
`BorderUIResource.EmptyBorderUIResource`(int top, int left, int bottom,
int right)

Class BorderUIResource.EtchedBorderUIResource

```
java.lang.Object
    |
    +--javax.swing.border.AbstractBorder
            |
            +--javax.swing.border.EtchedBorder
                    |
                    +--javax.swing.plaf.BorderUIResource.EtchedBorderUIResource
```

public static class **BorderUIResource.EtchedBorderUIResource**
                extends EtchedBorder
                implements UIResource

Constructors

`BorderUIResource.EtchedBorderUIResource`()
`BorderUIResource.EtchedBorderUIResource`(Color highlight, Color shadow)
`BorderUIResource.EtchedBorderUIResource`(int etchType)
`BorderUIResource.EtchedBorderUIResource`(int etchType, Color highlight,
Color shadow)

Class BorderUIResource.LineBorderUIResource

```
java.lang.Object
    |
    +--javax.swing.border.AbstractBorder
            |
            +--javax.swing.border.LineBorder
                    |
                    +--javax.swing.plaf.BorderUIResource.LineBorderUIResource
```

public static class **BorderUIResource.LineBorderUIResource**
                extends LineBorder
                implements UIResource

Constructors

`BorderUIResource.LineBorderUIResource`(Color color)
BorderUIResource.LineBorderUIResource(Color color, int thickness)

Class BorderUIResource.MatteBorderUIResource

```
java.lang.Object
    |
    +--javax.swing.border.AbstractBorder
            |
            +--javax.swing.border.EmptyBorder
                    |
                    +--javax.swing.border.MatteBorder
```

```
                      |
                      +--javax.swing.plaf.BorderUIResource.MatteBorderUIResource
public static class BorderUIResource.MatteBorderUIResource
                      extends MatteBorder
                      implements UIResource
```

Constructors

BorderUIResource.MatteBorderUIResource(Icon tileIcon)
BorderUIResource.MatteBorderUIResource(int top, int left, int bottom,
➥int right, Color color)
BorderUIResource.MatteBorderUIResource(int top, int left, int bottom,
➥int right, Icon tileIcon)

Class BorderUIResource.TitledBorderUIResource

```
        java.lang.Object
          |
          +--javax.swing.border.AbstractBorder
                  |
                  +--javax.swing.border.TitledBorder
                          |
                          +--javax.swing.plaf.BorderUIResource.TitledBorderUIResource
public static class BorderUIResource.TitledBorderUIResource
                      extends TitledBorder
                      implements UIResource
```

Constructors

BorderUIResource.TitledBorderUIResource(Border border)
BorderUIResource.TitledBorderUIResource(Border border, String title)
BorderUIResource.TitledBorderUIResource(Border border, String title,
int titleJustification, int titlePosition)
BorderUIResource.TitledBorderUIResource(Border border, String title,
int titleJustification, int titlePosition, Font titleFont)
BorderUIResource.TitledBorderUIResource(Border border, String title,
int titleJustification, int titlePosition, Font titleFont, Color titleColor)
BorderUIResource.TitledBorderUIResource(String title)

Class ButtonUI

```
        java.lang.Object
          |
          +--javax.swing.plaf.ComponentUI
                  |
                  +--javax.swing.plaf.ButtonUI
public abstract class ButtonUI
                      extends ComponentUI
```

Constructor

ButtonUI()

Class ColorChooserUI

```
java.lang.Object
  |
  +--javax.swing.plaf.ComponentUI
        |
        +--javax.swing.plaf.ColorChooserUI
```

public abstract class **ColorChooserUI**
                    extends ComponentUI

Constructor
ColorChooserUI()

Class ColorUIResource

```
java.lang.Object
  |
  +--java.awt.Color
        |
        +--javax.swing.plaf.ColorUIResource
```

public class **ColorUIResource**
         extends Color
         implements UIResource

Constructors
ColorUIResource(Color c)
ColorUIResource(float r, float g, float b)
ColorUIResource(int rgb)
ColorUIResource(int r, int g, int b)

Class ComboBoxUI

```
java.lang.Object
  |
  +--javax.swing.plaf.ComponentUI
        |
        +--javax.swing.plaf.ComboBoxUI
```

public abstract class **ComboBoxUI**
                    extends ComponentUI

Constructor
ComboBoxUI()

Methods
abstract boolean   **isFocusTraversable**(JComboBox c)
abstract boolean   **isPopupVisible**(JComboBox c)
abstract void   **setPopupVisible**(JComboBox c, boolean v)

Class ComponentUI

```
java.lang.Object
  |
  +--javax.swing.plaf.ComponentUI
```

```
public abstract class ComponentUI
                         extends Object
```

Constructor
```
ComponentUI()
```

Methods
```
boolean                contains(JComponent c, int x, int y)
static ComponentUI     createUI(JComponent c)
Accessible             getAccessibleChild(JComponent c, int i)
int                    getAccessibleChildrenCount(JComponent c)
Dimension              getMaximumSize(JComponent c)
Dimension              getMinimumSize(JComponent c)
Dimension              getPreferredSize(JComponent c)
void                   installUI(JComponent c)
void                   paint(Graphics g, JComponent c)
void                   uninstallUI(JComponent c)
void                   update(Graphics g, JComponent c)
```

Class DesktopIconUI
```
java.lang.Object
   |
   +--javax.swing.plaf.ComponentUI
         |
         +--javax.swing.plaf.DesktopIconUI
```
```
public abstract class DesktopIconUI
                         extends ComponentUI
```

Constructor
```
DesktopIconUI()
```

Class DesktopPaneUI
```
java.lang.Object
   |
   +--javax.swing.plaf.ComponentUI
         |
         +--javax.swing.plaf.DesktopPaneUI
```
```
public abstract class DesktopPaneUI
                         extends ComponentUI
```

Constructor
```
DesktopPaneUI()
```

Class DimensionUIResource
```
java.lang.Object
   |
```

```
        +--java.awt.geom.Dimension2D
                 |
                 +--java.awt.Dimension
                          |
                          +--javax.swing.plaf.DimensionUIResource
```

public class **DimensionUIResource**
        extends Dimension
        implements UIResource

Constructor
DimensionUIResource(int width, int height)

Class FileChooserUI

```
    java.lang.Object
      |
      +--javax.swing.plaf.ComponentUI
              |
              +--javax.swing.plaf.FileChooserUI
```

public abstract class **FileChooserUI**
          extends ComponentUI

Constructor
FileChooserUI()

Methods

abstract void	**ensureFileIsVisible**(JFileChooser fc, File f)
abstract FileFilter	**getAcceptAllFileFilter**(JFileChooser fc)
abstract String	**getApproveButtonText**(JFileChooser fc)
abstract String	**getDialogTitle**(JFileChooser fc)
abstract FileView	**getFileView**(JFileChooser fc)
abstract void	**rescanCurrentDirectory**(JFileChooser fc)

Class FontUIResource

```
    java.lang.Object
      |
      +--java.awt.Font
              |
              +--javax.swing.plaf.FontUIResource
```

public class **FontUIResource**
        extends Font
        implements UIResource

Class IconUIResource

```
    java.lang.Object
      |
      +--javax.swing.plaf.IconUIResource
```

public class **IconUIResource**
        extends Object
        implements Icon, UIResource, Serializable

Constructor
`IconUIResource`(Icon delegate)

Methods
int	**getIconHeight**()
int	**getIconWidth**()
void	**paintIcon**(Component c, Graphics g, int x, int y)

Class InsetsUIResource

```
java.lang.Object
   |
   +--java.awt.Insets
          |
          +--javax.swing.plaf.InsetsUIResource
```

public class **InsetsUIResource**
          extends Insets
          implements UIResource

Constructor
`InsetsUIResource`(int top, int left, int bottom, int right)

Class InternalFrameUI

```
java.lang.Object
   |
   +--javax.swing.plaf.ComponentUI
          |
          +--javax.swing.plaf.InternalFrameUI
```

public abstract class **InternalFrameUI**
                    extends ComponentUI

Constructor
`InternalFrameUI`()

Class LabelUI

```
java.lang.Object
   |
   +--javax.swing.plaf.ComponentUI
          |
          +--javax.swing.plaf.LabelUI
```

public abstract class **LabelUI**
                    extends ComponentUI

Constructor
`LabelUI`()

Class ListUI

```
java.lang.Object
   |
```

```
          +--javax.swing.plaf.ComponentUI
               |
               +--javax.swing.plaf.ListUI
public abstract class ListUI
                    extends ComponentUI
```

Constructor
`ListUI()`

Methods

abstract Rectangle	**getCellBounds**(JList list, int index1, int index2)
abstract Point	**indexToLocation**(JList list, int index)
abstract int	**locationToIndex**(JList list, Point location)

Class MenuBarUI

```
     java.lang.Object
        |
        +--javax.swing.plaf.ComponentUI
               |
               +--javax.swing.plaf.MenuBarUI
public abstract class MenuBarUI
                    extends ComponentUI
```

Constructor
`MenuBarUI()`

Class MenuItemUI

```
     java.lang.Object
        |
        +--javax.swing.plaf.ComponentUI
               |
               |--javax.swing.plaf.ButtonUI
                    |
                    +--javax.swing.plaf.MenuItemUI
public abstract class MenuItemUI
                    extends ButtonUI
```

Constructor
`MenuItemUI()`

Class OptionPaneUI

```
     java.lang.Object
        |
        +--javax.swing.plaf.ComponentUI
               |
               +--javax.swing.plaf.OptionPaneUI
public abstract class OptionPaneUI
                    extends ComponentUI
```

Constructor
`OptionPaneUI()`

Methods
```
abstract boolean    containsCustomComponents(JOptionPane op)
abstract void       selectInitialValue(JOptionPane op)
```

Class PanelUI

```
java.lang.Object
   |
   +--javax.swing.plaf.ComponentUI
            |
            +--javax.swing.plaf.PanelUI
```

```
public abstract class PanelUI
                    extends ComponentUI
```

Constructor
`PanelUI()`

Class PopupMenuUI

```
java.lang.Object
   |
   +--javax.swing.plaf.ComponentUI
            |
            +--javax.swing.plaf.PopupMenuUI
```

```
public abstract class PopupMenuUI
                    extends ComponentUI
```

Constructor
`PopupMenuUI()`

Class ProgressBarUI

```
java.lang.Object
   |
   +--javax.swing.plaf.ComponentUI
            |
            +--javax.swing.plaf.ProgressBarUI
```

```
public abstract class ProgressBarUI
                    extends ComponentUI
```

Constructor
`ProgressBarUI()`

Class ScrollBarUI

```
java.lang.Object
   |
   +--javax.swing.plaf.ComponentUI
            |
```

```
              +--javax.swing.plaf.ScrollBarUI
public abstract class ScrollBarUI
                        extends ComponentUI
```

Constructor
`ScrollBarUI()`

Class ScrollPaneUI

```
       java.lang.Object
         |
         +--javax.swing.plaf.ComponentUI
              |
              +--javax.swing.plaf.ScrollPaneUI
public abstract class ScrollPaneUI
                        extends ComponentUI
```

Constructor
`ScrollPaneUI()`

Class SeparatorUI

```
       java.lang.Object
         |
         +--javax.swing.plaf.ComponentUI
              |
              +--javax.swing.plaf.SeparatorUI
public abstract class SeparatorUI
                        extends ComponentUI
```

Constructor
`SeparatorUI()`

Class SliderUI

```
       java.lang.Object
         |
         +--javax.swing.plaf.ComponentUI
              |
              +--javax.swing.plaf.SliderUI
public abstract class SliderUI
                        extends ComponentUI
```

Constructor
`SliderUI()`

Class SplitPaneUI

```
       java.lang.Object
         |
         +--javax.swing.plaf.ComponentUI
              |
              +--javax.swing.plaf.SplitPaneUI
```

```
public abstract class SplitPaneUI
                        extends ComponentUI
```

Constructor
SplitPaneUI()

Methods
abstract void	**finishedPaintingChildren**(JSplitPane jc, Graphics g)
abstract int	**getDividerLocation**(JSplitPane jc)
abstract int	**getMaximumDividerLocation**(JSplitPane jc)
abstract int	**getMinimumDividerLocation**(JSplitPane jc)
abstract void	**resetToPreferredSizes**(JSplitPane jc)
abstract void	**setDividerLocation**(JSplitPane jc, int location)

Class TabbedPaneUI

```
java.lang.Object
   |
   +--javax.swing.plaf.ComponentUI
             |
             +--javax.swing.plaf.TabbedPaneUI
```

```
public abstract class TabbedPaneUI
                        extends ComponentUI
```

Constructor
TabbedPaneUI()

Methods
abstract Rectangle	**getTabBounds**(JTabbedPane pane, int index)
abstract int	**getTabRunCount**(JTabbedPane pane)
abstract int	**tabForCoordinate**(JTabbedPane pane, int x, int y)

Class TableHeaderUI

```
java.lang.Object
   |
   +--javax.swing.plaf.ComponentUI
             |
             +--javax.swing.plaf.TableHeaderUI
```

```
public abstract class TableHeaderUI
                        extends ComponentUI
```

Constructor
TableHeaderUI()

Class TableUI

```
java.lang.Object
   |
   +--javax.swing.plaf.ComponentUI
             |
             +--javax.swing.plaf.TableUI
```

```
public abstract class TableUI
                    extends ComponentUI
```

Constructor
TableUI()

Class TextUI

```
java.lang.Object
   |
   +--javax.swing.plaf.ComponentUI
        |
        +--javax.swing.plaf.TextUI
```

```
public abstract class TextUI
                    extends ComponentUI
```

Constructor
TextUI()

Methods

abstract void	**damageRange**(JTextComponent t, int p0, int p1)
abstract void	**damageRange**(JTextComponent t, int p0, int p1, ➥Position.Bias firstBias, Position.Bias secondBias)
abstract EditorKit	**getEditorKit**(JTextComponent t)
abstract int	**getNextVisualPositionFrom**(JTextComponent t, nt pos, ➥Position.Bias b, int direction, Position.Bias[] biasRet)
abstract View	**getRootView**(JTextComponent t)
abstract Rectangle	**modelToView**(JTextComponent t, int pos)
abstract Rectangle	**modelToView**(JTextComponent t, int pos, ➥Position.Bias bias)
abstract int	**viewToModel**(JTextComponent t, Point pt)
abstract int	**viewToModel**(JTextComponent t, Point pt, Position.Bias[] ➥biasReturn)

Class ToolBarUI

```
java.lang.Object
   |
   +--javax.swing.plaf.ComponentUI
        |
        +--javax.swing.plaf.ToolBarUI
```

```
public abstract class ToolBarUI
                    extends ComponentUI
```

Constructor
ToolBarUI()

Class ToolTipUI

```
java.lang.Object
   |
   +--javax.swing.plaf.ComponentUI
          |
          +--javax.swing.plaf.ToolTipUI
```

public abstract class **ToolTipUI**
                       extends ComponentUI

Constructor
ToolTipUI()

Class TreeUI

```
java.lang.Object
   |
   +--javax.swing.plaf.ComponentUI
          |
          +--javax.swing.plaf.TreeUI
```

public abstract class **TreeUI**
                       extends ComponentUI

Constructor
TreeUI()

Methods

abstract void	**cancelEditing**(JTree tree)
abstract TreePath	**getClosestPathForLocation**(JTree tree, int x, int y)
abstract TreePath	**getEditingPath**(JTree tree)
abstract Rectangle	**getPathBounds**(JTree tree, TreePath path)
abstract TreePath	**getPathForRow**(JTree tree, int row)
abstract int	**getRowCount**(JTree tree)
abstract int	**getRowForPath**(JTree tree, TreePath path)
abstract boolean	**isEditing**(JTree tree)
abstract void	**startEditingAtPath**(JTree tree, TreePath path)
abstract boolean	**stopEditing**(JTree tree)

Class ViewportUI

```
java.lang.Object
   |
   +--javax.swing.plaf.ComponentUI
          |
          +--javax.swing.plaf.ViewportUI
```

public abstract class **ViewportUI**
                       extends ComponentUI

Constructor
ViewportUI()

javax.swing.table

Interface TableCellEditor

```
public abstract interface TableCellEditor
                         extends CellEditor
```

This interface describes an editor that can be used to edit the cells of a Swing table.

Method

Component   **getTableCellEditorComponent**(JTable table, Object value, boolean isSelected, int row, int column)

Interface TableCellRenderer

```
public abstract interface TableCellRenderer
```

This interface describes the cell renderer of a Swing table.

Method

Component   **getTableCellRendererComponent**(JTable table, Object value, boolean isSelected, boolean hasFocus, int row, int column)

Interface TableColumnModel

```
public abstract interface TableColumnModel
```

This interface describes the data model for a column in a table.

Methods

void	**addColumn**(TableColumn aColumn)
void	**addColumnModelListener**(TableColumnModelListener x)
TableColumn	**getColumn**(int columnIndex)
int	**getColumnCount**()
int	**getColumnIndex**(Object columnIdentifier)
int	**getColumnIndexAtX**(int xPosition)
int	**getColumnMargin**()
Enumeration	**getColumns**()
boolean	**getColumnSelectionAllowed**()
int	**getSelectedColumnCount**()
int[]	**getSelectedColumns**()
ListSelectionModel	**getSelectionModel**()
int	**getTotalColumnWidth**()
void	**moveColumn**(int columnIndex, int newIndex)
void	**removeColumn**(TableColumn column)
void	**removeColumnModelListener** (TableColumnModelListener x)
void	**setColumnMargin**(int newMargin)
void	**setColumnSelectionAllowed**(boolean flag)
void	**setSelectionModel**(ListSelectionModel newModel)

Interface TableModel

`public abstract interface TableModel`

This interface describes the data model of a table.

Methods

void	**addTableModelListener**(TableModelListener l)
Class	**getColumnClass**(int columnIndex)
int	**getColumnCount**()
String	**getColumnName**(int columnIndex)
int	**getRowCount**()
Object	**getValueAt**(int rowIndex, int columnIndex)
boolean	**isCellEditable**(int rowIndex, int columnIndex)
void	**removeTableModelListener**(TableModelListener l)
void	**setValueAt**(Object aValue, int rowIndex, int columnIndex)

Class AbstractTableModel

```
java.lang.Object
   |
   |
   +--javax.swing.table.AbstractTableModel
```

```
public abstract class AbstractTableModel
                        extends Object
                        implements TableModel, Serializable
```

This class represents an abstract table model by implementing the table model. The class requires you to implement the following methods:

```
public int     getRowCount();
public int     getColumnCount();
public Object  getValueAt(int row, int column);
```

Field

protected EventListenerList	**listenerList**

Constructor

`AbstractTableModel()`

Methods

void	**addTableModelListener**(TableModelListener l)
int	**findColumn**(String columnName)
void	**fireTableCellUpdated**(int row, int column)
void	**fireTableChanged**(TableModelEvent e)
void	**fireTableDataChanged**()
void	**fireTableRowsDeleted**(int firstRow, int lastRow)
void	**fireTableRowsInserted**(int firstRow, int lastRow)
void	**fireTableRowsUpdated**(int firstRow, int lastRow)
void	**fireTableStructureChanged**()
Class	**getColumnClass**(int columnIndex)
String	**getColumnName**(int column)

boolean	**isCellEditable**(int rowIndex, int columnIndex)
void	**removeTableModelListener**(TableModelListener l)
void	**setValueAt**(Object aValue, int rowIndex, int columnIndex)

Class DefaultTableCellRenderer

```
java.lang.Object
   |
   +--java.awt.Component
         |
         +--java.awt.Container
               |
               +--javax.swing.JComponent
                     |
                     +--javax.swing.JLabel
                           |
                           +--javax.swing.table.DefaultTableCellRenderer
```

public class **DefaultTableCellRenderer**
        extends JLabel
        implements TableCellRenderer, Serializable

This class represents the default cell renderer to display cells of a table.

Inner Class Summary

static class	**DefaultTableCellRenderer.UIResource**

Field

protected static Border	**noFocusBorder**

Constructor

DefaultTableCellRenderer()

Methods

Component	**getTableCellRendererComponent**(JTable table, Object value, boolean isSelected, boolean hasFocus, int row, int column)
void	**setBackground**(Color c)
void	**setForeground**(Color c)
protected void	**setValue**(Object value)
void	**updateUI**()

Class DefaultTableCellRenderer.UIResource

```
java.lang.Object
   |
   +--java.awt.Component
         |
         +--java.awt.Container
               |
               +--javax.swing.JComponent
                     |
                     +--javax.swing.JLabel
```

```
        !
        !
      +--javax.swing.table.DefaultTableCellRenderer
             !
             !
             +--javax.swing.table.DefaultTableCellRenderer.UIResource
public static class DefaultTableCellRenderer.UIResource
              extends DefaultTableCellRenderer
              implements UIResource
```

This class represents the user interface resource for a cell renderer by implementing UIResource.

Constructor
`DefaultTableCellRenderer.UIResource()`

Class DefaultTableColumnModel

```
    java.lang.Object
      !
      !
      +--javax.swing.table.DefaultTableColumnModel
```

```
public class DefaultTableColumnModel
extends Object
implements TableColumnModel, PropertyChangeListener,
ListSelectionListener, Serializable
```

This class represents the standard implementation of the column model of the Swing table.

Fields

protected ChangeEvent	**changeEvent**
protected int	**columnMargin**
protected boolean	**columnSelectionAllowed**
protected EventListenerList	**listenerList**
protected ListSelectionModel	**selectionModel**
protected Vector	**tableColumns**
protected int	**totalColumnWidth**

Constructor
`DefaultTableColumnModel()`

Methods

void	**addColumn**(TableColumn aColumn)
void	**addColumnModelListener** (TableColumnModelListener x)
protected ListSelectionModel	**createSelectionModel**()
protected void	**fireColumnAdded**(TableColumnModelEvent e)
protected void	**fireColumnMarginChanged**()
protected void	**fireColumnMoved**(TableColumnModelEvent e)
protected void	**fireColumnRemoved**(TableColumnModelEvent e)
protected void	**fireColumnSelectionChanged** (ListSelectionEvent e)

TableColumn	**getColumn**(int columnIndex)
int	**getColumnCount**()
int	**getColumnIndex**(Object identifier)
int	**getColumnIndexAtX**(int xPosition)
int	**getColumnMargin**()
Enumeration	**getColumns**()
boolean	**getColumnSelectionAllowed**()
int	**getSelectedColumnCount**()
int[]	**getSelectedColumns**()
ListSelectionModel	**getSelectionModel**()
int	**getTotalColumnWidth**()
void	**moveColumn**(int columnIndex, int newIndex)
void	**propertyChange**(PropertyChangeEvent evt)
protected void	**recalcWidthCache**()
void	**removeColumn**(TableColumn column)
void	**removeColumnModelListener** (TableColumnModelListener x)
void	**setColumnMargin**(int newMargin)
void	**setColumnSelectionAllowed**(boolean flag)
void	**setSelectionModel**(ListSelectionModel newModel)
void	**valueChanged**(ListSelectionEvent e)

Class DefaultTableModel

```
java.lang.Object
   |
   +--javax.swing.table.AbstractTableModel
          |
          +--javax.swing.table.DefaultTableModel
```

public class **DefaultTableModel**
        extends AbstractTableModel
        implements Serializable

This class represents the standard implementation of a table data model.

Fields

protected Vector	**columnIdentifiers**
Vector	**dataVector**

Constructors

DefaultTableModel()
DefaultTableModel(int numRows, int numColumns)
DefaultTableModel(Object[][] data, Object[] columnNames)
DefaultTableModel(Object[] columnNames, int numRows)0
DefaultTableModel(Vector columnNames, int numRows)
DefaultTableModel(Vector data, Vector columnNames)

Methods

void	**addColumn**(Object columnName)
void	**addColumn**(Object columnName, Object[] columnData)
void	**addColumn**(Object columnName, Vector columnData)

```
void                          addRow(Object[] rowData)
void                          addRow(Vector rowData)
protected static Vector       convertToVector(Object[] anArray)
protected static Vector       convertToVector(Object[][] anArray)
int                           getColumnCount()
String                        getColumnName(int column)
Vector                        getDataVector()
int                           getRowCount()
Object                        getValueAt(int row, int column)
void                          insertRow(int row, Object[] rowData)
void                          insertRow(int row, Vector rowData)
boolean                       isCellEditable(int row, int column)
void                          moveRow(int startIndex, int endIndex, int toIndex)
void                          newDataAvailable(TableModelEvent event)
void                          newRowsAdded(TableModelEvent event)
void                          removeRow(int row)
void                          rowsRemoved(TableModelEvent event)
void                          setColumnIdentifiers(Object[] newIdentifiers)
void                          setColumnIdentifiers(Vector newIdentifiers)
void                          setDataVector(Object[][] newData,
                              Object[] columnNames)
void                          setDataVector(Vector newData, Vector columnNames)
void                          setNumRows(int newSize)
void                          setValueAt(Object aValue, int row, int column)
```

Class JTableHeader

```
java.lang.Object
   |
   +--java.awt.Component
         |
         +--java.awt.Container
               |
               +--javax.swing.JComponent
                     |
                     +--javax.swing.table.JTableHeader
```

```
public class JTableHeader
          extends JComponent
          implements TableColumnModelListener, Accessible
```

This class represents the column header of a Swing table.

Inner Class Summary
```
protected class              JTableHeader.AccessibleJTableHeader
```

Fields
```
protected TableColumnModel   columnModel
protected TableColumn        draggedColumn
protected int                draggedDistance
protected boolean            reorderingAllowed
```

protected boolean	**resizingAllowed**
Protected TableColumn	**resizingColumn**
protected JTable	**table**
protected boolean	**updateTableInRealTime**

Constructors
JTableHeader()
JTableHeader(TableColumnModel cm)

Methods

void	**columnAdded**(TableColumnModelEvent e)
int	**columnAtPoint**(Point point)
void	**columnMarginChanged**(ChangeEvent e)
void	**columnMoved**(TableColumnModelEvent e)
void	**columnRemoved**(TableColumnModelEvent e)
void	**columnSelectionChanged**(ListSelectionEvent e)
protected TableColumnModel	**createDefaultColumnModel**()
AccessibleContext	**getAccessibleContext**()
TableColumnModel	**getColumnModel**()
TableColumn	**getDraggedColumn**()
int	**getDraggedDistance**()
Rectangle	**getHeaderRect**(int columnIndex)
boolean	**getReorderingAllowed**()
boolean	**getResizingAllowed**()
TableColumn	**getResizingColumn**()
JTable	**getTable**()
String	**getToolTipText**(MouseEvent event)
TableHeaderUI	**getUI**()
String	**getUIClassID**()
boolean	**getUpdateTableInRealTime**()
protected void	**initializeLocalVars**()
protected String	**paramString**()
void	**resizeAndRepaint**()
void	**setColumnModel**(TableColumnModel newModel)
void	**setDraggedColumn**(TableColumn aColumn)
void	**setDraggedDistance**(int distance)
void	**setReorderingAllowed**(boolean b)
void	**setResizingAllowed**(boolean b)
void	**setResizingColumn**(TableColumn aColumn)
void	**setTable**(JTable aTable)
void	**setUI**(TableHeaderUI ui)
void	**setUpdateTableInRealTime**(boolean flag)
void	**updateUI**()

Class TableColumn

```
java.lang.Object
   |
   +--javax.swing.table.TableColumn
```

public class **TableColumn**

```
                  extends Object
                  implements Serializable
```

This class represents the table column by possessing all the properties of a table column.

Fields

```
static String                    CELL_RENDERER_PROPERTY
protected TableCellEditor        cellEditor
protected TableCellRenderer      cellRenderer
static String                    COLUMN_WIDTH_PROPERTY
static String                    HEADER_RENDERER_PROPERTY
static String                    HEADER_VALUE_PROPERTY
protected TableCellRenderer      headerRenderer
protected Object                 headerValue
protected Object                 identifier
protected boolean isResizable    Resizable flag
protected int                    maxWidth
protected int                    minWidth
protected int                    modelIndex
protected int                    resizedPostingDisableCount
protected int                    width
```

Constructors

```
TableColumn()
TableColumn(int modelIndex)
TableColumn(int modelIndex, int width)
TableColumn(int modelIndex, int width, TableCellRenderer cellRenderer,
TableCellEditor cellEditor)
TableColumn with modelIndex
```

Methods

```
void                             addPropertyChangeListener
                                 (PropertyChangeListener listener)
protected TableCellRenderer      createDefaultHeaderRenderer()
void                             disableResizedPosting()
void                             enableResizedPosting()
TableCellEditor                  getCellEditor()
TableCellRenderer                getCellRenderer()
TableCellRenderer                getHeaderRenderer()
Object                           getHeaderValue()
Object                           getIdentifier()
int                              getMaxWidth()
int                              getMinWidth()
int                              getModelIndex()
int                              getPreferredWidth()
boolean                          getResizable()
int                              getWidth()
void                             removePropertyChangeListener
                                 (PropertyChangeListener listener)
```

void	**setCellEditor**(TableCellEditor anEditor)
void	**setCellRenderer**(TableCellRenderer aRenderer)
void	**setHeaderRenderer**(TableCellRenderer aRenderer)
void	**setHeaderValue**(Object aValue)
void	**setIdentifier**(Object anIdentifier)
void	**setMaxWidth**(int maxWidth)
void	**setMinWidth**(int minWidth)
void	**setModelIndex**(int anIndex)
void	**setPreferredWidth**(int preferredWidth)
void	**setResizable**(boolean flag)
void	**setWidth**(int width)
void	**sizeWidthToFit**()

javax.swing.text

Interface AbstractDocument.AttributeContext

public abstract static interface **AbstractDocument.AttributeContext**

This interface describes a context object that allows the mutable attribute sets to be added or removed.

Methods

AttributeSet	**addAttribute**(AttributeSet old, Object name, Object value)
AttributeSet	**addAttributes**(AttributeSet old, AttributeSet attr)
AttributeSet	**getEmptySet**()
void	**reclaim**(AttributeSet a)
AttributeSet	**removeAttribute**(AttributeSet old, Object name)
AttributeSet	**removeAttributes**(AttributeSet old, AttributeSet attrs)

Interface AbstractDocument.Content

public abstract static interface **AbstractDocument.Content**

This interface describes the content of information in a document.

Methods

Position	**createPosition**(int offset)
void	**getChars**(int where, int len, Segment txt)
String	**getString**(int where, int len)
UndoableEdit	**insertString**(int where, String str)
int	**length**()
UndoableEdit	**remove**(int where, int nitems)

Interface AttributeSet

public abstract interface **AttributeSet**

This interface represents a read-only attribute set. An attribute set is basically a collection of keys with associated values.

Inner Classes

```
static interface    AttributeSet.CharacterAttribute
static interface    AttributeSet.ColorAttribute
static interface    AttributeSet.FontAttribute
static interface    AttributeSet.ParagraphAttribute
```

Fields

```
static Object NameAttribute
static Object ResolveAttribute
```

Methods

```
boolean        containsAttribute(Object name, Object value)
boolean        containsAttributes(AttributeSet attributes)
AttributeSet   copyAttributes()
Object         getAttribute(Object key)
int            getAttributeCount()
Enumeration    getAttributeNames()
AttributeSet   getResolveParent()
boolean        isDefined(Object attrName)
boolean        isEqual(AttributeSet attr)
```

Interface AttributeSet.CharacterAttribute

```
public abstract static interface AttributeSet.CharacterAttribute
```

This interface describes the type signature that needs to associate an attribute key to furnish character content.

Interface AttributeSet.ColorAttribute

```
public abstract static interface AttributeSet.ColorAttribute
```

This interface describes the type signature that needs to associate an attribute key to furnish color.

Interface AttributeSet.FontAttribute

```
public abstract static interface AttributeSet.FontAttribute
```

This interface describes the type signature that needs to associate an attribute key to furnish the font of a text.

Interface AttributeSet.ParagraphAttribute

```
public abstract static interface AttributeSet.ParagraphAttribute
```

This interface describes the type signature that needs to associate an attribute key to furnish a paragraph of content.

Interface Caret

```
public abstract interface Caret
```

This interface describes the features of a caret that is used in Document view to insert text.

Methods

void	addChangeListener(ChangeListener l)
void	deinstall(JTextComponent c)
int	getBlinkRate()
int	getDot()
Point	getMagicCaretPosition()
int	getMark()
void	install(JTextComponent c)
boolean	isSelectionVisible()
boolean	isVisible()
void	moveDot(int dot)
void	paint(Graphics g)
void	removeChangeListener(ChangeListener l)
void	setBlinkRate(int rate)
void	setDot(int dot)
void	setMagicCaretPosition(Point p)
void	setSelectionVisible(boolean v)
void	setVisible(boolean v)

Interface Document

public abstract interface **Document**

This interface describes the features of a document. The document is the content model used in a text component.

Fields

static String **StreamDescriptionProperty**
static String **TitleProperty**

Methods

void	addDocumentListener(DocumentListener listener)
void	addUndoableEditListener(UndoableEditListener listener)
Position	createPosition(int offs)
Element	getDefaultRootElement()
Position	getEndPosition()
int	getLength()
Object	getProperty(Object key)
Element[]	getRootElements()
Position	getStartPosition()
String	getText(int offset, int length)
void	getText(int offset, int length, Segment txt)
void	insertString(int offset, String str, AttributeSet a)
void	putProperty(Object key, Object value)
void	remove(int offs, int len)
void	removeDocumentListener(DocumentListener listener)
void	removeUndoableEditListener(UndoableEditListener listener)
void	render(Runnable r)

Interface Element

`public abstract interface` **`Element`**

This interface describes an element in a document.

Methods

AttributeSet	**getAttributes**()
Document	**getDocument**()
Element	**getElement**(int index)
int	**getElementCount**()
int	**getElementIndex**(int offset)
int	**getEndOffset**()
String	**getName**()
Element	**getParentElement**()
int	**getStartOffset**()
boolean	**isLeaf**()

Interface Highlighter

`public abstract interface` **`Highlighter`**

This interface describes an object that allows you to highlight a selection with a specified color.

Inner Classes

static interface	**Highlighter**.Highlight
static interface	**Highlighter**.HighlightPainter

Methods

Object	**addHighlight**(int p0, int p1, Highlighter.HighlightPainter p)
void	**changeHighlight**(Object tag, int p0, int p1)
void	**deinstall**(JTextComponent c)
Highlighter.Highlight[]	**getHighlights**()
void	**install**(JTextComponent c)
void	**paint**(Graphics g)
void	**removeAllHighlights**()
void	**removeHighlight**(Object tag)

Interface Highlighter.Highlight

`public abstract static interface` **`Highlighter.Highlight`**

This interface describes the object that contains the specified values of a highlight (see the interface methods).

Methods

int	**getEndOffset**()
Highlighter.HighlightPainter	**getPainter**()
int	**getStartOffset**()

Interface Highlighter.HighlightPainter

`public abstract static interface Highlighter.HighlightPainter`

This interface describes the renderer that is used to highlight certain content.

Method

```
void    paint(Graphics g, int p0, int p1, Shape bounds,
        JTextComponent c)
```

Interface Keymap

`public abstract interface Keymap`

This interface describes keymaps (name-value pairs).

Methods

```
void            addActionForKeyStroke(KeyStroke key, Action a)
Action          getAction(KeyStroke key)
Action[]        getBoundActions()
KeyStroke[]     getBoundKeyStrokes()
Action          getDefaultAction()
KeyStroke[]     getKeyStrokesForAction(Action a)
String          getName()
Keymap          getResolveParent()
boolean         isLocallyDefined(KeyStroke key)
void            removeBindings()
void            removeKeyStrokeBinding(KeyStroke keys)
void            setDefaultAction(Action a)
void            setResolveParent(Keymap parent)
```

Interface MutableAttributeSet

```
public abstract interface MutableAttributeSet
                        extends AttributeSet
```

This interface represents a set of unique attributes that can be subjected to mutation.

Methods

```
void    addAttribute(Object name, Object value)
void    addAttributes(AttributeSet attributes)
void    removeAttribute(Object name)
void    removeAttributes(AttributeSet attributes)
void    removeAttributes(Enumeration names)
void    setResolveParent(AttributeSet parent)
```

Interface Position

`public abstract interface Position`

This interface represents the position within a document.

Inner Class

```
static class    Position.Bias
```

Method

```
int    getOffset()
```

Interface Style

```
public abstract interface Style
                         extends MutableAttributeSet
```

This interface describes the collection of attributes to associate an element in a document.

Methods

```
void    addChangeListener(ChangeListener l)
String  getName()
void    removeChangeListener(ChangeListener l)
```

Interface StyledDocument

```
public abstract interface StyledDocument
                         extends Document
```

This interface represents a styled document.

Methods

```
Style    addStyle(String nm, Style parent)
Color    getBackground(AttributeSet attr)
Element  getCharacterElement(int pos)
Font     getFont(AttributeSet attr)
Color    getForeground(AttributeSet attr)
Style    getLogicalStyle(int p)
Element  getParagraphElement(int pos)
Style    getStyle(String nm)
void     removeStyle(String nm)
void     setCharacterAttributes(int offset, int length,
         AttributeSet s, boolean replace)
void     setLogicalStyle(int pos, Style s)
void     setParagraphAttributes(int offset, int length,
         AttributeSet s, boolean replace)
```

Interface TabableView

```
public abstract interface TabableView
```

This interface describes a view with its size depending on tabs.

Methods

```
float    getPartialSpan(int p0, int p1)
float    getTabbedSpan(float x, TabExpander e)
```

Interface TabExpander

```
public abstract interface TabExpander
```

This interface describes an object that implements the expansion of a tab.

Method
```
float    nextTabStop(float x, int tabOffset)
```

Interface ViewFactory
```
public abstract interface ViewFactory
```

This interface represents a factory to create the view of a certain portion of a document.

Method
```
View    create(Element elem)
```

Class AbstractDocument
```
      java.lang.Object
        |
        +--javax.swing.text.AbstractDocument
```
```
public abstract class AbstractDocument
                      extends Object
                      implements Document, Serializable
```

This class represents an abstract implementation of the interface Document.

Inner Classes
class	AbstractDocument.AbstractElement
static interface	AbstractDocument.AttributeContext
class	AbstractDocument.BranchElement
static interface	AbstractDocument.Content
class	AbstractDocument.DefaultDocumentEvent
static class	AbstractDocument.ElementEdit
class	AbstractDocument.LeafElement

Fields
protected static String	BAD_LOCATION
static String	BidiElementName
static String	ContentElementName
static String	ElementNameAttribute
protected EventListenerList	listenerList
static String	ParagraphElementName
static String	SectionElementName

Constructors
```
protected    AbstractDocument(AbstractDocument.Content data)
protected    AbstractDocument(AbstractDocument.Content data,
             AbstractDocument.AttributeContext context)
```

Methods
```
void                               addDocumentListener
                                   (DocumentListener listener)
void                               addUndoableEditListener
                                   (UndoableEditListener listener)
```

protected Element	**createBranchElement** (Element parent, AttributeSet a)
protected Element	**createLeafElement**(Element parent, AttributeSet a, int p0, int p1)
Position	**createPosition**(int offs)
void	**dump**(PrintStream out)
protected void	**fireChangedUpdate** (DocumentEvent e)
protected void	**fireInsertUpdate** (DocumentEvent e)
protected void	**fireRemoveUpdate** (DocumentEvent e)
protected void	**fireUndoableEditUpdate** (UndoableEditEvent e)
int	**getAsynchronousLoadPriority**()
protected AbstractDocument.AttributeContext	**getAttributeContext**()
Element	**getBidiRootElement**()
protected AbstractDocument.Content	**getContent**()
protected Thread	**getCurrentWriter**()
abstract Element	**getDefaultRootElement**()
Dictionary	**getDocumentProperties**()
Position	**getEndPosition**()
int	**getLength**()
abstract Element	**getParagraphElement**(int pos)
Object	**getProperty**(Object key)
Element[]	**getRootElements**()
Position	**getStartPosition**()
String	**getText**(int offset, int length)
void	**getText**(int offset, int length, Segment txt)
void	**insertString**(int offs, String str, AttributeSet a)
protected void	**insertUpdate** (AbstractDocument. DefaultDocumentEvent chng, AttributeSet attr)
protected void	**postRemoveUpdate** (AbstractDocument. DefaultDocumentEvent chng)
void	**putProperty**(Object key, Object value)
void	**readLock**()
void	**readUnlock**()
void	**remove**(int offs, int len)
void	**removeDocumentListener** (DocumentListener listener)
void	**removeUndoableEditListener** (UndoableEditListener listener)

protected void	**removeUpdate**(AbstractDocument. DefaultDocumentEvent chng)
void	**render**(Runnable r)
void	**setAsynchronousLoadPriority** (int p)
void	**setDocumentProperties** (Dictionary x)
protected void	**writeLock**()
protected void	**writeUnlock**()

Class AbstractDocument.ElementEdit

```
java.lang.Object
  |
  |
  +--javax.swing.undo.AbstractUndoableEdit
        |
        |
        +--javax.swing.text.AbstractDocument.ElementEdit
```

public static class **AbstractDocument.ElementEdit**
                extends AbstractUndoableEdit
                implements DocumentEvent.ElementChange

This class represents an implementation of editing of an element in a document.

Constructor
AbstractDocument.ElementEdit(Element e, int index, Element[] removed,
Element[] added)

Methods
Element[]	**getChildrenAdded**()
Element[]	**getChildrenRemoved**()
Element	**getElement**()
int	**getIndex**()
void	**redo**()
void	**undo**()

Class AbstractWriter

```
java.lang.Object
  |
  |
  +--javax.swing.text.AbstractWriter
```

public abstract class **AbstractWriter**
                extends Object

This class represents an abstract writer that actually writes the hierarchy of elements in a document.

Field
protected static char **NEWLINE**

Constructors
protected	**AbstractWriter**(Writer w, Document doc)
protected	**AbstractWriter**(Writer w, Document doc, int pos, int len)

```
protected        AbstractWriter(Writer w, Element root)
protected        AbstractWriter(Writer w, Element root, int pos, int len)
```

Methods

```
protected void              decrIndent()
protected Document          getDocument()
protected ElementIterator   getElementIterator()
protected String            getText(Element elem)
protected void              incrIndent()
protected void              indent()
protected boolean           inRange(Element next)
protected void              setIndentSpace(int space)
protected void              setLineLength(int l)
protected void              text(Element elem)
protected abstract void     write()
protected void              write(char ch)
protected void              write(String str)
protected void              writeAttributes(AttributeSet attr)
```

Class BoxView

```
java.lang.Object
   |
   +--javax.swing.text.View
        |
        +--javax.swing.text.CompositeView
             |
             +--javax.swing.text.BoxView
```

```
public class BoxView
          extends CompositeView
```

This interface represents the view of a text model that arranges its children into a box.

Constructor

```
BoxView(Element elem, int axis)
```

Methods

```
protected void              baselineLayout(int targetSpan, int axis,
                            int[] offsets, int[] spans)
protected SizeRequirements  baselineRequirements(int axis,
                            SizeRequirements r)
protected SizeRequirements  calculateMajorAxisRequirements(int axis,
                            SizeRequirements r)
protected SizeRequirements  calculateMinorAxisRequirements(int axis,
                            SizeRequirements r)
void                        changedUpdate(DocumentEvent e, Shape a,
                            ViewFactory f)
protected void              childAllocation(int index, Rectangle alloc)
protected boolean           flipEastAndWestAtEnds(int position,
                            Position.Bias bias)
float                       getAlignment(int axis)
```

int	**getHeight**()
float	**getMaximumSpan**(int axis)
float	**getMinimumSpan**(int axis)
protected int	**getOffset**(int axis, int childIndex)
float	**getPreferredSpan**(int axis)
int	**getResizeWeight**(int axis)
protected int	**getSpan**(int axis, int childIndex)
protected View	**getViewAtPoint**(int x, int y, Rectangle alloc)
int	**getWidth**()
void	**insertUpdate**(DocumentEvent e, Shape a, ViewFactory f)
protected boolean	**isAfter**(int x, int y, Rectangle innerAlloc)
protected boolean	**isAllocationValid**()
protected boolean	**isBefore**(int x, int y, Rectangle innerAlloc)
protected void	**layout**(int width, int height)
protected void	**layoutMajorAxis**(int targetSpan, int axis, int[] offsets, int[] spans)
protected void	**layoutMinorAxis**(int targetSpan, int axis, int[] offsets, int[] spans)
Shape	**modelToView**(int pos, Shape a, Position.Bias b)
void	**paint**(Graphics g, Shape allocation)
protected void	**paintChild**(Graphics g, Rectangle alloc, int index)
void	**preferenceChanged**(View child, boolean width, boolean height)
void	**removeUpdate**(DocumentEvent e, Shape a, ViewFactory f)
void	**replace**(int offset, int length, View[] elems)
void	**setSize**(float width, float height)
int	**viewToModel**(float x, float y, Shape a, Position.Bias[] bias)

Class ComponentView

```
java.lang.Object
   |
   |
   +--javax.swing.text.View
          |
          |
          +--javax.swing.text.ComponentView
```

public class **ComponentView**
            extends View

This interface represents a component decorator that implements the view interface.

Constructor
ComponentView(Element elem)

Methods
protected Component	**createComponent**()
float	**getAlignment**(int axis)

Component	**getComponent**()
float	**getMaximumSpan**(int axis)
float	**getMinimumSpan**(int axis)
float	**getPreferredSpan**(int axis)
Shape	**modelToView**(int pos, Shape a, Position.Bias b)
void	**paint**(Graphics g, Shape a)
void	**setParent**(View p)
void	**setSize**(float width, float height)
int	**viewToModel**(float x, float y, Shape a, Position.Bias[] bias)

Class CompositeView

```
java.lang.Object
   |
   +--javax.swing.text.View
         |
         +--javax.swing.text.CompositeView
```

public abstract class **CompositeView**
                    extends View

This interface represents the composite view of a text model that arranges children in a box.

Constructor
CompositeView(Element elem)

Methods

void	**append**(View v)
protected abstract void	**childAllocation**(int index, Rectangle a)
protected boolean	**flipEastAndWestAtEnds**(int position, Position.Bias bias)
protected short	**getBottomInset**()
Shape	**getChildAllocation**(int index, Shape a)
protected Rectangle	**getInsideAllocation**(Shape a)
protected short	**getLeftInset**()
protected int	**getNextEastWestVisualPositionFrom**(int pos, Position.Bias b, Shape a, int direction, Position.Bias[] biasRet)
protected int	**getNextNorthSouthVisualPositionFrom**(int pos, Position.Bias b, Shape a, int direction, Position.Bias[] biasRet)
int	**getNextVisualPositionFrom**(int pos, Position.Bias b, Shape a, int direction, Position.Bias[] biasRet)
protected short	**getRightInset**()
protected short	**getTopInset**()
View	**getView**(int n)
protected abstract View	**getViewAtPoint**(int x, int y, Rectangle alloc)
protected View	**getViewAtPosition**(int pos, Rectangle a)

int	**getViewCount**()
protected int	**getViewIndexAtPosition**(int pos)
void	**insert**(int offs, View v)
protected abstract boolean	**isAfter**(int x, int y, Rectangle alloc)
protected abstract boolean	**isBefore**(int x, int y, Rectangle alloc)
protected void	**loadChildren**(ViewFactory f)
Shape	**modelToView**(int p0, Position.Bias b0, int p1, Position.Bias b1, Shape a)
Shape	**modelToView**(int pos, Shape a, Position.Bias b)
void	**removeAll**()
void	**replace**(int offset, int length, View[] views)
protected void	**setInsets**(short top, short left, short bottom, short right)
protected void	**setParagraphInsets**(AttributeSet attr)
void	**setParent**(View parent)
int	**viewToModel**(float x, float y, Shape a, Position.Bias[] bias)

Class DefaultCaret

```
java.lang.Object
    |
    +--java.awt.geom.RectangularShape
            |
            +--java.awt.geom.Rectangle2D
                    |
                    +--java.awt.Rectangle
                            |
                            +--javax.swing.text.DefaultCaret
```

public class **DefaultCaret**
            extends Rectangle
            implements Caret, FocusListener, MouseListener,
            MouseMotionListener

This class represents the default implementation of Caret, which is basically a small piece of vertical line that blinks at the specified rate.

Fields

protected ChangeEvent	**changeEvent**
protected EventListenerList	**listenerList**

Constructor
DefaultCaret()

Methods

void	**addChangeListener**(ChangeListener l)
protected void	**adjustVisibility**(Rectangle nloc)
protected void	**damage**(Rectangle r)
void	**deinstall**(JTextComponent c)
protected void	**fireStateChanged**()
void	**focusGained**(FocusEvent e)

void	**focusLost**(FocusEvent e)
int	**getBlinkRate**()
protected JTextComponent	**getComponent**()
int	**getDot**()
Point	**getMagicCaretPosition**()
int	**getMark**()
protected Highlighter.HighlightPainter	**getSelectionPainter**()
void	**install**(JTextComponent c).
boolean	**isSelectionVisible**()
boolean	**isVisible**()
void	**mouseClicked**(MouseEvent e)
void	**mouseDragged**(MouseEvent e)
void	**mouseEntered**(MouseEvent e)
void	**mouseExited**(MouseEvent e)
void	**mouseMoved**(MouseEvent e)
void	**mousePressed**(MouseEvent e)
void	**mouseReleased**(MouseEvent e)
protected void	**moveCaret**(MouseEvent e)
void	**moveDot**(int dot)
void	**paint**(Graphics g)
protected void	**positionCaret**(MouseEvent e)
void	**removeChangeListener** (ChangeListener l)
protected void	**repaint**()
void	**setBlinkRate**(int rate)
void	**setDot**(int dot)
void	**setMagicCaretPosition**(Point p)
void	**setSelectionVisible**(boolean vis)
void	**setVisible**(boolean e)
String	**toString**()

Class DefaultEditorKit

```
java.lang.Object
   |
   +--javax.swing.text.EditorKit
         |
         +--javax.swing.text.DefaultEditorKit
```

public class **DefaultEditorKit**
            extends EditorKit

This class represents the default editor kit with plain text that can be edited by using minimal features, such as cut, copy, and paste.

Inner Classes

static class	**DefaultEditorKit.BeepAction**
static class	**DefaultEditorKit.CopyAction**
static class	**DefaultEditorKit.CutAction**
static class	**DefaultEditorKit.DefaultKeyTypedAction**
static class	**DefaultEditorKit.InsertBreakAction**

static class	**DefaultEditorKit.InsertContentAction**
static class	**DefaultEditorKit.InsertTabAction**
static class	**DefaultEditorKit.PasteAction**

Fields

static String	**backwardAction**
static String	**beepAction**
static String	**beginAction**
static String	**beginLineAction**
static String	**beginParagraphAction**
static String	**beginWordAction**
static String	**copyAction**
static String	**cutAction**
static String	**defaultKeyTypedAction**
static String	**deleteNextCharAction**
static String	**deletePrevCharAction**
static String	**downAction**
static String	**endAction**
static String	**endLineAction**
static String	**EndOfLineStringProperty**
static String	**endParagraphAction**
static String	**endWordAction**
static String	**forwardAction**
static String	**insertBreakAction**
static String	**insertContentAction**
static String	**insertTabAction**
static String	**nextWordAction**
static String	**pageDownAction**
static String	**pageUpAction**
static String	**pasteAction**
static String	**previousWordAction**
static String	**readOnlyAction**
static String	**selectAllAction**
static String	**selectionBackwardAction**
static String	**selectionBeginAction**
static String	**selectionBeginLineAction**
static String	**selectionBeginParagraphAction**
static String	**selectionBeginWordAction**
static String	**selectionDownAction**
static String	**selectionEndAction**
static String	**selectionEndLineAction**
static String	**selectionEndParagraphAction**
static String	**selectionEndWordAction**
static String	**selectionForwardAction**
static String	**selectionNextWordAction**
static String	**selectionPreviousWordAction**
static String	**selectionUpAction**
static String	**selectLineAction**
static String	**selectParagraphAction**

```
static String    selectWordAction
static String    upAction
static String    writableAction
```

Constructor
```
DefaultEditorKit()
```

Methods
```
Object           clone()
Caret            createCaret()
Document         createDefaultDocument()
Action[]         getActions()
String           getContentType()
ViewFactory      getViewFactory()
void             read(InputStream in, Document doc, int pos)
void             read(Reader in, Document doc, int pos)
void             write(OutputStream out, Document doc, int pos, int len)
void             write(Writer out, Document doc, int pos, int len)
```

Class DefaultEditorKit.BeepAction

```
java.lang.Object
   |
   |
   +--javax.swing.AbstractAction
          |
          |
          +--javax.swing.text.TextAction
                 |
                 |
                 +--javax.swing.text.DefaultEditorKit.BeepAction
```

```
public static class DefaultEditorKit.BeepAction
                extends TextAction
```

This class represents an action that creates a beep.

Constructor
```
DefaultEditorKit.BeepAction()
```

Method
```
void actionPerformed(ActionEvent e)
```

Class DefaultEditorKit.CopyAction

```
java.lang.Object
   |
   |
   +--javax.swing.AbstractAction
          |
          |
          +--javax.swing.text.TextAction
                 |
                 |
                 +--javax.swing.text.DefaultEditorKit.CopyAction
```

```
public static class DefaultEditorKit.CopyAction
                extends TextAction
```

This class reperesents an action to copy a selected region and place its contents on the system Clipboard.

Constructor
`DefaultEditorKit.CopyAction()`

Method
void   **actionPerformed**(ActionEvent e)

Class DefaultEditorKit.CutAction

```
java.lang.Object
   |
   +--javax.swing.AbstractAction
         |
         +--javax.swing.text.TextAction
               |
               +--javax.swing.text.DefaultEditorKit.CutAction
```

public static class **DefaultEditorKit.CutAction**
                    extends TextAction

This class represents an action to cut a selected region and place its contents on the system Clipboard.

Constructor
`DefaultEditorKit.CutAction()`

Create this object with the appropriate identifier.

Method
void   **actionPerformed**(ActionEvent e)

Class DefaultEditorKit.DefaultKeyTypedAction

```
java.lang.Object
   |
   +--javax.swing.AbstractAction
         |
         +--javax.swing.text.TextAction
               |
               +--javax.swing.text.DefaultEditorKit.DefaultKeyTypedAction
```

public static class **DefaultEditorKit.DefaultKeyTypedAction**
                    extends TextAction

This class represents the action object that is executed by default if a key-typed event without any keymap entry is received.

Constructor
`DefaultEditorKit.DefaultKeyTypedAction()`

Method
void   **actionPerformed**(ActionEvent e)

Class DefaultEditorKit.InsertBreakAction

```
java.lang.Object
   |
   +--javax.swing.AbstractAction
          |
          +--javax.swing.text.TextAction
                 |
                 +--javax.swing.text.DefaultEditorKit.InsertBreakAction
```
public static class **DefaultEditorKit.InsertBreakAction**
                  extends TextAction

This class represents an object that puts a line or paragraph break into a document. If there is any selection, it will be removed before the break is added.

Constructor
DefaultEditorKit.InsertBreakAction()

Method
void   **actionPerformed**(ActionEvent e)

Class DefaultEditorKit.InsertContentAction

```
java.lang.Object
   |
   +--javax.swing.AbstractAction
          |
          +--javax.swing.text.TextAction
                 |
                 +--javax.swing.text.DefaultEditorKit.InsertContentAction
```
public static class **DefaultEditorKit.InsertContentAction**
                  extends TextAction

This class represents an action object that puts information content into the document.

Constructor
DefaultEditorKit.InsertContentAction()

Method
void   **actionPerformed**(ActionEvent e)

Class DefaultEditorKit.InsertTabAction

```
java.lang.Object
   |
   +--javax.swing.AbstractAction
          |
          +--javax.swing.text.TextAction
                 |
                 +--javax.swing.text.DefaultEditorKit.InsertTabAction
```
public static class **DefaultEditorKit.InsertTabAction**
                  extends TextAction

This class represents an action object that positions a tab character in the document.

Constructor
`DefaultEditorKit.InsertTabAction`()

Method
void   **actionPerformed**(ActionEvent e)

Class DefaultEditorKit.PasteAction

```
java.lang.Object
   |
   +--javax.swing.AbstractAction
         |
         +--javax.swing.text.TextAction
               |
               +--javax.swing.text.DefaultEditorKit.PasteAction
```

public static class **DefaultEditorKit.PasteAction**
                    extends TextAction

This class represents the paste action to paste the contents from the system Clipboard into the selected region. If there is no selection, the content is placed before the caret.

Constructor
`DefaultEditorKit.PasteAction`()

Method
void   **actionPerformed**(ActionEvent e)

Class DefaultHighlighter

```
java.lang.Object
   |
   +--javax.swing.text.LayeredHighlighter
         |
         +--javax.swing.text.DefaultHighlighter
```

public class **DefaultHighlighter**
            extends LayeredHighlighter

This class represents the default implementation of a highlighter. The highlighter renders in a solid color.

Inner Class
static class   **DefaultHighlighter.DefaultHighlightPainter**

Field
static   **LayeredHighlighter.LayerPainter**

Constructor
`DefaultHighlighter`()

Methods

Object	**addHighlight**(int p0, int p1, Highlighter.HighlightPainter p)
void	**changeHighlight**(Object tag, int p0, int p1)
void	**deinstall**(JTextComponent c)
boolean	**getDrawsLayeredHighlights**()
Highlighter.Highlight[]	**getHighlights**()
void	**install**(JTextComponent c)
void	**paint**(Graphics g)
void	**paintLayeredHighlights**(Graphics g, int p0, int p1, Shape viewBounds, JTextComponent editor, View view)
void	**removeAllHighlights**()
void	**removeHighlight**(Object tag)
void	**setDrawsLayeredHighlights**(boolean newValue)

Class DefaultHighlighter.DefaultHighlightPainter

```
java.lang.Object
   |
   +--javax.swing.text.LayeredHighlighter.LayerPainter
            |
            +--javax.swing.text.DefaultHighlighter.DefaultHighlightPainter
```

public static class **DefaultHighlighter.DefaultHighlightPainter**
            extends LayeredHighlighter.LayerPainter

This class represents the default highlight painter that fills the highlighted area with a solid color.

Constructor

DefaultHighlighter.DefaultHighlightPainter(Color c)

Methods

Color	**getColor**()
void	**paint**(Graphics g, int offs0, int offs1, Shape bounds, JTextComponent c)
Shape	**paintLayer**(Graphics g, int offs0, int offs1, Shape bounds, JTextComponent c, View view)

Class DefaultStyledDocument

```
java.lang.Object
   |
   +--javax.swing.text.AbstractDocument
            |
            +--javax.swing.text.DefaultStyledDocument
```

public class **DefaultStyledDocument**
            extends AbstractDocument
            implements StyledDocument

This class represents the styled document that can be marked up with character and paragraph styles in a manner similar to the Rich Text Format.

Inner Classes

static class	**DefaultStyledDocument.AttributeUndoableEdit**
class	**DefaultStyledDocument.ElementBuffer**
static class	**DefaultStyledDocument.ElementSpec**
protected class	**DefaultStyledDocument.SectionElements**

Fields

protected DefaultStyledDocument.ElementBuffer	**buffer**
static int	**BUFFER_SIZE_DEFAULT**

Constructors

DefaultStyledDocument()
DefaultStyledDocument(AbstractDocument.Content c, StyleContext styles)
DefaultStyledDocument(StyleContext styles)

Methods

void	**addDocumentListener** (DocumentListener listener)
Style	**addStyle**(String nm, Style parent)
protected void	**create**(DefaultStyledDocument. ElementSpec[] data)
protected AbstractDocument.AbstractElement	**createDefaultRoot**()
Color	**getBackground**(AttributeSet attr)
Element	**getCharacterElement**(int pos)
Element	**getDefaultRootElement**()
Font	**getFont**(AttributeSet attr)
Color	**getForeground**(AttributeSet attr)
Style	**getLogicalStyle**(int p)
Element	**getParagraphElement**(int pos)
Style	**getStyle**(String nm)
Enumeration	**getStyleNames**()
protected void	**insert**(int offset, DefaultStyledDocument. ElementSpec[] data)
protected void	**insertUpdate**(AbstractDocument. DefaultDocumentEvent chng, AttributeSet attr)
void	**removeDocumentListener** (DocumentListener listener)
void	**removeStyle**(String nm)
protected void	**removeUpdate**(AbstractDocument. DefaultDocumentEvent chng)
void	**setCharacterAttributes** (int offset, int length, AttributeSet s, boolean replace)
void	**setLogicalStyle**(int pos, Style s)
void	**setParagraphAttributes** (int offset, int length, AttributeSet s, boolean replace)
protected void	**styleChanged**(Style style)

Class DefaultStyledDocument.AttributeUndoableEdit

```
java.lang.Object
   |
   +--javax.swing.undo.AbstractUndoableEdit
        |
        |
        +--javax.swing.text.DefaultStyledDocument.AttributeUndoableEdit
```

public static class   **DefaultStyledDocument.AttributeUndoableEdit**
                        extends AbstractUndoableEdit

This class represents an undoadable edit that is used to memorize the changes in the attribute set of an element.

Fields

protected AttributeSet	**copy**
protected Element	**element**
protected boolean	**isReplacing**
protected AttributeSet	**newAttributes**

Constructor

DefaultStyledDocument.AttributeUndoableEdit(Element element,
AttributeSet newAttributes, boolean isReplacing)

Methods

void	**redo**()
void	**undo**()

Class DefaultStyledDocument.ElementSpec

```
java.lang.Object
   |
   |
   +--javax.swing.text.DefaultStyledDocument.ElementSpec
```

public static class **DefaultStyledDocument.ElementSpec**
extends Object

This class represents the specification for building the elements of a document.

Fields

static short	**ContentType**
static short	**EndTagType**
static short	**JoinFractureDirection**
static short	**JoinNextDirection**
static short	**JoinPreviousDirection**
static short	**OriginateDirection**
static short	**StartTagType**

Constructors

DefaultStyledDocument.ElementSpec(AttributeSet a, short type)
DefaultStyledDocument.ElementSpec(AttributeSet a, short type, char[] txt,
int offs, int len)
DefaultStyledDocument.ElementSpec(AttributeSet a, short type, int len)

Methods

char[]	**getArray**()
AttributeSet	**getAttributes**()
short	**getDirection**()
int	**getLength**()
int	**getOffset**()
short	**getType**()
void	**setDirection**(short direction)
void	**setType**(short type)
String	**toString**()

Class ElementIterator

```
java.lang.Object
   |
   |
   +--javax.swing.text.ElementIterator
```

public class **ElementIterator**
          extends Object
          implements Cloneable

This class represents an element iterator to implement iterations over a tree of elements.

Constructors

ElementIterator(Document document)
ElementIterator(Element root)

Methods

Object	**clone**()
Element	**current**()
int	**depth**()
Element	**first**()
Element	**next**()
Element	**previous**()

Class FieldView

```
java.lang.Object
   |
   |
   +--javax.swing.text.View
          |
          |
          +--javax.swing.text.PlainView
                 |
                 |
                 +--javax.swing.text.FieldView
```

public class **FieldView**
          extends PlainView

This class represents the view for single-line editing of plain text.

Constructor

FieldView(Element elem)

Methods

```
protected Shape          adjustAllocation(Shape a)
protected FontMetrics    getFontMetrics()
float                    getPreferredSpan(int axis)
int                      getResizeWeight(int axis)
void                     insertUpdate(DocumentEvent changes,
                         Shape a, ViewFactory f)
Shape                    modelToView(int pos, Shape a, Position.Bias b)
void                     paint(Graphics g, Shape a)
void                     removeUpdate(DocumentEvent changes,
                         Shape a, ViewFactory f)
int                      viewToModel(float fx, float fy, Shape a,
                         Position.Bias[] bias)
```

Class GapContent

```
java.lang.Object
   |
   +--javax.swing.text.GapVector
          |
          +--javax.swing.text.GapContent
```

public class **GapContent**
        extends javax.swing.text.GapVector
        implements AbstractDocument.Content, Serializable

This class represents an implementation of the interface `AbstractDocument.Content` to represent gap content as observed in emacs editor.

Constructors

GapContent()
GapContent(int initialLength)

Methods

```
protected Object         allocateArray(int len)
Position                 createPosition(int offset)
protected int            getArrayLength()
void                     getChars(int where, int len, Segment chars)
protected Vector         getPositionsInRange(Vector v, int offset, int length)
String                   getString(int where, int len)
UndoableEdit             insertString(int where, String str)
int                      length()
UndoableEdit             remove(int where, int nitems)
protected void           resetMarksAtZero()
protected void           shiftEnd(int newSize)
protected void           shiftGap(int newGapStart)
protected void           shiftGapEndUp(int newGapEnd)
protected void           shiftGapStartDown(int newGapStart)
protected void           updateUndoPositions(Vector positions, int offset,
                         int length)
```

Class IconView

```
java.lang.Object
   |
   +--javax.swing.text.View
          |
          +--javax.swing.text.IconView
```

public class **IconView**
        extends View

This class represents the view of a decorative icon, by implementing the interface View.

Constructor

IconView(Element elem)

Methods

float	**getAlignment**(int axis)
float	**getPreferredSpan**(int axis)
Shape	**modelToView**(int pos, Shape a, Position.Bias b)
void	**paint**(Graphics g, Shape a)
void	**setSize**(float width, float height)
int	**viewToModel**(float x, float y, Shape a, Position.Bias[] bias)

Class JTextComponent

```
java.lang.Object
   |
   +--java.awt.Component
          |
          +--java.awt.Container
                 |
                 +--javax.swing.JComponent
                        |
                        +--javax.swing.text.JTextComponent
```

public abstract class **JTextComponent**
        extends JComponent
        implements Scrollable, Accessible

This class represents the parent of all text components used in Swing.

Inner Classes

class	**JTextComponent.AccessibleJTextComponent**
static class	**JTextComponent.KeyBinding**

Inner Classes Inherited from Class javax.swing.JComponent

JComponent.AccessibleJComponent

Fields

static String	**DEFAULT_KEYMAP**
static String	**FOCUS_ACCELERATOR_KEY**

Constructor
JTextComponent()

Methods

void	**addCaretListener**(CaretListener listener)
static Keymap	**addKeymap**(String nm, Keymap parent)
void	**copy**()
void	**cut**()
protected void	**fireCaretUpdate**(CaretEvent e)
AccessibleContext	**getAccessibleContext**()
Action[]	**getActions**()
Caret	**getCaret**()
Color	**getCaretColor**()
int	**getCaretPosition**()
Color	**getDisabledTextColor**()
Document	**getDocument**()
char	**getFocusAccelerator**()
Highlighter	**getHighlighter**()
Keymap	**getKeymap**()
static Keymap	**getKeymap**(String nm)
Insets	**getMargin**()
Dimension	**getPreferredScrollableViewportSize**()
int	**getScrollableBlockIncrement**(Rectangle visibleRect, int orientation, int direction)
boolean	**getScrollableTracksViewportHeight**()
boolean	**getScrollableTracksViewportWidth**()
int	**getScrollableUnitIncrement**(Rectangle visibleRect, int orientation, int direction)
String	**getSelectedText**()
Color	**getSelectedTextColor**()
Color	**getSelectionColor**()
int	**getSelectionEnd**()
int	**getSelectionStart**()
String	**getText**()
String	**getText**(int offs, int len)
TextUI	**getUI**()
boolean	**isEditable**()
boolean	**isFocusTraversable**()
boolean	**isOpaque**()
static void	**loadKeymap**(Keymap map, JTextComponent.KeyBinding[] bindings, Action[] actions)
Rectangle	**modelToView**(int pos)
void	**moveCaretPosition**(int pos)
protected String	**paramString**()
void	**paste**()
protected void	**processComponentKeyEvent**(KeyEvent e)
void	**read**(Reader in, Object desc)
void	**removeCaretListener**(CaretListener listener)
static Keymap	**removeKeymap**(String nm)

void	**removeNotify**()
void	**replaceSelection**(String content)
void	**select**(int selectionStart, int selectionEnd)
void	**selectAll**()
void	**setCaret**(Caret c)
void	**setCaretColor**(Color c)
void	**setCaretPosition**(int position)
void	**setDisabledTextColor**(Color c)
void	**setDocument**(Document doc)
void	**setEditable**(boolean b)
void	**setEnabled**(boolean b)
void	**setFocusAccelerator**(char aKey)
void	**setHighlighter**(Highlighter h)
void	**setKeymap**(Keymap map)
void	**setMargin**(Insets m)
void	**setOpaque**(boolean o)
void	**setSelectedTextColor**(Color c)
void	**setSelectionColor**(Color c)
void	**setSelectionEnd**(int selectionEnd)
void	**setSelectionStart**(int selectionStart)
void	**setText**(String t)
void	**setUI**(TextUI ui)
void	**updateUI**()
int	**viewToModel**(Point pt)
void	**write**(Writer out)

Class JTextComponent.KeyBinding

```
java.lang.Object
   |
   +--javax.swing.text.JTextComponent.KeyBinding
```

public static class **JTextComponent.KeyBinding**
                extends Object

This class represents the catalog for creating key bindings.

Fields
String	**actionName**
KeyStroke	**key**

Constructor
JTextComponent.KeyBinding(KeyStroke key, String actionName)

Class LabelView

```
java.lang.Object
   |
   +--javax.swing.text.View
         |
         +--javax.swing.text.LabelView
```

public class **LabelView**

```
                    extends View
                    implements TabableView
```

This class represents the label view for a styled text.

Constructor
LabelView(Element elem)

Methods

View	**breakView**(int axis, int p0, float pos, float len)
void	**changedUpdate**(DocumentEvent e, Shape a, ViewFactory f)
View	**createFragment**(int p0, int p1)
float	**getAlignment**(int axis)
int	**getBreakWeight**(int axis, float pos, float len)
protected Font	**getFont**()
protected FontMetrics	**getFontMetrics**()
int	**getNextVisualPositionFrom**(int pos, Position.Bias b, Shape a, int direction, Position.Bias[] biasRet)
float	**getPartialSpan**(int p0, int p1)
float	**getPreferredSpan**(int axis)
float	**getTabbedSpan**(float x, TabExpander e)
void	**insertUpdate**(DocumentEvent e, Shape a, ViewFactory f)
Shape	**modelToView**(int pos, Shape a, Position.Bias b)
void	**paint**(Graphics g, Shape a)
protected void	**setPropertiesFromAttributes**()
protected void	**setStrikeThrough**(boolean s)
protected void	**setSubscript**(boolean s)
protected void	**setSuperscript**(boolean s)
protected void	**setUnderline**(boolean u)
int	**viewToModel**(float x, float y, Shape a, Position.Bias[] biasReturn)

Class LabelView2D

```
      java.lang.Object
         |
         |
      +--javax.swing.text.View
             |
             |
             +--javax.swing.text.LabelView2D
```

public class **LabelView2D**
            extends View

This class represents a label view in two dimensions.

Constructor
LabelView2D(Element elem)

Methods

View	**breakView**(int axis, int p0, float pos, float len)
void	**changedUpdate**(DocumentEvent e, Shape a, ViewFactory f)
View	**createFragment**(int p0, int p1)
float	**getAlignment**(int axis)

int	**getBreakWeight**(int axis, float pos, float len)
protected Font	**getFont**()
protected FontMetrics	**getFontMetrics**()
int	**getNextVisualPositionFrom**(int pos, Position.Bias b, Shape a, int direction, Position.Bias[] biasRet)
float	**getPreferredSpan**(int axis)
void	**insertUpdate**(DocumentEvent e, Shape a, ViewFactory f)
Shape	**modelToView**(int pos, Shape a, Position.Bias b)
void	**paint**(Graphics g, Shape a)
void	**removeUpdate**(DocumentEvent changes, Shape a, ViewFactory f)
protected void	**setPropertiesFromAttributes**()
protected void	**setStrikeThrough**(boolean s)
protected void	**setSubscript**(boolean s)
protected void	**setSuperscript**(boolean s)
protected void	**setUnderline**(boolean u)
String	**toString**()
int	**viewToModel**(float x, float y, Shape a, Position.Bias[] biasReturn)

Class LayeredHighlighter

```
java.lang.Object
   |
   +--javax.swing.text.LayeredHighlighter
```

public abstract class **LayeredHighlighter**
                     extends Object
                     implements Highlighter

This class represents the layered highlighter that is used by view objects such as label view.

Inner Class
static class   **LayeredHighlighter.LayerPainter**

Constructor
LayeredHighlighter()

Method
abstract void   **paintLayeredHighlights**(Graphics g, int p0, int p1, Shape viewBounds, JTextComponent editor, View view)

Class LayeredHighlighter.LayerPainter

```
java.lang.Object
   |
   +--javax.swing.text.LayeredHighlighter.LayerPainter
```

public abstract static class **LayeredHighlighter.LayerPainter**
                             extends Object
                             implements Highlighter.HighlightPainter

This class represents the layered highlight renderer.

Constructor
`LayeredHighlighter.LayerPainter()`

Method
abstract Shape	**paintLayer**(Graphics g, int p0, int p1, Shape viewBounds, JTextComponent editor, View view)

Class ParagraphView

```
java.lang.Object
   |
   +--javax.swing.text.View
          |
          +--javax.swing.text.CompositeView
                 |
                 +--javax.swing.text.BoxView
                        |
                        +--javax.swing.text.ParagraphView
```

```
public class ParagraphView
        extends BoxView
        implements TabExpander
```

This class represents the view of a paragraph composed of lines of characters with multiple fonts and colors and components and icons embedded in it.

Field
protected int	**firstLineIndent**

Constructor
`ParagraphView(Element elem)`

Methods
protected void	**adjustRow**(javax.swing.text.ParagraphView.Row r, int desiredSpan, int x)
View	**breakView**(int axis, float len, Shape a)
protected SizeRequirements	**calculateMinorAxisRequirements**(int axis, SizeRequirements r)
void	**changedUpdate**(DocumentEvent changes, Shape a, ViewFactory f)
protected int	**findOffsetToCharactersInString**(char[] string, int start)
protected boolean	**flipEastAndWestAtEnds**(int position, Position.Bias bias)
float	**getAlignment**(int axis)
int	**getBreakWeight**(int axis, float len)
protected int	**getClosestPositionTo**(int pos, Position.Bias b, Shape a, int direction, Position.Bias[] biasRet, int rowIndex, int x)
protected View	**getLayoutView**(int index)
protected int	**getLayoutViewCount**()

protected int	**getNextNorthSouthVisualPositionFrom**(int pos, Position.Bias b, Shape a, int direction, Position.Bias[] biasRet)
protected float	**getPartialSize**(int startOffset, int endOffset)
protected float	**getTabBase**()
protected TabSet	**getTabSet**()
protected View	**getViewAtPosition**(int pos, Rectangle a)
protected int	**getViewIndexAtPosition**(int pos)
void	**insertUpdate**(DocumentEvent changes, Shape a, ViewFactory f)
protected void	**layout**(int width, int height)
protected void	**loadChildren**(ViewFactory f)
float	**nextTabStop**(float x, int tabOffset)
void	**paint**(Graphics g, Shape a)
void	**removeUpdate**(DocumentEvent changes, Shape a, ViewFactory f)
protected void	**setFirstLineIndent**(float fi)
protected void	**setJustification**(int j)
protected void	**setLineSpacing**(float ls)
protected void	**setPropertiesFromAttributes**()

Class PasswordView

```
java.lang.Object
  |
  +--javax.swing.text.View
        |
        +--javax.swing.text.PlainView
              |
              +--javax.swing.text.FieldView
                    |
                    |--javax.swing.text.PasswordView
```

public class **PasswordView**
         extends FieldView

This class represents the view of a password field.

Constructor
PasswordView(Element elem)

Methods

protected int	**drawEchoCharacter**(Graphics g, int x, int y, char c)
protected int	**drawSelectedText**(Graphics g, int x, int y, int p0, int p1)
protected int	**drawUnselectedText**(Graphics g, int x, int y, int p0, int p1)
Shape	**modelToView**(int pos, Shape a, Position.Bias b)
int	**viewToModel**(float fx, float fy, Shape a, Position.Bias[] bias)

Class PlainDocument

```
java.lang.Object
  |
```

```
         +--javax.swing.text.AbstractDocument
            ¦
            ¦
         +--javax.swing.text.PlainDocument
public class PlainDocument
         extends AbstractDocument
```

This class represents a plain document with element structure as lines of text.

Fields
```
static String    lineLimitAttribute
static String    tabSizeAttribute
```

Constructors
```
PlainDocument()
protected PlainDocument(AbstractDocument.Content c)
```

Methods
```
protected AbstractDocument.AbstractElement    createDefaultRoot()
Element                                       getDefaultRootElement()
Element                                       getParagraphElement(int pos)
protected void                                insertUpdate(AbstractDocument.
                                              DefaultDocumentEvent chng,
                                              AttributeSet attr)
protected void                                removeUpdate(AbstractDocument.
                                              DefaultDocumentEvent chng)
```

Class PlainView
```
      java.lang.Object
         ¦
         ¦
      +--javax.swing.text.View
            ¦
            ¦
         +--javax.swing.text.PlainView
public class PlainView
         extends View
         implements TabExpander
```

This class represents the view for simple multiline text.

Field
```
protected FontMetrics metrics
```

Constructor
```
PlainView(Element elem)
```

Methods
```
void               changedUpdate(DocumentEvent changes, Shape a,
                   ViewFactory f)
protected void     drawLine(int lineIndex, Graphics g, int x, int y)
protected int      drawSelectedText(Graphics g, int x, int y, int p0, int p1)
protected int      drawUnselectedText(Graphics g, int x, int y, int p0,
                   int p1)
```

protected Segment	**getLineBuffer**()
float	**getPreferredSpan**(int axis)
protected int	**getTabSize**()
void	**insertUpdate**(DocumentEvent changes, Shape a, ViewFactory f)
Shape	**modelToView**(int pos, Shape a, Position.Bias b)
float	**nextTabStop**(float x, int tabOffset)
void	**paint**(Graphics g, Shape a)
void	**preferenceChanged**(View child, boolean width, boolean height)
void	**removeUpdate**(DocumentEvent changes, Shape a, ViewFactory f)
int	**viewToModel**(float fx, float fy, Shape a, Position.Bias[] bias)

Class Position.Bias

```
java.lang.Object
    |
    +--javax.swing.text.Position.Bias
```

public static final class **Position.Bias**
                      extends Object

This class represents the enumeration object that indicates the bias to a position in the model.

Fields

static Position.Bias	**Backward**
static Position.Bias	**Forward**

Method

String	**toString**()

Class Segment

```
java.lang.Object
    |
    +--javax.swing.text.Segment
```

public class **Segment**
             extends Object

This class represents a segment of an array of characters. The segment represents a fragment of text.

Fields

char[]	**array**
int	**count**
int	**offset**

Constructors

Segment()
Segment(char[] array, int offset, int count)

Method

```
String      toString()
```

Class SimpleAttributeSet

```
java.lang.Object
   ¦
   ¦
   +--javax.swing.text.SimpleAttributeSet
```

```
public class SimpleAttributeSet
          extends Object
          implements MutableAttributeSet, Serializable, Cloneable
```

This class represents a simple implementation of mutable attribute set by using a hashtable.

Field

```
static AttributeSet    EMPTY
```

Constructors

```
SimpleAttributeSet()
SimpleAttributeSet(AttributeSet source)
```

Methods

```
void           addAttribute(Object name, Object value)
void           addAttributes(AttributeSet attributes)
Object         clone()
boolean        containsAttribute(Object name, Object value)
boolean        containsAttributes(AttributeSet attributes)
AttributeSet   copyAttributes()
boolean        equals(Object obj)
Object         getAttribute(Object name)
int            getAttributeCount()
Enumeration    getAttributeNames()
AttributeSet   getResolveParent()
int            hashCode()
boolean        isDefined(Object attrName)
boolean        isEmpty()
boolean        isEqual(AttributeSet attr)
void           removeAttribute(Object name)
void           removeAttributes(AttributeSet attributes)
void           removeAttributes(Enumeration names)
void           setResolveParent(AttributeSet parent)
String         toString()
```

Class StringContent

```
java.lang.Object
   ¦
   ¦
   +--javax.swing.text.StringContent
```

```
public final class StringContent
              extends Object
              implements AbstractDocument.Content, Serializable
```

This class represents an implementation of string content that is useful for small documents.

Constructors
StringContent()
StringContent(int initialLength)

Methods

Position	**createPosition**(int offset)
void	**getChars**(int where, int len, Segment chars)
protected Vector	**getPositionsInRange**(Vector v, int offset, int length)
String	**getString**(int where, int len)
UndoableEdit	**insertString**(int where, String str)
int	**length**()
UndoableEdit	**remove**(int where, int nitems)
protected void	**updateUndoPositions**(Vector positions)

Class StyleConstants

```
java.lang.Object
    |
    +--javax.swing.text.StyleConstants
```

public class **StyleConstants**
        extends Object

This class represents a collection object for commonly used style constants.

Inner Classes

static class	**StyleConstants.CharacterConstants**
static class	**StyleConstants.ColorConstants**
static class	**StyleConstants.FontConstants**
static class	**StyleConstants.ParagraphConstants**

Fields

static int	**ALIGN_CENTER**
static int	**ALIGN_JUSTIFIED**
static int	**ALIGN_LEFT**
static int	**ALIGN_RIGHT**
static Object	**Alignment**
static Object	**Background**
static Object	**BidiLevel**
static Object	**Bold**
static Object	**ComponentAttribute**
static String	**ComponentElementName**
static Object	**ComposedTextAttribute**
static Object	**FirstLineIndent**
static Object	**FontFamily**
static Object	**FontSize**
static Object	**Foreground**
static Object	**IconAttribute**
static String	**IconElementName**

```
static Object    Italic
static Object    LeftIndent
static Object    LineSpacing
static Object    ModelAttribute
static Object    NameAttribute
static Object    Orientation
static Object    ResolveAttribute
static Object    RightIndent
static Object    SpaceAbove
static Object    SpaceBelow
static Object    StrikeThrough
static Object    Subscript
static Object    Superscript
static Object    TabSet
static Object    Underline
```

Methods

```
static int        getAlignment(AttributeSet a)
static Color      getBackground(AttributeSet a)
static int        getBidiLevel(AttributeSet a)
static Component  getComponent(AttributeSet a)
static float      getFirstLineIndent(AttributeSet a)
static String     getFontFamily(AttributeSet a)
static int        getFontSize(AttributeSet a)
static Color      getForeground(AttributeSet a)
static Icon       getIcon(AttributeSet a)
static float      getLeftIndent(AttributeSet a)
static float      getLineSpacing(AttributeSet a)
static float      getRightIndent(AttributeSet a)
static float      getSpaceAbove(AttributeSet a)
static float      getSpaceBelow(AttributeSet a)
static TabSet     getTabSet(AttributeSet a)
static boolean    isBold(AttributeSet a)
static boolean    isItalic(AttributeSet a)
static boolean    isStrikeThrough(AttributeSet a)
static boolean    isSubscript(AttributeSet a)
static boolean    isSuperscript(AttributeSet a)
static boolean    isUnderline(AttributeSet a)
static void       setAlignment(MutableAttributeSet a, int align)
static void       setBackground(MutableAttributeSet a, Color fg)
static void       setBidiLevel(MutableAttributeSet a, int o)
static void       setBold(MutableAttributeSet a, boolean b)
static void       setComponent(MutableAttributeSet a, Component c)
static void       setFirstLineIndent(MutableAttributeSet a, float i)
static void       setFontFamily(MutableAttributeSet a, String fam)
static void       setFontSize(MutableAttributeSet a, int s)
static void       setForeground(MutableAttributeSet a, Color fg)
static void       setIcon(MutableAttributeSet a, Icon c)
static void       setItalic(MutableAttributeSet a, boolean b)
```

```
static void          setLeftIndent(MutableAttributeSet a, float i)
static void          setLineSpacing(MutableAttributeSet a, float i)
static void          setRightIndent(MutableAttributeSet a, float i)
static void          setSpaceAbove(MutableAttributeSet a, float i)
static void          setSpaceBelow(MutableAttributeSet a, float i)
static void          setStrikeThrough(MutableAttributeSet a, boolean b)
static void          setSubscript(MutableAttributeSet a, boolean b)
static void          setSuperscript(MutableAttributeSet a, boolean b)
static void          setTabSet(MutableAttributeSet a, TabSet tabs)
static void          setUnderline(MutableAttributeSet a, boolean b)
String               toString()
```

Class StyleConstants.CharacterConstants

```
java.lang.Object
   |
   +--javax.swing.text.StyleConstants
          |
          +--javax.swing.text.StyleConstants.CharacterConstants
```

public static class **StyleConstants.CharacterConstants**
                    extends StyleConstants
                    implements AttributeSet.CharacterAttribute

This class represents a collection object for character constants such as size, font type, and so on.

Fields

```
static Object    Background
static Object    BidiLevel
static Object    Bold
static Object    ComponentAttribute
static Object    Family
static Object    Foreground
static Object    IconAttribute
static Object    Italic
static Object    Size
static Object    StrikeThrough
static Object    Subscript
static Object    Superscript
static Object    Underline
```

Class StyleConstants.ColorConstants

```
java.lang.Object
   |
   +--javax.swing.text.StyleConstants
          |
          +--javax.swing.text.StyleConstants.ColorConstants
```

public static class **StyleConstants.ColorConstants**
                    extends StyleConstants

```
                    implements AttributeSet.ColorAttribute,
                    AttributeSet.CharacterAttribute
```

This class represents a collection object for color constants.

Fields

```
static Object    Background
static Object    Foreground
```

Class StyleConstants.FontConstants

```
        java.lang.Object
          |
          |
          +--javax.swing.text.StyleConstants
                    |
                    |
                    +--javax.swing.text.StyleConstants.FontConstants
```

```
public static class StyleConstants.FontConstants
                    extends StyleConstants
                    implements AttributeSet.FontAttribute,
                    AttributeSet.CharacterAttribute
```

This class represents a collection object for font constants.

Fields

```
static Object    Bold
static Object    Family
static Object    Italic
static Object    Size
```

Class StyleConstants.ParagraphConstants

```
        java.lang.Object
          |
          |
          +--javax.swing.text.StyleConstants
                    |
                    |
                    +--javax.swing.text.StyleConstants.ParagraphConstants
```

```
public static class StyleConstants.ParagraphConstants
                    extends StyleConstants
                    implements AttributeSet.ParagraphAttribute
```

This class represents a collection object for the paragraph constants.

Fields

```
static Object    Alignment
static Object    FirstLineIndent
static Object    LeftIndent
static Object    LineSpacing
static Object    Orientation
static Object    RightIndent
static Object    SpaceAbove
static Object    SpaceBelow
static Object    TabSet
```

Class StyleContext

```
java.lang.Object
   |
   +--javax.swing.text.StyleContext
```

public class **StyleContext**
        extends Object
        implements Serializable, AbstractDocument.AttributeContext

This class represents style context.

Inner Classes

| class | **StyleContext.NamedStyle** |
| class | **StyleContext.SmallAttributeSet** |

Field

static String   **DEFAULT_STYLE**

Constructor

StyleContext()

Methods

AttributeSet	**addAttribute**(AttributeSet old, Object name, Object value)
AttributeSet	**addAttributes**(AttributeSet old, AttributeSet attr)
void	**addChangeListener**(ChangeListener l)
Style	**addStyle**(String nm, Style parent)
protected MutableAttributeSet	**createLargeAttributeSet** (AttributeSet a)
protected StyleContext.SmallAttributeSet	**createSmallAttributeSet** (AttributeSet a)
Color	**getBackground**(AttributeSet attr)
protected int	**getCompressionThreshold**()
static StyleContext	**getDefaultStyleContext**()
AttributeSet	**getEmptySet**()
Font	**getFont**(AttributeSet attr)
Font	**getFont**(String family, int style, int size)
FontMetrics	**getFontMetrics**(Font f)
Color	**getForeground**(AttributeSet attr)
static Object	**getStaticAttribute**(Object key)
static Object	**getStaticAttributeKey**(Object key)
Style	**getStyle**(String nm)
Enumeration	**getStyleNames**()
void	**readAttributes** (ObjectInputStream in, MutableAttributeSet a)
static void	**readAttributeSet** (ObjectInputStream in, MutableAttributeSet a)

void	**reclaim**(AttributeSet a)
static void	**registerStaticAttributeKey** (Object key)
AttributeSet	**removeAttribute**(AttributeSet old, Object name)
AttributeSet	**removeAttributes**(AttributeSet old, AttributeSet attrs)
AttributeSet	**removeAttributes**(AttributeSet old, Enumeration names)
void	**removeChangeListener** (ChangeListener 1)
void	**removeStyle**(String nm)
String	**toString**()
void	**writeAttributes** (ObjectOutputStream out, AttributeSet a)
static void	**writeAttributeSet** (ObjectOutputStream out, AttributeSet a)

Class StyledEditorKit

```
java.lang.Object
   |
   +--javax.swing.text.EditorKit
          |
          +--javax.swing.text.DefaultEditorKit
                 |
                 +--javax.swing.text.StyledEditorKit
```

public class **StyledEditorKit**
          extends DefaultEditorKit

This class represents a styled editor kit that provides the basic editing features of styled text.

Inner Classes

static class	**StyledEditorKit.AlignmentAction**
static class	**StyledEditorKit.BoldAction**
static class	**StyledEditorKit.FontFamilyAction**
static class	**StyledEditorKit.FontSizeAction**
static class	**StyledEditorKit.ForegroundAction**
static class	**StyledEditorKit.ItalicAction**
static class	**StyledEditorKit.StyledTextAction**
static class	**StyledEditorKit.UnderlineAction**

Constructor

StyledEditorKit()

Methods

```
Object              clone()
Document            createDefaultDocument()
protected void      createInputAttributes(Element element,
MutableAttributeSet set)
void                deinstall(JEditorPane c)
Action[]            getActions()
Element             getCharacterAttributeRun()
MutableAttributeSet getInputAttributes()
ViewFactory         getViewFactory()
void                install(JEditorPane c)
```

Class StyledEditorKit.AlignmentAction

```
java.lang.Object
  |
  +--javax.swing.AbstractAction
        |
        +--javax.swing.text.TextAction
              |
              +--javax.swing.text.StyledEditorKit.StyledTextAction
                    |
                    +--javax.swing.text.StyledEditorKit.AlignmentAction
```

```
public static class StyledEditorKit.AlignmentAction
                extends StyledEditorKit.StyledTextAction
```

This class represents an action to set paragraph alignment.

Constructor
```
StyledEditorKit.AlignmentAction(String nm, int a)
```

Method
```
void    actionPerformed(ActionEvent e)
```

Class StyledEditorKit.BoldAction

```
java.lang.Object
  |
  +--javax.swing.AbstractAction
        |
        +--javax.swing.text.TextAction
              |
              +--javax.swing.text.StyledEditorKit.StyledTextAction
                    |
                    +--javax.swing.text.StyledEditorKit.BoldAction
```

```
public static class StyledEditorKit.BoldAction
                extends StyledEditorKit.StyledTextAction
```

This class represents an action object to toggle the bold attribute.

Constructor
`StyledEditorKit.BoldAction()`

Method
`void     actionPerformed(ActionEvent e)`

Class StyledEditorKit.FontFamilyAction

```
java.lang.Object
   |
   +--javax.swing.AbstractAction
         |
         +--javax.swing.text.TextAction
               |
               +--javax.swing.text.StyledEditorKit.StyledTextAction
                     |
                     +--javax.swing.text.StyledEditorKit.FontFamilyAction
```

`public static class StyledEditorKit.FontFamilyAction`
`                extends StyledEditorKit.StyledTextAction`

This class represents an action to set the font family.

Constructor
`StyledEditorKit.FontFamilyAction(String nm, String family)`

Method
`void     actionPerformed(ActionEvent e)`

Class StyledEditorKit.FontSizeAction

```
java.lang.Object
   |
   +--javax.swing.AbstractAction
         |
         +--javax.swing.text.TextAction
               |
               +--javax.swing.text.StyledEditorKit.StyledTextAction
                     |
                     +--javax.swing.text.StyledEditorKit.FontSizeAction
```

`public static class StyledEditorKit.FontSizeAction`
`                extends StyledEditorKit.StyledTextAction`

This class represents an action object to assign font size.

Constructor
`StyledEditorKit.FontSizeAction(String nm, int size)`

Method
`void     actionPerformed(ActionEvent e)`

Class StyledEditorKit.ForegroundAction

```
java.lang.Object
  |
  +--javax.swing.AbstractAction
        |
        +--javax.swing.text.TextAction
              |
              +--javax.swing.text.StyledEditorKit.StyledTextAction
                    |
                    +--javax.swing.text.StyledEditorKit.ForegroundAction
```

public static class **StyledEditorKit.ForegroundAction**
                    extends StyledEditorKit.StyledTextAction

This class represents an action to assign foreground color.

Constructor
StyledEditorKit.ForegroundAction(String nm, Color fg)

Method
void   **actionPerformed**(ActionEvent e)

Class StyledEditorKit.ItalicAction

```
java.lang.Object
  |
  +--javax.swing.AbstractAction
        |
        +--javax.swing.text.TextAction
              |
              +--javax.swing.text.StyledEditorKit.StyledTextAction
                    |
                    +--javax.swing.text.StyledEditorKit.ItalicAction
```

public static class **StyledEditorKit.ItalicAction**
                    extends StyledEditorKit.StyledTextAction

This class represents an action to toggle the italic attribute.

Constructor
StyledEditorKit.ItalicAction()

Method
void   **actionPerformed**(ActionEvent e)

Class StyledEditorKit.StyledTextAction

```
java.lang.Object
  |
  +--javax.swing.AbstractAction
        |
        +--javax.swing.text.TextAction
              |
              +--javax.swing.text.StyledEditorKit.StyledTextAction
```

```
public abstract static class StyledEditorKit.StyledTextAction
                            extends TextAction
```

This class represents an action object that contains some convenience methods for changing character- or paragraph-level attributes.

Constructor
```
StyledEditorKit.StyledTextAction(String nm)
```

Methods
```
protected JEditorPane          getEditor(ActionEvent e)
protected StyledDocument       getStyledDocument(JEditorPane e)
protected StyledEditorKit      getStyledEditorKit(JEditorPane e)
protected void                 setCharacterAttributes(JEditorPane editor,
                               AttributeSet attr, boolean replace)
protected void                 setParagraphAttributes(JEditorPane editor,
                               AttributeSet attr, boolean replace)
```

Class StyledEditorKit.UnderlineAction

```
java.lang.Object
  |
  +--javax.swing.AbstractAction
        |
        +--javax.swing.text.TextAction
              |
              +--javax.swing.text.StyledEditorKit.StyledTextAction
                    |
                    +--javax.swing.text.StyledEditorKit.UnderlineAction
```

```
public static class StyledEditorKit.UnderlineAction
                    extends StyledEditorKit.StyledTextAction
```

This class represents an action object to toggle the underline attribute.

Constructor
```
StyledEditorKit.UnderlineAction()
```

Method
```
void    actionPerformed(ActionEvent e)
```

Class TableView

```
java.lang.Object
  |
  +--javax.swing.text.View
        |
        +--javax.swing.text.CompositeView
              |
              +--javax.swing.text.BoxView
                    |
                    +--javax.swing.text.TableView
```

```
public abstract class TableView
                extends BoxView
```

This class is an implementation of the interface View to represent a table.

Inner Classes

```
class     TableView.TableCell
class     TableView.TableRow
```

Constructor

```
TableView(Element elem)
```

Methods

protected SizeRequirements	**calculateMinorAxisRequirements**(int axis, SizeRequirements r)
protected TableView.TableCell	**createTableCell**(Element elem)
protected TableView.TableRow	**createTableRow**(Element elem)
protected View	**getViewAtPosition**(int pos, Rectangle a)
protected void	**layoutColumns**(int targetSpan, int[] offsets, int[] spans, SizeRequirements[] reqs)
protected void	**layoutMinorAxis**(int targetSpan, int axis, int[] offsets, int[] spans)
protected void	**loadChildren**(ViewFactory f)

Class TabSet

```
        java.lang.Object
          |
          |
        +--javax.swing.text.TabSet
public class TabSet
            extends Object
            implements Serializable
```

This class represents a tab set that is composed of several tab stops.

Constructor

```
TabSet(TabStop[] tabs)
```

Methods

TabStop	**getTab**(int index)
TabStop	**getTabAfter**(float location)
int	**getTabCount**()
int	**getTabIndex**(TabStop tab)
int	**getTabIndexAfter**(float location)
String	**toString**()

Class TabStop

```
        java.lang.Object
          |
          |
        +--javax.swing.text.TabStop
```

```
public class TabStop
              extends Object
              implements Serializable
```

This class represents a tab stop.

Fields

```
static int    ALIGN_BAR

static int    ALIGN_CENTER
static int    ALIGN_DECIMAL
static int    ALIGN_LEFT
static int    ALIGN_RIGHT
static int    LEAD_DOTS
static int    LEAD_EQUALS
static int    LEAD_HYPHENS
static int    LEAD_NONE
static int    LEAD_THICKLINE
static int    LEAD_UNDERLINE
```

Constructors

```
TabStop(float pos)
TabStop(float pos, int align, int leader)
```

Methods

```
boolean    equals(Object other)
int        getAlignment()
int        getLeader()
float      getPosition()
int        hashCode()
String     toString()
```

Class TextAction

```
java.lang.Object
   |
   +--javax.swing.AbstractAction
         |
         +--javax.swing.text.TextAction
```

```
public abstract class TextAction
                  extends AbstractAction
```

This class represents an action that is used for key bindings shared among several text components.

Constructor

```
TextAction(String name)
```

Methods

```
static Action[]              augmentList(Action[] list1, Action[] list2)
protected JTextComponent     getFocusedComponent()
protected JTextComponent     getTextComponent(ActionEvent e)
```

Class Utilities

```
java.lang.Object
  |
  +--javax.swing.text.Utilities
```

public class **Utilities**
        extends Object

This class represents a collection of utility methods to handle various text-related functions.

Constructor
Utilities()

Methods

static int	**drawTabbedText**(Segment s, int x, int y, Graphics g, TabExpander e, int startOffset)
static int	**getBreakLocation**(Segment s, FontMetrics metrics, int x0, int x, TabExpander e, int startOffset)
static int	**getNextWord**(JTextComponent c, int offs)
static Element	**getParagraphElement**(JTextComponent c, int offs)
static int	**getPositionAbove**(JTextComponent c, int offs, int x)
static int	**getPositionBelow**(JTextComponent c, int offs, int x)
static int	**getPreviousWord**(JTextComponent c, int offs)
static int	**getRowEnd**(JTextComponent c, int offs)
static int	**getRowStart**(JTextComponent c, int offs)
static int	**getTabbedTextOffset**(Segment s, FontMetrics metrics, int x0, int x, TabExpander e, int startOffset)
static int	**getTabbedTextOffset**(Segment s, FontMetrics metrics, int x0, int x, TabExpander e, int startOffset, boolean round)
static int	**getTabbedTextWidth**(Segment s, FontMetrics metrics, int x, TabExpander e, int startOffset)
static int	**getWordEnd**(JTextComponent c, int offs)
static int	**getWordStart**(JTextComponent c, int offs)

Class View

```
java.lang.Object
  |
  +--javax.swing.text.View
```

public abstract class **View**
            extends Object
            implements SwingConstants

This class represents the view of a certain portion of a document.

Fields

static int	**BadBreakWeight**
static int	**ExcellentBreakWeight**
static int	**ForcedBreakWeight**
static int	**GoodBreakWeight**

```
static int      X_AXIS
static int      Y_AXIS
```

Constructor
View(Element elem)

Methods

View	**breakView**(int axis, int offset, float pos, float len)
void	**changedUpdate**(DocumentEvent e, Shape a, ViewFactory f)
View	**createFragment**(int p0, int p1)
float	**getAlignment**(int axis)
AttributeSet	**getAttributes**()
int	**getBreakWeight**(int axis, float pos, float len)
Shape	**getChildAllocation**(int index, Shape a)
Container	**getContainer**()
Document	**getDocument**()
Element	**getElement**()
int	**getEndOffset**()
float	**getMaximumSpan**(int axis)
float	**getMinimumSpan**(int axis)
int	**getNextVisualPositionFrom**(int pos, Position.Bias b, Shape a, int direction, Position.Bias[] biasRet)
View	**getParent**()
abstract float	**getPreferredSpan**(int axis)
int	**getResizeWeight**(int axis)
int	**getStartOffset**()
View	**getView**(int n)
int	**getViewCount**()
ViewFactory	**getViewFactory**()
void	**insertUpdate**(DocumentEvent e, Shape a, ViewFactory f)
boolean	**isVisible**()
Shape	**modelToView**(int p0, Position.Bias b0, int p1, Position.Bias b1, Shape a)
Shape	**modelToView**(int pos, Shape a)
abstract Shape	**modelToView**(int pos, Shape a, Position.Bias b)
abstract void	**paint**(Graphics g, Shape allocation)
void	**preferenceChanged**(View child, boolean width, boolean height)
void	**removeUpdate**(DocumentEvent e, Shape a, ViewFactory f)
void	**setParent**(View parent)
void	**setSize**(float width, float height)
int	**viewToModel**(float x, float y, Shape a)
abstract int	**viewToModel**(float x, float y, Shape a, Position.Bias[] biasReturn)

Class WrappedPlainView

```
java.lang.Object
   |
   +--javax.swing.text.View
       |
```

```
+--javax.swing.text.CompositeView
    |
    |
    +--javax.swing.text.BoxView
        |
        |
        +--javax.swing.text.WrappedPlainView
```
public class **WrappedPlainView**
                extends BoxView
                implements TabExpander

This class represents the view of plain text that does line wrapping. The plain text must be using only a single font and color.

Constructors
WrappedPlainView(Element elem)
WrappedPlainView(Element elem, boolean wordWrap)

Methods
protected int	**calculateBreakPosition**(int p0, int p1)
void	**changedUpdate**(DocumentEvent e, Shape a, ViewFactory f)
protected void	**drawLine**(int p0, int p1, Graphics g, int x, int y)
protected int	**drawSelectedText**(Graphics g, int x, int y, int p0, int p1)
protected int	**drawUnselectedText**(Graphics g, int x, int y, int p0, int p1)
protected Segment	**getLineBuffer**()
float	**getMaximumSpan**(int axis)
float	**getMinimumSpan**(int axis)
float	**getPreferredSpan**(int axis)
protected int	**getTabSize**()
void	**insertUpdate**(DocumentEvent e, Shape a, ViewFactory f)
protected void	**loadChildren**(ViewFactory f)
float	**nextTabStop**(float x, int tabOffset)
void	**paint**(Graphics g, Shape a)
void	**removeUpdate**(DocumentEvent e, Shape a, ViewFactory f)
void	**setSize**(float width, float height)

Class BadLocationException

```
java.lang.Object
    |
    +--java.lang.Throwable
        |
        +--java.lang.Exception
            |
            +--javax.swing.text.BadLocationException
```
public class **BadLocationException**
                extends Exception

This class represents an exception that is thrown if you attempt to reference a location that does not exist.

Constructor
`BadLocationException`(String s, int offs)

Method
int `offsetRequested`()

Class ChangedCharSetException

```
java.lang.Object
  |
  +--java.lang.Throwable
       |
       +--java.lang.Exception
            |
            +--java.io.IOException
                 |
                 +--javax.swing.text.ChangedCharSetException
```

```
public class ChangedCharSetException
          extends IOException
```

This class represents an exception that is thrown when the Charset is changed.

Constructor
`ChangedCharSetException`(String charSetSpec, boolean charSetKey)

Methods
String `getCharSetSpec`()
boolean `keyEqualsCharSet`()

javax.swing.text.html

Class BlockView

```
java.lang.Object
  |
  +--javax.swing.text.View
       |
       +--javax.swing.text.CompositeView
            |
            +--javax.swing.text.BoxView
                 |
                 +--javax.swing.text.html.BlockView
```

```
public class BlockView
          extends BoxView
```

This class represents a view to present a block of text with CSS specifications.

Constructor
`BlockView`(Element elem, int axis)

Methods

float	**getAlignment**(int axis)
AttributeSet	**getAttributes**()
int	**getResizeWeight**(int axis)
protected StyleSheet	**getStyleSheet**()
void	**paint**(Graphics g, Shape allocation)
protected void	**setPropertiesFromAttributes**()

Class CSS

```
java.lang.Object
   |
   +--javax.swing.text.html.CSS
```

public class **CSS**
            extends Object

This class represents CSS attributes. The view implementations of HTML documents use CSS attributes to determine how to render the content of information.

Inner Class

static class	**CSS.Attribute**

Constructor

CSS()

Methods

static CSS.Attribute[]	**getAllAttributeKeys**()
static CSS.Attribute	**getAttribute**(String name)

Class CSS.Attribute

```
java.lang.Object
   |
   +--javax.swing.text.html.CSS.Attribute
```

public static final class **CSS.Attribute**
                            extends Object

This inner (and final) class represents the definitions to be used as keys on attribute sets that hold CSS attributes.

Fields

static CSS.Attribute	**BACKGROUND**
static CSS.Attribute	**BACKGROUND_ATTACHMENT**
static CSS.Attribute	**BACKGROUND_COLOR**
static CSS.Attribute	**BACKGROUND_IMAGE**
static CSS.Attribute	**BACKGROUND_POSITION**
static CSS.Attribute	**BACKGROUND_REPEAT**
static CSS.Attribute	**BORDER**
static CSS.Attribute	**BORDER_BOTTOM**
static CSS.Attribute	**BORDER_BOTTOM_WIDTH**
static CSS.Attribute	**BORDER_COLOR**

static CSS.Attribute	**BORDER_LEFT**
static CSS.Attribute	**BORDER_LEFT_WIDTH**
static CSS.Attribute	**BORDER_RIGHT**
static CSS.Attribute	**BORDER_RIGHT_WIDTH**
static CSS.Attribute	**BORDER_STYLE**
static CSS.Attribute	**BORDER_TOP**
static CSS.Attribute	**BORDER_TOP_WIDTH**
static CSS.Attribute	**BORDER_WIDTH**
static CSS.Attribute	**CLEAR**
static CSS.Attribute	**COLOR**
static CSS.Attribute	**DISPLAY**
static CSS.Attribute	**FLOAT**
static CSS.Attribute	**FONT**
static CSS.Attribute	**FONT_FAMILY**
static CSS.Attribute	**FONT_SIZE**
static CSS.Attribute	**FONT_STYLE**
static CSS.Attribute	**FONT_VARIANT**
static CSS.Attribute	**FONT_WEIGHT**
static CSS.Attribute	**HEIGHT**
static CSS.Attribute	**LETTER_SPACING**
static CSS.Attribute	**LINE_HEIGHT**
static CSS.Attribute	**LIST_STYLE**
static CSS.Attribute	**LIST_STYLE_IMAGE**
static CSS.Attribute	**LIST_STYLE_POSITION**
static CSS.Attribute	**LIST_STYLE_TYPE**
static CSS.Attribute	**MARGIN**
static CSS.Attribute	**MARGIN_BOTTOM**
static CSS.Attribute	**MARGIN_LEFT**
static CSS.Attribute	**MARGIN_RIGHT**
static CSS.Attribute	**MARGIN_TOP**
static CSS.Attribute	**PADDING**
static CSS.Attribute	**PADDING_BOTTOM**
static CSS.Attribute	**PADDING_LEFT**
static CSS.Attribute	**PADDING_RIGHT**
static CSS.Attribute	**PADDING_TOP**
static CSS.Attribute	**TEXT_ALIGN**
static CSS.Attribute	**TEXT_DECORATION**
static CSS.Attribute	**TEXT_INDENT**
static CSS.Attribute	**TEXT_TRANSFORM**
static CSS.Attribute	**VERTICAL_ALIGN**
static CSS.Attribute	**WHITE_SPACE**
static CSS.Attribute	**WIDTH**
static CSS.Attribute	**WORD_SPACING**

Methods

String	**getDefaultValue**()
boolean	**isInherited**()
String	**toString**()

Class FormView

```
java.lang.Object
    |
    +--javax.swing.text.View
            |
            +--javax.swing.text.ComponentView
                    |
                    +--javax.swing.text.html.FormView
```

```
public class FormView
            extends ComponentView
            implements ActionListener
```

This class represents a form view for form elements, inputs, text area, and selections.

Inner Class

protected class   **FormView.MouseEventListener**

Fields

static String   **RESET**
static String   **SUBMIT**

Constructor

FormView(Element elem)

Methods

void	**actionPerformed**(ActionEvent evt)
protected Component	**createComponent**()
protected void	**imageSubmit**(String imageData)
protected void	**submitData**(String data)

Class HTML

```
java.lang.Object
    |
    +--javax.swing.text.html.HTML
```

```
public class HTML
            extends Object
```

This class represents objects that contain constants to be used in HTML documents.

Inner Classes

static class   **HTML.Attribute**
static class   **HTML.Tag**
static class   **HTML.UnknownTag**

Field

static String   **NULL_ATTRIBUTE_VALUE**

Constructor

HTML()

Methods

```
static HTML.Attribute[]     getAllAttributeKeys()
static HTML.Tag[]           getAllTags()
static HTML.Attribute       getAttributeKey(String attName)
static int                  getIntegerAttributeValue(AttributeSet attr,
                            HTML.Attribute key, int def)
static HTML.Tag             getTag(String tagName)
```

Class HTML.Attribute

```
java.lang.Object
   ¦
   +--javax.swing.text.html.HTML.Attribute
```

```
public static final class HTML.Attribute
                          extends Object
```

This inner class represents an HTML attribute.

Fields

```
static HTML.Attribute       ACTION
static HTML.Attribute       ALIGN
static HTML.Attribute       ALINK
static HTML.Attribute       ALT
static HTML.Attribute       ARCHIVE
static HTML.Attribute       BACKGROUND
static HTML.Attribute       BGCOLOR
static HTML.Attribute       BORDER
static HTML.Attribute       CELLPADDING
static HTML.Attribute       CELLSPACING
static HTML.Attribute       CHECKED
static HTML.Attribute       CLASS
static HTML.Attribute       CLASSID
static HTML.Attribute       CLEAR
static HTML.Attribute       CODE
static HTML.Attribute       CODEBASE
static HTML.Attribute       CODETYPE
static HTML.Attribute       COLOR
static HTML.Attribute       COLS
static HTML.Attribute       COLSPAN
static HTML.Attribute       COMMENT
static HTML.Attribute       COMPACT
static HTML.Attribute       CONTENT
static HTML.Attribute       COORDS
static HTML.Attribute       DATA
static HTML.Attribute       DECLARE
static HTML.Attribute       DIR
static HTML.Attribute       DUMMY
static HTML.Attribute       ENCTYPE
static HTML.Attribute       ENDTAG
static HTML.Attribute       FACE
```

```
static HTML.Attribute      FRAMEBORDER
static HTML.Attribute      HALIGN
static HTML.Attribute      HEIGHT
static HTML.Attribute      HREF
static HTML.Attribute      HSPACE
static HTML.Attribute      HTTPEQUIV
static HTML.Attribute      ID
static HTML.Attribute      ISMAP
static HTML.Attribute      LANG
static HTML.Attribute      LANGUAGE
static HTML.Attribute      LINK
static HTML.Attribute      LOWSRC
static HTML.Attribute      MARGINHEIGHT
static HTML.Attribute      MARGINWIDTH
static HTML.Attribute      MAXLENGTH
static HTML.Attribute      METHOD
static HTML.Attribute      MULTIPLE
static HTML.Attribute      N
static HTML.Attribute      NAME
static HTML.Attribute      NOHREF
static HTML.Attribute      NORESIZE
static HTML.Attribute      NOSHADE
static HTML.Attribute      NOWRAP
static HTML.Attribute      PROMPT
static HTML.Attribute      REL
static HTML.Attribute      REV
static HTML.Attribute      ROWS
static HTML.Attribute      ROWSPAN
static HTML.Attribute      SCROLLING
static HTML.Attribute      SELECTED
static HTML.Attribute      SHAPE
static HTML.Attribute      SHAPES
static HTML.Attribute      SIZE
static HTML.Attribute      SRC
static HTML.Attribute      STANDBY
static HTML.Attribute      START
static HTML.Attribute      STYLE
static HTML.Attribute      TARGET
static HTML.Attribute      TEXT
static HTML.Attribute      TITLE
static HTML.Attribute      TYPE
static HTML.Attribute      USEMAP
static HTML.Attribute      VALIGN
static HTML.Attribute      VALUE
static HTML.Attribute      VALUETYPE
static HTML.Attribute      VERSION
static HTML.Attribute      VLINK
static HTML.Attribute      VSPACE
static HTML.Attribute      WIDTH
```

Method

```
String    toString()
```

Class HTML.Tag

```
java.lang.Object
   |
   +--javax.swing.text.html.HTML.Tag
```

```
public static class HTML.Tag
                      extends Object
```

This class represents an HTML tag.

Fields

static HTML.Tag	**A**
static HTML.Tag	**ADDRESS**
static HTML.Tag	**APPLET**
static HTML.Tag	**AREA**
static HTML.Tag	**B**
static HTML.Tag	**BASE**
static HTML.Tag	**BASEFONT**
static HTML.Tag	**BIG**
static HTML.Tag	**BLOCKQUOTE**
static HTML.Tag	**BODY**
static HTML.Tag	**BR**
static HTML.Tag	**CAPTION**
static HTML.Tag	**CENTER**
static HTML.Tag	**CITE**
static HTML.Tag	**CODE**
static HTML.Tag	**COMMENT**
static HTML.Tag	**CONTENT**
static HTML.Tag	**DD**
static HTML.Tag	**DFN**
static HTML.Tag	**DIR**
static HTML.Tag	**DIV**
static HTML.Tag	**DL**
static HTML.Tag	**DT**
static HTML.Tag	**EM**
static HTML.Tag	**FONT**
static HTML.Tag	**FORM**
static HTML.Tag	**FRAME**
static HTML.Tag	**FRAMESET**
static HTML.Tag	**H1**
static HTML.Tag	**H2**
static HTML.Tag	**H3**
static HTML.Tag	**H4**
static HTML.Tag	**H5**
static HTML.Tag	**H6**
static HTML.Tag	**HEAD**
static HTML.Tag	**HR**

static HTML.Tag	**HTML**
static HTML.Tag	**I**
static HTML.Tag	**IMG**
static HTML.Tag	**IMPLIED**
static HTML.Tag	**INPUT**
static HTML.Tag	**ISINDEX**
static HTML.Tag	**KBD**
static HTML.Tag	**LI**
static HTML.Tag	**LINK**
static HTML.Tag	**MAP**
static HTML.Tag	**MENU**
static HTML.Tag	**META**
static HTML.Tag	**NOFRAMES**
static HTML.Tag	**OBJECT**
static HTML.Tag	**OL**
static HTML.Tag	**OPTION**
static HTML.Tag	**P**
static HTML.Tag	**PARAM**
static HTML.Tag	**PRE**
static HTML.Tag	**S**
static HTML.Tag	**SAMP**
static HTML.Tag	**SCRIPT**
static HTML.Tag	**SELECT**
static HTML.Tag	**SMALL**
static HTML.Tag	**STRIKE**
static HTML.Tag	**STRONG**
static HTML.Tag	**STYLE**
static HTML.Tag	**SUB**
static HTML.Tag	**SUP**
static HTML.Tag	**TABLE**
static HTML.Tag	**TD**
static HTML.Tag	**TEXTAREA**
static HTML.Tag	**TH**
static HTML.Tag	**TITLE**
static HTML.Tag	**TR**
static HTML.Tag	**TT**
static HTML.Tag	**U**
static HTML.Tag	**UL**
static HTML.Tag	**VAR**

Constructors

protected	**HTML.Tag**(String id)
protected	**HTML.Tag**(String id, boolean causesBreak, boolean isBlock)

Methods

boolean	**breaksFlow**()
true.boolean	**isBlock**()
boolean	**isPreformatted**()
String	**toString**()

Class HTML.UnknownTag

```
java.lang.Object
   |
   +--javax.swing.text.html.HTML.Tag
           |
           +--javax.swing.text.html.HTML.UnknownTag
```

public static class **HTML.UnknownTag**
                      extends HTML.Tag
                      implements Serializable

This inner class represents an unknown tag.

Constructor
HTML.UnknownTag(String id)

Methods
boolean   **equals**(Object obj)
int   **hashCode**()

Class HTMLDocument

```
java.lang.Object
   |
   +--javax.swing.text.AbstractDocument
           |
           +--javax.swing.text.DefaultStyledDocument
                   |
                   +--javax.swing.text.html.HTMLDocument
```

public class **HTMLDocument**
             extends DefaultStyledDocument

This class represents the content model for HTML, which supports both browsing and editing.

Inner Classes
class   **HTMLDocument.BlockElement**
class   **HTMLDocument.HTMLReader**
static class   **HTMLDocument.Iterator**
class   **HTMLDocument.RunElement**

Field
static String   **AdditionalComments**

Constructors
HTMLDocument()
HTMLDocument(AbstractDocument.Content c, StyleSheet styles)
HTMLDocument(StyleSheet styles)

Methods
protected void   **create**(DefaultStyledDocument.
                                            ElementSpec[] data)

protected Element	**createBranchElement**(Element parent, AttributeSet a)
protected AbstractDocument.AbstractElement	**createDefaultRoot**()
protected Element	**createLeafElement**(Element parent, AttributeSet a, int p0, int p1)
URL	**getBase**()
HTMLDocument.Iterator	**getIterator**(HTML.Tag t)
boolean	**getPreservesUnknownTags**()
HTMLEditorKit.ParserCallback	**getReader**(int pos)
HTMLEditorKit.ParserCallback	**getReader**(int pos, int popDepth, int pushDepth, HTML.Tag insertTag)
StyleSheet	**getStyleSheet**()
int	**getTokenThreshold**()
protected void	**insert**(int offset, DefaultStyledDocument.ElementSpec[] data)
protected void	**insertUpdate**(AbstractDocument.DefaultDocumentEvent chng, AttributeSet attr)
void	**processHTMLFrameHyperlinkEvent**(HTMLFrameHyperlinkEvent e)
void	**setBase**(URL u)
void	**setPreservesUnknownTags**(boolean preservesTags)
void	**setTokenThreshold**(int n)

Class HTMLDocument.Iterator

```
java.lang.Object
   |
   +--javax.swing.text.html.HTMLDocument.Iterator
```

public abstract static class **HTMLDocument.Iterator**
                        extends Object

This class represents an iterator (which is not thread safe) to iterate over a particular type of tag.

Constructor
HTMLDocument.Iterator()

Methods

abstract AttributeSet	**getAttributes**()
abstract int	**getEndOffset**()
abstract int	**getStartOffset**()
abstract HTML.Tag	**getTag**()
abstract boolean	**isValid**()
abstract void	**next**()

Class HTMLEditorKit

```
java.lang.Object
   |
   +--javax.swing.text.EditorKit
           |
           +--javax.swing.text.DefaultEditorKit
                   |
                   +--javax.swing.text.StyledEditorKit
                           |
                           +--javax.swing.text.html.HTMLEditorKit
```

public class **HTMLEditorKit**
             extends StyledEditorKit

This class represents an editor kit for HTML version 3.2. Note that the applet tag is not supported.

Inner Classes

static class	**HTMLEditorKit.HTMLFactory**
static class	**HTMLEditorKit.HTMLTextAction**
static class	**HTMLEditorKit.InsertHTMLTextAction**
static class	**HTMLEditorKit.LinkController**
static class	**HTMLEditorKit.Parser**
static class	**HTMLEditorKit.ParserCallback**

Fields

static String	**BOLD_ACTION**
static String	**COLOR_ACTION**
static String	**DEFAULT_CSS**
static String	**FONT_CHANGE_BIGGER**
static String	**FONT_CHANGE_SMALLER**
static String	**IMG_ALIGN_BOTTOM**
static String	**IMG_ALIGN_MIDDLE**
static String	**IMG_ALIGN_TOP**
static String	**IMG_BORDER**
static String	**ITALIC_ACTION**
static String	**LOGICAL_STYLE_ACTION**
static String	**PARA_INDENT_LEFT**
static String	**PARA_INDENT_RIGHT**

Constructor

HTMLEditorKit()

Methods

Object	**clone**()
Document	**createDefaultDocument**()
protected void	**createInputAttributes**(Element element, MutableAttributeSet set)
void	**deinstall**(JEditorPane c)
Action[]	**getActions**()
String	**getContentType**()

```
protected HTMLEditorKit.Parser   getParser()
StyleSheet                       getStyleSheet()
ViewFactory                      getViewFactory()
void                             insertHTML(HTMLDocument doc, int offset,
                                 String html, int popDepth, int pushDepth,
                                 HTML.Tag insertTag)
void                             install(JEditorPane c)
void                             read(Reader in, Document doc, int pos)
void                             setStyleSheet(StyleSheet s)
void                             write(Writer out, Document doc,
                                 int pos, int len)
```

Class HTMLEditorKit.HTMLFactory

```
java.lang.Object
    |
    +--javax.swing.text.html.HTMLEditorKit.HTMLFactory
```

```
public static class HTMLEditorKit.HTMLFactory
                extends Object
                implements ViewFactory
```

This inner class represents a factory to build views for HTML content.

Constructor
```
HTMLEditorKit.HTMLFactory()
```

Method
```
View create(Element elem)
```

Class HTMLEditorKit.HTMLTextAction

```
java.lang.Object
    |
    +--javax.swing.AbstractAction
            |
            +--javax.swing.text.TextAction
                    |
                    +--javax.swing.text.StyledEditorKit.StyledTextAction
                            |
                            +--javax.swing.text.html.HTMLEditorKit.HTMLTextAction
```

```
public abstract static class HTMLEditorKit.HTMLTextAction
                extends StyledEditorKit.StyledTextAction
```

This inner class represents an abstract action that supports certain methods to include HTML in an existing document.

Constructor
```
HTMLEditorKit.HTMLTextAction(String name)
```

Methods
```
protected int          elementCountToTag(HTMLDocument doc, int offset,
                       HTML.Tag tag)
```

```
protected Element          findElementMatchingTag(HTMLDocument doc, int offset,
                           HTML.Tag tag)
protected Element[]        getElementsAt(HTMLDocument doc, int offset)
protected HTMLDocument     getHTMLDocument(JEditorPane e)
protected HTMLEditorKit    getHTMLEditorKit(JEditorPane e)
```

Class HTMLEditorKit.InsertHTMLTextAction

```
java.lang.Object
   |
   +--javax.swing.AbstractAction
       |
       +--javax.swing.text.TextAction
           |
           +--javax.swing.text.StyledEditorKit.StyledTextAction
               |
               +--javax.swing.text.html.HTMLEditorKit.HTMLTextAction
                   |
                   +--javax.swing.text.html.HTMLEditorKit.InsertHTMLTextAction
public static class HTMLEditorKit.InsertHTMLTextAction
                   extends HTMLEditorKit.HTMLTextAction
```

This class represents an action object that can be used to insert HTML into an existing HTML document.

Fields

```
protected HTML.Tag    addTag
protected HTML.Tag    alternateAddTag
protected HTML.Tag    alternateParentTag
protected String      html
protected HTML.Tag    parentTag
```

Constructors

HTMLEditorKit.InsertHTMLTextAction(String name, String html, HTML.Tag parentTag, HTML.Tag addTag)
HTMLEditorKit.InsertHTMLTextAction(String name, String html, HTML.Tag parentTag, HTML.Tag addTag, HTML.Tag alternateParentTag, HTML.Tag alternateAddTag)

Methods

```
void             actionPerformed(ActionEvent ae)
protected void   insertAtBoundry(JEditorPane editor, HTMLDocument doc,
                 int offset, Element insertElement, String html,
                 HTML.Tag parentTag, HTML.Tag addTag)
protected void   insertHTML(JEditorPane editor, HTMLDocument doc, int offset,
                 String html, int popDepth, int pushDepth, HTML.Tag addTag)
```

Class HTMLEditorKit.LinkController

```
java.lang.Object
  |
  +--java.awt.event.MouseAdapter
         |
         +--javax.swing.text.html.HTMLEditorKit.LinkController
```

public static class **HTMLEditorKit.LinkController**
                extends MouseAdapter
                implements Serializable

This class represents an object to watch the associated component and fire hyperlink events when necessary.

Constructor
HTMLEditorKit.LinkController()

Methods
protected void   **activateLink**(int pos, JEditorPane html)
void   **mouseClicked**(MouseEvent e)

Class HTMLEditorKit.Parser

```
java.lang.Object
  |
  +--javax.swing.text.html.HTMLEditorKit.Parser
```

public abstract static class **HTMLEditorKit.Parser**
                        extends Object

This inner class represents a parser.

Constructor
HTMLEditorKit.Parser()

Method
abstract void   **parse**(Reader r, HTMLEditorKit.ParserCallback cb,
                  boolean ignoreCharSet)

Class HTMLEditorKit.ParserCallback

```
java.lang.Object
  |
  +--javax.swing.text.html.HTMLEditorKit.ParserCallback
```

public static class **HTMLEditorKit.ParserCallback**
                extends Object

This inner class represents the parser callbacks.

Constructor
HTMLEditorKit.ParserCallback()

Methods

```
void      flush()
void      handleComment(char[] data, int pos)
void      handleEndTag(HTML.Tag t, int pos)
void      handleError(String errorMsg, int pos)
void      handleSimpleTag(HTML.Tag t, MutableAttributeSet a, int pos)
void      handleStartTag(HTML.Tag t, MutableAttributeSet a, int pos)
void      handleText(char[] data, int pos)
```

Class HTMLFrameHyperlinkEvent

```
java.lang.Object
   |
   +--java.util.EventObject
          |
          +--javax.swing.event.HyperlinkEvent
                 |
                 +--javax.swing.text.html.HTMLFrameHyperlinkEvent
```

public class **HTMLFrameHyperlinkEvent**
        extends HyperlinkEvent

This class represents an event to notify registered listeners that a link has been activated in a frame.

Constructors

```
HTMLFrameHyperlinkEvent(Object source, HyperlinkEvent.EventType type,
URL targetURL, Element sourceElement, String targetFrame)
HTMLFrameHyperlinkEvent(Object source, HyperlinkEvent.EventType type,
URL targetURL, String targetFrame)
HTMLFrameHyperlinkEvent(Object source, HyperlinkEvent.EventType type,
URL targetURL, String desc, Element sourceElement, String targetFrame)
HTMLFrameHyperlinkEvent(Object source, HyperlinkEvent.EventType type,
URL targetURL, String desc, String targetFrame)
```

Methods

```
Element   getSourceElement()
String    getTarget()
```

Class HTMLWriter

```
java.lang.Object
   |
   +--javax.swing.text.AbstractWriter
          |
          +--javax.swing.text.html.HTMLWriter
```

public class **HTMLWriter**
        extends AbstractWriter

This class represents a writer for HTML documents.

Constructors

HTMLWriter(Writer w, HTMLDocument doc)
HTMLWriter(Writer w, HTMLDocument doc, int pos, int len)

Methods

protected void	**closeOutUnwantedEmbeddedTags**(AttributeSet attr)
protected void	**comment**(Element elem)
protected void	**emptyTag**(Element elem)
protected void	**endTag**(Element elem)
protected boolean	**isBlockTag**(AttributeSet attr)
protected boolean	**matchNameAttribute**(AttributeSet attr, HTML.Tag tag)
protected void	**selectContent**(AttributeSet attr)
protected void	**startTag**(Element elem)
protected boolean	**synthesizedElement**(Element elem)
protected void	**text**(Element elem)
protected void	**textAreaContent**(AttributeSet attr)
void	**write**()
protected void	**write**(String content)
protected void	**writeAttributes**(AttributeSet attr)
protected void	**writeEmbeddedTags**(AttributeSet attr)
protected void	**writeOption**(Option option)

Class InlineView

```
java.lang.Object
   |
   +--javax.swing.text.View
          |
          +--javax.swing.text.LabelView
                 |
                 +--javax.swing.text.html.InlineView
```

public class **InlineView**
          extends LabelView

This class represents an object that displays inline element styles based on CSS attributes.

Constructor

InlineView(Element elem)

Methods

AttributeSet	**getAttributes**()
protected StyleSheet	**getStyleSheet**()
boolean	**isVisible**()
protected void	**setPropertiesFromAttributes**()

Class ListView

```
java.lang.Object
   |
   +--javax.swing.text.View
          |
```

```
              +--javax.swing.text.CompositeView
                    |
                    +--javax.swing.text.BoxView
                          |
                          +--javax.swing.text.html.BlockView
                                |
                                +--javax.swing.text.html.ListView
```

public class **ListView**
        extends BlockView

This class represents a view object that displays an HTML list.

Constructor
ListView(Element elem)

Methods
float	**getAlignment**(int axis)
void	**paint**(Graphics g, Shape allocation)
protected void	**paintChild**(Graphics g, Rectangle alloc, int index)

Class MinimalHTMLWriter

```
  java.lang.Object
      |
      +--javax.swing.text.AbstractWriter
              |
              +--javax.swing.text.html.MinimalHTMLWriter
```

public class **MinimalHTMLWriter**
        extends AbstractWriter

This class represents a minimal HTML writer.

Constructors
MinimalHTMLWriter(Writer w, StyledDocument doc)
MinimalHTMLWriter(Writer w, StyledDocument doc, int pos, int len)

Class ObjectView

```
  java.lang.Object
      |
      +--javax.swing.text.View
              |
              +--javax.swing.text.ComponentView
                      |
                      +--javax.swing.text.html.ObjectView
```

public class **ObjectView**
        extends ComponentView

This class represents a component view decorator.

Constructor
ObjectView(Element elem)

Method
```
protected Component    createComponent()
```

Class Option
```
java.lang.Object
  |
  +--javax.swing.text.html.Option
```
public class **Option**
        extends Object

This class represents option elements.

Constructor
```
Option(AttributeSet attr)
```

Methods
```
AttributeSet      getAttributes()
String            getLabel()
String            getValue()
boolean           isSelected()
void              setLabel(String label)
protected void    setSelection(boolean state)
String            toString()
```

Class ParagraphView
```
java.lang.Object
  |
  +--javax.swing.text.View
       |
       +--javax.swing.text.CompositeView
            |
            +--javax.swing.text.BoxView
                 |
                 +--javax.swing.text.ParagraphView
                      |
                      +--javax.swing.text.html.ParagraphView
```
public class **ParagraphView**
        extends ParagraphView

This class represents a view of Paragraph by using CSS attributes.

Constructor
```
ParagraphView(Element elem)
```

Methods
```
protected SizeRequirements    calculateMinorAxisRequirements(int axis,
                              SizeRequirements r)
void                          changedUpdate(DocumentEvent e, Shape a,
                              ViewFactory f)
```

AttributeSet	**getAttributes**()
float	**getMaximumSpan**(int axis)
float	**getMinimumSpan**(int axis)
float	**getPreferredSpan**(int axis)
protected StyleSheet	**getStyleSheet**()
boolean	**isVisible**()
void	**setParent**(View parent)
protected void	**setPropertiesFromAttributes**()

Class StyleSheet

```
java.lang.Object
   |
   +--javax.swing.text.StyleContext
          |
          +--javax.swing.text.html.StyleSheet
```

public class **StyleSheet**
        extends StyleContext

This class represents a style sheet that is used to translate an HTML document into a visual representation.

Inner Classes

static class	**StyleSheet.BoxPainter**
static class	**StyleSheet.ListPainter**

Constructor

StyleSheet()

Methods

void	**addRule**(String rule)
Color	**getBackground**(AttributeSet a)
StyleSheet.BoxPainter	**getBoxPainter**(AttributeSet a)
AttributeSet	**getDeclaration**(String decl)
Font	**getFont**(AttributeSet a)
Color	**getForeground**(AttributeSet a)
static int	**getIndexOfSize**(float pt)
StyleSheet.ListPainter	**getListPainter**(AttributeSet a)
float	**getPointSize**(int index)
float	**getPointSize**(String size)
Style	**getRule**(HTML.Tag t, Element e)
Style	**getRule**(String selector)
AttributeSet	**getViewAttributes**(View v)
void	**loadRules**(Reader in, URL ref)
void	**setBaseFontSize**(int sz)
void	**setBaseFontSize**(String size)
Color	**stringToColor**(String str)
AttributeSet	**translateHTMLToCSS**(AttributeSet htmlAttrSet)

Class StyleSheet.BoxPainter

```
java.lang.Object
   |
   +--javax.swing.text.html.StyleSheet.BoxPainter
```

public static class **StyleSheet.BoxPainter**
                                  extends Object
                                  implements Serializable

This inner class represents an object that handles CSS formatting of HTML documents.

Methods

float   **getInset**(int side, View v)
void   **paint**(Graphics g, float x, float y, float w, float h, View v)

Class StyleSheet.ListPainter

```
java.lang.Object
   |
   +--javax.swing.text.html.StyleSheet.ListPainter
```

public static class **StyleSheet.ListPainter**
                                  extends Object
                                  implements Serializable

This class also represents an object to handle CSS formatting of HTML documents.

Methods

void   **paint**(Graphics g, float x, float y, float w, float h, View v, int item)

javax.swing.tree

Interface MutableTreeNode

public abstract interface **MutableTreeNode**
                            extends TreeNode

This interface defines the design level abstraction for a mutable or changeable tree node. A mutable tree node can be subjected to the addition or removal of nodes.

Methods

void   **insert**(MutableTreeNode child, int index)
void   **remove**(int index)
void   **remove**(MutableTreeNode node)
void   **removeFromParent**()
void   **setParent**(MutableTreeNode newParent)
void   **setUserObject**(Object object)

Interface RowMapper

public abstract interface **RowMapper**

This interface describes a mapper that translates the tree path data into the rows of the tree.

Method

```
int[]     getRowsForPaths(TreePath[] path)
```

Interface TreeCellEditor

```
public abstract interface TreeCellEditor
                         extends CellEditor
```

This interface describes the cell editor for a tree. You need to define the attributes of the editor component in the supported method that returns the component.

Method

```
Component   getTreeCellEditorComponent(JTree tree, Object value,
              boolean isSelected, boolean expanded, boolean leaf, int row)
```

Interface TreeCellRenderer

```
public abstract interface TreeCellRenderer
```

This interface describes the cell renderer of a tree node. You need to define the attributes of the renderer component in the supported method that returns the component.

Method

```
Component   getTreeCellRendererComponent(JTree tree, Object value,
              boolean selected, boolean expanded, boolean leaf, int row,
              boolean hasFocus)
```

Interface TreeModel

```
public abstract interface TreeModel
```

This interface describes the data model for a tree object. The interface is useful when building custom tree models.

Methods

```
void        addTreeModelListener(TreeModelListener l)
Object      getChild(Object parent, int index)
int         getChildCount(Object parent)
int         getIndexOfChild(Object parent, Object child)
Object      getRoot()
boolean     isLeaf(Object node)
void        removeTreeModelListener(TreeModelListener l)
void        valueForPathChanged(TreePath path, Object newValue)
```

Interface TreeNode

```
public abstract interface TreeNode
```

This interface describes the tree node.

Methods

```
Enumeration   children()
boolean       getAllowsChildren()
TreeNode      getChildAt(int childIndex)
```

```
int          getChildCount()
int          getIndex(TreeNode node)
TreeNode     getParent()
boolean      isLeaf()
```

Interface TreeSelectionModel

```
public abstract interface TreeSelectionModel
```

This interface describes the model to hold the selection data of a tree.

Fields

```
static int   CONTIGUOUS_TREE_SELECTION
static int   DISCONTIGUOUS_TREE_SELECTION
static int   SINGLE_TREE_SELECTION
```

Methods

```
void         addPropertyChangeListener(PropertyChangeListener listener)
void         addSelectionPath(TreePath path)
void         addSelectionPaths(TreePath[] paths)
void         addTreeSelectionListener(TreeSelectionListener x)
void         clearSelection()
TreePath     getLeadSelectionPath()
int          getLeadSelectionRow()
int          getMaxSelectionRow()
int          getMinSelectionRow()
RowMapper    getRowMapper()
int          getSelectionCount()
int          getSelectionMode()
TreePath     getSelectionPath()
TreePath[]   getSelectionPaths()
int[]        getSelectionRows()
boolean      isPathSelected(TreePath path)
boolean      isRowSelected(int row)
boolean      isSelectionEmpty()
void         removePropertyChangeListener(PropertyChangeListener listener)
void         removeSelectionPath(TreePath path)
void         removeSelectionPaths(TreePath[] paths)
void         removeTreeSelectionListener(TreeSelectionListener x)
void         resetRowSelection()
void         setRowMapper(RowMapper newMapper)
void         setSelectionMode(int mode)
void         setSelectionPath(TreePath path)
void         setSelectionPaths(TreePath[] paths)
```

Class AbstractLayoutCache

```
java.lang.Object
   |
   +--javax.swing.tree.AbstractLayoutCache
```

```
public abstract class AbstractLayoutCache
```

```
extends Object
implements RowMapper
```

This class represents an abstract cache for the tree arrangement such as node dimensions, height of rows, tree model, and tree selection model.

Inner Class

static class   **AbstractLayoutCache.NodeDimensions**

Fields

protected AbstractLayoutCache.NodeDimensions	**nodeDimensions**
protected boolean	**rootVisible**
protected int	**rowHeight**
protected TreeModel	**treeModel**
protected TreeSelectionModel	**treeSelectionModel**

Constructor

AbstractLayoutCache()

Methods

abstract Rectangle	**getBounds**(TreePath path, Rectangle placeIn)
abstract boolean	**getExpandedState**(TreePath path)
TreeModel	**getModel**()
AbstractLayoutCache.NodeDimensions	**getNodeDimensions**()
protected	**Rectangle** getNodeDimensions(Object value, int row, int depth, boolean expanded, Rectangle placeIn)
abstract TreePath	**getPathClosestTo**(int x, int y)
abstract TreePath	**getPathForRow**(int row)
int	**getPreferredHeight**()
int	**getPreferredWidth**(Rectangle bounds)
abstract int	**getRowCount**()
abstract int	**getRowForPath**(TreePath path)
int	**getRowHeight**()
int[]	**getRowsForPaths**(TreePath[] paths)
TreeSelectionModel	**getSelectionModel**()
abstract int	**getVisibleChildCount**(TreePath path)
abstract Enumeration	**getVisiblePathsFrom**(TreePath path)
abstract void	**invalidatePathBounds**(TreePath path)
abstract void	**invalidateSizes**()
abstract boolean	**isExpanded**(TreePath path)
protected boolean	**isFixedRowHeight**()
boolean	**isRootVisible**()
abstract void	**setExpandedState**(TreePath path, boolean isExpanded)
void	**setModel**(TreeModel newModel)
void	**setNodeDimensions** (AbstractLayoutCache.NodeDimensions nd)
void	**setRootVisible**(boolean rootVisible)

void	**setRowHeight**(int rowHeight)
void	**setSelectionModel**(TreeSelectionModel newLSM)
abstract void	**treeNodesChanged**(TreeModelEvent e)
abstract void	**treeNodesInserted**(TreeModelEvent e)
abstract void	**treeNodesRemoved**(TreeModelEvent e)
abstract void	**treeStructureChanged**(TreeModelEvent e)

Class AbstractLayoutCache.NodeDimensions

```
java.lang.Object
   |
   +--javax.swing.tree.AbstractLayoutCache.NodeDimensions
```

public abstract static class **AbstractLayoutCache.NodeDimensions**
                         extends Object

This is an inner class that is used by the abstract cache for tree arrangement.

Constructor
AbstractLayoutCache.NodeDimensions()

Method

abstract Rectangle	**getNodeDimensions**(Object value, int row, int depth, boolean expanded, Rectangle bounds)

Class DefaultMutableTreeNode

```
java.lang.Object
   |
   +--javax.swing.tree.DefaultMutableTreeNode
```

public class **DefaultMutableTreeNode**
           extends Object
           implements Cloneable, MutableTreeNode, Serializable

This class represents a default implementation of the mutable tree node.

Fields

protected boolean	**allowsChildren**
protected Vector	**children**
static Enumeration	**EMPTY_ENUMERATION**
protected MutableTreeNode	**parent**
protected Object	**userObject**

Constructors
DefaultMutableTreeNode()
DefaultMutableTreeNode(Object userObject)
DefaultMutableTreeNode(Object userObject, boolean allowsChildren)

Methods

void	**add**(MutableTreeNode newChild)
Enumeration	**breadthFirstEnumeration**()
Enumeration	**children**()
Object	**clone**()

```
Enumeration              depthFirstEnumeration()
boolean                  getAllowsChildren()
TreeNode                 getChildAfter(TreeNode aChild)
TreeNode                 getChildAt(int index)
TreeNode                 getChildBefore(TreeNode aChild)
int                      getChildCount()
int                      getDepth()
TreeNode                 getFirstChild()
DefaultMutableTreeNode   getFirstLeaf()
int                      getIndex(TreeNode aChild)
TreeNode                 getLastChild()
DefaultMutableTreeNode   getLastLeaf()
int                      getLeafCount()
int                      getLevel()
DefaultMutableTreeNode   getNextLeaf()
DefaultMutableTreeNode   getNextNode()
DefaultMutableTreeNode   getNextSibling()
TreeNode                 getParent()
TreeNode[]               getPath()
protected TreeNode[]     getPathToRoot(TreeNode aNode, int depth)
DefaultMutableTreeNode   getPreviousLeaf()
DefaultMutableTreeNode   getPreviousNode()
DefaultMutableTreeNode   getPreviousSibling()
TreeNode                 getRoot()
TreeNode                 getSharedAncestor(DefaultMutableTreeNode aNode)
int                      getSiblingCount()
Object                   getUserObject()
Object[]                 getUserObjectPath()
void                     insert(MutableTreeNode newChild, int childIndex)
boolean                  isLeaf()
boolean                  isNodeAncestor(TreeNode anotherNode)
boolean                  isNodeChild(TreeNode aNode)
boolean                  isNodeDescendant(DefaultMutableTreeNode anotherNode)
boolean                  isNodeRelated(DefaultMutableTreeNode aNode)
boolean                  isNodeSibling(TreeNode anotherNode)
boolean                  isRoot()
Enumeration              pathFromAncestorEnumeration(TreeNode ancestor)
Enumeration              postorderEnumeration()
Enumeration              preorderEnumeration()
void                     remove(int childIndex)
void                     remove(MutableTreeNode aChild)
void                     removeAllChildren()
void                     removeFromParent()
void                     setAllowsChildren(boolean allows)
void                     setParent(MutableTreeNode newParent)
void                     setUserObject(Object userObject)
String                   toString()
```

Class DefaultTreeCellEditor

```
java.lang.Object
  |
  +--javax.swing.tree.DefaultTreeCellEditor
```

public class **DefaultTreeCellEditor**
   extends Object
   implements ActionListener, TreeCellEditor, TreeSelectionListener

This class represents the default editor component to be used in a tree cell.

Inner Classes

class	**DefaultTreeCellEditor.DefaultTextField**
class	**DefaultTreeCellEditor.EditorContainer**

Fields

protected Color	**borderSelectionColor**
protected boolean	**canEdit**
protected Component	**editingComponent**
protected Container	**editingContainer**
protected Icon	**editingIcon**
protected Font	**font**
protected TreePath	**lastPath**
protected int	**lastRow**
protected int	**offset**
protected TreeCellEditor	**realEditor**
protected DefaultTreeCellRenderer	**renderer**
protected Timer	**timer**
protected JTree	**tree**

Constructors

DefaultTreeCellEditor(JTree tree, DefaultTreeCellRenderer renderer)
DefaultTreeCellEditor(JTree tree, DefaultTreeCellRenderer renderer,
TreeCellEditor editor)

Methods

void	**actionPerformed**(ActionEvent e)
void	**addCellEditorListener**(CellEditorListener l)
void	**cancelCellEditing**()
protected boolean	**canEditImmediately**(EventObject event)
protected Container	**createContainer**()
protected TreeCellEditor	**createTreeCellEditor**()
protected void	**determineOffset**(JTree tree, Object value, boolean isSelected, boolean expanded, boolean leaf, int row)
Color	**getBorderSelectionColor**()
Object	**getCellEditorValue**()
Font	**getFont**()
Component	**getTreeCellEditorComponent**(JTree tree, Object value, boolean isSelected, boolean expanded, boolean leaf, int row)

```
protected boolean        inHitRegion(int x, int y)
boolean                  isCellEditable(EventObject event)
protected void           prepareForEditing()
void                     removeCellEditorListener(CellEditorListener l)
void                     setBorderSelectionColor(Color newColor)
void                     setFont(Font font)
protected void           setTree(JTree newTree)
boolean                  shouldSelectCell(EventObject event)
protected boolean        shouldStartEditingTimer(EventObject event)
protected void           startEditingTimer()
boolean                  stopCellEditing()
```

Class DefaultTreeCellRenderer

```
java.lang.Object
   |
   +--java.awt.Component
           |
           +--java.awt.Container
                   |
                   +--javax.swing.JComponent
                           |
                           +--javax.swing.JLabel
                                   |
                                   +--javax.swing.tree.DefaultTreeCellRenderer
```

```
public class DefaultTreeCellRenderer
            extends JLabel
            implements TreeCellRenderer
```

This class represents the default cell renderer for a Swing tree.

Fields

```
protected Color          backgroundNonSelectionColor
protected Color          backgroundSelectionColor
protected Color          borderSelectionColor
protected Icon           closedIcon
protected Icon           leafIcon
protected Icon           openIcon
protected boolean        selected
protected Color          textNonSelectionColor
protected Color          textSelectionColor
```

Constructor

```
DefaultTreeCellRenderer()
```

Methods

```
Color       getBackgroundNonSelectionColor()
Color       getBackgroundSelectionColor()
Color       getBorderSelectionColor()
Icon        getClosedIcon()
```

Icon	getDefaultClosedIcon()
Icon	getDefaultLeafIcon()
Icon	getDefaultOpenIcon()
Icon	getLeafIcon()
Icon	getOpenIcon()
Dimension	getPreferredSize()
Color	getTextNonSelectionColor()
Color	getTextSelectionColor()
Component	getTreeCellRendererComponent(JTree tree, Object value, boolean sel, boolean expanded, boolean leaf, int row, boolean hasFocus)
void	paint(Graphics g)
void	setBackground(Color color)
void	setBackgroundNonSelectionColor(Color newColor)
void	setBackgroundSelectionColor(Color newColor)
void	setBorderSelectionColor(Color newColor)
void	setClosedIcon(Icon newIcon)
void	setFont(Font font)
void	setLeafIcon(Icon newIcon)
void	setOpenIcon(Icon newIcon)
void	setTextNonSelectionColor(Color newColor)
void	setTextSelectionColor(Color newColor)

Class DefaultTreeModel

```
java.lang.Object
   |
   +--javax.swing.tree.DefaultTreeModel
```

public class **DefaultTreeModel**
        extends Object
        implements Serializable, TreeModel

This class represents the default data model for a tree.

Fields

protected boolean	asksAllowsChildren
protected EventListenerList	listenerList
protected TreeNode	root

Constructors

DefaultTreeModel(TreeNode root)
DefaultTreeModel(TreeNode root, boolean asksAllowsChildren)

Methods

void	addTreeModelListener(TreeModelListener l)
boolean	asksAllowsChildren()
protected void	fireTreeNodesChanged(Object source, Object[] path, int[] childIndices, Object[] children)
protected void	fireTreeNodesInserted(Object source, Object[] path, int[] childIndices, Object[] children)
protected void	fireTreeNodesRemoved(Object source, Object[] path, int[] childIndices, Object[] children)

protected void	**fireTreeStructureChanged**(Object source, Object[] path, int[] childIndices, Object[] children)
Object	**getChild**(Object parent, int index)
int	**getChildCount**(Object parent)
int	**getIndexOfChild**(Object parent, Object child)
TreeNode[]	**getPathToRoot**(TreeNode aNode)
protected TreeNode[]	**getPathToRoot**(TreeNode aNode, int depth)
Object	**getRoot**()
void	**insertNodeInto**(MutableTreeNode newChild, MutableTreeNode parent, int index)
boolean	**isLeaf**(Object node)
void	**nodeChanged**(TreeNode node)
void	**nodesChanged**(TreeNode node, int[] childIndices)
void	**nodeStructureChanged**(TreeNode node)
void	**nodesWereInserted**(TreeNode node, int[] childIndices)
void	**nodesWereRemoved**(TreeNode node, int[] childIndices, Object[] removedChildren)
void	**reload**()
void	**reload**(TreeNode node)
void	**removeNodeFromParent**(MutableTreeNode node)
void	**removeTreeModelListener**(TreeModelListener l)
void	**setAsksAllowsChildren**(boolean newValue)
void	**setRoot**(TreeNode root)
void	**valueForPathChanged**(TreePath path, Object newValue)

Class DefaultTreeSelectionModel

```
java.lang.Object
   |
   +--javax.swing.tree.DefaultTreeSelectionModel
```

public class **DefaultTreeSelectionModel**
        extends Object
        implements Cloneable, Serializable, TreeSelectionModel

This class represents the default tree selection model.

Fields

protected SwingPropertyChangeSupport	**changeSupport**
protected int	**leadIndex**
protected TreePath	**leadPath**
protected int	**leadRow**
protected EventListenerList	**listenerList**
protected DefaultListSelectionModel	**listSelectionModel**
protected RowMapper	**rowMapper**
protected TreePath[]	**selection**
static String	**SELECTION_MODE_PROPERTY**
protected int	**selectionMode**

Constructor

DefaultTreeSelectionModel()

Methods

void	**addPropertyChangeListener**(PropertyChangeListener listener)
void	**addSelectionPath**(TreePath path)
void	**addSelectionPaths**(TreePath[] paths)
void	**addTreeSelectionListener**(TreeSelectionListener x)
protected boolean	**arePathsContiguous**(TreePath[] paths)
protected boolean	**canPathsBeAdded**(TreePath[] paths)
protected boolean	**canPathsBeRemoved**(TreePath[] paths)
void	**clearSelection**()
Object	**clone**()
protected void	**fireValueChanged**(TreeSelectionEvent e)
TreePath	**getLeadSelectionPath**()
int	**getLeadSelectionRow**()
int	**getMaxSelectionRow**()
int	**getMinSelectionRow**()
RowMapper	**getRowMapper**()
int	**getSelectionCount**()
int	**getSelectionMode**()
TreePath	**getSelectionPath**()
TreePath[]	**getSelectionPaths**()
int[]	**getSelectionRows**()
protected void	**insureRowContinuity**()
protected void	**insureUniqueness**()
boolean	**isPathSelected**(TreePath path)
boolean	**isRowSelected**(int row)
boolean	**isSelectionEmpty**()
protected void	**notifyPathChange**(Vector changedPaths, TreePath oldLeadSelection)
void	**removePropertyChangeListener**(PropertyChangeListener listener)
void	**removeSelectionPath**(TreePath path)
void	**removeSelectionPaths**(TreePath[] paths)
void	**removeTreeSelectionListener**(TreeSelectionListener x)
void	**resetRowSelection**()
void	**setRowMapper**(RowMapper newMapper)
void	**setSelectionMode**(int mode)
void	**setSelectionPath**(TreePath path)
void	**setSelectionPaths**(TreePath[] pPaths)
String	**toString**()
protected void	**updateLeadIndex**()

Class FixedHeightLayoutCache

```
java.lang.Object
  |
  +--javax.swing.tree.AbstractLayoutCache
        |
        +--javax.swing.tree.FixedHeightLayoutCache
```

```
public class FixedHeightLayoutCache
            extends AbstractLayoutCache
```

This class represents a layout cache that is of fixed size.

Constructor
```
FixedHeightLayoutCache()
```

Methods

Rectangle	**getBounds**(TreePath path, Rectangle placeIn)
boolean	**getExpandedState**(TreePath path)
TreePath	**getPathClosestTo**(int x, int y)
TreePath	**getPathForRow**(int row)
int	**getRowCount**()
int	**getRowForPath**(TreePath path)
int	**getVisibleChildCount**(TreePath path)
Enumeration	**getVisiblePathsFrom**(TreePath path)
void	**invalidatePathBounds**(TreePath path)
void	**invalidateSizes**()
boolean	**isExpanded**(TreePath path)
void	**setExpandedState**(TreePath path, boolean isExpanded)
void	**setModel**(TreeModel newModel)
void	**setRootVisible**(boolean rootVisible)
void	**setRowHeight**(int rowHeight)
void	**treeNodesChanged**(TreeModelEvent e)
void	**treeNodesInserted**(TreeModelEvent e)
void	**treeNodesRemoved**(TreeModelEvent e)
void	**treeStructureChanged**(TreeModelEvent e)

Class TreePath

```
java.lang.Object
   |
   +--javax.swing.tree.TreePath
```

```
public class TreePath
            extends Object
            implements Serializable
```

This class represents the path to a tree node.

Constructors

protected	**TreePath**()
	TreePath(Object singlePath)
	TreePath(Object[] path)
protected	**TreePath**(Object[] path, int length)
protected	**TreePath**(TreePath parent, Object lastElement)

Methods

boolean	**equals**(Object o)
Object	**getLastPathComponent**()

```
TreePath     getParentPath()
Object[]     getPath()
Object       getPathComponent(int element)
int          getPathCount()
int          hashCode()
boolean      isDescendant(TreePath aTreePath)
TreePath     pathByAddingChild(Object child)
String       toString()
```

Class VariableHeightLayoutCache

```
java.lang.Object
    |
    +--javax.swing.tree.AbstractLayoutCache
          |
          +--javax.swing.tree.VariableHeightLayoutCache
```

public class **VariableHeightLayoutCache**
        extends AbstractLayoutCache

This class represents a layout cache that is of variable size.

Constructor
VariableHeightLayoutCache()

Methods
```
Rectangle      getBounds(TreePath path, Rectangle placeIn)
boolean        getExpandedState(TreePath path)
TreePath       getPathClosestTo(int x, int y)
TreePath       getPathForRow(int row)
int            getPreferredWidth(Rectangle bounds)
int            getRowCount()
int            getRowForPath(TreePath path)
int            getVisibleChildCount(TreePath path)
Enumeration    getVisiblePathsFrom(TreePath path)
void           invalidatePathBounds(TreePath path)
void           invalidateSizes()
boolean        isExpanded(TreePath path)
void           setExpandedState(TreePath path, boolean isExpanded)
void           setModel(TreeModel newModel)
void           setNodeDimensions(AbstractLayoutCache.NodeDimensions nd)
void           setRootVisible(boolean rootVisible)
void           setRowHeight(int rowHeight)
void           treeNodesChanged(TreeModelEvent e)
void           treeNodesInserted(TreeModelEvent e)
void           treeNodesRemoved(TreeModelEvent e)
void           treeStructureChanged(TreeModelEvent e)
```

Class ExpandVetoException

```
java.lang.Object
    |
```

```
        +--java.lang.Throwable
            ¦
            +--java.lang.Exception
                ¦
                +--javax.swing.tree.ExpandVetoException
public class ExpandVetoException
            extends Exception
```

This class represents an exception that is thrown whenever there is an abnormal or unusual condition while expanding or collapsing a tree path.

Field
```
protected TreeExpansionEvent event
```

Constructors
```
ExpandVetoException(TreeExpansionEvent event)
ExpandVetoException(TreeExpansionEvent event, String message)
```

javax.swing.undo

Interface StateEditable
```
public abstract interface StateEditable
```

This interface describes the objects to have the undoable or redoable edit states.

Field
```
static String    RCSID
```

Methods
```
void    restoreState(Hashtable state)
void    storeState(Hashtable state)
```

Interface UndoableEdit
```
public abstract interface UndoableEdit
```

This interface describes an undoable edit operation and is implemented by an edit object that can be undoable.

Methods
```
boolean    addEdit(UndoableEdit anEdit)
boolean    canRedo()
boolean    canUndo()
void       die()
String     getPresentationName()
String     getRedoPresentationName()
String     getUndoPresentationName()
boolean    isSignificant()
void       redo()
boolean    replaceEdit(UndoableEdit anEdit)
void       undo()
```

Class AbstractUndoableEdit

```
java.lang.Object
  |
  +--javax.swing.undo.AbstractUndoableEdit
```

public class **AbstractUndoableEdit**
        extends Object
        implements UndoableEdit, Serializable

This abstract class represents an undoable edit by implementing the methods that return Boolean values in the corresponding interface.

Fields

protected static String   **RedoName**
protected static String   **UndoName**

Constructor

AbstractUndoableEdit()

Methods

boolean	**addEdit**(UndoableEdit anEdit)
boolean	**canRedo**()
boolean	**canUndo**()
void	**die**()
String	**getPresentationName**()
String	**getRedoPresentationName**()
String	**getUndoPresentationName**()
boolean	**isSignificant**()
void	**redo**()
boolean	**replaceEdit**(UndoableEdit anEdit)
String	**toString**()
void	**undo**()

Class CompoundEdit

```
java.lang.Object
  |
  +--javax.swing.undo.AbstractUndoableEdit
        |
        +--javax.swing.undo.CompoundEdit
```

public class **CompoundEdit**
        extends AbstractUndoableEdit

This class represents an undoable compound edit, which is basically a collection of multiple undoable edits.

Field

protected Vector   **edits**

Constructor

CompoundEdit()

Methods

boolean	**addEdit**(UndoableEdit anEdit)
boolean	**canRedo**()
boolean	**canUndo**()
void	**die**()
void	**end**()
String	**getPresentationName**()
String	**getRedoPresentationName**()
String	**getUndoPresentationName**()
boolean	**isInProgress**()
boolean	**isSignificant**()
protected UndoableEdit	**lastEdit**()
void	**redo**()
String	**toString**()
void	**undo**()

Class StateEdit

```
java.lang.Object
   |
   +--javax.swing.undo.AbstractUndoableEdit
          |
          +--javax.swing.undo.StateEdit
```

public class **StateEdit**
        extends AbstractUndoableEdit

This class represents a generic edit for objects that undergo a change in state.

Fields

protected StateEditable	**object**
protected Hashtable	**postState**
protected Hashtable	**preState**
protected static String	**RCSID**
protected String	**undoRedoName**

Constructors

StateEdit(StateEditable anObject)
StateEdit(StateEditable anObject, String name)

Methods

void	**end**()
String	**getPresentationName**()
protected void	**init**(StateEditable anObject, String name)
void	**redo**()
protected void	**removeRedundantState**()
void	**undo**()

Class UndoableEditSupport

```
java.lang.Object
   |
   +--javax.swing.undo.UndoableEditSupport
```

public class **UndoableEditSupport**
         extends Object

This class represents an undoable edit support, which is used for managing UndoableEdit listeners.

Fields

protected CompoundEdit   **compoundEdit**
protected Vector   **listeners**
protected Object   **realSource**
protected int   **updateLevel**

Constructors
UndoableEditSupport()
UndoableEditSupport(Object r)

Methods

protected void   **postEdit**(UndoableEdit e)
void   **addUndoableEditListener**(UndoableEditListener l)
void   **beginUpdate**()
protected CompoundEdit   **createCompoundEdit**()
void   **endUpdate**()
int   **getUpdateLevel**()
void   **postEdit**(UndoableEdit e)
void   **removeUndoableEditListener**(UndoableEditListener l)
String   **toString**()

Class UndoManager

```
java.lang.Object
   |
   +--javax.swing.undo.AbstractUndoableEdit
        |
        +--javax.swing.undo.CompoundEdit
             |
             +--javax.swing.undo.UndoManager
```

public class **UndoManager**
         extends CompoundEdit
         implements UndoableEditListener

This class represents an undo manager, which is a subclass of CompoundEdit.

Constructor
UndoManager()

Methods

boolean	**addEdit**(UndoableEdit anEdit)
boolean	**canRedo**()
boolean	**canUndo**()
boolean	**canUndoOrRedo**()
void	**discardAllEdits**()
protected UndoableEdit	**editToBeRedone**()
protected UndoableEdit	**editToBeUndone**()
void	**end**()
int	**getLimit**()
String	**getRedoPresentationName**()
String	**getUndoOrRedoPresentationName**()
String	**getUndoPresentationName**()
void	**redo**()
protected void	**redoTo**(UndoableEdit edit)
void	**setLimit**(int l)
String	**toString**()
protected void	**trimEdits**(int from, int to)
protected void	**trimForLimit**()
void	**undo**()
void	**undoableEditHappened**(UndoableEditEvent e)
void	**undoOrRedo**()
protected void	**undoTo**(UndoableEdit edit)

Class CannotRedoException

```
java.lang.Object
   |
   +--java.lang.Throwable
          |
          +--java.lang.Exception
                 |
                 +--java.lang.RuntimeException
                        |
                        +--javax.swing.undo.CannotRedoException
```

public class **CannotRedoException**
             extends RuntimeException

This class represents an exception that is thrown when a redo operation cannot be performed on an undoable edit.

Constructor

CannotRedoException()

Class CannotUndoException

```
java.lang.Object
   |
   +--java.lang.Throwable
         |
         +--java.lang.Exception
               |
               +--java.lang.RuntimeException
                     |
                     +--javax.swing.undo.CannotUndoException
```

public class **CannotUndoException**
        extends RuntimeException

This class represents an exception that is thrown when an undo operation cannot be performed on an undoable edit.

Constructor
CannotUndoException()

APPENDIX B

AWT Event Classes Quick Reference

This appendix contains the quick reference material on AWT event classes and event listeners. These interfaces or classes are used by some of the Swing components. For example, Swing buttons also fire the events of type ActionEvent. The corresponding listener of type ActionListener is registered with the event source.

Package Summary

The java.awt.event package contains interfaces and classes for dealing with different types of events fired by AWT and Swing components.

Interfaces

```
ActionListener
AdjustmentListener
AWTEventListener
ComponentListener
ContainerListener
FocusListener
InputMethodListener
ItemListener
KeyListener
MouseListener
MouseMotionListener
TextListener
WindowListener
```

Classes

ActionEvent

AdjustmentEvent

ComponentAdapter

ComponentEvent

ContainerAdapter

ContainerEvent

FocusAdapter

FocusEvent

InputEvent

InputMethodEvent

InvocationEvent

ItemEvent

KeyAdapter

KeyEvent

MouseAdapter

MouseEvent

MouseMotionAdapter

PaintEvent

TextEvent

WindowAdapter

WindowEvent

Interface and Class Details

Interface ActionListener

public abstract interface **ActionListener**
                        extends EventListener

This interface describes an action listener. The implementing class is capable of receiving the events of type ActionEvent.

Method

void   **actionPerformed**(ActionEvent e)

Interface AdjustmentListener

public abstract interface **AdjustmentListener**
                        extends EventListener

This interface describes an adjustment listener. The implementing class is capable of receiving the events of type AdjustmentEvent.

Method

void   **adjustmentValueChanged**(AdjustmentEvent e)

Interface AWTEventListener

public abstract interface **AWTEventListener**
                        extends EventListener

This interface describes an object that is capable of monitoring AWT events. The objects of the implementation class are capable of receiving events of type AWTEvent and are registered with the Toolkit by using the method addAWTEventListener(). Normally you do not have to use this interface.

Method

void   **eventDispatched**(AWTEvent event)

Interface ComponentListener

```
public abstract interface ComponentListener
                extends EventListener
```

This interface describes a listener that is capable of receiving component events. These events notify the listener about the moving, resizing, showing, and hiding of components in a layout.

Methods

void	**componentHidden**(ComponentEvent e)
void	**componentMoved**(ComponentEvent e)
void	**componentResized**(ComponentEvent e)
void	**componentShown**(ComponentEvent e)

Interface ContainerListener

```
public abstract interface ContainerListener
                extends EventListener
```

This interface describes a listener object that is capable of receiving container events.

Methods

void	**componentAdded**(ContainerEvent e)
void	**componentRemoved**(ContainerEvent e)

Interface FocusListener

```
public abstract interface FocusListener
                extends EventListener
```

This interface describes a listener object that is capable of receiving focus events.

Methods

void	**focusGained**(FocusEvent e)
void	**focusLost**(FocusEvent e)

Interface InputMethodListener

```
public abstract interface InputMethodListener
                extends EventListener
```

This interface describes a listener object that is capable of receiving input method events. The input method events are fired by text components when a caret position changes or input method text changes.

Methods

void	**caretPositionChanged**(InputMethodEvent event)
void	**inputMethodTextChanged**(InputMethodEvent event)

Interface ItemListener

```
public abstract interface ItemListener
                        extends EventListener
```

This interface describes a listener object that is capable of receiving item events.

Method

```
void                    itemStateChanged(ItemEvent e)
```

Interface KeyListener

```
public abstract interface KeyListener
                        extends EventListener
```

This interface describes a key listener that is capable of receiving events when a key is pressed, released, or typed.

Methods

```
void                    keyPressed(KeyEvent e)
void                    keyReleased(KeyEvent e)
void                    keyTyped(KeyEvent e)
```

Interface MouseListener

```
public abstract interface MouseListener
                        extends EventListener
```

This interface describes a listener capable of receiving events when a mouse is pressed, released, or clicked, and also when a mouse enters or exits a component.

Methods

```
void                    mouseClicked(MouseEvent e)
void                    mouseEntered(MouseEvent e)
void                    mouseExited(MouseEvent e)
void                    mousePressed(MouseEvent e)
void                    mouseReleased(MouseEvent e)
```

Interface MouseMotionListener

```
public abstract interface MouseMotionListener
                        extends EventListener
```

This interface describes a listener that is capable of receiving mouse motion events.

Methods

```
void                    mouseDragged(MouseEvent e)
void                    mouseMoved(MouseEvent e)
```

Interface TextListener

```
public abstract interface TextListener
                    extends EventListener
```

This interface describes the listener class that is capable of receiving events when a text value changes in a component.

Method

```
void                    textValueChanged(TextEvent e)
```

Interface WindowListener

```
public abstract interface WindowListener
                    extends EventListener
```

This interface describes a listener object that is capable of receiving events that are fired when a window is opened, closed, iconified, deiconified, and so on.

Methods

```
void                    windowActivated(WindowEvent e)
void                    windowClosed(WindowEvent e)
void                    windowClosing(WindowEvent e)
void                    windowDeactivated(WindowEvent e)
void                    windowDeiconified(WindowEvent e)
void                    windowIconified(WindowEvent e)
void                    windowOpened(WindowEvent e)
```

Class ActionEvent

```
java.lang.Object
   |
   +—java.util.EventObject
          |
          +—java.awt.AWTEvent
                 |
                 +—java.awt.event.ActionEvent
```

```
public class ActionEvent
          extends AWTEvent
```

This class represents an action event that is fired whenever an action is performed on a component.

Fields

```
static int              ACTION_FIRST
static int              ACTION_LAST
static int              ACTION_PERFORMED
static int              ALT_MASK
static int              CTRL_MASK
```

```
static int           META_MASK
static int           SHIFT_MASK
```

Constructors

```
ActionEvent(Object source, int id, String command)
ActionEvent(Object source, int id, String command, int modifiers)
```

Methods

```
String               getActionCommand()
int                  getModifiers()
String               paramString()
```

Class AdjustmentEvent

```
java.lang.Object
  |
  + — java.util.EventObject
         |
         + — java.awt.AWTEvent
                |
                + — java.awt.event.AdjustmentEvent

public class AdjustmentEvent
            extends AWTEvent
```

This class represents an event that is fired whenever a component's adjustable value is changed.

Fields

```
static int           ADJUSTMENT_FIRST
static int           ADJUSTMENT_LAST
static int           ADJUSTMENT_VALUE_CHANGED
static int           BLOCK_DECREMENT
static int           BLOCK_INCREMENT
static int           TRACK
static int           UNIT_DECREMENT
static int           UNIT_INCREMENT
```

Constructor

```
AdjustmentEvent(Adjustable source, int id, int type, int value)
```

Methods

```
Adjustable           getAdjustable()
int                  getAdjustmentType()
int                  getValue()
String               paramString()
```

Class ComponentAdapter

```
java.lang.Object
   |
   +—java.awt.event.ComponentAdapter
```

Direct known subclasses:

```
BasicSliderUI.ComponentHandler, BasicTreeUI.ComponentHandler,
JViewport.ViewListener
```

```
public abstract class ComponentAdapter
                      extends Object
                      implements ComponentListener
```

This is an adapter class that can be subclassed to receive component events.

Constructor

ComponentAdapter()

Methods

```
void                    componentHidden(ComponentEvent e)
void                    componentMoved(ComponentEvent e)
void                    componentResized(ComponentEvent e)
void                    componentShown(ComponentEvent e)
```

Class ComponentEvent

```
java.lang.Object
   |
   +—java.util.EventObject
         |
         +—java.awt.AWTEvent
               |
               +—java.awt.event.ComponentEvent
```

```
public class ComponentEvent
            extends AWTEvent
```

This class represents a component event that is fired whenever a component is moved, resized, and so on.

Fields

```
static int              COMPONENT_FIRST
static int              COMPONENT_HIDDEN
static int              COMPONENT_LAST
static int              COMPONENT_MOVED
static int              COMPONENT_RESIZED
static int              COMPONENT_SHOWN
```

Constructor

`ComponentEvent`(Component source, int id)

Methods

Component	**getComponent**()
String	**paramString**()

Class ContainerAdapter

```
java.lang.Object
    ¦
    +—java.awt.event.ContainerAdapter
```

```
public abstract class ContainerAdapter
                 extends Object
                 implements ContainerListener
```

This class represents an adapter class that can be subclassed to receive container events.

Constructor

`ContainerAdapter`()

Methods

void	**componentAdded**(ContainerEvent e)
void	**componentRemoved**(ContainerEvent e)

Class ContainerEvent

```
java.lang.Object
    ¦
    +—java.util.EventObject
         ¦
         +—java.awt.AWTEvent
              ¦
              +—java.awt.event.ComponentEvent
                   ¦
                   +—java.awt.event.ContainerEvent
```

```
public class ContainerEvent
extends ComponentEvent
```

This class represents a container event that is fired whenever a component is added to or removed from a container.

Fields

static int	**COMPONENT_ADDED**
static int	**COMPONENT_REMOVED**
static int	**CONTAINER_FIRST**
static int	**CONTAINER_LAST**

Constructor

`ContainerEvent`(Component source, int id, Component child)

Methods

Component	`getChild`()
Container	`getContainer`()
String	`paramString`()

Class FocusAdapter

```
java.lang.Object
   |
   +— java.awt.event.FocusAdapter
```

public abstract class **FocusAdapter**
               extends Object
               implements FocusListener

This is an adapter class that can be subclassed to receive focus events.

Constructor

`FocusAdapter`()

Methods

void	`focusGained`(FocusEvent e)
void	`focusLost`(FocusEvent e)

Class FocusEvent

```
java.lang.Object
  |
  +— java.util.EventObject
       |
       +— java.awt.AWTEvent
            |
            +— java.awt.event.ComponentEvent
                 |
                 +— java.awt.event.FocusEvent
```

public class **FocusEvent**
        extends ComponentEvent

This class represents a focus event that is fired whenever a component gains or loses the keyboard focus.

Fields

static int	**FOCUS_FIRST**
static int	**FOCUS_GAINED**
static int	**FOCUS_LAST**
static int	**FOCUS_LOST**

Constructors

FocusEvent(Component source, int id)
FocusEvent(Component source, int id, boolean temporary)

Methods

boolean	**isTemporary**()
String	**paramString**()

Class InputEvent

```
java.lang.Object
   |
   +—java.util.EventObject
         |
         +—java.awt.AWTEvent
               |
               +—java.awt.event.ComponentEvent
                     |
                     +—java.awt.event.InputEvent
```

public abstract class **InputEvent**
                    extends ComponentEvent

This class represents a base class for the input events of components.

Fields

static int	**ALT_GRAPH_MASK**
static int	**ALT_MASK**
static int	**BUTTON1_MASK**
static int	**BUTTON2_MASK**
static int	**BUTTON3_MASK**
static int	**CTRL_MASK**
static int	**META_MASK**
static int	**SHIFT_MASK**

Methods

void	**consume**()
int	**getModifiers**()
long	**getWhen**()
boolean	**isAltDown**()
boolean	**isAltGraphDown**()
boolean	**isConsumed**()
boolean	**isControlDown**()
boolean	**isMetaDown**()
boolean	**isShiftDown**()

Class InputMethodEvent

```
java.lang.Object
    |
    +—java.util.EventObject
            |
            +—java.awt.AWTEvent
                    |
                    +—java.awt.event.InputMethodEvent
```

public class **InputMethodEvent**
        extends AWTEvent

This class represents an input method event that is fired whenever the text being composed undergoes a change.

Fields

static int	**CARET_POSITION_CHANGED**
static int	**INPUT_METHOD_FIRST**
static int	**INPUT_METHOD_LAST**
static int	**INPUT_METHOD_TEXT_CHANGED**

Constructors

InputMethodEvent(Component source, int id, AttributedCharacterIterator text,
        int committedCharacterCount, TextHitInfo caret,
        TextHitInfo visiblePosition)
InputMethodEvent(Component source, int id, TextHitInfo caret,
        TextHitInfo visiblePosition)

Methods

void	**consume**()
TextHitInfo	**getCaret**()
Int	**getCommittedCharacterCount**()
AttributedCharacterIterator	**getText**()
TextHitInfo	**getVisiblePosition**()
boolean	**isConsumed**()
String	**paramString**()

Class InvocationEvent

```
java.lang.Object
    |
    +—java.util.EventObject
            |
            +—java.awt.AWTEvent
                    |
                    +—java.awt.event.InvocationEvent
```

public class **InvocationEvent**
        extends AWTEvent
        implements ActiveEvent

This class represents an invocation event that is capable of invoking the run() method in a thread.

Fields

protected boolean	**catchExceptions**
static int	**INVOCATION_DEFAULT**
static int	**INVOCATION_FIRST**
static int	**INVOCATION_LAST**
protected Object	**notifier**
protected Runnable	runnable

Constructors

protected **InvocationEvent**(Object source, int id, Runnable runnable,
        Object notifier, boolean catchExceptions)

InvocationEvent(Object source, Runnable runnable)

InvocationEvent(Object source, Runnable runnable, Object notifier,
            boolean catchExceptions)

Methods

void	**dispatch**()
Exception	**getException**()
String	**paramString**()

Class ItemEvent

```
java.lang.Object
   |
   +—java.util.EventObject
        |
        +—java.awt.AWTEvent
             |
             +—java.awt.event.ItemEvent
```

public class **ItemEvent**
        extends AWTEvent

This class represents an item event that is fired by a component whenever an item is selected or deselected in an item-selectable component.

Fields

static int	**DESELECTED**
static int	**ITEM_FIRST**
static int	**ITEM_LAST**
static int	**ITEM_STATE_CHANGED**
static int	**SELECTED**

Constructor

`ItemEvent`(ItemSelectable source, int id, Object item, int stateChange)

Methods

Object	`getItem`()
ItemSelectable	`getItemSelectable`()
Int	`getStateChange`()
String	`paramString`()

Class KeyAdapter

```
java.lang.Object
   |
   +— java.awt.event.KeyAdapter
```

public abstract class **KeyAdapter**
        extends Object
        implements KeyListener

This class represents an adapter class that can be subclassed to receive events whenever the keyboard is operated.

Constructor

KeyAdapter()

Methods

void	**keyPressed**(KeyEvent e)
void	**keyReleased**(KeyEvent e)
void	**keyTyped**(KeyEvent e)

Class KeyEvent

```
java.lang.Object
   |
   +— java.util.EventObject
          |
          +— java.awt.AWTEvent
                 |
                 +— java.awt.event.ComponentEvent
                        |
                        +— java.awt.event.InputEvent
                               |
                               +— java.awt.event.KeyEvent
```

public class **KeyEvent**
    extends InputEvent

This class represents an event that is fired whenever a keystroke occurs on the keyboard.

Fields

static char	CHAR_UNDEFINED
static int	KEY_FIRST
static int	KEY_LAST
static int	KEY_PRESSED
static int	KEY_RELEASED
static int	KEY_TYPED
static int	VK_0
static int	VK_1
static int	VK_2
static int	VK_3
static int	VK_4
static int	VK_5
static int	VK_6
static int	VK_7
static int	VK_8
static int	VK_9
static int	VK_A
static int	VK_ACCEPT
static int	VK_ADD
static int	VK_AGAIN
static int	VK_ALL_CANDIDATES
static int	VK_ALPHANUMERIC
static int	VK_ALT
static int	VK_ALT_GRAPH
static int	VK_AMPERSAND
static int	VK_ASTERISK
static int	VK_AT
static int	VK_B
static int	VK_BACK_QUOTE
static int	VK_BACK_SLASH
static int	VK_BACK_SPACE
static int	VK_BRACELEFT
static int	VK_BRACERIGHT
static int	VK_C
static int	VK_CANCEL
static int	VK_CAPS_LOCK
static int	VK_CIRCUMFLEX
static int	VK_CLEAR
static int	VK_CLOSE_BRACKET
static int	VK_CODE_INPUT
static int	VK_COLON
static int	VK_COMMA
static int	VK_COMPOSE
static int	VK_CONTROL
static int	VK_CONVERT
static int	VK_COPY
static int	VK_CUT
static int	VK_D
static int	VK_DEAD_ABOVEDOT

static int	VK_DEAD_ABOVERING
static int	VK_DEAD_ACUTE
static int	VK_DEAD_BREVE
static int	VK_DEAD_CARON
static int	VK_DEAD_CEDILLA
static int	VK_DEAD_CIRCUMFLEX
static int	VK_DEAD_DIAERESIS
static int	VK_DEAD_DOUBLEACUTE
static int	VK_DEAD_GRAVE
static int	VK_DEAD_IOTA
static int	VK_DEAD_MACRON
static int	VK_DEAD_OGONEK
static int	VK_DEAD_SEMIVOICED_SOUND
static int	VK_DEAD_TILDE
static int	VK_DEAD_VOICED_SOUND
static int	VK_DECIMAL
static int	VK_DELETE
static int	VK_DIVIDE
static int	VK_DOLLAR
static int	VK_DOWN
static int	VK_E
static int	VK_END
static int	VK_ENTER
static int	VK_EQUALS
static int	VK_ESCAPE
static int	VK_EURO_SIGN
static int	VK_EXCLAMATION_MARK
static int	VK_F
static int	VK_F1
static int	VK_F10
static int	VK_F11
static int	VK_F12
static int	VK_F13
static int	VK_F14
static int	VK_F15
static int	VK_F16
static int	VK_F17
static int	VK_F18
static int	VK_F19
static int	VK_F2
static int	VK_F20
static int	VK_F21
static int	VK_F22
static int	VK_F23
static int	VK_F24
static int	VK_F3
static int	VK_F4
static int	VK_F5
static int	VK_F6
static int	VK_F7

```
static int          VK_F8
static int          VK_F9
static int          VK_FINAL
static int          VK_FIND
static int          VK_FULL_WIDTH
static int          VK_G
static int          VK_GREATER
static int          VK_H
static int          VK_HALF_WIDTH
static int          VK_HELP
static int          VK_HIRAGANA
static int          VK_HOME
static int          VK_I
static int          VK_INSERT
static int          VK_INVERTED_EXCLAMATION_MARK
static int          VK_J
static int          VK_JAPANESE_HIRAGANA
static int          VK_JAPANESE_KATAKANA
static int          VK_JAPANESE_ROMAN
static int          VK_K
static int          VK_KANA
static int          VK_KANJI
static int          VK_KATAKANA
static int          VK_KP_DOWN
static int          VK_KP_LEFT
static int          VK_KP_RIGHT
static int          VK_KP_UP
static int          VK_L
static int          VK_LEFT
static int          VK_LEFT_PARENTHESIS
static int          VK_LESS
static int          VK_M
static int          VK_META
static int          VK_MINUS
static int          VK_MODECHANGE
static int          VK_MULTIPLY
static int          VK_N
static int          VK_NONCONVERT
static int          VK_NUM_LOCK
static int          VK_NUMBER_SIGN
static int          VK_NUMPAD0
static int          VK_NUMPAD1
static int          VK_NUMPAD2
static int          VK_NUMPAD3
static int          VK_NUMPAD4
static int          VK_NUMPAD5
static int          VK_NUMPAD6
static int          VK_NUMPAD7
static int          VK_NUMPAD8
static int          VK_NUMPAD9
```

static int	VK_O
static int	VK_OPEN_BRACKET
static int	VK_P
static int	VK_PAGE_DOWN
static int	VK_PAGE_UP
static int	VK_PASTE
static int	VK_PAUSE
static int	VK_PERIOD
static int	VK_PLUS
static int	VK_PREVIOUS_CANDIDATE
static int	VK_PRINTSCREEN
static int	VK_PROPS
static int	VK_Q
static int	VK_QUOTE
static int	VK_QUOTEDBL
static int	VK_R
static int	VK_RIGHT
static int	VK_RIGHT_PARENTHESIS
static int	VK_ROMAN_CHARACTERS
static int	VK_S
static int	VK_SCROLL_LOCK
static int	VK_SEMICOLON
static int	VK_SEPARATER
static int	VK_SHIFT
static int	VK_SLASH
static int	VK_SPACE
static int	VK_STOP
static int	VK_SUBTRACT
static int	VK_T
static int	VK_TAB
static int	VK_U
static int	VK_UNDEFINED
static int	VK_UNDERSCORE
static int	VK_UNDO
static int	VK_UP
static int	VK_V
static int	VK_W
static int	VK_X
static int	VK_Y
static int	VK_Z

Constructors

KeyEvent(Component source, int id, long when, int modifiers, int keyCode)

KeyEvent(Component source, int id, long when, int modifiers, int keyCode,
     char keyChar)

Methods

char	getKeyChar()
Int	getKeyCode()

static String	**getKeyModifiersText**(int modifiers)
static String	**getKeyText**(int keyCode)
Boolean	**isActionKey**()
String	**paramString**()
void	**setKeyChar**(char keyChar)
void	**setKeyCode**(int keyCode)
void	**setModifiers**(int modifiers)

Class MouseAdapter

```
java.lang.Object
    |
    +-java.awt.event.MouseAdapter
```

```
public abstract class MouseAdapter
                    extends Object
                    implements MouseListener
```

This class represents an adapter that can be subclassed to receive mouse events.

Constructor

```
MouseAdapter()
```

Methods

void	**mouseClicked**(MouseEvent e)
void	**mouseEntered**(MouseEvent e)
void	**mouseExited**(MouseEvent e)
void	**mousePressed**(MouseEvent e)
void	**mouseReleased**(MouseEvent e)

Class MouseEvent

```
java.lang.Object
    |
    +-java.util.EventObject
            |
            +-java.awt.AWTEvent
                    |
                    +-java.awt.event.ComponentEvent
                            |
                            +-java.awt.event.InputEvent
                                    |
                                    +-java.awt.event.MouseEvent
```

```
public class MouseEvent
          extends InputEvent
```

This class represents a mouse event that is fired when the mouse buttons are operated or the mouse is dragged.

Fields

static int	**MOUSE_CLICKED**
static int	**MOUSE_DRAGGED**
static int	**MOUSE_ENTERED**
static int	**MOUSE_EXITED**
static int	**MOUSE_FIRST**
static int	**MOUSE_LAST**
static int	**MOUSE_MOVED**
static int	**MOUSE_PRESSED**
static int	**MOUSE_RELEASED**

Constructor

MouseEvent(Component source, int id, long when, int modifiers, int x,
        int y, int clickCount, boolean popupTrigger)

Methods

int	**getClickCount**()
Point	**getPoint**()
Int	**getX**()
Int	**getY**()
Boolean	**isPopupTrigger**()
String	**paramString**()
void	**translatePoint**(int x, int y)

Class MouseMotionAdapter

```
java.lang.Object
   |
   +—java.awt.event.MouseMotionAdapter
```

public abstract class **MouseMotionAdapter**
                extends Object
                implements MouseMotionListener

This is an adapter class that can be subclassed to receive mouse events.

Constructor

MouseMotionAdapter()

Methods

void	**mouseDragged**(MouseEvent e)
void	**mouseMoved**(MouseEvent e)

Class PaintEvent

```
java.lang.Object
   |
   +—java.util.EventObject
       |
```

```
+ — java.awt.AWTEvent
      |
      + — java.awt.event.ComponentEvent
            |
            + — java.awt.event.PaintEvent
```

public class **PaintEvent**
          extends ComponentEvent

This class represents a paint event that is used to ensure that the paint() and update() methods are serialized for the event queues.

Fields

static int	**PAINT**
static int	**PAINT_FIRST**
static int	**PAINT_LAST**
static int	**UPDATE**

Constructor

PaintEvent(Component source, int id, Rectangle updateRect)

Methods

Rectangle	**getUpdateRect**()
String	**paramString**()
void	**setUpdateRect**(Rectangle updateRect)

Class TextEvent

```
java.lang.Object
   |
   + — java.util.EventObject
         |
         + — java.awt.AWTEvent
               |
               + — java.awt.event.TextEvent
```

public class **TextEvent**
          extends AWTEvent

This class represents an event that is fired whenever the text is changed in a text component.

Fields

static int	**TEXT_FIRST**
static int	**TEXT_LAST**
static int	**TEXT_VALUE_CHANGED**

Constructor

TextEvent(Object source, int id)

Method

```
String                    paramString()
```

Class WindowAdapter

```
java.lang.Object
    |
    + — java.awt.event.WindowAdapter
public abstract class WindowAdapter
                      extends Object
                      implements WindowListener
```

This class represents an adapter that can be subclassed to receive window events.

Constructor

```
WindowAdapter()
```

Methods

```
void                    windowActivated(WindowEvent e)
void                    windowClosed(WindowEvent e)
void                    windowClosing(WindowEvent e)
void                    windowDeactivated(WindowEvent e)
void                    windowDeiconified(WindowEvent e)
void                    windowIconified(WindowEvent e)
void                    windowOpened(WindowEvent e)
```

Class WindowEvent

```
java.lang.Object
    |
    + — java.util.EventObject
            |
            + — java.awt.AWTEvent
                    |
                    + — java.awt.event.ComponentEvent
                            |
                            + — java.awt.event.WindowEvent
public class WindowEvent
             extends ComponentEvent
```

This class represents a window event that is fired when a window is opened, closed, iconified, deiconified, and so on.

Fields

```
static int              WINDOW_ACTIVATED
static int              WINDOW_CLOSED
static int              WINDOW_CLOSING
static int              WINDOW_DEACTIVATED
```

```
static int          WINDOW_DEICONIFIED
static int          WINDOW_FIRST
static int          WINDOW_ICONIFIED
static int          WINDOW_LAST
static int          WINDOW_OPENED
```

Constructor

WindowEvent(Window source, int id)

Methods

```
Window              getWindow()
String              paramString()
```

APPENDIX C

Important AWT Classes for Swing

Package Summary

This portion of the reference contains the important interfaces and classes from the AWT package java.awt that are commonly required in Swing programs. The following is the list of these classes and interfaces.

Interfaces

Classes

Interface and Class Details

Interface LayoutManager

public abstract interface **LayoutManager**

This interface represents the abstract layout manager. The implementation classes define the methods for specific layout models to be used in a container.

Methods

void	**addLayoutComponent**(String name, Component comp)
void	**layoutContainer**(Container parent)
Dimension	**minimumLayoutSize**(Container parent)
Dimension	**preferredLayoutSize**(Container parent)
void	**removeLayoutComponent**(Component comp)

Interface LayoutManager2

```
public abstract interface LayoutManager2
                         extends LayoutManager
```

This is an interface to be implemented by layout classes that lay out containers based on certain layout constraints.

Methods

void	**addLayoutComponent**(Component comp, Object constraints)
float	**getLayoutAlignmentX**(Container target)
float	**getLayoutAlignmentY**(Container target)
void	**invalidateLayout**(Container target)
Dimension	**maximumLayoutSize**(Container target)

Class Component

```
java.lang.Object
   |
   +--java.awt.Component
```

```
public abstract class Component
                     extends Object
                     implements ImageObserver, MenuContainer, Serializable
```

This is the parent component of all AWT components. The class is also in the hierarchy of base classes for the Swing components. Thus, you can exercise the methods from this class on Swing components.

Fields

static float	**BOTTOM_ALIGNMENT**
static float	**CENTER_ALIGNMENT**
static float	**LEFT_ALIGNMENT**
static float	**RIGHT_ALIGNMENT**
static float	**TOP_ALIGNMENT**

Constructor

protected	**Component**()

Methods

boolean	**action**(Event evt, Object what)
void	**add**(PopupMenu popup)
void	**addComponentListener**(ComponentListener l)

void	**addFocusListener**(FocusListener l)
void	**addInputMethodListener**(InputMethodListener l)
void	**addKeyListener**(KeyListener l)
void	**addMouseListener**(MouseListener l)
void	**addMouseMotionListener**(MouseMotionListener l)
void	**addNotify**()
void	**addPropertyChangeListener** ➥(PropertyChangeListener listener)
void	**addPropertyChangeListener**(String propertyName, ➥PropertyChangeListener listener)

Rectangle	**bounds**()
	//Deprecated. As of JDK version 1.1, replaced by
	//getBounds().

int	**checkImage**(Image image, ImageObserver observer)
int	**checkImage**(Image image, int width, int height, ➥ImageObserver observer)
protected AWTEvent	**coalesceEvents**(AWTEvent existingEvent, AWTEvent ➥newEvent)
boolean	**contains**(int x, int y)
boolean	**contains**(Point p)
Image	**createImage**(ImageProducer producer)
Image	**createImage**(int width, int height)

void	**deliverEvent**(Event e)
	//Deprecated. As of JDK version 1.1, replaced by
	//dispatchEvent(AWTEvent e).

void	**disable**()
	//Deprecated. As of JDK version 1.1, replaced by
	//setEnabled(boolean).

protected void	**disableEvents**(long eventsToDisable)
void	**dispatchEvent**(AWTEvent e)
void	**doLayout**()

void	**enable**()
	//Deprecated. As of JDK version 1.1, replaced by
	//setEnabled(boolean).

void	**enable**(boolean b)
	//Deprecated. As of JDK version 1.1, replaced by
	//setEnabled(boolean).

protected void	**enableEvents**(long eventsToEnable)
void	**enableInputMethods**(boolean enable)
protected void	**firePropertyChange**(String propertyName, Object ➥oldValue, Object newValue)
float	**getAlignmentX**()
float	**getAlignmentY**()
Color	**getBackground**()
Rectangle	**getBounds**()
Rectangle	**getBounds**(Rectangle rv)
ColorModel	**getColorModel**()
Component	**getComponentAt**(int x, int y)

Component	**getComponentAt**(Point p)
ComponentOrientation	**getComponentOrientation**()
Cursor	**getCursor**()
DropTarget	**getDropTarget**()
Font	**getFont**()
FontMetrics	**getFontMetrics**(Font font)
Color	**getForeground**()
Graphics	**getGraphics**()
int	**getHeight**()
InputContext	**getInputContext**()
InputMethodRequests	**getInputMethodRequests**()
Locale	**getLocale**()
Point	**getLocation**()
Point	**getLocation**(Point rv)
Point	**getLocationOnScreen**()
Dimension	**getMaximumSize**()
Dimension	**getMinimumSize**()
String	**getName**()
Container	**getParent**()
java.awt.peer.ComponentPeer	**getPeer**()
	//Deprecated. As of JDK version 1.1, programs
	//should not directly manipulate peers.
	//Replaced by boolean isDisplayable().
Dimension	**getPreferredSize**()
Dimension	**getSize**()
Dimension	**getSize**(Dimension rv)
Toolkit	**getToolkit**()
Object	**getTreeLock**()
int	**getWidth**()
int	**getX**()
int	**getY**()
boolean	**gotFocus**(Event evt, Object what)
	//Deprecated. As of JDK version 1.1, replaced by
	//processFocusEvent(FocusEvent).
boolean	**handleEvent**(Event evt)
	//Deprecated. As of JDK version 1.1, replaced by
	//processEvent(AWTEvent).
boolean	**hasFocus**()
void	**hide**()
	//Deprecated. As of JDK version 1.1, replaced by
	//setVisible(boolean).
boolean	**imageUpdate**(Image img, int flags, int x, int y, int w, int h)
boolean	**inside**(int x, int y)
	//Deprecated. As of JDK version 1.1, replaced by
	//contains(int, int).
void	**invalidate**()
boolean	**isDisplayable**()
boolean	**isDoubleBuffered**()

boolean	**isEnabled**()
boolean	**isFocusTraversable**()
boolean	**isLightweight**()
boolean	**isOpaque**()
boolean	**isShowing**()
boolean	**isValid**()
boolean	**isVisible**()
boolean	**keyDown**(Event evt, int key)
	//Deprecated. As of JDK version 1.1, replaced by
	//processKeyEvent(KeyEvent).
boolean	**keyUp**(Event evt, int key)
	//Deprecated. As of JDK version 1.1, replaced by
	//processKeyEvent(KeyEvent).
void	**layout**()
	//Deprecated. As of JDK version 1.1, replaced by
	//doLayout().
void	**list**()
void	**list**(PrintStream out)
void	**list**(PrintStream out, int indent)
void	**list**(PrintWriter out)
void	**list**(PrintWriter out, int indent)
Component	**locate**(int x, int y)
	//Deprecated. As of JDK version 1.1, replaced by
	//processMouseEvent(MouseEvent).
Point	**location**()
	//Deprecated. As of JDK version 1.1, replaced by
	//getLocation().
boolean	**lostFocus**(Event evt, Object what)
	//Deprecated. As of JDK version 1.1, replaced by
	//processFocusEvent(FocusEvent).
Dimension	**minimumSize**()
	//Deprecated. As of JDK version 1.1, replaced by
	//getMinimumSize().
boolean	**mouseDown**(Event evt, int x, int y)
	//Deprecated. As of JDK version 1.1, replaced by
	//processMouseEvent(MouseEvent).
boolean	**mouseDrag**(Event evt, int x, int y)
	//Deprecated. As of JDK version 1.1, replaced by
	//processMouseMotionEvent(MouseEvent).
boolean	**mouseEnter**(Event evt, int x, int y)
	//Deprecated. As of JDK version 1.1, replaced by
	//processMouseEvent(MouseEvent).
boolean	**mouseExit**(Event evt, int x, int y)
	//Deprecated. As of JDK version 1.1, replaced by
	//processMouseEvent(MouseEvent).
boolean	**mouseMove**(Event evt, int x, int y)
	//Deprecated. As of JDK version 1.1, replaced by
	//processMouseMotionEvent(MouseEvent).

boolean	**mouseUp**(Event evt, int x, int y)
	//Deprecated. As of JDK version 1.1, replaced by
	//processMouseEvent(MouseEvent).

void	**move**(int x, int y)
	//Deprecated. As of JDK version 1.1, replaced by
	//setLocation(int, int).

void	**nextFocus**()
	//Deprecated. As of JDK version 1.1, replaced by
	//transferFocus().

void	**paint**(Graphics g)
void	**paintAll**(Graphics g)
protected String	**paramString**()

boolean	**postEvent**(Event e)
	//Deprecated. As of JDK version 1.1, replaced by
	//dispatchEvent(AWTEvent).

Dimension	**preferredSize**()
	//Deprecated. As of JDK version 1.1, replaced by
	//getPreferredSize().

boolean	**prepareImage**(Image image, ImageObserver observer)
boolean	**prepareImage**(Image image, int width, int height, ➥ImageObserver observer)
void	**print**(Graphics g)
void	**printAll**(Graphics g)
protected void	**processComponentEvent**(ComponentEvent e)
protected void	**processEvent**(AWTEvent e)
protected void	**processFocusEvent**(FocusEvent e)
protected void	**processInputMethodEvent**(InputMethodEvent e)
protected void	**processKeyEvent**(KeyEvent e)
protected void	**processMouseEvent**(MouseEvent e)
protected void	**processMouseMotionEvent**(MouseEvent e)
void	**remove**(MenuComponent popup)
void	**removeComponentListener**(ComponentListener l)
void	**removeFocusListener**(FocusListener l)
void	**removeInputMethodListener** ➥(InputMethodListener l)
void	**removeKeyListener**(KeyListener l)
void	**removeMouseListener**(MouseListener l)
void	**removeMouseMotionListener** ➥(MouseMotionListener l)
void	**removeNotify**()
void	**removePropertyChangeListener** ➥(PropertyChangeListener listener)
void	**removePropertyChangeListener**(String ➥propertyName, PropertyChangeListener ➥listener)
void	**repaint**()
void	**repaint**(int x, int y, int width, int height)
void	**repaint**(long tm)
void	**repaint**(long tm, int x, int y, int width, int height)

void	**requestFocus**()

void	**reshape**(int x, int y, int width, int height)
	//Deprecated. As of JDK version 1.1, replaced by
	//setBounds(int, int, int, int).

void	**resize**(Dimension d)
	//Deprecated. As of JDK version 1.1, replaced by
	//setSize(Dimension d).

void	**resize**(int width, int height)
	//Deprecated. As of JDK version 1.1, replaced by
	//setSize(int, int).

void	**setBackground**(Color c)
void	**setBounds**(int x, int y, int width, int height)
void	**setBounds**(Rectangle r)
void	**setComponentOrientation** ➥(ComponentOrientation o)
void	**setCursor**(Cursor cursor)
void	**setDropTarget**(DropTarget dt)
void	**setEnabled**(boolean b)
void	**setFont**(Font f)
void	**setForeground**(Color c)
void	**setLocale**(Locale l)
void	**setLocation**(int x, int y)
void	**setLocation**(Point p)
void	**setName**(String name)
void	**setSize**(Dimension d)
void	**setSize**(int width, int height)
void	**setVisible**(boolean b)

void	**show**()
	//Deprecated. As of JDK version 1.1, replaced by
	//setVisible(boolean).

void	**show**(boolean b)
	//Deprecated. As of JDK version 1.1, replaced by
	//setVisible(boolean).

Dimension	**size**()
	//Deprecated. As of JDK version 1.1, replaced by
	// getSize().

String	**toString**()
void	**transferFocus**()
void	**update**(Graphics g)
void	**validate**()

Class Container

```
java.lang.Object
    |
    +--java.awt.Component
          |
          |
          +--java.awt.Container
public class Container
          extends Component
```

This class is a generic container in the Abstract Windowing Toolkit (AWT). This class is the parent class for the Swing parent JComponent. Because the class JComponent extends Container, the Swing components can behave like containers.

Constructor

Container()

Methods

Component	**add**(Component comp)
Component	**add**(Component comp, int index)
void	**add**(Component comp, Object constraints)
void	**add**(Component comp, Object constraints, int index)
Component	**add**(String name, Component comp)
void	**addContainerListener**(ContainerListener l)
protected void	**addImpl**(Component comp, Object constraints, int index)
void	**addNotify**()
int	**countComponents**()
	//Deprecated. As of JDK version 1.1, replaced by
	//getComponentCount().
void	**deliverEvent**(Event e)
	//Deprecated. As of JDK version 1.1, replaced by
	//dispatchEvent(AWTEvent e).
void	**doLayout**()
Component	**findComponentAt**(int x, int y)
Component	**findComponentAt**(Point p)
float	**getAlignmentX**()
float	**getAlignmentY**()
Component	**getComponent**(int n)
Component	**getComponentAt**(int x, int y)
Component	**getComponentAt**(Point p)
int	**getComponentCount**()
Component[]	**getComponents**()
Insets	**getInsets**()
LayoutManager	**getLayout**()
Dimension	**getMaximumSize**()
Dimension	**getMinimumSize**()
Dimension	**getPreferredSize**()
Insets	**insets**()
	//Deprecated. As of JDK version 1.1, replaced by
	//getInsets().
void	**invalidate**()
boolean	**isAncestorOf**(Component c)
void	**layout**()
	//Deprecated. As of JDK version 1.1, replaced by
	//doLayout().
void	**list**(PrintStream out, int indent)
void	**list**(PrintWriter out, int indent)

Component	**locate**(int x, int y)
	//Deprecated. As of JDK version 1.1, replaced by
	//getComponentAt(int, int).
Dimension	**minimumSize**()
	//Deprecated. As of JDK version 1.1, replaced by
	//getMinimumSize().
void	**paint**(Graphics g)
void	**paintComponents**(Graphics g)
protected String	**paramString**()
Dimension	**preferredSize**()
	//Deprecated. As of JDK version 1.1, replaced by
	//getPreferredSize().
void	**print**(Graphics g)
void	**printComponents**(Graphics g)
protected void	**processContainerEvent**(ContainerEvent e)
protected void	**processEvent**(AWTEvent e)
void	**remove**(Component comp)
void	**remove**(int index)
void	**removeAll**()
void	**removeContainerListener**(ContainerListener l)
void	**removeNotify**()
void	**setFont**(Font f)
void	**setLayout**(LayoutManager mgr)
void	**update**(Graphics g)
void	**validate**()
protected void	**validateTree**()

Class FlowLayout

```
java.lang.Object
   |
   +--java.awt.FlowLayout
```

public class **FlowLayout**
        extends Object
        implements LayoutManager, Serializable

This class represents the layout manager called flow layout. When the layout is assigned to a container, the components are added from left to right and top to bottom when no component can be added in the same row.

Fields

static int	**CENTER**
static int	**LEADING**
static int	**LEFT**
static int	**RIGHT**
static int	**TRAILING**

Constructors

```
FlowLayout()
FlowLayout(int align)
FlowLayout(int align, int hgap, int vgap)
```

Methods

void	**addLayoutComponent**(String name, Component comp)
int	**getAlignment**()
int	**getHgap**()
int	**getVgap**()
void	**layoutContainer**(Container target)
Dimension	**minimumLayoutSize**(Container target)
Dimension	**preferredLayoutSize**(Container target)
void	**removeLayoutComponent**(Component comp)
void	**setAlignment**(int align)
void	**setHgap**(int hgap)
void	**setVgap**(int vgap)
String	**toString**()

Class BorderLayout

```
      java.lang.Object
         |
         |
      +--java.awt.BorderLayout

public class BorderLayout
            extends Object
            implements LayoutManager2, Serializable
```

This layout represents the layout manager called border layout. When this layout manager is assigned to a container, components can be added in the four geographical locations North, South, East, and West and the Center location.

Fields

static String	**AFTER_LAST_LINE**
static String	**AFTER_LINE_ENDS**
static String	**BEFORE_FIRST_LINE**
static String	**BEFORE_LINE_BEGINS**
static String	**CENTER**
static String	**EAST**
static String	**NORTH**
static String	**SOUTH**
static String	**WEST**

Constructors

```
BorderLayout()
BorderLayout(int hgap, int vgap)
```

Methods

void	**addLayoutComponent**(Component comp, Object constraints)
void	**addLayoutComponent**(String name, Component comp)
	//Deprecated. As of JDK version 1.1, replaced by
	//addLayoutComponent(Component, Object).
int	**getHgap**()
float	**getLayoutAlignmentX**(Container parent)
float	**getLayoutAlignmentY**(Container parent)
int	**getVgap**()
void	**invalidateLayout**(Container target)
void	**layoutContainer**(Container target)
Dimension	**maximumLayoutSize**(Container target)
Dimension	**minimumLayoutSize**(Container target)
Dimension	**preferredLayoutSize**(Container target)
void	**removeLayoutComponent**(Component comp)
void	**setHgap**(int hgap)
void	**setVgap**(int vgap)
String	**toString**()

Class GridLayout

```
java.lang.Object
   |
   +--java.awt.GridLayout
```

public class **GridLayout**
        extends Object
        implements LayoutManager, Serializable

This class represents the layout manager called grid layout. Components can be added in a grid pattern when this type of layout is assigned to a container.

Constructors

GridLayout()
GridLayout(int rows, int cols)
GridLayout(int rows, int cols, int hgap, int vgap)

Methods

void	**addLayoutComponent**(String name, Component comp)
int	**getColumns**()
int	**getHgap**()
int	**getRows**()
int	**getVgap**()
void	**layoutContainer**(Container parent)
Dimension	**minimumLayoutSize**(Container parent)
Dimension	**preferredLayoutSize**(Container parent)
void	**removeLayoutComponent**(Component comp)
void	**setColumns**(int cols)
void	**setHgap**(int hgap)

```
void          setRows(int rows)
void          setVgap(int vgap)
String        toString()
```

Class CardLayout

```
java.lang.Object
   ¦
   +--java.awt.CardLayout
```

public class **CardLayout**
          extends Object
          implements LayoutManager2, Serializable

This class represents the layout manager called card layout. Components can be added to different cards overlapping each other when this layout manager is assigned to a container. Only one card can be visible at a time.

Constructors

CardLayout()
CardLayout(int hgap, int vgap)

Methods

```
void          addLayoutComponent(Component comp, Object constraints)
void          addLayoutComponent(String name, Component comp)
void          first(Container parent)
int           getHgap()
float         getLayoutAlignmentX(Container parent)
float         getLayoutAlignmentY(Container parent)
int           getVgap()
void          invalidateLayout(Container target)
void          last(Container parent)
void          layoutContainer(Container parent)
Dimension     maximumLayoutSize(Container target)
Dimension     minimumLayoutSize(Container parent)
void          next(Container parent)
Dimension     preferredLayoutSize(Container parent)
void          previous(Container parent)
void          removeLayoutComponent(Component comp)
void          setHgap(int hgap)
void          setVgap(int vgap)
void          show(Container parent, String name)
String        toString()
```

Class GridBagLayout

```
java.lang.Object
   ¦
   +--java.awt.GridBagLayout
```

public class **GridBagLayout**
          extends Object
          implements LayoutManager2, Serializable

This class represents the layout manager called grid bag layout. When this layout manager is assigned to a container, various components can be added based on the specified constraints. The constraints are represented by a constraints object of type GridBagConstraints. The components need not be of the same size and can be aligned, anchored, and padded as required.

Fields

double[]	columnWeights
int[]	columnWidths
protected Hashtable	comptable
protected GridBagConstraints	defaultConstraints
protected java.awt.GridBagLayoutInfo	layoutInfo
protected static int	MAXGRIDSIZE
protected static int	MINSIZE
protected static int	PREFERREDSIZE
int[]	rowHeights
double[]	rowWeights

Constructor

GridBagLayout()

Methods

void	addLayoutComponent(Component comp, Object constraints)
void	addLayoutComponent(String name, Component comp)
protected void	AdjustForGravity(GridBagConstraints constraints, Rectangle r)
protected void	ArrangeGrid(Container parent)
GridBagConstraints	getConstraints(Component comp)
float	getLayoutAlignmentX(Container parent)
float	getLayoutAlignmentY(Container parent)
int[][]	getLayoutDimensions()
protected java.awt.GridBagLayoutInfo	GetLayoutInfo(Container parent, int sizeflag)
Point	getLayoutOrigin()
double[][]	getLayoutWeights()
protected Dimension	GetMinSize(Container parent, java.awt.GridBagLayoutInfo info)
void	invalidateLayout(Container target)
void	layoutContainer(Container parent)
Point	location(int x, int y)
protected GridBagConstraints	lookupConstraints(Component comp)
Dimension	maximumLayoutSize(Container target)

Dimension	**minimumLayoutSize**(Container parent)
Dimension	**preferredLayoutSize**(Container parent)
void	**removeLayoutComponent**(Component comp)
void	**setConstraints**(Component comp, GridBagConstraints constraints)
String	**toString**()

Class GridBagConstraints

```
java.lang.Object
   |
   +--java.awt.GridBagConstraints
```

public class **GridBagConstraints**
        extends Object
        implements Cloneable, Serializable

This class represents the constraints objects. This class provides various constants to specify the constraints for components that are laid out according to the grid bag layout.

Fields

int	**anchor**
static int	**BOTH**
static int	**CENTER**
static int	**EAST**
int	**fill**
int	**gridheight**
int	**gridwidth**
int	**gridx**
int	**gridy**
static int	**HORIZONTAL**
Insets	**insets**
int	**ipadx**
int	**ipady**
static int	**NONE**
static int	**NORTH**
static int	**NORTHEAST**
static int	**NORTHWEST**
static int	**RELATIVE**
static int	**REMAINDER**
static int	**SOUTH**
static int	**SOUTHEAST**
static int	**SOUTHWEST**
static int	**VERTICAL**
double	**weightx**
double	**weighty**
static int	**WEST**

Constructors

GridBagConstraints()
GridBagConstraints(int gridx, int gridy, int gridwidth, int gridheight,
↪double weightx, double weighty, int anchor, int fill, Insets insets,
↪int ipadx, int ipady)

Method

Object   **clone**()

APPENDIX D

Accessibility Quick Reference

Package Summary

The javax.accessibility package supports interfaces and classes that abridge user-interface components and an assistive technology system that provides access to those components.

Interfaces

```
Accessible
AccessibleAction
AccessibleComponent
AccessibleHypertext
AccessibleSelection
AccessibleText
AccessibleValue
```

Classes

```
AccessibleBundle
AccessibleContext
AccessibleHyperlink
AccessibleResourceBundle
AccessibleRole
AccessibleState
AccessibleStateSet
```

Interface and Class Details

Interface Accessible

public abstract interface **Accessible**

This interface is implemented by all components that support accessibility.

Method

AccessibleContext **getAccessibleContext()**

Interface AccessibleAction

public abstract interface **AccessibleAction**

This interface describes the mechanism for an assistive technology system to communicate with an object to perform some action. The interface can also determine the
actions of an object.

Methods

```
boolean   doAccessibleAction(int i)
int       getAccessibleActionCount()
String    getAccessibleActionDescription(int i)
```

Interface AccessibleComponent

public abstract interface **AccessibleComponent**

This interface describes the mechanism for an assistive technology system to decide
and assign the graphical representation of an object. Any component that is rendered
on the screen should implement this interface.

Methods

```
void        addFocusListener(FocusListener l)
boolean     contains(Point p)
Accessible  getAccessibleAt(Point p)
Color       getBackground()
Rectangle   getBounds()
Cursor      getCursor()
Font        getFont()
FontMetrics getFontMetrics(Font f)
Color       getForeground()
Point       getLocation()
Point       getLocationOnScreen()
Dimension   getSize()
boolean     isEnabled()
boolean     isFocusTraversable()
boolean     isShowing()
boolean     isVisible()
```

```
void         removeFocusListener(FocusListener l)
void         requestFocus()
void         setBackground(Color c)
void         setBounds(Rectangle r)
void         setCursor(Cursor cursor)
void         setEnabled(boolean b)
void         setFont(Font f)
void         setForeground(Color c)
void         setLocation(Point p)
void         setSize(Dimension d)
void         setVisible(boolean b)
```

Interface AccessibleHypertext

```
public abstract interface AccessibleHypertext
                         extends AccessibleText
```

This interface describes the mechanism for an assistive technology to access hypertext through the attributes and its location. It also provides the means of dealing with hyperlinks.

Methods

```
AccessibleHyperlink  getLink(int linkIndex)
int                  getLinkCount()
int                  getLinkIndex(int charIndex)
```

Interface AccessibleSelection

```
public abstract interface AccessibleSelection
```

This interface describes the mechanism for an assistive technology to determine the current selections.

Methods

```
void        addAccessibleSelection(int i)
void        clearAccessibleSelection()
Accessible  getAccessibleSelection(int i)
int         getAccessibleSelectionCount()
boolean     isAccessibleChildSelected(int i)
void        removeAccessibleSelection(int i)
void        selectAllAccessibleSelection()
```

Interface AccessibleText

```
public abstract interface AccessibleText
```

This interface describes the accessible text and is implemented by all classes that display text content.

Fields

```
static int    CHARACTER
static int    SENTENCE
static int    WORD
```

Methods

```
String        getAfterIndex(int part, int index)
String        getAtIndex(int part, int index)
String        getBeforeIndex(int part, int index)
int           getCaretPosition()
AttributeSet  getCharacterAttribute(int i)
Rectangle     getCharacterBounds(int i)
int           getCharCount()
int           getIndexAtPoint(Point p)
String        getSelectedText()
int           getSelectionEnd()
int           getSelectionStart()
```

Interface AccessibleValue

```
public abstract interface AccessibleValue
```

This interface describes the mechanism for an assistive technology system to decide and assign the numerical values.

Methods

```
Number    getCurrentAccessibleValue()
Number    getMaximumAccessibleValue()
Number    getMinimumAccessibleValue()
boolean   setCurrentAccessibleValue(Number n)
```

Class AccessibleBundle

```
    java.lang.Object
      ¦
      +—javax.accessibility.AccessibleBundle
public abstract class AccessibleBundle
                      extends Object
```

This class serves as the superclass of AccessibleState and AccessibleRole and is used to maintain strongly typed enumeration.

Field

```
protected String    key
```

Constructor

```
AccessibleBundle()
```

Methods

```
String              toDisplayString()
String              toDisplayString(Locale locale)
protected String    toDisplayString(String resourceBundleName, Locale locale)
String              toString()
```

Class AccessibleContext

```
java.lang.Object
    |
    +— javax.accessibility.AccessibleContext
public abstract class AccessibleContext
                    extends Object
```

This class represents the accessible context that is the basic information provided by the accessible objects.

Fields

```
static String           ACCESSIBLE_ACTIVE_DESCENDANT_PROPERTY
static String           ACCESSIBLE_CARET_PROPERTY
static String           ACCESSIBLE_CHILD_PROPERTY
static String           ACCESSIBLE_DESCRIPTION_PROPERTY
static String           ACCESSIBLE_NAME_PROPERTY
static String           ACCESSIBLE_SELECTION_PROPERTY
static String           ACCESSIBLE_STATE_PROPERTY
static String           ACCESSIBLE_TEXT_PROPERTY
static String           ACCESSIBLE_VALUE_PROPERTY
static String           ACCESSIBLE_VISIBLE_DATA_PROPERTY
protected String        accessibleDescription
protected String        accessibleName
protected Accessible    accessibleParent
```

Constructor

```
AccessibleContext()
```

Methods

```
void addPropertyChangeListener(PropertyChangeListener listener)
void firePropertyChange(String propertyName, Object oldValue, Object newValue)
AccessibleAction getAccessibleAction()
abstract Accessible getAccessibleChild(int i)
abstract int getAccessibleChildrenCount()
AccessibleComponent getAccessibleComponent()
String  getAccessibleDescription()
abstract int getAccessibleIndexInParent()
String getAccessibleName()
Accessible getAccessibleParent()
abstract AccessibleRole getAccessibleRole()
AccessibleSelection getAccessibleSelection()
```

```
abstract AccessibleStateSet getAccessibleStateSet()
AccessibleText getAccessibleText()
AccessibleValue getAccessibleValue()
abstract Locale getLocale()
void removePropertyChangeListener(PropertyChangeListener listener)
void setAccessibleDescription(String s)
void setAccessibleName(String s)
void setAccessibleParent(Accessible a)
```

Class AccessibleHyperlink

```
    java.lang.Object
       |
       +--javax.accessibility.AccessibleHyperlink
public abstract class AccessibleHyperlink
                        extends Object
                        implements AccessibleAction
```

This class represents the accessible hyperlink in a hypertext document.

Constructor

AccessibleHyperlink()

Methods

```
abstract boolean  doAccessibleAction(int i)
abstract Object   getAccessibleActionAnchor(int i)
abstract int      getAccessibleActionCount()
abstract String   getAccessibleActionDescription(int i)
abstract Object   getAccessibleActionObject(int i)
abstract int      getEndIndex()
abstract int      getStartIndex()
abstract boolean  isValid()
```

Class AccessibleResourceBundle

```
    java.lang.Object
       |
       +--java.util.ResourceBundle
              |
              +--java.util.ListResourceBundle
                     |
                     +--javax.accessibility.AccessibleResourceBundle
public class AccessibleResourceBundle
             extends ListResourceBundle
```

This class represents the resource bundle that holds localized strings used for accessibility.

Constructor

AccessibleResourceBundle()

Method

`Object[][]` **`getContents()`**

Class AccessibleRole

```
java.lang.Object
   |
   +— javax.accessibility.AccessibleBundle
       |
       +— javax.accessibility.AccessibleRole
```

public class **AccessibleRole**
          extends AccessibleBundle

This class represents the accessible role that determines the role of a component. See the list of roles in the fields of this class.

Fields

static AccessibleRole	**ALERT**
static AccessibleRole	**AWT_COMPONENT**
static AccessibleRole	**CHECK_BOX**
static AccessibleRole	**COLOR_CHOOSER**
static AccessibleRole	**COLUMN_HEADER**
static AccessibleRole	**COMBO_BOX**
static AccessibleRole	**DESKTOP_ICON**
static AccessibleRole	**DESKTOP_PANE**
static AccessibleRole	**DIALOG**
static AccessibleRole	**DIRECTORY_PANE**
static AccessibleRole	**FILE_CHOOSER**
static AccessibleRole	**FILLER**
static AccessibleRole	**GLASS_PANE**
static AccessibleRole	**INTERNAL_FRAME**
static AccessibleRole	**LABEL**
static AccessibleRole	**LAYERED_PANE**
static AccessibleRole	**LIST**
static AccessibleRole	**MENU**
static AccessibleRole	**MENU_BAR**
static AccessibleRole	**MENU_ITEM**
static AccessibleRole	**OPTION_PANE**
static AccessibleRole	**PAGE_TAB**
static AccessibleRole	**PAGE_TAB_LIST**
static AccessibleRole	**PANEL**
static AccessibleRole	**PASSWORD_TEXT**
static AccessibleRole	**POPUP_MENU**
static AccessibleRole	**PROGRESS_BAR**
static AccessibleRole	**PUSH_BUTTON**
static AccessibleRole	**RADIO_BUTTON**
static AccessibleRol	**ROOT_PANE**
static AccessibleRole	**ROW_HEADER**
static AccessibleRole	**SCROLL_BAR**
static AccessibleRole	**SCROLL_PANE**

static AccessibleRole	**SEPARATOR**
static AccessibleRole	**SLIDER**
static AccessibleRole	**SPLIT_PANE**
static AccessibleRole	**SWING_COMPONENT**
static AccessibleRole	**TABLE**
static AccessibleRole	**TEXT**
static AccessibleRole	**TOGGLE_BUTTON**
static AccessibleRole	**TOOL_BAR**
static AccessibleRole	**TOOL_TIP**
static AccessibleRole	**TREE**
static AccessibleRole	**UNKNOWN**
static AccessibleRole	**VIEWPORT**
static AccessibleRole	**WINDOW**

Constructor

protected   **AccessibleRole**(String key)

Class AccessibleState

```
java.lang.Object
   ¦
   +—javax.accessibility.AccessibleBundle
        ¦
        +—javax.accessibility.AccessibleState
```

public class **AccessibleState**
        extends AccessibleBundle

This class represents the accessible state of a component. See the list of states under the fields of this class.

Fields

static AccessibleState	**ACTIVE**
static AccessibleState	**ARMED**
static AccessibleState	**BUSY**
static AccessibleState	**CHECKED**
static AccessibleState	**COLLAPSED**
static AccessibleState	**EDITABLE**
static AccessibleState	**ENABLED**
static AccessibleState	**EXPANDABLE**
static AccessibleState	**EXPANDED**
static AccessibleState	**FOCUSABLE**
static AccessibleState	**FOCUSED**
static AccessibleState	**HORIZONTAL**
static AccessibleState	**ICONIFIED**
static AccessibleState	**MODAL**
static AccessibleState	**MULTI_LINE**
static AccessibleState	**MULTISELECTABLE**
static AccessibleState	**OPAQUE**
static AccessibleState	**PRESSED**

static AccessibleState	**RESIZABLE**
static AccessibleState	**SELECTABLE**
static AccessibleState	**SELECTED**
static AccessibleState	**SHOWING**
static AccessibleState	**SINGLE_LINE**
static AccessibleState	**TRANSIENT**
static AccessibleState	**VERTICAL**
static AccessibleState	**VISIBLE**

Constructor

protected   **AccessibleState**(String key)

Class AccessibleStateSet

```
java.lang.Object
   |
   +—javax.accessibility.AccessibleStateSet
```

public class **AccessibleStateSet**
       extends Object

This class represents the set of accessible states of a component.

Field

protected Vector **states**

Constructors

AccessibleStateSet()
AccessibleStateSet(AccessibleState[] states)

Methods

boolean	**add**(AccessibleState state)
void	**addAll**(AccessibleState[] states)
void	**clear**()
boolean	**contains**(AccessibleState state)
boolean	**remove**(AccessibleState state)
AccessibleState[]	**toArray**()
String	**toString**()

INDEX

A

C

K

T

X-Y-Z

Other Related Titles

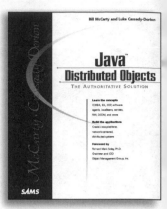

Java 1.2 Class Libraries Unleashed
Krishna Sankar
ISBN: 078971292X
$49.99 US/$71.95 CAN

Mitchell Waite Signature Series Data Structures and Algorithms in Java
Robert Lafore
ISBN: 1571690956
$49.99 US/$71.95 CAN

Java 1.2 Unleashed
Jamie Jaworski
ISBN: 1575213893
$49.99 US/$71.95 CAN

Mitchell Waite Signature Series Object-Oriented Programming in Java
Stephen Gilbert; Bill McCarty
ISBN: 1571690867
$59.99 US/$85.95 CAN

JFC Unleashed
Michael Foley; Mark McCulley
ISBN: 0789714663
$39.99 US/$57.95 CAN

Java Distributed Objects
Bill McCarty
ISBN: 0672315378
$49.99 US/$71.95 CAN

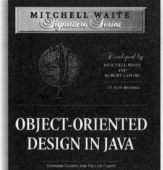

Mitchell Waite Signature Series Object-Oriented Design in Java
Stephen Gilbert; Bill McCarty
ISBN: 1571691340
$49.99 US/$71.95 CAN

www.samspublishing.com